Personality Traits

This second edition of the bestselling textbook *Personality Traits* is an essential text for students doing courses in personality and differential psychology and also of   coherent, up-to-date overview for researchers and practitioners. Th   ors have updated the volume throughout, incorporating the latest re   in the field, and added three new chapters on personality across th   n, health and applications of personality assessment. Personali   h has been transformed by recent advances in our understanding   ality traits. This book reviews the origins of traits in biological a   rocesses, and their consequences for cognition, stress and ph   ental health. Contrary to the traditional view of personality   s a collection of disconnected theories, *Personality Traits* p   ntegrated account, linking theory-driven research with applic   linical and occupational psychology. The new format of the   ding many additional features, makes it even more accessibl   r friendly.

GERALD MATTHE   essor of Psychology at the University of Cincinnati and has   held faculty positions at the Universities of Aston and Dund   co-authored several volumes, including *Attention and Emo   Clinical Perspective* (1994) which won the 1998 British Psycho   Society Book Award, and has published many articles in the area   ality research.

IAN J. DEARY is   of Differential Psychology at the University of Edinburgh. He i   a registered medical practitioner and member of the Royal Colleg   ychiatrists. He has written extensively on personality and intellig   nd won the 2002 British Psychological Society Book Award for *Lo   Down on Human Intelligence* (2000).

MARTHA C. WHI   N is a Lecturer in Psychology at the University of Edinburgh. Her r   h is directed towards personality, cardiovascular disease, aging and   ic health. She has published articles in medical and psychological journals that include *The Lancet* and *Psychosomatic Medicine*.

Personality Traits

SECOND EDITION

GERALD MATTHEWS
University of Cincinnati

IAN J. DEARY
University of Edinburgh

MARTHA C. WHITEMAN
University of Edinburgh

CAMBRIDGE
UNIVERSITY PRESS

PUBLISHED BY THE PRESS SYNDICATE OF THE UNIVERSITY OF CAMBRIDGE
The Pitt Building, Trumpington Street, Cambridge, United Kingdom

CAMBRIDGE UNIVERSITY PRESS
The Edinburgh Building, Cambridge, CB2 2RU, UK
40 West 20th Street, New York, NY 10011–4211, USA
477 Williamstown Road, Port Melbourne, VIC 3207, Australia
Ruiz de Alarcón 13, 28014 Madrid, Spain
Dock House, The Waterfront, Cape Town 8001, South Africa

http://www.cambridge.org

First published 1998. Reprinted 1999, 2000, 2002
Second edition 2003

Printed in the United Kingdom at the University Press, Cambridge

Typefaces Times 10/13 pt. Formata   *System* LATEX 2_ε [TB]

A catalogue record for this book is available from the British Library

Library of Congress Cataloguing in Publication data
Matthews, Gerald.
Personality traits / Gerald Matthews, Ian J. Deary, Martha C. Whiteman. – 2nd edn.
    p.   cm.
Includes bibliographical references and index.
ISBN 0 521 83107 5 – ISBN 0 521 53824 6 (pb)
1. Personality.   I. Deary, Ian J.   II. Whiteman, Martha C.   III. Title.
BF698.M3434   2003
155.2′3 – dc21   2003046259

ISBN 0 521 83107 5 hardback
ISBN 0 521 53824 6 paperback

The publisher has used its best endeavours to ensure that URLs for external websites
referred to in this book are correct and active at the time of going to press. However, the
publisher has no responsibility for the websites and can make no guarantee that a site will
remain live or that the content is or will remain appropriate.

To my wife, Diana – GM

To my parents,
Hugh and Isobelle Deary – IJD

To my parents,
Jim Pollard and Allene Grossman
Sally Pollard and Bill Grossman – MCW

Contents

Figures

Tables

Boxes

Preface to the first edition

The stimuli for writing this book were private and public. In our conversations with colleagues in other areas of psychology we have noticed a lack of awareness of recent advances and retreats in personality psychology. In parallel with these conversations, we noticed that textbooks on personality and sections on personality in general psychology texts frequently failed to reflect what was happening in the research journals and at personality conferences. Many psychologists, we found, were under the impression either that traits had perished under Mischel's broadsword in 1968, or that trait theorists were still discussing how many angels were perched on their particular pinhead. Personality texts, more surprisingly, seemed stuck in an arcane formula, variously described as a Dutch Auction or a Hall of Fame. Thus, the typical book on personality has a number of more or less free-standing chapters on 'approaches to personality' handed down largely by great names: Freud, Jung, Maslow, Erikson, Horney, Sullivan, May, Kelly, Rogers. What many of these approaches shared was a lack of current, and often past, academic interest and a lack of empirical evidence or even testability. Within the Hall of Fame, traits appeared as one or two dusty portraits, neither more nor less distinguished than the other works on offer, though perhaps with a little less depth.

The typical book reviewing personality does not adequately represent current personality research. It offers a parallel world where knowledge does not progress and where stories pertaining to human personality are collected irrespective of their validity. The version of traits offered is frequently a straw man that entails a rigidity and narrowness not seen among living trait researchers. One still sees situationism and interactionism portrayed as alternatives to trait models, whereas the truth is that there are no credible situationists who deny the existence of traits and no trait theorists who deny the power of the situation. Situationism and trait theories are complementary, not alternatives, and interactionism is the description of the emergent approach consequent on recognising these truths. This does not deny that some researchers will devote their careers more to studying traits or situations, and there is more than one way to become an interactionist. It is a truism verging on cliché to say that behaviour is multifactorially determined and that there is a reciprocity between the person and the environment. However, this richness may only be captured by systematic empirical research that stakes out the lawful personological and situational (and interactional) factors influencing behaviour.

An accurate exposition of scientific research on personality must break the common mould from which many personality texts have been cast; it must explain to the reader why some personality theories and constructs should be dropped from our consideration, and others need to be recognised as having become married. This book is about contemporary personality research, one which is aware of the historical roots of the field but focuses on constructs with a future as well as a past. Although the treatment of personality is centred on traits, it recognises other empirical approaches. The book makes no expansionist claims for traits, but does assert that other aspects of research on personality may be seen from the vantage point of the trait theorist and may be used in tandem with traits.

The book is not wholly or even largely concerned with the narrow psychometrics of personality traits. As is the case with cognitive abilities, psychometric studies provide a possible classificatory scheme for personality traits that has to look elsewhere for validation. Therefore, whereas some attention must be given to the dimensionality of personality traits, most of the evidence for the validity of traits will come from what we call horizontal and vertical validation. Horizontal validation includes such efforts as finding the same factorial structure for a trait scheme in different groups (sexes, cultures, ages), and finding convergent and discriminant validity when the traits are compared with other related and unrelated psychometric constructs. Vertical validity may look up or down. Upward vertical validation involves finding real-life correlates of trait differences, such as occupational and other life successes and failures, social behaviours, and susceptibility to clinical conditions. Downward vertical validity concerns finding the psychological and biological underpinnings of traits, and involves a variety of approaches from cognitive to psychobiological. Therefore, the richness of psychological research involving traits includes differential, biological, cognitive and social techniques. Thus, whereas the sine qua non of the personality researcher must be a minimum level of psychometric knowledge, the personality researcher must be eclectic in validating traits.

The structure of the book reflects the validational structure outlined above. Part 1 of the book charts the trait domain and attempts to clarify the boundaries between the most agreed upon dimensions. It also examines the relationship between trait theory and its supposed alternatives in the domain of personality. Part 2 deals with the causes of traits, both biological and social. Part 3 concerns some of the consequences of trait differences. Again, it is important to emphasise that, whereas a replicable and generalisable psychometric structure for personality traits is necessary for a theory of personality, it is not sufficient. Sufficiency arises when the origins of traits have been established in valid constructs that lie outside the trait domain, and where there are replicable, significant and objective real-life outcomes of traits in terms of human behaviour. The book gives an idea of the empirical mass of trait theories of personality; compared with other psychological constructs we think that trait theory has come near to the status of a paradigm in psychological research. Not the least impressive fact about traits is that their influence may be carried in the genetic material.

The book builds an eclectic picture of human personality around traits. It is a call to those interested in human individuality to come and stand on some 'solid ground on the wetlands of personality' (Costa and McCrae, 1995); as such it welcomes all other empirical approaches to personality. Therefore, the reader will see an attempt to reconcile trait theory with the often-neglected work on abnormal personality, with state research, with social psychology, with situationism, and so forth. Because we have adopted an eclectic approach, some chapters or sections will begin with a description of the explanatory principles of an area of psychological research, and only then move on to the association of that area with trait theory. We contend that all empirical research on personality must ultimately be woven into a comprehensive account of the person, and that perhaps trait theory is a reasonable platform from which to begin. In the treatment of individual topics, the book, because of its breadth, is frequently selective, though never intentionally unrepresentative. Our aim has been to offer the general flavour of an area as well as a dip into some specific noteworthy studies. We have attempted to provide a comprehensive scientific account of contemporary personality research with traits centre stage, and with a strong supporting cast. This has been successfully accomplished in part elsewhere, though usually such books have been written at the level of the research monograph or have had a focus on a narrower range of traits (Eysenck, 1982; Eysenck and Eysenck, 1985; Brody, 1989; Zuckerman, 1991; Costa and McCrae, 1993). The level of the material has been pitched to appeal to interested senior undergraduates, postgraduate students, and career psychologists who wish to catch up on the contemporary scientific study of personality.

Preface to the second edition

The first edition of this book was motivated by the authors' perception that research on personality traits had reached a 'critical mass', that would justify a textbook focusing on the trait as an organising construct for understanding personality. We are gratified by the success of the first edition, which satisfied the need for a book on personality based on modern scientific research. Since the publication of the first edition, other authors appear to be distancing themselves from the traditional Hall of Fame text that we criticised initially. It is a relief to see the Hall of Fame approach receding into the distance so that the teaching of personality can be based on empirical data rather than historical relics.

We appreciate the feedback that we received from colleagues concerning the first edition. These comments helped to shape both the content and organisation of this new edition. We encourage academic faculty, practitioners and students to continue to share their opinions of the text with us. So far as content is concerned, the challenge has been to keep pace with the surge of new data and theorising on traits. In consequence, all chapters have been updated, and readers will note that a high proportion of the studies cited are recent. To better keep up with new developments, we invited a new author to join the original duo: Dr Whiteman brings expertise in health, epidemiology and lifespan aspects of personality.

Recent research confirms our original contention that trait research is becoming ever more interwoven into mainstream psychology. Focal topics as diverse as behaviour genetics, stress and abnormality simply cannot be understood without reference to traits. Several fields of inquiry have seen the extension and elaboration of research that we highlighted in the first edition. Recent psychometric studies largely take the Five Factor model as a reference point, even when seeking to fractionate or collapse its dimensions. The trend towards integration of trait psychology and social-cognitive psychology has accelerated, for example with the important new work on how Agreeableness relates to social behavior. We have also expanded our coverage of self-efficacy. In other cases, we have added much new material to develop more fully topics such as sex differences, brain-imaging studies, molecular genetics, psychopathy and traits in occupational psychology. We have added three new chapters to review in more depth personality across the lifespan, traits and health, and the practical applications of personality trait assessment. Other new research areas include psychophysiological studies inspired by recent work on reinforcement sensitivity, schizotypy, spirituality and the controversial but influential construct of emotional intelligence.

From its inception, the book has aimed to meet the needs of both the researcher requiring an introductory survey of traits, and the student of personality. Thus, we have also responded to feedback on the use of the book for teaching. The layout and structure are better geared to teaching needs: including summaries, space for notes, and more boxes on special topics. In addition, the new chapter on practical application is intended to emphasise the real-world utility of personality assessment (and its limitations), for the benefit of the practitioner.

As a closing thought, it is satisfying to see a valid edifice of personality psychology rising ever higher from its solid foundation in the rigorous assessment of stable traits. The flourishing dialogue between trait psychologists and social psychologists – traditional adversaries – is especially welcome: both sides have much to learn from one another. However, this undoubted success brings new challenges and issues. We have referred already to the potentially overwhelming volume of new research, which raises special difficulties for theory. How can we have a unified theory of personality traits that explains findings from so many disparate subdisciplines, ranging from molecular genetics to high-level social cognitive processes? We have sketched out some tentative suggestions for theory development in the concluding chapter. It is important also to maintain boundaries between core personality research and other disciplines. Social psychology and personality are often seen as a single field, but are there aspects of social psychology that should be sharply differentiated from personality? The possible evolutionary basis for human nature has been much debated of late, but perhaps it is unwise to merge evolutionary psychology with personality. We continue to anticipate the maturation of a trait-based personality science, but we also perceive a need for clarifying the scope of this science. We hope that this text continues to assist both students and working psychologists in grasping the basic principles and findings of research on personality traits.

Gerald Matthews
Ian Deary
Martha Whiteman

1

The nature of personality traits

1 The trait concept and personality theory

Everyday conceptions of traits

The idea of personality traits may be as old as human language itself. Aristotle (384–322 BC), writing the Ethics in the fourth century BC, saw dispositions such as vanity, modesty and cowardice as key determinants of moral and immoral behaviour. He also described individual differences in these dispositions, often referring to excess, defect and intermediate levels of each. His student Theophrastus (371–287 BC) wrote a book describing thirty 'characters' or personality types, of which a translator remarked that Theophrastus's title might better be rendered 'traits' (Rusten, 1993). Basic to his whole enterprise was the notion that individual good or bad traits of character may be isolated and studied separately.

Contemporary English is replete with terms used to describe personal qualities. Table 1.1 shows some examples: the five words rated by American college students as the most and least favourable words in Anderson's (1968) survey of 555 personality terms, together with five words given a neutral rating. Allport and Odbert (1936) identified almost 18,000 English personality-relevant terms; more words than Shakespeare used! Nouns, sentences and even actions may also have personality connotations (Hofstee, 1990). The language of personality description permeates our everyday conversation and discourse.

Everyday conceptions of personality traits make two key assumptions. First, traits are stable over time. Most people would accept that an individual's behaviour naturally varies somewhat from occasion to occasion, but would maintain also that there is a core of consistency which defines the individual's 'true nature': the unchangeable spots of the leopard. In other words, there are differences between individuals that are apparent across a variety of situations. We might expect a student we have noted as a 'worrier' to be unusually disturbed and worried in several different contexts such as examinations, social occasions and group discussions. Stability distinguishes traits from more transient properties of the person, such as temporary mood states. Second, it is generally believed that traits directly influence behaviour. If a person spontaneously breaks into cheerful song, we might 'explain' the behaviour by saying that he or she has a happy disposition. Such lay explanations are, of course, on shaky ground because of their circularity. Aristotle

Table 1.1 *Ratings of likeableness of some favourable, neutral and unfavourable traits*

Favourable traits		Neutral traits		Unfavourable traits	
Trait	Rating	Trait	Rating	Trait	Rating
Sincere	5.73	Quiet	3.11	Dishonest	0.41
Honest	5.55	Impulsive	3.07	Cruel	0.40
Understanding	5.49	Changeable	2.97	Mean	0.37
Loyal	5.47	Conservative	2.95	Phony	0.27
Truthful	5.45	Hesitant	2.90	Liar	0.26

Note Each word was rated on a 0–6 scale by 100 US college students
Source Anderson, 1968

suggested a more subtle, reciprocal causal hypothesis: that it is through actions that dispositions develop, which in turn influence actions.

> It is by refraining from pleasures that we become temperate, and it is when we have become temperate that we are most able to abstain from pleasures. (Thomson's, 1976, translation of the *Ethics*, 1104a: 33–35)

One of the major tasks for a scientific psychology of traits is to distinguish internal properties of the person from overt behaviours, and to investigate the causal relationships between them. To avoid circularity, it is essential to seek to identify the underlying physiological, psychological and social bases of traits, which are the true causal influences on behaviour.

Scientific conceptions of traits

This book places the concept of the trait at centre stage in the scientific study of human personality because, 'if there is to be a speciality called personality, its unique and therefore defining characteristic is traits' (Buss, 1989). There is a large gap between the everyday concept of a trait, and a concept that is scientifically useful. Several distinct steps are necessary for developing a science of traits. The first step is the measurement and classification of traits. The simplest technique for personality measurement is just to ask the person to rate how well trait adjectives such as those shown in Table 1.1 apply to himself or herself. We can also ask questions about behaviours that are thought to relate to personality. Measures of the extraversion–introversion trait typically ask whether the person enjoys parties, meeting people and other social activities, for example. We can also have a person who knows the respondent well, such as a spouse or close friend, provide ratings of his or her personality. Traits need not be measured solely by verbal report: real-world actions and behaviour in the laboratory may be assessed too (Cattell, 1973). We would expect an extraverted person to belong to many clubs and societies, for example. Experimental tests of typically extraverted behaviours may also be devised, such as amount of laughter at jokes and willingness to respond rapidly but inaccurately. In practice, however, personality measures based on objective

Table 1.2 *Examples of experimental studies showing correspondences between traits and objective behavioural measures*

Study	Trait	Behavioural measure
Carment, Miles and Cervin (1965)	Extraversion	More time spent talking
Edman, Levander and Schalling (1983)	Impulsivity	Faster reaction time
De Julio and Duffy (1977)	Neuroticism	Greater distance from experimenter chosen
Ganzer (1968)	Test anxiety	More time spent looking away from the task during testing
Newman, Patterson and Kosson (1987)	Psychopathy	More persistence in gambling when consistently losing

behavioural tests have had only limited success, and few have been validated (see Kline, 1993). Verbal report has been the preferred method of trait assessment used by personality researchers.

As we have seen already there is a huge number of words which may be used to describe personality. Many of these words have rather similar meanings: precise, careful, meticulous and painstaking would all seem to relate to some common quality of conscientiousness. Such overlapping traits can be grouped together as a broad aspect or dimension of personality. The question then becomes: what is the number of broad dimensions needed to describe the main elements of any individual personality? Much research effort has been devoted to drawing up classificatory schemes of fundamental personality dimensions: estimates of the number required range from three to thirty or so.

There is no guarantee that people's self-descriptions are accurate. The second step in personality research is to test whether and how traits relate to behaviours. Table 1.2 gives some examples of correlations obtained empirically between personality traits and objectively assessed behavioural measures. In each case, the data imply that the person's self-ratings or questionnaire responses are at least partially accurate. Traits may also be useful in applied settings, in predicting a person's job performance, or the response of a patient to therapy, for example. A related research question is the consistency of behaviour in various situations. The implicit assumption of the trait approach is that people do in fact tend to behave consistently in different settings, an assumption which has been vigorously challenged, as we shall see in chapter 2.

A science of personality traits requires a final, but difficult step: development of a satisfactory theory of personality traits. We may be able to assess people's levels of extraversion and other traits, and show that our assessment predicts some aspects of their behaviour, but in themselves these observations tell us nothing about why the personality dimension predicts behaviour. One difficulty is that personality may be represented at a variety of levels of psychological description. For example, extraversion might be associated with simple properties of the central nervous system, such as the excitability of individual neurones, or with style of information processing, or with acquired social knowledge and beliefs. We can only distinguish these broad possibilities by the normal, somewhat laborious scientific methods of formulating specific hypotheses and testing them rigorously against experimental and observational evidence.

There are also some more subtle conceptual problems to be overcome. There is some question over whether we can ever develop a general scientific theory of traits at all. The idiographic approach to personality (e.g., Lamiell, 1981) considers that all aspects of personality are fundamentally unique and idiosyncratic to each individual, so that no generalised theoretical statements are possible. In this book, we adopt the alternative nomothetic approach, which assumes that we can arrive at general hypotheses concerning stable individual differences through the normal scientific method. We cannot, of course, expect such hypotheses to predict all or even most of the person's behaviour; the uniqueness of individuals seems secure.

Causal primacy. There is uncertainty too over the causal status of traits. Suppose we have a person who obtains a high score on a measure of neuroticism, and also shows clinical symptoms of mild depression. Did neuroticism cause depression, did depression cause neuroticism, or are both qualities independently influenced by some additional causal factor such as a stressful life event? A traditional assumption of trait theorists has been the *causal primacy* of traits. Although, as suggested by Aristotle, there is probably some reciprocity of causal influence between traits and behaviours, it has often been supposed that the dominant direction of causality is from trait to behaviour. For example, Brody (1994) stated that 'I assume that personality traits are causal. They are genotypically influenced latent characteristics of persons that determine the way in which individuals respond to the social world they encounter.' That is, although measures of traits such as questionnaire scores are not causal agents themselves, they validly index underlying physiological or psychological structures which directly influence behaviour. One of the pioneering trait psychologists, Gordon Allport (1937), saw traits as organised mental structures, varying from person to person, which initiate and guide behaviour.

There are two important qualifications to this general principle. First, as Hettema and Deary (1993) pointed out, the explaining of behaviour requires different levels of analysis, including genetics, physiology, learning and social factors. Allport's notion that all the various manifestations of traits can be explained at a single level of 'mental structure' is simplistic. Hence, causal models of trait action will vary depending on the level investigated, although the ultimate research aim is to develop a trait theory that will interrelate the various levels. Second, the causal effects of traits on behaviour may be indirect. As discussed in chapter 2, traits interact with situational factors to produce transient internal conditions or states, which may sometimes be a more direct influence on behaviour than the trait. For example, trait anxiety may interact with an immediate situational threat to generate transient state anxiety, which in turn disrupts ongoing information processing and impairs performance (Spielberger, 1966).

Inner locus. A second traditional assumption is that of the *inner locus* of traits. The most important traits, such as extraversion and neuroticism (a broad tendency to experience negative emotions), are assumed by some to relate to some fundamental, core quality of the person, which might be influenced substantially by genetic factors (Eysenck, 1967; McCrae et al., 2000). Again, even within theories that are sympathetic to the traditional view of traits, there has been some modification of the basic view. For example, Cattell and Kline (1977) distinguished 'surface' traits, which are simply clusters of overt responses which tend to be associated, from 'source' traits, which are deeper properties of the person with causal effects on behaviour. Modern developments of traditional theory seek to identify and explain underlying sources of consistency in behaviour, whether these are conceived of as genetic, physiological or cognitive in nature. The process of relating operationally defined measures such as questionnaire scores to theory is often referred to as construct validation, and is discussed further below.

Both assumptions of traditional trait theory – their causal primacy and inner locus – have been challenged more radically. The alternative to causal primacy is the view that traits are a construction with no independent causal status. For example, Buss and Craik (1983) argued that traits are simply descriptions of natural categories of acts. Wright and Mischel (1987) characterised traits as conditional statements of situation–behaviour contingencies. Furthermore, traits may be jointly constructed by two or more people in social interaction, according to the social dynamics of the situation (Hampson, 1988). Social psychological approaches to traits tend also to abandon the inner locus assumption. Even if traits represent genuine psychological structures, these structures may be no more than the superficial mask the person presents to the outside world, in order to present a socially acceptable self-image to other people. Such challenges to traditional views of traits are explored in more detail in chapters 5 and 8.

The upshot of these considerations is that there is no generally accepted scientific theory of traits. Some trait theorists have tended to take the relatively easy option of focusing on the dimensional structure and measurement of traits rather than investigating their underlying nature (Goldberg, 1993). However, it should be clear from the preceding discussion that we cannot accept trait descriptions at face value, and that there may be various qualitatively different types of explanation for consistencies in self-reports and behaviours. In recent years progress has been made in developing psychobiological information processing, and social psychological trait theories which are partly complementary and partly competing accounts. One of the major aims of this book is to show that trait psychology requires these theoretical endeavours as well as its traditional concern with psychometrics. Development of successful theories is necessary for the study of traits to take its rightful place as a fundamental area of psychological science.

A brief history of traits

The scientific study of traits develops two aspects of common-sense discourse on personality. First, it formalises the tendency in natural language to use trait descriptors of individuals. Second, it formalises the popular awareness that there are generalities of personality, such that individuals of a similar disposition may be grouped together. This tendency is seen in folk psychology: astrology has twelve personality-based sun signs, and there is a Chinese custom of ascribing certain aspects of personality to the year in which a person was born; for instance, those born in the years of the cow are said to be conscientious and hardworking. Traits emerged from folk psychology and medicine, and from natural language. The history of traits is a story which may be told in various ways: through tracing the counterparts to extraversion and neuroticism identified in different epochs (Eysenck and Eysenck, 1969; Eysenck, 1981), or through emphasising the evolution of the currently dominant five factor model of personality (Goldberg, 1993). We confine ourselves to highlighting three aspects of the history of traits: the influence of classical thinking, the earliest scientific work on traits, and the emergence of current models of personality.

The four humours

Amongst the earliest progenitors of present-day trait theories, apart from Aristotle and Theophrastus, were Hippocrates (ca. 460–377 BC) and Galen of Pergamum (AD 130–200) (Stelmack and Stalikas, 1991). The Hippocratic conception of the aetiology of physical illnesses was based upon the theory of humours, or bodily fluids, notably blood, phlegm, black bile and yellow bile. It was in the writings of Galen, a Greek physician, that the humours became the bases of temperaments. Galen's temperamental terms, melancholic (tending towards low mood), choleric (tending toward anger), phlegmatic (tending towards stolid calmness) and sanguine (tending towards optimism and confidence), survive in today's English. When the humours were blended in a balanced fashion, an optimal temperament resulted:

> in his soul he is in the middle of boldness and timidity, of negligence and impertinence, of compassion and envy. He is cheerful, affectionate, charitable and prudent. (Stelmack and Stalikas, 1991, p. 259)

Imbalance led to physical illness, but also to mental disturbance. For example, the melancholic temperament, associated with feelings of depression and anxiety, resulted from an excess of black bile. In the seventeenth century, Burton's (1837; originally published 1621) description of the melancholic character has some resemblance to the high neuroticism scorer on a present-day personality questionnaire,

> that which is a flea-biting to one causeth unsufferable torment to another; and which one by his singular moderation and well-composed carriage can happily overcome, a second is no whit able to sustain; but, upon every small occasion of misconceived abuse, injury, grief, disgrace, loss, cross, rumour etc. (if solitary,

or idle) yields so far to passion, that his complexion is altered, his digestion hindred, his sleep gone, his spirits obscured, and his heart heavy, his hypocondries misaffected; wind, crudity, on a sudden overtake him, and he himself overcome with melancholy. (vol. 1, p. 140)

The humoral terms exist today merely as descriptive metaphors. Their aetiological significance did not long outlast the Middle Ages. Immanuel Kant recast the four humoral temperaments along the dimensions of 'feeling' and 'activity' to yield a typology of four simple temperaments that emphasised their psychological nature. The humoral terms also appear in the writings of the father of modern psychology, Wilhelm Wundt. Wundt described the four temperamental types in terms of two dimensions: strong–weak emotions versus changeable–unchangeable activity. The relationships between the humoral terms and the schemes of temperament classification devised by Kant and Wundt are shown in figure 1.1. Stelmack and Stalikas (1991) described the relationship between these schemes and the present-day dimensions of neuroticism and extraversion as 'uncanny'. However,

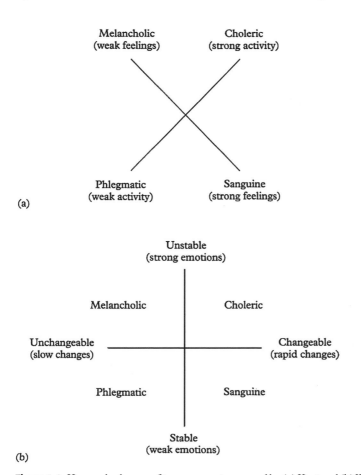

Figure 1.1 Humoral schemes of temperament proposed by (a) Kant and (b) Wundt

any veracity they have is owed to shrewd psychological observation and not the classical theory of the humours.

Beginnings of the science of traits

Three ingredients were required for the initiation of scientific research on traits: systematic data collection, statistical techniques for data analysis, and development of testable theories. These prerequisites became available around the beginning of the twentieth century. Of key importance were the new techniques of correlation and, somewhat later, factor analysis (Gorsuch, 1983). Before the introduction of factor analysis there was no objective method for reducing the huge numbers of trait terms to a manageable number of broad dimensions. Thurstone's (1947) introduction of multiple factor analysis proved particularly influential, and the systematic use of factor analysis began the modern research era in personality.

The first empirical studies

The raw materials, or stimuli, for some early researchers were gathered from the dictionary. Sir Francis Galton (1884) was prescient in hypothesising that individual differences in personality might be represented in natural language terms, and trawling Roget's Thesaurus for character-descriptive terms. This was later dubbed the 'lexical hypothesis', for which De Raad (2000) provides a history. Pioneers of empirical personality research included the Dutch psychologists Heymans and Wiersma who, in a series of papers between 1906 and 1909, obtained ratings of character for large numbers of subjects and attempted to reduce these to smaller numbers of factors or dimensions. They employed a statistical method that was conceptually related to factor analysis, though much more crude, and obtained three factors. Eysenck (1970) identified the first dimension with emotionality, and the other two with introversion–extraversion.

After Spearman's (1904) epoch-making study of mental ability, in which he discovered general intelligence and introduced an embryonic form of factor analysis, similar techniques were used under his supervision to analyse character. Webb (1915) collected detailed ratings of mental qualities on 194 students at a teacher training college and 140 younger schoolboys. The individual rating items were collected under the headings of intellect, emotions, sociality, activity, and self qualities. Webb used such statistical techniques as were available to deduce that, after general intelligence had been extracted, a second general factor of character could be identified. This second factor was called 'persistence of motives' or 'will'. There are many aspects of Webb's study which make it a good source of data: the subject sample was large, the ratings were performed consistently, by more than one rater, for each subject over an extended period of time, and the range of personality qualities assessed was broad. As a result, it has been re-analysed at intervals since its publication: these re-analyses are documented by Eysenck (1970). A comprehensive re-analysis showed that five or six factors existed in Webb's data, and trait researchers consider them to be very similar to modern dimensions of personality (Deary, 1996).

The beginnings of trait theory

In addition to minimally adequate statistical procedures for dealing with traits, and some conception of where to begin to search for trait stimuli, there was a contemporaneous theoretical development of trait psychology. In part, this theoretical development was driven by an awareness of the fact that trait psychology was perforce beginning with commonsense terms in everyday use. Allport (1937) commented that:

> To use trait terms, but to use them cautiously, is, then, our lot. Nor need we fear them simply because they bear the age-long sanction of common sense.

Carr and Kingsbury's article from 1938 addressed many core issues of trait psychology at a conceptual level. They emphasised the predictive nature of traits, i.e., knowing the traits of an individual was predictive of that person's likely future behaviour. Moreover, they articulated the notion that traits were not directly observable – traits may only be inferred from behaviour. This continues to be the view of prominent trait theorists. For example, McCrae et al. (2000, p. 175) stated,

> Traits cannot be directly observed, but rather must be inferred from patterns of behaviour and experience that are known to be valid trait indicators.

Carr and Kingsbury emphasised the need for trait scales in order to compare individuals on a given characteristic. They lamented the blind progress of trait psychology and its lack of 'principles of orientation in reference to the concept'. This last continued to be one of the most contentious issues in the theory of traits (Pervin, 1994). One of their closing comments is ironic when one reflects on the pre-eminence of the dimensions of neuroticism (emotional stability) and introversion–extraversion today,

> We may note that abnormal and clinical psychology have evinced no interest in the popular traits, but have developed a new set of traits that are supposed to possess a distinctive value for their purposes. We refer to such traits as introversion and extraversion, submission and ascendancy, emotional stability, mal-adjustment, and integration. Perhaps a systematic psychology should likewise be concerned with the development and study of a set of new traits that are relevant to its purposes.

Perhaps the most comprehensive contribution to the conceptual development of trait psychology, and of personality psychology more generally, is Allport's (1937) book, *Personality: a Psychological Interpretation*. Much of present-day trait psychology may be considered as empirical footnotes to Allport's chapters 9–12, where he laid out the tasks for, and difficulties facing, the personality psychologist.

Allport's resounding 'Resume of the Doctrine of Traits' began with the famous sentence,

> In everyday life, no one, not even a psychologist, doubts that underlying the conduct of a mature person there are characteristic dispositions or traits.

In addition to the common traits that are emphasised in the present book (indicative of the nomothetic approach), Allport also emphasised those traits which are more specific to individuals and that are not prone to distribute normally in the population (indicating that an idiographic approach is necessary also). Allport's account of traits was able to embrace many disparate approaches. Thus, in addition to accommodating differential psychologists, his overall definition of traits moved Murray (1938) to indicate that his 'needs' – identified by a depth psychology approach using biographical interviews and projective tests – could also be conceptualised as traits, such as need for achievement (nAch).

Psychometric approaches to identifying personality dimensions

Questionnaire construction and psychometrics

Contemporary views of traits are intimately related to the processes of measurement and assessment necessary to identify basic personality dimensions. Typically, the trait researcher has some hypothesis about the number and nature of the principal dimensions, and designs a questionnaire to measure them. Subsequent work investigates how useful a measuring device the questionnaire actually is, and modifies the questionnaire items in response to any shortcomings detected.

The initial development of a satisfactory questionnaire for measuring traits is not easy. Care must be taken in the composition of items: they must be easily understood and unambiguous, applicable to all respondents, and unlikely to cause offence (see Angleitner and Wiggins, 1986). There should also be some systematic sampling of the various expressions of the personality trait of interest. It is important also to check that items are not strongly contaminated by response sets or biases, such as social desirability, yea-saying or extreme responding (see also chapter 13). However carefully the questionnaire has been designed, it is still necessary to assess its adequacy formally, by application of psychometrics, the science of psychological measurement. Psychometrics provides statistical techniques which tell us how good a measuring tool a particular questionnaire is, just as we might assess the accuracy of a thermometer or balance in the physical sciences. The sophistication of modern techniques and the number-crunching power afforded by computers provide the contemporary researcher with powers of data analysis far beyond those envisaged by the pioneering trait researchers. Today's researcher is in some danger of becoming a sorcerer's apprentice though, as the increasing availability of powerful statistical packages raises the risk of misapplication and abuse of statistics. Hence, understanding traits requires at least a rudimentary grasp of psychometrics. In this section, we provide a brief, non-technical overview of some of the key psychometric techniques applied to personality assessment. Of particular concern is factor analysis, because of its use in investigations of the fundamental structure of personality traits. For a more detailed review of psychometric statistics and personality measurement, Kline's (1993, 2000) accessible books are recommended. The reader should also note the importance of the Pearson correlation coefficient (r) in psychometrics. A thorough grasp of this statistic and its limitations is invaluable in understanding research on personality traits. Howell (2002) and Jensen (1980) offer good introductory accounts of Pearson's r.

Psychometrics of single scales

Any single trait scale must be satisfactory with respect to three essential criteria: *reliability*, *stability* and *validity* (for more detailed accounts, see Anastasi and Urbina, 1997; Cronbach, 1990; Jensen, 1980; and chapter 13).

Reliability. This refers to the accuracy with which the questionnaire measures a given quality. At this stage, we are not committing ourselves to specifying what that quality actually is. Reliability may be assessed by administering two alternative measures of the trait to a sample of subjects, and computing the correlation between them. If the correlation is high, the quality can be assessed consistently and the scale is reliable or *internally consistent*. If not, the two supposedly equivalent forms are not assessing the same quality, the scale is unreliable, and the items must be revised. The Cronbach alpha statistic is a widely used measure of reliability calculated from a single set of test items. It is, in effect, the correlation of the test with itself. In general, alpha tends to increase both as inter-item correlation increases, and as the number of items on the test increases.

Stability. Reliability should be distinguished from stability, which is the test–retest correlation of the scale over a given time interval. Personality is expected to change slowly as the person grows older, but it is expected that stabilities of trait measures will be fairly high over periods of a year or more. If we have a scale that is reliable, but has a low test–retest correlation, we may be assessing a mood or some other transient quality of the person, rather than a genuine trait.

Validity. The third essential quality for a personality questionnaire is validity: it must be shown that the measure actually does assess what it purports to assess. A scale may be reliable but not valid. For example, a fortune teller might use a highly consistent method for inferring a person's future from the lines on their palm, but the consistency of the technique would be no guarantee that the fortune teller's predictions were accurate. The most straightforward and convincing method for assessing validity is referred to as *criterion* or *predictive validity*. The trait measure is correlated with some independent index of a quality associated with the trait, as in the studies listed in table 1.2. Other external criteria frequently used in personality research include measures of job performance and behaviour, psychophysiological functioning and clinical abnormality. Establishing predictive validity is important in the early part of questionnaire development and in applied settings. However, the ultimate goal of theory-driven trait research is to establish *construct validity*. The essence of construct validity is that correlations between the trait and external criteria are predicted in advance from an adequate scientific theory, rather than from common sense or a superficial analysis of trait characteristics. For example, we could use a psychobiological theory of personality to predict how a particular trait should correlate with measures of autonomic functioning, such as heart rate. Construct validity arises out of the total web of empirical data and theoretical analysis which builds up around a trait, sometimes referred to as its *nomological network* (Eysenck, 1981). The difficulties of construct validity are those of establishing scientific truth. Even 'good' theories are never fully satisfactory, and require periodic modification of hypotheses and concepts as new research findings are obtained (see Lakatos, 1976). Hence, construct validity is always somewhat provisional, and may be reduced or enhanced by fresh research. There are various other forms of validity, but they are of less importance than predictive and construct validity.

Psychometrics of multiple traits: factor analysis

The methods just described may be used to obtain a satisfactory scale for measuring a single trait, such as extraversion or agreeableness. However, we cannot arrive at a satisfactory model of personality simply by accumulating different traits. Inevitably, some of the traits will be positively correlated, and it will be uncertain whether the traits concerned are genuinely distinct, or simply different aspects of some unitary trait. The technique most widely used for the simultaneous identification of multiple traits is factor analysis, described in more detail by Gorsuch (1983) and, in a text for beginners, by Kline (1994). The input to a factor analysis is the matrix representing all possible correlations between the various items making up a questionnaire or questionnaires. The aim is to simplify the correlation matrix, by identifying one or more underlying dimensions or factors which account for most of the variation in individuals' item scores. Factors are defined by the individual items which correlate with or 'load' on them.

Let us look at an example of a simple factor-analysis, using trait data taken from a study by Matthews and Oddy (1993). One thousand and ten people working in British business occupations rated themselves on a set of personality-descriptive adjectives. Table 1.3 shows the correlation matrix for ratings on twelve of these adjectives, divided into three sets. Each set of four adjectives was thought to relate to a different broad personality trait: Conscientiousness, Agreeableness and Intellectance (self-rated intelligence and intellectual interest). The pattern of correlations seems to accord with this expectation. For example, correlations between the four conscientiousness items are moderately large, ranging from 0.35 to 0.54. Correlations between the conscientiousness items and the other adjectives are considerably smaller, ranging from 0.01 to 0.25. That is, if a person is hardworking, it is likely that they are also industrious, conscientious and meticulous, but we

Table 1.3 *Correlations between trait descriptive adjectives thought to relate to conscientiousness, agreeableness and intellectance (n = 1,010)*

Trait adjective	1	2	3	4	5	6	7	8	9	10	11	12
1 Hardworking	1.00											
2 Industrious	0.54	1.00										
3 Conscientious	0.47	0.47	1.00									
4 Meticulous	0.38	0.35	0.41	1.00								
5 Compassionate	0.24	0.12	0.21	0.16	1.00							
6 Tender-hearted	0.16	0.06	0.17	0.14	0.59	1.00						
7 Loving	0.21	0.12	0.19	0.15	0.42	0.51	1.00					
8 Mild	0.08	0.01	0.10	0.14	0.24	0.40	0.25	1.00				
9 Brainy	0.15	0.20	0.12	0.12	0.08	0.09	0.10	−0.06	1.00			
10 Knowledgeable	0.19	0.25	0.18	0.12	0.05	0.01	0.07	0.01	0.45	1.00		
11 Wise	0.22	0.21	0.25	0.22	0.14	0.13	0.15	0.07	0.38	0.38	1.00	
12 Intelligent	0.14	0.21	0.17	0.09	0.03	−0.00	0.10	−0.13	0.62	0.48	0.39	1.00

Source Matthews and Oddy, 1993

cannot predict whether they will also be agreeable or intellectual. Intuitively, we might say that there is an underlying dimension of conscientiousness, associated with all four related adjectives, together with distinct dimensions of agreeableness and intellectance. Factor analysis aims to show whether such intuitions are actually in agreement with the data, by re-describing the data in terms of hypothetical underlying constructs or factors. Its end-point is a listing of the correlations between each factor and each of the initial variables. Hence, if there is a 'conscientiousness' factor it should correlate with each of the four conscientiousness items, but it should be largely uncorrelated with the remaining items.

Table 1.4 shows the factor matrix obtained following extraction of three factors. The first factor is defined mainly by the intellectance items, the second by the conscientiousness items, and the third by the agreeableness items. We can now describe individuals' personalities in terms of three dimensions rather than twelve. (For the knowledgeable reader, we have run a principal components analysis, followed by varimax rotation. Note that there is a technical difference between 'factor analysis' and 'principal components analysis', which is not important in the present context.) Techniques exist for calculating factor scores that would describe any individual's intellectance, conscientiousness and agreeableness. Together, the three factors explain 59% of the variance in the original correlation matrix. This considerable gain in economy of description is bought at a moderate cost in loss of information about individual item responses. The assumption of factor analysis is that the information discarded is trivial, largely error and item-specific variance.

In a non-technical exposition of this kind, we cannot adequately explain the actual computation of the factor matrix (see Jensen, 1980; and Kline, 1993, 1994 for more detailed but accessible accounts). In brief, there are two stages to the

Table 1.4 *Factor solution obtained from correlational data of table 1.3*

	Factor 1	Factor 2	Factor 3
Hardworking	0.12	0.77	0.14
Industrious	0.19	0.78	−0.03
Conscientious	0.11	0.76	0.14
Meticulous	0.05	0.68	0.13
Compassionate	0.07	0.15	0.76
Tender-hearted	0.04	0.05	0.86
Loving	0.13	0.12	0.71
Mild	−0.12	0.05	0.60
Brainy	0.82	0.04	0.03
Knowledgeable	0.73	0.15	−0.02
Wise	0.62	0.21	0.15
Intelligent	0.84	0.07	−0.06

Note Factor solution obtained from principal components analysis, followed by varimax rotation

analysis, each of which produces a factor solution. The second-stage solution (shown in table 1.4) is usually preferred to the first-stage solution (not shown). At the first stage, the general principle is that the first factor extracted explains as much of the variation in data as possible. For the correlations shown in table 1.3, the first factor explains 28% of the variance. The next factor extracted then explains as much as possible of the remaining variance: 18% in the example. Subsequent factors are extracted on the same basis, with the third factor extracted from the table 1.3 data explaining 13% of the variance. In personality research, the principle of grabbing as much variance as possible for each successive factor does not usually give psychologically meaningful results. (The position is different in research on ability tests, where the first factor is typically an approximation to *g* or general intelligence.) The second stage of the analysis capitalises on the fact that there is an infinite number of mathematically equivalent factor matrices which may be extracted from a given correlation matrix. We can recompute the factor matrix to explain exactly the same amount of variance using different values for the factor loadings. This re-computation is referred to as rotation, because it can be illustrated geometrically (e.g., Kline, 1993, chapter 8). The principle used to guide rotation is that of simple structure, the assumption that the most meaningful factor solution is the one for which factor interpretation is most clearcut. The various methods of rotation aim to maximise the number of loadings which are either 1.0 or 0.0, so we can say unequivocally whether or not a given variable is associated with a given factor. The factor matrix shown in table 1.4 has been rotated, and approximates to simple structure: large loadings are all 0.60 or more, whereas small loadings do not exceed 0.21. Rotation re-assigns variance across factors more evenly: the three factors shown in table 1.4 explain 20%, 20% and 19% of the variance, respectively.

Limitations of factor analysis

No factor analysis should ever be accepted uncritically. Three questions should always be asked. The first is whether the data are actually suitable for factor analysis. Since the technique is based on Pearson correlation, its validity depends on whether the original correlations are satisfactory. For example, correlation does not represent non-linear relationships validly, and correlations will be reduced if measures are unreliable or if the range of variable scores is restricted (Jensen, 1980). It is important that there are sufficient items which relate to or 'mark' each hypothesised personality dimension. Factor analysis also requires large sample sizes, particularly when there are many items and when loadings of items on factors are expected to be small.

The second question is how much the results depend on the particular methods of analysis used. Factor analysis should really be seen as a family of related techniques, and the exact choice of method may profoundly influence the eventual solution. In the example of factor analysis described previously, the 'orthogonal' rotation that was used forced the factors to be independent, that is, uncorrelated. However, we could also have chosen an 'oblique' rotation that allowed the factors to be correlated if that gave better simple structure. Another key choice is the number of factors extracted (Zwick and Velicer, 1986). There is a number of rules for deciding how many factors should be extracted from a set of items, but none is definitive.

The third, and most difficult, question is what the results actually mean. Critics of factor analysis point out that the mathematical equivalence of alternative factor solutions make all of them suspect. This criticism is probably overstated. As we shall see, use of the simple structure criterion for rotation has led to real progress in identifying scientifically useful personality measures. The essential point is that factor analysis does no more than indicate structural relationships among sets of variables. Construct validity must be established for factorial dimensions just as it must for single scales, by relating factorial measures to external criteria, and developing a testable scientific theory.

Further techniques of factor analysis

The techniques discussed so far are *exploratory*: the researcher relies on simple structure or some other theory-neutral, empirical criterion to determine the eventual factor solution rather than any hypothesised target solution. Thus, exploratory factor analysis can only suggest hypotheses. A newer approach, *confirmatory factor analysis* (Jöreskog, 1973), allows hypothesis testing, because the pattern of factor loadings for a given set of items tested on a subject sample is specified in advance. The factor analysis calculates the factor solution which is closest to the hypothesised factor matrix, and computes the goodness of fit between actual and hypothesised matrices. The researcher can then gauge whether or not the data provide an acceptable fit to the initial hypothesis. Confirmatory factor analysis is part of a larger group of techniques known as *structural modelling* (Bentler, 1995; Byrne, 2000). The researcher may specify any set of relationships between directly observed variables, and unmeasured or latent factors, and test whether the hypothetical model fits the data. Unlike conventional factor analysis, structural modelling may formally test for fit among competing models, so it is particularly useful for establishing construct validity.

If the investigator chooses an oblique rotation, which allows derived personality factors to be correlated, an intriguing possibility arises. If the factors are in fact correlated, we can run a further factor analysis of the correlations between the factors themselves. This second factor analysis will then identify *second-order* or secondary factors. For example, in cognitive ability research the initial factor analysis of test scores often gives us a set of 'primary' abilities, such as verbal, mathematical and spatial abilities, which are all positively intercorrelated. Factoring the correlations between these somewhat specific abilities then defines broader, higher-order ability factors, such as general intelligence or *g*. Similarly, in personality research, we may obtain secondary, or broader, personality factors by factoring correlated primary, or narrower, personality trait measures. In the next section of this chapter, we review attempts to establish a comprehensive set of primary trait dimensions, which could be used to provide a detailed description of an individual's personality. In the following section, we look at efforts to describe personality in terms of secondary traits such as extraversion and neuroticism.

Primary factors of personality: the 16PF and other questionnaires

The Sixteen Personality Factor Questionnaire (16PF)

Discussion of primary traits must begin with the work of Raymond B. Cattell. The Cattellian project is one of the most ambitious ever undertaken in psychology. It seeks to explain individual differences in every area of life from psychometrically sound measures of ability, motivation, personality and mood. Massive quantities of data have been generated by this enterprise (see, e.g., Cattell, 1971; Cattell and Kline, 1977), along with several widely used questionnaires and tests. Cattell (e.g., 1946) began his personality research with the lexicon of trait-descriptive words, but shifted the main focus of his work to questionnaire items early in his research career. He eventually identified twenty-three fundamental primary factors, one of which is an ability factor, general intelligence. The sixteen most robust of these dimensions are measured by the Sixteen Personality Factor Questionnaire (16PF: Cattell, Eber and Tatsuoka, 1970), which has been extensively used in research and applied settings over several decades. Cattell et al.'s (1970) version of the 16PF became a standard personality measure, but attracted a number of psychometric criticisms. Internal consistencies of some of the scales were low, and several investigators (e.g., Barrett and Kline, 1982; Matthews, 1989) were unable to recover the Cattellian primary factors from factor analysis of the 16PF.

The latest version of the 16PF, the 16PF5 (Conn and Rieke, 1994), features improved internal consistency, with a mean Cronbach alpha for the sixteen scales of 0.74, although some alphas remain relatively modest (less than 0.70). However, internal consistency may have been increased at the cost of loss of comparability with previous 16PF versions. 51 per cent of the 16PF5 items are new or substantially revised, and correlations between equivalent scales on the 16PF5 and the previous version of the 16PF (Cattell et al., 1970) are small or modest in most cases (less than 0.6 for eleven scales, and less than 0.4 for four scales). The 16PF has a hierarchical factor structure, such that secondary factors may be derived from the intercorrelations of the sixteen primary factors (Chernyshenko, Stark and Chan, 2001). As we shall see subsequently, there is some correspondence between the 16PF secondaries and the personality factors of the five factor model, sometimes called the Big Five. Table 1.5 provides descriptions of the 16PF scales, together with examples of historical and literary figures who exemplify the qualities assessed. These should not be taken too seriously, in the absence of actual questionnaire data. The table also gives 16PF5 alpha coefficients. Note that in this and subsequent tables we adopt the common convention of omitting the decimal point from reliability and correlation coefficients.

Extensive evidence on the predictive validity of the various versions of the 16PF has been obtained. We provide two examples here. Barton, Dielman and Cattell (1971) found significant correlations between several 16PF primary scales and achievement in various school subjects. The high achiever at this level of education is outgoing (A+), conscientious (G+), venturesome (H+), self-assured (O−), and self-controlled (Q3+). None of the personality traits predicts achievement as much as intelligence (B) does, but other, similar research (Cattell and Butcher, 1968) shows that personality predicts achievement even when intelligence is statistically controlled. Figure 1.2 shows mean levels of the traits for three occupational groups, which differ as we might expect. Note the social reserve of physicists (low A and H), the high sensitivity (I) and imaginativeness (M) of artists, and the calmness of airline hostesses (high C, low Q4). A large study of the 16PF5 among Church of England clergy showed that, within this occupational group, many of the usual gender differences were reversed: female clergy were less outgoing (A), more emotionally stable (C), more dominant (E), less rule-conscious (G), less emotionally sensitive (I), less apprehensive (O), and more open to change (Q1) (Musson, 2001). The 16PF is also useful for discriminating various clinical groups from one another and from normal subjects.

Although the 16PF has good predictive validity, doubts remain about the construct validity of the 16PF scales. Cattell (1973) provides detailed descriptions of qualities associated with the scales, which include references to experimental and psychophysiological data. However, there has been little attempt to use this

Table 1.5 *The fifteen personality traits assessed by the 16PF, with examples of famous individuals exemplifying the traits, and 16PF5 alpha coefficients*

Trait	Trait descriptions High	Low	Famous individuals High	Low	Alpha
A	Outgoing Warmhearted	Reserved Detached	Falstaff	Greta Garbo	69
C	Unemotional Calm	Emotional Changeable	Washington	Hamlet	78
E	Assertive Dominant	Humble Cooperative	Genghis Khan	Jesus	66
F	Cheerful Lively	Sober Taciturn	Groucho Marx	Clint Eastwood	72
G	Conscientious Persistent	Expedient Undisciplined	Mother Teresa	Casanova	75
H	Venturesome Socially bold	Shy Retiring	Columbus	Sylvia Plath	85
I	Tough-minded Self-reliant	Tender-minded Sensitive	James Bond	Robert Burns	77
L	Suspicious Sceptical	Trusting Accepting	De Gaulle	Pollyanna	74
M	Imaginative Bohemian	Practical Conventional	Van Gogh	Henry Ford	74
N	Shrewd Discreet	Forthright Straightforward	Machiavelli	Joan of Arc	75
O	Guilt-prone Worrying	Resilient Self-assured	Dostoevsky	Stalin	78
Q1	Radical Experimental	Conservative Traditional	Karl Marx	Queen Victoria	64
Q2	Self-sufficient Resourceful	Group-dependent Affiliative	Copernicus	Marilyn Monroe	78
Q3	Controlled Compulsive	Undisciplined Lax	Margaret Thatcher	Mick Jagger	71
Q4	Tense Driven	Relaxed Tranquil	Macbeth	Buddha	76

Note Dimension B (Intelligence) is omitted. Examples of famous individuals are partly taken from Cattell (1973)

Sources Cattell, 1973; Conn and Rieke, 1994

descriptive information on scale correlates to derive detailed, testable hypotheses concerning the nature of the psychological constructs associated with the scales. Cattell's (1983) favoured theoretical approach is the construction of linear equations which predict behaviour from individual difference measures. However, most psychologists would see this approach as essentially descriptive; the nature of the constructs linked to behaviour remains obscure.

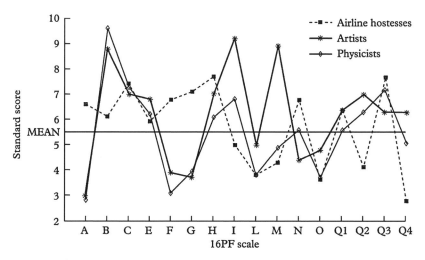

Figure 1.2 Mean scores obtained on the 16PF by three occupational groups
Source Cattell and Kline, 1977

Other systems of primary factors

Several other questionnaires attempt to assess primary traits comprehensively but most suffer from deficiencies more serious than those of the 16PF (see Kline, 1993, for a review). Perhaps the most popular is the California Psychological Inventory (CPI: Gough, 1987; Gough and Bradley, 1996) which assesses eighteen traits with moderately good reliability, and is widely used in industry. However, development of the CPI made no reference to factor analysis. Instead, the method of *criterion-keying* was used: items were chosen on the basis of their ability to discriminate criterion groups. This method has the serious disadvantage that scales may not correspond to those obtained by factor analysis, and, in the absence of systematic experimental studies, construct validity is lacking (see Kline, 1993). A more recent questionnaire is the Occupational Personality Questionnaire (Saville et al., 1984), which measures thirty-one traits relevant to personnel recruitment and selection, career development and training. Reliability of the scales is good, although, like the CPI, the thirty-one-trait model is not explicitly based on factor analysis. A recent re-analysis of the OPQ standardisation data (Matthews and Stanton, 1994) concluded that only about twenty dimensions could be identified through factor analysis of the items, although correspondences between these dimensions and the traits hypothesised by Saville et al. (1984) were good. There is also encouraging evidence for the validity of the OPQ traits (Saville et al., 1996).

Higher-order factors: the 'Big Five' or the 'Gigantic Three'?

In this section we describe two prominent personality schemes which advocate the usefulness of higher-order secondary factors, describing personality

Table 1.6 *Traits associated with the three dimensions of Eysenck's model of personality*

Neuroticism	Anxious, depressed, guilt feelings, low self-esteem, tense, irrational, shy, moody, emotional
Extraversion	Sociable, lively, active, assertive, sensation seeking, carefree, dominant, surgent, venturesome
Psychoticism	Aggressive, cold, egocentric, impersonal, impulsive, antisocial, unempathetic, creative, tough-minded

in broad, abstract terms. Within these schemes each dimension may be assumed to be significantly related to hundreds of basic trait terms. The proper identification of such higher-order factors, their validation, the discovery of their origins, and the demonstration of their value in predicting behaviour are the chief goals of trait researchers.

H. J. Eysenck's three factor model

According to the personality theory of Eysenck (1967, 1997), there are three broad personality factors, named neuroticism, extraversion–introversion, and psychoticism. These factors are assessed using a self-report questionnaire in which the testee is required to answer 'yes' or 'no' to a number of questions. The questionnaire has evolved through several different versions, culminating in the Eysenck Personality Questionnaire-Revised (EPQ-R: Eysenck and Eysenck, 1991). The EPQ-R, like some of its predecessors, also contains a 'Lie scale' intended to measure subjects' tendencies to 'fake good' when completing the questionnaire. Although Eysenck's higher-order dimensions are intended to be statistically uncorrelated, there are slight positive correlations, especially among male subjects, between psychoticism and the other two scales (Eysenck and Eysenck, 1991). The distribution of neuroticism and extraversion scores in the population approximates to a normal curve, whereas psychoticism scores are markedly skewed towards low scores.

Some of the lower-level traits captured by Eysenck's three dimensions are shown in table 1.6. Eysenck and Eysenck (1991) describe the typical extravert – a high scorer on the introversion-extraversion scale – as someone who is sociable, craves excitement, takes chances, is fond of practical jokes, is not always reliable, and can at times lose his temper. Their characterisation of the typical introvert is someone who is quiet and retiring, is fond of books rather than people, is serious, keeps feelings under close control, is reliable and has high ethical standards. The high neuroticism (N) scorer is someone who tends towards anxiety and depression, worries, has bad sleep and psychosomatic disorders, allows emotions to affect judgement, and is preoccupied with things that might go wrong. Unlike the high neuroticism scorer, the low N scorer recovers quickly after an emotionally upsetting experience and is generally calm and unworried.

A high scorer on psychoticism, according to Eysenck and Eysenck (1991), is solitary, often troublesome, sometimes cruel, unempathic, aggressive, and has unusual tastes. This dimension overlaps with concepts such as schizoid and antisocial personality disorders within the psychiatric sphere. However, Eysenck emphasises that both neuroticism and psychoticism are normal personality traits, even though these might predispose to neurotic and psychotic disorders, respectively, in a very few individuals. Because of the obvious pejorative connotations of neuroticism and psychoticism, Eysenck has suggested that these might be replaced with emotionality and tough-mindedness versus superego control, respectively. Given Eysenck's long-standing antipathy towards psychoanalysis it is ironic to see that his scheme contains a term partly attributable to Jung (introversion–extraversion) and a Freudian term (superego).

Eysenck (1993) emphasised that it is the nomological network in which a dimension is embedded that provides its validity. This network must specify the psychometric properties of the dimension, but also its biological and psychophysiological bases, its cultural invariance, its relationship to social behaviour and illness, and its role in psychological research. Amongst Eysenck's substantial contributions to personality research was his formulation of theories of the biological bases of his personality dimensions (Eysenck, 1967). The assumption that phenotypic personality traits are linked to biological processes moulded by natural selection can also be found in the schemes of Cloninger (1987) and Zuckerman (1991). The degree to which these theories have stood up to empirical testing will be the subject of a later chapter.

Costa and McCrae's five factor model

So much recent consensus has been achieved about a possible five factor model for personality that researchers sometimes use the term, 'The Big Five' (De Raad, 2000). However, it would be more appropriate to speak of the big fives, since there is no single set of identical dimensions agreed upon by all researchers (De Raad and Perugini, 2002). In this sub-section we shall describe the five dimensional model of Costa and McCrae. We justify this on the basis of the huge amount of empirical research that has been done by Costa and McCrae and others in an effort to integrate their five factors with many other personality schemes (O'Connor, 2002). Secondly, their model forms the basis of a widely used measurement scale, the NEO-Personality Inventory-Revised (NEO-PI-R: Costa and McCrae, 1992a), developed from earlier questionnaires.

The NEO-PI-R is made up of 240 questions, forty-eight for each of the five dimensions or 'domains'. The response to each question is made on a five-point scale from 'strongly agree' to 'strongly disagree'. Each dimension is composed of six facets – lower-level traits – each of which is assessed by eight questions. The five broad dimensions are called Neuroticism, Extraversion, Openness, Agreeableness and Conscientiousness (N, E, O, A and C). Table 1.7 lists the facets that make up each of these broad domains.

Table 1.7 *Trait facets associated with the five domains of the Costa and McCrae five factor model of personality*

Neuroticism	Anxiety, angry hostility, depression, self-consciousness, impulsiveness, vulnerability
Extraversion	Warmth, gregariousness, assertiveness, activity, excitement seeking, positive emotions
Openness	Fantasy, aesthetics, feelings, actions, ideas, values
Agreeableness	Trust, straightforwardness, altruism, compliance, modesty, tender-mindedness
Conscientiousness	Competence, order, dutifulness, achievement striving, self-discipline, deliberation

The development of the five factor model of Costa and McCrae has been driven partly by rational and partly by statistical concerns. From a wide range of personality researchers' results they have decided upon the domains they wished to measure and then constructed scales to assess them, which are then subjected to factor analysis. Block's (1995) view was that N and E arose from Cattellian analyses, O was built up from embryonic status, and C and A were 'grafted' on in view of results from lexical approaches to personality (De Raad, 2000). He believes that the creation of facet scales required 'intelligent arbitrariness'. Costa and McCrae (1992a) sought to convince others that there was considerable agreement among many seemingly different personality schemes, by correlating their scales with those from many other well-known personality instruments. About half of the common variance in most personality inventories can be accounted for by the five factor model, and the factor structures of almost all personality inventories can be reproduced from knowing their associations with the five factors (O'Connor, 2002). This indicates that the five factor model might be a comprehensive account of human personality differences. Unlike Eysenck's dimensions, the domains of Costa and McCrae were not explicitly related to psychiatric concepts and had no prior bases in biological theory. However, the five factors have recently been viewed as genetically influenced, universal aspects of human nature, which promotes them from mere descriptions of phenotype to expressions of genotypes. McCrae et al. (2000) stated that, 'personality traits are more expressions of human biology than products of life experience'.

Personality inventories are not personality theories. Questionnaires are revised typically every five to ten years, if at all. The details of personality theory are in principle subject to alteration as every new relevant research report is produced, although major theoretical propositions are more enduring. Therefore, the tests outlined above should be considered as the best attempts to date to capture the three and five factor models, respectively; they should not be treated as being equivalent to the theoretical dimensions themselves. It will be the task of the remainder of the book to arrive at a conclusion about the status of current theories concerning the most important dimensions of personality.

Current conceptions of personality structure

The differences between the three and five factor models is probably the most significant disagreement in trait psychology. This may appear surprising, for the sixteen factor model of Cattell, for instance, appears at first sight to offer a larger chasm for the sceptic to peer into. In this section we shall demonstrate that important differences between the many, superficially very different, personality schemes are often more apparent than real. An appreciation of the irreducible consistency that can be found in psychometric personality research rests on various types of evidence, a summary of which will be presented below.

Any attempt at an overview must be clear about which level of traits is being assessed. We shall focus mostly on the highest level of secondary traits and compare the three and five factor models. The sixteen Cattellian dimensions are not relevant to such discussions, because they represent correlated, primary-level traits which can be reduced to a smaller number of orthogonal higher-order dimensions (Chernyshenko et al., 2001). Narrower trait concepts, such as the Type A personality do not profess to cover the main areas of human inter-individual differences and make no attempt to give a broad-based conception of personality. In addition, we shall see that narrow traits are often closely correlated with dimensions from more inclusive personality theories.

Why has the five factor model achieved such prominence, and why did Costa and McCrae (1993) state:

> The five factor model has provided a unified framework for trait research; it is the Christmas tree on which the findings of stability, heritability, consensual validation, cross-cultural invariance and predictive utility are hung like ornaments.

And why did De Raad and Perugini (2002) state:

> The Big Five model has aquired the status of a reference model . . . its five main constructs capture so much of the subject matter of personality psychology.

The answer is that similar five factor solutions to the problem of personality have arrived from a number of disparate sources.

The consensus from the lexical approach

The first source is the 'lexical approach' which has sought to find the clusters of personality descriptors that exist in natural language. A detailed history of the lexical approach to personality is given by De Raad (2000) and Saucier and Goldberg (2001). The key premises of the lexical approach were enumerated by Saucier and Goldberg (2001).

1 Personality language refers to phenotypes and not genotypes.
2 Important phenotypic attributes become encoded in the natural language.

3 The degree of representation of an attribute in language has some correspondence with the general importance of the attribute.

4 The lexical perspective provides an unusually strong rationale for the selection of variables in personality research. Heavily used predicates in the natural language are a powerful indicator of salient psychological phenomena.

5 Person-description and the sedimentation of important differences in language both work primarily through the adjective function.

6 The structure of person-descriptions in phrases and sentences is closely related to that based on single words.

7 The science of personality differs from other disciplines in ways that make the lexical perspective particularly germane in this scientific context, yet not in others.

8 The most important dimensions in aggregated personality judgements are the most invariant and universal dimensions – those that replicate across samples of targets, targets of description, and variations in analytic procedures, as well as across languages.

In a landmark series of studies, Tupes and Christal (1961; reprinted 1992) analysed the correlational patterns of trait terms in eight different samples of subjects and found five robust factors, which were little affected by differences in samples, situations, raters, and the extent of the rater's knowledge of the subject being rated. An earlier re-analysis of Cattell's rating data using personality trait terms (Fiske, 1949) found five factors, a conclusion confirmed by more recent re-analyses (Digman and Takemoto-Chock, 1981). Norman (1963) showed that five similar factors could be recovered from personality ratings made by the subject's peers. Table 1.8 summarises correspondences between the Costa and McCrae dimensional scheme, and studies of trait term ratings. As we shall see in chapter 2, five similar factors have been identified in studies of trait ratings in languages other than English, such as Italian, Polish and Hungarian (Ostendorf and Angleitner, 1994). The most comprehensive recent experimental studies have been conducted by Goldberg (1990, 1993; Saucier and Goldberg, 2001), who stated that:

> it now seems reasonable to conclude that analyses of any reasonably large samples of English trait adjectives in either self- or peer descriptions will elicit a variant of the Big Five factor structure, and therefore that virtually all such terms can be represented within this model. In other words, trait adjectives can be viewed as blends of five major features, features that relate in a gross way to Power, Love, Work, Affect, and Intellect. (Goldberg, 1990)

There is even quite good replication of lower level aspects of personality between German and English adjectives (Saucier and Ostendorf, 1999). Large samples were used to classify 500 adjectives in each language by Big Five domains. These were then factor-analysed within domains and the correspondences of the words checked by bilingual raters. The following groups of subcomponents replicated across

Table 1.8 *Studies of rating data demonstrating the Big Five*

Study	Data	Big Five dimension				
		E	N	C	A	O
Fiske (1949)	Self-, observer and peer ratings	Confident self-expression	Emotional control	Conformity	Social adaptability	Inquiring intellect
Borgatta (1964)	Self- and peer ratings (two samples)	Assertiveness	Emotionality	Responsibility	Likeability	Intelligence
Norman (1963)	Self- and peer ratings	Extraversion	Emotional stability	Conscientiousness	Agreeableness	Culture
Smith (1967)	Peer ratings	Extraversion	Emotionality	Strength of character	Agreeableness	Refinement
Digman and Takemoto-Chock (1981)	Re-analysis of data obtained by Cattell, Tupes and Christal and others	Extraversion vs introversion	Ego strength vs emotional disorganisation	Will to achieve	Friendly compliance vs hostile non-compliance	Intellect
Goldberg (1990)	Self-ratings	Surgency	Emotional stability	Conscientiousness	Agreeableness	Intellect

the two languages: adventurous, sociable, unrestrained, assertive; warm, gentle, modest, generous; non-irritable, non-secure, non-emotional; creative, intellectual, perceptive; industrious, decisive, orderly, reliable.

Saucier and Goldberg (2001) described lexical approaches to personality structure as emic; that is, the research progresses by using the native descriptors found in each language. The other approach – etic – imports (via translations) structures embedded in personality questionnaires from another language, usually English. They found that a 'big three' of agreeableness, extraversion and conscientiousness emerged from a larger range of languages than did a 'big five' that regularly emerged in Anglo-Germanic studies. They make a strong case for investigating further the greater cultural variability of emic-derived traits as compared with etic-derived traits, such as those based on translations of the NEO-PI-R (McCrae and Costa, 1997). Perugini and Di Blas (2002) used a combination of etic and emic methods in an Italian setting and provide an interesting discussion as to why etic rather than emic methods tend more neatly to replicate the five factors in different cultures.

Finally, factors resembling the Big Five were recovered from the pioneering study of Webb (1915), described earlier. Deary (1996) extracted six factors from Webb's data, which are shown in table 1.9. Five relate to personality, and one to intelligence. The marked degree of correspondence between this solution and present-day schemes was endorsed by independent experts in personality trait research. Webb deserves recognition for providing the first data set to contain factors close to contemporary dimensions, even if he was unable to extract them.

For those interested in obtaining items used in the lexical model of personality, Goldberg has developed public domain adjective scales to measure the five lexical personality factors. In addition, his team provided public domain personality items to assess the five factors in the 'international personality item pool' (http://www.ipip.ori.org/ipip/; Goldberg, 1999).

The consensus from questionnaire studies

The second source of data supportive of a consensual five factor model of personality traits is studies which compare more than one questionnaire or personality model on the same subject sample. Joint factor analyses of two or more questionnaires have clarified the confusion arising from the very large number of available personality tests with some success. The five factor model quite comprehensively captures the variance shared by different theory-based personality questionnaires (O'Connor, 2002). It is easiest to summarise this large body of research with reference to the Costa and McCrae five factor model as encapsulated in the NEO-PI-R. The NEO-PI-R manual shows the impressive correspondences between the domains and facets of the five factor model and factors from the Guildford-Zimmerman Temperament Survey, the Minnesota Multiphasic Personality Inventory, the Revised California Personality Inventory, and other questionnaires too numerous to list. The five Costa and McCrae factors also appear to be

Table 1.9 *A new factor analysis of Webb's (1915) trait rating data*

Factor 1 (Will?)
Desire to impose his will on other people (as opposed to tolerance)
Offensive manifestation of self-esteem (superciliousness)
Eagerness for admiration
Readiness to become angry
Esteem of himself as a whole
Belief in his own powers
Occasional liability to extreme anger

Factor 2 (Extraversion?)
Degree of bodily activity in pursuit of pleasures (games, etc.)
Extent of mental work bestowed upon pleasures (games, etc.)
Degree of corporate spirit (in whatever body interest is taken)
Fondness for large social gatherings
Wideness of his influence
Desire to be liked by his associates

Factor 3 (Conscientiousness?)
Degree to which he works with distant objects in view (as opposed to living from 'hand to mouth')
Extent of mental work bestowed upon usual studies
Conscientiousness (keenness of interest in the goodness and wickedness of actions)
Interest in religious beliefs and ceremonies (regardless of denomination)
Pure-mindedness (extent to which he shuns telling or hearing stories of immoral meaning)
Trustworthiness (keeping his word or engagement, performing his duty)

Factor 4 (Agreeableness?)
Desire to be liked by his associates
Readiness to accept the sentiments of his associates
Impulsive kindness
Readiness to recover from anger

Factor 5 (Intelligence?)
Quickness of apprehension
Originality of ideas
Degree of sense of humour
Profoundness of apprehension
Intensity of his influence on his special intimates
Wideness of his influence (i.e., the extent to which he makes his influence felt among any of his fellows whenever he speaks or acts)

Factor 6 (Low neuroticism?)
(−) Occasional liability to extreme depression
General tendency to be cheerful (as opposed to being depressed and low-spirited)
(−) Tendency to quick oscillation between cheerfulness and depression (as opposed to permanence of mood)
Degree of bodily activity during business hours
Tendency not to abandon tasks in the face of obstacles

Note Items within a factor are given in order of strength of loading, with the most influential items first. Those preceded by a (−) are negatively loaded on the factor, i.e., the opposite of that quality relates to the factor.

broadly compatible with factors from the personality models of Cattell, Comrey and Eysenck (Noller, Law and Comrey, 1987; Boyle, 1989), Wiggins (McCrae and Costa, 1989), Murray (Costa and McCrae, 1988), the Jungian Myers-Briggs Type Inventory (McCrae and Costa, 1989) and the Occupational Personality Questionnaire (Matthews and Stanton, 1994). The NEO-PI-R's five factor structure is replicated in its translations into several languages (McCrae and Costa, 1997; McCrae et al., 1998; McCrae et al., 2000).

In a very large study of Cattell's 16PF scales, involving over 17,000 subjects, Krug and Johns (1986) found five second-order factors: Extraversion, Neuroticism, Tough Poise, Independence and Control. The latest version of the 16PF, the 16PF5, explicitly allows the questionnaire to be scored for five secondary factors. Data provided in the 16PF5 technical manual (Conn and Rieke, 1994) on correlations between the 16PF5 and NEO-PI-R facet scales show imperfect convergence with the Big Five. There is a fairly good correspondence between Extraversion and Neuroticism scales, and between Control and NEO-PI-R Conscientiousness, and moderate correlations between Tough Poise and facets of Openness (ranging from -0.17 to -0.53). Cattell's Independence cannot be clearly identified with any of the NEO-PI-R five factors, and, conversely, there is no clear equivalent of Agreeableness among the 16PF secondary factors. On the other hand, Hofer and Eber (2002, p. 405) considered:

> Global factors extracted at the second-order level of the 16PF Questionnaire are highly similar to factors known as the Big Five.

In a comparison between the 16PF and the NEO-PI-R they found the following large correlations (the 16PF factor is named first): Extraversion vs Introversion $=$ 0.65; Anxiety vs Neuroticism $=$ 0.75; Tough-mindedness vs Openness $=$ 0.56; Self-control vs Conscientiousness $=$ 0.66. Independence correlated -0.42 with Agreeableness and 0.36 with Extraversion.

In general, there is a reasonable degree of congruence between the five factor model and personality factors from a wide range of schemes devised by different authors with different theoretical orientations. There appear to be some difficulties with specific instruments, such as the 16PF5. Conceivably, these are due to sub-optimal sampling of the personality domain, leading to distorted personality factors. Alternatively, some of the five factor model dimensions may require revision.

Remaining doubts: psychometric and theoretical issues

Costa and McCrae (1992b) summarised the evidence for the validity of the five factor model by stating the 'four ways the five factors are basic'. These were: (1) that longitudinal and cross-sectional studies have shown five robust factors to be enduring behavioural dispositions; (2) traits associated with the five factors emerge from different personality systems and from studies of natural language; (3) the five factors are found in different age, sex, race and language groups; and (4) heritability studies demonstrate some biological basis for each of the five factors. Since then, they have added to these with evidence, for example, of cross-cultural similarities in the ageing trajectories of the five factors and asserted that the five factors are a human universal, with the traits being primarily genetically influenced (McCrae and Costa, 1997; McCrae et al., 1999; McCrae et al., 2000).

Thus, can a strong case be made for the five factor model? There is no single five factor model. There are multiple questionnaires that have slightly different versions of five factors, there are questionnaires with fewer and more than five factors, and there are adjective scales with five and potentially more and fewer factors. This book is not principally concerned with psychometric structure; its aim is to examine the validity of some traits that achieve broad consensus, and to explore the usefulness of the trait approach for advancing our understanding of human personality variability. Those who wish to explore further the variety of instruments on offer that assess personality along five, or more, or fewer, dimensions should consult the excellent resource provided by De Raad and Perugini (2002; see box 1.1).

Box 1.1 Instruments for measuring the Big Five

It would take more of anyone's lifetime than would be wise to investigate all extant personality measurement instruments. An excellent guide to the state of five factor model assessment, and the variations on the theme, was provided by De Raad and Perugini (2002) in their edited book *Big Five Assessment*. They open with a useful introductory essay on the five factor model, including descriptions of the domains, applications in research and construct validity. There follow many chapters on different ways to assess the five factors and some others. Below, the authors of the relevant chapters are indicated, as are the instruments to which they refer. Where the instrument is not explicitly based on the mainstream five factor model(s), the personality trait names are given.

Five factor assessments, mostly questionnaires, are described by,

- Saucier and Goldberg (the development of marker scales)
- Costa, McCrae and Jonsson (the NEO Personality Inventory)
- Hendriks, Hofstee and De Raad (the Five Factor Personality Inventory)
- Barbaranelli and Caprara (the Big Five Questionnaire)
- Mervielde and De Fruyt (the Hierarchical Personality Inventory for Children)
- Trull and Widiger (the Structured Interview for the Five Factor Model of Personality)
- Paunonen and Ashton (the nonverbal assessment of personality with NPQ and FF-NPQ)
- Schmit, Kihm and Robie (the Global Personality Inventory)
- Tsaousis (the Traits Personality Questionnaire).

Five factor assessments, by adjective scales, are described by,

- Wiggins and Tobst (Interpersonal Adjectives Scales; English)
- Perugini and Di Blas (Big Five Marker Scales; Italian)
- Kashiwagi (Japanese Adjectives List)
- Hill, Williams and Bassett (Adjective check list; English)

Other instruments discussed in some detail, including their relation to the five factor model, are (with factors in parentheses) described by,

- Hogan and Hogan: The Hogan Personality Inventory (Adjustment, Ambition, Sociability, Likeability, Prudence, Intellectance, and School Success)
- Jackson and Tremblay: the Six Factor Personality Questionnaire (Extraversion, Agreeableness, Independence, Openness to Experience, Methodicalness, Industriousness)
- Zuckerman: the Zuckerman-Kuhlman Personality Questionnaire (this has three, four, five and six factor solutions)
- Hofer and Eber: Cattell Sixteen Personality Factor Questionnaire (its second order structure is Extraversion, Anxiety, Tough-mindedness, Independence, Self-Control)
- McNulty and Harkness: the PSY-5 scales from the Minnesota Multiphasic Personality Inventory (Aggressiveness, Psychoticism, Disconstraint, Neuroticism, Introversion)
- Barrett: the Professional Personality Questionnaire (Insecurity, Conscientious, Introversion, Tender-minded, Unconventional).

There are anomalies and dissenters to be considered. Psychometric criticisms of the five factor model have focused on three issues: (1) the Big-Five-like factors obtained by different investigators are not necessarily equivalent, (2) five broad trait factors may be insufficient, and (3) five factors may be too many. Comparative studies of different Big Five measures indicate that they are not completely interchangeable. For example, Goldberg (1992) correlated lexically defined factors with the NEO-PI scales, and obtained correlations between supposedly equivalent measures ranging from 0.46 to 0.69. Although correspondence between equivalent measures is fairly good, it is markedly lower than would normally be required for parallel versions of a scale. The lowest correlation of 0.46 here was between lexical and questionnaire measures of Openness, the Big Five factor which has been the most difficult to define precisely. Openness tends also to be called intellect, culture or imagination in lexical systems, and these are not necessarily close enough to be considered synonymous (Digman and Takemoto-Chock, 1981). Saucier and Goldberg (2001) showed many deviations from a strict five factor model in different languages, with interesting two, three (often), four, five (often) and seven factor models in certain instances.

Zuckerman et al. (1993; Zuckerman, 2002) describe an 'Alternate 5', which differs from the standard five factor model conceptually and psychometrically.

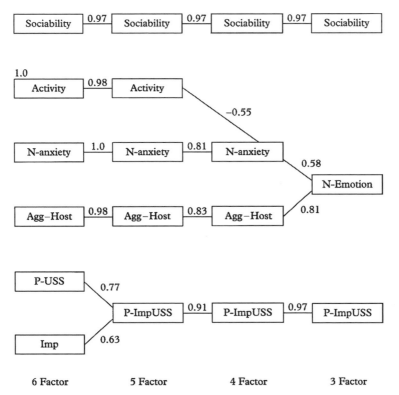

Figure 1.3 A hierarchy of factor solutions (three, four, five and six factor analyses) with factor score correlations across levels
Notes (N = neuroticism, Agg–Host = aggression–hostility, Emotion = emotionality, P-USS = psychopathy–unsocialised sensation seeking, Imp = impulsivity, P-ImpUSS = psychopathy–impulsive unsocialised sensation seeking).
Source Zuckerman et al., 1991

In addition to sociability (extraversion) and neuroticism-anxiety, Zuckerman et al. identify traits of aggression-hostility and impulsive sensation seeking, which correspond approximately to low agreeableness and low conscientiousness respectively. Zuckerman et al. also drop the openness dimension, and replace it with an activity factor. Zuckerman et al. (1991) argued that a hierarchy of factor solutions may be obtained, depending on the number of factors the researcher chooses to extract. Figure 1.3 shows the six, five, four and three factor solutions extracted in this study. The three factor solution resembles the Eysenckian superfactor system, with Sociability, N-emotion and P-ImpUSS corresponding to E, N and P respectively. Whereas Zuckerman et al.'s (1993) work indicates some broad alignments of standard and alternate five factor models and the Eysenckian system, there are also differences in the narrower traits which relate to corresponding dimensions. For example, Eysenck has tended to relate some aspects of impulsivity to E and some to P. However, as figure 1.3 shows, in Zuckerman et al.'s (1991) system impulsivity is a core constituent of the P-ImpUSS dimension. Zuckerman's scales were compared in a group of Spanish students with five factor model factors from the Goldberg adjectives and the NEO-PI-R, and with the Eysenck factors from the EPQ-R (Aluja et al., 2002). Again, no one factor structure could definitively be preferred above others. A three factor solution was similar to Eysenck's. A four factor solution, apart from E and N, found two factors: conscientiousness+psychoticism+impulsive sensation seeking; and agreeableness+aggression/hostility. The five factor model added openness (a combination of openness from the NEO and intellect from the Goldberg adjectives) to the four factor solution. Other pulls towards fewer than five factors are that the Multidimensional Personality Questionnaire, as well as Eysenck's system, emphasises three higher-order personality dimensions, of positive emotionality, negative emotionality and constraint (Patrick et al., 2002).

Some theorists have argued that five factors are too few to represent the major dimensions of personality. Hogan (1986; Hogan and Hogan, 2002) developed the Hogan Personality Inventory in which extraversion is replaced by two factors, sociability and ambition (see box 1.1). In a further approach towards finding the correct numbers of factors Brand (Brand and Egan, 1989; Brand, Egan and Deary, 1993; Brand 1994) conducted a conceptual review of a number of personality theories and suggested that, after intelligence is considered, there are five broad personality factors; these are Neuroticism, Energy (like Extraversion), Conscientiousness, Affection and Will. Affection and Will, in this scheme, represent a slight rotation of the Openness and Agreeableness dimensions of Costa and McCrae. Therefore, Brand's scheme is somewhat at odds with others in recommending that, if intelligence is added as a personality domain, there should be six factors and not five. This possible solution to the differences over the nature of the fifth factor is not unlike that proposed by Digman and Takemoto-Chock (1981). Matthews and Oddy (1993) presented factor analyses of trait ratings which support the view that self-rated intelligence is a distinct aspect of personality. The fifth factor of the Big Five – openness or intellect – continues to be the source of controversy; recently, several papers devoted to the topic failed to resolve its nature (De Raad and Van Heck, 1994). A strong case may be made for its social relevance, though (McCrae, 1996). In addition, there is evidence in various languages for a 'big seven' model of personality that includes factors of positive and negative valence in addition to factors closely resembling the standard Big Five (Almagor, Tellegen and Waller, 1995; Benet and Waller, 1995). McCrae and Costa (1995) found the two valence dimensions to be related to Big Five personality factors. They conclude that they are related to self-appraisal and social evaluation, but do not constitute core personality traits. There is a research vogue for asking which, if any, replicable factors lie beyond the Big Five. Suggestions include honesty, negative valence, religiousness, machiavellianism, and so on, but all are disputed (Saucier and Goldberg, 1998; Paunonen and Jackson, 2000; Ashton and Lee, 2002). In the specific evolutionarily important area of sexuality, seven dimensions were reported – sexual attractiveness, relationship exclusivity, gender orientation, sexual restraint, erotophilic disposition, emotional investment, and sexual orientation – and described as 'reapportionment of general personality variation' (Schmitt and Buss, 2000).

Turning to theoretical criticisms, Block (1995) voiced an important worry about the prestructuring of data sets from which five personality traits emerge. Wittingly or unwittingly, the variables included in factor analyses might have been selected to contain different subsets of redundant variables, which then cluster together to 'define' the five factors. Support for the five factor model from lexical data might thus result from the gathering together of five groups of synonyms related to personality, with the exclusion of many other relevant terms. Goldberg and Saucier (1995) pointed out that discoveries of five personality factors emerged from data sets where no prestructuring or selection has taken place. For example, no prestructuring can have taken place with Webb's data set described previously (Deary, 1996). A large study of trait terms in which prestructuring was explicitly avoided resulted in a clear five factor model similar to that obtained in previous studies (Saucier and Goldberg, 1996; Saucier and Ostendorf, 1999).

H. J. Eysenck (1991, 1992a) criticised the five factor models of personality. He suggested that the criteria enumerated by Costa and McCrae for accepting the five factor model are necessary but not sufficient for determining the important dimensions of personality, although they have demonstrated that one of Eysenck's own instruments – the Eysenck Personality Profiler – may yield a five factor solution (Costa and McCrae, 1995a). He argued that agreeableness and conscientiousness are primary level traits which are both facets of his higher-order factor Psychoticism, which is a possible interpretation of the three factor solution of Aluja et al.'s (2002) data. Additionally, he suggested that Openness forms a part of Extraversion and (low) Conscientiousness a part of Neuroticism. Eysenck further points to the meta-analysis of factor analytic studies carried out by Royce and Powell (1983) which he takes to indicate a three factor model similar to his own. Eysenck suggests that the five factor model lacks a nomological or theoretical network and is, therefore, arbitrary; he contrasted this with the theoretical basis of his psychoticism dimension which has roots in mental illness phenomena.

There is a contrast between the emphasis of five factor models on a taxonomy or descriptive scheme as the centrepiece of trait theory, and Eysenck's avowedly reductionistic scheme, which sees traits as expressions of partly heritable nervous system variance. However, though some advocates continue to emphasise that the five factors are assessments of phenotypes (Saucier and Goldberg, 2001), others have taken the view that the five factors are indicators of underlying, genetically influenced dispositions that are universal aspects of human nature (McCrae et al., 2000). Similarly to Eysenck's, the work of Zuckerman et al. (1993) and of Cloninger (1987) was in part motivated by a desire to obtain factors which are more closely related to psychobiological processes than are the standard five. Cloninger (1987) discusses brain systems supporting factors of novelty seeking, harm avoidance and reward dependence, as measured by his Tridimensional Personality Questionnaire. There is, in fact, much shared variance among the traits described by Eysenck, Zuckerman and Cloninger (Zuckerman and Cloninger, 1996). Table 1.10

Table 1.10 *Correspondences between primary traits in four systems*

Costa and McCrae	Eysenck	Zuckerman	Cloninger
Extraversion	Extraversion	Sociability	Harm avoidance
Neuroticism	Neuroticism	Neuroticism–anxiety	Harm avoidance
Conscientiousness	Psychoticism	Impulsive sensation seeking	Novelty seeking
Agreeableness	—	Aggression–hostility	Co-operativeness
Openness	—	—	—
—	—	Activity	—
—	—	—	Reward dependence
—	—	—	Self-determination
—	—	—	Spirituality

Note A minus sign indicates that the trait is negatively related to the trait in the first lefthand column in the row
Source Adapted from Zuckerman, 1995

shows Zuckerman's (1995) view of the strongest inter-trait associations, together with the correspondences between the three biologically based models and a Big Five model. The correspondences shown are not exhaustive. For example, as previously described, Eysenck (1992a) relates Openness to Extraversion and Agreeableness to low Psychoticism. Ultimately, declarations by the originators as to whether personality trait systems were conceived as indicators of biological systems or mere summaries of phenotypic variance is of little relevance to current research. Later chapters will show that genetic, environmental and physiological research is as much directed at one type of system as it is at the other.

Some critics have expressed serious doubts concerning not just the five factor model, but trait theory itself (Block, 1995). Pervin (1994) resurrected doubts about whether traits could ever be explanatory, as opposed to merely descriptive constructs, and viewed the trait approach as fundamentally flawed in addressing personality dynamics and organisation. Doubts of this kind, and rejoinders to them, will be considered in the next chapter. Moreover, studies of the genetic architecture of traits, discussed in chapter 6, in part allay these concerns. For the present, we may distinguish two strands of trait theory. Eysenck and Eysenck (1985) claim that the surest means for demonstrating the scientific validity of traits is to verify predictions derived explicitly from theory, through experimentation. Experimental tests of the biologically based theory favoured by Eysenck are discussed further in chapter 7. However, nomological networks are not obliged to be biological in nature. A second theoretical strand is exemplified by McCrae and Costa's (1995) original view that traits are hypothetical psychological constructs, which are influenced by biology, but are not tightly coupled to neural processes (see McCrae et al., 2000, for an update). They emphasise the expression of traits through culturally conditioned adaptations which relate to social-cognitive variables. In chapters 8 and 12 we explore the possible contributions of experimental social and cognitive research to trait theory.

We may conclude that trait psychology is in a healthy state, with signs of growing agreement on the structure of human personality. However, although some old combatants may have signed an armistice, there remain significant conflicts between partisans of the various perspectives described in this chapter. With this proviso, a cautious view of the current consensus is as follows. Extraversion and Neuroticism stimulate no detectable controversy; they are almost universally represented in psychometric personality systems. Conscientiousness and Agreeableness are the objects of a little more doubt, and a higher-order factor such as Psychoticism might challenge their status. Additionally, different systems have rotated these dimensions slightly differently to give them altered emphases. It might be argued that the Gigantic Three and Big Five simply reflect different levels of description, and so are not fundamentally incompatible (cf. Boyle, 1989). The most problematic issue is the status of Openness. There is some dispute over whether there is a distinction between dimensions of Intellect/Culture and Openness, and whether Openness should be ranked as a 'Big Five' factor at all. It is unlikely that such issues will be resolved entirely from psychometric studies. As we shall see in subsequent chapters, the development of theories of the psychological and/or physiological and/or social bases of traits is essential for establishing them as scientifically useful constructs.

Conclusions

1. Trait terms abound in the everyday language of person description. People use them to differentiate people's styles of behaviour. Historically, thinkers who tried logically to seek taxomomies of personal styles resorted to traits. But there is a difference between lay and pre-science conceptions of personality traits and a science of traits.

2. The history of the science of personality traits is contained mostly within the twentieth century. That time saw the growth of the psychometric techniques that support the deriving and validating of traits; the emergence of competing and complementary approaches to personality; the survival of trait and cognitive-behavioural approaches as the viable scientific ways to study personality; the growth of many apparently disparate trait systems, with respect to both the number and nature of traits they contained; and the eventual converging consensus around a relatively small number of broad personality domains.

3. To conduct and understand scientific studies of personality traits requires some understanding of psychometrics, the statistical methods applied to scales. Correlation and factor analyses are the everyday tools of the trait-oriented personality psychologist. In addition to substantive development in the content of personality trait theories, there have been developments in psychometrics too.

Correlation was available at the start of the twentieth century, multiple factor analysis in the first half, and confirmatory factor analytic techniques emerged in the later decades of the century.

4. Trait systems of personality exist at the primary and broader trait levels. Broader traits are often called dimensions or domains. An influential model from the last two decades of the twentieth century to date is the five factor model, which recognises personality variation along the lines of neuroticism, extraversion, openness/intellect, agreeableness, and conscientiousness. There is no single five factor model. Lexical versions sometimes find different numbers and types of traits in different cultures. Questionnaire-based versions differ somewhat depending on the questionnaire. Some influential theories of personality have more or fewer than five traits. Nevertheless, just as complete consensus should not be claimed, neither should differences be exaggerated. Most personality theories and instruments have large overlaps with concepts contained in the five factor model.

5. Personality trait systems are descriptions of phenotypes. Validating these systems requires finding out the causes and the consequences of personality traits.

Further reading

De Raad, B. and Perugini, M. (2002) *Big Five Assessment*. Seattle, WA: Hogrefe and Huber.
Saucier, G. and Goldberg, L. R. (2001) Lexical studies of indigenous personality factors: premises, products and prospects. *Journal of Personality*, 69, 847–79.

2 Persons, situations and interactionism

In chapter 1, we introduced the essentials of trait theory. We saw how personality might be characterised in terms of broad dimensions related to a variety of behaviours, including responses to personality questionnaires. We saw, too, that psychometrics provides statistical tools for identifying these dimensions, and that the use of techniques such as factor analysis has provided the beginnings of a consensus on personality structure. In this chapter, we shall discuss the unreliability of predicting behaviour for an isolated situation, in contrast to the reliable predictions we can make across many situations. We also discuss interactionism: the inter-relationships between personality traits and situations that have an impact on the expression of behaviour. Finally, we explore the cross-cultural generality of trait structure.

Traits and situations

If the aim of psychology is to explain behaviour, then personality traits succeed as constructs only insofar as they make a contribution to this end. Hence, the success of the trait approach requires that (1) individuals can be described in terms of their levels on valid and enduring dispositions, and (2) individual differences in these dispositions can predict a substantial proportion of the variance in behaviour. An alternative or complementary view, inspired by the successes of learning theory (Dollard and Miller, 1950), is that human behaviour is largely dependent on the situation. The so-called person–situation controversy derives from distinguishing two stark alternatives, that human behaviour is the result of either enduring dispositions or of the situation (Carson, 1989). It is hard to find a radical advocate for either position within the respective research communities, though it is true that researchers often emphasise one or the other influence on behaviour (Buss, 1989; Pervin, 1985, 2002). The study of both influences, the relative contribution of the person and the situation towards behaviour, is called interactionism, the approach to which most personality researchers subscribe, if implicitly, but few make a serious attempt to employ (Ekehammar, 1974).

The situationist critique of traits

The criticisms that traits, however consistent as self-descriptions, are poor at predicting behaviours was most loudly and elegantly trumpeted from Mischel's (1968) seminal book *Personality and Assessment*, although Pervin (1985) refers to similar debates in the 1930s and 1950s. Moskowitz and Schwartz (1982) captured Mischel's contribution concisely by stating that he had shown that knowledgeable informants form trait-like conceptions of others. These conceptions, he believed, are strongly influenced by the semantic structure of language and are not affected by situation-specific information that would contradict the concept of traits. That is, if the informants have no access to language to describe others' behaviours except by using trait-like concepts, then it follows that their descriptions of others will be in terms of traits – which are, by their nature, cross-situational. Mischel goes on to argue that personality does not exist in the form of cross-situational behavioural dispositions (i.e., traits), as suggested by the low cross-situational consistency of moral behaviours in the classic study of Hartshorne and May (1928). If personality does not exist in the form of traits and if informants can provide information only in the form of these dispositional descriptions, then the information provided by knowledgeable informants must have low validity. If trait conceptions are not situation specific, they cannot correlate strongly with behaviours counted in specific situations. Thus, from Mischel's perspective, it is not surprising that trait ratings have low validity correlations (below 0.30) when the raters are making observations of behaviour.

Note what Mischel's (1968) situationist critique claims and what it does not (see Bem and Allen, 1974). First, it allows that people do form consistent impressions of other people. Second, it admits that these impressions can predict some of the reliable variance in behaviour, but usually less than 9 per cent. Third, Mischel argues that 'real' personality dispositions must lie in behavioural consistencies from one situation to the next, but that these consistencies are not found. Fourth, he is prepared to allow that traits will be validated if informants' impressions are found to predict behaviour reliably. This is not the wholesale denial of traits that some have uncritically taken it to be (Lewis and Appleby, 1988); rather, it is a challenge to trait theorists to consider the scientific status and real-life applicability of traits and to appreciate the contribution that a given situation can make to people's behaviours.

Testing consistency in empirical studies

There is a straightforward criticism of Mischel's (1968) situationist critique, and his claim that traits are unable to predict much of the variance in a given situation. If we examine, say, Eysenck's (e.g., 1969) trait theory, we see that accurate prediction in a single given situation is not the basis for Eysenck's model (see figure 2.1). It is only after observing an individual in many situations that we form impressions about their habitual response patterns, which we intuitively correlate to produce a trait-like impression. Other trait theorists such as Allport (1961) and Cattell (1983) have stated explicitly that any given trait may fail to predict behaviour in a single situation; it is only by behavioural aggregation that we can make trait claims.

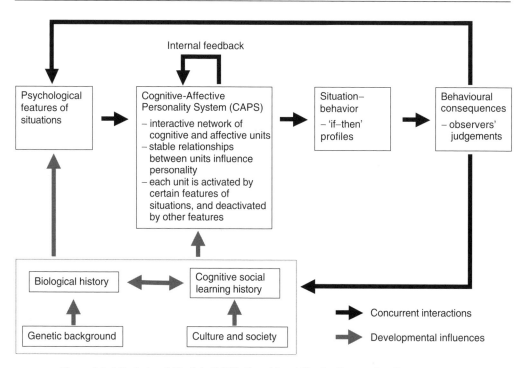

Figure 2.1 Mischel and Shoda's (1995) Cognitive-Affective Personality System (CAPS)

Thus, the situationist claim that traits could neither predict nor be inferred from individual situations attacks a straw man (Epstein, 1977).

Therefore, testing the veridicality of traits requires a researcher to test how people act over a series of relevant situations. Two points about the predictive validity of traits are important here: first, that they should be able to predict behaviour generally, as observed over a number of situations, and second, that the situation should be relevant to the trait. Take the example of neuroticism. If we wish to use a neuroticism scale to predict a person's behaviour, it would not be sensible to study that person in just one situation, or to study an irrelevant situation. In order to demonstrate that people with higher N levels show more apparent anxiety prior to a stressful event, the researcher should examine anxiety before an important examination, not before going to the cinema – unless a control condition is desired! Second, behaviour of subjects should be observed before several examinations, in order to minimise error variance and uncontrollable situational variables such as the student's liking for a given subject, health on the day of the exam, and so on. In the next section, we look at studies that demonstrate the importance of aggregating situations, and the relevance of the situation.

Epstein (1977) asked subjects to rate and describe their positive and negative emotions, impulses, behaviours and situations for over two weeks. Although the correlation between single days was as low as suggested by the work of Mischel

(1968) and Bem (1972) suggested, the reliability of measures in each of these categories ranged from 0.40 to 0.88, with a median of 0.72 when odd and even days were correlated for data collected for between twenty-four and thirty-four days. Another message of this study was that, in all of the above categories, a certain minimum frequency of occurrence and variance was required to achieve high reliability, whether it was between behaviours and emotions. Epstein reckoned that, given the frequent assertion that there is a 0.30 barrier for cross-situational reliability coefficients, the findings of this study are no less than dramatic. Personality, behaviour, and even situations as scored by judges independent of the subjects, were all highly reliable when aggregated over several days; the low predictive validity coefficients claimed by the situationists for personality variables were imposed by error of measurement as the result of single observations. Therefore, the procedure that others have employed all but guarantees reliability coefficients to be low. It may be concluded that those who have argued that personality is unstable have simply not used procedures that can establish its stability. As Eysenck (1981) pointed out, aggregation of data actually provides quite good evidence for cross-situational consistency in studies such as that of Hartshorne and May (1928) which purport to show situation specificity of behaviour.

Similarly, when personality is assessed through judges' ratings, large numbers of behavioural observations may be needed for the behavioural consistency and predictive validity of traits to appear (Moskowitz and Schwartz, 1982). Moskowitz (1988) studied the reliability of ratings and behaviour counts of friendliness and dominance in forty-three subjects who visited a laboratory on six occasions in order to conduct a problem-solving exercise with one partner. Correlating ratings (inferred traits) of friendliness and dominance made in one situation with only one other situation gave coefficients of 0.26 and 0.12, respectively; both were non-significant, but of the order expected from the criticisms of Mischel. The same analyses performed on behaviour counts gave coefficients of 0.37 ($p<0.05$) for friendliness and 0.06 for dominance. However, when generalisability (using coefficient alpha) was calculated using the six situations the ratings values for friendliness and dominance were 0.68 ($p<0.001$) and 0.44 ($p<0.01$), respectively. The value for behaviour counts for friendliness was 0.78 ($p<0.001$) and for dominance, 0.28 (ns). She concluded that there were high levels of cross-situational generality for behaviour count and ratings measures of friendliness (aggregated over six laboratory situations), and moderate levels of generality for ratings of dominance.

Further, using data from only five situations to predict friendliness ratings or behaviour counts in a single situation, multiple R values of 0.50 and 0.57 were obtained for ratings and behaviour counts, respectively (both $p<0.01$). For dominance, the expression of relevant behaviours was affected by whether the subject knew the partner they were with in the situation. The use of abstract qualities such as friendliness also seems to raise behavioural consistency. Funder and Colvin (1991) showed cross-situational consistencies typically of 0.4–0.6 for behaviours coded by meaning, but substantially smaller consistencies for specific instances of behaviours. For example, 'humour' is more consistent than 'joke-telling'.

Consistency of behaviour: the role of context

Later work by Mischel has in fact made use of trait constructs to predict behaviours with remarkable success. As might be expected, he uses behavioural dispositions in a particular way – one that takes the context into account and may be seen as a form of interactionism (Wright and Mischel, 1987). As an alternative to theories that see traits as causal agents or as mere summaries of observed behaviours (e.g., Buss and Craik, 1983), Mischel sees a trait statement as the 'conditional probability of a category of behaviours in a category of contexts'. It is hard to imagine any trait theorist taking exception to this definition, and the present authors consider it to be a good, mainstream definition of a trait, stripped of beliefs about the origin of the trait. In particular, the point that traits most reliably express themselves in situations that are suited to their expression is accepted by most, if not all, personality trait theorists. That is, it is difficult to express extraversion whilst marching with other soldiers in a parade, but much easier to express it at a party. What is remarkable about Mischel and colleagues' research is the care with which it is formulated and executed, and the high level of predictive validity that it provides for personality traits from this once champion of situationism.

Wright and Mischel (1987) asked raters to assess children on the traits of 'aggression' and 'withdrawal'. Several different observers watched the children's actual behaviours over a period of time. The raters were also asked to judge how demanding the situation was for the child, in comparison to the child's competence. The hypotheses were complex: that children with high levels of a trait would show more behaviours that were central to that trait ('feature-centrality'), and that correlations between traits and behaviours would be especially high if the situation was a demanding one for the child. Feature-centrality needs explanation: with regard to aggression, one 'feature-central' behaviour would be a threat issued to another child. The feature-central threatening behaviour would be expected to show higher correlations with aggression than would a non-feature-central trait such as distractability. Table 2.1 shows some typical results from Wright and Mischel's study. As hypothesised, children with given levels of a trait showed more trait-relevant behaviours. The correlations are especially strong when the demand level of the situation is high, and when the rated behaviour is central to the trait concept, although correlations are substantial for feature-central behaviours even in low-demand situations. Ratings of traits made by others do predict objectively observed behaviours. Wright and Mischel's study is a success for trait theory, situationism and interactionism all at once: traits were highly predictive of behaviours, the relevance of the situation made a difference to the behavioural scores, and there was also a significant trait–situation interaction. Thus, highly aggressive children displayed more overall feature-central behaviours such as pushing and shoving, which further increased as the demands of the situation rose.

Table 2.1 *Correlations between judgements of children and their social behaviour as a function of feature centrality in the judgement and level of situation-competency demand*

Centrality of features	Sample feature	Situation demand level		
		Low	Medium	High
	Aggression			
1 Low	Distractible	35	28	34
2	Feels angry	42	51	59
3	Acts impulsively	49	54	65
4 High	Threatens others	45	57	67
	Withdrawal			
1 Low	Cries	19	30	22
2	Unusual movements	42	32	44
3	Feels sad	41	33	52
4 High	Unassertive	46	32	65

This model of interactionism has continued to develop, and Mischel and colleagues have conceptualised personality as a dynamical system (Mischel and Shoda, 1995; Shoda, LeeTiernan, and Mischel, 2002). These authors' Cognitive-Affective Personality System (CAPS) describes affects, goals, expectancies, beliefs, competencies, and self-regulatory plans and strategies as the basic units of personality (see figure 2.1). The outcome of these interacting units is typically of an *if . . . then . . .* form: e.g., *if* you encounter someone you know, *then* behave in a friendly manner. The individual's repertoire of if–then connections provides a unique behavioural signature or profile for that person. Typically, these outcomes are then highly contextually dependent: e.g., showing friendly behaviour towards acquaintances, but not to strangers or work colleagues. Furthermore, the various units are always subject to change as a consequence of social interaction. Thus, CAPS suggests a view of consistency that differs from trait theory in proposing many more personality units, whose control over behaviour is linked to specific situational features, on a person-by-person basis. Nevertheless, the model assumes some personality stability, that produces consistency in how the individual behaves in specific situations. As with trait models, it assumes personality develops from both biological and cognitive-social influences, a point to be elaborated in subsequent chapters.

Mendoza-Denton et al. (2001) studied person by situation interactions by asking subjects to describe themselves in 'if–then' terms ('I am. . . . . when. . . .') after they had performed a task for which they were given either positive or negative feedback. In doing so, the subjects were less likely to put themselves on extreme ends of dimensions (as they might using standard personality inventories), and less likely to misattribute – or overgeneralise – success or failure to *themselves,*

rather than to the specific situation. In addition, the 'if–then' framework also reduced the likelihood that subjects would attribute reasons for others' behaviour to
stereotypes. This 'dynamical system' has also been modelled using computer sim-
ulations of interactions between 'dyads' (pairs) (Shoda, LeeTiernan and Mischel,
2002). The models suggest that one pair member's behaviour serves as a situation
for the other, so that displayed 'personality' is actually a function of interpersonal
relationships. That is, behaviour stems in part from traits, but whether a trait is
manifested is conditional upon both the situation and on interpersonal dynamics.
Although not expressed in the same terms, this idea is borne out in applied fields
of research, too. For example, while behaviours in certain crime *situations* are
consistent across individuals, people's traits alone do not predict criminal involvement (Alison et al., 2002). Other studies have also shown that 'driver stress' is
predicted from situational factors such as traffic congestion and time pressure of
the journey (Hennessy, Wiesenthal and Kohn, 2000), together with dispositional
stress vulnerabilities that are specific to driving (Matthews, 2002).

Johnson (1999) offers a critique of CAPS that suggests that this model promises
rather more than it actually delivers. He suggests that description of personality in
terms of many very narrow traits, such as if–then contingencies, may not offer the
advantages claimed by Mischel and Shoda (1995), by comparison with broad traits
such as the Big Five. Broad traits may have as much explanatory power as narrow
ones, and are equally subject to situational moderation. Indeed, assessment of the
'behavioural signature' may fall into the same trap of poor reliability as the early
studies of behavioural consistency, discussed in chapter 2. Studies of behavioural
signatures use from one to six data points to assess each if–then relationship, which
is likely to be insufficient. Finally, Johnson questions the theoretical contribution
of CAPS, pointing out that its constructs tend to be common-sense notions of
desires, beliefs and abilities relabelled using contemporary psychological jargon.
Despite these criticisms, however, CAPS is at the leading edge of social-cognitive
approaches to personality stability and consistency, and future empirical work is
likely to reveal how much the model adds to conventional trait approaches to
predicting individual differences in behaviour.

Implications of the situationist controversy for trait research

The above discussion of Mischel's situationist critique and its evolution into a form
of interactionism point to a realistic view of traits that most trait theorists probably
always held anyway. Although the late 1960s and 1970s are sometimes seen as
the situationist zenith, trait research has never really slowed since its inception,
despite psychological zeitgeists coming and going (Buss, 1989). Sometimes the
psychological community seems reluctant to abandon a good street fight, and the
intermittent resumption of the supposed person versus situation debate has tried
the patience of those who created much of the furore (Mischel and Peake, 1982;
Bem, 1983). This is despite the fact that there are no important personality theorists
who believe that only person or situation factors contribute to behaviour. The trait

Table 2.2 *Factors in an experimental situation that favour the importance of traits or manipulations in accounting for behaviour differences*

Issue	Manipulations become important	Traits become important
Context	Novel, formal, public	Familiar, informal, private
Instructions	Detailed, complete	General or none
Choice	Little or none	Considerable
Duration	Brief	Extensive
Response	Narrowly defined	Broadly defined

Source From Buss (1989)

manifesto of Eysenck and Eysenk (1980) does, in fact, give considerable weight to the power of the situation, and allows for person–situation interactions via intervening variables, just as Mischel seems to have given up radical situationism and become frankly interactionist (Carson, 1989). The extent to which behaviour is better predicted from broad, narrow or contextualised traits remains open (e.g., Johnson, 1999), but, as Allport (1937) anticipated, it is likely that we need trait constructs at different levels of generality.

In addition, situations alone may only be modestly predictive of behaviour, even when situational effects are shown to be statistically significant. When sample sizes are even quite modest, a very small p-value can hide a small effect size. Funder and Ozer (1983) re-examined some key manipulations in social psychology and found an average correlational effect size equivalent of less than 0.4. Furthermore, it is easy to load the dice in favour of the person or situation by appropriate choice of methods (Buss, 1989). Table 2.2 shows the features of an experimental set-up that can be used to manipulate the importance of traits or situations.

The overall message is clear: aggregation is needed across situations or across times, after which reliable trait ratings and behavioural dispositions will be found (Buss, 1989). However, it is worth picking over the bones of the person–situation controversy to assess its lasting implications for the study of traits. Kenrick and Funder (1988) provide an insightful list of the hypotheses related to traits thrown up by situationism, shown in Table 2.3 in order of their anti-trait power, with the most pessimistic hypotheses first. The first and strongest anti-trait hypothesis is that personality is in the eye of the beholder. This view is falsified by the impressive agreement between self and peer ratings of personality discussed previously. Kenrick and Funder provide a list of studies where different raters' estimates of a target subject's personality were compared. Arranged around the dimensions of intelligence, likeability, self-control, sociability, adjustment and dominance, when psychometrically adequate scales were used, the correlations were typically greater than 0.5. The second hypothesis states that traits arise because there are shared assumptions about which words go together. However, this cannot explain how people would make similar trait judgements about a given individual, how the same trait structures arise in different languages and cultures, or why the same trait dimensions arise from adjectival scales and questionnaire studies (see chapter 1). The

Table 2.3 *Hierarchy of hypotheses from the person-situation controversy, arranged from most to least pessimistic*

Critical assumptions	Hypotheses
Solipsism over consensus	1. Personality is in the eye of the beholder.
Consensus without discrimination	2. Agreement between raters is an artifact of the semantic structure of the language used to describe personality.
	3. Agreement is an artifact of base-rate accuracy (rater's tendency to make similar guesses about what people in general are like).
Discriminative consensus without behavioural referents	4. Differential agreement is an artifact of the shared use of invalid stereotypes.
	5. Observers are in cahoots with one another; that is, their agreement results from discussion rather than accurate observation.
Differential agreement about behaviour without internal traits	6. Raters see targets only within a limited range of settings and mistake situational effects for traits.
	7. Compared with situational pressures, cross-situational consistencies in behaviour are too weak to be important.

Source From Kenrick and Funder (1989)

third hypothesis states that raters make guesses about what people in general are like when they rate individuals on traits; thus more people would be rated as 'tidy' than 'obsessionally neat'. However, such response tendencies cannot explain different raters' agreements about target subjects' individual differences in trait levels.

The fourth hypothesis enumerated by Kenrick and Funder (1988) suggests that raters' agreement arises out the their shared focus on some obvious characteristic of the individual (weight, hair colour, race, etc.) and the subsequent shared application of stereotypical personality traits to the stereotype. Note that this is the first of the hypotheses that can potentially explain inter-rater agreement in personality trait differences. Contrary to this hypothesis, inter-rater agreements are stronger for people who know the target subject better. When a single observation is made, raters who know the subject tend to agree with one another and with the subject him/herself, but 'stranger' raters agree with neither each other nor the subject (Funder and Colvin, 1988). These authors also found strong support for the hypothesis that the more visible a trait was considered to be, the stronger the inter-judge agreement was on a target subject's level on the trait. Extraversion items appeared particularly visible and neuroticism items much less so. With regard to the hypothesis that traits arise out of the raters' discussions of the target person's personality (hypothesis 5 in table 2.3), Kenrick and Funder (1988) provide ample evidence to show that: (a) informants with no contact make equally similar judgements to those who have contact; (b) the better agreement found in the more easy-to-observe traits goes against this hypothesis, since the less easy-to-observe traits are just as easy to discuss; and (c) informants' ratings are more influenced by a subject's behaviour than their discursive self-accounts.

Situationist hypothesis 6 in table 2.3 states that informants adduce traits based on a limited range of situations; for example, students are often used to make peer ratings, yet they might see different behaviours than family members do during the vacation. This is refuted by the fact that parents' ratings agree with fellow students' ratings in college samples (Kenrick and Stringfield, 1980). The last hypothesis states that the 0.3 correlation barrier between personality traits and behaviours means that traits are relatively unimportant. However, we have already seen that correlations higher than this can be found when behaviours are aggregated and when the situation is relevant to the trait (e.g., Wright and Mischel, 1987). Kenrick and Funder's (1988) conclusions are that the best predictive validity coefficients may be obtained from traits when we use:

(a) raters who are familiar with the person being rated
(b) multiple behavioural observations
(c) multiple observers
(d) dimensions that are publicly observable
(e) behaviours that seem relevant to the dimension in question (p. 31).

Some have seen the person–situation debate as a fruitless power struggle between trait and social psychology (Kihlstrom, 1987), but, as Kenrick and Funder (1988) indicate, the controversy may have been useful in generating these guidelines for improving predictive validity. Endler and Parker (1992) agree that the battle lines drawn between trait theory and situationism had the cleansing effect that comes with criticism-inspired self-reflection, but they also think that many personality researchers have failed to learn the lessons or even consider the criticisms that were once so prominent.

Funder (2001) notes that there is still a great need for research that balances out the 'personality triad' of the person, the situation and behaviour. As he points out, the person variable, largely through the work of trait theorists and aided by the low cost and convenience of self-report questionnaires, is very well researched. However, actual behaviours are much less well described and documented, with notable exceptions (especially in relation to measuring personality in children). The characteristics of situations are, empirically, poorly understood: researchers have not tested which aspects of a situation are the important ones in determining behaviour change. In addition, the practice of attributing variance unexplained by personality or behaviour to the situation hides the problem that the remaining variance may be due to personality or behavioural variables not measured, rather than to situation variables that were not measured. It also tells us nothing about which aspects of the situation are most important. The debate between situationist and personality research, however, has now brought about co-operation and collaboration and more fruitful ways of understanding the interaction between persons and situations.

Interactionism

Almost all contemporary trait psychologists subscribe to interactionism, the view that both the person and the situation, and their mutual interaction, are important. Interactionist conceptions of personality were evident in the writings of Kantor and Lewin (see Ekehammer, 1974), but contemporary interactionist formulations appear to have originated independently of these forerunners (Mischel, 1973; Magnusson and Endler, 1977). Ekehammer's analysis of the emergence and re-emergence of interactionism in personality research sees present-day interactionism as having grown out of criticisms of trait psychology. Moreover, Carson (1989) described Mischel-inspired situationist–trait controversy as having ended in an international draw with the publication in 1973 of Bower's superb analysis of the issues. Finally, Epstein's (1977) conclusion vis-à-vis the person-situation debate was that person and situation variables could be important in accounting for behavioural variance, as could their interactions.

The studies by Wright and Mischel (1987) and Mendoza-Denton et al. (2001) that were discussed above are good examples of thorough interactionist research, where the person and situation are studied in conjunction, and clearly formulated hypotheses are tested. A further, somewhat simpler, example is provided by studies of extraversion and performance. There are many tasks for which there is no clear main effect for extraversion; its effect on performance is entirely dependent on situational factors. For example, Revelle, Amaral and Turriff (1976) showed that in a stimulating environment (time pressure and drinking a caffeinated beverage), extraverts performed better than introverts on a verbal ability test. However, when the environment was non-stimulating (no time pressure or caffeine), introverts outscored extraverts. The dependence of extraversion effects on environmental factors is discussed further in chapter 12. A comprehensive account of person–situation interaction would seem to require some more general model for classifying and measuring situations: this has proved to be a thorny problem, as discussed in Box 2.1.

It would be too complacent to state that 'we are all now "interactionists"' (Bem, 1972): Endler and Parker (1992) lament that the influence of interactionism has been rhetorical, changing what people say about their research rather than altering the way they go about it; their view is that the crisis in personality still has to be addressed. In addition, they characterise modern trait research as atheoretical and populated largely with bandwagon-jumpers. They cite with approval authors such as Stam (1987), who have characterised situationist researchers' attempts to conduct interactional studies as simplistic and mechanistic. In agreement with this, Endler and Parker's (1991) and Carson's (1989) surveys of contemporary personality research show a continued dominance of studies in classrooms and

Box 2.1 Taxonomies of situations: towards measurement models?

Systematic study of person x situation interaction requires that the critical aspects of the situation may be measured with the same precision as traits themselves. However, it is a familiar lament that researchers do not have good measurement models for the situation. Ten Berge and De Raad (1999) have reviewed attempts to develop a taxonomy for situations. One approach is to develop taxonomies on theoretical grounds. For example, if we have a theory of anxiety that tells us that loss of control, physical danger and social criticism are three distinct types of external threat, we could assess specific situations for presence of these situational features. Alternatively, we could proceed in a more empirical fashion, by having people rate situations for various qualities, and then deriving coherent clusters of situational attributes by factor analysis. Research has employed both strategies, with mixed success, and limited convergence between different taxonomies. Ten Berge and De Raad (1999) endorse an approach adopted by Van Heck (1989) that was based on a lexical approach. He investigated the clustering of nouns that could be used to describe a situation, but did not refer to inner, psychological constructs, including personality traits. This empirical strategy produced ten categories of situation, listed below, although Van Heck's (1989) taxonomy has not provided any generally applicable measurement instrument for use in research.

These categories have some plausibility as situational modifiers of trait effects on behaviour. For example, as we will see, high neuroticism persons are especially sensitive to interpersonal conflict (see chapter 9): presence of this situational feature may act something like a switch that 'turns on' behaviours linked to high N. However, we might also wonder if these categories adequately reflect the meanings that people 'read into' situations: for example, intimacy may be rewarding to some persons but threatening to others. As Ten Berge and De Raad (1999) state, what is lacking is a taxonomy that would integrate trait and situation factors, so as to identify (and measure) those situations that maximize the behavioural expression of a given trait.

Van Heck's (1989) taxonomy of situations

1. Interpersonal conflict
2. Joint working; exchange of thoughts, ideals and knowledge
3. Intimacy and interpersonal relations
4. Recreation
5. Travelling
6. Rituals
7. Sport
8. Excesses
9. Serving
10. Trading

laboratories, use of questionnaires, emphasis on college students, and lack of use of structural modelling techniques to elucidate processes.

Carson (1989) described the research of Wright and Mischel (1987) as mechanistic interactionism, an impoverished genus of the species when compared with dynamic interactionism – a criticism which has been in part addressed with continuing research by Mischel and researchers associated with him. Mechanistic interactionism is concerned with the structural aspects of people in situations, dynamic interactionism with process. Thus, whereas analysis of variance techniques are preferred tools of mechanistic interactionists, the process-oriented dynamic interactionists make use of path analyses and hypothesis testing procedures made available by structural equation modelling. Combining study design with structural models allows the cycle of person–environment interactions and changes over time in these interactions to be examined simultaneously. In addition, such studies lessen or remove the sometimes false distinction between independent and dependent variables. Endler (1983) describes his rich conception of human behaviour as follows:

> A function of a continuous multidirectional process of person-by-situation interactions; cognitive, motivational and emotional factors have important determining roles on behaviour, regarding the person side; and the perception or psychological meaning that the situation has for the person is an essential determining factor of behaviour. (p. 160)

Hettema and Kenrick's (1989) formulations are commended for progressing beyond the mere correlations (often between self-reported traits and other self-report scales) of the trait researcher, or the static ANOVA of the pseudo-interactionist. In fact, some of Endler's own interactionist research on anxiety has been successful in showing that specific facets of trait anxiety in specific situations produce predicted rises in specific facets of state anxiety (Endler, Edwards and Vitelli, 1991) as discussed further in chapter 4. It is not clear, though, in what ways this transcends models such as Mischel and Wright's – the analysis of the person construct may be more fine grained, but it is no more 'dynamic' or process oriented. Such impressive demonstrations of the predictive power of traits contrasts with the tendency of some interactionist writers to make vague, holistic statements, sometimes truisms, that afford the empirical scientist little purchase for theory formulation. For example, it is not clear what is to be done by acknowledging, as Magnusson (1988) states:

> the characteristic way in which the individual develops, in interaction with the environment, depends on and influences that continuous reciprocal process of interaction among subsystems of psychological and biological factors. (p. 21)

Situationism and interactionism are not alternatives to trait approaches and neither denies the importance of traits. Situationists recognise the importance of people's stable dispositions, and some interactionists are really just those who combine trait and situation variables. Others would prefer a more subtle and comprehensive form of interactionism that emphasises the developmental and dynamic aspects of behaviour of people in the environment, despite the difficulties of such an enterprise. In the meantime, even if much research on traits is atheoretical and of limited practical use (Endler and Parker, 1992) or trivial and non-cumulative (Carson, 1989), the point that traits can predict behaviours, especially if aspects of the situation are taken into account, should be accepted and recognised as progress.

Are traits universal across cultures?

We saw in chapter 1 that one of the criteria that broad traits should meet is cultural universality (Costa and McCrae, 1992b) – in effect, cross-situational universality of trait structure. There are a priori arguments why we might expect structural models of traits to replicate across cultures. If traits do have a biological basis, then they should be a property of homo sapiens rather than of any particular culture, although the way the biological substrate is expressed in behaviour may be culture bound. Irrespective of biology, it is likely that different cultures face somewhat similar adaptive challenges. All people must cope with threats to well-being, form social relationships with others, obtain a livelihood, and so forth. Goldberg (1990) has loosely related the Big Five to Power, Love, Work, Affect and Intellect (i.e., E, A, C, N and O). It is likely that these five areas of life may be identified in all or most cultures, even if there are important cross-cultural differences. More generally still, Pinker (1994) has suggested that Western culture is rediscovering the concept of human nature. The twentieth century was characterised by what Pinker called the Standard Social Science Model (SSSM), which states that human behaviour is wholly or largely determined by culture-bound social learning (popularly, but wrongly, described as 'conditioning'). Pinker claims that anthropologists have overstated the malleability of behaviour, and have frequently ignored similarities between cultures. If our species does have a common 'human nature', which may be biologically influenced, we might expect that individual difference dimensions should show some similarities across cultures.

Nevertheless, there are potential obstacles to establishing trait universality. Cultural specificity may be strong enough to substantially alter the relative importance of traits. For example, given that cultures differ in the value placed upon achievement motivation (McClelland, 1961), it might be that Conscientiousness is less salient in some non-Western societies than it is in our own, or that C is not expressed through achievement striving. As discussed in chapter 8, we can measure a distinctive 'Protestant work ethic' (Furnham, 1990) trait related to Western cultural values. Conversely, other traits might be more important in societies other than our own. For example, Bond (1979; 2000) discusses a 'filial piety' or 'Chinese tradition' trait found in Chinese cultures, which places high value upon respect for parents and upholding Chinese ways. In addition, a sixth factor – Interpersonal Relatedness – was obtained in factor analyses of the NEO-PI-R and the Chinese

Personality Assessment Inventory (Cheung et al., 2001). Hence, we cannot, a priori, be confident that the Western 'Big Five' is assessing universal traits as opposed to traits that reflect the preoccupations of our culture. In addition, there are methodological difficulties in translating Western questionnaires into the languages of other cultures, because item content, and differences in compliance of responding, is culture-bound. One of the versions of the 16PF includes items asking, variously, about interest in improvements in production and marketing, in Indian murders, in photography and in becoming a research chemist!

In the next section, we review empirical studies of the cross-cultural generality of two major descriptive frameworks for personality, the Eysenckian three and the Big Five. We focus on questions of dimensional structure. This is a distinct issue from that of cross-cultural differences in mean scores on trait dimensions, though comparison of means is sensible only if commonality of dimensional structure is established (see Lynn and Martin, 1995, for a survey of data). Triandis (1997) describes the structural approach as 'etics'. This contrasts with 'emics', in which traits specific to individual cultures are identified. There has also been considerable research on generality of factor structure across different groups within the same culture, such as comparisons across sex, age, and different ethnic groups. Box 2.2 summarises studies of sex differences. Normally, factor structure is highly replicable across different demographic groups (e.g., Costa, McCrae and Dye, 1991). In the sections that follow, we concentrate on etics first, and emics second – both are important in building our understanding of personality cross-culturally.

Cross-cultural research on traits

The most comprehensive program of cross-cultural research is that of Sybil Eysenck and her colleagues, who have translated the EPQ into many different languages and tested for factor replicability. Eysenck and Eysenck (1982) summarise studies conducted in twenty-five countries, including non-Western countries such as Bangladesh, Brazil, Japan and Uganda. In each case, four factors were extracted, and the similarity of the factor structure to the UK data was computed using a recognised method of factor comparison. In general, it appeared that the same four factors of E, N, P and L were extracted from each data set, showing a high level of cross-cultural replicability. Some difficulties were apparent in measurement of P, with internal consistency (alpha) falling to values as low as 0.4 or 0.5 in some countries, especially Nigeria and Egypt. Similar results have been obtained in subsequent studies, with the most recent using Eysenck et al.'s (1985) EPQ-R. Although the EPQ-R was intended to improve the reliability and distribution of P scores, internal consistency of P dimensions obtained in other cultures remains moderate. Eysenck, Barrett and Barnes (1993) report alphas of 0.66 (males) and 0.62 (females) in a Canadian sample. They suggest that reluctance of high P subjects to participate in studies may contribute to the low internal consistency. The Junior EPQ also shows good cross-cultural replicability, as shown in a study of Iranian and English children (Eysenck, Makaremi and Barrett, 1994).

Box 2.2 Are there sex differences in personality traits?

There are theoretical reasons to hypothesise that men and women will display differences in personality traits. These hypotheses arise from biological and social models of personality: that men and women differ because of biologically/evolutionarily-based innate temperamental or hormonal differences; or that personality differences appear because men and women class themselves into gender roles (Feingold, 1994; Costa, Terracciano and McCrae, 2001). The main questions, therefore, have arisen around Agreeableness (nurturance) and emotional expression (N), both of which are thought to be higher in women, and dominance (A and E), thought to be higher in men. In addition, differences might be expected between traditional or collectivist cultures (e.g., Pakistan or China), and individualistic cultures (e.g., Europe or USA).

The two meta-analyses of Feingold (1994) and Costa, Terracciano and McCrae (2001) collated findings of studies on personality traits from many different age groups and nations. The answer to the question 'are there sex differences in personality traits?' is: 'yes,' and these differences, while small-to-medium in effect size, are in line with expectations. The first of the meta-analyses reported that, across cultures (Canada, China, Finland, Germany, Poland and Russia), males score higher on assertiveness measures, whereas females score higher on anxiety, trust and tender-mindedness (Feingold, 1994). The second of the meta-analyses studied a much broader array of traits, and a wider range of cultures, including Africa, South America, and central and eastern Asia (Costa, Terracciano and McCrae, 2001). Costa and colleagues reported that women were higher in negative affect, submissiveness and nurturance; men were higher in dominance and were less concerned with feelings than with ideas. Some cultures showed greater differences than others; contrary to expectation, individualistic cultures showed wider sex differences than collectivistic cultures. Overall, however, the two meta-analyses, covering hundreds of studies, show that there are consistent sex differences in personality – in emotional (N), agreeableness and dominance-related traits – both within and across cultures.

There is a smaller, but impressive, corpus of research on other questionnaires, such as Costa and McCrae's NEO questionnaires. Translations of the NEO-PI-R into German, Portuguese, Hebrew, Chinese, Korean and Japanese have closely replicated the five factor structure found among North Americans (McCrae et al., 1996; McCrae and Costa, 1999), and in a review of studies in twenty-six cultures, and 23,031 subjects, McCrae (2001) reported that intercultural factor analysis retrieved structures similar to the Big Five in almost all samples. Silva et al. (1994) and Avia et al. (1995) recovered the Big Five factors from the Spanish translation of the NEO-PI questionnaire (Silva et al., 1994), the precursor to the NEO-PI-R. The validity of the Spanish Big Five was also similar to the American Five, with respect to other self-report measures of personality, clinical disorders and risk-related behaviours. However, some difficulties were also apparent. Silva et al. (1994) factor-analysed the facet scales of E, N and O (see table 1.7), and A and C scale scores (because the NEO-PI has no A and C facet scales). They found that extraversion facets in particular tended to load on factors other than the E factor. For example, Assertiveness and Activity tended to load on C. Silva et al. (1994) indicate similar problems in both North American and German data. An Italian study (Caprara, Barbaranelli and Comrey, 1995) also reported only partial support for the Big Five. A joint factor analysis was conducted on the NEO-PI scales and the Comrey Personality scales (1994), from which eight factors were extracted, five of which corresponded fairly well to the Big Five. Additional factors related to trust-defensiveness, activity and masculinity–femininity, and had some loadings from the NEO-PI scales. Paunonen et al. (1992) studied subjects from Canada, Finland, Poland and Germany who had completed Jackson's Personality Research Form as well as a non-verbal measure of traits based on ratings of trait-related line drawings. They found that the Big Five factor structure replicated across both measures in all four countries.

The lexical approach to trait assessment has stimulated attempts to recover the Big Five in languages other than English. Comparison of languages is not straightforward. Trait concepts are expressed through a variety of word classes (nouns, adjectives, etc.) whose nature, usage and frequency vary from language to language. There are important differences even between related languages such as English and German (Angleitner, Ostendorf and John, 1990). For example, German allows complex concepts to be expressed as single words made up as a compound of more basic words. Angleitner (1990) gives us an example: 'freundschaftlich', meaning 'acts as one would expect a friend to act', a concept which cannot be expressed in a single word in English. Other languages do not even have adjectives and express adjectival meaning through other constructions (Szirmak and De Raad, 1994). Yang and Bond (1990) have shown that there is only a modest similarity between Big Five solutions obtained from indigenous Chinese words, and from translations of American Big Five markers. Unfortunately, such difficulties largely preclude direct factor comparison across cultures.

A number of studies have tackled linguistic difficulties through careful taxonomic analysis and sampling of the language concerned. In general, these studies have found a good, but imperfect, fit to the English language Big Five. For example, De Raad (1992) extracted a fairly clear Big Five from Dutch personality adjectives, but found that noun and verb data were best characterised by four and two factor solutions respectively. An Italian adjectival Big Five obtained by Caprara and Perugini (1994) showed only a moderate degree of correspondence to the English language Big Five. In place of Intellect and Openness, the fifth factor was one of 'Conventionality', contrasting words such as unconventional, rebellious and critical with servile, puritan and obedient. The position is similar for non-Indo-European languages. Szirmak and De Raad (1994) obtained good equivalents to N, E, C and A in a study of Hungarian trait adjectives, but the fifth factor was one of 'Integrity': veracious and just versus swollen-headed and hypocritical. Marker adjectives for Intellect tended to load on E and N factors. Saucier and Goldberg (1996) have called language a 'conceptual' reservoir with respect to personality. They conclude that the lexical five factor model has been found in English, German, Czech and Dutch, and is quite strong in Hungarian, Russian and Filipino.

In emics (Triandis, 1997), the focus is on identifying culture-specific traits. Such research may use indigenous measures alongside Big Five measures. In doing so, it becomes apparent that there are within-culture traits that are not tapped by the Big Five. For instance, the concept of wisdom and characterisation of a wise person are quite different in Chinese than American people (Yang, 2001). Other investigations have revealed important differences in values and outlook: happiness in Taiwanese students was strongly related to social integration and human-heartedness; in British students this was not so (Lu, Gilmour and Kao, 2001). Subjective well-being and happiness are two constructs that appear to be quite sensitive to cultural influences, and are particularly different between collectivist and individualistic cultures (Schimmack et al., 2002). However, while some characterise subjective well-being as a trait (e.g., Deneve and Cooper, 1998), others would view it as a state rather than a trait, and would not expect it to fall within the five factor structure (see chapter 4).

Cross-cultural generality of traits: conclusions

In summary, studies of the EPQ provide the strongest evidence for cross-cultural generality of broad traits, but the method adopted does not directly address the issue of whether the Eysenckian traits are the most important in each culture. Even if we can measure equivalent E dimensions in each culture, it does not follow that E is of equal importance across cultures (although it is plausible that E is universally important as well as replicable). Lexical studies of the Big Five go further towards identifying the major traits within different cultures through systematic sampling of personality language. However, both lexical and questionnaire studies tend to show fairly good but imperfect correspondence between 'Big Fives' from different cultures. It is a problem with lexical studies that in cases where there is replication, that replication has only been sought using the same model (i.e., either the Eysenckian 3 or the FFM), therefore making it difficult to say whether the glass is half empty or half full in this case. Should we be impressed by the many correspondences established, or should we be critical of the differences between lexical factor solutions – all tested using the same model – across different cultures? At the least, the Eysenck and Big Five structural models provide good starting points for investigating broad traits in non-English-language cultures. Further progress will require further direct testing of these models against models that include culture-specific traits.

Conclusions

1. During the height of situationist research, it appeared that trait theory was unsupportable. However, the debate that followed from the important criticisms of the situationists eventually extended and strengthened trait research, and led to the important finding that while traits were poor predictors of behaviour in one-off situations, they were, as they should be, very good predictors of behaviour aggregated across many situations.

2. The existence of a trait predisposes people to act and react in certain ways that become apparent over time. Both self-report and rater-report methods of trait measurement make use of this aggregation of behaviour in different situations, and result in reliable and valid measures of traits.

3. At the same time, situational factors play an important role in moderating the impact of traits on behaviour, as recognised by interactionism which is the basis for almost all contemporary research. There is continuing debate over how these situational factors should be characterised, and how best to capture dynamic interaction between person and situation.

4. The existence of the five factor structure of traits is found consistently across cultures, giving further evidence that personality traits may be universal psycho-biological constructs. This position is modified, however, by evidence that there are culture-specific traits that are not well described by the five factor model. In addition, the expression of traits may be modified both by situational and cultural constraints.

5. Future research would benefit from better characterisation of situations and behaviours, so that becomes possible to identify the important behaviour-modifying elements of situations, and enable us to make better predictions about trait expression in different types of situations.

Further reading

McCrae, R. R. (2001) Trait psychology and culture: exploring intercultural comparisions. *Journal of Personality*, 69 (6), 819–46.

Pervin, L. A. (2002) *Current controversies and issues in personality* (3rd edn). New York: Wiley.

3 Personality across the life span

The previous two chapters introduced the idea of traits and discussed interactions between situations and behaviour, and that behaviour, when aggregated across situations, provides evidence for the existence of traits. In addition, we saw that the basic structure of traits in different cultures (a special kind of situation) is, by and large, reliable and replicable. In this chapter, we discuss how personality develops over the life span, particularly with regard to traits. How stable are our personalities as we go from childhood to adulthood, and during adulthood? In this chapter, first, we discuss traits and their stability in adulthood. Second, we introduce the concept of temperament and its relationship to personality traits. Finally, we look at the evidence that childhood temperaments are related to adult personality traits.

Trait stability

For a trait to be valid, it must have a degree of stability over time. A quality that is shifting, or that depends on the situation at hand, cannot accurately predict behaviour during a future event (i.e., it cannot account for reliable variance in that event), nor can it have a stable biological basis in the individual. Without some stability of individual differences, the theory of traits fails in its entirety. As with other aspects of trait theory, the problem of demonstrating stability is a bit like pulling yourself up by your shoelaces: the demonstration of stability is best done using validated trait assessments. However, stability is one of the key properties we wish to know before stating that a trait is valid.

Before examining stability data, a few definitions are necessary. First, stability is not the same as reliability, although it is necessary to have reliability in order to have stability. Reliability is, effectively, the internal consistency of the trait assessment over a short time period, whereas stability is measured in terms of years or decades. Second, there are two types of stability. One type is stability of mean trait levels; groups of people as a whole may or may not show changes in mean score on a trait without reference to individual differences. That is, if we conducted a study to compare a group of older people and a group of younger people on the trait of extraversion, we might find that the older people have a lower mean level of extraversion than the younger people. However, this does not tell us anything about how stable extraversion is in any given individual in that sample.

To know that, we would have had to have personality trait measures on the same individuals at two points in time, or more.

The other type of stability relates to individual differences in trait levels, which may or may not be stable regardless of any change in mean trait level. For example, it is quite possible to have a situation where the mean level of a trait remains the same in a population sample, but where there are no stable individual differences. Perhaps some people within the group scored higher than they did before, and others lower, although the mean level of the trait remains the same. In addition, it is possible to have a situation in which there are very stable individual differences and where the sample as a whole has risen or fallen considerably on their mean score on a trait. This could occur if, for instance, many people remain within two to three points of their previous score – showing individual stability – but it happens that all of them have decreased by two to three points. There might also be differences among traits in their stability levels (perhaps extraversion is more stable than neuroticism), and there might be important aspects of personality that change rather than remain stable through time.

As to the question of stability in mean levels of traits: between the ages of eighteen and thirty, mean trait levels of neuroticism, extraversion and openness have been found to decrease slightly, whereas agreeableness and conscientiousness increase slightly. After age thirty the same pattern of changes are observed over time, but to a lesser extent (McCrae et al., 2000). Overall, mean levels of personality traits appear to change very little after the age of thirty. In the remainder of the chapter, the principal issue we are addressing is the stability of individual differences – rather than group differences – over time.

Empirical studies of stability

The estimated stability of traits prior to the 1970s was often considered to be quite low (e.g, Neugarten, 1964). However, by the late 1960s Mischel (1968) discussed a number of studies that provided evidence of impressive long-term stability in personality trait scores, and stated that 'the trait-descriptive categories and personality labels with which individuals describe themselves on questionnaires and trait-rating scales seem to be especially long lasting' (Mischel, 1968, p. 35). Costa and McCrae (1977) reported ten-year stability coefficients for extraversion ranging from 0.70 to 0.84, while those for anxiety and neuroticism fell between 0.58 and 0.69. Leon et al. (1979) studied Minnesota Multiphasic Personality Inventory (MMPI) scores in seventy males over thirty years. The average stability coefficient was greater than 0.40, with a thirty-year re-test correlation for social extraversion as high as 0.74. We illustrate further research by looking at a few of the most comprehensive projects.

Costa, McCrae and Arenberg (1980) used the Guildford Zimmerman Temperament Survey (GZTS) in a study of over 400 largely middle-class male graduates who formed part of the Baltimore Longitudinal Study of Ageing (BLSA). Different age groups – young, middle-aged and old – showed no differences in personality trait stability. The six-year stability of the ten GZTS scales ran from 0.71 to 0.83, with a mean of 0.77. The twelve-year stability of the scales ran from 0.68 to 0.83, with a mean of 0.73. Taking scale reliability into account, the estimated twelve-year stabilities for the scales ran from 0.80 for emotional stability to 1.0 for ascendance. The general activity, friendliness and personal relations scales were used to give a (low) neuroticism level. The six- and twelve-year stabilities of extraversion were 0.82 and 0.78, respectively, and were 0.74 and 0.70 for neuroticism. Costa and McCrae (1992c) reported twenty-four-year stability on the GZTS for a sub-sample; the coefficients for the ten scales ranged from 0.61 to 0.71, with a median of 0.65. Correcting for the reliability of the scales, the estimated twenty-four-year stability rose to between 0.70 and 0.87.

Conley (1985) developed the multitrait-multimethod theory of Campbell and Fiske (1959) to obtain stability estimates that were not dependent on the use of a specific personality measure. By assessing different traits using two methods (self- and other-ratings) on different occasions, Conley argued that three key aspects of traits could be demonstrated: that a trait can be observed under more than one experimental condition; that a trait can be differentiated from other traits; and that individual differences in traits are stable over time. Conley (1985) tested 300 middle-class engaged couples who were first studied in 1935–8 (E. L. Kelly, 1955), and who rated each other's traits. Ratings were also made by acquaintances. In 1954–5 189 couples were tested again, and 183 men and 205 women were re-tested in 1980–1. The subjects were in their early twenties when first tested, and in their late sixties on the third occasion. The Personality Rating Scale (PRS) of Kelly was used on the first and second occasions, and the Cornell Medical Index on the third occasion. The PRS was factor analysed and showed the following traits across men and women: neuroticism, social extraversion, impulse control (like conscientiousness) and agreeableness. Therefore, factors similar to four of the Big Five factors were assessed.

Conley's (1985) main results are shown in Table 3.1. The first line of correlations in the table is an estimate of the inter-rater reliability for each trait based upon the five acquaintances that rated each subject at time 1. The second, fourth, sixth and eighth lines of the table demonstrate that different traits do not have substantial cross-correlations, which argues for the distinctiveness of the traits – and the fact that any stability is not a mere artifact of the method used. Line 3 demonstrates the agreement among self, partner and acquaintances for each trait at the same occasion, and shows good agreement for neuroticism and social extraversion, modest agreement for impulse control, and limited agreement for agreeableness. Line 5 has the agreement of the same person (self or partner) on the same trait across almost twenty years; again the stability is good for neuroticism and social extraversion, and slightly lower for impulse control and agreeableness.

Line 7 of table 3.1 is the most important of all. It has the correlations for the same traits in the same people – but rated by different people – across twenty years. That is, the self-assessed trait in 1935 is correlated with the partner's assessment in 1954, and vice-versa. For neuroticism, social extraversion and impulse control,

Table 3.1 *Inter-trait correlations obtained by Conley (1985)*

	Neuroticism		Social Extraversion		Impulse Control		Agreeableness	
	m	w	m	w	m	w	m	w
1. $T_s M_s O_s$	76	77	70	66	59	67	64	50
2. $T_d M_s O_s$	07	05	06	06	07	07	07	08
3. $T_s M_d O_s$	48	39	52	48	36	38	27	25
4. $T_d M_d O_s$	07	11	11	11	08	10	08	11
5. $T_s M_s O_d$	50	39	47	52	32	43	33	46
6. $T_d M_s O_d$	08	07	08	12	10	15	10	08
7. $T_s M_d O_d$	43	30	36	41	30	29	16	17
8. $T_d M_d O_d$	08	10	11	11	09	11	09	09

Note m = men, w = women
T = trait (s = same trait, d = different trait)
M = method (s = same rater, d = different raters)
O = occasion (s = same occasion, d = different occasion/i.e., 1935 vs 1954)
Source Conley (1985)

the correlations range from around 0.3 to over 0.4. For agreeableness, the correlations for men and women are 0.16 and 0.17, respectively. Conley concluded that

> for each of the three traits [of] neuroticism, social extraversion and impulse control, a substantial proportion of the longitudinal stability variance is generalisable across methods of assessment. Furthermore, these three traits remain distinct over the decades of adulthood, and their discriminant validity over time is as impressive as their convergent validity over time.

Studies of the Big Five and Eysenck traits

Studies based explicitly on the Big Five and Eysenck traits (as opposed to traits that may fall outside these models) confirm stability. Costa and McCrae (1988) presented data for the six-year self-rated stabilities of neuroticism, extraversion and openness in 398 men and women; they were 0.83, 0.82 and 0.83 respectively. When corrected for the scale reliabilities the estimated six-year stability of neuroticism was 0.95, of extraversion, 0.90, and of openness, greater than 0.95. The three-year correlations for agreeableness and conscientiousness in a sub-sample of 360 participants were 0.63 and 0.79 respectively, confirming that agreeableness tends to be less stable than other traits. The stability of trait ratings made by others was of a similar magnitude to self-ratings, confirming that it is not just self-perceptions that remain stable over time. A later study of personality ratings using the NEO Personality Inventory with a seven-year delay found the following stability coefficients: neuroticism, 0.67; extraversion, 0.81; openness, 0.84; agreeableness, 0.63; conscientiousness, 0.78 (Costa and McCrae, 1992c). Costa and

McCrae (1994; 2000) combined data from several longitudinal studies of traits, using a variety of instruments, with time intervals varying from six to thirty years. Median stability coefficients for the Big Five traits in these studies were as follows: neuroticism, 0.64; extraversion, 0.64; openness, 0.64; agreeableness, 0.64; and conscientiousness, 0.67.

Eysenck's factors appear to have similar stability levels to those mentioned above. The six-year stability coefficients of the Eysenck Personality Questionnaire dimensions in 225 Dutch, middle-aged men and women were: psychoticism, 0.61; extraversion, 0.84; neuroticism, 0.73; and lie scale, 0.75 (Sanderman and Ranchor, 1994). Stability of the Eysenck Personality Questionnaire was examined by Wilson, Deary and Maran (1991) in eighty-nine ear, nose and throat patients who were followed up after an average delay of two and a half years. They found stability coefficients for neuroticism, extraversion and the lie scale of 0.60, 0.64, and 0.54, respectively, but the psychoticism scale over the same period was close to zero (0.02). Stabilities may be even higher when correlations are corrected to take into account the reliabilities of the trait assessments. Conley's (1984) review of neuroticism, extraversion and impulse control traits found stabilities of 0.6 over ten years, 0.4 over twenty years and 0.3 over thirty years or more. However, much of the apparent instability was due to period-free reliability. When this was taken into account the annual stability of the three traits was 0.98; as a result, the estimated stability over forty years was 0.45.

Schuerger, Zarella and Hotz (1989) re-analysed personality stability from 106 sources involving eighty-nine studies that made use of at least one of the following instruments: the High School Personality Inventory, the 16PF, the Minnesota Multiphasic Personality Inventory, the Myers-Briggs Type Inventory, the California Personality Inventory, the Guildford-Zimmerman Temperament Scales, the Edwards Personal Preference Schedule and the Omnibus Personality Inventory. Anxiety (like neuroticism) and extraversion scales were derived from each instrument and their homogeneity adjusted to an average length of fifty items. Figure 3.1 shows the stability of anxiety, extraversion and all scales in this large review. There appears to be an exponential decay in stability over time, which eventually reaches a stable asymptote, at about 0.6 for extraversion, and rather less for anxiety and the average of all scales. Patient and prisoner groups showed lower stability than normals. Scale homogeneity and length of scale made important contributions to stabilities.

Stability: further issues

Large-scale reviews and large single studies offer overwhelming evidence for the stability of personality traits over many years. Extraversion appears to be particularly stable, with good evidence for the high stability of neuroticism, openness and conscientiousness. Agreeableness would appear to be less stable. Some puzzles remain, such as the greater stability of extraversion compared with that of neuroticism. Costa and McCrae (1977) suggest that temporary stresses have an

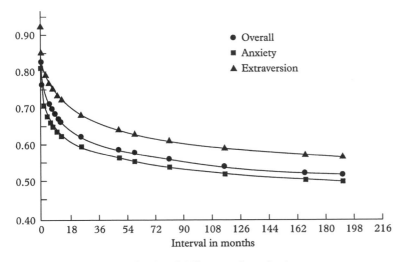

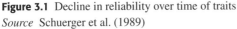

Figure 3.1 Decline in reliability over time of traits
Source Schuerger et al. (1989)

effect on neuroticism levels or that people with high neuroticism levels change slightly through therapy or the counselling of friends. However, such intuitively plausible suggestions are not necessarily correct. As discussed further in chapter 12, extraversion and neuroticism have been found, in prospective studies, to influence future numbers of objectively measured positive and negative life events, rather than the reverse (Magnus et al. 1993). In an eighteen-year longitudinal study, depression was not found to have a recurrent effect on neuroticism scores, even though the individual differences in the personality traits were highly stable over the duration of the study (Duggan et al. 1991).

It is unclear, despite the evidence for the stability of traits over time, whether there may in fact be systematic changes in personality. McCrae (1993) argued that change in personality over time in normal adults might be a result of measurement error. He recommended that further studies be conducted on personality change, particularly studies that involve children, patients who have received interventions or therapy after illnesses, and older people. For example, Asendorpf (1992) has shown that stability in children's non-family environment (e.g., at school) affects the stability of their inhibition scores, and personality changes in people with Alzheimer's disease have been documented (Siegler et al, 1991). Studies have also shown that some traits change in line with predictions from Erikson's (1963) developmental stage theory (trust versus mistrust, identity versus identity diffusion and intimacy versus isolation), although the 'growth'-oriented scales show stabilities similar to other traits. Some of the most important developments in exploring trait stability from childhood onwards have been in long-term longitudinal studies of childhood temperament linked to adulthood personality traits, and in retrospective studies of adults who also have archival data on personality from their childhood. It is to temperament and the stability of personality from childhood to adulthood that we turn next.

Temperament

A construct similar to that of traits is 'temperament'. Bates (1987) provides a definition of temperament that captures its distinctive characteristics: biologically rooted individual differences in behaviour tendencies that are present early in life and are relatively stable across various kinds of situations and over the course of time. To some extent, temperament research is simply the investigation of traits in infancy and childhood, but it does have distinctive features. First, because infants cannot complete questionnaires, temperament research makes greater use of objective behavioural measures, and of observer ratings of behaviour. Parents or teachers may complete questionnaires on the child's behaviour, or temperament may be assessed through structured observation (see Bates, 1987). McCrae et al. (2000) argue that the distinction between temperament and trait research is that the goals and methods in the two traditions differ: researchers of temperament are interested in the process and mechanism of temperamental dispositions; trait researchers tend to focus on the consequences and correlates of traits (such as conscientiousness and job performance or health).

Second, although temporal stability of temperament is expected, the concept is embedded in processes of developmental change resulting from maturation and learning. Hence, the salience and behavioural expression of temperament may vary with age, and test–re-test correlations between specific temperament measures taken at different ages are often modest, especially in infancy (Bates, 1987; Lewis, 2000). For example, inhibition of approach, which may relate to anxious personality, develops only after an age of six months or so, when the child may become hesitant in grasping a novel toy (Rothbart, 1988). In longitudinal studies of inhibition, different measures must be used at different ages. In a study by Kagan, Reznick and Sidman (1988), discussed further in chapter 7, inhibition at twenty-one months was assessed on the basis of behavioural signs such as clinging to the mother, cessation of vocalisation and reluctance to approach unfamiliar stimuli. At seven and a half years, inhibition was measured using a composite of spontaneous comments made by the child to other (unfamiliar) children and adults and the time the child chose to spend apart from other children. The correlation between aggregate indices of inhibition at the two times was 0.67, showing continuity between behaviours at the two ages, although the specific behaviours themselves differed.

There are two distinct strands of research on temperament. The first, pioneered by Thomas and Chess (1977), is based on developmental psychology. The distinction between personality and temperament is rather fuzzy, and some researchers (e.g., Buss and Plomin, 1984) see temperaments as simply the sub-class of personality traits that are inherited. The second strand originates in Eastern Europe and the former Soviet Union, and seeks to use Pavlovian accounts of fundamental properties of the central nervous system as the basis for explaining individual differences in temperament. The most comprehensive theory of temperament of this type (Strelau, 1983) draws a sharp distinction between temperament as biological in nature, and personality as a product of socialisation. In the remainder of this

Table 3.2 *Components of temperament described by Buss and Plomin (1984)*

Temperament	Component
Emotionality	
– Fear	Sympathetic activation
	Apprehension, worry
	Fear face
	Escape, avoidance
– Anger	Sympathetic activation
	Transient hostility
	Angry face, pout
	Angry aggression
– Distress	
Activity	Tempo
	Vigour
	Endurance
Sociability	Tendency to affiliate
	Responsivity when with others

section on temperament, we review some of the constructs developed by these two approaches, and their relationship to traits.

Measures of temperament

Buss and Plomin (1984) distinguished between three basic temperaments referred to as 'EAS' or emotionality, activity and sociability, which break down into more specific components, as shown in table 3.2. Temperament was assessed using the EAS Temperament Survey (EAS-TS), which measures emotionality through the basic emotions of fear and anger, together with distress in the more recent version of the questionnaire. These components meet several criteria for valid dimensions of temperament listed by Buss and Plomin (1984); they are heritable, stable, predictive of adult personality, and adaptive in the evolutionary sense. Buss and Plomin also argued that the EAS temperaments are evident in other primates.

Various other descriptive frameworks have been proposed. Thomas and Chess (1977) listed nine dimensions, and Derryberry and Rothbart (1988) proposed no fewer than nineteen, but most of these dimensions appear to relate conceptually to the EAS temperaments. For example, the (negative) emotionality temperament (Buss and Plomin, 1984) may also relate to constructs such as negative versus positive emotionality, difficultness, low adaptability (Thomas and Chess, 1977), and low ego resiliency (Block and Block, 1980). Marin, Wisenbaker and Hattunen (1994) reviewed twelve large sample factor analyses of instruments based on the Thomas and Chess dimensions. They proposed a seven factor model, comprising dimensions of activity level, negative emotionality, task persistence, adaptability/agreeableness, inhibition, rhythmicity and threshold. However, such results tend to be less consistent across different methods than for adult personality. Martin et al. (1994) found that more dimensions (five to seven) were identified in studies using parent ratings than in studies using teacher ratings (three or four). A review of 119 studies of cross-method correlations suggested that inter-correlations between parent, teacher and self-ratings range from 0.20 to 0.27 (Achenbach, McConaughy and Howell, 1987). There is considerable evidence from longitudinal studies supporting the validity of various temperamental measures as predictors of subsequent behaviours; for example, excessive emotionality is predictive of subsequent behavioural problems (Eisenberg, Fabes and Loyola, 1997; Southam-Gerow and Kendall, 2002).

Rothbart's (e.g., Rothbart and Bates, 1998) model of temperament has three principal elements: a measurement model distinguishing different dimensions of temperament, an account of the biological bases for the dimensions, and an account of how temperament influences emotional behaviours and self-regulation. The Children's Behavior Questionnaire (CBQ: Rothbart et al. 2001) is completed by a caregiver, and assesses fifteen primary temperament dimensions, in children aged three to seven, with good or adequate reliability. Factor analyses of these intercorrelated dimensions identified three nearly independent higher-order factors: Negative Affectivity (e.g., discomfort, fear, anger, sadness), Extraversion/Surgency (e.g., high intensity pleasure, activity, impulsivity) and Effortful control (e.g., inhibitory control, attentional focusing, low intensity pleasure). An Infant Behavior Questionnaire (IBQ: Rothbart, Derryberry and Hershey, 2000) measures some related dimensions from the caregiver's reports of behaviours in infants, in the laboratory. Rothbart et al. (2000) showed, in a small sample of twenty-six, that these behaviours showed moderate stability from infancy to seven years. Furthermore, laboratory behaviours measured at thirteen and a half months predicted aspects of temperament at age seven. Several studies reviewed by Kochanska, Coy and Murray (2002) have validated the Rothbart et al. (2001) dimensions as predictors of self-regulative behaviour; for example, effortful control tends to relate to greater compliance with the mother's requests.

Rothbart and Bates (1998) link negative affect and extraversion to largely subcortical brain systems for punishment/avoidance and reward/approach respectively, sometimes described as behavioural inhibition and activation systems (BIS and BAS: see chapter 7). Rothbart also recognises differences between different components, e.g., between fear and anger as elements of negative affectivity. Beyond this psychobiological orthodoxy, Rothbart (e.g., Posner and Rothbart, 2000) has also emphasised the importance of high-level attentional networks that control both cognition and emotion. The Effortful control component of temperament is substantially defined by resistance to distraction, and may be supported by an anterior attentional system that affords executive control of attention, a system that continues to develop anatomically throughout childhood (Rothbart and Bates, 1998).

Much of the theoretical thrust of the above approaches to temperament is concerned with the interplay between biological predispositions and socialisation.

Few would disagree with Kagan's (1989) general statement that the child must learn to exercise voluntary control over its temperamental inclinations. 'Human behaviour is, some of the time, the product of the imposition of deliberative processes on the invisible, uncontrollable forces that both biology and history have created' (Kagan, 1989, p. 674). However, there are various perspectives on the nature of control mechanisms. Derryberry and Rothbart (1988) emphasise the in-built regulative mechanisms that the child inherits as part of the package of temperament-related functions. They see self-regulatory functions such as attention, approach and inhibition as serving to modulate reactive functions such as the arousal of motor activity, affect and physiological systems. In contrast, Thomas and Chess (1977) emphasise the social interaction between child and caregiver, and the match or goodness of fit between the child's temperament and the caregiver's style of interaction with the child. For example, if the child is temperamentally active, the success of caregiving may hinge on channelling that activity into acceptable pursuits. However, as Chess and Thomas (1984) point out, 'poorness of fit' does not necessarily lead to maladjustment. Speculatively, it is possible that innate self-regulation mechanisms may sometimes compensate for poor quality interaction with parents.

Conversely, poor self-regulation exacerbates problems: children whose temperament is characterised by high emotional intensity react to adult anger with distress and aggressive behaviour, perpetuating a dysfunctional cycle of interaction (Davies and Cummings, 1995). Results of studies that tested for interaction between temperament and parenting behaviours are rather mixed and inconsistent (Bates and McFadyen-Ketchum, 2000). However, it seems that fearful children benefit from gentle rather than harsh forms of control, and temperamentally unco-operative children are less likely to develop conduct problems if the mother uses more restrictive parenting control. In shaping the development of their children, parents to some extent respond to children's biologically influenced temperament. Constitutional temperament and the socialisation experiences provided by the environment interact to shape personality development.

The neo-Pavlovian tradition

Temperament research in the neo-Pavlovian tradition derives from the hypothesis of Pavlov, Teplov and Nebylitsyn (see Mangan, 1982, for a review) that the central nervous system (cns) has general, formal characteristics, and that these characteristics can be assessed both psychophysiologically and behaviourally (through conditioning, for example). For instance, individuals differ on their 'strength of excitation' of the nervous system, that is, the length of time that the cns maintains its responses in the face of intense or prolonged stimuli. The strength of excitation can be measured by techniques such as testing the effect of an extra, intense stimulus on a person's visual threshold (Mangan, 1982). At a behavioural level, strength of the nervous system may be inferred from the ability to maintain performance on a task under high levels of stimulation. Presumably, heavy-metal guitarists have

Table 3.3 *Scales of the Formal Characteristics of Behaviour–Temperament Inventory*

Scale	Temperamental characteristics
Briskness	Tendency to react quickly, maintain a high tempo of activity and to shift response easily when surroundings change
Perseverance	Tendency to continue and repeat behaviour after cessation of evoking stimuli
Sensory Sensitivity	Ability to react to sensory stimuli of low stimulative value
Emotional Reactivity	Tendency to react to affective stimuli with high emotional sensitivity and low emotional endurance
Endurance	Ability to react adequately in situations requiring long-lasting or high stimulative activity and tolerance of external stimulation
Activity	Tendency to undertake behaviour of high stimulative value or which provides strong stimulation from surroundings

Source Strelau and Zawadki (1995)

strong (or pharmacologically fortified) nervous systems. Strength of the nervous system may be one of the bases of extraversion (Gray, 1964), as extraverts appear to tolerate stimulation better than introverts (Eysenck and Eysenck, 1985). Sensory threshold studies (Shigehisa and Symons, 1973) are consistent with this hypothesis.

In an extended programme of research, Strelau (e.g., 1983; Strelau and Zawadzki, 1995; Strelau, 2001) has developed a temperament theory based on Pavolvian concepts. He acknowledges that it is often difficult to distinguish temperament and personality clearly, but lists five discriminating features:

1 Determinants of development: temperament is biologically based, whereas personality is shaped by social processes such as social learning.
2 Developmental stages: temperament appears in infancy, but personality gradually develops during childhood, and continues to change in the adult.
3 Species specificity: temperament characterises all mammals, but personality is exclusively human.
4 Behavioural characteristics: temperament relates to formal characteristics such as the energy or rapidity of response, but personality relates to the meaningful content of actions.
5 Regulative functions: temperament modifies specific behaviours, but personality relates to central integrative functions that ensure that behaviours are consistent and that goal-directed activities maintain their personal relevance.

Strelau developed a series of questionnaires that attempted to measure the Pavlovian constructs, and from these he formulated his own theory of temperament. Table 3.3 lists the scales of Strelau and Zawadzki's (1995) Formal Characteristics of Behaviour–Temperament Inventory (FCB–TI). Briskness and perseverance are, naturally, time-related behaviours; the remaining scales (e.g., endurance) are energy-related behaviours. Endurance is the scale that related most closely to the strength of excitation of the cns. Strelau and his associates have reported a number of studies linking temperament scales to Pavlovian behavioural and psychophysiological measures (e.g., Strelau, 1983; Klonowicz, 1987). Results of these studies are, so far, inconclusive, with several failures to obtain predicted relationships between questionnaire measures of strength of the nervous system and Pavlovian measures (Strelau, 1991). One source of difficulty is that the various Pavlovian indices of strength may be poorly inter-correlated (Strelau, 1991). It is debatable whether Pavlovian constructs are just difficult to measure, or fundamentally misconceived. As we shall see in chapter 7, there are also some problems with the construct of cortical arousal.

The relationship between temperament and personality

At a conceptual level, the relationship between personality and temperament is often confusing. Temperament is sometimes considered to be synonymous with personality, as in psychobiological trait theories (Cloninger, 1987), or temperament may be considered to be a subset of personality (its biological components), or the two types of construct may be considered to be conceptually distinct, if strongly related (Strelau, 1983; 2001). The personality–temperament relationship may also be tackled psychometrically: there are often substantial correlations between neo-Pavlovian constructs and traits such as extraversion and neuroticism (Mangan, 1982). Strelau and Zawadzki (1995) report the most comprehensive study, factor analysing the FCB together with the EPQ, NEO-FFI, EAS-TS and various other personality and temperament scales in a sample of 919 Poles. Table 3.4 shows some of the factor loadings. The NEO-FFI loadings show that the factors resemble the Big Five, although some of the variance in C relates to a low P/high A factor. An additional factor, not shown in table 3.4, related to the rather narrow quality of rhythmicity of behaviour. The neuroticism factor appears to account for a substantial amount of the variance in both the FCB-TI measures and in the three sub-scales of Buss and Plomins' (1984) Emotionality dimension. Extraversion relates to EAS-TS Activity and Sociability and to FCB-TI Activity.

Although Strelau and Zawadzki's (1995) results establish measurement overlap between temperament and personality measures, a number of questions remain open. On the basis of factor analysis, one might argue that temperament scales are just providing alternate measures of personality traits, or, alternatively, that the NEO-FFI and EPQ-R dimensions should be related to temperament rather than personality. A further possibility is that temperament and personality traits are distinct, but highly correlated because personality development is influenced by temperament. Implications of data are also limited by the use of an adult sample. Temperament and personality may be more sharply distinguished in children, even if they tend to converge in adults. The five factor model is quite well supported in studies of both parents' and teachers' ratings of children (Robins, John and Caspi, 1994; Mervielde, Buyst and De Fruyt, 1995), but factor analytic studies such as that of Mervielde, Buyst and De Fruyt (1995) have not tried to distinguish between

Table 3.4 *Selected loadings of personality and temperament scales on five factors*

		Factor				
		I	II	III	IV	V
FCB-TI	Briskness	−38	57			
	Perseverance	69				
	Sensory Sensitivity				69	
	Emotional Reactivity	79				
	Endurance	−59		47		
	Activity	71				
EAS-TS	Activity	56	46			
	Sociability	70				
	Fearfulness	70				
	Distress	79				
	Anger	64			−33	
EPQ-R	Extraversion	79				
	Neuroticism	84				
	Psychoticism			−77		
NEO-FFI	N	76				
	E		86			
	O				77	
	A				80	
	C		55	54		

Note We have omitted one factor related to rhythmicity, and loadings for scales of two additional temperament measures. Fearfulness, Distress and Anger represent Emotionality on the EAS-TS
Source Strelau and Zawadkzi (1995)

personality and temperament. Strelau (2001) sees temperament as inextricably linked with the concepts of traits, and sees temperament as a distinct biological level of explanation for individual differences. However, there is insufficient empirical evidence to judge whether this level of reductionism is necessary. As we shall see in chapter 7, most psychobiological researchers are content to link personality directly to biology.

Temperament, personality and stability: longitudinal studies

Results from some impressively data-rich longitudinal studies from around the world have become available towards the start of the twenty-first century. Such studies provide important insights into the development of personality from birth through to adulthood. For example, the New Zealand based Dunedin

Box 3.1 Does personality change in old age?

Little work has been carried out on the Big Five factors, but distress and anxiety, aspects of neuroticism, in old age are much more widely studied. In one such study, the Longitudinal Aging Study Amsterdam (LASA) of men and women aged fifty-five to eighty-five, 2,165 participants were followed up for three years (De Beurs et al., 2000). At baseline, the predictors of being anxious were being female, having hearing or eyesight problems and concurrent significant life events. Over the three years, levels of neuroticism on the Dutch Personality Inventory predicted chronic anxiety; after controlling for neuroticism, it was found that, independently of other life events and decline in cognitive function, the death of one's partner was predictive of increased levels of anxiety. Such personality changes in reaction to distressing life events fits in with Baltes (1987) life span view of personality development as arising from interactions between biological, social and psychological factors (McFadden, 1999). Erik Erikson's theory of psychosocial development, in the tradition of ego psychology, has emphasised the development of individuals as they enter different stages of life. While aspects of his ideas have been tested empirically, showing predicted increases in trust and intimacy (see chapter 5), some of the changes predicted by his model have not been demonstrated. The widely discussed increase in life span in Western countries means that research in personality change and stability into old age, during times of highly prevalent physical changes, is a high priority.

Study has studied the temperament and personality development of 1,037 boys and girls from their birth in 1972–3, and is continuing to follow up the sample (Caspi, 2000; Roberts, Caspi and Moffitt, 2000). The California based Terman Life-Cycle Study has provided data on the personality and life course of a sample of over 1,500 intellectually gifted children (e.g., Martin and Friedman, 2000). An international group of researchers has combined personality data from German, British, Spanish, Czech and Turkish samples of adolescents and adults to provide information on personality development (McCrae et al., 2000). There are fewer studies of traits in old age, but in box 3.1 we describe some types of work that have been carried out in samples of older people.

The Dunedin Study is a prospective and longitudinal study that collected information on the same individuals on several occasions: birth, age 3, 5, 7, 9, 11, 13, 15, 18 and 21 (Caspi, 2000). Because it was a carefully sampled birth cohort, it is representative of the general population, and it has not suffered from high attrition: 97 per cent of the study sample were tested at the latest wave, when they were twenty-six. The first waves of testing were designed to assess the children's temperament type: well-adjusted, undercontrolled, or inhibited. Well-adjusted children ($n=405$) were able to control themselves, were self-confident,

Box 3.2 Early temperament and criminal behaviour

The Dunedin longitudinal study of temperament and personality development studied children from birth, into adolescence and beyond (Caspi, 2000). At age three, children were classified into three temperament groups: undercontrolled ($n=106$), inhibited ($n=80$) or well-adjusted ($n=405$). At age twenty-one, the participants filled in the Self-Report Delinquency Interview (Moffitt et al., 1994). This scale asks about criminal-type behaviours in the past twelve months such as burglary, assault or vandalism. Children who had been undercontrolled at age three were significantly more likely to report being involved in such behaviours at age twenty-one. In addition, independently obtained criminal convictions data showed that 14 per cent of undercontrolled children had more than one conviction by the age of twenty-one, in comparison to 6 per cent of well-adjusted children and 7 per cent of inhibited children. Moreover, the undercontrolled children were also less likely to report that their social setting would inhibit criminal behaviour: their 'perceived social deterrents to crime' scores were significantly lower than either the inhibited or well-adjusted children. Personality disorders were also more prevalent in undercontrolled children: 7 per cent were diagnosed with antisocial personality disorder by the age of twenty-one versus approximately 3 per cent in the other two groups. It should be noted that only a small proportion of children of any temperament type were involved in criminal activities, and that associations do not imply that the temperament itself, rather than the situational context of the family or peer group (perhaps affecting temperament measures even at age three), *causes* the criminal behaviour. However, the findings indicate that early childhood temperament could act as a marker for possible problem behaviours later on.

and were not overly upset by new people or situations. Undercontrolled children ($n=106$) were impulsive, restless, easy to distract and emotionally labile. Inhibited children ($n=80$) were fearful, hesitant socially and were upset by new people and situations. The initial data on temperaments were then analysed in relation to childhood development and personality at ages eighteen and twenty-one. Using well-adjusted children as the comparison group, Caspi reported that children in the 'undercontrolled' category were more likely to have behavioural problems throughout childhood and into adolescence; inhibited types did not suffer from behavioural problems but tended to deal with problems by internalising them.

At age eighteen, the Dunedin study subjects were assessed on the Multidimensional Personality Questionnaire (MPQ), which measures eight factors, including 'control', 'alienation', 'well-being', and 'social closeness' (Caspi, 2000; Roberts, Caspi and Moffitt, 2000). The three temperamental types showed quite different personality profiles at ages eighteen, twenty-one and twenty-six. Undercontrolled children, when adolescents, scored low on control and harm avoidance but high on aggression and alienation, and were rated by others as untrustworthy and low in conscientiousness. Inhibited children as adolescents were high on control and harm avoidance and low on aggression and social potency (dominance), and were rated by others as lacking in self-confidence and energy. In addition, the childhood temperaments were predictive of 'real-life' outcomes such that undercontrolled children were more likely to have participated in criminal behaviour and to have relationship difficulties. These results are described in more detail in box 3.2. The effect sizes were small-to-moderate; the temperaments could predict a statistically significant, moderate amount of variance in personality and behaviours in adolescence and early adulthood.

The research team also examined the case for temperament/personality change: whether there were indicators of maturing in personality from age eighteen to twenty-six (Roberts, Caspi and Moffitt, 2000). In adolescents who were low in self-control, well-being or social closeness, there were reliable and consistent 'maturing-type' changes in these traits from age eighteen to age twenty-six: self-control, well-being and social closeness increased, and aggression decreased. Adolescents who already displayed high maturity at age eighteen were least likely to undergo further personality changes as they entered their twenties. Overall, however, most of the participants showed reliable changes (changes not attributable to errors of measurement) on at least one of the eight dimensions.

Caspi and colleagues (2000) conclude that, while their study provides evidence that childhood temperament does predict some of the variance in behaviours and personality in later childhood and adolescence, the data 'suggest that a strict temperament interpretation of personality development is incorrect'. However, they note that, as with IQ, our methods of assessing temperament in childhood may be subject to error, thereby decreasing the predictive power of temperament. They do, however, find it encouraging that there is evidence of personality maturation between the ages of eighteen and twenty-six. Their data indicate that temperament and personality measures in childhood and adolescence are good predictors of temperament, personality and behaviour in the short term (two to three years) but the farther away in time the assessment is made, the lower its predictive power. In a later review, Caspi and Roberts (2001) discuss some of the influences on developmental personality change, such as family circumstances and peer group norms, and note that their longitudinal findings from the Dunedin Study suggest only modest continuity from childhood to adulthood.

Lewis (2001) points out that the modest size of correlations such as those reported by Caspi indicates that very little of the variance in later personality is accounted for by earlier measures of temperament. Further, he argues that characteristics in children are not consistent in different contexts (such as at school and at home), and that the rating of children, because of observer bias, is prone to error. For example, with depression, teachers, parents and clinicians give quite different ratings of children, all of which are different from the child's own assessment. Therefore, postulated influences on change or stability of individual differences may differ depending on the characteristic measured. Using the most consistent rater to try to reduce measurement error does not address the problem that the characteristic may indeed vary by context, and that inconsistency of ratings is not a measurement error at all. In addition, apparent consistency of temperament may be an artifact of recall bias of the raters, who will have constructed their own view of the child (this artifact may also be apparent in adults, when rating themselves on personality scales). In addition, contrary to the idea that characteristics are stable, Lewis explains that attachment, depression and fearfulness in children all vary according to family circumstances – that they are not fixed by a given point in childhood (Lewis, 2001). However, it may well be that depression or attachment, which could be viewed as states rather than traits, are much more prone to measurement error and change over time than other characteristics. These are important points to consider in the design and interpretation of studies, particularly regarding measurements and underlying assumptions about the models being tested. As we saw in chapter 2, progress is now being made on being able to incorporate both persons and situations into personality research – progress that also needs to be made into temperament research.

In McCrae et al.'s (2000) study of German, British, Spanish, Czech and Turkish groups on the NEO-FFI personality scale, the Czech, British, German, Turkish samples contained adolescents as well as adults. The study was focused on mean trait stability or change rather than individual trait stability or change. As a whole, personality data from the five nations showed good internal consistency on the extraversion, neuroticism and conscientiousness scales. On aggregating the data, they found that there were declines in neuroticism, extraversion and openness from ages eighteen to thirty, and increases in agreeableness and conscientiousness. In fourteen to eighteen year olds, neuroticism and extraversion were higher still than in eighteen to twenty-two year olds.

Unlike the Dunedin study data, the personality data from the Terman Life Cycle study were retrospectively gathered from archival sources. In the original Terman study, the 1,528 gifted children were rated by their teachers and parents on temperament measures (Terman and Oden, 1947). To validate these measures against the Big Five factors, Martin and Friedman (2000) recruited a new sample of children and a new sample of adults. The children were rated by parents according to the Terman criteria on temperament, as well as on the NEO-PI-R. The adult sample was asked to complete the NEO-PI-R. In the childhood sample, the NEO-PI-R five factors correlated modestly with the temperament measures (e.g., 'social dependency' with conscientiousness, r=0.55; 'cheerfulness-humour' with agreeableness, r=0.31). Having converted the temperament measures into Big Five factors, Martin and Friedman then examined the correlations between the Terman sample's childhood scores with their adulthood NEO-PI-R scores: correlation coefficients ranged from around 0.14 (between NEO-PI assertiveness and childhood 'sociability', re-labelled extraversion) to 0.55 (between NEO-PI gregariousness and childhood extraversion). Effect sizes of the correlations between childhood temperament and adulthood personality were small to moderate, as we would expect from studies such as the Dunedin study. This study importantly suggests that data from archival sources can be used to create childhood personality variables that resemble the Big Five. Such data, while not able to replace prospective, longitudinal studies of temperament and personality, do help open up the field for further retrospective data collection to enhance the understandably few long-term, longitudinal studies that exist.

Together, the three studies – the individual-level, prospective data from the Dunedin study, the mean-level group data across nations, and the archival data – suggest that there is some reliable stability within childhood on temperament and personality measures, and reliable changes in personality measures from adolescence to adulthood. Childhood temperament – to a certain extent – can predict some behavioural outcomes in adolescence; more mature adolescents are less likely to show personality changes as they enter adulthood. As we have seen from the extensive studies on stability of personality in adulthood, there is much less evidence to show reliable changes in personality within adulthood. Indeed, in their review of personality development research, Caspi and Roberts (2001) conclude that: (1) personality continuity from childhood to adulthood is modest; and (2) while personality traits do not become fixed at a given age in adulthood, consistency over time, rather than change, is the norm.

Conclusions

1. Empirical studies show that major traits, especially in adulthood, are remarkably stable over time, and it is difficult to detect patterns of systematic change. Traits typically appear to have resilience in the face of the normal events of a life, especially after age thirty. In adulthood, it may take major events such as mental illness to induce substantial trait change.

2. It is often desirable to assess traits by aggregating measures taken at different points in time, because this method will tap into behaviours that are most consistent. However, major trait measures are robust enough that it is valid to measure traits just once in many different types of investigations. For example, cross-sectional and longitudinal studies of the relationships between personality traits and emotional or health outcomes have capitalised on this, as we shall see in later chapters.

3. Temperament has been presented as a separate conceptualisation from the trait concept, but, as we have seen, there is a convergence between temperamental and personality trait constructs in adulthood. Constitutional temperament interacts with socialisation (environmental experiences) to shape personality development. Nonetheless, long-term, longitudinal developmental studies have shown us that childhood temperament does predict some reliable variance in personality traits and various behavioural outcomes in late adolescence. However, there are still problems with ratings of characteristics in children, depending on

the characteristic in question and the rater, and this continues to have implications for how we study personality development in childhood.

4. In general, the research on traits has tended to strengthen and validate the trait construct, showing general trait stability in adulthood, and modest correlations between childhood temperament and adult personality traits. Perhaps it is most correct to conclude that while personality traits can be described as stable, they cannot be described as rigid.

Further reading

Caspi, A. and Roberts, B. W. (2001) Personality development across the life course: the argument for change and continuity. *Psychological Inquiry*, 12, 49–66.

McCrae, R. R., Costa, P. T., Ostendorf, F., Angleitner, A., Hrebickova, M., Avia, M. D., Sanz, J., Sanchez-Bernardos, M. L., Kusdil, M. E., Woodfield, R., Saunders, P. R. and Smith, P. B. (2000) Nature over nurture: temperament, personality, and life span development. *Journal of Personality and Social Psychology*, 78, 173–186.

4   Stable traits and transient states

Introduction: the place of states in trait theory

Traits refer to stabilities of behaviour and beliefs about our enduring dispositions. However, we must also take into account the variation over time of the person's 'state of mind' or 'transient internal conditions' (Eysenck and Eysenck, 1980). Since antiquity, philosophers such as Aristotle and Cicero distinguished temporary emotional states from stable dispositions. Someone whose personality is characterised by trait anxiety is not usually anxious the whole time. The high trait anxious person may experience feelings of anxiety more often and more intensely than the low trait anxious person, but, even so, periods of feeling anxious alternate with periods of more relaxed states of mind (Spielberger, 1966). Similarly, even extraverts may occasionally wish for solitude, and introverts may sometimes be in a party mood. Short-lasting, unstable general characteristics of the person, such as a temporary feeling of anxiety or sociability, are known as states. In principle, states may refer to any reliably measurable characteristic, but, typically, state variables refer to conscious, verbally reportable qualities such as moods.

Interest in dimensions of mood goes back to Wilhelm Wundt (1897), but, in the behaviourist epoch, the field languished until the 1950s and 1960s. Nowlis (1965) developed a pioneering adjective checklist, requiring the person to rate how well each adjective corresponded to their present mood. Although Nowlis hypothesised twelve dimensions of mood, subsequent work has reduced dimensionality to as few as two or three fundamental constructs. Subsequent research on mood has seen argument over the number and nature of fundamental mood dimensions, echoing contentions about personality structure. At around the same time, Spielberger (1966) developed a scale for the emotional state of anxiety, using questions about the person's thoughts and feelings, rather than single adjectives. Emotions are often conceptualised as discrete categories of experience, but Spielberger's work suggested that anxiety, at least, could be assessed as a continuous dimension.

Spielberger (e.g., 1966, 1972; Spielberger et al., 1999) also addressed the relationship between states and traits in the context of anxiety. How exactly do temporary feelings of anxiety (the state) relate to anxiety-prone personality (the trait)? Spielberger characterised trait anxiety as a general predisposition to experience transient states of anxiety. State anxiety was defined primarily by introspective verbal report, as consciously perceived feelings of tension and apprehension, but was expected also to relate to arousal of the autonomic nervous system. Spielberger, Gorsuch and Lushene (1970) developed a widely used questionnaire, the State-Trait Anxiety Inventory (STAI), which includes scales for both trait and state anxiety. Items on the trait scale concern the person's usual feelings, whereas state items inquire about the person's feelings at the time of completing the questionnaire. Trait and state measures are generally modestly positively correlated, confirming that, probabilistically, high trait anxious individuals tend to experience higher state anxiety than low state anxious individuals (Zeidner, 1998; Endler and Kocovski, 2001). However, state anxiety is also influenced by situational factors; even a very low trait anxious person is likely to experience state anxiety if the situation is sufficiently threatening, such as encountering a masked man with a knife in a dark alley. Hence, traits and situational threats interactively affect states, which are the more direct influence on behaviour.

This chapter reviews dimensional models of subjective state, and their relationships with personality traits. We will review the following issues:

Differentiating traits and states. Traits and states can be assessed separately, depending on the stability of the measurement. We will list psychometric criteria for distinguishing the two types of construct. Beyond assessment issues, states may mediate the effects of traits on behaviour. In chapter 2, we discussed the interaction of trait and situational variables. We will look in more detail at Spielberger's (1966; Spielberger et al., 1999) state-trait theory of anxiety, that sees states as transmitting or *mediating* the behavioural consequences of traits, in interaction with situations.

Dimensional structure of states. Individual differences in states are of interest in their own right. Just as we can use techniques such as factor analysis to identify the principal trait dimensions, such as the Big Five, so too we can attempt to determine the main dimensions of mental states. We will review psychometric studies of mood, and of other attributes of state, and the experimental studies that validate measures of the main dimensions.

Effects of traits on states. Empirical studies show that traits and states are often correlated. In particular, extraversion tends to relate to positive mood, and neuroticism to negative mood. We will review studies that suggest some direct correspondence of these trait and state constructs, together with evidence suggesting an interactionist perspective may be more appropriate.

Trait-state models

Zuckerman's criteria for state measures

Spielberger's state-trait model of anxiety illustrates informally the distinction between states and traits. However, we also need more formal psychometric criteria, so that we can assess whether a questionnaire is in fact measuring a trait or state. Next, we present a formal set of criteria proposed by Zuckerman (1976), having re-worded them somewhat and illustrated their application to distinguishing trait and state anxiety.

1 Trait and state tests should have high internal consistency. Trait tests should show high retest reliability, but state tests should not.

The assumption here is that traits are stable over time, but states tend to fluctuate; hence, a measurement of how anxious a person feels on any one occasion gives only a poor indication of their state anxiety a day or a week later. Thus, the trait and state measures are distinguished not only by their content and/or the instructions given to subjects, but also by the formal psychometric property of test–retest reliability (stability) over durations of a day or more. For example, for the STAI, Spielberger et al. (1999) quote typical stability coefficients of around 0.8 for trait anxiety and 0.33 for state anxiety.

2 Trait and state tests that purport to measure the same construct should correlate to a low degree, but valid trait tests should correlate moderately with the aggregate mean of a series of state tests completed on different occasions.

Because states fluctuate, the trait is typically rather weakly related to any single administration of the state measure. Suppose though that we assess state anxiety on several occasions and compute the mean for each subject. This mean provides an index of the person's typical level of state anxiety, which should be more strongly related to trait anxiety than to any single state anxiety measure. Zuckerman (1976) provides empirical data which support this contention. He argues that traits may simply represent averages of states over time. This view of traits suggests structural equivalence between traits and states; there should be a corresponding trait dimension for every state. Aggregation of single-occasion data is, as discussed in chapter 2, a well-established tactic for increasing the predictive validity of traits.

3 A valid trait test should correlate more highly with related trait measures than with other state tests. In contrast, a state test should correlate more highly with other concurrent state measures than with trait measures.

This criterion emphasises that conceptually related trait and state constructs, such as trait and state anxiety, are psychometrically distinct. For example, trait anxiety should be more strongly related to similar traits, such as neuroticism, than to state anxiety. Conversely, state anxiety should be more strongly related to other concurrently assessed negative mood measures than to trait anxiety.[1]

4 State but not trait measures should be sensitive to immediate conditions that are expected to affect the relevant construct.

Experimental manipulations of threat should influence state anxiety. However, the trait scale aims to measure only the stable predisposition to threat, which is the same regardless of the degree of threat afforded by the immediate environment. Ideally, therefore, trait anxiety scores should be unaffected by the level of immediate threat. As Eysenck and Eysenck (1980) also point out, the state change response to immediate conditions may be moderated by traits, as discussed further below.

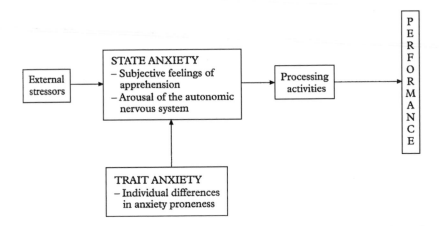

Figure 4.1 A state-trait model for detrimental effects of anxiety on information-processing and performance
Source Eysenck (1982)

Causal status of states as mediating variables

Trait-state models are important because they tell us something about how traits influence behaviour, i.e., about cause and effect. A basic principle of these models is that trait effects on behaviour are mediated by states, i.e., that states have a more direct effect on behaviour than do traits. Figure 4.1 shows a simplified version of Spielberger's (1966) model proposed by Eysenck (1982) as an explanation for anxiety effects on performance. The effects of trait anxiety are indirect; the trait, together with situational factors such as external stressors, influences the state, but it is the state which directly influences internal processing activities, and hence behaviour. Suppose we have two individuals, one high and one low trait anxious, but both having the same elevated STAI state anxiety score. We might then predict that both should tend to perform equally poorly due to their high state anxiety (other factors being equal). Both individuals should show the same behavioural impairment, despite their differences in personality. This prediction succeeds fairly well for certain kinds of anxiety-induced performance impairment. For example, state anxiety is more reliably associated with short term memory impairment than is trait anxiety (Eysenck, 1982).

However, issues of causality and mediation are frequently problematic, in the psychology of traits as in other disciplines. States may sometimes mediate trait effects, but sometimes it is not so simple to trace the causal path from trait to state to behaviour. In some situations, behavioural differences between high and low trait anxious individuals are found even if they are matched for state anxiety. As we shall see in chapter 12, anxiety relates to selective attention for threat stimuli, and, in this instance, trait anxiety is a stronger predictor of measures of attention than state anxiety (M. W. Eysenck, 1992). Trait anxious subjects may anticipate potential threats even if they are not actually experiencing state anxiety, leading to a 'hypervigilant' scanning of the environment for threat. Extraversion and neuroticism appear to be linked to cognitive biases in processing affective information that are not mediated by mood (Zelenski and Larsen, 2002). The effects of traits on behaviour may also be mediated by the skills and learned responses the individual brings to a particular context. For example, high N and high trait anxiety individuals may learn to avoid social situations, leading to poorer social skills and shyness (Cheek and Melchior, 1990). Similarly the 'test anxiety' that some students experience in examination settings can be assessed as a trait that is correlated with performance impairment (Zeidner, 1998).

However, there appear to be at least two causal paths for this effect. In some students, the anxiety state does seem to cause performance impairments, mediating the effect of trait anxiety (Sarason, 1984; Zeidner, 1998). In others, state anxiety is raised because they are poorly prepared, and it is lack of preparation and learning rather than anxiety which is the main cause of their poor performance (Mueller, 1992). Thus, states are one important factor that mediate trait effects on performance, but other causal mechanisms may operate also.

Theories of state mediation

Addressing the causality issue requires a theory of how traits, states and behaviour may be interrelated. In particular, we would like to know whether states act as indices or markers for underlying biological or cognitive processes which are the true causal factors. For example, state anxiety might be a marker for brain processes initiated by signals of threat (Gray, 1991), or for information-processing associated with threat anticipation. (As we shall see in chapter 12, the information-processing hypothesis is better supported by the empirical data than physiological theories.) A good theory would explain how traits influence states and behaviours in terms of specific mechanisms, rather than just describing a probabilistic trait–state relationship without insight into its origins.

In fact, theories in this area are quite varied, and both psychobiological and cognitive explanations have attracted interest. Traits may indeed operate through influencing the way the brain responds to stimuli, as further discussed in chapter 7. For example, Eysenck (1967) proposed that extraversion–introversion relates to arousability of the reticular formation and cerebral cortex, such that the cortex tends to be in a higher state of arousal in introverts than in extraverts. It may be individual differences in cortical arousal state that are responsible for emotional and behavioural differences between extraverts and introverts. It is claimed that moderate levels of arousal promote optimal mood, so we might expect that extraverts would be happiest in stimulating environments, whereas introverts would feel best in low-arousal settings.

An alternative biological theory (Gray, 1987; Pickering et al., 1997) distinguishes various brain systems that include a Behavioural Activation System (BAS), controlling sensitivity to reward stimuli, and a Behavioural Inhibition System (BIS), controlling sensitivity to punishment stimuli. The BAS may influence positive emotional states. As we shall discuss shortly, it may be more easily activated in extraverts than in introverts, so that extraverts tend to be more cheerful and exuberant than introverts. Again, on the state-trait principle, these differences in emotional state may be responsible for behavioural differences between extraverts and introverts. In addition, activity of the BIS may be experienced as negative emotion. Trait anxiety and neuroticism have been linked to greater sensitivity of the BIS, so that these traits make the person prone to negative affects such as anxiety and depression (see chapter 7).

From the neuroscience perspective, traits correspond to brain systems whose states may not be directly observable: mood reflects the unconscious operations of sub-cortical brain structures. Hence, we cannot necessarily use a state questionnaire to evaluate the activity of these systems. Instead, we may need to use psychophysiological indices of state, or infer state change from experimental data, although both these approaches have methodological difficulties (Matthews and Gilliland, 1999; see also chapter 7). However, the general state–trait principle applies. Traits may relate to biases in the neural machinery which controls the activation of brain arousal and/or motivation systems. Activation of these systems has two concurrent effects: first, a change in subjective state, and, second, a change in behaviour. For example, in Gray's (1991) anxiety theory, activation of the BIS leads to both increased anxiety, and to behaviours such as orienting towards possible threats. Hence, subjective state change is not directly linked to behavioural change: both are outputs of the same underlying brain system.

An alternative explanation refers to cognition: states may reflect how the person evaluates and acts upon some external situation. The complete version of Spielberger's (1966) state-trait model of anxiety, shown in figure 4.2, was one of the first cognitive models. The central causal construct is the person's *cognitive appraisal* of the situation, which independently influences both state anxiety and defence mechanisms for anticipating threat, which, in contemporary terms, we might conceptualise as coping responses (Zeidner and Endler, 1996). In this model, trait anxiety is associated with tendencies to appraise situations as threatening, perhaps leading to an exaggerated sense of danger. The effects of trait anxiety on behaviour are mediated by cognitive appraisal, but appraisal influences behaviour both through elevating state anxiety, and through influencing the person's choice of action for coping with the threatening situation. Much research on emotion supports the hypothesis that affect is closely linked to appraisals (Scherer, 2001). Of course, cognitive and biological explanations may be complementary rather than exclusive, as discussed further below.

Contemporary research on affect and cognition frequently refers to Lazarus's (1999) transactional model of emotion and stress. Lazarus sees the person as being in continuous dynamic interaction with the external environment, with emotions indexing the reciprocal relationship between person and environment. Thus, moods may reflect not only how the environment influences the person (indexed by appraisals), but also the person's attempts to handle demands and opportunities by acting on the environment (indexed by coping strategies). As we shall see, investigating appraisal and coping as possible mediating factors has been useful in the study of both mood (see below) and stress (see chapter 9). However, transactional theory parts company from trait theory in that, at times, it appears that

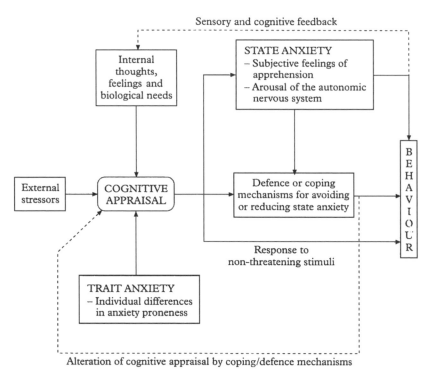

Figure 4.2 A state-trait model of anxiety in which cognitive appraisal plays a central role
Source adapted from Spielberger (1966)

emotion reflects some holistic integration of environmental and person factors, which precludes separating these component parts. As Parkinson et al. (1996) discuss, such notions are difficult to test empirically. In the trait context, the more useful inference is that trait and environmental factors may be correlated. People's efforts to cope influence their exposure to environments that may influence their moods, as when a sensation-seeker chooses to engage in some risky activity like sky-diving. To some extent, the influences of traits should be understood within this environmental context.

The final point to make about theory is that psychobiological and cognitive accounts of traits and states are not necessarily incompatible (Corr, 2000). Matthews (2000) suggests that there are three levels of description that may be useful (these levels are described formally by cognitive science): the biological, the cognitive-architectural and the (self-)knowledge level. Figure 4.3 illustrates how these different levels might apply to personality effects on mood (Matthews, Derryberry and Siegle, 2000). First, moods may reflect individual differences in the activation of brain systems, as in Gray's (1991) personality theory. Second, moods may be linked to specific symbolic computations (i.e., information-processing), as described by appraisal theory: e.g., coding a stimulus as threatening directly produces feelings of anxiety. Third, as in transactional theory, moods may index a higher-level personal meaning, reflecting contextual factors and personal beliefs

- **Neural**

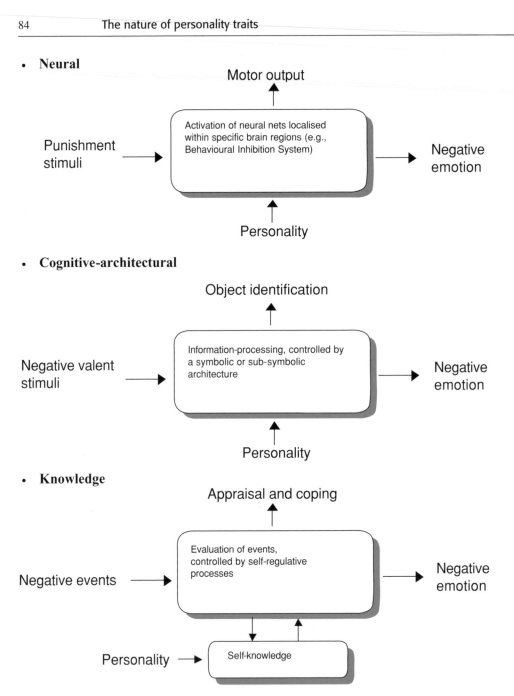

- **Cognitive-architectural**

- **Knowledge**

Figure 4.3 Schematic outlines of alternative cognitive science explanations for personality–emotion associations
Source Matthews et al. (2000)

(self-knowledge) as well as the immediate coding of the event. All three levels of explanation might potentially explain data on personality and mood; determining which level works best requires the normal scientific process of building and testing theories based on one or other type of construct. For example, if it was shown that moods correlated strongly with some neural state, we might not need to refer to information-processing or self-knowledge at all.

State dimensions: affect, mood and self-report arousal

In contrast to studies of traits, there have been few attempts to derive a comprehensive structural framework for state research. There are no major psychometric barriers towards doing so; Cattell (1973) describes factor-analytic techniques which aim to distinguish traits and states through analysis of longitudinal data. He also indicates the importance of distinguishing states from trait change over periods of months or years. Curran and Cattell (1974) developed the Eight State Questionnaire (8SQ) through factor analysis, but high inter-scale correlations have tended to discourage researchers from using it. In general, researchers who have developed state measures have had more specific aims of assessing a single dimension, such as state anxiety, or of developing a comprehensive dimensional model of one particular aspect of state, such as mood or subjective arousal.

Traditionally, psychological experience is divided into three domains of affect, cognition and motivation (Hilgard, 1980). The majority of research has been directed towards affect; i.e., moods and subjective arousal states (we will return to cognitive and motivational states subsequently). Moods are distinguished from emotions in that they are not explicitly linked to specific objects or events, so that they may persist in the absence of specific triggering events (Matthews, 1992b; Parkinson et al., 1996). It is often assumed that there are relatively few fundamental dimensions of mood, whereas the structure of emotions may be complex. There are various techniques for mood assessment (Mackay, 1980), although in recent years the most common technique has been the mood adjective checklist, which requires the respondent to rate the applicability of descriptive adjectives to their current mood (Parkinson et al., 1996). Of course, as with any self-report, the validity of people's introspections is open to question. Arguably, people may have limited awareness of their own moods, although mood checklists typically assess the more salient features of affective state, such as happiness and tension, rather than the more subtle emotions. State measures may be less sensitive to failures of introspection than trait measures because they require an immediate assessment of conscious state, rather than accessing typical beliefs and behaviours from long-term memory.

In addition, as with traits, social pressures may lead people to distort their responses, consciously or unconsciously. However, recent research (e.g., Lucas et al., 1996; Schimmack, Böckenholt and Reisenzein, 2002) using multivariate modelling techniques has concluded that the influence of response bias on mood ratings seems to be minor, at most. There may be a place for alternate, objective indices of affect using techniques such as psychophysiology and measuring facial expression. Unfortunately, as Parkinson et al. (1996) point out, none of these techniques has proved very sensitive or discriminating, and different indices often fail to converge. Indeed, autonomic reactivity may be linked to the degree of effort applied to mood-regulation rather than to mood per se (Gendolla and Krüsken, 2001). Thus, self-reports will provide the main medium of assessment into the foreseeable future.

In this section, we review the principal dimensional models of mood. The first family of models proposes that there are just two dimensions; a second set of models is based on three dimensions. We will look also at how we can place the various negative emotions within these very parsimonious models, and we will briefly review evidence on the validity of mood scales. We focus here on the structure of mood in non-clinical populations. There is an important literature on the assessment of moods such as anxiety and depression in clinical samples, but this work has been more concerned with validating specific constructs (e.g., ensuring that depression scales discriminate depressed patients from other groups) than with comprehensive structural models.

Two mood dimensions: energy and tension

There may be as few as two or three fundamental dimensions of mood. Thayer (1978, 1989, 1996, 2001) developed the Activation–Deactivation Adjective Check-list (AD-ACL) to assess two dimensions of subjective arousal, currently referred to as energetic arousal (EA) and tense arousal (TA). EA contrasts feelings of vigour and energy with tiredness and fatigue, whereas TA contrasts tension and nervous-ness with relaxation and calmness. These are *bipolar* dimensions, in that each one proposes a spectrum of states anchored at each end of the spectrum by states pre-sumed to be incompatible. For example, one cannot be simultaneously energised and tired. Thayer suggests that the two arousal dimensions represent the activity of underlying biopsychological systems. Energetic arousal is associated with readi-ness for vigorous action, and muscular-skeletal activation. Tense arousal reflects a preparatory-emergency system, activated by some real or imagined danger that prepares the person for both 'fight or flight' and inhibiting ongoing activity to maintain readiness for reacting to threat. Thayer's research is notable for its use of careful experimental studies to show that energy and tension have different origins and antecedents.

A somewhat similar two-dimensional model of mood has been proposed by Watson (Watson and Tellegen, 1985; Watson, 2000). Rather than focus exclu-sively on self-report arousal, Watson and his colleagues aimed to cover the full range of moods, including those that have no particular connotation of high or low arousal. Their factor-analytic studies identified two orthogonal dimensions labeled Positive Affect (PA) and Negative Affect (NA), measured by the Positive and Negative Affect Scale (PANAS: Watson and Clark, 1988). PA (rather like en-ergetic arousal) contrasts feelings of elation with lethargy and dullness, whereas NA (like tense arousal) contrasts negative emotions such as anxiety and anger with contented, serene states. According to Watson, PA and NA reflect the activity of two biobehavioural systems that integrate subjective, cognitive, biological and behavioural aspects. PA is linked to a dopaminergic Behavioural Facilitation System (BFS), that strongly resembles Gray's BAS, whereas NA is presumed to reflect Gray's BIS. It is important to realise that Watson and his colleagues have not conducted any psychophysiological studies in support of these claims, and so these biological bases may seem rather conjectural. We return to Gray's personality theory in chapter 7.

Subsequently, Watson and Clark (1997) developed an explicitly hierarchical model, such that PA and NA are higher-order factors, each defined by a set of more narrowly defined affects: fear, sadness, guilt and hostility (NA), and joviality, self-assurance and attentiveness (PA). These affects are measured by the expanded PANAS (PANAS-X: Watson and Clark, 1997) that also measures further specific affects of shyness, fatigue, serenity and surprise. By analogy with Thayer, one might expect fatigue to represent the negative pole of PA, and serenity the negative end of the NA spectrum, but in fact, correlations between the additional affects and NA and PA are complex (Watson, 2000), indicating a need for further psychometric investigation. Indeed, Watson et al. (1999) acknowledge that the fit of the PA–NA model to data is imperfect.

So far, we have seen a reasonably good convergence between the Thayer and Watson models, with some differences in detail. Cox and Mackay (1985) also proposed a similar scheme, with dimensions of arousal (EA/PA) and stress (TA/NA). However, there is another way of constructing a two-dimensional model, proposed by Russell (1979; Russell and Feldman Barrett, 1999). This model essentially rotates the Thayer axes through forty-five degrees to obtain new dimensions of activation and pleasure. Activation indexes the total amount of arousal experienced, both energetic and tense, whereas pleasure refers to the balance of positive moods over negative moods. Evidence for this model comes from studies analysing the meanings that people attach to affective terms. Studies using multidimensional scaling and semantic differential techniques suggested that valence of evaluation (i.e., positive or negative) and activation were the main sources of word meaning. Diener et al. (1985) propose a somewhat similar scheme with dimensions of intensity of affect, similar to arousal, and frequency of affect, similar to pleasure.

One advantage of the Russell scheme is that it avoids what seems like a shortcoming of the PA–NA model, i.e., that a person could apparently experience strong positive and negative mood simultaneously (remembering that PA and NA are independent dimensions). It seems implausible that one could be both happy and depressed, at the same instant in time. There is indeed extensive evidence that the intercorrelation of PA and NA is close to zero in various circumstances (Watson, 2000). It has been claimed that this apparent independence is an artifact of response style, and, in fact, the true correlation between PA and NA approaches -1, so that positive and negative moods are the two poles of a single continuum (Green, Salovey and Truax, 1999). However, sophisticated multivariate studies that separate mood and response style variance have failed to substantiate this view, although

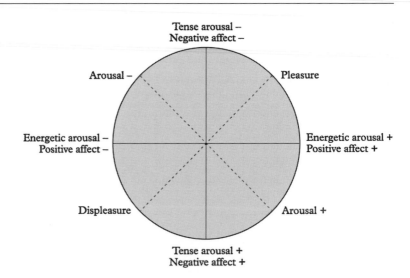

Figure 4.4 Two-dimensional models of mood

these studies have shown that the format used for response may have some modest biasing effects (Schimmack et al., 2002). Nevertheless, the extent of compatibility between positive and negative affect requires further attention.

Assuming a two-dimensional model of mood, what are we to make of these two different rotations of the axes, proposed by (1) Russell (1979) and (2) Watson and Tellegen (1985) and Thayer (1989)? One view is that the issue is really rather minor, in that both descriptive schemes refer to the same dimensional space, and are mathematically equivalent (Larsen and Diener, 1992; Yik and Russell, 2001). Thus, both schemes can be represented as a *circumplex*, a structure in which mood descriptors are placed around the diameter of a circle, and the angular disparity between descriptors represents their correlation (the smaller the angle, the larger the correlation). Figure 4.4 shows the approximate alignment of the various two-dimensional models in their common dimensional space. Note the ambiguity of the word 'arousal' revealed by these analyses. As there are mood words all around the circumplex, perhaps it is just a matter of convenience where we put the axes. Another view is that the axes should be placed to correspond to whatever two under-lying psychological or physiological systems are actually driving the experience of mood. From this point of view, the Thayer-Watson orientation seems preferable, given that both researchers link their dimensions to underlying biobehavioural systems (albeit with limited evidence). Psychometric evidence may also favour the energy (PA) and tension (NA) axes, given that it is hard to obtain a reliable scale for Russell's general activation dimension (Watson et al., 1999; Schimmack and Grob, 2000).

Three-dimensional models: separating pleasure from arousal

There is no doubt that the two-dimensional models are the most popular in the USA, but, in Europe, three-dimensional models have often been preferred (Schimmack

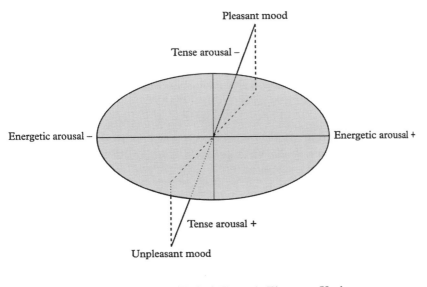

Pleasant mood

Tense arousal −

Energetic arousal −   Energetic arousal +

Tense arousal +

Unpleasant mood

- - - -   Projection of the Hedonic Tone axis (Pleasant vs Unpleasant
          mood) onto the plane defined by the Energetic and Tense
          arousal dimensions

Figure 4.5 A three-dimensional model of mood
Source Matthews et al. (1990)

and Grob, 2000). Such models go back to Wundt's (1897) introspection that affects vary along three separate dimensions: pleasure–displeasure, tension–relaxation and excitement–calm. As Schimmack and Grob (2000) point out, factor-analytic studies in the United Kingdom, Scandinavia and Germany have found three dimensions rather similar to those proposed by Wundt. For example, Matthews, Jones and Chamberlain (1990) suggested that, rather than attaching feelings of happiness and depression to the Thayer arousal dimensions, a third dimension related to the overall pleasantness of mood should be distinguished. Hence, Matthews et al. proposed three dimensions: EA, TA and hedonic tone (HT) or pleasantness. TA relates to feelings of anxiety, whereas the lower end of the HT dimension is defined by anger, depression and unpleasant mood. The three dimensions are oblique, in that there is a moderate positive correlation between EA and HT, and a moderate negative correlation between TA and HT. The three-dimensional model is shown in Figure 4.5; the HT dimension (pleasant vs unpleasant mood) is at an angle to the plane defined by the EA and TA dimensions, such that its projection onto the plane roughly corresponds to the Russell (1979) pleasure dimension. The three-dimensional model may also be helpful in resolving the issue of whether positive and negative affects may coexist. It does indeed identify pairs of opposed states that are mutually incompatible (e.g. pleasant and sad mood). However, energetic and tense arousal states can coexist, for example, in challenging situations such as competing in a sports event or giving a public address (cf. Thayer, 1989). In experimental studies, short, time-pressured high workload tasks requiring working memory seem to elicit both types of arousal (Matthews, Campbell et al., 2002).

Schimmack and Grob (2000) suggest that the reason for the discrepancy between American and European researchers is methodological: Europeans have been more willing to entertain oblique factor solutions, with correlated axes, whereas US researchers have favoured orthogonal solutions. In two studies using American college student samples, Schimmack and Grob (2002) fitted various structural equation models to mood data. In both studies, a three-dimensional PAT (Pleasure–Awake–Tension) model provided a good fit (with pleasure positively correlated with wakefulness, and negatively correlated with tension). Furthermore, fit for two-dimensional models was appreciably lower. A further study (Schimmack and Reisenzein, 2003) conducted a different kind of test, to see whether Thayer's (1989) energy and tension dimensions can, in fact, be reduced to mixtures of general activation and valence of evaluation, as two-dimensional models claim. They reasoned that, if this were the case, energy and tension should be positively correlated, once variance associated with valence was removed from both dimensions, because the reliable part of the remaining variance of each scale would reflect activation. They performed this test, using structural equation modeling techniques, and found that there was actually no residual correlation between energy and tension, with valence statistically controlled. Again, the two-dimensional model is seen as inadequate to explain the data: the arousal associated with energy is distinct from the arousal associated with tension. However, Schimmack and Grob (2000) caution that, while three dimensions may be superior, they do not explain all the variance, and may need further refinement. Rather as with trait models, there is a growing consensus over the nature of mood 'superfactors' (i.e., two or three dimensions), and some uncertainty over what a more fine-grained description should look like.

Differentiating negative emotions

Dimensional models of mood take a parsimonious view of negative affects, reducing them to a single dimension in the Watson and Tellegen (1985) model, or to tension and unpleasant mood in three dimensional models (Matthews et al., 1990; Schimmack and Grob, 2000). However, theories of emotion frequently propose multiple 'basic' emotions that include various negative affects. Oatley and Johnson-Laird (1996) point out that fear, sadness, anger and disgust are almost always distinguished by emotion theorists as discrete categories. There has also been interest in more complex, 'social' emotions such as shame, guilt and embarrassment. How can we reconcile this multifaceted view of negative emotion with dimensional models of mood? One possibility is to develop a hierarchical model such as that of Watson and Clark (1997), although their 'primary' affect scales do not exactly correspond to those of basic emotions theory. For example, anger is grouped with disgust and contempt to define a hostility factor, that contributes to overall negative affect. In the clinical domain, Bedford and Deary (1997) showed that questionnaire data could be modelled with a general factor of distress, together with two lower-level factors of anxiety and depression.

Another possibility is to supplement broad affective dimensions with more fine-grained models of specific emotions. Spielberger's work on anger states provides a good example. Spielberger et al. (1983) developed a State-Trait Anger Scale by analogy with the STAI. People high in trait Anger perceive a wider range of situations as anger-provoking, and also experience more intense elevations of state Anger. Spielberger was especially interested in how anger, as an element of Type A personality, may increase vulnerability to chronically elevated blood pressure or hypertension (see also chapter 10). Some correlations between state Anger and hypertension have indeed been reported (see Spielberger et al., 1991). However, in contrast to work on anxiety and performance, the most consistent criterion validity has been obtained with an additional trait-like measure, Anger-In, which relates to frequency of experiencing but not expressing angry feelings (Spielberger et al., 1991). Anger-Out, the frequency of aggressive behaviours motivated by angry feelings, does not seem to predict hypertension. Thus, it is not just the state but how it is expressed that may be important for mediating personality effects on health. Hence, a more recent questionnaire, the State-Trait Anger Expression Inventory (STAXI: Forgays, Forgays and Spielberger, 1997; Spielberger et al., 1999) discriminates three state-anger factors: Feeling Angry (similar to state anger per se), Feel Like Expressing Anger – Verbal (e.g., feeling like screaming) and Feel Like Expressing Anger – Physical (e.g., feeling like hitting someone). It is expected that high scores on Feeling Angry coupled with low scores on the two expression of anger states should be related to hypertension.

Another example is provided by Endler's (e.g., Endler et al., 1991; Endler and Kocovski, 2001) work on multiple dimensions of anxiety. By contrast with Spielberger's (1966) single dimensions of trait and state anxiety, Endler sees both aspects of anxiety as multidimensional. Endler et al. (1991) identified four distinct trait anxiety facets related to the threats posed by social evaluation, physical danger, ambiguous situations and daily routines, together with two facets of state anxiety, cognitive-worry and autonomic-emotional (see Figure 4.6). State-anxiety response depends on the match or congruence between trait anxiety and situational threat; for example, physical-danger trait anxiety moderates state response to physical threats.

Thus, as in the case of trait measures, we may need different levels of analysis of state, depending on the research context. Two- and three-dimensional models explain much of the variance in mood states, and offer a parsimonious general scheme that lends itself to straightforward assessment. At the same time, these models do not fully explain the variance, although they may provide a basic affective core to the full range of emotional states (Reisenzein, 1994). In some research settings, we may wish to focus in more detail on specific affects such as anger (Spielberger et al., 1999) and anxiety (Endler and Kocovski, 2001). There is also room for further development of hierarchical models that distinguish primary, narrowly defined affective constructs from secondary, broad constructs such as positive and negative affect. Such efforts have been held back by naiveté in sampling affective constructs; that is, factor analysts have often been rather negligent in sampling

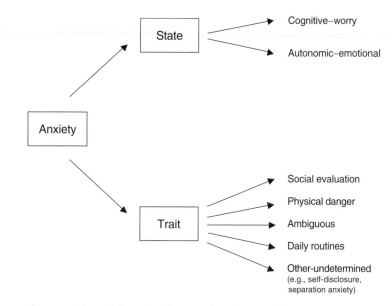

Figure 4.6 A multidimensional state-trait anxiety model
Source Endler and Kocovski (2001)

temporary states other than basic mood descriptors. As an example, there may be states that are essentially social in nature, that should be sampled separately from basic moods (Sjoberg et al., 1979). These authors saw anger and hostility as relating to the social domain. Other 'social state' constructs might include dominance–submission, trust and love, together with other 'social emotions' such as guilt. Another sampling issue is how to differentiate motivational and cognitive aspects of state from mood, an issue we address in the next section.

Validity of mood scales

There has been extensive research on antecedents of mood which, as Zuckerman's (1976) fourth criterion specifies, is essential for establishing the validity of states. A full review of this work is beyond our present scope (see Thayer, 1989; Matthews, 1992; Parkinson et al., 1996), but we will outline some of the main findings. Two methods predominate. First, it is straightforward to run experimental studies that expose participants to some pleasurable or noxious event, and assess the change in mood that results. The second method is more naturalistic, in that moods may be measured in everyday contexts, and then related to daily events. Subjects may be asked to keep a diary, over several weeks, that records moods and salient events, or they may be given a watch that is pre-set to cue the person to record their current mood and activity at random times (Diener and Larsen, 1984; see Watson, 2000, for a review).

Evidence concerning the Thayer (1989, 1996, 2001) dimensions of energetic and tense arousal is particularly impressive. Both these dimensions correlate with

Table 4.1 *Examples of how different types of factor relate to changes in energetic and tense arousal*

Type of factor	Examples	Energy	Tension
Drug	Caffeine	Raised	None or raised
	Nicotine	Raised	Lowered
Biological rhythm	Time of day	Highest mid-day	Little effect
	Menstrual cycle	Complex findings	Raised in pre-menstruum
Physical exercise	Swimming	Raised	Lowered
	Singing		
Autosuggestion	Velten technique	Mood change depends on suggestions made	
	Hypnosis		
Everyday life events	Social events	Raised	Little effect
	Arguments	Lowered	Raised

Note See Clark and Watson (1988), Matthews (1988), Thayer (1989), Matthews and Ryan (1994), Quinlan et al. (2000) and Valentine and Evans (2001) for references to specific studies

indices of autonomic arousal (Thayer, 1978). Table 4.1 illustrates some of the types of factor which influence these elements of mood in experimental studies, or which relate to mood in diary studies. Moderate physical exercise is perhaps the easiest way of elevating energetic arousal (Thayer, 2001; Valentine and Evans, 2001). Other manipulations seem to primarily influence hedonic tone. For example, Gendolla and Krüsken (2001) showed that both a music manipulation (a sad cello piece vs upbeat easy listening) and a mood-induction based on fantasising about positive and negative scenarios influenced scores on the hedonic tone scale of the UMACL (Matthews et al., 1990). Neurological influences on mood are demonstrated by drug studies, although it is often difficult to map subjective states onto specific brain systems (Thayer, 1989, 1995).

Medical conditions are also important influences on mood. Deary and his colleagues have provided some biological evidence for the validity of mood dimensions using a powerful experimental manipulation. In three studies (Hepburn et al., 1995; Gold et al., 1995) they showed that the experimental induction of hypoglycaemia in humans in a laboratory could increase tense arousal and concurrently reduce energetic arousal. Gold et al. also showed a reduction in hedonic tone. These researchers have suggested that energetic arousal is lowered by reduced glucose availability in the cerebral cortex, and that tense arousal may be caused by the effect of hypoglycaemia on central autonomic function and the resultant release of adrenalin. This latter hypothesis was supported in a controlled study of subjects who had had their adrenal glands removed, and so were unable to release adrenalin following central autonomic stimulation induced by hypoglycaemia. These individuals showed no increase in tense arousal, but the expected decrease in energetic arousal (Hepburn et al., 1996) was found. A third study (McCrimmon, Frier and Deary, 1999) showed that mood change induced by hypoglycaemia led to more negative appraisals of life events, demonstrating the inter-relationship of moods and cognitions. Another line of evidence for biological influences on mood comes from studies of sleep disturbance, which tends to lower energetic arousal and hedonic tone, and increase tense arousal (Martin et al., 1996; Martin et al., 1997). On the basis of psychophysiological data, Martin et al. (1997, p. 1600) concluded that 'changes in hedonic tone and tense arousal could be autonomically mediated, whereas changes in energetic arousal are due to cortical stimulation'.

Cognitive influences on mood are demonstrated most directly by mood change following verbal suggestion. Various techniques are effective for inducing positive or negative moods (see Gerrards-Hesse, Spies and Hesse, 1995, for a review). For example, the Velten technique requires the subject to read aloud mood-evocative sentences, such as 'It's great to be alive', 'My future is so bright I've got to wear shades', and 'I wish I could be myself, but nobody likes me when I am.' Correlational data also show associations between moods and cognitions. In three studies, Matthews and Falconer (2000, 2002) and Matthews et al. (2000) found that each state factor related to multiple, independent cognitive variables, including: for task engagement, high task-focus and low avoidance; for distress, high workload, threat appraisal and emotion-focus; and for worry, high emotion-focus and low avoidance. Everyday moods probably reflect a mixture of biological, cognitive and social influences. Overall, data are broadly consistent with Thayer's view that moods are underpinned by broad, integrated biobehavioural systems, but cognitive and social factors have important moderating effects.

Mood has been validated primarily as a dependent variable. However, there is increasing evidence for mood effects on behaviour, implying that mood is capable of mediating effects of personality and environmental factors, consistent with the trait-state model. The evidence is most clearcut in studies of performance. Happy and depressed moods are associated with a variety of mood-congruent biases in memory and judgement, such as better recall for information whose affective content matches the person's mood (Bower and Forgas, 2000). Mood-congruent effects are found with naturally occurring moods as well as those that are induced experimentally. Matthews, Pitcaithly and Mann (1995) report data suggesting that the hedonic tone/pleasantness dimension relates to mood-congruent bias more strongly than either energy or tension. Energy is associated with enhanced performance on a range of attentionally demanding tasks (Matthews and Davies, 1998, 2001), demonstrating that mood may affect both the overall efficiency of information-processing, and influence processing qualitatively through the mood-congruence phenomenon. Conversely, the detrimental effects of state anxiety are well known, although they appear to relate to worry states rather than tension or negative affect per se (Zeidner, 1998).

Beyond mood: additional state domains

It is not unusual for state researchers to stray beyond the strict confines of mood and affect in scale development. For example, Watson and Clark (1997) include Attentiveness as one of three facets of positive affect, although being attentive refers to a state of cognition, rather than an affect such as happiness. However, other researchers have investigated cognitive states as reflecting a distinct sphere or domain of experience. Motivational states may also be important, although they have been rather neglected, in favour of trait constructs such as need achievement. There is indeed a longstanding view that mental activities can be divided into three components of affect (and emotion), motivation (or 'conation') and cognition (or thought). Nineteenth-century Scottish psychologists, such as Alexander Bain, played a leading role in developing this 'trilogy of mind': for reviews of its impact in the modern age, see Hilgard (1980) and Mayer, Frasier Chabot and Carlsmith (1997). The trilogy may provide an a priori scheme for sampling temporary states, distinguishing moods as affective states from motivational and cognitive states.

Cognitive aspects of state

Anxiety researchers have long been aware that anxiety states have both cognitive and affective components. Morris and Liebert (1969) divided anxiety items into those associated with the cognitive state of worry, and those related to the affective state of tension. Worry items were more predictive of performance impairment than tension items. As discussed further in chapter 12, it may be that worry, but not tension, is associated with a diversion of attention or effort from the task at hand to processing associated with the worrying thoughts. Endler et al. (1991) reported large-scale factor analyses which confirm the existence of two dimensions of state anxiety, which they call cognitive–worry and autonomic–emotional. Cognitive components of state anxiety may be broken down still further. As part of an extensive programme of research on test anxiety, Sarason and his colleagues (e.g. Sarason et al., 1995) developed a state measure of interfering thoughts, termed the Cognitive Interference Questionnaire (CIQ). The CIQ assesses the frequency with which the person experiences thoughts about the test taken and about personal concerns, and the general tendency for the mind to wander.

The CIQ is a prototypical cognitive-state measure. Any given cognition expresses a specific proposition, which, because of its specificity, is not to be considered as a 'state' as defined above. What the CIQ attempts to assess is the overall frequency of potentially distracting cognitions. It does so because Sarason believes that overall frequency of cognitive interference is a general attribute of the person's psychological functioning which relates to important criteria such as test performance. From this perspective, the detailed propositional content of the individual's cognitions may be de-emphasised or disregarded. The utility of the state construct is shown by validation evidence that relates cognitive interference to objective performance impairment (Sarason et al., 1986; Zeidner, 1998; see chapter 12).

Further scales assess other general attributes of the person's cognitions. Heatherton and Polivy (1991) developed a state measure of self-esteem, the person's beliefs about their own worth and competence. Their measure has three internally consistent, inter-correlated subscales related to self-esteem concerning performance,

Table 4.2 *Three secondary factors assessed by the Dundee Stress State Questionnaire (DSSQ)*

Task Engagement	Distress	Worry
Energetic arousal	Tense arousal	Self-consciousness
Interest motivation	Low hedonic tone	Low self-esteem
Success motivation	Low confidence/perceived control	Cognitive interference (task-related)
Concentration		Cognitive interference (task-irrelevant)

Note Some primary scales have additional, minor loadings on other secondary factors
Source Matthews and Campbell (1998); Matthews, Campbell et al. (2002)

social functioning and appearance. Experimental studies showed that the scales were appropriately sensitive to manipulations such as experimentally induced failure experiences. Another example is Sedikides's (1992) state measure of self-consciousness; the extent to which the person's attention is focused on internal self-related processes, as opposed to external stimuli. As we shall see in chapter 9, trait self-consciousness is an important construct in stress research. We cannot, of course, assume that cognitive-state measures provide a direct measure of information-processing. They depend on introspection, and, as such, are subject to bias. However, careful empirical validation and theory development may allow us to use them as indices of underlying constructs, just as we can use trait measures without necessarily assuming that the person's self-reports are veridical (Cattell, 1973; Matthews et al., 2002).

Subjective states and the 'trilogy of mind'

Matthews (Matthews et al., 1999; Matthews, Campbell and Falconer, 2001; Matthews, Campbell et al., 2002) used the trilogy of mind as a foundation for building on existing models of mood states, sampling motivational and cognitive constructs within the context of human performance settings. Constructs were required to be genuine 'states' – i.e., generalised and pervasive qualities of experience – rather than specific beliefs or goals. Exploratory factor analyses first identified eleven robust 'primary' factors defined by item-level data; each was linked to one (and only one) of the three domains defined by the trilogy. In addition to the three fundamental dimensions of mood (Matthews et al., 1990), two dimensions of motivation and six of cognition were obtained. The Dundee Stress State Questionnaire (DSSQ: Matthews et al., 1999) assesses these dimensions, with good reliability. These primary dimensions were themselves correlated, and further, second-order factor-analyses identified three higher-order factors labelled Task Engagement, Distress and Worry. Table 4.2 shows how the primary-state factors defined these broader complexes of subjective states. The factor solution was robust in data obtained before and after performance, in student and nonstudent samples, and in British and North American samples (Matthews et al., 2002).

Experimental studies showed that the state factors were sensitive to different stress factors. For example, sustained monotony lowers task engagement, high workload provokes distress, and failure seems to maintain worry (Matthews and Desmond, 2002; Matthews et al., 2002). Matthews et al. (2002) suggest that the factors represent the dominant transactional themes of the performance setting. Task engagement (including positive affect) may index commitment to effort, distress (including negative affect) may relate to overload of cognition, and worry may be a sign of personal self-reflection. In support of these ideas, Matthews, Campbell et al. (2002) showed that, in occupational samples, state response was systematically related to the person's appraisals and coping strategies in the workplace. For example, supportive work environments raised task engagement, whereas high workload and use of emotion-focused coping were associated with distress.

The Matthews, Campbell et al. (2002) three-factor solution is attractive because it builds on and extends current conceptions of state. Task Engagement and Distress somewhat resemble positive and negative affect, and these factors tend to align with Thayer's (2001) energy and tension dimensions. However, the factor definitions show that, at this higher-order level, the factors are not pure mood factors, but integrate mood with aspects of cognition and motivation. The distinction between Distress and Worry factors corresponds to the contrast drawn in anxiety research between anxious emotion and worry (Zeidner, 1998), which is revealed as a fundamental distinction. The worry factor is defined by cognitive primary dimensions only, and is largely independent of mood: both two- and three-dimensional models of mood fail to capture this important element of subjective experience. Thus, the three-factor model of higher-order states represents the most comprehensive attempt at describing the complete universe of subjective states, though it, too, is limited, in that it neglects 'social' states such as dominance–submission. Further research is needed to determine whether or not there are specifically social factors of state, or whether existing state factors also have social facets.

To summarise, research on moods and subjective states provides a progressively more differentiated set of mood dimensions that may be linked to traits. The most parsimonious models distinguish just two dimensions: energy and tension (Thayer, 1996), or positive affect and negative affect (Watson, 2000). Other work suggests various refinements. There may be three fundamental mood dimensions, with pleasantness differentiated from the two Thayer (1996) dimensions (Schimmack and Grob, 2000). Moods may be just one sphere of a larger universe of subjective states, including motivational and cognitive states, cohering around the Task Engagement, Distress and Worry dimensions identified by Matthews et al. (1999, 2002). In the next section, we shall see that most state research is based on two-dimensional models, but there is increasing interest in other approaches.

Traits and states: empirical studies

If moods are intrinsically changeable, it might seem that personality traits could not be strongly related to mood. However, individual differences in mood provide a good example of the influence of aggregation of data, as discussed in chapter 2. Although moods vary considerably from day to day, it seems as though people have different typical or baseline levels of mood, around which momentary moods fluctuate (Diener and Larsen, 1984). Watson (2000) has shown that, if average mood over a fourteen-day period is calculated, this value correlates at about 0.8 with average mood over the next fourteen days, although the day-to-day correlation between mood assessments is only about 0.4. The more days over which mood values are aggregated, the stronger the test–retest correlation. Watson (2000) also reviews studies of the stability of typical mood over longer time periods, concluding that long-term stabilities (six months to seven and a half years) typically fall into the 0.35 to 0.55 range. That is, typical mood shows appreciable stability, though to a lesser degree than traits, and many respondents show substantial change in characteristic affect levels over these timespans. Box 4.1 describes work on subjective well-being, that has shown how overall life satisfaction and happiness are influenced by personality. Hence, we can look for correlations between traits and both momentary mood assessments in a specific setting and characteristic mood.

Box 4.1 Secrets of happiness: subjective well-being

Subjective Well-being (SWB) refers to people's overall contentment with their lives, including components of cognitive judgement of life satisfaction, high pleasant emotion, and low negative emotion (see Diener et al., 1999 for a review). Extensive research has used various reliable self-report scales for well-being to investigate the sources of life-long happiness. Individual differences in SWB are moderately stable over time, though less so than traits (typical ten-year stabilities are about 0.4). Several lines of evidence suggest that SWB is more than just an evaluation of current life circumstances. For example, demographic factors and external circumstances play only a minor role in SWB. Even money and employment status often have little effect, although it seems that materialistic people need to be rich to be happy (Diener and Biswas-Diener, 2002). SWB also tends to be lower in economically underdeveloped nations, but recessions and booms within nations have little effect. Conversely, personality plays a major role in SWB. A meta-analysis (DeNeve and Cooper, 1998) found that low neuroticism was the strongest predictor of SWB, but, as we might expect from the personality studies reviewed in this chapter, traits are differentially related to the different SWB components. Both extraversion and agreeableness relate most strongly to its positive-affective component, for example. The constitutional basis of SWB is confirmed by behaviour-genetic studies suggesting that a substantial part of SWB, or at least its temporally stable components, is heritable (Lucas and Diener, 2000).

The substantial effects of personality on subjective well-being does not mean that people cannot take steps to increase trait happiness. As previously discussed, Thayer (1996, 2001) has drawn up guidelines for improving mood; systematic practice of these techniques is likely to produce long-lasting benefits. Similarly, Larsen and Buss (2002) summarise methods for increasing happiness, as follows:

1. *Spend time with other people, particularly friends, family and loved ones.* Social interaction is typically mood-enhancing.
2. *Seek challenge and meaning at work.* Work that is challenging, but within the person's capabilities, is the most satisfying.
3. *Look for ways to be helpful to others.* Helping people enhances self-esteem, and takes one's mind off personal problems.
4. *Enjoy pleasurable leisure activities.* Making time for one's favourite hobbies and activities is beneficial.
5. *Stay in shape.* Many empirical studies show that exercise improves not just physical health, but also mental well-being.
6. *Have a plan, but be open to new experiences.* Life needs a certain amount of organisation, but it is important also to be flexible and spontaneous when circumstances allow.
7. *Be optimistic.* Focusing attention on the positive side of life enhances happiness.
8. *Don't let things get blown out of proportion.* Happy people are able to step back and see things in perspective, which facilitates constructive approaches to dealing with problems.

It is probably also true that personality influences how easily the individual can carry out these strategies; being optimistic and keeping things in proportion may not come naturally to the high N person, for example. Nevertheless, research summarised by Larson and Buss (2002) suggests that making efforts of these kinds will make a difference for most people.

Many personality traits may be implicated in mood response in specific circumstances. For example, optimism–pessimism is associated with mood in demanding performance settings (Helton et al., 1999), and sensation seeking predicts the extent to which daily physical pleasures (such as food and sex) lead to greater satisfaction (Oishi, Schimmack and Diener, 2001). Traits that are linked to a specific context are often the best predictors of mood in that context; for example, driver-stress-vulnerability traits predict mood during vehicle driving more reliably than do general traits (Dorn and Matthews, 1995). In this chapter, however, we will focus on the broad traits of the Five Factor Model (FFM).

The two broad traits which we might expect to relate most strongly to mood are neuroticism (N) and extraversion (E). As discussed in chapter 1 (see table 1.6), most of the narrow traits related to the broad N factor are associated with unpleasant affective states such as anxiety, depression, tension, moodiness and so forth. The affective content of E is less striking, but some of the narrow traits contributing to the construct, such as being carefree, lively and active, do have connotations of positive affect and energy. Costa and McCrae (1992) explicitly include 'positive emotions' as one of the facets of the extraversion scale on the NEO-PI-R (see table 1.7). Similarly, Nemanick and Munz (1997) showed that trait PA and trait NA could be modelled as distinct personality variables that mediated the effects of E and N on mood. Some authors have argued that mood and personality may relate to common brain structures. Thayer (1989), for example, suggests that E and energetic arousal are associated with a common arousal system, as are N and tense arousal. Gray's (1991) personality theory seems to suggest that extraversion might relate to positive mood, whereas neuroticism should relate to negative mood. Such ideas are a development of psychobiological theories of personality, discussed further in chapter 7.

Correlational studies: extraversion and neuroticism

The associations between E, N and mood have been extensively studied. There is little dispute that N is consistently associated with higher tension/negative affect, whereas E relates to higher energy/positive affect (Emmons and Diener, 1986; Thayer, 1989; Watson, 2000). In addition, extraverts tend to experience more pleasant moods, whereas high neuroticism scorers are prone to unpleasant mood (Matthews, Jones and Chamberlain, 1990; Williams, 1989). There has been some debate over the specificity of these trait–state associations. Sometimes, N relates to reduced positive affect, and E to reduced negative affect (Vittersø, 2001; Yik and Russell, 2001). The greater propensity of high N subjects to negative moods is part of a general susceptibility to stress symptoms, discussed further in chapter 9. Given the high correlation between N and trait anxiety, the correlation between trait and state anxiety may also reflect the stress vulnerability of high N subjects.

Table 4.3 shows some illustrative examples of studies of E, N and mood, using a variety of instruments, and both two- and three-dimensional mood assessments (Matthews and Gilliland, 1999). Studies are divided into those in which participants simply completed questionnaires, and those in which the environment was experimentally controlled as part of a mood-induction or performance study. The striking feature of the data are the variability of correlation magnitudes across studies. The Watson and Clark (1992) and Meyer and Shack (1989) studies showed E–PA and N–NA correlations as high as 0.6 or so, suggesting a high degree of overlap between related trait and state constructs. These authors claimed that N and E are essentially affect-related dimensions, which should be re-labelled Negative Emotionality and Positive Emotionality respectively. However, studies conducted in controlled laboratory environments, following task performance, show trait–state correlations of considerably smaller magnitude. For example, in the Matthews et al. (1990, 1999, 2002) studies, the N–TA correlation is consistently about 0.25, and the E–PA correlation did not exceed 0.13.

Table 4.3 *Data from illustrative studies of personality and mood*

Study	n	Sample	Scales	Energy (PA)		Tension (NA)		Hedonic Tone (Happiness)	
				N	E	N	E	N	E
Questionnaire-based studies									
Costa and McCrae (1980)	575	Community	EPI PAS/NAS	−11**	16**	35**	−01	—	—
Emmons and Diener (1986)	72	Students	EPI ACL	−02	34**	32**	24**	—	—
Meyer and Shack (1989)	231	Students	EPQ ACL	−19*	50**	54**	−11	—	—
Watson and Clark (1992)	532	Students	NEO-PI PANAS	−25**	62**	52**	−21**	—	—
Studies using experimentally controlled situations									
Larsen and Ketelaar (1991)[1]	70	Students	EPQ ACL	−03	10	29**	−12	—	—
Adan and Guàrdia (1997)[2]	578	Students	EPI UMACL	−20**	18**	26**	−08	−27**	24**
Matthews, Jones et al. (1990a)	158	Students	EPI UMACL	−25**	13	23*	−15	−24**	12
Matthews et al. (1999)[2]	636	Students	EPQ-R UMACL	−06	10*	27**	−18**	−20**	18**
Matthews et al. (in press)[2]	328	Occupational	EPQ-R UMACL	−22**	11	27**	−11	−18**	07

Note

[1] Neutral mood induction

[2] Data re-analysed

ACL = unpublished adjective checklist

Correlation coefficients multiplied × 100, *p<.05, **p<.01

NEO-PI = NEO Personality Inventory

PA = Positive Affect, NA = Negative Affect, EPI = Eysenck Personality Inventory, EPQ(-R) = Eysenck Personality Questionnaire(-Revised), PAS = Positive Affect Scale, NAS = Negative Affect Scale, PANAS = Positive and Negative Affect Schedule, UMACL = UWIST Mood Adjective Checklist

What explains these discrepancies? Dorn and Matthews (1995) suggest that two factors may influence the magnitude of correlations between personality and mood. First, the shorter the time-frame over which mood is assessed, the smaller the correlation between personality and mood (Watson, 2000). Studies showing strong E–PA and N–NA correlations (e.g. Watson and Clark, 1992) are usually those that have used long time-frames or have asked for a trait-like rating of typical mood. However, trait-like ratings also introduce the risk of artifacts due to the retrospective nature of the report, including moods at the time of reporting, expectations, and bias associated with personality (Fisher, 2002). In particular, happy memories are more accessible to extraverts than to introverts, whereas negative memories are more easily retrieved by neurotic subjects (Mayo, 1989).

Artifacts apart, the use of a longer time-frame may, in effect, aggregate mood data, leading to a more trait-like estimate, which should correlate more highly with personality than a state index. Watson (2000) reports a study in which 379 college student respondents each provided an estimate of at least thirty daily mood ratings. Students rated daily mood in the evening, so these ratings were still not based on true momentary mood, but they provide a better indication of mood states than a rating of 'typical' feelings. Ratings were averaged to yield an average daily mood score on PA and NA. The correlation between NA and N was 0.43 (18 per cent of the variance); that between PA and E was 0.36 (13 per cent of the variance). These more modest associations are more in line with the values found in controlled experimental studies, though still a bit higher. However, aggregation cannot fully explain the discrepancy between samples. A subsample (n=111) of the student participants in the Matthews et al. (1999) study performed a working memory task on repeated occasions. An aggregate mood index was found as the mean of eight different state measures, for each mood scale used. Correlations between E and N and the aggregate mood indices could then be compared with their correlations with the mean single-occasion mood indices. In fact, aggregation had modest effects. It increased the correlation between E and energy trivially, from 0.10 to 0.14, and the correlation between N and tension rather more, from 0.33 to 0.47. Even when aggregated, correlations between personality and mood are small (E) or moderate (N) in the performance context.

Another important factor is that situations and contexts may influence the personality–mood correlation. In Watson and Clark's studies (1992) undergraduates completed questionnaires to obtain course credit, and it may be that mood data collected in this context simply reflect personality-dependent reactions to the characteristic events of student life (Dorn and Matthews, 1995). In contrast, data reported by Matthews et al. (1990, 1999, 2002) and Dorn and Matthews (1995) were collected from carefully controlled performance-testing settings, in which the influence of everyday events on mood may have been attenuated. High correlations between N and NA/TA in Watson and Clark's data may result from the academic evaluation to which students are subjected, which high N subjects are likely to find stressful. Similarly, extraverts may enjoy the social opportunities afforded by the student lifestyle more than introverts, and they may seek out pleasurable social interaction more actively, so that personality and environmental influences on mood are confounded.

Delineating person × situation interaction in studies of mood has proved problematic, with inconsistent results reported in different studies (Moskowitz and Coté, 1995; Lucas and Diener, 2000). One daily diary study (Pavot, Fujita and Diener, 1990) suggested additive effects of personality and situation: extraversion and being in a social situation (as opposed to being alone). Both factors related to happier mood, but there was no interaction betweeen personality and situation. By contrast, another diary-based study showed plausible moderator effects of situations on relationships between extraversion, emotional stability and mood

(Brandstätter, 1994, 2001). 'Mood' here reflects the predominance of positive over negative moods. Effects of emotional stability were confined to situations where the person was alone or with relatives and friends; this trait did not predict mood in situations involving family, or acquaintances and strangers. Extraversion was positively related to mood when socialising in leisure situations, but not when alone. Extraversion related to mood at work only in situations involving strangers or acquaintances. These data match experimental data showing only weak associations between E and mood, in that laboratory studies typically have the person 'working' alone. Brandstätter (2001) suggests that extraverts have stronger social motives and higher social skills that become more salient during leisure than during work.

Beyond positive and negative affectivity: other traits, other states

Studies of the mood correlates of the C, A and O dimensions are much more infrequent, possibly because robust associations are rarely found. McCrae and Costa (1991) found small but significant relationships between these dimensions and affect. Both C and A tended to be associated with high positive affect but low negative affect, whereas O was associated with high positive affect and high negative affect. Few of these correlations exceed ± 0.2 in magnitude, and the O–affect correlations were particularly small. McCrae and Costa suggest that C and A relate to achievement-related and social success, respectively, which leads to greater well-being. Matthews et al. (1999) found that C related to higher energy and lower tension, A to lower tension and higher hedonic tone, and O (in contrast to McCrae and Costa, 1991) to higher energy, lower tension and higher hedonic tone. Correlations did not exceed ± 0.3. Using trait-like rather than state-like measures of affect, Watson and Clark (1992) obtained broadly similar findings, with O being weakly related to lower levels of negative affect. A and C related to specific lower-level aspects of the broad affect dimensions. C was associated mainly with an 'Attentiveness' scale (which might be better seen as a cognitive rather than an affective dimension), and A was associated with lower hostility (which has interpersonal aspects). A has also been found to relate to positive mood experienced during agreeable behaviour (Coté and Moskowitz, 1998), and to negative mood during interpersonal conflict (Suls, Martin and David, 1998), indicating the role of situational moderator effects. In general, when E and N are controlled, the ability of the remaining Big Five dimensions to predict additional variance in mood is modest.

Matthews et al. (1999, 2002) investigated how the Eysenck traits relate to the broader affective–motivational–cognitive state factors measured by the DSSQ, illustrated in Table 4.2. In the two data sets summarised in Table 4.2, N correlated at 0.28 with distress and 0.22 with worry in the student sample. Equivalent correlations in the occupational sample were 0.29 and 0.15. E correlated −0.21 with distress in the student sample, and −0.10 (NS) in the occupational sample. Matthews et al. (1999) also reported data on the Big Five, in a subset of the student sample. C was modestly related to higher task engagement, and lower distress and worry, whereas both A and O were associated with lower distress. Consistent with the data using the EPQ, N was related to higher distress and worry, and E to lower distress. Thus, at this level of analysis, subjective states seem to be modestly related to each of several broad personality factors. Narrow, 'midlevel' traits may play an additional role. Zeidner's (1998) literature review identifies several traits that may predict state anxiety states in evaluative settings, including trait anger, the impatience/irritability component of Type A personality, low self-esteem, low self-efficacy and pessimism. Further research is needed to test whether these traits remain predictive with N controlled.

Finally, one might wonder if there is some direct dimensional correspondence or structural equivalence between traits and states. That is, does the existence of the FFM as a model of personality imply that the structure of states should follow the same model? Watson and Clark (1992) proposed that the E and N traits correspond directly to positive and negative affect respectively (although we saw some difficulties with this hypothesis), but there is little evidence for clear state equivalents of the Big Five C, O and A dimensions. Deinzer et al. (1995) report a study of a short version of the NEO-PI-R and other trait measures which used a theory based on structural equation modelling to distinguish matched trait and state factors. This modelling approach provides a powerful methodology for decomposing scores on personality questionnaires into trait and state components, provided that individuals are tested on the questionnaire on at least two occasions. So far, though, it has been rarely employed in empirical research.

Also, the assumption of matching trait and state dimensions may be incorrect. The structure of anxiety appears to be different at trait and state levels, for example. Deffenbacher (1980) points out that worry and emotionality items tend to cluster together as elements of trait test anxiety, but separate at the state level. Similarly, the content of Endler et al.'s (1991) four trait anxiety dimensions (social evaluation, physical danger, ambiguous situations and daily routines) does not relate in any simple way to their two state dimensions of cognitive–worry and autonomic–emotional. It is possible that further work will find major state dimensions related to, say, task motivation (C), curiosity (O) and social orientation (A) which will correlate with the appropriate traits, and define a state Big Five. Alternatively, it may be that there is no simple mapping of traits into states, and different descriptive principles must be sought for the two kinds of variable.

Experimental studies

Another important source of evidence on relationships between trait and state comes from experimental studies of mood induction. Blackburn, Cameron and Deary (1990) used a version of the popular Velten technique intended to increase state depression. They showed that N was significantly positively correlated with the magnitude of increase in depression, but E was unrelated to state change. Larsen and Ketelaar (1989, 1991) used a guided imagery procedure requiring subjects to imagine vividly positive, negative and neutral scenarios. These included events

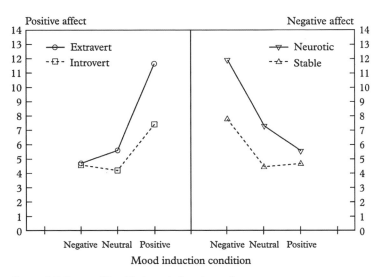

Figure 4.7 Personality effects on induced mood
Source Larsen and Ketelaar (1991)

such as winning a lottery (positive), visiting a supermarket (neutral) and having a close friend die of a painful and incurable disease (negative). Consistent with the correlational data, extraverts tended to show greater increases than introverts in positive affect under the positive mood induction, whereas N was associated with greater negative affect when a negative mood was induced (see figure 4.7). Rusting and Larsen (1997, 1999) report a further replication study, although they found that both N and (low) E independently predicted negative affect response to the negative mood induction. Zelenski and Larsen (1999) used emotive slides to induce mood, and showed that a reward-sensitivity trait (related to extraversion) correlated with induced happiness ($r=0.39$, $n=86$), whereas a punishment-sensitivity trait (related to neuroticism) correlated with induced disgust, anxiety and gloom (range of rs: 0.39–0.42). Two studies using emotive film-clips have also provided broadly similar results (Gross, Sutton and Ketelaar, 1998; Morrone et al., 2000). However, two studies failed to confirm that E related to positive emotional reactivity and N to negative emotional reactivity (Bunce, Larsen and Cruz, 1993; Berenbaum and Williams, 1995): these studies related E to response to negative stimuli and N to response to positive stimuli.

Thus, as with the correlational data, there is a clear general trend linking E to positive affect and N to negative affect, but also a smaller number of exceptions to that trend. The typical finding (e.g. Larsen and Ketelaar, 1991) is open to a variety of interpretations. The mood-induction data are often taken to support a psychobiological account of personality effects (e.g., Morrone et al., 2000), but there is no direct evidence. Perhaps, brain reward systems in extraverts are more sensitive to the positive (internal) signals afforded by the positive induction, and, likewise, a punishment system is responsible for the greater negative mood response of high N persons. Equally, extraverts may have greater access to positive information in long-term memory to be integrated into the image, or greater facility in cognitive elaboration of that information. Personality may also affect active regulation of moods, i.e., voluntary, strategic attempts to change mood (Larsen, 2000; Thayer, 1996, 2001). Thayer, Newman and McClain (1994) found that introverts are more likely than extraverts to use withdrawal from social interaction as a strategy for dealing with bad moods, but extraverts are more prone to use exercise to enhance energy. Thus, although the mood-induction studies have tended to neglect mediating mechanisms, they converge with the correlational data, in suggesting how personality may moderate the mood changes that people experience in response to everyday positive and negative events.

Studies of the relationship between trait and state anxiety show the importance of contextual factors. Hodges (1968) demonstrated that trait anxiety is positively related to increase in state anxiety when stress is imposed through the threat to self-esteem posed by failure on a task, but not when the stressor is physical in nature (electric shock). Findings of this kind suggest that trait anxiety is primarily related to sensitivity to ego threat (Eysenck, 1982). However, it is too simplistic to suppose that trait anxiety moderates stress-induced increases in anxiety in certain contexts only. As previously described, Endler et al. (1991) discriminated multiple anxiety traits relating to different types of threatening context (social evaluation, physical danger, ambiguous situations and daily routines). Each trait dimension should predict state anxiety increase in the appropriate setting. This prediction has been fairly successful (see Endler, 1997; Endler and Kocovski, 2001 for reviews of studies). For example, in a physical threat situation (parachute jumping) the physical danger trait predicted state anxiety, whereas in a social evaluation situation (an equestrian competition) the social evaluation trait predicted state response.

In fact, the prediction of state anxiety is still more complex because the key factor is not so much the objective nature of the setting, but the way it is appraised by the individual subject. For example, one person might see the primary threat of going to the dentist as being the physical pain inflicted, whereas another might focus on the social threat of appearing cowardly. Endler and his colleagues (e.g. Busch, King and Guttman, 1994) reported a series of studies in which a composite predictor of state anxiety change was calculated by weighting trait anxiety scores by the individual's perception of the four types of threat. The composite predictor was consistently more predictive than any of the anxiety trait variables of the state anxiety change resulting from stressors such as taking an examination or dental treatment.

Explaining the state correlates of extraversion and neuroticism

Thus far, we have established some fairly consistent associations between traits and states, especially between E–PA-energy-happiness, and N–NA-tension-unhappiness. However, trait–state intercorrelation varies with contextual factors including the external situation (Brandstätter, 2001), the person's appraisal of the situation (Busch et al., 1994) and levels of reward and punishment stimuli (Rusting and Larsen, 1999). How can we explain these associations? In fact, there are several different interpretations of the associations between E and N, as traits, and mood. One distinction that is made is whether the source of correlation is *temperamental* or *instrumental* (Costa and McCrae, 1980; Lucas and Diener, 2000). The temperamental explanation is that affect is central to the E and N traits, so that personality necessarily entails individual differences in mood (Watson and Clark, 1992). The instrumental explanation is that personality influences situational engagement, and consequently mood. For example, extraversion may be linked to positive affect because extraverts have more social involvement, which in turn tends to elicit positive mood.

Lucas and Diener (2000) favour the temperamental explanation. Instrumental theories, they claim, predict that controlling for situational factors should eliminate associations between personality and mood, but this hypothesis has not been substantiated. For example, although social participation correlates with both extraversion and positive mood, this situational factor does not fully mediate the association between extraversion and mood. Box 4.2 discusses in more detail one of the studies that has investigated the interrelationship of extraversion, mood and social activity (Argyle and Lu, 1990). Conversely, at the trait level, there appears to be quite strong convergence between E and PA. So far as N is concerned, it is hard to see why high-N persons should seek out situations that make them unhappy, again favouring a temperamental explanation. Thus, like Watson (2000), Lucas and Diener (2000) favour Gray's hypothesis, that E relates to sensitivity to reward signals, and N to sensitivity to punishment signals, as an explanation for temperamental influences on mood. They argue that extraverts' preference for social situations is a *consequence* not a *cause* of positive affectivity, in that extraverts' higher reward sensitivity makes it more likely that they will seek out social situations, which are primarily rewarding.

However, the case in favour of a temperamental explanation is not quite as clearcut as Lucas and Diener (2000) and Watson (2000) suggest, especially in the case of E and PA. These authors seem to assume that all social participation is equally uplifting, which may not be correct. Perhaps, extraverts are better able to select or manage social situations that elevate positive mood, explaining why extraverts are happier than introverts in social situations. Lucas and Diener (2000) cite the Pavot et al. (1990) study that showed extraverts were happier than introverts even when alone. However, Brandstätter's (1994, 2001) data failed to replicate this result. The difficulty may be that classifying situations as 'social' or 'alone' is too crude to identify the critical situational modifiers. Assuming that extraverts prefer more stimulating environments than introverts, there may be some solitary environments, such as watching a horror film alone, that are sufficiently arousing that they provoke higher levels of positive affect in extraverts than in introverts. Conversely, familiar or routine social situations may be de-arousing. Farthofer and Brandstätter (2001) showed that in a sample of crane drivers and operators working in a steel plant, extraversion was related to mood in work but not leisure situations. They argued that the work was highly arousing, because of environmental factors

Box 4.2 Extraversion, social activity and positive mood

One of the most consistent predictors of elevated energy, positive affect and pleasantness of mood in naturalistic studies is social interaction with others (e.g., Watson et al., 1992). Extraversion also correlates with both positive mood and social activity, especially active participation in dating, party-going and socialising over drinks (Watson et al., 1992). Could it be that social participation actually contributes to the more positive moods of extraverts? Argyle and Lu (1990a) showed that about half of the greater happiness of extraverts could be explained by their greater participation in social activities. In a further study, Argyle and Lu (1990b) suggested that it may be social competence which explains the extraversion–happiness link. They developed the simple model shown in Figure B.4.2.1 in which extraversion effects are partially mediated by social skills related to assertiveness. Possibly, assertiveness allows extraverts to have more satisfying interactions with others (cf. Brandstätter, 1994, 2000), which would encourage greater social participation. However, as Figure B.4.2.1 shows, assertion does not fully explain the extraversion–happiness association. The causal network may also be more complex. It is conceivable that happiness promotes assertiveness and interest in social interaction, for example. All the studies cited here used trait-like mood/happiness measures, rather than measuring state mood in situ. Nevertheless, there are reasonable grounds for supposing that lifestyle differences may contribute to relationships between extraversion and mood.

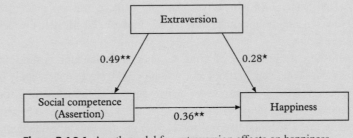

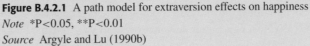

Figure B.4.2.1 A path model for extraversion effects on happiness
Note *P<0.05, **P<0.01
Source Argyle and Lu (1990b)

such as noise, and the inherent risks of working with molten steel. Analysis of diary data indeed showed that extraverts were only happier than introverts in high-risk work situations. Hence, most current studies do not really do justice to situational variability, and a more fine-grained analysis of situational moderators is required.

A second weakness of the argument for temperament is that it is based mainly on the shortcomings of the instrumental explanation, rather than on direct evidence that associations between traits and states are mediated by brain reward and punishment systems. As we will see in chapter 7, the evidence for Gray's theory of brain motivation systems is mixed (Matthews and Gilliland, 1999). To give one example, it is often supposed that the behavioural activation or facilitation system linked to E is dopaminergic in nature (Depue and Collins, 1999). If this system is more reactive in extraverts, then dopaminergic drugs should produce more positive moods in extraverts than in introverts. Corr and Kumari (2000) tested this prediction, using the UWIST Mood Adjective Checklist (Matthews et al., 1990) to assess mood. In fact, extraversion had no moderating effect on mood response to the drug amphetamine. Instead, the critical personality factor was psychoticism (P): lower-P individuals had relatively more positive responses to the drug. These findings suggest that, contrary to much theorising on personality and mood, it may be P rather than E that should be related to dopaminergic functioning.

An alternative, interactionist framework for relating traits to states is provided by Lazarus's (1991) view that (emotional) states provide an 'on-line' index of the person's current state of adaptation or maladaptation to their environment. States describe how the person stands in relation to environmental demands and pressures, so that anxiety signals personal threat, depression signals irrevocable loss, and so forth. Matthews, Derryberry and Siegle (2000) suggest that traits may bias the cognitive processes that govern adaptive status, i.e. appraisal of external demands and personal competence, and choice of strategy for coping with demands. As we shall see in chapter 9, there is extensive evidence linking both E and N to appraisal and coping. Matthews, Derryberry and Siegle (2000) reported that a correlation of 0.41 ($n = 108$) between N and distress was no longer significant with cognitive factors controlled: the state–trait association appeared to be mediated by factors including threat appraisal and emotion-focused coping. Similarly, a significant correlation of 0.29 between N and worry was mediated by emotion-focused and avoidant coping. E was unrelated to task engagement in this study, but this state factor correlated with cognitive factors including challenge appraisal and task-focused coping. Hence, trait–state relationships may be a consequence of traits biasing the person's situational cognitions of external demands. Future research will undoubtedly focus in more detail on mechanisms mediating between traits and individual differences in moods and states. It may well transpire that multiple biological and cognitive mechanisms play a role in the emotional consequences of traits.

Conclusions

1. State variables are important both as correlates of traits, and as potential mediators of associations between traits and behaviour. Research on states has focused on psychometric criteria for differentiating traits and states, dimensional models for states, and inter-relationships between traits and states.

2. Both trait and state measures must be internally consistent and valid. However, by contrast with trait scales, state measures should show only moderate test–retest reliability over periods of a day or more. Scores should also be sensitive to situational manipulations. States are an important aspect of trait theory, because they may sometimes mediate the behavioural consequences of traits, as described by state–trait models. The nature of the mediating processes is open to debate. One possibility is that trait effects are biologically mediated. For example, positive and negative moods might reflect the activity levels of brain reward and punishment systems, respectively. A second possibility is that effects might be cognitively mediated: moods may reflect the person's situational appraisals, and their choice of strategy for coping with external pressures. Personality traits might relate to individual differences in both neural function and information-processing that control individual differences in mood states.

3. Factor-analytic studies of mood suggest that there are only a small number of fundamental dimensions. Thayer (2001) identified energetic arousal and tense arousal as basic dimensions; another scheme (Watson and Tellegen, 1985) called similar dimensions positive affect and negative affect. Rotating these axes through 45 degrees gives alternative dimensions of pleasure and activation. Other studies (e.g., Schimmack and Grob, 2000) have extracted three factors, adding a pleasantness factor to energetic and tense arousal dimensions, within a correlated-factor model. Further differentiation of affects, especially negative affects, may be necessary to fully explain the variance in states. Both two- and three-dimensional models provide a useful basis for research. There is extensive validation evidence from experimental and naturalistic studies that shows that different mood dimensions are sensitive to different biological and cognitive-social influences. The validity of mood scales is also shown by studies that relate mood to objective performance indices.

4. The study of states includes cognitive and motivational states, as well as mood states, as described by the 'trilogy of mind'. Cognitive states have received more attention, and scales have been developed to measure constructs such as cognitive interference and self-esteem. Recently, Matthews et al. (in press) have presented a comprehensive state model for performance settings that differentiates three second-order factors of task engagement, distress and worry. The first two factors integrate cognitive, motivational and affective aspects of state, whereas worry is exclusively cognitive.

5. Extraversion and neuroticism are the traits most reliably associated with mood and, in the case of N, with the cognitive states that define worry. Both correlational and experimental studies tend to link E to positive affect (energy) and N to negative affect (tension). One view is that E represents temperamental positive affect, whereas N represents temperamental negative affect. These temperaments have been linked to brain reward and punishment systems, respectively. However, the temperament hypothesis may not fully explain the

variation of associations between personality and mood across different situations ('situational moderation'), especially in the case of E. There is some evidence that personality effects may be mediated by cognitive factors (appraisal and coping), suggesting a transactional perspective on trait–state associations. Further research in this area should focus more closely on possible mediating mechanisms.

Note

1. This criterion also illustrates a broad psychometric principle, that of convergent–divergent validity. Scales should correlate strongly with related constructs (convergent validity), but weakly, at most, with unrelated constructs (divergent validity).

5 Alternatives to trait theory

Thus far, we have outlined the general case for approaching the study of personality via the trait concept. Before developing this argument, we must look briefly at the relationship between trait theories and other approaches to personality, such as psychoanalysis and humanistic psychology. There are two main reasons for so doing. First, trait theory has not developed in isolation from alternative theories. Allport (1937), for example, explicitly stated that his trait theory was an attempt to unify the diverse personality theories of this day. It is important to identify, first, those features of trait theories which are distinctive from other approaches, and, second, areas of common ground between trait theories and the alternatives. An issue of particular importance is consistency of behaviour. As we shall see, the idea of temporal stability in behaviour and mental life is not exclusive to trait psychology. Second, our thesis in this book is that trait psychology is becoming the dominant paradigm for personality research. This chapter offers some reasons why the trait approach may be more successful than competing ones, such as its use of the scientific method, and its ability to accommodate empirical data on behavioural consistency and stability.

Some disclaimers are necessary at this point. This chapter is not an attempt at a general survey of personality theory, and we assume the reader has an introductory knowledge of the main strands of personality research, such as psychoanalysis. Any of the standard texts on the Hall of Fame of influential personality psychologists (e.g., Hall and Lindzey, Phares, Engler) will suffice to provide the necessary background. The structure of the chapter reflects the broad issues introduced in the previous paragraph, and we refer to specific theories as they relate to these issues. Hence, there is no attempt to provide a name check for all the members of the Hall of Fame. First, we describe how we might conceptualise traits within psychodynamic theory, referring mainly to Freud's psychoanalysis. Second, we review recent studies of unconscious processes that use rigorous experimental methods, and consider what light they may shed on personality. Third, we survey phenomenological and humanistic approaches to personality, such as those of Rogers and Maslow. We also consider how some humanistic themes have been picked up in contemporary studies of motivational dispositions and positive psychology.

Traits in psychodynamic theory

The contribution of psychoanalysis

Psychoanalysis began with the theories of Sigmund Freud, and has spawned a family of 'psychodynamic' personality theories with various common elements. At a theoretical level, these include the importance of unconscious processes, sexual gratification or other basic motives, and childhood experience. Methodologically, Freudian and post-Freudian psychodynamic theories emphasise the importance of the detailed study of individuals, and especially the clues they provide to the workings of the unconsciousness, for example, in dreams, parapraxes, the relationship with the analyst, free association, responses to ambiguous stimuli, and so forth. Because few of Freud's contemporaries and successors set out their conceptual system as clearly as he did, we shall primarily use Freudian theory to illustrate the main features of the psychodynamic approach to personality.

A fundamental attribute of psychoanalysis is that the basis for personality is the energy associated with basic biological drives or id. The sexual component of these drives, the libido, is of special importance. During development, parts of this energy become detached from the id to form the reality-oriented ego, and the superego or 'conscience'. The psyche has a kind of internal economy, such that a fixed quantity of energy is invested in various mental structures. Energy fixation or cathexis takes place at more fine-grained levels also. Attachment and re-attachment of libido to the various erogenous zones is associated with the stages of psychosexual development (oral, anal, phallic, latency and genital) and with associated complexes, notably the Oedipus complex. At a still more differentiated level, libido may be fixated on specific stimuli, such as people, or on cherished ideas and causes. This process may lead to perversions such as fetishisms. Personality derives in part from the pattern of investment of energy. We might see a gluttonous and licentious individual such as Shakespeare's Falstaff as someone in whom much of the libidinal energy remains within the id. In religious leaders, such as the Pope, a large proportion of the libido is invested in the superego.

However, personality is not simply derived from a free choice between libidinal alternatives, because, in modern society, there is a deep-rooted tendency for different personality structures to be in conflict with one another. The id's immediate need for gratification (the pleasure principle) often transgresses the ego's need to maintain security in the objective world (the reality principle). As the long catalogue of politicians shamed by sexual misadventure shows, the id sometimes wins the struggle with the ego. Likewise, both ego and id may be at odds with the moral dictates of the superego.

The most important consequence of these conflicts is that important areas of psychic experience, such as unacceptable wishes, become unconscious. However, unconscious does not mean inactive. Unconscious wishes continue to seek fulfilment, leading to defence mechanisms such as projection and reaction-formation.

Many defence mechanisms are essentially a compromise between the id's need to find an outlet for sexual and/or aggressive desires, and the needs of the ego and superego to thwart desires which threaten reality-adjustment or moral rules. Defence mechanisms are often unsuccessful because maintaining them requires libido and itself distorts behaviour. The ego typically reacts to repressed libido with neurotic anxiety; the person's own desires are seen as a source of threat. Adjustment requires sublimation, finding socially acceptable substitute behaviours, such as a person with sadistic desires becoming a butcher or surgeon.

Correspondences between psychodynamic and trait approaches to personality structure

Thus far, we have identified four principal ideas: libidinal energy as the basis for personality, energy-based personality structures, conflict between structures, and unconsciousness as a defence against unacceptable desires. Leaving aside for the moment the scientific validity of these ideas, we may ask how they relate to trait psychology. The energetic metaphor remains influential, in the form of arousal theories which propose that personality results from individual differences in the excitability of brain systems (see chapter 7). Ironically, given the sexual connotations of 'arousal', the contemporary concept is largely asexual; sexual arousal is a rather special case of a more general activating response. Some of Freud's successors moved in a similar direction, with Jung (1948) replacing libido with a more general psychic or life energy. However, contemporary neuropsychology does not favour a unitary psychic energy. The general trend is towards ever finer discrimination of multiple systems which may be independently aroused or de-aroused (e.g., Robbins, 1986).

At the level of personality structure, there is no doubt that psychoanalysis has been useful, for labelling purposes at least, to trait theorists. Cattell (1973) labelled one of his primary factors (C) Ego Strength and another (G) as Superego, though he rejected any general correspondence between psychometric and psychoanalytic personality constructs. Brand (1994) relates each of his modified Big Five factors to Freudian constructs, while retaining intelligence as a purely intellectual factor. Extraversion is linked to energy and relatively free expression of the desires of the id. This identification is plausible, in that extraverts appear to enjoy more varied and extensive sexual experiences than introverts (see Eysenck and Eysenck, 1985). Neuroticism relates to weakness of the ego, and Conscientiousness to the relatively primitive methods used by the superego to maintain social conformity, such as adherence to traditional values. Conversely, Eysenck's P dimension might be linked to superego weakness, and Eysenck himself has used this terminology. To explain the remaining two Big Five dimensions, Brand (1994) refers to two concepts introduced at a relatively late stage of Freud's (1920) theorising, eros and thanatos, the so-called life and death instincts. Brand's affection dimension (emotional Openness) relates to eros, and his will dimension (low Agreeableness) to thanatos. In other words, the 'niceness' to others which characterises the high A individual is simply the lack of the destructive, aggressive drives associated with thanatos.

A further example of convergence between psychoanalytic and trait theories comes from work on depression. In psychoanalytic theory 'anaclitic' depression refers to feelings of helplessness and abandonment, whereas 'introjective' depression is associated with feelings of inferiority, guilt and worthlessness (Blatt and Maroudas, 1992). The two types of depression are said to arise from, respectively, inadequate maternal care and parental criticism of the child's early attempts at asserting independence. As Blatt and Maroudas (1992) discuss, cognitive personality research appears to have rediscovered this distinction in the guise of trait measures. A dimension of sociotropy (Beck et al., 1983) corresponds to the anaclitic or dependent type of depression, whereas Beck et al.'s autonomy dimension relates to the introjective or self-critical type. A further twist is that both dimensions are substantially correlated with neuroticism, which may be responsible for their associations with clinical criteria (Coyne and Whiffen, 1995). The relationship between neuroticism and depression is discussed further in chapter 9.

The Big Five are in evidence in post-Freudian psychodynamic theory also. Horney (1950) discriminated three broad interpersonal styles of moving towards others (self-effacement), moving against others (expansion) and moving away from others (resignation) which appear to correspond to a mixture of high A and low C, low A and high C, and low E respectively. Self-effacement and expansion might also be seen as contrasting low and high Psychoticism. Horney's scheme of things also includes an analogue of N: basic anxiety derived from all-pervading feelings of vulnerability and loneliness. As mentioned in chapter 1, the Jungian personality characteristics measured by the MBTI correspond to four of the Big Five (McCrae and Costa, 1989), although there is little contact between Jung's somewhat mystical personality theory and trait psychology. More recently, Loevinger (e.g., 1997) has identified a series of stages of ego development which relate to personality and style of interpersonal interaction. These stages have clear Big Five connotations. For example, there is a Conscientious stage, and an earlier Self-Protective stage associated with low A characteristics such as wariness of others and manipulation in relationships. As with other stage models, there is an implicit value judgement that, in adults, characteristics associated with later stages are better than those of earlier stages, which is not a part of the Big Five.

The two remaining 'big ideas' of psychoanalysis mentioned above, conflict between structures and the importance of the unconscious, have found fewer direct applications in trait theory. Theorists such as Eysenck (e.g., 1992b) have tended to see psychopathology as derived from single personality traits such as neuroticism or psychoticism, although the expression of pathology is moderated by extraversion. Conflict has been more important in motivation theory, as expressed, for example, by the hypothesis that 'resultant' achievement motivation represents the difference between approach and avoidance tendencies (McClelland, 1985). As we shall see below, the conflict theme has also been developed within

Table 5.1 *Examples of empirical psychoanalytic research*

Concept	Research
Unconscious processes	Subliminal presentation of motivational stimuli e.g. 'Beating Dad is OK' may activate Oedipal reactions
Defensive processes	Investigations of relationships between pathological defensiveness and mental health
'Attachment' to significant others	Security of attachment in childhood and adult social functioning: does childhood insecurity lead to later difficulties in forming close relationships?
Ego development	Stages of ego development, and their dependence mode of interpersonal interaction

Note See Westen and Gabbard (1999) for references to original research

phenomenological approaches to personality. Westen and Gabbard (1995) point out the rediscovery by experimental psychology of the unconscious, as exemplified by distinctions such as implicit and explicit knowledge. They suggest that the questionnaire measures which form the basis for trait theory neglect unconscious knowledge, and provide impoverished descriptions of the person compared to those provided by psychodynamic analyses of the individual. The emphasis of trait theory on biological bases for personality has discouraged interest in distinctions between conscious and unconscious processes. More recently, however, the influx of cognitive psychological concepts into personality psychology has led to renewed interest in this area (see chapter 12).

Empirical studies of psychoanalysis and personality

There is undoubtedly some overlap between the personality constructs used in psychoanalytic and trait approaches. In itself, this is unsurprising, and, from the Big Five perspective, supports the pervasiveness of the Five (Costa and McCrae, 1992b). The more interesting questions are whether psychoanalysis helps to explain the underlying psychology of the Big Five, and whether we should develop personality constructs and measures tightly linked to Freudian theory. The scientific acceptability of psychoanalysis has been much debated, and various positions have emerged. One school of thought argues that the key ideas of psychoanalysis are simply not scientifically testable (Popper, 1957), another that some hypotheses can be tested and are false (Grünbaum, 1984; Eysenck, 1985). The reliability and validity of Freud's methods, such as free association, have also been criticised (Macmillan, 1997, 2001). Box 5.1 assesses the limited utility of dreams as a guide to personality. Clearly, if psychoanalysis is untestable, wrong or based on nonscientific methods it cannot contribute to personality theory. The case in favour of empirical verification of psychoanalysis has been put by Westen (1999; Westen and Gabbard, 1991). He argues that there is experimental support for a number of fundamental tenets of psychoanalysis, as illustrated in table 5.1. However, even within psychoanalysis, some have admitted that the personality theory – Freud's

Box 5.1 Dreams: Royal road or blind alley?

Freud famously saw dreams as a 'royal road' to understanding the psyche. Decoding the manifest dream revealed the latent unconscious material that threatened the ego. Unfortunately, there is little evidence that substantiates traditional Freudian interpretations of dream images, although perhaps the skilled clinician may obtain clues to pathology on an idiographic basis. If anything, dreams may simply reflect conscious preoccupations; for example, individuals with panic disorder appear to be vulnerable to nightmares (Schredl et al., 2001). One influential theory of dreams (Crick and Mitchison, 1995) proposes that they are no more than the process of removing unneeded memories. If so, the interpreter of dreams is much like a private investigator searching someone's trash for clues. The search may turn up occasional revelations, but the great majority of the material is the psychological equivalent of fishbones and potato peelings.

Studies of traits have focused on quantity of dreaming, i.e., dream recall frequency (DRF), indexed by self-reports of number of dreams recalled per month. Freudian theory predicts that the trait of repression, discussed in this chapter, should be negatively correlated with DRF. Conversely, we might expect a positive correlation with overt anxiety or neuroticism. In fact, these hypotheses have received little empirical support (see Schredl, Nuernberg and Weiler, 1995; Blagrove and Akehurst, 2000): personality correlates of DRF are inconsistent from study to study, and are often non-significant. As Blagrove and Akehurst (2000) conclude, the main influences on DRF may be physiological rather than psychological. Another line of research is suggested by studies that show more creative persons report a higher DRF (Schredl et al., 1995). However, Schredl (2002) failed to find any correlation between DRF and Openness to Experience, which may relate to creative inclinations, or, indeed, any of the Big Five. Of course, DRF is a crude measure of dreaming experience, and use of more fine-grained indices may be more productive. In addition, sleep and dreaming may be disturbed in clinical patients (Schredl et al., 2001). So far, though, the data do not suggest that measures of dreaming can tell us much about normal personality.

metapsychology – is invalid and that only the core aspects of his clinical psychology are retained (Holt, 1985).

An intermediate position is advocated by Kline (1981), who finds empirical support for some Freudian propositions, but not others. For example, Kline (1981) suggests that there are distinct dimensions of 'oral' and 'anal' character which can be reliably and validly measured, by questionnaire, or (less reliably) by projective measures. The anal character is associated with qualities related to obsessionality such as rigidity and obstinacy. However, there is no evidence that this aspect of personality relates to childhood events at the anal stage of development, such as toilet training, so it is unclear that the Freudian interpretation of this obsessional personality trait adds to our understanding of it. In general, obsessional traits appear to be a mixture of high C and low O (Kline and Lapham, 1991; Kline, 1993). A related trait, authoritarianism, is discussed further in chapter 8.

One of the difficulties in assessing work in this area is deciding what level of supportive evidence is required to reach a judgement that psychoanalytic theory is basically in good shape. Even supporters of psychoanalysis such as Westen (1999) accept that some of Freud's views were incorrect. The question which arises is what degree of error in psychoanalysis forces us to abandon the approach, and to formulate an alternative which still captures whatever positive features of psychoanalysis there may be. Such philosophical issues will not be pursued further here (see Kuhn, 1962, and Lakatos, 1970, for discussion of scientific 'paradigm-shifts'). In general, trait theorists have been unconvinced by psychoanalysis, and there is, in general, little acceptable scientific study of Freudian or post-Freudian concepts and systems. It may be that some of the major concerns of psychoanalysis will contribute to the understanding of personality traits. However, it may be necessary to divest theories of research findings such as those of table 5.1 of their psychoanalytic trappings for progress to be made.

The unconscious: contemporary studies

In recent years, interest in the unconscious has revived through two developments in cognitive psychology: one a theoretical advance, the other a methodology. The theoretical development is the theory of automatic and controlled processing (Schneider, Dumais and Shiffrin, 1977). It distinguishes two qualitatively distinct modes of information-processing (which may or may not grade into one another). Automatic processing is unconscious, effortless and driven by external stimuli, without volition. Controlled processing is partly accessible to consciousness, effortful and voluntary, in being driven by a strategy. With sufficient practice, even complex mental activities may be accomplished automatically. The theory seems to reinforce the Freudian notion that much of mental life operates outside awareness.

The methodology is the use of subliminal stimuli to investigate cognitive processes. Subjects are presented with a briefly presented target stimulus, followed by a masking stimulus that prevents conscious awareness of stimulus presentation, provided the presentation time of the target is sufficiently short (often less than 50 ms). A typical application is the 'priming' paradigm, in which the subliminal stimulus is presented prior to a consciously perceived stimulus that requires some response. The subliminal stimulus may bias or prime response to that stimulus. For example, the 'lexical decision' task requires the person to decide whether strings of letters are valid English words or not. Recognition is faster when the word is preceded by a semantically related word, even if this priming word is subliminal: for example, NURSE speeds recognition of DOCTOR (Neely, 1991). The relevance to personality is that studies show priming of social attitudes and behaviours. For example, subliminal presentation of African-American faces to white American subjects increases the level of their hostile attitudes and verbal behaviours in an experimental setting (Chen and Bargh, 1997). As aggression is part of the stereotype attached to African-Americans, it is supposed that unconscious activation of this stereotype increases hostility. Perhaps there is a parallel here with the Freudian concept of repression of socially unacceptable thoughts (i.e, racist thoughts). In this section, we look, first, at some illustrations of empirical studies, and, second, at their implications for studies of personality traits.

Experimental studies of the unconscious

A recent review (Kihlstrom, 1999) of unconscious (or implicit) processing has demonstrated its pervasiveness. Studies of *perception* demonstrate that the meaning of a subliminal stimulus can be encoded without it being conscious recognition. It should be noted that studies of subliminal stimuli are fraught with methodological difficulties (Holender, 1986). Although the effects are real, they are often of small magnitude, and subjects' self-reports of awareness are not reliable (Kunimoto, Miller and Pashler, 2001). Studies of implicit *memory* are based on demonstrations that subjects' behaviour is affected by a previous encounter, even if they have no conscious recollection of it (Schacter, 1996). For example, in lexical decision, prior exposure to the word speeds response, even when the exposure has been forgotten. Implicit *thought* is demonstrated by studies showing that people can solve certain types of problems without being able to articulate what they did. Kihlstrom (1999) also points to instances of implicit emotion and motivation. The person may have feelings and urges that they cannot explain.

One area of research is concerned with repression of unacceptable material. In an early experiment, McGinnies (1949) briefly presented subjects with taboo words (such as sexual words) and neutral words. He found that the minimum time at which the word could be consciously recognised (the 'recognition threshold') was of longer duration for taboo words. It was claimed that taboo words evoked anxiety, which in turn initiated psychological defence, blocking perceptual processing. The study appears to provide an experimental confirmation of one aspect of Freudian theory. More recent work (reviewed by Kitayama, 1997) has replicated the McGinnies finding, and shown that the emotional content of the word does indeed influence perceptual threshold. It is not the case the subjects are simply more reluctant to report taboo words (response bias).

However, these studies also call into question the Freudian view that unconscious processing is motivated and purposive (see Kitayama, 1997). For example, 'defence' is not restricted to taboo words: both positive and negative words produce the same elevation of recognition threshold. The effect also varies with factors such as word length and frequency, which are of no motivational relevance. In fact, as Kitayama's studies show, the key factor is the accessibility of the perceptual code.

According to his affect-amplification model, both positive and negative emotions tend to amplify attentive processing, facilitating recognition of accessible codes, but impairing recognition of codes that are hard to access (e.g., briefly presented, short, unusual words). Thus, effects of word content on recognition thresholds have nothing to do with Freudian defence. Instead, they are the 'result of an interaction between affective and cognitive pathways commonly involved in any ordinary processes of perceiving and thinking' (Kitayama, 1997, p. 239).

Evidence for the operation of defence mechanisms comes from studies of individual differences. 'Repressors' are a group of people who obtain low trait anxiety scores, but are high in 'social desirability'; that is, they respond defensively to criticism. Studies show that repressors have, for example, poorer memory for unpleasant events, deficits in emotional self-disclosure, and avoidance of threatening material (Weinberger and Davidson, 1994). Again, however, it is unclear whether 'repression' operates as described by Freud. In reviewing the literature, Caprara and Cervone (2000) point to some discrepancies. For example, repressors have poorer recall of positive experiences as well as negative experiences. In fact, memory differences may be a consequence of differences in the ways that repressors and nonrepressors encode information in the first place. There also seem to be some advantages to repression: Furnham, Petrides and Spencer-Bowdage (2002) found that repressors were quite high in self-esteem, life satisfaction and use of 'healthy' coping styles. Indeed, perhaps the repressor personality has conscious as well as unconscious aspects. More generally, Caprara and Cervone (2000) reach three reasonable conclusions on defence mechanisms. First, there is good evidence for their existence. Second, mechanisms underlying defence are only partially understood, but they may reflect interactions among basic, normal affective and cognitive processes. Third, there is no evidence for the Freudian concept of some unconscious ego-protection mechanism that protects against unacceptable emotional feelings.

Another line of research (reviewed by Bargh, 1997) is concerned with priming effects. Several studies show that attitudes and behaviours can be primed by appropriate cues, even if the subject is unaware of the cue. For example, subjects subliminally exposed to aggressive words are more likely to rate other people as aggressive, in an experimentally controlled setting (Bargh and Pietromonaco, 1982). Bargh, Chen and Burrows (1996) primed subjects with words suggesting a stereotype for old people (e.g., bingo, Miami), and showed this manipulation influenced how slowly they walked away when leaving the experiment, demonstrating behavioural change. Chartrand and Bargh (2002) discuss studies suggesting unconscious motivations. They argue that goals produce much the same effects on behaviour irrespective of whether they are explicit, or primed by contextual factors. For example, one of their studies showed that subjects could be primed to process sentences so as to either form an impression or to memorise them.

Bargh (1997) and Chartrand (Chartrand and Bargh, 2002) conclude that much of mental life proceeds unconsciously. However, they differ from Freud in suggesting that unconscious processing simply handles routine mental activities, leaving consciously accessible processing to handle novel and complex situations. Thus, the unconscious is not a seething morass of repressed desires, but an adaptive system with distinct cognitive, affective and motivational aspects. Its main disadvantage is that lack of awareness is associated with lack of control, so that the person cannot correct processing that may be undesired, such as stereotypical beliefs. In short, the unconscious is important, but not for the reasons given by Freud. As Kihlstrom (1999, p. 208) states, with perhaps just a little hyperbole, 'Modern research on cognition and the cognitive unconscious owes nothing whatsoever to Freud and that is also the case with modern research on emotion and the emotional unconscious.'

Implications for trait theory

The topic of the unconscious is again prominent in many contemporary reviews of personality. For example, Pervin (2002) refers to the unconscious as 'a topic of enormous theoretical and methodological importance to the field of personality psychology' (p. 209), with 'tremendous implications for the assessment of personality' (p. 210). Is this really so? There are some reasons for caution. The evidence reviewed comes from carefully controlled laboratory studies, in which even small effects of, for example, priming manipulations, may be detected. The real-world relevance of these effects remains to be demonstrated. People are, perhaps, generally aware of those motives and thoughts that are important to them. Mayer and Merckelbach (1999) showed that subliminal stimuli had no effects on strong emotions. The theoretical implications of whether processing is unconscious or conscious is also uncertain. Clore and Ortony (2000) suggest that unconscious processing is based on an associative 'reinstatement' mechanism that retrieves prototypical meanings for the stimulus concerned. Thus, subliminal presentation of stimuli does not involve some separate unconscious system. Instead, it strips the stimulus representation of the contextual, episodic information that would normally be encoded with it, so that the person does not explicitly recognise the stimulus. A final reason for caution is that much work on the unconscious does not directly relate to personality at all. As Todorov and Bargh (2002, p. 54) state, 'research on these [unconscious] determinants is an extension of the social psychology tradition of discovering the situational causes of behavior'.

At the same time, there is scope for integrating experimental studies of the unconscious with work on personality traits. At an empirical level, we can investigate whether traits predict individual differences in unconscious processing. Two examples will show the potential interest of studies of this kind. Chartrand and Bargh (1999) investigated what they called the 'chameleon effect': the tendency towards unconscious mimicry of the nonverbal behaviours of the other people one interacts with, such as postures, mannerisms and facial expressions. They showed that people high in dispositional empathy exhibited the chameleon effect to a greater extent than low empathic individuals. As empathy is an aspect of agreeableness, this process might contribute to differences in social behaviour shown by persons high or low in this trait, which we discuss in chapter 8. A second example concerns studies of subliminal threat stimuli. Several studies have shown that such stimuli seem to attract the attention of subjects high or low in trait anxiety, as further discussed in chapter 12. Again, similar effects are seen with supraliminal stimuli, implying that it is more useful to think in terms of processing mechanisms rather than consciousness. Furthermore, effects of subliminal stimuli seem to be moderated by conscious expectancies and other contextual factors (Fox, 1996; Matthews and Wells, 2000). It is important that traits influence unconscious processing, but we may be able to see similar outcomes in studies of conscious processes.

In terms of theory, an important contribution of work on the unconscious is the idea of 'chronically accessible constructs', i.e., those that come to mind spontaneously, when, for example, the subject is asked to rate the personality of others (Higgins, King and Mavin, 1982). For example, some people are biased towards thinking about people in terms of how kind they are, while others focus on shyness. Chronically accessible constructs meet some of the criteria for traits. They are considered stable over time, and to influence cognition across different situations. Unfortunately, studies in this area have neglected trait measures: it is unclear whether thinking about people as kind or unkind relates to being kind oneself. Indeed, Cervone and Caprara (2000) suggest that constructs should be approached idiographically. However, Todorov and Bargh (2002) suggest that dispositional aggression may be a consequence of chronically accessible constructs representing a history of exposure to violent events. It seems that aggressive children tend, automatically, to attribute hostile intentions to others, for example. More generally, the idea is that personality may relate to unconscious knowledge structures developed through social learning that generate consistent biases in cognition and behaviour. We return to this idea in more detail on chapter 8.

Humanistic and phenomenological approaches

We have seen that there is no fundamental conflict between psychoanalysis and trait theory. In principle, trait theory might even be enriched by incorporation of the sources of consistency described by psychoanalytic theory, although in practice scientifically acceptable support for the psychoanalytic view of personality has been disappointing. A more radical challenge to the assumptions of trait theory is posed by humanistic and phenomenological approaches to personality. There are a variety of approaches of this kind, but they all emphasise the importance and uniqueness of the individual's subjective experience and the self as actively shaping experienced reality and personality. At one level, phenomenological personality theories are directly opposed to trait theories in their emphasis on the idiographic study of personality, on a case by case basis. At the extreme, there is little basis for any sort of dialogue between psychologists favouring idiographic and trait approaches, because their assumptions are so much at variance. Existential psychology (Binswanger, 1963), for example, rejects the view that behaviour has unseen causes; psychology must deal with immediate conscious phenomena. However, if there are no latent causes of experience, there is no basis

Table 5.2 *A survey of idiographic methods*

1. Quantitative single case study	Measurement of time spent on different activities during the day by a particular person
2. Qualitative single case study	Reconstruction and interpretation of events leading up to an episode of mental illness
3. Intra-individual correlation study	Correlating asthma attacks with presence of precipitating factors in a single individual
4. Single-case experimental study	Systematic comparison of effects of different treatments on a single clinical patient
5. Idiographic personality measurement	Determination of the rebellious acts a person may perform, followed by assessment of the frequency of rebelliousness during various activities during a fixed time period
6. Idiographic prediction	Use of past patterns of behaviour to predict clinical prognosis for a clinical patient
7. Configurational analysis	Assessment of patterns of subjective experience behaviour which co-occur in an individual

Note See Runyan (1983) for references to original research

for psychological stability, and the trait concept is meaningless. Indeed, existential psychology denies the validity of the natural-science approach on which nomothetic trait theories are based. A distaste for 'pure data-grubbing', in Bannister and Fransella's (1989) revealing phrase, is common even among variants of phenomenological psychology which make use of quantitative measures.

However, compromises are also possible. Allport's (1937) trait theory aimed to synthesise a nomothetic, explanatory theory of common traits with an idiographic account of individual traits. Allport diverged from contemporary trait theory in seeing individual traits as being more 'real' psychologically than common traits, which he described as merely the measurable aspects of complex individual traits (Allport, 1937, p. 299). Allport also saw consistency as a feature of both common and individual traits; there is no contradiction between consistency of behaviour or experience and the idiographic approach. It is possible to do systematic idiographic research: table 5.2 summarises Runyan's (1983) survey of idiographic methods. Bem and Allen (1974) have suggested that consistency is best understood idiographically; some people are consistent some of the time in some situations.

Like psychoanalysis, phenomenological and humanistic personality theories are based on a set of key themes or big ideas. They largely reject the energy metaphor and fixed structural differentiation of personality systems such as id and ego. They also differ from both psychoanalysis and most trait theories in emphasising subjective experience, including awareness of the self. The self is also important as an agent which actively constructs the person's mental life: a distinction is sometimes drawn between self-as-object and self-as-doer (Smith, 1950). Like psychoanalysis, these theories admit the importance of conflict, but see conflict as arising out of maladaptive or unwise conceptions of the self or the individual's place in the world. The final theme is that of a fundamental motivation towards personal development, sometimes termed self-actualisation. This latter emphasis on the development – even progression or maturation – of personality in adulthood is not generally a part of the trait tradition (Erikson, 1982).

Investigating the self

To the trait theorist, the more interesting strands of phenomenological research are those which aim to investigate the self using quantitative data. Some theorists have developed systematic means for investigating the organisation of the individual's self-awareness. Rogers (1951) used the Q-sort technique in which subjects sort cards containing self-descriptive statements into piles according to their self-relevance. The technique goes beyond conventional personality ratings in that the cards may be sorted with respect to various aspects of the self. For example, the first sorting might be for a simple self-description ('the actual self') and the second for a description of how one would ideally like to be ('the ideal self'). The cards may be made more or less idiographic in application, by using the same statements across a variety of respondents, or by tailoring them to the individual. Rogers also used rating scales and content analysis of self-statements, as well as qualitative interpretations of verbalisations in his investigations of the self.

More recent research has made considerable efforts to develop social-cognitive models of self-concepts which can be tested experimentally. Kihlstrom and Canter (1984) see self-concepts as 'prototypes', fundamental concepts represented as nodes in a network also containing more specific concepts. The self has also been described as a 'schema', an organised cognitive structure representing key elements of self-beliefs (see Markus and Cross, 1990). Both approaches allow for considerable differentiation of self-concept; one may have multiple selves according to context. To the extent that schemas or other knowledge structures reside in long-term memory, they provide a source of consistency in behaviour. The self-knowledge approach also converges with the study of unconscious processes, through experimental priming paradigms, for example, as previously discussed. Models of this kind have some promise for improved understanding of traits, although contemporary theorists differ in the extent to which they see self-schemas as nomothetic or idiographic, as discussed further in chapter 8. As in Rogers's original work, the researcher may choose to focus on either elements of the self common to people in general, or on the uniqueness of the self of the individual.

The self-construction of personality

Another strand of phenomenological theory emphasises the self as an agent actively constructing experienced reality. A pioneer in this area was Kelly (1955), whose personal construct theory describes the person as interpreting experience in terms of their own unique construct dimensions. (The idea of 'chronically accessible constructs', previously described, is a contemporary version of Kelly's theory.) Each person, in effect, develops his or her own private theories of the self and others, and different people may construe the same event using quite different dimensions. He devised the repertory grid technique, still quite widely used to investigate personal constructs (see Bannister and Fransella, 1989). Constructs also have an interpersonal character, in that people may enact many different roles, in which constructs are derived from perceptions of another's constructs. The person's ability to shift from role to role gives behaviour a fluidity and impermanence at variance with the trait theory perspective. The closest parallel in contemporary research is provided by social constructionism, which we discuss further in chapter 8.

Conflict and pathology

The importance of conflict in phenomenological personality theory was expressed most directly in Rogers's (1951) concept of the congruence between the self-concept and the actual organism itself. Psychopathology is associated with reduced or distorted awareness of the actual experiences of the organism. There is some evidence for this position derived from Q-sort studies (e.g., Butler and Haigh, 1954). In emotionally disturbed individuals, the self- and ideal-sorts are often uncorrelated; the actual self does not resemble the personality to which the individual aspires. However, there are methodological difficulties with such studies associated with defensiveness; the disturbed person may distort the actual self to present a more positive impression. More recent work on the self has also used the discrepancy concept. Higgins (1989) describes various sources of discrepancy which may lead to anxiety or depression, as described further in chapter 9. Watson and Randolph (2001) showed that discrepancies between actual and ideal selves predicted neuroticism. However, their measures of 'self-image disparity' were more predictive when based on idiographic as opposed to conventional, non-idiographic constructs. Conceivably, self-discrepancy might also relate to 'schizoid' traits and vulnerability to schizophrenia, as proposed by Laing (1965). One Q-sort study confirmed that schizophrenics may have more contradictory elements in their self-concepts (Gruba and Johnson, 1974).

Self-actualisation

The final major theme relates to the humanistic orientation of phenomenological theories, that people have a tendency towards personal development and fulfilment, sometimes referred to as self-actualisation (Rogers, 1951). The best-known expression of this idea is Maslow's (1971) view that self-actualisation is a fundamental motivation, most potent when more primitive motivations such as attaining physical security are satisfied. Self-actualisation is most apparent phenomenologically; the non-actualised individual may feel de-personalised and detached from life experiences, whereas the actualised person experiences a sense of wholeness, fulfilment and richness of awareness. It is hard to relate such concepts to trait

Box 5.2 Measurement of individual differences in basic needs

Studies of basic human needs and motives form a counterpart to studies of basic personality traits. As with traits (Costa and McCrae, 1992), it is assumed that there are motives that are culturally universal, that are physiologically based, and that have various, wide-ranging psychological and social consequences (e.g., Baumeister and Leary, 1995). This idea was a familiar part of twentieth-century psychology. In the 1930s, lists of twenty to thirty basic propensities or needs were drawn up by McDougall and Murray respectively. These lists included some obvious biologically based motives (e.g., sex and fear), together with those that related to more social-psychological motivations, such as needs for achievement and dominance. Some of these constructs failed to spark much interest (e.g., the propensity to migrate), but three social motives became central to the psychology of motivation: the need for achievement (n Ach), the need for power over others (n Pow), and the need for affiliation (n Aff), i.e., seeking out relationships with others (e.g., McAdams, 1999).

Traditionally, needs have been measured using projective tests, such as the Thematic Apperception Test (TAT: see McClelland, 1985). This test requires the respondent to tell a short story about ambiguous pictures, that can be scored for motivational content. A story containing themes of personal striving would indicate high n Ach, for example. Studies showed that such techniques could be used to assess individuals with some reliability on multiple, largely independent, dimensions (Bowen, 1973). However, most researchers focused on only a small number of needs: McClelland's (e.g., 1985) work on n Ach became especially well known. By contrast with trait theory, the development of comprehensive structural models of needs, based on psychometrically sound measurement, was largely neglected (though see Cattell and Kline, 1977).

Superficially, it might appear that there is considerable overlap between basic needs and personality traits, which often have motivational connotations. For example, achievement motivation would seem to relate to conscientiousness, power to extraversion, and affiliation to agreeableness. However, the TAT appears to measure something different from standard traits. TAT measures of n Ach are independent from self-reports of achievement striving (similar to those contributing to Conscientiousness trait scales), but nevertheless have predictive validity for criteria such as career success (McClelland, 1985; Spangler, 1992). McClelland believed that self-reports indicated short-term, voluntary choice of goals, whereas projective measures assessed less conscious motives that shaped the course of life over longer time periods.

A recent study by Sokolowski et al. (2000) shows how the classic work of McClelland and others can be placed on an increasingly sound basis psychometrically. They used a modification of the TAT, the 'Multi-Motive Grid' (MMG), that comprises fourteen pictures relating to achievement-arousing, affiliation-arousing, and power-arousing situations. For each picture, the subject rates agreement with twelve statements representing the three motive domains (see table B.5.1), allowing data to be scored nomothetically. The statements also distinguish between positive motivations ('hopes') and negative motivations ('fears'). Various analyses reported by Sokolowski et al. (2000), including confirmatory factor analyses, discriminated multiple motive dimensions in line with initial expectations. Further analyses and studies showed that the scales were reliable, distinct from standard personality traits, and predicted external criteria appropriately. This study may represent an important step on the journey towards a comprehensive psychometric model of basic needs that would complement trait models.

Table B.5.3 *Statements describing hopes and fears relating to three motive domains*

Motive Domain	Hope	Fear
Achievement	Feeling confident to succeed	Wanting to postpone a difficult task
Power	Trying to influence other people	Anticipating losing standing
Affiliation	Hoping to get in touch with other people	Being afraid of being rejected by others

Source Sokolowski et al., 2000

theory, which emphasises the similarity of personality structure across the lifespan. If there is, as Maslow (1971) suggests, almost an ontogenetic trend towards self-fulfilment, it is an aspect of personality which trait theory does not capture. However, there is little rigorous evidence in favour of such a developmental 'force'. Humanistic approaches also have moral concerns alien to the natural science basis for trait theory. They aim to see the person as a whole (rather than as a collection of mechanistic components), to put the investigator and the investigated on an equal footing, and in some instances, to encourage social and political change. Thus, in many respects, the themes of phenomenological approaches are antagonistic to the concerns of trait psychology. These approaches may make an independent contribution to the understanding of personality, but it is difficult to see how they can add to understanding of traits.

Contemporary studies of self-directed motivation

The most enduring legacy of humanistic psychology may be its emphases on self-directed agency and the positive side of human experience. Contemporary researchers continue to investigate what Maslow (1970) termed growth needs, contrasted with deficiency needs such as hunger and thirst (see Box 5.2 for an account of needs measurement). A particularly influential idea is that people are innately motivated towards mastery of the physical and social environment; i.e., even if the person is not subject to some deficiency, he or she will strive towards personal competence (White, 1959). A contemporary theory of this kind has been articulated by Deci and Ryan (2000). Their *self-determination theory* distinguishes three innate needs that support personal growth and harmony between the personal and social worlds. The need for competence refers to a basic mastery motive, similar to White's competence motive. The need for relatedness refers to the desire to feel connected to others, within loving and caring relationships. The need for autonomy refers to motives to self-organise experience and behavior, and to engage in activities concordant with one's sense of self; in short to experience oneself as having free will. The theory has not been without its critics. Carver and Scheier (2000) point out that self-integration and self-coherence may equally well be the outcome of tension-reduction as an autonomous motive. They also suggest that Ryan and Deci's needs may be secondary to more basic approach and avoidance motives (similar to the BAS and BIS described in chapter 4). Ryan and Deci (2000) provide a rejoinder to this critique.

Self-determination theory is primarily concerned with showing that social contexts that enhance competence, relatedness and autonomy tend to promote positive affect, mental health and performance. Deci and Ryan (2000) are ambivalent about individual differences. They state that innate differences in the need strength, such as those discussed in Box 5.2, are not the most fruitful place to focus attention, as individual differences in motives may reflect past experience. A strong need for control may be a compensation for past powerlessness. On the other hand, they also review studies that have operationalised the level of satisfaction of the three needs as traits. For example, Reis et al. (2000) found that trait indices of competence, relatedness and autonomy, as well as measures of day-to-day fluctuation, were related to well-being in a two-week daily diary study. Sheldon and Kasser (2001) claim that empirical studies, such as those just reviewed, show that well-being depends on striving for authentic, self-concordant reasons and orienting towards intrinsic values such as intimacy, community and growth, rather than extrinsic values such as status, money and image.

It is a pity that these studies neglected traits, such as neuroticism, that predict similar criteria (see chapter 4). There is also some conceptual overlap with the Big Five. We might link relatedness to Agreeableness, competence to Conscientiousness, and, more tentatively, autonomy to Emotional Stability and Openness. In any event, this line of research signals a need to look more closely at the overlap between traits and stable motivational tendancies.

The work of Deci and Ryan (2000) may be seen as part of a larger psychological movement towards *positive psychology*, which has a humanistic tendency, along with a greater dedication to rigorous research methods. Positive psychology represents a reaction to what is perceived as an excessive focus on negative aspects of functioning, such as the traditional 'disease model' of clinical psychology, with its emphasis on damage repair. By contrast, positive psychology seeks to promote personal and societal growth, and the fulfilment of human potential. According to Seligman and Csikszentmihalyi (2000, p. 5):

The field of positive psychology at the subjective level is about valued subjective experiences: well being, contentment, and satisfaction (in the past); hope and optimism (for the future); and flow and happiness (in the present). At the individual level, it is about positive individual traits; the capacity for love and vocation, courage, interpersonal skill, aesthetic sensibility, perseverance, forgiveness, originality, future mindedness, spirituality, high talent, and wisdom. At the group level, it is about the civic virtues and institutions that move individuals towards better citizenship; responsibility, nurturance, altruism, civility, moderation, tolerance, and work ethic.

Seligman and Csikszentmihalyi (2000) acknowledge their debt to Maslow and Rogers, but point out the lack of a cumulative research base for traditional humanistic psychology. Hence, much existing research on constructs such as optimism, well-being and attributional style is being recast within this new movement (see Snyder and Lopez, 2000, for a review). The aim is to distance positive psychology from crystal healing, aromatherapy, reaching the inner child and other new-age expressions of humanism. Some contemporary humanistic psychologists concur on the need for empirical science. Sheldon and Kasser (2001) claim support for humanistic psychology on the basis of research evidence that well-being depends on striving for authentic, self-concordant reasons and orienting towards intrinsic values such as intimacy, community, and growth, rather than extrinsic values such as status, money, and image. Thus, we are likely to see a new wave of empirical research on positive human qualities. In chapter 13, we review the new individual difference construct of emotional intelligence, which is seen as an important element of positive psychology (Salovey, Mayer and Caruso, 2001).

What are the implications of positive psychology for the study of traits? The quotation above includes some constructs familiar to trait psychologists, as well as some that are less well known. Perhaps, positive traits are indeed under-represented in contemporary trait models. On the other hand, the sceptic could reasonably require that reliable and valid scales for constructs such as 'capacity for love' are developed before it is concluded that current models are incomplete. Some more general reservations about positive psychology have been expressed. Lazarus (2003) points out that 'God needs Satan', and vice versa: negative and positive aspects of life experiences are inextricably intertwined, and to try to separate them as branches of psychological science is foolish. For example, suffering can lead to personal development.

In addition, some aspects of positive experience may relate not to high-minded personal growth but to subcortical brain systems sensitive to reward (Matthews and Zeidner, in press; see chapter 5). Thus, positive psychology may need better definition as a subdiscipline, but it does offer the hope of a more scientific approach to the concerns of humanistic psychology, which may have implications for understanding positive dispositions. However, this scientific approach may require the abandonment of precisely those basic tenets that are most cherished by its proponents, such as the idiographic nature of the person's self constructs, and the somewhat mystical drive to self-actualisation.

Conclusions

1. Sigmund Freud's psychodynamic theory of personality makes four key assumptions relevant to trait theory. First, personality reflects fixation of instinctual energy ('libido') to psychological structures and objects. Second, stable traits may reflect the structures most strongly fixated, such as id, ego and superego, and the psychosexual stages of development. Third, the pressures of objective reality and culture are prone to generate conflict between personality structures. Fourth, defence mechanisms provide an unconscious means for protecting the ego from such conflicts, but may themselves influence personality. There has been some interest in matching Freudian constructs to traits, for example, extraversion to expression of the id, and neuroticism to ego weakness. However, it is unclear that making these correspondences adds to our understanding of traits. A general problem is the suspect scientific basis for psychoanalysis, whose propositions may be either untestable, or testable but incorrect.

2. Recent cognitive-psychological studies have given the unconscious a higher profile as a research topic. Much 'automatic' processing appears to be inaccessible to consciousness. It may be investigated through studies using subliminal stimuli, which may influence emotion and motivation. Research seems to confirm some empirical phenomena suggested by psychoanalysis, such as difficulty in perceiving near-threshold taboo words ('perceptual defence') and the operation of unconscious defence mechanisms. However, most researchers have found that Freudian concepts are not useful in explaining empirical data on these phenomena, preferring to develop new models of how basic cognitive and emotional processes interact. This new wave of studies of unconscious processes may be relevant to trait psychology, as a source of new paradigms for exploring trait effects. Unconscious self-knowledge may also be a source of behavioural consistency, as further explored in chapter 8.

3. Humanistic and phenomenological theories of personality, such as those of Carl Rogers and Abraham Maslow make assumptions that are not congenial to trait psychology. These theories promote idiographic understanding of personality, based especially on understanding personal experience. However, some themes touch upon the concerns of trait psychology. These include a focus on the self, which, in more recent work, has been investigated empirically. Conflict between different aspects of the self as a source of pathology may also be an idea worth pursuing. Maslow's humanistic psychology sees personal growth and self-actualisation as a fundamental drive, implying a developmental view of adult perspective that does not cohere with the normal stability of traits. Recent work on motivation deals with similar ideas rather more rigorously, for example, by investigating motives towards self-determination. Such motives may be related to traits. Such work is part of a more general 'positive psychology'

movement, which may lead to increased interest in positive traits and their social implications. However, the theoretical coherence of positive psychology as the basis for studying traits has been challenged. In general, the alternatives to trait theory reviewed here may make an independent contribution to understanding personality, but, so far, their contribution to understanding traits has been limited. Future research on the unconscious and self-determination motives, for example, may lead to greater integration.

II

Causes of personality traits

6 Genes, environments and personality traits

Introduction

    The structure of personality traits shows consistency across different groups of people in different cultures. Furthermore, traits are stable across time, and there is evidence to indicate that some of them may have a tractable biological basis. Therefore, it seems reasonable to enquire to what extent individual differences in personality traits are caused by genetic and environmental factors.

    There is the tendency to see this as a difficult area, because biometric behaviour geneticists and molecular genetics researchers both use advanced statistical techniques and specialised jargon. This chapter to introduces, in a non-technical way, the main study designs and findings in these areas. Studies of twins and adopted people can indicate the relative proportions of genetic and environmental influence on personality traits. Molecular genetic studies indicate which individual genes might influence personality. Genetics researchers make some surprising contributions. For example, genetic studies can make a contribution to the study of personality change, and even the genetic contribution to personality traits may change with age or over time. Genetic studies are just as informative about the environmental factors that influence personality traits. Plomin, Asbury and Dunn (2001) commented that 'behavioural-genetic research provides the best available evidence for the importance of environmental influences' (p. 225).

    Once it has been established that traits are in part inherited, we might start to wonder how genetic variability in personality relates to the evolutionary processes that have influenced human nature (Buss, 1999). At present, there are no good answers to this question, although it is likely that future research will increasingly inter-relate the genetics and evolutionary psychology of traits. Box 6.1 describes some possible research strategies for making such connections.

Three basic designs

Genetic and environmental research on personality traits – and on other psychological and physical traits – is based on three simple research designs: twin studies, adoption studies and molecular genetic studies (Bouchard and Loehlin, 2001; Plomin et al., 2001). Each may be elaborated upon to ask more complex questions. Twin and adoption studies are called 'genetically informative' and are carried

Box 6.1 Towards an evolutionary psychology of traits

The human mind contains many complex psychological mechanisms that are selectively activated, depending on cultural contexts. (Buss, 2001, p. 955)

Evolutionary psychology is a fairly new approach to the whole of psychology that seeks to explain behaviour in terms of *adaptations* that have evolved through natural selection (Tooby and Cosmides, 1992). An adaptation is a neuropsychological mechanism that confers a selective advantage in some specific situation or set of situations, increasing the likelihood that the organism survives, reproduces or raises offspring that are themselves likely to survive and reproduce. It is assumed that there are many specific adaptations, each one keyed to solving some particular adaptive problem. For example, taste-perception mechanisms, such as detecting and liking sweetness, assist the person in eating nutritious items, and avoiding those that are non-nutritious or toxic. The evolutionary basis for such basic survival mechanisms is uncontroversial. There has been more debate over whether evolutionary psychology can explain more complex social behaviours such as aggression, cooperation and intimate relationships. There is also debate as to whether mental traits might be a result of sexual selection rather than natural selection; that is, trait differences might relate to mate attraction and retention rather than adaptation to environments (Miller, 2001).

Evolutionary psychology is primarily concerned with the human species, i.e., those adaptations that all humans require in order to maintain fitness. It has also had a special interest in sex differences. Personality differences between men and women (see chapter 3) may reflect the different adaptive problems the two sexes were called upon to solve during the prehistoric epochs in which our species evolved (Buss, 1999). To give a rather crude example, adaptations for hunting might have been especially important for men, whereas adaptations for nurturing children might have been more important for women than for men. Might such differences in part explain gender differences in aggression and agreeableness?

Gender differences might also reflect the differing reproductive strategies of men and women. For example, women are said to be especially concerned with their partner's ability to provide for a child, whereas men are supposedly concerned with the woman's fertility and fidelity (because of the 'risk' of raising another man's child). These hypotheses generate testable predictions – for example, that men should be more distressed by sexual infidelity than women – that have been tested with some success (Buss, 1999). Such explanations have been criticised on various grounds. For example, gender differences might reflect culturally set social roles rather than genetically influenced adaptations (Eagly and Wood, 1999). More generally, there is a concern that evolutionary hypotheses are hard to falsify, because the multiplicity of possible adaptations lends itself to post hoc explanation. Like Freudian theory, the problem with evolutionary theory might be that it can explain too much rather than too little. Also, the adaptive problems people are designed to solve are those of the Paleolithic period, during which our species first appears in the fossil record. Our knowledge of the hunter-gatherer lifestyle of our ancestors is fragmentary, and lends itself to speculation.

Individual differences have been rather neglected by evolutionary psychology (MacDonald, 1998). The most parsimonious view is that variation in traits such as personality characteristics simply reflects random variation of no adaptive significance; i.e., they confer a colourful variety to human minds, but not survival or reproductive advantage. Buss and Greiling (1999) have set out some more systematic sources of individual variation that might be linked to traits, although there is no well-articulated theory of traits such as the Big Five (though see MacDonald, 1998). For example, it is well established that a species may support several distinct 'frequency-dependent' adaptive strategies, in equilibrium. According to Mealey (1995), human societies may support a small proportion of antisocial or psychopathic individuals who exploit the cooperative and affiliative behaviors of others; e.g., befriending someone prior to borrowing a large sum of money, never to be repaid. If there are few such individuals, the general level of trust makes it easy for them to prosper. Too many psychopaths increases suspicion, which makes it more difficult for them to survive, so that, over the generations, the proportion remains more or less constant. Perhaps such a mechanism explains heritable variation in traits such as psychoticism, further discussed in chapter 11, although it appears to suggest a typology rather than a continuum of psychopathic behaviour.

A second mechanism described by Buss and Greiling (1999) is that individuals may choose between adaptive strategies according to their inherited characteristics, so that physically strong individuals, for example, are more likely to be aggressive. (The idea is reminiscent of early theories of 'somatotype' that aimed to link personality to physical build, with only limited success.) Buss and Greiling also present evolutionary accounts of environmental influences on personality. For example, as discussed in chapter 8, personality may be influenced by how the child 'attaches' to care-givers: a secure attachment promotes dispositional well-being. Perhaps the quality of early care triggers different adaptive mechanisms. The insecurity of the poorly attached child may in fact reflect an adaptive mechanism that generates behaviours that are adaptive when parents are neglectful, such as badgering adults for attention.

At this time, it is premature to say how successful evolutionary psychology will ultimately prove to be in explaining variation in personality traits. However, its growing popularity means that it is likely to generate empirical tests that will pit evolutionary explanations against those of other disciplines such as social psychology. Whatever the outcome, such tests are likely to be informative about the origins of individual differences in personality. Even the leading theorists in evolutionary psychology recognise that the enterprise is only beginning, and that a crucial step lies in validating the central construct of a mental adaptation.

Reasonable criteria have been developed for identifying adaptations that evolved to fulfil many survival and social functions. However, these criteria are not very applicable to adaptations that evolved as fitness indicators to deter predators, intimidate rivals, or attract mates. If evolutionary psychology does not expand its view of adaptation, these fitness indicators will continue to be overlooked. Since these fitness indicators are likely to encompass exactly those mental traits that show the highest individual differences and most dramatic display behaviours, analysis of these indicators may have the most immediate relevance to applied areas such as education, economics, clinical psychology and human mate choice. The development of new and better criteria for identifying psychological adaptations, including fitness indicators, should be a major step in evolutionary psychology's methodological maturation over the coming years (Miller, 2000, p. 72).

out because typical families are not useful for indicating the relative effects of genes and the environment. Children are usually brought up by people with whom they share both genes and environment, so their influences cannot be partitioned. Twin and adoption studies overcome this confounding of genes and environments. Molecular genetic studies can ask whether individual differences in genes are related to individual differences in personality traits. Whereas twin and adoption studies can discover whether genes are involved, molecular genetic studies can discover which genes are involved. The core concepts in the three basic designs are now described.

Twin studies

Experimental designs using twins ask this simple question: on average, are two people who have 100 per cent of their genes in common more alike in their personality trait scores than two people who have 50 per cent of their genes in common (Segal, 1999)?

There are two types of twin: monozygotic (MZ; identical) and dizygotic (DZ; non-identical). An ovum fertilised by a sperm is a zygote. Monozygotic twins arise from the separation into two of the same fertilised ovum, whereas dizygotic twins arise from two separate ova simultaneously fertilised by different sperm. Monozygotic twins have the same genes. Same sex dizygotic twins share, on average, 50% of their genes, the same as any two same-sex siblings born to the same biological parents. Monozygotic twins are always the same sex; dizygotic twins can be the same or different in sex.

To conceive how this can help to understand whether there is a genetic contribution to personality differences, imagine the following experiment. Take 100 pairs of monozygotic twins and 100 pairs of dizygotic twins. Assume that only same-sex dizygotic twins are chosen. Members of each twin pair are raised in the same family. All 400 members of these 200 twin pairs complete a questionnaire to measure extraversion. Correlation is used to discover if pairs of monozygotic twins are, on average, more alike with regard to extraversion than pairs of dizygotic twins. Correlation usually involves two columns of numbers that refer to two measurements taken on the same people. For example, people's heights and weights might be measured to see if they correlate. Here, the first column of data has the extraversion score of the first member of each twin pair. The second column of data has the extraversion score of the second member of each twin pair. Correlation here is used to find out how similar members of twin pairs tend to be in their scores. This gives two correlations: one for monozygotic twins and one for dizygotic twins. If genes contribute to extraversion differences the expected result is that the correlation for dizygotic twins is higher than that for monozygotic twins.

An example of such data is found in Jang et al. (2002). They report data on monozygotic and dizygotic twins from Canada and Germany who completed the NEO-Personality Inventory-Revised. For the six facets of extraversion the mean correlations between monozygotic twins were 0.47 for both Canadian and German samples. The corresponding correlations for dizygotic twins were 0.22 and 0.21. This represents good replication across countries and these correlations may be used as the basis for further analyses.

The amount of the difference between these two correlations can indicate how much genes contribute to extraversion differences. A simple estimate of the proportion of the trait variance contributed by genetic factors may be obtained by doubling the difference between the MZ and DZ correlation. To explain this, imagine the unlikely instance in which a trait could be measured without error and in which the genetic contribution was 100 per cent. One would expect the MZ twin pairs to correlate at 1.0 and the DZ twin pairs to correlate at 0.5. Therefore 2 X (1–0.5) gives 1.0, or 100 per cent of the variance.

There are more complex analyses using twin studies, and they involve assumptions that can be questioned. For example, it is assumed that the only difference between the monozygotic and dizygotic twins is their degree of genetic resemblance. The key to twin studies is the simple difference in the correlation between monozygotic twin pairs and dizygotic twin pairs.

Adoption studies

Experimental designs using adopted people ask this simple question: when an adopted child grows up does its personality resemble more closely (1) the adopted parents with whom it spent its life, or (2) its biological parents it might never have met?

To understand how adoption studies can help to find out whether genes contribute to personality trait scores, consider the following situation. A mother offers a baby for adoption just after birth. The child is raised to adulthood by a biologically unrelated family. This adopted family has a child of their own. This produces a situation where there is a child in the family who shares genes and environment with the mother and a child who shares only environment. There is a biological mother who shares genes but not environment with a child who was adopted by another family. Imagine that 100 such families are traced by a researcher. Assume that all parents and children (when grown) fill in a questionnaire measuring extraversion. Correlations can be done to examine whether genetic similarity increases personality similarity. The column of extraversion scores for the adopted mothers can be correlated with scores from their adopted and biological child. The children in each family shared the same lifetime environment. They differ only in genetic relatedness to their mother. Therefore, if, on average, the biological children's scores correlate higher with their mothers' scores than the adopted children's scores, that is evidence for genetic similarity causing similarity in personality trait scores.

Other comparisons can be performed. If there is more than one biological child within each family then it can be asked whether biologically related siblings resemble each other more than their adopted sibling. It can be asked whether biological mothers come to resemble their adopted offspring (whom they might never have seen during their growing up) just as much as mothers who bear and raise their children.

There are assumptions within such comparisons that need to be questioned, and there are complexities in these studies that have not been raised here. The key to adoption studies is the relative similarity of adopted children to various members of their adopted and biological families.

Molecular genetic (quantitative trait loci, QTL) studies

Experimental designs in the area of molecular genetics ask this simple question: do people with one version of a gene have significant differences in personality trait scores than people who have a different version?

The following imaginary experiment explains how one type of molecular genetic study might be conducted. It is known that a gene has two versions, A and B. The gene codes for a protein that influences the metabolism of chemical X. Some published evidence points to chemical X being related to extraversion scores. A researcher recruits people to find whether those with versions A and B differ in their extraversion scores. DNA is prepared from white blood cells obtained in a blood sample. The DNA is analysed and each person is found to have either the A or B version of the gene. The A and B versions of the gene are used in a t test as two levels of an independent variable to compare extraversion scores. If the test is significant then there is evidence to link specific genetic variability with personality differences.

There are complexities in studies of this type that are not addressed here. The key to them is that variability in specific genes can be examined as a possible source of personality variability.

We now turn to actual studies that have used these basic genetic designs. Extraversion is used as an exemplar personality trait.

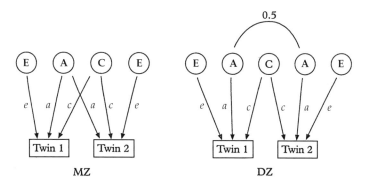

Figure 6.1 A model of the contributions of genetic (A), common environment (C) and unshared environment (E) factors to phenotypic personality trait scores, in MZ and DZ twins

Twin studies

Using personality test scores on twins to discover the relative contribution of genetic and environmental factors involves some initial premises. There are two broad contributions to personality differences: genetic effects and environmental effects. Environmental effects can be divided into those shared by family members and those unique even to individual siblings within the same family. Researchers in behavioural genetics use these and further assumptions to construct models of the personality trait correlations between MZ and DZ twin pairs. The statistical modelling techniques are accessibly described in Plomin et al. (2001, pp. 349–60).

Figure 6.1 demonstrates the above assumptions by indicating the contributions to measured personality trait scores. The contributions to the personality trait scores of MZ twins are given by the same additive genetic factor (A), because they share 100 per cent of each other's genes. The contribution of the shared or common environment factor (C) is assumed to be identical for the two twins. Lastly, the contribution of the unshared environment (E) is assumed to be entirely independent in the two twins, shown by the fact that each of the identical twins has his/her own E. This unshared environmental factor captures aspects of the environment that is unique to each twin, and also includes error variance. Comparing the left-hand and right-hand sides of figure 6.1 reveals only one difference between the models for monozygotic and dizygotic twins. Instead of having the same genetic source of variance, the A contributions for DZ twins are correlated at only 0.5, reflecting the fact that they share only 50 per cent of their genes.

The constraints represented in figure 6.1 can be used quantitatively to model the personality trait scores obtained from pairs of MZ and DZ twins. The starting points for a behavioural genetic model are the personality scores of MZ and DZ twins and the correlations between members of MZ and DZ twin pairs. The contributions to trait scores come from the A, C and E sources identified in figure 6.1.

The relative strengths of these effects are given by the sizes of the parameters that lie alongside the arrows: 'a' represents the relative size of the genetic effect, 'c' the shared environment effect and 'e' the unshared environment effect. Each can take values between 0 to 1. They can be squared to obtain the percentage of variance that they contribute to any given outcome. Therefore, the sum of the squares of a, c and e must equal 1, because predictors cannot account for more than 100 per cent of the variance in an outcome.

The values of the a, c and e parameters can be adjusted by model-fitting statistical packages to give the best fit to the correlations found in MZ and DZ twins, i.e., the parameter estimates are forced to have the same values in the MZ and DZ twins. It can be asked whether these parameter estimates fit other data, such as those from adoption and family studies, and whether we must relax the assumption that all parameters are equal in MZ and DZ twins. Using these parameters, figure 6.1 can be used to derive expressions for the correlations between twin pairs on personality traits. Take the MZ twins first. To calculate the correlation between twin pairs the paths that connect the twins must be added. A 'path' is the product of any series of arrows that connect the twins. Therefore, the correlation for MZ twins is given by $(a \times a) + (c \times c)$, or $a^2 + c^2$. In the same manner, the correlation between the DZ twins can be worked out by following the paths between the two DZ twins in figure 6.1. Therefore, the DZ correlation is $(a \times 0.5 \times a) + (c \times c)$, or $0.5\ a^2 + c^2$.

What is being tested when a model like that represented figure 6.1 is constructed? The model in figure 6.1 is stating the following: a genetic factor makes a greater than zero contribution to twin similarity and is twice as strong in MZ as in DZ twins; a shared environment factor makes a significant contribution to twin similarity and is equally strong in MZ and DZ twins; and unshared environmental factors have significant effects in both MZ and DZ twins. For a model to be considered successful, the pathways it includes must make significant contributions to the personality variance, and the model must explain most of the covariance in trait scores. The latter demand can be examined using a chi-square test to see if the remaining covariance after the model has been fitted is still significant. Model testing – discovering whether an empirical data set has a structure that is close to our theory – has the advantage that it is explicit and allows alternative hypotheses to be tested competitively. More importantly, it provides a way of testing whether the same estimates of genetic and environmental contribution can be found in subsequent studies, even when they use different designs.

A gene-environment model of extraversion in five twin studies

Loehlin (1992) used the model in figure 6.1 to examine the genetic and environmental influences on extraversion data gathered from five large twin studies conducted in five different countries: the UK (Eaves, Eysenck and Martin, 1989), USA (Loehlin and Nichols, 1976), Sweden (Floderus-Myrhed, Pedersen and Rasmuson, 1980), Australia (Martin and Jardine, 1986) and Finland (Rose et al., 1988). He found a range of estimates of heritability ($a^2 \times 100$) for extraversion between

54 per cent and 80 per cent in men and 56 per cent and 70 per cent in women. That is, all of the studies indicated that over half of the variability in extraversion scores arises from genetic sources. The same model could be accepted across all male samples, but not in females. Note how important and stringent a test of the genetic and environmental contributions to extraversion this is: not only did Loehlin search for a genetic/environmental model to fit any one of these large samples, he tried to find a single model to fit all of them, despite the differences in the studies (e.g., use of different questionnaire measures of extraversion).

Therefore, high and consistent personality trait heritabilities arise from different studies, at least for extraversion. What of the environmental contributions? Here there was an odd result: the estimate for the shared environment contribution (c^2) was significantly negative. That is, sharing the same family environment tended to bring about significant dissimilarities in extraversion. These contributions were small, accounting for only 6 per cent to 24 per cent of the variance in extraversion scores, with a mean of 14.3 per cent. Loehlin (1992) found the occurrence of a negative shared environmental effect to be counterintuitive, and his examination of this conundrum provides a helpful way of addressing some of the complexities that must be introduced to the simple twin study model. It is an easy expedient to change figure 6.1, so that one co-twin has a positive 'c' value and the other a negative value. This would be called a contrast effect, whereby one co-twin would be treated within the family as an extravert and the other as an introvert. This does not alter the fit of the model, but alters the shared family environment variance to a positive value by assuming that families cause sibling differences in personality, rather than inducing similarities. In fact, for some personality dimensions, including extraversion, the present authors find this possible induction of children into different 'roles' quite plausible.

There are ways to account for the data other than assuming this 'sibling competition' effect within families. To introduce these, first consider the raw MZ and DZ correlations for extraversion in Loehlin's (1992) data. For the five large twin studies mentioned above, Loehlin's best estimates of the male MZ and DZ correlations are 0.48 and 0.18, respectively, and 0.53 and 0.19 for the females' correlations. As expected, the MZ correlations are higher than the DZ correlations. In fact they are more than twice as high. Something is needed to capture the fact that, given only twice the genetic similarity over DZ twins, MZ twins are more than twice as alike on extraversion. This disproportionately high correlation between MZ twins is a common finding in personality trait data (Eaves et al., 1998). Two factors could explain this: non-additive genetic variance, and unequal MZ–DZ environments.

Non-additive genetic variance

The foregoing analysis of extraversion scores assumed that the genetic contribution to the similarity of MZ twins was twice as great as that for DZ twins. This is the additive genetic assumption: that there is a linear increase in trait similarity as the proportion of genes shared by two individuals increases. Simply, it assumes that, if MZ twins are twice as genetically similar as DZ twins, then they will be twice as similar in personality. However, there are two well-recognised ways in which this assumption might be incorrect.

The first is genetic dominance. Genetic theory predicts that, whereas MZ twins share 100 per cent of the gene-dominance effects, DZ twins share only 25 per cent. If there are significant dominance effects in the genetic contribution to extraversion, therefore, the assumption that the DZ genetic similarity is half that of the MZ twins will be false.

The other non-linear genetic effect is epistasis. Some traits arise out of the combined interacting effects of multiple genes. A particular configuration of multiple genes (from diverse sites across different chromosomes) may be needed to produce certain phenotypes (Lykken et al., 1992, provide a discussion of this phenomenon, called emergenesis). In the case of MZ twins these configurations will be identical, whereas DZ twins will be unlikely to share many if any such multigene configurations. Therefore, epistasis provides another mechanism that would violate the assumption of purely additive genetic effects in extraversion.

Both of these well-recognised genetic effects, therefore, predict that MZ twins will be more than twice as similar than DZ twins in personality scores, assuming that genetic variance in personality traits is the combined effect of many genes, i.e., is polygenetic.

Loehlin (1992) altered figure 6.1 by eliminating the 'c' parameter and replacing it with a genetic dominance parameter that was identical for MZ twins and correlated at 0.25 for DZ twins. This fitted the extraversion data just as well as the model with a negative shared-environment factor, but had the interesting effect of reducing the additive genetic effect to 24 per cent and estimating the genetic dominance effect at about 24 per cent. The additive genetic effect (a^2) is the narrow heritability of a trait, and the sum of the additive and the non-additive genetic effects is the broad heritability. In this case, the narrow heritability of extraversion would be 24 per cent and the broad heritability, 48 per cent. Instead of including a dominance effect, Loehlin (1992) introduced an epistasis parameter, which was identical in the MZ twins, but uncorrelated in the DZ twins. This gave a narrow heritability estimate of 36 per cent, an epistasis effect estimate of 12 per cent and a broad heritability estimate, therefore, of 48 per cent. The problem for the twin design used in isolation is that there is no way for the researcher to choose the best model from the three described above – i.e., those with negative shared-environment, genetic-dominance or epistasis effects (Plomin et al., 2001, pp. 349–60). All of the models fit well, and all suggest a large contribution from the genes, but they point to rather different reasons for the relative sizes of the MZ and DZ correlations; and they suggest quite different additive genetic contributions.

The equal environments assumption

Introducing non-additive genetic effects challenged the assumption that only additive genetic variance contributes to personality differences. A further assumption of the model in figure 6.1 is that the similarity of the shared environment (the size of the 'c' parameter) is the same for MZ and DZ twins. This is called the equal environments assumption (Plomin et al., 2001, pp. 80–2). However, identical twins might be provided with environments that are more similar than non-identical twins. Figure 6.1 can be altered to take account of this, and the 'c' parameters allowed to be different for MZ and DZ twins. Loehlin (1992) found that the model with unequal MZ–DZ shared environment contributions fitted just as well as the others discussed above. The extraversion correlations found in MZ and DZ twins are, therefore, compatible with a situation where narrow heritability accounts for 36 per cent of extraversion variance, and shared-environment effects account for 12 per cent of the variance in MZ twins and zero per cent in DZ twins. Before accepting this model, however, it would be necessary to establish that more similar treatment in childhood is related to similar personality scores in adulthood. Loehlin and Nichols (1976) addressed this possibility in the national Merit Twin Study: MZ twins did indeed have greater environmental similarities than DZ twins. Of course, there is a problem of cause and effect here: greater similarity in personality could lead to greater similarity in the resulting environment or vice versa. To decide on the causal direction, Loehlin and Nichols examined the correlation between personality and treatment similarity, and found little association. Other researchers, studying other traits, have found that the equal environments assumption holds (Bouchard and Propping, 1993).

It is possible that twins might be a special group whose results might not generalise to the general population. There is evidence against this possibility (Krueger, Bouchard and McGue, 2002), and DZ twins are as similar in personality as non-twin siblings (Eaves et al., 1998). The twin study design does not allow researchers to choose between importantly different gene–environment models. Therefore, other research designs are used.

Other research designs

Adoption studies

The shared-environment and additive genetic effects are confounded in normal families, because normal parents provide the family environment for their children as well as sharing 50 per cent of their genes. Adoption studies provide another natural experiment for behaviour geneticists. Parents who have their own biological children as well as adopted children provide the family environment for both types of child, but share genes with only their biological children. There are three adoption studies in which children were adopted away at an early age and where the adults and their grown-up children were given the same personality scale. These were conducted in the UK (Eaves, Eysenck and Martin, 1989; with 150 families), in Minnesota (Scarr et al., 1981; with 115 families) and Texas (Loehlin, Willerman and Horn, 1985; with 220 families). They tested personality using the Eysenck

Table 6.1 *Correlations between adopted children (age 16 years) and adopted, biological and control parents from the Colorado Adoption project*

	Adoptive parents	Biological parents	Control parents	Genetic effect	Family environment
Emotionality	.12	.01	−.06	.00	.03
Activity	.01	.17	.08	.20	−.02
Sociability	−.05	.15	.17	.27	−.01
Impulsivity	−.01	.08	.00	.07	−.03

Source Plomin et al. (1998)

Personality Questionnaire, the Eysenck Personality Inventory and the California Personality Inventory, respectively. Loehlin (1992) analysed these data together to discover whether the same environmental–genetic model can be fitted. For extraversion, at least, this is true. Moreover, a good fit was obtained for a model which set additive genetic effects at 35 per cent and shared environment (family effects) at zero per cent. This is similar to the case in the twin studies, where a well-fitting model for extraversion put additive genetic effects at 36 per cent and included dominance or epistatic or special MZ environment effects. Not all studies agree, and twin studies sometimes give apparently clearer results than adoption studies. The Colorado adoption project tested the 16-year-old adoptees, their adoptive and biological parents, and control parents, on the EASI temperament survey (Plomin et al., 1998). The resulting correlations are shown in table 6.1. They provide only weak evidence for genetic contributions, with the larger effects on the traits of sociability and activity. The authors concluded that the effects of genes on personality were mostly non-additive and their subtitle suggested that, in this adoption study of this personality instrument at this age there was 'not much nature or nurture'.

Adoption and twin studies, therefore, provide a similar message overall, though heritability estimates are lower from adoption than twin studies (Bouchard and Loehlin, 2001). Exceptions and variability among studies must be recognised. With regard to extraversion, children grow to resemble their biological parents, but not their adoptive parents. Growing up in the same family does not make a person resemble their siblings or their parents unless one is related to them genetically. As was found with twin studies, some assumptions of the adoption studies should be made explicit. First, genetic effects on extraversion at the ages the children were tested might differ from those at the parents' ages. Loehlin (1992) tested this assumption and found that the genetic effects could be assumed to be identical. Second, it is assumed that there is no selective placement of adoptive children with respect to extraversion, which appears to be true. Third, it is assumed that people do not marry others who have similar levels of extraversion; in fact, there appears to be no so-called assortative mating for extraversion (Eaves et al., 1998; Bouchard and Loehlin, 2001).

Twin-family studies

The hypotheses offered by twin and family studies may be combined to provide another behaviour genetic study design. Consider two MZ twins who have children. The child of an MZ twin will be as closely related to the parent as to the co-twin (his or her uncle or aunt). In the absence of shared environment effects, therefore, the personality correlations between a twin and his or her nephew or niece should be the same as that between the twin and his own children. In addition, the children born to the co-twins should have personality correlations as strong as half-siblings rather than cousins. Two studies collected data relevant to these hypotheses. One was conducted in Sweden (Price et al., 1982) and one in the USA (Loehlin, 1986). Loehlin (1992) analysed these data together. First, the weighted mean correlation between MZ twins for extraversion in these studies was 0.43. The correlation between twins and their own and co-twin's children were, respectively, 0.22 and 0.21, confirming the expectation that an MZ twin's child resembles the co-twin as much as the parent. Model fitting to these data suggested additive genetic effects accounting for about 37 per cent of extraversion variance and epistasis effects of about 14 per cent. Family environment made no contribution. These estimates agree closely with twin and adoption studies. Combined analyses of data on US twins, their spouses, parents, siblings and children, and twin data from Australia and Finland – involving over 42,000 people – confirm the contribution of additive genetic and epistatic genetic effects on extraversion differences (Eaves et al., 1998). These data also confirm the lack of a contribution from the shared family environment. Box 6.2 discusses a twin family study of other personality traits.

Box 6.2 A twin family study

Tambs et al. (1991) conducted a twin-family study of the Eysenck Personality Questionnaire. They examined data from MZ twins and their families (150 families with 811 subjects). A model with only additive genetic effects fits quite well to the data for extraversion, neuroticism and the lie scale. For extraversion the fit was significantly better when non-additive genetic variance or negative cultural transmission terms were added. The additive genetic contribution to extraversion was 29 per cent and the non-additive contribution 24 per cent, making a broad heritability of 53 per cent. The variance apparently attributable to genetic dominance and/or epistasis may be due to special MZ environment factors, however. For neuroticism, no model improved on the additive genetic model with a narrow and broad heritability of 36 per cent. Psychoticism had a narrow heritability of 3 per cent, a broad heritability of 39 per cent, and specific cultural transmission path from fathers to daughters. This result, and the low reliability and internal consistency of psychoticism (Heath, Cloninger and Martin, 1994), must call into question the validity of this factor.

Table 6.2 *Extraversion correlations in four studies of separated twins*

	Finland		Sweden		USA		UK	
	r	pairs	*r*	pairs	*r*	pairs	*r*	pairs
MZ apart	38	30	30	95	34	44	61	42
MZ together	33	47	54	150	63	217	42	43
DZ apart	12	95	04	220	–07	27		
DZ together	13	135	06	204	18	114		

Source Loehlin, 1992.

Separated-twin studies

Another way of trying to tease out the effects of genes and the environment on personality is to study twins who were separated in early life and who grew up in different family environments. By comparing the personality likenesses of MZ and DZ twins reared apart and together we might be able to choose between models which include non-additive genetic effects and specially similar MZ twin environments as explanations for the particular similarity found among MZ twins. Four studies examined separated MZ twins and three of these include DZ twins. They were conducted in Finland (Langinvainio et al., 1984), Sweden (Pedersen et al., 1988), the USA (Tellegen et al., 1988) and the UK (Shields, 1962). Most of the twins across all studies were separated in the first year of life. Some had had contact in adult life prior to their personality tests being administered. The study of twins reared apart was criticised by Joseph (2001) who contended that the typical research design used lacks adequate control.

Because these represent such a rare and hard-to-collect set of data it is worthwhile examining the raw correlations (see table 6.2). The most obvious result is, again, that the correlations between MZ twins are greater than twice those among DZ twins. Moreover, whereas in the two largest studies the correlations among MZ twins reared together are greater than for those reared apart, the other two studies show the reverse trend. With regard to model fitting, these four studies were anomalous when compared with the other designs discussed above (Loehlin, 1992). For extraversion, a model with 37 per cent additive genetic effects, 14 per cent epistasis and zero per cent shared environment – which is congruent with all of the diverse study designs and samples discussed above – did not fit these data well. In fact, the model that included these parameters had the following values: additive genetic effects = 4 per cent, shared environment = 12 per cent, and epistasis effects = 39 per cent, i.e., the broad heritability is high but the narrow heritability is very low. In modelling these data sets the shared environment factor could not be set at zero. A model with unequal DZ/MZ environments and non-additive genetic effects also fitted the data well.

Modelling all study designs together

A powerful test of a definitive environmental–genetic model for extraversion is to try to fit a single model to all of the above data sets: four twin studies, three adoption studies, two twin-family studies and four studies of separated twins. This entails the stringent assumption that, across diverse study designs and subject samples, and using different extraversion scales, the parameter sizes for genetic and environmental effects can be assumed to be equal. Loehlin (1992) modelled extraversion data from these studies using six parameters: additive genetic effects, non-additive (epistatic) genetic effects, shared environment effects for male and female MZ twins, and shared-environment effects for male and female siblings (including DZ twins). Note the new assumption that male and female MZ twins and siblings might be differentially affected by their shared environment. A model with these parameters fits acceptably and gives contributions to extraversion variance as follows: 33 per cent additive genetic, 5 per cent non-additive genetic, 10 per cent and 15 per cent shared environment for male and female MZ twins, and 3 per cent and 4 per cent for male and female siblings. The variance left over represents unshared environmental effects and error variance. Shared environment factors could be discarded for all relationships except MZ twins without worsening the model fit.

Some tentative conclusions may be made about the genetic and environmental influences on extraversion. Additive genetic variance and unshared (non-family related) environment effects are usually substantial, with the former contributing between 35 per cent to 39 per cent of personality variance. When MZ twins are included epistasis effects are required and/or the assumption of unequal MZ/DZ environments to get a good model fit. Shared environment effects are below 5 per cent for all relationships except MZ twins, and may even be negative. The unexplained variance is usually around or above 50 per cent and contains variance attributable to non-shared environment, gene-environment interactions and errors of measurement (from Loehlin, 1992, and see also Plomin et al., 2001, chapter 12).

Genes, environment and multiple personality traits

Most studies of genetic and environmental contributions to personality traits include a number of traits. One twin study example is the German Observational Study of Adult Twins, which examined personality traits based on the five factor model (Borkenau et al., 2001). Unusually, it employed peer-reports of personality trait scores and personality ratings based on video-recorded behaviours as well as self-reports. The results from the peer-reports are shown in table 6.3. The correlations between monozygotic twins' ratings are always higher than those between dizygotic twins, often more than twice as high. The genetic contributions

Table 6.3 *Genetic and environmental influences of peer-rated personality trait scores in German monozygotic and dizygotic twins*

	Correlation between MZ twins	Correlation between DZ twins	a^2	c^2	e^2
Extraversion	.42	.13	.41	.00	.59
Agreeableness	.37	.11	.35	.00	.65
Conscientiousness	.45	.20	.44	.00	.56
Neuroticism	.38	.02	.33	.00	.67
Openness	.47	.28	.40	.07	.52

Source Borkenau et al. (2001)

Table 6.4 *Genetic and environmental contributions (percentage variance) to the Big Five personality dimensions*

(a) Models assuming unequal MZ/DZ environments

	a^2	c_{mz^2}	c_{s^2}
Extraversion	36	15	0
Neuroticism	31	17	5
Agreeableness	28	19	9
Conscientiousness	28	17	4
Culture	46	5	5

(b) Models assuming non-additive genetic effects

	a^2	i^2	c_{s^2}
Extraversion	32	17	2
Neuroticism	27	14	7
Agreeableness	24	11	11
Conscientiousness	22	16	7
Culture	43	2	6

Note a^2 = additive genetic effects; c_{mz^2} = shared environment of MZ twins; c_{s^2} = shared environment of any siblings; i^2 = epistasis. Remaining variance (100 minus row totals) is due to individual (unshared) environment and error
Source Loehlin, 1992

range from 33 to 44 per cent, the shared environment makes very little contribution, and non-shared environment is the largest contributor for all traits.

Loehlin (1992) fitted models to mixed data sets that used all of the Big Five dimensions of personality. For neuroticism he drew data from the same studies as those used to model extraversion. For agreeableness, conscientiousness and culture the data were patchier with respect to the studies included and the scales used. The results of these analyses are shown in table 6.4, which gives a summary of the genetic and environmental effects on some major personality traits. There

Table 6.5 *Broad heritabilities of self-report measures of the Big Five factors*

	Loehlin (1992 review)	Jang et al. (Canada)	Waller (US)	Loehlin (US)	Riemann et al. (Germany)
Extraversion	.49	.53	.49	.57	.56
Agreeableness	.35	.41	.33	.51	.42
Conscientiousness	.38	.44	.48	.52	.53
Neuroticism	.41	.41	.42	.58	.52
Openness	.45	.61	.58	.56	.53
MZ pairs		123	313	490	660
DZ pairs		127	91	317	304

Source Bouchard and Loehlin (2001). References for column headers: Loehlin (1992); Jang, Livesley and Vernon (1996); Waller (1999); Loehlin (1998); Riemann, Angleitner and Strelau (1997)

is no way to choose between models which assume non-additive genetic effects and those which assume unequal MZ–DZ/sibling shared environmental effects, so both solutions have been included. If the unequal environments assumption is made, the additive genetic effects have a range of 28 to 46 per cent with a mean of 34 per cent. The shared environment effect on MZ twins ranges from 5 to 17 per cent with a mean of 15 per cent, and that of ordinary siblings ranges from zero to 9 per cent with a mean of 5 per cent. If the non-additive genetic effects are assumed, the broad heritability estimates (additive plus other genetic effects) range from 35 to 49 per cent with a mean of 42 per cent. The shared-environment effects range from 2 to 11 per cent with a mean of 7 per cent. By implication, non-shared-environment effects may be large for all of the five dimensions. Bouchard's (1994) summary of the data from the Minnesota Study of Twins Reared Apart provided similar conclusions, with broad heritabilities of the Big Five personality dimensions ranging from around 30 per cent for agreeableness to about 50 per cent for Neuroticism. Extraversion and Agreeableness, however, showed very large non-additive genetic effects, with narrow heritabilities of less than 10 per cent. Similar estimates for the range of heritabilities of the Big Five traits are given by Plomin et al. (2001, p. 239) in a re-analysis of a large German study of MZ and DZ twins (Riemann, Angleitner and Strelau, 1997). Finally, a summary of the twin-study-derived broad heritabilities (additive and non-additive genetic effects) for self-report indicators of the five factor model traits shows considerable agreement that up to around half of the variance is caused by genetic factors (table 6.5; Bouchard and Loehlin, 2001). The contributions of non-additive genetic effects were not consistent between studies. Most showed little or no effect for shared environment.

The studies discussed above are based almost exclusively on self-reports of personality. However, Heath et al. (1992) reported comparable genetic effects for Eysenck's neuroticism and extraversion factors whether the traits were self- or co-twin rated. The German observational study of MZ and DZ twins shows substantial genetic influences on peer-reports of all Big Five traits, though genetic contributions to extraversion and agreeableness were considerably lower than those for self-reports (Riemann, Angleitner and Strelau, 1997; Plomin et al., 2001, p. 239; Borkenau et al., 2001).

A massive study of the genetic and environmental contributions to neuroticism differences examined twins and their extended families in the USA and Australia. Over 45,000 subjects provided data (Lake et al., 2000). The proposed best model included genetic influences (additive and non-additive), non-shared environment, and a small influence of assortative mating. There was no evidence of substantial influences from shared environment or special MZ twin environments.

Further issues in genetic research

The environment

The above studies add a lot of weight to the claim that genetic factors contribute substantially to the causation of individual differences in personality traits. However, while accepting current estimates of heritability for personality traits, Endler (1989) issued four cautions about the behaviour genetic study of personality. First, he urged:

> all behavior is dependent on both heredity and environment, and heredity and environment are not additive, but interactive. The two proportions are 100 per cent heredity and 100 per cent environment. Trying to obtain variance proportions of heredity and environment in personality is like asking how much the area of a rectangle is due to length and how much due to width.

To a degree this first criticism is misplaced. Certainly, there are genetic and environmental factors without which a person cannot survive and without which a personality cannot express itself. However, behaviour genetics can get at that part of human expression which shows individual differences and can apportion the causes of these differences to genetic and environmental effects using the strategies discussed above.

With regard to whether there are genotype-environment interaction effects in the production of personality phenotypes, this has been tested in only a limited way. Bergeman et al. (1988) tested the possibility that 'individuals of different genotypes may respond differently to specific environments'. They examined ninety-nine pairs of Swedish identical twins reared apart from the Swedish Adoption Twin Study of Ageing who had been given personality scales and the Family Environment Scale (FES). The significance of the product of genotype and environment factors was examined after the main effects of genes and environment had been statistically controlled. The genetic effect was calculated using the co-twin's personality score, and the environment effect was calculated using the FES. Significant genotype-environment interactions were found for eleven of the forty-eight analyses performed, and such interactions tended to account for about 7 per cent of the total variance in personality trait scores. For extraversion, those with a low extraversion genotype brought up in a low controlling environment had significantly higher extraversion scores than those with low extraversion genotypes brought up in a highly controlling environment. Those with genotypes for high extraversion were not affected by the environment. For neuroticism, it was found that people with high genotypes for neuroticism scored lower on neuroticism in an active environment, but people with low genotypes for neuroticism scored higher in an active environment. A study of genotype-environment interaction based on a molecular genetic analysis is described in box 6.2.

Second, Endler (1989) cautioned that correlation does not imply causation. This is of course true, but it is a criticism that, when explored, may strengthen the effect of genes on personality. Whereas we might hypothesise that similar environments might bring about personality similarities, Bouchard et al. (1990) concluded from their studies of twins reared together and apart that 'MZA [MZ twins reared apart] twins are so similar in psychological traits because their identical genomes make it probable that their effective environments are similar'. Thus, they explain, genetic differences and similarities drive developing individuals to seek out different and similar environments, respectively (gene–environment covariance), and genetically different people attend to

Box 6.3 Gene–environment interaction and the cycle of violence in maltreated children

Maltreated children are more likely to become adult criminals. Not all maltreated children become offenders. The reason for this variability in outcome given similar treatment was sought in the Dunedin Multidisciplinary Health and Development Study which examined over 500 males from a birth cohort of over 1,000 children at regular intervals from birth to age twenty-six with almost no attrition (Caspi et al., 2002). They tested the idea that environmental factors were dependent on genetic susceptibility. The gene examined was one which showed individual differences (polymorphism) and coded for the enzyme monoamine oxidase A (MAOA). MAOA metabolises brain transmitter substances such as serotonin, noradrenalin and dopamine. The authors provided animal and human evidence to suggest that genetically mediated MAOA differences might be linked to aggressive behaviours, and that genetic differences might interact with childhood maltreatment.

They established the status of each subject on a variable number tandem repeat (VNTR) polymorphism at the promoter of the MAOA gene. Maltreatment was recorded in childhood between age three and eleven years. Four outcomes were assessed in later years: DSM-IV adolescent conduct disorder, police convictions for violent crimes, personality disposition toward violence, and third-person reports of antisocial personality disorder. These four measures were highly interrelated. With regard to a composite measure of antisocial behaviour as an outcome they found a significant interaction between childhood maltreatment level and MAOA genotype (which influences MAOA activity) (figure B.6.3.1). The influence of childhood maltreatment was weaker among males with high MAOA activity. The interaction was found for all four measures of antisocial behaviour. In this group 85 per cent of males who had a low-activity MAOA-associated genotype and severe maltreatment as children developed at least one of the indicators of antisocial behaviour.

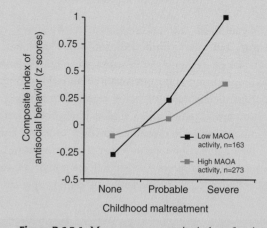

Figure B.6.3.1 Means on a composite index of antisocial behaviour as a function of monoaomine oxidase A (MAOA) activity – based on genotype – and a history of maltreatment in childhood
Source Caspi et al. (2002)

different aspects of the same experience and respond differently to it (gene–environment interaction). The tendency for personality to play a role in the selection and shaping of environments was confirmed in a review (Reiss et al., 2000). Neuroticism and extraversion are significant predictors of life events (Magnus et al., 1993). Controllable life events, which are traditionally thought to assess environmental influences, show substantial genetic variance which is entirely shared with the genetic influence on personality traits (Saudino et al., 1997). Jang, Vernon and Livesley (2001, p. 241) concluded: 'Heritable factors, such as personality and depression, influence the types of environments sought or encountered', reversing the easy causal assumption that shared environment may be causal to personality differences.

Third, Endler (1989) stated that the impact of the environment on personality cannot be assessed until we have systematic psychometrically sound measures of environmental characteristics. Hoffman (1991) has also insisted that valid, quantitative assessments of the shared environment are needed before its effects are deemed negligible. Again, this is true: those instruments that exist at present to assess the environment, such as the Family Environment Scale (FES), are largely retrospective and impressionistic, and might themselves be influenced by genetic effects. Chipuer et al. (1993) showed that, for two out of three of the dimensions of the FES, there were additive genetic effects specific to those dimensions, and there were additional genetic effects shared with extraversion and with extraversion and neuroticism. Therefore, estimates of the family environment are significantly caused by genetic factors, and some of this genetic influence is shared with personality. Estimates of the environment come contaminated by variance which they are intended to explain (Bouchard and Loehlin, 2001).

Environmentalists have lagged behind geneticists in the evidence they have provided and in the sophistication with which they have researched personality differences. For example, Hoffman (1991) suggested that identical twins might become similar in personality because they look alike and therefore are treated alike. However, not only might the causal chain be reversed – such that it is similar personality that brings about similar treatment and not vice versa – there is little evidence for any impact of treatment effects on later personality (Loehlin, 1992; Bouchard, 1993; Plomin, Asbury and Dunn, 2001). Hoffman (1991) insisted also that the environmentalist does not expect to find that the child becomes a clone of the parent. For example, an overprotective parent might bring about a dependent child, and a threatening parent might raise an anxious child. With so much good evidence for broad heritability effects, the onus is on environmentalists to make clear hypotheses about the effects of specific environmental factors on personality and test them. This is rarely done (Reiss et al., 2000).

Endler's fourth criticism is that personality assessments are based on questionnaires, not on biological or genetic markers. True, it is not known yet whether phenotypic personality traits are isomorphic with identifiable biological processes. Molecular genetic investigations are already making progress here (Cloninger, Adolfsson and Svrakic, 1996). Moreover, newer methods in behaviour genetics may be used to distinguish the genetic and environmental sources tapped by different trait instruments from the trait measures themselves (e.g., Heath, Cloninger and Martin, 1994; Jang, Vernon and Livesley, 2001). Genetic covariance research has found that the genetic structure of traits in the five factor model resembles the phenotypic structure (McCrae et al., 2001). These results refute a temperament–character distinction in personality traits. The structure of the non-shared environment correlation matrix produced a two factor model, with factors of 'love' and 'work'. McCrae and colleagues suggested that these high-order factors might act as environmental modulators on the five genetically influenced traits, but the validity of these higher-order traits and the nature of any modulation are not established.

In most behaviour–genetic studies of personality traits the largest single influence originates from the non-shared environment. Shared genes bring about similarities in family members' personality trait scores, not shared experiences. The unique environments they experience have a large effect on their individuality. Correspondingly, the amount of attention and research that non-shared environment received from researchers was scant. Plomin has long emphasised the importance of non-shared environment on personality differences and has encouraged research on this cause of individual differences (Plomin and Daniels, 1987; Plomin, Asbury and Dunn, 2001). He confirmed the following assertions concerning non-shared environment: it needs to be distinguished from error of measurement; shared

Table 6.6 *Categories of environmental influences that cause children in the same family to differ*

Categories	Examples
Error of measurement	Test–re-test reliability
Non-shared environment	
Nonsystematic	Accidents, differential prenatal effects, illness, trauma
Systematic	
Family composition	Birth order, sex differences
Sibling interaction	Differential treatment or perceptions
Parent–child relations	Differential treatment or perceptions
Extrafamilial	Differential experiences with peers, friends, teachers, sports, other activities and interests, education, occupations, spouses, family life

Source Plomin, Asbury and Dunn (2001)

environment may have more effect in extreme situations, such as abusive families; perceptions of environment may be an important source of non-shared experience; non-shared environment may involve chance, in the sense of idiosyncratic experiences, including prenatal events (Plomin, Asbury and Dunn, 2001, p. 226). He explained that genotype–environment interaction and correlation do not account for non-shared environment because they cannot explain why identical twins are different. He suggested a three step outline for research programmes that might investigate the large effect of non-shared environment on personality: document, using valid measures, the experiences specific to each child in the family; document the association between differential experiences and differential personality trait outcomes; and investigate whether any associations are causal (Plomin, Asbury and Dunn, 2001, p. 226). Table 6.6 describes sources on non-shared environmental influences. Some researchers almost despair of non-shared-environments effects ever coming under the control of systematic scientific investigation (Turkheimer and Waldron, 2000).

One obvious and under-appreciated conclusion from the importance of non-shared environment is that studies of personality development should include more than one child per family. This point should be obvious because the key claim about non-shared environments is that they make siblings differ. The Nonshared Environment in Adolescent Development (NEAD) project has attempted logically to apply the three step outline, as described in Box 6.3 (Reiss et al., 2000). Despite its sensitive design it has not identified systematic non-shared environment effects. A small, longitudinal study of MZ twins found that stressors in childhood and adolescence were associated with personality trait differences in agreeableness, openness and conscientiousness at age twenty-nine (Torgersen and Janson, 2002). These authors question the convention of denoting shared environmental effects as unshared when their result is to make siblings dissimilar. An alternative to there being systematic effects of non-shared environment on personality development

Box 6.4 The nonshared environment in adolescent development (NEAD) project

720 families were recruited. Each had two same-sex children aged between ten and eighteen years. Three years apart, two visits lasting two hours were made by researchers. Family environment was assessed by questionnaires and interviews given to the parents and their children, and the families were video-recorded to show interactions among members. There was evidence of non-shared experiences, for example in reports of children's reports of their parents' negativity toward them. Once such evidence of non-shared experiences has been identified, the next step is to investigate whether this relates to differences in behavioural outcomes between children. One example is that negative parental behaviour to one child (controlling for the treatment given by parents to the other child) is associated with antisocial behaviour and depression (Reiss et al., 2000). The third step is to ask whether the non-shared environment effect (in this case parental negativity) is causally related to the children's differences in outcomes (antisocial behaviour and depression). The technique used to examine this was genetic covariance. The finding was that the associations were mediated not by non-shared environment, but by genetic factors: 'differential parental treatment of siblings reflects genetically influenced differences between the siblings. As implausible as this finding might seem on first encounter, it is part of the second great discovery of genetic research at the interface of nature and nurture – genetics contributes substantially to experience. The NEAD quest for nonshared environment led to genotype-environment correlation; that is, children select, modify, construct, and reconstruct their experiences in part on the basis of their genetic propensities' (Plomin, Asbury and Dunn, 2001, p. 231). The conclusion is that, even in this well-designed project, more thinking will have to be done before non-shared-environment effects can be detected and found to be causal. One obvious step is to look to sources beyond the family setting.

is that non-genetic sources of influence are largely due to chance idiosyncratic events. This is supported by studies which suggest that, after removing method bias, only the genetic and not the non-shared environment contributions resemble the phenotypic structure of personality traits (McCrae et al., 2001).

Personality change

Genetic studies tend to be equated in people's minds with static aspects of the person, but genetic approaches can be used to examine personality change and development. Plomin and Nesselroade (1990) suggested that heritability of personality may change over development, with some evidence for higher heritabilities at older ages, though the heritability of extraversion and neuroticism may decline

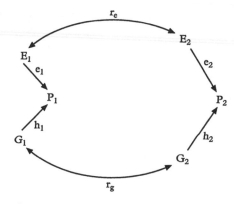

Figure 6.2 Environmental (E) and genetic (G) mediators of phenotypic (P) change and stability from time 1 to time 2

Note e_1 and e_2 and h_1 and h_2, respectively describe the magnitude of the environmental and genetic effects on the phenotype (P) at times 1 and 2. r_e and r_g, respectively, describe the correlations between these environmental genetic influences at times 1 and 2

from late adolescence to age 30 (Viken et al., 1994). Even if the heritability estimates are the same at two ages, the genes affecting a trait need not be the same. Figure 6.2 illustrates the possible mediators of the change/stability of a phenotype – say a personality trait score – from time 1 to time 2. There are environmental and genetic determinants of the trait score at time 1 and similar determinants at time 2. By gathering longitudinal data on MZ and DZ twins the correlation between the genetic contributions at time 1 and time 2 may be estimated. Using such models there is little evidence of genetic mediation of personality change in adulthood but some evidence for such effects in childhood (Plomin and Nesselroade, 1990). Similarly, McGue, Bacon and Lykken (1993) found that stability of personality was associated with genetic effects and change with environmental factors.

Genetic covariation

Traditional biometric, behaviour genetic approaches using twin and adoption studies seemed likely to be replaced by molecular genetic studies. There might be only so many times one could replicate and refine heritability estimates on personality trait scores. The future would lie in finding the actual genetic variability that contributed to personality differences. One reason that traditional approaches continue to be useful is that researchers have found other applications for biometric studies.

One important advance is in the study of genetic covariation. It is usually asked whether a trait shows any genetic influence. An extension to the behaviour genetic method affords asking whether the genetic influences on two related traits are shared, and to what degree. Imagine two traits A and B are correlated in the population, and that they both have some genetic basis. It can be asked whether the genetic influences on the two traits show some overlap. The effect of a gene on two or more phenotypic outcomes is called pleiotropy. Traditional biometric genetic designs can be extended in this way to find out whether genetic influences contribute to the correlation between the two traits. The method used to conduct these studies involves an extension of the usual twin studies. The basis of examining genetic covariation is the difference in the similarity between MZ and DZ twins. A basic heritability study examines the correlation between twin pairs on a single trait. In genetic covariance the correlations examined are those between one twin's scores on trait A and the second twin's scores on trait B.

Genetic covariation studies have special importance in psychiatry. Many psychiatric disorders have some genetic basis. Personality traits are thought to be predisposing influences that can affect whether people develop particular psychiatric states. It is interesting to ask whether the genetic influence on personality traits overlaps with the genetic influence on psychiatric disorders. Clear descriptions of studies of genetic covariation are found in Bouchard and Loehlin (2001); Jang, Vernon and Livesley (2001); Plomin et al. (2001).

A study on personality and alcohol dependence provides an example of this type of research (Slutske et al., 2002). Over 3,000 Australian twin pairs were assessed on the psychiatric states of alcohol dependence and conduct disorder. The personality trait of behavioural undercontrol correlated with both of these states. The genetic sources of behavioural undercontrol accounted for 40 per cent of the genetic variation in alcohol dependence and conduct disorder, and 90 per cent of the genetic-based risk that was shared by the two psychiatric states. This shows that genetic influences on a personality trait contribute to genetic predisposition to important psychiatric states.

Studies of genetic covariation may be used to provide leads in searching for the biological basis of personality differences, something which has proved elusive to physiological (chapter 7) and molecular genetic study designs (see below). A twin-based study of genetic covariation found that 8 per cent of the additive genetic influences on monoamine oxidase activity were shared with genetic contributions to individual differences in neuroticism (Kirk et al., 2001; figure 6.3). Monoamine oxidase is an enzyme affecting serotonin metabolism, and that shared genetic influence suggests a possible causal link between this brain transmitter system and neuroticism differences.

Studies of genetic covariation can assist in refining personality trait models themselves. Because these studies can discover whether measured, phenotypic variables share genetic origins, they can be applied to the facets of personality traits. It may be asked, for example, whether all of the six facets of neuroticism within the NEO-PI-R have shared genetic influences. At an even finer analysis, it can be asked whether each of the items within each facet of a personality trait has common genetic influences. It was suggested that scales could be improved by including items with common genetic influences, leading to so-called 'genetically crisp scales' (Jang, Vernon and Livesley, 2001, p. 237). There are further possibilities for this type of analysis for the development of personality scales. Genetic covariation studies can provide a correlation between traits that assess

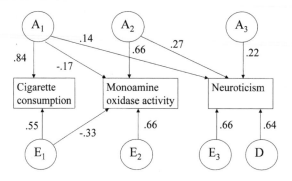

Figure 6.3 Path diagram showing latent genetic and environmental influences (circles) on the measured phenotypes (rectangles) of cigarette smoking, monoamine oxidase activity and neuroticism.

Note A1, A2 and A3 are additive genetic sources of variation, whereas E1, E2 and E3 are non-shared environmental sources and D represents non-additive genetic effects influencing only Eysenck Personality Questionnaire-Neuroticism scores. Numbers by paths are path coefficients and must be squared to obtain proportions of variance of the measured variable accounted for by the latent variable. Proportion of variance in neuroticism explained by genes influencing monoamine oxidase activity (A2) after adjustment for smoking (A1) is 0.27^2, or about 8 per cent.

Source Redrawn from Kirk et al. (2001)

the degree to which the genetic influences on the trait covary. This is called the genetic correlation. Similarly, a non-shared environmental correlation can be calculated for the association between traits. This allows matrices of genetic and environmental correlations to be produced and subjected to factor analysis. The factor structure of, say, facets of a personality scale can be compared with respect to their phenotypic, genetic and environmental structures. One example of this type of analysis, using data from Canadian and German MZ and DZ twins, analysed the items and the facets of the NEO-PI-R. There were multiple genetic and environmental factors discovered within each personality domain and the factors were common to the facets within the domain (Jang et al., 2002). This lends support to the facet groups that comprise the NEO-PI-R domains and suggests that each personality domain has multiple genetic influences. The same research group has indicated that the genetic influences on the five factor model might cohere more closely with the phenotypic structure of personality than do the non-shared environmental influences (McCrae et al., 2001). Concordance between the aetiological structure of personality and the phenotypic structure was found in a large-scale analysis of the negative emotionality, positive emotionality and constraint dimensions of Tellegen's Multidimensional Personality Questionnaire (Krueger, 2000).

With its contributions to the relation between personality and psychiatric states, to the biological basis of personality, and to the genetic and environmental architecture of personality traits, studies involving genetic covariation methods are among the most influential and informative investigations in personality.

Molecular genetic studies of personality

Traditional biometric behaviour genetic studies have proved informative about personality. The major personality traits and some others have a substantial heritable component. The environmental variance appears largely to be in the non-shared aspect of the environment, though it has proven elusive (Plomin, Asbury and Dunn, 2001), and might be composed more substantially of error and bias than was supposed (McCrae et al., 2001). What are the bases and mechanisms of the genetic effects? Behaviour genetic studies may only begin this search, not end it. They can sketch the architecture of the inheritance of personality. The biochemical mediators of behavioural consistency will be revealed by the leads given by molecular genetic studies of personality.

A revolution has occurred in genetics, brought about by technology for physical manipulation of DNA pieces. Our genetic code is contained in twenty-three pairs of chromosomes made of deoxyribosenucleic acid (DNA). It may be thought of as a very long string of code that uses a four-letter alphabet. The human genome project has provided some drafts of this code. That is, they have literally printed the sequence of the code letters (DNA base pairs) from the start of chromosome one to the end of the sex chromosomes. Most locations on human DNA have the same base pair – building units of DNA – in all people. If we set out the code of various people's DNA then most letters in most locations would be the same. Some DNA locations have variants which are the basis of individual differences in our DNA sequences. Different people have a different base pair at that point in their DNA code. These variations are called polymorphisms, meaning 'many forms'. Put simply, variations at a given chromosome locus may be treated as levels of an independent variable. If a DNA locus has two variants, it may be asked whether people with one or other variant score higher or lower on a personality trait.

Phenotypic characteristics of living things can thus be associated with specific variations at specific sites on chromosomes. Take a hypothetical example. Suppose that there is a disease X that we know is genetically mediated because it has a particular pattern of inheritance. If we can show that people who have a particular variant of a given piece of DNA are more likely to develop the disease then we can say that part of the genetic predisposition to the disease arises from a particular DNA message. The first successes in human biology in this area have been in the many hundreds of diseases, such as familial Alzheimer's disease, whose genetic predispositions have been located to specific gene loci. However, it has proved difficult to find the gene loci for psychiatric syndromes such as schizophrenia (Sawa and Snyder, 2002) and bipolar affective disorder (Berrettini, 2001), in part because such conditions do not have clear phenotypic characterisations, the pattern of inheritance is often unclear, and several genes may be involved.

Personality researchers face similar problems to researchers addressing the molecular genetics of psychiatric syndromes. First, we have to be clear that the correct phenotypes are being investigated, as emphasized by Jang, Vernon and Livesley's (2001) view that the phenotype of personality remains 'elusive'. Certainly, the modest consensus around the five factor model has come at a convenient time, but there are rival descriptive schemes and there is some indication that the heritability of personality might lie within narrower traits (Loehlin, 1992; McCrae et al., 2001). Therefore, the first concern for molecular genetic researchers in personality will be which dimensions to study.

The second problem is how to proceed. One way is to find a candidate gene and to compute a statistical association between that locus and the phenotypic characteristic being studied. The gene itself need not be assessed. An accessible nearby gene may be used, such as a blood group gene. The nearer that two genes lie on the chromosome the more likely they are to be inherited together. A statistical association can be calculated between the likelihood of having the given gene and the likelihood of having the particular phenotype, say an illness. This type of study is called a linkage study and tends to be successful in cases where the phenotype has a well-understood mode of inheritance and where 'cases' can be separated clearly from 'non-cases'. Personality traits do not meet these criteria. The linkage approach has been fruitful with many diseases, but led to blind alleys in psychiatric research where unreplicated links between genes and disorders have been frequent. Useful hints for further research may be obtained from unusual families with rare disorders. For example, Brunner et al. (1993) discovered that, in a large family in which several of the males had disturbed regulation of impulsive aggression, there was a single mutation in the structural gene for the enzyme monoamine oxidase A. This is an enzyme that is involved in the breakdown of the monoamine neurotransmitters. In the males in question the enzyme deficiency was complete, leading the researchers to speculate that, given the wide range of monoamine oxidase A activity in the population, there might be an association with aggressive behaviour and relative deficiency of the enzyme.

An alternative to the linkage approach is to examine the statistical relation between polymorphisms in a gene of interest and whether or not people have a disorder. This is called an association study. The idea is to assess relative proportions of people with and without a given behavioural condition, who possess a particular DNA sequence. For example, 40 per cent of people with late-onset Alzheimer's disease (distinct from the much rarer early onset form that was mentioned earlier) have a particular allele called Apo-E4, whereas only 15 per cent of control subjects have it (Deary, 2000, chapter 9).

Personality traits are not discrete entities that people possess or lack. They are quantitative traits with, for the most part, a normal distribution of scores in populations. They do not have a well-understood mode of inheritance. The prevailing assumption is that personality traits will be the result of the action and interactions of many genes. Small effects from any one gene cannot be detected by standard examination of family pedigrees in linkage studies. The molecular genetic approach applied to personality traits and other behavioural phenotypes such as cognitive abilities is called Quantitative Trait Loci (Bouchard and Loehlin, 2001; Jang, Vernon and Livesley, 2001; Plomin et al., 2001). Researchers using QTL approaches make the assumption that variance in phenotypic characteristics is influenced by many genes, each of which has a small influence such as contributing a few per cent of the variance, or even less than one per cent. The first apparent successes of the QTL approach applied to personality traits linked dopamine with novelty seeking and serotonin with neuroticism (Ebstein, Benjamin and Belmaker, 2000; Jang, Vernon and Livesley, 2001).

A significant association was reported between novelty seeking tendencies, one of Cloninger's three biologically based traits (see chapter 11), and variations at the D4 dopamine receptor gene (Cloninger, Adolfsson and Svrakic, 1996). This association was replicated across two studies, one of which used Cloninger's Tridimensional Personality Questionnaire (TPQ: Ebstein et al., 1996). The other study used the TPQ and Costa and McCrae's NEO-PI-R to index the five factors and their facets (Benjamin et al., 1996). Certain variants of the dopamine receptor gene were significantly associated with TPQ novelty seeking and NEO-PI-R extraversion and conscientiousness. Only the warmth, excitement-seeking and positive-emotion facets of extraversion and the deliberation facet of conscientiousness were associated with the D4 dopamine receptor (D4DR) allelic variation. Though the association with the excitement-seeking facet suggests a replication of Ebstein et al.'s (1996) finding with TPQ novelty seeking, the additional associations between the gene and the other extraversion and conscientiousness facets complicate the narrow interpretation of this finding. About 10 per cent of the genetic variance of novelty seeking was accounted for in this single genetic site. A number of studies failed to replicate the finding (e.g., Malhotra et al., 1996; Pogue-Geile et al., 1998), and there exist a mixture of studies with positive and negative findings. Schmidt et al. (2002) provide a summary of these mixed findings and report a significant association in children aged four between their mothers' reports of aggression and D4DR variation. The relationship between the dopamine D4 receptor variation and novelty-seeking trait scores in adults, if it exists, might occur only in interaction with variation in other genes related to brain monoamine transmitter–receptor systems (Benjamin et al., 2000).

A second apparent success for molecular genetic techniques linked neuroticism to the neurotransmitter serotonin (also called 5-hydroxytryptamine or 5-HT), which has been implicated in anxiety and depressive disorders. A single gene on chromosome 17 codes for the 5-HT transporter (5-HTT), which regulates re-uptake of 5-HT at the synapses where it is released. Two alleles of this transporter gene have been found, one long (l) and one short (s). This genetic variation is said to occur in the 5-HT transporter-linked polymorphic region (5HTTLPR) (Deary et al., 1999). The short allele was associated with higher neuroticism levels, in a study of 505 subjects, whether measured by the NEO-PI or Cattell's 16PF (Goldman, 1996; Lesch et al., 1996). The allele was also associated with anxiety, angry hostility, depression and impulsiveness facets of NEO-PI neuroticism, and with estimated scores for Cloninger's harm avoidance trait. The gene accounted for 3 to 4 per cent of total neuroticism variance, and 7 to 9 per cent of the genetic variance. Attempts to replicate the association between the 5HTTLPR anxiety- and depression-related personality traits had mixed results, with some studies confirming the findings (e.g., Greenberg et al., 2000) and some not (Deary et al., 1999). Some have concluded that the inconsistency in these results is partly caused by the use of Cloninger's personality scales which are said to have poorer psychometric properties than, for example, the NEO-PI-R scales (Herbst et al., 2001; Jang, Vernon and Livesley, 2001). An fMRI study supported this site of genetic variability's being involved in emotion-based personality differences. People with the short allele of the 5HT-TLPR showed greater neuronal activity in the amygdala in response to fear-related stimuli (Hariri et al., 2002).

This field of personality research is still at the stage of producing interesting initial reports and then attempting to replicate the findings. A recent meta-analytic review of forty-six studies (Munafo et al., 2003) illustrates some of the difficulties involved. It reported that the most robust finding was the association between the 5HTTLPR polymorphism and what the authors term 'avoidance' traits, such as anxiety. The meta-analysis also linked alleles for the dopamine receptors to 'approach' traits, such as novelty seeking. However, whether or not the various associations between traits and polymorphisms reached significance was highly dependent on the exact technical assumptions made in conducting these analyses. The authors caution that associations are likely to be of small magnitude, and may vary with sex, age and ethnicity. Future research may also examine the role of the environment at the molecular level: an example of genotype-environment interaction demonstrated using molecular genetic research is given in Box 6.3.

Conclusions

1. Investigations into the genetic and environmental influences on personality traits use biometric (twin, adoption and family) studies and molecular genetic techniques. Biometric studies have established that there is a substantial (additive and non-additive) genetic contribution to most of the recognised major personality dimensions and also to some lower level personality facets.

2. Shared (family) environment has little influence on personality. The broad source of variance that is termed non-shared environment typically contributes substantially to personality, but its effects are not understood. It contains non-systematic sources of variance and measured non-shared environment differences have not been related to personality differences.

3. Studies of genetic covariation represent an advance on heritability studies. They are being used to define and validate personality phenotypes, to clarify the genetic and environmental architecture of personality traits, to discover genetic

links shared by personality traits and psychiatric states and disorders, and to discover shared genetic influences between personality traits and physiological variability.

4. The certainty with which some additive genetic variance has been established for the major secondary-level personality traits augurs well for future molecular genetic studies of personality. Molecular genetic studies of personality to date mostly concern the possible links between novelty seeking and the dopamine receptor and neuroticism and the 5HT transporter. They have not provided replicable associations between genetic and personality variability, but they indicate how the genetics of personality and the psychobiology of personality will become part of the same topic, because molecular genetic studies are informative about biological mechanisms.

5. Molecular, as well as biometric, genetic studies of personality traits may reveal the links between personality traits and susceptibility to some forms of mental illness and distress. Molecular genetic studies of personality are suited to examining gene-environment interactions in personality development.

7   The psychophysiology of traits

Introduction: neuropsychological approaches to personality

In this chapter we discuss the hypothesis that personality is an expression of individual differences in brain function. There are several reasons for linking personality traits to neural systems. First, there is the evidence from behaviour genetics discussed in the last chapter. If personality traits are partially inherited, then there must necessarily be a biological influence on traits, encoded within the person's DNA. Of course, the influence of the genotype on brain physiology is likely to be influenced by interaction with the environment. Second, there is striking evidence for radical personality change resulting from brain damage (see Powell, 1981; and Zuckerman, 1991, 1999 for reviews). Damage to the frontal lobes of the cerebral cortex is notorious for disruption of personality; the person may become unstable, impulsive and even aggressive (depending on the exact region damaged). Third, there is evidence that traits correlate with psychophysiological indicators of brain functioning, such as the electrical activity of the brain and the increase in heart rate when the person is exposed to stress. Such observations suggest that we might develop neuropsychological theories of personality traits. Such theories should describe how individual differences in the functioning of specific brain systems influence individual differences in behaviour.

However, there are various difficulties involved in building a neuropsychological theory of personality traits. First, the complexity of the task is daunting. Personality may be related to a multitude of different brain structures, ranging from primitive systems controlling wakefulness and alertness (in the brainstem) to systems for higher cognitive functions such as language and thought (in the neocortex). Typically, researchers attempt to simplify the problem by picking out some key brain systems for special attention. Second, the empirical evidence may be correlational and open to different interpretations. Psychophysiological response and higher-order cognition are closely linked. For example, if you are driving to the airport and you recall that you left a fire burning in your house, you will probably experience physiological arousal responses such as a racing heart: the thought precedes the response. In other words, physiological response reflects both a direct output of unconscious, low-level neural processes and high-level thought. If we find a correlation between neuroticism and cardiac response to stress, we then have two possible explanations. Do high-N persons possess brain systems that automatically generate higher levels of physiological reactivity to stress? Or does the person high in N react to demanding or disturbing events with more negative thoughts, that in turn drive the physiological response? Both possibilities seem plausible (and may indeed coexist).

A final difficulty is conceptual (Matthews, 2000, 2001). Can variation in the electrochemical functioning of nerve cells directly explain variation in complex behaviours such as social interaction? Think of the brain as functioning like a computer, with a physical substrate or hardware (e.g., silicon chips) that supports symbolic programs or software. How the programs work is dependent on the physical hardware, and damage to the chips will interfere with program execution. But if we want to understand how a program like a spreadsheet or word processor works, we need a description in terms of software, not hardware. That is, we need to describe the logical structure of the program, such as the way it represents the columns of a spreadsheet as program variables. Even though everything the system does is governed by physics, understanding its operations requires an analysis of its logical operations, not the physical processes themselves. Similarly, even if personality does have a biological basis, explaining behaviour may require us to analyse it in terms of 'software' (information-processing) rather than 'hardware' (neurons). More generally, we may need to explain personality at multiple levels of abstraction from physical reality. Sometimes we may indeed be able to link behaviour directly to some neural process, whereas in other contexts higher-level explanations may work better. In this chapter, we will largely set aside these potential difficulties, and consider how psychophysiological techniques have been used to explore the neural foundations of personality.

The assumptions of physiological theories are shown in figure 7.1 (cf., Gray, 1981). Genes (and environment) are responsible for individual differences in the various systems of the brain, which in turn influence behaviour and adjustment. In some cases, the brain–behaviour link may be quite direct, for example, in controlling the intensity of emotion felt in response to some challenging event. However, theory also includes indirect links; for example, people whose brains are slow to become aroused may actively seek stimulation to maintain some optimal level of arousal (Eysenck, 1981). In addition, individual differences in brain function influence the person's *learning*, i.e., how slowly or rapidly the person forms associations between stimuli, or between stimuli and responses. Thus, complex, seemingly culturally shaped behaviours may also reflect the influence of brain systems that bias the learning process.

The chapter is organised as follows. First, we explore in more detail the theoretical basis for a neuropsychology of personality. We will emphasise especially the possibility that personality relates to the general sensitivity of brain systems controlling cortical arousal, or sensitivity to motivational signals. Next, we review the range of measurement techniques used in psychophysiological research. Using these techniques to probe brain functioning requires some methodological sophistication, so we provide examples of personality studies that demonstrate how these

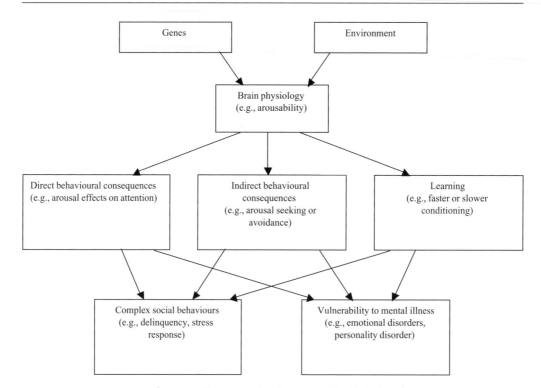

Figure 7.1 Some causal paths assumed by biological theories of personality

measurements are taken in practice. In the final sections of the book, we return to the theoretical insights gained from psychophysiological studies, reviewing, first, work on arousal, and, second, work on motivational bases for personality. These concepts have been used to unify a wide range of psychophysiological and behavioural studies, and merit special attention. We consider a variety of studies of the empirical links between arousal and extraversion, neuroticism and other traits, and their theoretical implications. We conclude with an overview of the achievements and limitations of the psychophysiological approach.

Ground-plans for neuropsychological theory

Neuropsychological theories tend to have a number of common building blocks. The first is what Gray (1987) has termed a conceptual nervous system, i.e., a ground-plan of the most important brain systems. Because of the complexity of the brain, the theorist must pick out a few key neural systems as the basis for theory. What do we mean by a system? Essentially, a system is a functional component of the brain that may be supported by several distinct anatomical structures. Minimally, we need to identify these structures and the neurotransmitters associated with the main neural pathways of the system, because variation in neurotransmitter function may relate to personality. The neurotransmitters which

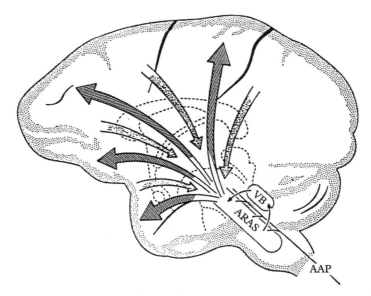

Figure 7.2 Eysenck's (1983) model for the hypothetical physiological basis of extraversion (reticular formation–cortical arousal) and neuroticism (limbic system or visceral brain)

have been of most interest to trait theorists include serotonin, acetylcholine and the catecholamines, such as noradrenalin (norepinephrine) and dopamine. The second component of theory is a description of the behavioural functions of the key systems, such as controlling fight/flight or consummatory responses. The third component is a hypothesis concerning personality differences in system operation and function. From these building blocks, the theorist can then predict how personality should influence psychophysiological response, behaviour and reaction to psychobiological manipulations such as drug treatments.

Eysenck's (1967) arousal theory

Two influential neuropsychological theories of personality follow this ground-plan for theory development (Eysenck, 1967; Gray, 1981). Eysenck (1967, 1981, 1997) related personality to two neural systems (figure 7.2). The first is a cortico-reticular loop including the cerebral cortex, the thalamus and the ascending reticular activating system (ARAS). Feedback between the various structures allows this circuitry to be seen as a single system. It is excited by incoming sensory stimulation, transmitted by the ascending afferent pathways, but the level of excitation is regulated by cortical processing. Its function is to support information-processing. Activity of the cortico-reticular loop is associated with increased cortical arousal. According to Eysenck, this system provides the neural substrate for extraversion–introversion: it is hypothesised to be more readily activated in introverts than in extraverts, so that introverts are more easily aroused, and tend to show higher levels of cortical arousal. These predicted personality differences in arousability, and in characteristic tonic cortical arousal, generate testable predictions, because arousal is believed to influence observable behaviours such as conditioning and performance. Eysenck (e.g., 1994) emphasises the use of the 'drug postulate' in theory-testing. Introverts should behave like subjects given stimulant drugs, whereas extraverts should behave like subjects given depressants. For example, stimulants appear to increase rate of conditioning in simple associative and operant paradigms. Consistent with the theory, introverts too show faster conditioning, at least in some paradigms (Martin and Levey, 1981).

Because of the importance of the arousal concept, we look in detail at predictions from arousal-based theories in later sections. Broadly, however, we can explain the general characteristics of extraverts and introverts on the basis of a further hypothesis, that intermediate levels of arousal are subjectively pleasant, but low or high arousal is experienced as unpleasant. Because extraverts tend to be chronically low in arousal, they tend to seek out sources of stimulation to raise their arousal to the desired moderate level. Thus, extraverts tend to be venturesome and daring, and particularly drawn to social stimulation. Conversely, introverts tend to be over-aroused, and so avoid stimulation by engaging in behaviours such as solitary reading.

The second neural circuit in Eysenck's (1967) conceptual nervous system is a viscero-cortical loop interconnecting the cerebral cortex with the 'visceral brain', comprising structures such as those of the limbic system. The function of the system is to control subjective and autonomic emotional response, particularly in potentially stressful environments. The system is more excitable in people with high neuroticism than in emotionally stable people. Hence, high N scorers are more likely than low N scorers to become autonomically aroused, and to experience distress and agitation when subjected to stress.

An alternative conceptual nervous system: Gray (1991)

Gray's (1981, 1991; Gray and McNaughton, 2000) neurophysiological theory is based on a different conceptual nervous system, described in more detail than that of Eysenck. The theory has undergone a variety of modifications over the years. Here we outline the best-known version; later in this chapter we describe some recent changes. Gray's theory is distinctive not only for its neuropsychology, but because Gray believes that the causal axes of personality differ from those proposed by Eysenck. Rather than E and N, Gray refers to dimensions of anxiety (Anx) and impulsivity (Imp), which are rotated through 60 degrees in factor space, with respect to the Eysenck dimensions, as shown in figure 7.3. Anx is thus mainly high N, with an element of introversion (low E), whereas Imp is mainly high E, with some neuroticism. Gray retains the psychoticism construct, but, again, suggests it may not exactly align with the Eysenck P dimension. In particular, a part of the Imp dimension relates to Eysenckian P.

Gray begins with five brain systems established from animal research, controlling arousal, reward, behavioural inhibition, consummatory response and fight/

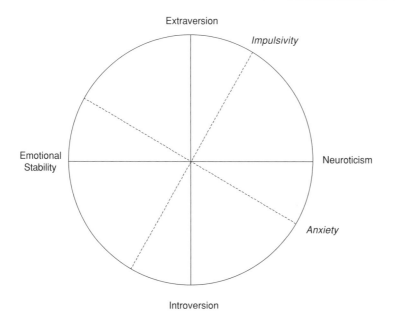

Figure 7.3 Gray's axes (broken lines) as aligned with Eysenck's axes (solid lines) (alignment with Eysenck psychoticism dimension not shown)

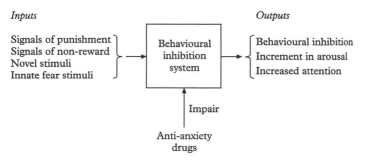

Figure 7.4 Functional properties of Gray's (1982) behavioural inhibition system

flight. The systems of most importance for personality are the behavioural inhibition, reward and fight/flight systems. The behavioural inhibition system (BIS) is made up of a variety of structures, including the hippocampus, septum, and parts of the limbic system and frontal lobes of the cerebral cortex. Its function is to interrupt ongoing behaviour and prepare the organism to deal with certain potentially threatening stimuli: signals of punishment and non-reward, novel stimuli and innate fear stimuli. It inhibits response, orients attention to the potential threat, and raises arousal. These functional properties of the BIS are shown in figure 7.4. According to Gray the system is more readily activated in people of anxious personality (neurotic introverts), so that the anxious person is generally threat-sensitive.

The reward system, also described as the behavioural activation system (BAS), has the function of controlling approach to potentially beneficial stimuli. Anatomically, it is based upon various forebrain structures that use the neurotransmitter dopamine, such as the dorsal and ventral striatum. It is considered to be the substrate for impulsivity, considered by Gray to be a mixture of high N, high E and high P. Hence, impulsive people show impulsive behaviour, not because they are under-aroused, but because their sensitivity to reward signals makes them particularly likely to engage in approach behaviour. Like the BIS, the BAS also tends to produce arousal, so that motivating stimuli are generally arousing. Finally, the fight/flight system is sensitive to unconditioned aversive stimuli, so that it controls behaviours related to rage and panic. It is associated with structures known to control negative emotion such as the amygdala, medial hypothalamus and the central gray matter of the midbrain. It is related primarily to psychoticism; presumably, in high P individuals, rage tends to dominate panic.

The complexity of personality: Zuckerman's (1991) model

A third theorist, Marvin Zuckerman (1991, 1995, 1999), criticises theories such as those of Eysenck and Gray because they assume *isomorphism* between personality traits and brain systems. For example, Eysenck (1967) assumes (1) that the only brain system influencing extraversion is the reticulo-cortical loop, and (2) that the reticulo-cortical loop influences only extraversion and not other personality dimensions. Zuckerman argues that the complexity of the brain is such that any personality trait may relate to several brain systems, and any given brain system may contribute to two or more personality traits. He points out also that brain systems are typically functionally inter-dependent, and that associations between activity of systems and traits may be non-linear. For example, extraversion may be associated with moderate levels of activity in catecholamine systems, whereas introverts might show either high or low levels of catecholaminergic activity.

Figure 7.5 reproduces Zuckerman's (1991) representation of a model for his alternative Big Five, discussed in chapter 1. It will be apparent that the model is too complex to be discussed in full in this book, but some of its features are worth highlighting. Zuckerman's view of extraversion is somewhat similar to Gray's in that he relates it to brain systems associated with sensitivity to reward, particularly dopaminergic circuits, which also tend to increase motor activity. The finding that genetic variations for the dopamine D4 receptor are associated with extraversion differences confirms this aspect of Zuckerman's model (see chapter 6). Zuckerman's model of the neuroticism trait incorporates sensitivity to punishment and emotional or adrenergic arousal. He also implicates other brain systems in controlling neuroticism and anxiety, such as the benzodiazepine (BZ) receptors responsible for the anxiety-relieving effects of drugs like valium. His model requires modification to accommodate the link between neuroticism and genetic variation in the serotonin transporter gene.

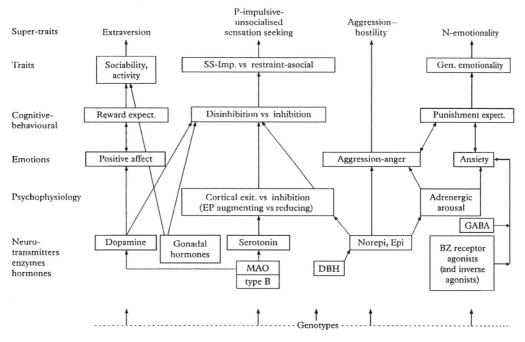

Figure 7.5 Zuckerman's (1991) psychobiological model for personality

We can convey the flavour of the Zuckerman (1991) model by outlining its view of the psychobiology of the cluster of traits referred to as P-impulsive-unsocialised sensation seeking, which is somewhat similar to Eysenck's P dimension. The primary behavioural characteristic of the high scorer on the dimension is a lack of behavioural restraint, who becomes particularly disinhibited when the situation has a potential for both reward and punishment, such as the opportunity to steal a car. However, disinhibition is influenced by a number of distinct physiological systems. These may include arousability of noradrenergic and dopaminergic neural pathways by intense stimulation, low levels of serotonin, high levels of the sex hormone testosterone, and low levels of the enzyme monoamine oxidase (MAO). Thus, we are unlikely to find a single biological 'mark of Cain' which will identify the potential criminal or psychopath. Instead, the predisposition to engage in antisocial behaviour arises out of the interaction between several different functional systems.

From brain to behaviour: testing neuropsychological theories

Theories such as those of Eysenck, Gray, Zuckerman and Cloninger (see chapter 1) appear to have at least some potential for explaining personality and its expression in behaviour. We may use the biological model to predict how personality will influence behaviour in various contexts. For example, we can derive from

Eysenckian theory the prediction that introverts should show stronger conditioning when stimuli are weak, but not when stimuli are intense (Levey and Martin, 1981). Gray's (1981) theory, however, implies that personality effects vary not so much with stimulus intensity, but with its motivational signal value: high impulsives should condition more strongly to signals of reward, low impulsives to signals of punishment. We consider such behavioural predictions in later chapters of the book. The second research strategy is to test how personality and situational variables influence psychophysiological measures, such as those related to arousal.

Having outlined some of the more ambitious biological accounts of personality trait variation, we shall describe psychophysiological techniques used in personality studies. For each technique we present an example of an actual study, described in sufficient detail to illustrate its use. A full review of the evidence on psychophysiological correlates of personality is beyond the scope of this book (see Zuckerman, 1991, 1999). We confine ourselves to the relatively straightforward techniques of 'online' assessment of cns and ans activity. A further class of techniques, beyond the scope of this book, is concerned with biochemical assessment of levels of metabolites of brain neurotransmitters, and of circulating hormones. Evidence from neurotransmitter-based studies has not consistently supported Cloninger's theories (Bond, 2001). Evidence provided by biochemical techniques is complex, and somewhat inconsistent, but of particular relevance to Zuckerman's (1991) model.

Psychophysiological techniques: an outline and examples

Electroencephalography (EEG)

By positioning electrodes on the surface of the scalp it is possible to detect the small electrical potentials that are produced by the living brain. By amplifying these signals, the continuous electrical potential differences between brain areas can be measured and displayed in real time. The record of the potential differences between any one pair of electrodes appears like a chaotic squiggle (figure 7.6). However, with changes in conscious state, there are predictable changes in the EEG record. As with any other continuous line that varies with respect to its deviation from a zero line on the X axis, the EEG can be described in terms of the frequencies that make up the waveform.

Generally, the frequency of the EEG becomes greater and the amplitude decreases as the person becomes more awake and alert, as shown in figure 7.7. A person who is awake and in a relaxed state with eyes closed will have an EEG whose frequency is about eight to twelve Hertz (Hz). The record of this so-called alpha rhythm is relatively regular over large areas of the scalp, and the alpha rhythm of different brain areas is said to be 'synchronised'. When a person becomes more alert, when the eyes are open and especially if some effortful, attention-demanding

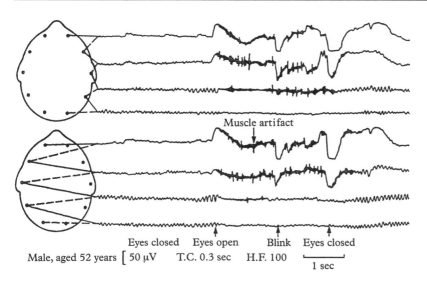

Muscle artifact

Eyes closed   Eyes open   Blink   Eyes closed

Male, aged 52 years ⌈ 50 μV   T.C. 0.3 sec   H.F. 100   1 sec

Figure 7.6 Normal adult EEG. Note the alpha rhythm which is prominent over the rear parts of the head when the eyes are closed
Source Pryse-Phillips (1969)

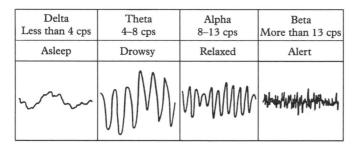

Delta Less than 4 cps	Theta 4–8 cps	Alpha 8–13 cps	Beta More than 13 cps
Asleep	Drowsy	Relaxed	Alert

Figure 7.7 Brain waves classified by frequency

task like mental arithmetic is performed, the frequency of the EEG becomes faster, typically 13–30Hz. This band of frequencies is known as the beta rhythm, and it is less constant across different areas of the scalp and, by inference, the brain. This phenomenon is known as desynchronisation. In contrast, when individuals are drowsy, or during meditation, the frequency slows and the theta waveform appears. It has a frequency of 4–8 Hz. During sleep the delta waveform (less than 4 Hz) appears.

An example of a relatively early study which attempted to associate personality differences and features of the EEG was by Gale, Coles and Blaydon (1969), who tested twelve extravert and twelve introvert undergraduates, assessing extraversion with the EPI. Subjects reclined on a bed in a sound-proofed cubicle, their heads surrounded by a large cube (open at the base) of black card with constant illumination. EEG was recorded from the occipital part of the head. Each subject had EEG recorded for ten two-minute periods, with the eyes closed or open in alternate periods. The EEGs obtained from extraverts and introverts differed in two respects. First, within the alpha range of activity, introverts had a mean dominant frequency of electrical activity (10.80 Hz, SD 1.68) that was higher than that of the extraverts (10.25 Hz, SD 1.50 Hz). Second, extraverts had higher 'mean integrated output' for the theta (4.5–6.5 Hz), alpha (8–13 Hz), and beta (14.5–20 Hz) bands. Within the beta and theta bands, the significant effect of personality was obtained only for the condition where eyes were closed, and for the alpha band only for eyes open. The results were interpreted as offering some support to Eysenck's (1967) hypothesis that extraverts were less cortically aroused than introverts, because 'an inverse relation between alpha amplitude and arousal (within the waking stage) is generally accepted' (p. 220). The report of the study contains numerous cautions about the interpretability of EEG parameters in terms of psychological constructs, such as arousal.

Brain average evoked potentials (EPs)

A person's EEG response to the same stimulus repeated several times over looks very different. This is because each individual record of the brain's electrical activity contains the specific electrical activity evoked by the stimulus, and super-imposed background activity. If one averages a large number of brain electrical responses to a given stimulus the only constant pattern across the responses should be the specific electrical activity evoked by the stimulus, and the noise, being random, should cancel itself out. Averaging the EEG records following each successive presentation of the same stimulus does indeed provide a wave pattern which has a predictable shape.

Typical average evoked potentials to simple stimuli are shown in figure 7.8. Following stimulus onset there is an identifiable negative potential at about 140 ms.

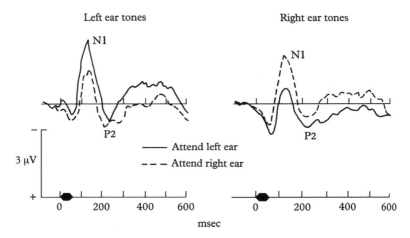

Figure 7.8 Early components of the auditory event-related potential recorded at central electrode (Cz), showing effects of attention on N1 and P2 waves
Source (Coles, Gratton and Fabiani, 1990)

This is called the N140 or the N1. There is a positive deflection at about 200 ms after stimulus onset: the P200 or P2. The N1–P2 complex is related to perception and identification of a stimulus. As figure 7.8 shows, the size of the N1 waveform varies with the attention paid to the stimulus. If, instead of asking a subject to listen to a series of similar tones, we ask a subject to note the instances of differently pitched tones that occur relatively rarely in a series of stimuli, we can alter the EP in an interesting way. Such a task is called an 'oddball' paradigm. We can distinguish the brain's electrical response to the common (ignored) and rarer (attended to) stimuli. Only the rarer 'oddball' tones elicit a prominent positive deflection of the EP at 300 ms or more after stimulus onset. This is P300 or P3, and is one of the most studied of all EP measures within psychology (Picton and Hillyard, 1988; Stelmack and Houlihan, 1995). We can quantify EPs by measuring (1) amplitude, the displacement of the component from a designated baseline in microvolts, and (2) latency, the time after stimulus onset, in milliseconds (ms), of the peak of the component.

As an example of brain evoked potential research in the field of personality traits, we will present Stenberg's (1994) study of extraversion and the P300 response elicited by attention to pictures. Forty young adults' personality traits were tested using the EPI, and the subjects were divided into low, medium and high extraversion groups. Subjects looked at pictures on a computer screen. In one condition they responded only to white pictures (colour task), in a second condition only to animal pictures (semantic task), and in a third task only to white animals (colour + semantic task). Because subjects were responding to some stimuli and ignoring others, there was a P300 component for all three tasks, at about 400–500 ms after stimulus onset. The amplitude of the P300 deflection was largest for the high-extraversion group, and lowest for the low-extraversion group. Extraversion scores of the subjects were correlated with the average amplitude of the P300 across all three tasks for the midline parietal electrode, and the size of the effect was 0.36. P300 amplitude is often seen as an index of updating of working memory, implying that extraversion is associated with the brain processes supporting this cognitive activity. As discussed in chapter 12, extraverts often perform better on short-term memory tasks also. Later we discuss data from functional magnetic resonance brain imaging that provides further evidence for a link between extraversion-related traits and the brain's response to a working memory task (Gray and Braver, 2002).

Electrodermal activity

Many types of emotional arousal involve an increase in the activity of the autonomic nervous system, including sweat gland activity. When sweat glands are activated there is a reduction of the electrical resistance of the skin. The electrical conductance/resistance of the skin may be measured by placing two electrodes on the surface of the skin and passing a small current between them. The site of the electrodes is usually the palmar surface of two fingers. During states of autonomic arousal, such as anxiety, the conductance of the skin decreases and the resistance rises. It is possible to assess both (1) the mean level of skin conductance over a period of time, and (2) changes in skin conductance in response to transient psychological events. The first of these is the Skin Conductance Level (SCL) and the latter is the Skin Conductance Response (SCR).

The study used as an example of research using electrodermal activity examined Zuckerman's (1979) sensation seeking dimension. Smith et al. (1989) hypothesised that the behaviour associated with high sensation seeking might be partly mediated via the reticulo-cortical activation system and the catecholamine system associated with a brainstem structure called the locus coeruleus, which activates a variety of other brain structures. Hence, high and low sensation seekers might be differentiated using measures of psychophysiological arousal. Prior to their study, results had been mixed, but Smith et al. noted that successful studies tended to use groups with extreme sensation seeking scores and highly arousing or novel stimulation. Hence, Smith et al. (1989) examined electrodermal activity (as an index of psychophysiological arousal) in two groups who were at extreme opposite ends of the sensation seeking scale, and used stimuli of varying capacity to generate arousal. They tested 500 students on the Zuckerman Sensation Seeking Scale, and selected twenty-four high scorers (HSS) and twenty-four low scorers (LSS).

Subjects heard and repeated words which represented neutral, sexual or violent categories. The sexual and violent words were rated according to their 'intensity' levels: 'affection' and 'anger' were used as low intensity stimuli, 'condom' and 'bomb' as medium intensity, and 'masturbate' and 'slaughter' as high intensity. Skin conductance level (SCL) was examined prior to each response. Skin conductance response (SCR) was collected after the presentation of stimulus words. There were no significant effects of sensation seeking on the SCL to any stimuli. For SCRs to initial presentations of stimuli there were no differences between HSS and LSS subjects at low intensity level, but differences became significant at the higher levels of stimulus intensity (figure 7.9a). The pattern of personality differences remained similar when averaged across all trials (figure 7.9b). The SCR amplitude of the HSS subjects becomes progressively greater than that of the LSS subjects as the intensity level increases. In general, sexual words caused bigger SCRs than violent words, and more intense words caused bigger SCR changes than less intense words. Smith et al. (1989) concluded that, 'high sensation seekers are the more aroused or arousable group, and this positive correlation between sensation seeking and psychophysiological arousal is enhanced at higher intensities of stimulation' (p. 677). How this result fits more widely into psychophysiological research on personality will be explored below.

Heart rate

Heart rate is controlled by both sympathetic and parasympathetic divisions of the autonomic nervous system. It is possible to examine (1) the mean heart rate and its variability over a period of time (tonic aspects of heart rate), and (2) transient

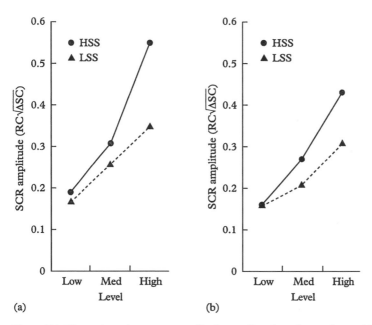

Figure 7.9 Electrodermal response amplitude as a function of sensation seeking and stimulus intensity level, for initial stimuli (left panel), and all stimuli (right panel)

Note HSS = High sensation seeking, LSS = Low sensation seeking

Source Smith et al. (1989)

(phasic) changes in heart rate in response to stimuli. A remarkable example of the association between heart rate and aspects of personality response was reported by Kagan, Reznick and Snidman (1988). They conducted a longitudinal study of behavioural inhibition in 400 children from age twenty-one months to seven and a half years. They were interested in comparing the 10 to 15 per cent of children who become quiet, vigilant and affectively subdued in novel situations with the 10 to 15 per cent of children who are spontaneous and relaxed in unfamiliar circumstances. Kagan et al. envisaged this response difference in children to be similar to adult introversion–extraversion differences. They selected twenty-eight extremely inhibited and thirty extremely uninhibited children at age twenty-one months by examining videotapes of the children's responses to unfamiliar women and objects in unfamiliar laboratory rooms. The children were subsequently seen at four, five and a half and seven and a half years of age, where the cohort fell to forty-one subjects. There was a moderately high correlation between the inhibition ratings of children at twenty-one months and seven and a half years.

The authors suggested that behavioural withdrawal in animals is related to greater arousal in hypothalamic and limbic brain sites. Therefore, the authors searched for evidence of greater arousal in systems that originated in these areas to explain behavioural inhibition in children. Such systems, they suggested, included

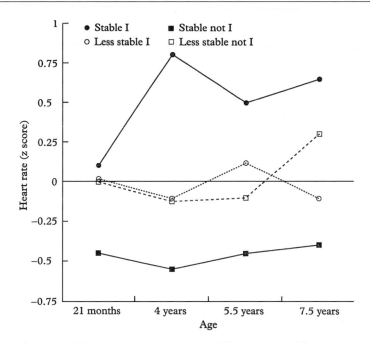

Figure 7.10 Mean heart rate (z score) for children at each of four assessments
Note Children were classified as stable or not stable, and inhibited (I) or unin-
hibited (not I)
Source Kagan et al. (1988)

the sympathetic branch of the autonomic nervous system. To assess sympathetic
reactivity, Kagan et al. (1988) assessed heart rate, and other measures. Children's
heart rates were measured at baseline (non-stressful) states and during cognitive
tasks (moderately stressful) at each of the four testing periods. Individual differences in heart rate were stable from twenty-one months to seven and a half years.
As figure 7.9 shows, children who were consistently inhibited (the stable I group)
tended to have higher heart rates at all four testing sessions. Conversely, consistently uninhibited children (the stable not I group) showed the lowest heart rates.
Correlations between inhibition and heart rate were 0.4 at twenty-one months
and 0.3 at seven and a half years. In addition, more inhibited children tended
to increase their heart rate – by about ten more beats per minute – in response
to a cognitively stressful task. Kagan et al. (1988) suggested that inhibited individuals have a lower threshold for limbic-hypothalamic arousal when faced with
novelty or unexpected change in the environment. They speculated further that
the basis for this altered threshold might be in the central noradrenergic system,
which is associated with sympathetic reactivity. These data appear to be consistent with Gray's (1982) anxiety theory, which associates anxiety with behavioural
inhibition.

Functional brain imaging techniques

Positron emission tomography (PET), single photon emission tomography (SPET), and functional magnetic resonance imaging (fMRI) are functional brain imaging techniques that have been put to use to discover whether there are correlations between personality traits and aspects of brain metabolism.

In both PET and SPET techniques, the subject is injected with or may inhale a radioactive tracer substance that is taken up by the actively metabolising cells of the brain. The amount of the tracer which is taken up by the cells is closely correlated with the amount of metabolism being carried out by these cells. The tracer substance gives off particles as a result of radioactive decay, which may then be registered by an appropriate particle – positron or photon – detector. The subject's head is placed in a scanning detector device, information from which can be used to recreate the pattern of radioactive emission from the subject's brain. In PET scanning the radioactive tracer substance is often a glucose analogue, and the brain scan which results from this technique can offer a picture of the differential metabolism carried out by the various parts of the brain which have been scanned. In SPET scanning the substance used is often exametazime, which is taken up by the brain areas in direct proportion to their blood flow, which is closely yoked to brain metabolic rate. Though brain scanning techniques are sophisticated, the experimental hypotheses are rudimentary, i.e., that some areas of the brain might be more active in certain types of personality than others.

Functional magnetic resonance imaging (fMRI) involves no radioactive compounds and is becoming the most common method to explore the brain's response to cognitive and emotional stimuli. There are different methods of conducting functional magnetic resonance imaging. A common one used in psychological research is called blood oxygen level dependent fMRI. The assumptions in this type of brain imaging are as follows. A cognitive and/or emotional task changes neural activity. This is associated with local changes in neural metabolism that are associated with local changes in brain blood flow. The flow of oxygenated haemoglobin to active areas is in excess of the metabolic demands. Therefore, oxyhaemoglobin is found in excess over deoxyhaemoglobin. These compounds have different magnetic characteristics that can be identified by fMRI and a spatio-temporal map of the brain's response to the task can be produced. That is, researchers can provide an illustration showing the probability that certain brain areas are more or less active during a certain type of mental work. Another type of approach can take this further and show the correlation between activation in certain brain areas during certain types of mental work and characteristics of the person, such as personality traits (Canli et al., 2001; Gray and Braver, 2002). A clear description of the principles behind fMRI is given by Heeger and Ress (2002), and applications in psychology are discussed by D'Esposito et al. (1999).

Haier et al. (1987) performed PET brain scans on eighteen patients with generalised anxiety disorders and nine normal controls. The radioactive tracer used in the experiment was 18F-deoxyglucose. There were significant associations between EPQ extraversion and brain glucose use in various brain areas, mostly in the right hemisphere (specifically, the cingulate gyrus, putamen, caudate nucleus, hippocampal gyrus and parahippocampal gyrus). There were significant associations with neuroticism and glucose use in the pons and inferior temporal areas. These results highlight some clear limitations of studies using brain scanning techniques. The number of brain areas which may be identified is usually very large, and the numbers of subjects in scanning studies tend to be small, because of the cost and labour intensive nature of the procedure. Moreover, the inclusion of patient groups with psychiatric problems is not ideal for the investigation of normal personality.

As an example of a SPET scan study, Ebmeier et al. (1994) examined cerebral blood flow in fifty-one subjects. Personality was assessed using the EPQ. The regions of the brain that were studied are shown in figure 7.9. As may be seen, there were fifteen brain areas in each hemisphere, giving at least thirty variables from the scanning procedure. Ebmeier et al. (1994) reasoned that it is unlikely that so many brain areas act independently, and principal components analysis with rotation found four oblique brain blood flow factors which were designated as 'functional brain systems'; these are shown in figure 7.11. Therefore, each subject was given a score for the blood flow in each brain system and this was correlated with personality variables. Extraversion correlated at 0.46 (P<.001) with tracer uptake and, by inference, brain metabolism, in the brain system that comprised the anterior and posterior cingulate areas (factor 2 in the figure). The results remained significant after correction for multiple testing and age.

The study by Ebmeier et al. (1995) is suggestive of a relationship between extraversion and brain mechanisms for emotion, but it is questionable whether this result is consistent with either the Gray (1987) or Zuckerman (1991) models of extraversion and positive emotion. The cingulum is linked to systems controlling anxiety by Gray (1987), and, indeed, cingulectomy tends to reduce neuroticism without affecting extraversion (Zuckerman, 1991). The cingulate cortex is also involved in cognitive control and attention (Bush et al., 2000). It was also associated with extraversion in Haier et al.'s (1987) and Johnson et al.'s (1999) PET studies, and with behavioural activation in an fMRI study by Gray and Braver (2002) as discussed below. Johnson et al. (1999) concluded, overall, extraverts had lower blood flow than introverts, supporting Eysenck's ideas. This study, combined with others, suggests that frontal cortical regions are active in introverts, while more posterior regions are active in extraverts. Moreover, findings of this study suggest that a circuit involving the frontal lobes, the striatum, and the thalamus plays an integral role in modulating individual differences in extraversion.

fMRI studies attempt to describe the cerebral activation signatures of the major personality traits. Gray and Braver (2002) tested fourteen healthy people on Carver and White's (1994) trait scales for Gray's (1991) behavioural inhibition (BIS) and behavioural activation (BAS) systems. Subjects performed a working-memory task (the n-back task) while their brains were imaged using fMRI procedure. They found

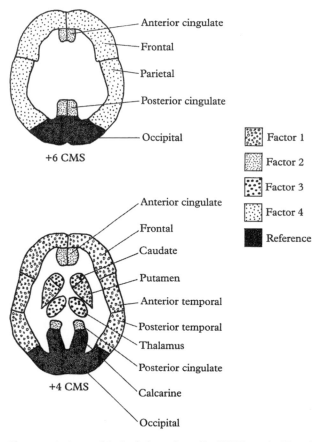

Factor 1
Factor 2
Factor 3
Factor 4
Reference

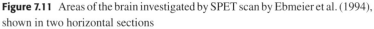

Figure 7.11 Areas of the brain investigated by SPET scan by Ebmeier et al. (1994), shown in two horizontal sections

that individual differences on the BAS were associated with lower activation – in response to performing the working-memory task – in the posterior regions of the anterior cingulate cortex. The results were interpreted in terms of personality being related to cognitive control. In agreement with other research (Lieberman and Rosenthal, 2001), they also found that people with high BAS scores were more accurate on the n-back working-memory task. With the numbers of subjects involved, this study may only be considered indicative. Nevertheless, it adumbrates a hopeful future for unravelling the mechanisms of personality differences by studying brain imaging, cognitive processes and traits, and binding them within a theoretical framework. The authors argue that these results are relevant to theories of extraversion which emphasise the appetitive-approach aspects of extraversion. Another fMRI study of personality traits has argued that emotional processing biases are the neural signature of neuroticism and extraversion (Canli et al., 2001; see Box 7.1).

Box 7.1 Personality and emotion: a functional imaging study

Canli and colleagues (2001) argued that functional imaging studies have revealed the localised brain areas that respond to emotional stimuli. Moreover, they argued that neuroticism and extraversion differences are related to emotional experience. Therefore, they set out to discover whether individual differences in the traits of neuroticism and extraversion moderated the brain responses to emotional stimuli. Fourteen healthy women were asked to pay attention to pictures. Some of the pictures were designed to be linked to negative emotional states, representing crying, anger, guns, spiders and a cemetery. Other pictures were linked to positive emotional states, representing happiness, puppies, ice cream and sunset. Personality traits were tested using the NEO Five Factor Inventory. The authors found that there were strong positive correlations – from 0.79 to 0.86 – between extraversion scores and brain activation to positive emotional stimuli in the amygdala, caudate, middle frontal gyrus, and putamen. There were strong negative correlations between neuroticism scores and brain activation to negative emotional stimuli in the middle frontal gyrus (−0.75) and middle temporal gyrus (−0.79). This is a small study, and may be considered a pilot examination of an interesting idea, that processing biases are the neural signature of neuroticism and extraversion. The results are in accordance with the importance of negative emotions to the concept of neuroticism, and the part that positive emotions play in the theory of extraversion.

Personality and arousal: towards an integrated theory?

The arousal concept

Thus far, we have looked at somewhat isolated examples of studies of the psychophysiology of personality. We turn now to the issue of whether the empirical data supports a broader theoretical picture of the kind advanced by Eysenck's (1967) arousal theory. Even if this particular theory is incorrect, arousal is of special interest to personality psychologists because this concept appears to provide the basis for integrating individual differences in physiology, subjective experience and behaviour (Anderson, 1990; Johnson et al., 1999). According to Duffy (1962), 'arousal' refers to a continuum of states of activity of the organism, ranging from deep sleep to highly aroused states of excitement or agitation. The primary means for tracking the individual's position on the arousal continuum are psychophysiological, though researchers also use the subjective measures of alertness and wakefulness discussed in chapter 4. Thus, highly aroused subjects should show a characteristic electroencephalogram, with a predominance of high-frequency beta waves, and a lack of lower frequency alpha and theta waves. They should also show symptoms of autonomic nervous system activation, such as increased heart rate and skin conductance, as the organism prepares for 'fight or flight'.

Arousal is the central explanatory construct in Eysenck's theory but many researchers have identified problems with traditional arousal theory (e.g., Duffy, 1962), which may limit its usefulness for personality theory. Matthews and Amelang (1993) described the problems of arousal theory as empirical, psychometric, methodological and conceptual. Empirically, predictions from arousal theory in both psychophysiological and behavioural domains often fail to be confirmed (Matthews, 1985; Neiss, 1988; Matthews et al., 2000). Such predictive failures do not necessarily imply that the underlying theory is incorrect. For example, if arousal is not measured reliably, the theory will be difficult to test successfully. As discussed in chapter 1, it is important that individual difference measures are internally consistent – that alternative measures of a construct correlate with one another. However, the arousal construct fails this psychometric test; very often alternate arousal measures such as heart rate and skin conductance fail to inter-correlate (e.g., Fahrenberg et al., 1983). One explanation for psychometric problems may be methodological, that the specific measures taken are not valid indicators of cortical arousal. Lacey (1967) introduced the important notion of response specificity: there are individual differences in the sensitivity of peripheral systems to arousal level. One person might show increased heart rate but not increased skin conductance when aroused, and another the reverse. Another methodological problem, particularly for ans measures, is that the measure is sensitive to other influences in addition to arousal, which may not be well controlled, such as motor activity in the case of heart rate. Thus, the proponent of arousal theory may argue that arousal is a satisfactory concept; it is just difficult to measure validly. A newer approach to arousal is to construe it as brain activation in functional brain imaging studies. One such study claims to have supported Eysenck's arousal hypothesis of introversion–extraversion (Johnson et al., 1999).

Some researchers have also criticised arousal on conceptual grounds, however. Arousal appears to be a multidimensional rather than a unidimensional construct (Thayer, 1989). There are various neurotransmitter systems that originate in the brainstem and ascend to the cerebral cortex and other forebrain structures, which may differ in their functional significance (Panicker and Parasuraman, 1998). Gray (1982) suggests that the operation of the BIS varies according to whether it receives arousing inputs from cholinergic, noradrenergic or serotonergic pathways. Table 7.1 lists some of these different systems and how their 'arousal' affects psychological functioning in animals (Panicker and Parasuraman, 1998; Robbins, 1998). Even these systems may be fractionated; Robbins (1998) differentiates multiple noradrenergic and dopaminergic pathways that control different aspects of behaviour. Thus, as Robbins (1998) concludes, unitary conceptions of arousal may have outlived their usefulness, and, therefore, we should try to link personality traits to these more specific brain systems. Nevertheless, arousal theories continue to inspire psychophysiological research, and there are ample data that may allow

Table 7.1 *A highly simplified description of some different systems for 'arousal'*

Neurotransmitter system	Function
Noradrenaline: Ascending pathways from locus coeruleus to cortex	Maintenance of attention under stress
Dopamine: Mesolimbic and mesostriatal pathways	Activation of cognitive and motor output
Acetylcholine: Pathways from basal forebrain to cortex and other structures	Enhancement of stimulus processing at the cortical level
Serotonin: Pathways from raphé nuclei to cortex and other structures	Behavioural inhibition and cortical de-arousal

Note Based on Robbins, 1998; Panicker and Parasuraman, 1998

us to decide whether or not they are empirically useful, in linking personality and brain function.

Predicting relationships between personality and arousal

Eysenck's (1967) personality theory predicts that extraverts should be less aroused than introverts, and high-neuroticism scorers should be more aroused than emotionally stable individuals. However, two riders must be attached to these predictions. The first, which is particularly important in studies of extraversion, derives from an extra hypothesis which has assumed more importance in Eysenck's (e.g., 1981, 1997) later work. This is the hypothesis of transmarginal inhibition or TMI, the idea that under high levels of stimulation the cns becomes paradoxically de-aroused, as a protection against over-stimulation. Because of their greater arousability, introverts show TMI and de-arousal at lower levels of stimulation than extraverts. Hence, introverts should only be more aroused than extraverts under moderate levels of stimulation; extraverts may actually be more aroused than introverts if levels of stimulation are high enough to generate TMI. The second qualification is that neuroticism will only consistently relate to arousal under conditions of emotional stress; otherwise the limbic system remains inactive regardless of personality. Hence, it may be insufficient to simply correlate arousal with personality measures; situational factors which may have a moderating effect should be controlled or manipulated also. Next, we briefly review the empirical evidence on the relationship between psychophysiological arousal indices and extraversion, neuroticism and other traits.

Studies of extraversion, the EEG and evoked potentials

Eysenck's (1967) arousal theory predicts that extraverts should show the patterning of the EEG associated with lower arousal compared to introverts. Many studies have tested this basic prediction, often by measuring alpha power only. Reviews by Gale (e.g., 1981; Gale and Edwards, 1986) and O'Gorman (1984) provide 'head-counts' of studies with respect to support for Eysenck's (1967) hypothesis. O'Gorman (1984) classified nineteen out of thirty-nine studies as supporting the prediction that extraverts are less aroused, ten studies showed no significant difference between extraverts and introverts, and ten studies showed results in the opposite direction to prediction. Recent, methodologically sound studies continue to provide conflicting evidence. For example, Hagemann et al. (1999) failed to find any association between extraversion and the EEG, whereas Gale et al. (2001) found that extraverts showed higher levels of alpha (i.e., lower arousal) in frontal, temporal and occipital sites. The latter authors suggest use of a meaningful, engaging task – in their case, rating photographs for emotional content – is needed to find consistent finding. To confuse the issue further, a recent Russian study (Knyazev, Slobodskaya and Wilson, 2002) obtained a significant *negative* correlation between extraversion and EEG alpha, although extraversion was positively associated with theta power, which might suggest lower arousal in extraverts. Hence, although there are some positive findings (e.g., Gale et al., 1969, 2001), EEG work provides only limited evidence in favour of a negative association between extraversion and arousal.

Both O'Gorman and Gale have drawn attention to the variable methodological quality of the studies. Possibly it is the poorly conducted studies which are responsible for the inconsistency. In fact, both reviewers agree that even well-conducted studies show inconsistency of outcome, although O'Gorman (1984) did show that studies using psychometrically adequate measures of extraversion such as the EPI or EPQ seemed more likely to support Eysenck's hypothesis. Matthews and Amelang (1993) point out that the typical sample size of EEG studies, comprising perhaps thirty or forty subjects, simply lacks the statistical power reliably to detect small or moderate relationships between extraversion and the EEG. These authors' study of 180 subjects showed that EPI extraversion was significantly correlated, but at only 0.16, with power of low frequency activity (delta/theta) as the Eysenck hypothesis predicts (but not with alpha or beta).

A further reason for the inconsistency of the EEG data is that the extraversion–arousal relationship may vary with the amount of stimulation provided by the environment. Gale (1981; Gale et al., 2001) suggests that if the environment is unstimulating extraverts will find it sufficiently unpleasant to take steps to arouse themselves, distorting the experimental results. Similarly, in stimulating environments introverts will be susceptible to TMI, so that extraverts may tend to show greater arousal. Gale's (1981) review of the data did find some indication that extraverts were more likely to be less aroused in moderately stimulating settings, although O'Gorman (1984) disagrees with this interpretation of the evidence. Studies which have set out to test Gale's (1981) hypothesis directly have failed to support it (O'Gorman and Malisse, 1984; Matthews and Amelang, 1993).

Stelmack (1981, 1990; Stelmack and Houlihan, 1995) provides selective reviews of studies of extraversion and evoked potentials. As with EEG studies,

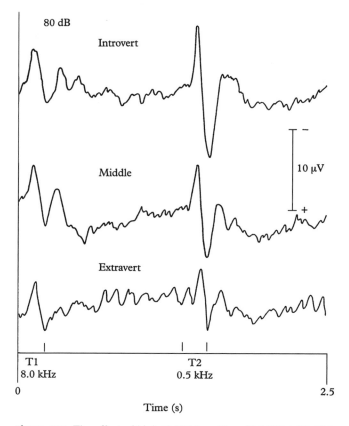

Figure 7.12 The effect of high (8 KHz) and low (0.5 KHz) 80 dB tones on the auditory evoked potentials of introvert, middle and extravert subjects
Source Stelmack, 1990

results are inconsistent. However, Stelmack's (1990) own EP work shows some consistent effects: greater amplitude of response in introverts during the first 100–200 ms after stimulus presentation, as shown in figure 7.12. In this study, introverts show a waveform of greater amplitude than extraverts following a low-frequency tone of 0.5 KHz, but there is no personality effect for the potential evoked by a high-frequency tone of 8.0 KHz. Stelmack (1990) interprets this greater reactivity of introverts as consistent with the Eysenck theory. It seems to correspond to psychophysical data suggesting greater sensory sensitivity in introverts (e.g., Shigehisa and Symons, 1973). Extraversion also appears to predict longer latency of brainstem evoked responses (BERs) developing within 10 ms of presentation of an auditory click stimulus, indicating reduced sensory reactivity in extraverts (Bullock and Gilliland, 1993). It appears to be Wave V of the BER that relates most consistently to extraversion (Swickert and Gilliland, 1998; Cox-Fuenzalida, Gilliland and Swickert, 2001). Wave V may be generated by the inferior colliculus, where the auditory pathway may converge on the ascending reticular activating system, so these findings are consistent with arousal theory.

Effects of extraversion on later components of the evoked potential have also been reported. Such components are believed to be associated with more 'cognitive' processes such as updating working memory. We have already described the Stenberg (1994) study, showing larger amplitude P3 waves in extraverts, but other studies (e.g., Daruna, Karrer and Rosen, 1985; Stelmack and Houlihan, 1995) have demonstrated larger amplitude P3 waves in introverts. The effect appears to vary with subject gender and exposure to the task (Polich and Martin, 1992), and failures to replicate have also been reported (see Stelmack and Houlihan, 1995). The effect may, as Stenberg (1994) suggests, vary with task stimuli and demands. Daruna et al. (1985) showed that the magnitude of the effect varied with an attentional manipulation, suggesting that it may be difficult to discriminate arousal- and attention-related effects in this EP paradigm. There is also evidence for TMI effects: Brocke, Tasche and Beauducel (1997) found that extraverts showed lower amplitude P3s than introverts in quiet, but higher amplitude in white noise.

Extraversion and the autonomic nervous system

As in the case of electrocortical studies, ans research has looked for simple correlations between extraversion and tonic arousal, interactive effects of extraversion and level of stimulation, and extraversion effects on the response evoked by specific stimuli. We shall focus in this section on the most popular research method, studies of electrodermal activity. Other response systems, such as the cardiovascular and pupillary systems have also been investigated (see Stelmack, 1981, 1990). Tonic arousal may be reflected in both increased skin conductance level (SCL) or in a higher rate of 'spontaneous' skin conductance responses (SCRs). Reviews of extraversion effects on these measures (Stelmack, 1990, 1997; Zuckerman, 1991) have tended to conclude that they do not consistently support the arousal hypothesis. Rather more promising results have been obtained in studies manipulating the level of stimulation experimentally. Fowles, Roberts and Nagel (1977) measured SCL during presentation of tones following performance of a learning task. Extraverts tended to show greater arousal than introverts in the most stimulating conditions, particularly when tones were of high intensity and the task performed was difficult. Smith (1983) reports comparable effects using the stimulant drug caffeine as a moderator variable. Extraverts show the expected effect of increased SCL following caffeine ingestion, whereas introverts fail to show tonic SCL increase, possibly because caffeine induces TMI in introverts.

Studies of event-related SCRs, reviewed by Stelmack (1990, 1997), show that extraversion effects depend on the level of stimulation. Extraversion effects are typically non-significant with low-intensity (<60 dB) auditory stimuli, but introverts show larger SCRs with moderate-intensity stimuli (75–90 dB). With higher-intensity auditory stimuli, extraverts may actually show greater SCRs than introverts, consistent with the TMI hypothesis. Caffeine has a similar moderating effect to noise intensity, with introverts showing greater SCRs when given a

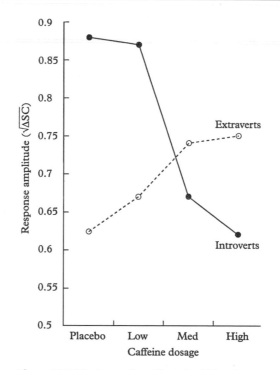

Figure 7.13 The interactive effect of caffeine dosage and extraversion on initial electrodermal response amplitude
Source Smith et al., 1983

placebo, and extraverts showing increasing SCR magnitude with increasing caffeine dosage, as shown in figure 7.13 (Smith et al., 1983). Arousal is said to block habituation of the SCR on repeated presentation of stimuli, so that introverts should habituate more rapidly than extraverts. Habituation studies have provided mixed results, although failures to find slower habituation in introverts may reflect methodological factors such as the method for assessment of habituation rate (Smith et al., 1990).

Neuroticism and arousal

The majority of studies of neuroticism present a fairly consistent picture in failing to show associations between this personality trait and electrocortical and ans arousal (e.g., Hagemann et al., 1999), although there are occasional findings suggestive of higher arousal in high scorers on the neuroticism scale (see Eysenck, 1994b). Studies of the EEG fail to show any reliable correlation between neuroticism and arousal, although neuroticism may moderate extraversion effects (Gale, 1981), and some authors discern a trend towards higher arousal in high N persons (Gale et al., 2001). There have been sporadic reports of associations between neuroticism and EP measures (e.g., Stelmack et al., 1993), but it is hard to discern any clear pattern to such findings. The most comprehensive review of electrodermal activity studies (Naveteur and Freixa i Baqué, 1987) provides little evidence for either neuroticism/trait anxiety or state anxiety relating consistently to any tonic SCL, rate of spontaneous SCRs, or amplitude and rate of habituation of event-related SCRs. Their own work (Naveteur and Freixa i Baqué, 1992) actually shows greater electrodermal activity in low trait anxious subjects, particularly under stressful conditions. Studies of neuroticism, trait anxiety and cardiac activity show a mixture of positive and negative outcomes (e.g., Huwe, Hennig and Netter, 1998; Dishman et al., 2000). Wilken et al. (2000) suggest that trait anxious subjects may show paradoxically reduced electrodermal response to stressors due to TMI, because they are already highly aroused, but this hypothesis has not been substantiated as convincingly as in the case of extraversion–introversion.

The failure of neuroticism studies to support the Eysenck (1967) arousal hypothesis is often attributed to the laboratory environment being insufficiently emotionally stressful to activate the viscero-cortical circuit. Fahrenberg (1991) discusses a series of fairly large-scale studies run by himself and his colleagues which manipulated stress in various ways, and assessed a variety of EEG and ans measures. These studies failed to confirm the prediction that subjects with high neuroticism levels would show greater physiological activation during stress. One concern about this work is that neuroticism was also only slightly correlated with self-report tension, a finding which contrasts with some of the mood studies reviewed in chapter 4. More work is needed to determine the exact circumstances under which neurotic individuals are particularly stress prone before the arousal hypothesis can be conclusively dismissed.

Psychoticism, impulsivity and sensation seeking

Individual differences in arousal have also been investigated in the context of the cluster of traits associated with Zuckerman's (1991) P-ImpUSS dimension. Studies by O'Gorman and Lloyd (1987) and Matthews and Amelang (1993) showed a positive association between narrow impulsivity and power in the alpha band, a result suggestive of lower arousal in impulsive individuals. However, Matthews and Amelang also found a significant correlation of -0.16 between psychoticism and alpha, implying that different P-ImpUSS traits may be differently related to electrocortical arousal. Sensation seeking itself does not seem to be reliably related to EEG measures, but high sensation seekers show increasingly large amplitude N1–P1 EPs to increasingly intense stimuli, a pattern known as augmenting (Zuckerman, 1991). Low sensation seekers show the opposite, reducing pattern: amplitude tends to decline with increasing stimulus intensity. Impulsiveness may also relate to EPs, although different impulsiveness dimensions appear to correlate with different electrocortical measures (Barrett, 1987). Different paradigms have shown both positive and negative associations between sensation seeking and P3 amplitudes (Wang and Wang, 2001).

Studies relating P-ImpUSS dimensions to electrodermal measures mostly fail to provide strong results, although there are some exceptions. There is a tendency for sensation seeking to be associated with lower tonic skin conductance level, although findings are not very consistent (Gatzke-Kopp et al., 2002). The Smith et al. (1989) experiment described previously shows greater augmenting of electrodermal response with increasing stimulus intensity in high sensation seekers, a result broadly comparable with EP studies. A study by Zahn et al. (1994) showed an interesting dissociation between extraversion and impulsivity. During a Reaction Time (RT) task, amplitude of spontaneous SCRs were positively related to impulsivity but negatively related to extraversion. Zuckerman (1991) reviews studies showing a tendency for high sensation seekers to show stronger SCRs to the initial stimulus in a sequence, which may be a personality difference in reaction to novelty.

Overall, it is hard to argue that there is any general, strong relationship between P-ImpUSS and arousal, although there may be associations between narrower traits related to P-ImpUSS and arousal. However, the augmenting response to strong stimulation evident in both EP and electrodermal studies may be a more important feature of this aspect of personality. Cortical excitability in response to high intensity stimuli is an important component of Zuckerman's (1991) psychobiological model of P-ImpUSS (see figure 7.5). At a behavioural level, the augmentation response may provide the disinhibited individual with the capacity to tolerate strong stimulation and stress. However, if the disinhibited person actually seeks out intense stimuli, there is a risk of maladaptive behaviours ensuing. The more antisocial forms of disinhibition may be associated with arousal seeking through aggressive or criminal behaviour such as football hooliganism or 'joy-riding' in stolen cars.

Traits and arousal: conclusions

Despite the energy with which investigators have attempted to demonstrate relationships between personality and arousal, results of the studies reviewed are patchy, at best. Matthews and Gilliland (1999) drew four conclusions concerning arousal theory from their literature review. First, many studies have failed to establish or replicate the personality–arousal relationships predicted by the Eysenck (1967) theory, especially when tonic arousal indices are used. At the same time, there is a modest trend towards extraverts being lower in cortical arousal (e.g., Gale et al., 2001; Stelmack, 1997). It is possible that the indifferent replicability of findings represents methodological weaknesses in some studies (Gale et al., 2001), and the insufficient power to detect small associations typical of most studies. Second, studies of certain phasic arousal responses provide more convincing support for Eysenck (1967), although findings are still somewhat inconsistent. One of the more consistent findings is in increased amplitude of early components (e.g., N1) of the EP in introverts, although careful attention to experimental parameters is needed (Doucet and Stelmack, 2000). Introverts also typically show greater amplitude phasic SCRs to certain kinds of moderate intensity stimuli. Recent work is also going beyond traditional arousal measures to identify further psychophysiological correlates. For example, Stelmack and Pivik (1996) showed that extraversion relates to decreased spinal motoneural recovery, which may relate to both dopaminergic activity and to behavioural evidence for higher motor responsiveness in extraverts (Doucet and Stelmack, 2000).

Third, in electrodermal activity (EDA) studies, there are fairly consistent moderating effects of level of stimulation and arousal on the extraversion–arousal association, consistent with the TMI hypothesis (Smith, 1983). At high levels of stimulation, extraverts are more responsive than introverts. However, although these findings are consistent with the Eysenck (1981) theory, the problem is that the level of stimulation needed to induce TMI is never specified a priori in these studies, so that hypothesis-testing is done on a post hoc basis, which is unsatisfactory. For example, in studies in which extraverts are less aroused than introverts irrespective of level of stimulation, the researcher can always claim that the level of stimulation was insufficient to induce TMI. However, the empirical findings provide a basis for establishing psychophysiological findings which generalise across response systems, and for addressing anomalies. For example, it is unclear why extraversion and caffeine interact in their influence on electrodermal activity (Smith, 1983), but appear to have additive effects on BERs (Bullock and Gilliland, 1993).

Fourth, although N appears to play some role in psychophysiological response, it does not conform in any simple way to that predicted by arousal theory (e.g., Fahrenberg, 1987). Again, it is possible that existing research has so far failed to identify the key moderating variables that must be controlled to obtain consistent results. It is possible too, that, as with extraversion, inhibitory processes may contribute to variance that is uncontrolled in many studies of neuroticism and trait anxiety (Wilken et al., 2000).

Personality and sensitivity to motivational stimuli

Increasingly, Gray's (e.g., 1991) personality theory is seen as a worthy competitor to Eysenck's (1981, 1997). As described previously, it states that high Anx individuals (neurotic introverts) are especially sensitive to punishment signals, mediated by the BIS, whereas high Imp individuals (stable extraverts) are sensitive to reward signals, mediated by the BAS. It has also received impetus from behavioural studies that show interactive effects of personality and motivational variables. For example, there is a general tendency for extraverts to learn better in rewarding conditions, whereas introverts learn better in punishing situations (Pickering, Diaz and Gray, 1995).

Gray's theory, often described as Reinforcement Sensitivity Theory (RST) (Corr, 2002) may be testable through psychophysiological research. It is convenient to divide research here into two waves. The first wave refers to basic tests of personality effects on response to motivational signals. We expect to see greater autonomic and central nervous system response to punishment cues in high Anx individuals, for example. In fact, these studies provide rather mixed results, some of which are clearly inconsistent with the original Gray theory (Matthews and Gilliland, 1999; Corr, 2001). There are also difficulties in deciding how to measure the Imp construct (see Box 7.2). Thus, a second wave of research is attempting to derive and test more subtle hypotheses that take into account interactions between BIS and BAS (Corr, 2002). This recent research also aims to accommodate recent theoretical revisions to Gray's theory (Gray and McNaughton, 2000).

Box 7.2 Impulsivity: a problem variable for psychophysiology

The impulsivity trait is a major focus for Gray's personality theory. It is said to correlate most strongly with extraversion, with some admixture of neuroticism and psychoticism. However, the best measure of the construct for hypothesis-testing has long been a source of contention. Some researchers contrast neurotic extraverts with stable introverts, whereas others use one of the many published scales for impulsivity, which often include various subscales, and may measure different constructs. Still others use one of several scales that have appeared in recent years that purport to measure Gray's BIS and BAS (e.g., Zelenski and Larsen, 1999). The lack of a standard, validated measure of Gray's impulsivity construct may contribute to the inconsistency of the psychophysiological data (Corr, 2001).

A recent study (Whiteside and Lynam, 2001) suggests the source of the difficulty: impulsivity may not be a homogeneous construct at all. The authors factor-analysed 17 of the most widely used impulsivity scales and subscales, along with selected NEO-PI-R facet scales, including four directly related to impulsivity, in a sample of over 400 young adults. They extracted four orthogonal 'impulsivity' factors, briefly described below, together with a separate extraversion factor:

Factor 1 (Lack of Premeditation). Defined by several standard impulsivity scales, dysfunctional impulsivity, and lack of deliberation (NEO-PI-R facet). Typical item: 'I usually think carefully before doing anything' (negative loading item).

Factor 2 (Urgency). Defined mainly by NEO-PI-R neuroticism facets, including impulsiveness. Typical item: 'When I am upset I often act without thinking.'

Factor 3 (Lack of Perseverance). Defined mainly by NEO-PI-R facets relating to Conscientiousness; e.g., (lack of) self-discipline. Typical item: 'I tend to give up easily.'

Factor 4 (Sensation seeking). Defined by scales for sensation seeking and venturesomeness, including NEO-PI-R excitement seeking. Typical item: 'I quite enjoy taking risks.'

Factor 5 (Extraversion). Defined by all six NEO-PI-R extraversion facets, e.g., warmth, gregariousness, positive emotions.

They conclude that each factor represents a distinct aspect of personality, and it is erroneous to consolidate them under the single term 'impulsivity'. Beyond the demonstration that verbal labels may be misleading, the study also raises some searching questions for Gray's RST. Which impulsivity construct is to be linked to the BAS? How does the theory accommodate the factorial independence of extraversion from the four 'impulsivity' factors? How can we differentiate biologically based impulsivity from those components that seem primarily cognitive (failure to plan and premeditate)? We offer no answers here, but note that successful psychophysiological tests of RST will require a clearer mapping of traits onto biological systems.

Initial studies

Psychophysiological studies have tested RST using both central and autonomic system indices. Although some studies have used autonomic indices, such as changes in heart rate (e.g., De Pascalis, Fiore and Sparita, 1996; De Pascalis and Speranza, 2000), we focus here on EEG studies. Of course, we might wonder whether EEG activity actually provides good measures of the activity of the BIS and BAS, as opposed to other brain systems. Remember that, according to Gray (1991), both the BIS and BAS tend to activate the separate arousal mechanism. That is, any kind of motivational stimulus tends to produce arousal, and so we can use arousal responses to test the theory. Thus, in an EEG study, we expect to see high levels of electrical activity (e.g., beta waves, increased amplitude evoked potentials) in two subject groups: high impulsives presented with reward signals, and high anxiety individuals presented with punishment signals. In fact, it is the data obtained from studies of reward that are most important in testing Gray's theory against Eysenck's. So, we expect that both high Imp/reward and high Anx/punishment groups will show increased EEG arousal. Eysenck's (1967) theory makes the same prediction for the high Anx/punishment group. Because high Anx is strongly correlated with high N, these subjects will, according to the theory, respond to punishment signals with increased activity in the cortico-limbic circuit that supports N, and hence with higher cortical arousal. On the other hand, the Eysenck theory predicts that low impulsives (similar to introverts) ought to show greater response than high impulsives (similar to extraverts) to both reward and punishment signals. Thus, the behaviour of high impulsives presented with reward signals should differentiate the two theories: compared with low impulsives, do they show relatively low EEG arousal (Eysenck prediction) or high arousal (Gray prediction)?

Several studies have used motivational manipulations. Stenberg (1992) observed the effects on the EEG of manipulations of positive and negative imagery. Consistent with both theories, high Anx subjects showed higher levels of beta waves in the negative imagery condition. However, high Imp subjects did not show any enhancement of response to positive imagery, and, overall, Stenberg concluded that, consistent with Eysenck (1967), Imp was related more to low arousal in general, than response to imagery. De Pascalis and Speranza (2000) used positive, negative and neutral words as cues in a task requiring spatial attention. Similar to Stenberg (1994), extraverts showed greater P3 amplitude, but there was no effect of whether positive or negative words were presented, as RST would predict. Neuroticism failed to influence P3 at all.

Bartussek (e.g., Bartussek et al., 1996) has reported a series of studies of evoked potentials, that set out to test RST using motivational manipulations such as presenting positive and negative words, and signals indicating gains and losses during a gambling task. For example, Bartussek et al. (1996, study 1) presented subjects with positive, neutral and negative adjectives. They were required either to count the number of letters in the word, or to rate its subjective emotional content. The key prediction from RST is that high impulsives should show enhanced response when rating the emotional content of positive words, especially from frontal electrode sites that pick up the activity of frontal cortex. Areas of frontal cortex are implicated in emotional response. In fact, in this study, as in others conducted by Bartussek, the prediction was not confirmed. Instead, extraverts showed a greater frontal P3 response to both positive and negative stimuli, relative to neutral stimuli, whereas introverts' response seemed indifferent to emotional content. Other complex interactions between personality, electrode sight and stimulus type were also inconsistent with RST. Simplifying somewhat, Bartussek et al. (1996, p. 312) arrive at the following general conclusion:

> However, Gray's theory could not be confirmed in either of the experiments. No differential susceptibility of introverts to negative stimuli, and of extraverts to positive stimuli could be found. In both experiments, it seemed rather that extraverts are more susceptible to *all* emotional stimuli regardless of the emotional valence.

Revisions to RST

It is generally accepted that psychophysiological studies provide only weak support to Gray's (1991) personality theory, as originally formulated (e.g., Corr, 2001; Matthews and Gilliland, 1999, 2001). Studies of learning and conditioning force a similar conclusion. One of the most thorough series of studies was conducted by Corr, Pickering and Gray (1995). These studies looked at both associative learning (stimulus–stimulus conditioning) and instrumental learning (stimulus–response conditioning), and produced some unexpected results. For example, in one study, subjects were rewarded or punished, by gaining or losing small sums of money during learning associations between stimuli. RST predicts that impulsives (and, hence, extraverts) should show faster conditioning when rewarded for correct responses. In fact, extraversion was unrelated to conditioning in rewarding conditions, but introverts learnt faster when punished for mistakes, although, according to RST, it should be N rather than E that controls aversive learning. Other studies from Corr's (2001, 2002) laboratory have also shown associations between E/impulsivity and response to punishment stimuli, and associations between N/trait anxiety and response to reward stimuli, i.e., the 'wrong' personality trait controls response, with respect to RST. Interactive effects of Imp and Anx on learning have also been reported (Zinbarg and Mohlmann, 1998), although these two traits are supposed to relate to independent systems (i.e., BAS and BIS).

In response to such difficulties, Corr (2001, 2002) has proposed a revised version of RST, that he describes as a 'joint-systems' hypothesis. He refers to the original RST as a 'separate-systems' hypothesis: that is, Anx controls response to punishment stimuli irrespective of the person's level of impulsivity, and Imp controls response to reward irrespective of anxiety. The new formulation supposes that the BIS and BAS may interact in their effects. Corr (2002) sets out some conditions under which the two systems do, or do not, interact. The revised theory also accommodates changes to the animal model made by Gray and McNaughton (2000). For example, although BIS and BAS were originally said to be sensitive to motivational *signals* only (i.e., conditioned stimuli), both signals and primary reinforcers (i.e., unconditioned stimuli) are now claimed to activate these systems. The theory also places more emphasis on the fight–flight system as the primary mediator of aversive stimuli, with the BIS activated mainly during approach–avoidance conflict. The details of the theory are beyond the scope of this chapter, but we will outline some circumstances under which interaction is said to take place, giving rise to personality effects not predicted by RST.

According to Corr (2002), the joint-systems hypothesis applies when stimuli are relatively weak (as is often the case in laboratory experiments). In this case, Anx may impair BAS functioning, as well as having its main, facilitative effect on the BIS. Similarly, Imp may antagonise the BIS, as well as facilitating the BAS. This hypothesis can explain Corr et al.'s (1995) findings with associative learning, in which punishments (loss of small sums of money) were minor. The joint-systems hypothesis supposes that high Imp antagonises the BIS response to these minor losses. Hence, introverts (low Imp) show better aversive conditioning than extraverts (high Imp), even though Imp is primarily linked to the BAS.

Corr (2002) presents a psychophysiological study that supports the joint-subsystems hypothesis. In this study, participants viewed slides including emotional material (e.g., mutilated bodies and pleasant outdoor scenes). Periodically, 50 ms bursts of loud white noise (100 db (A)) were presented, which elicited a startle response, including an eyeblink. Its intensity was measured by electromyographic (EMG) recording that picked up the muscular response in the muscle that produces the eyeblink. In general, positive emotion attenuates the response, whereas negative emotion increases response magnitude. Corr et al. showed that Imp and Anx moderated the size of the EMG response to slides of differing emotional content, but effects were more complex than those predicted by the original, separate-systems version of RST. For negative slides, the strongest response was seen in the high Anx/low Imp group, and the weakest response in the low Anx/high

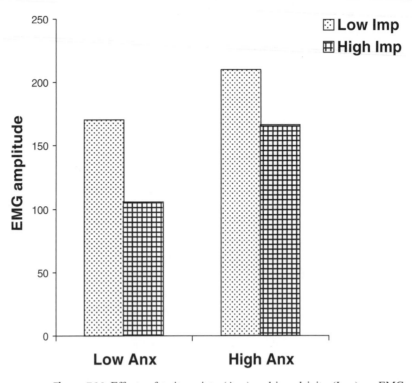

Figure 7.14 Effects of trait anxiety (Anx) and impulsivity (Imp) on EMG eye
blink response
Source Corr (2002)

Imp group (see figure 7.14). Here, response strength should index BIS activity. The
effect of Anx may be attributed to its facilitative effects on BIS, but, in addition,
it seems that high Imp antagonises the BIS, reducing response to the negative
stimulus. For positive slides, the revised theory predicted that response should be
greatest in subjects high in Imp (facilitation of BAS), but low in Anx (low antagonism of BAS). This prediction was not confirmed: response was greatest in the
low Imp/low Anx group. Corr et al. suggest that the aversive nature of the startle
paradigm may interfere with response to positive stimuli.

Reinforcement sensitivity theory: conclusions

There is little doubt that traits influence psychophysiological response to both
motivational signals (e.g., a negative feedback message) and primary reinforcers
(e.g., a loud noise burst). Such observations have stimulated interest in Gray's
RST as an explanation for personality effects. At the same time, studies have often
failed to support predictions from RST (Matthews and Gilliland, 1999, 2001). In
particular, high impulsives (and extraverts) do not show any *generalised* sensitivity
to reward signals, although they may do in some circumstances. Corr's (2001, 2002)

revision of RST provides an interesting attempt to deal with some of the empirical difficulties, and provides a rationale for the interactive effects of Imp and Anx often observed in studies. It is premature to state how successful this revision will be. However, we can see a general parallel with arousal theory. That theory also evolved as a result of conflicting results, to include the idea of TMI as a process that might lead to paradoxical elevation of arousal in extraverts. On the positive side, this modification provided a better fit to the data, but it also introduced greater complexity, and greater scope for post hoc rationalisation of results, through arbitrary decisions on whether TMI was or was not operative in any particular study. Similarly, Corr's (2001) notion of motivational systems sometimes interacting, and sometimes operating independently, explains some of the data, but it may also give the researcher too much latitude in fitting data to theory post hoc. Nevertheless, it remains a novel approach that will generate further experimental studies.

Psychophysiology: where next?

The tension we have explored in this chapter is that between the elegant conceptual models proposed by Eysenck, Gray and others, and the messy reality of empirical psychophysiological research. Three key issues emerge: obtaining replicable results, linking results to neuroscience theories, and linking results to broader personality theories that do not rely exclusively on biological explanations.

The first theme of this field of research has been a protracted struggle to find experimental paradigms which provide consistent results. However, there are indeed some paradigms that give tolerably consistent results, using a variety of measures including the brainstem auditory evoked potential (Cox-Fuenzalida et al., 2001), some standard evoked potential components (Stelmack and Houlihan, 1995) and phasic electrodermal response (Smith, 1983). In each case, careful attention to methods and environmental factors is important for replicability, as discussed in the early sections of this chapter. Often, personality effects are moderated by factors such as level of stimulation or task demands, consistent with the interactionist perspective discussed in chapter 2. Thus, although progress often seems slow, several decades of research have isolated some consistent associations between personality and brain function. New brain-imaging techniques may well bring further advances, although advanced technology is no panacea for the general methodological and conceptual difficulties of the field.

A second theme is that none of the leading theories receive more than limited support from psychophysiological theories. Several reviewers (e.g. Matthews and Gilliland, 1999; Stelmack, 1997) have concurred in finding some support for Eysenck's (1967, 1981, 1997) arousal theory, especially when level of stimulation is controlled. At the same time, continuing failures to replicate findings in many paradigms and the small magnitude of associations between personality and psychophysiological variables remains a source of concern (Matthews and Gilliland, 1999). Tests of Eysenck's (1967) theory of neuroticism have been less successful.

Table 7.2 *Two types of correlate of extraversion*

'Cortico-reticular' extraversion	'Dopaminergic' extraversion
Low cortical arousability	Decreased motoneuronal excitability
Low autonomic arousability	Conditioning to reward
Insensitivity to TMI	Faster movement time
Poor eyelid conditioning	Multiple channel detection
High sensory threshold	Subjective energy

There is a striking disjunction between the patchy and inconsistent findings from psychophysiological paradigms, and the very robust correlates of N found in studies of mood (see chapter 4) and stress (see chapter 9). It is tempting to conclude that an important component of N is cognitive, i.e., the high N person's negative beliefs and ineffective coping strategies produce stress outcomes (perhaps including psychophysiological response, sometimes). Matthews and Amelang (1993) suggest that, although the psychophysiology of personality is a potentially rewarding area of study, it may be unwise to make individual differences in arousal the central explanatory construct in personality theory. It is also troubling that contemporary neuroscience is increasingly rejecting arousal theory in favour of a more differentiated view of multiple activating systems (e.g., Robbins, 1998).

Gray's (1991; Gray and McNaughton, 2000) RST highlights the role of motivational variables in moderating the expression of personality. Empirically, the major traits do indeed interact with motivational factors, but it is unclear whether RST provides the best explanation for these findings. As Eysenck and Eysenck (1985) pointed out, motivational manipulations often induce arousal changes, which may be the key factor in personality studies. The continuing evolution of the theory, involving some major changes to its basic assumptions, also makes it hard to evaluate its account of the evidence. At an empirical level, researchers have yet to find a really consistent psychophysiological paradigm for demonstrating effects consistent with the theory (Matthews and Gilliland, 1999), although the electromyographic startle response may be promising (Corr, 2002). It is probably safest to treat RST as a work-in-progress, and await further studies that will show whether its latest version is usefully predictive of personality effects (cf., Corr, 2002).

Matthews and Gilliland (1999) concluded that extraversion seems to relate to at least two different sets of psychophysiological and behavioural correlates, as illustrated in table 7.2. One set of correlates is equivalent to Eysenck's 'cortico-reticular' extraversion, whereas a second set of correlates, 'dopaminergic' extraversion, bears some resemblance to Gray's Behavioural Activation System. These differing aspects of extraversion mesh with Zuckerman's (1991) view that traits and neural systems are non-isomorphic: several independent systems may influence extraversion. Conversely, systems may contribute to more than one trait; for example, low cortical arousability may also contribute to psychoticism.

The third issue we highlight is whether biological theories of personality are sufficient to explain the various behavioural consequences of traits; the hope expressed in figure 7.1. An alternative viewpoint is that cognitive and social-cognitive models may provide more predictive power. Matthews and Gilliland (1999, 2001) suggest several reasonable conclusions that might be drawn, depending on the researcher's theoretical preferences:

1 Either the Eysenck or Gray theory might be essentially correct. Future improvements in recording techniques and methodology will eventually vindicate one of these theories.

2 We may agree with Eysenck and Gray that neuroscience provides the key to personality, but adopt more complex physiological models (e.g., Zuckerman, 1991), in which traits reflect the integrated action of several discrete brain systems. We might also add that future research might place more emphasis on cortical mechanisms, such as circuits controlling attention (Matthews, Derryberry and Siegle, 2000). Of course, such models are more difficult to test in empirical study.

3 Revelle (1993) suggests that cognitive processes should be seen as more direct influences on behaviour than neural processes. Thus, to explain effects of extraversion on an attentionally demanding task, it may be most straightforward to refer to the cognitive processes described by theories of attention, such as allocating resources or capacity (see chapter 12). However, these processes are themselves dependent on neural functioning, and may be described in terms of cognitive neuroscience.

4 The final possibility is that we may never be able to reduce all the behavioural expressions of personality traits to neural processes (Matthews and Gilliland, 2001). Instead, we may need to use different explanations, depending on the behaviour of interest, as described in the introduction to this chapter. From this perspective, the aim for the future is to decide which behaviours are most amenable to neural explanation. There are good prospects for psychophysiological research on relatively primitive behaviours and processes, such as associative conditioning (Corr, 2002), and developmental processes that shape temperament (see Zeidner et al., 2003).

Conclusions

1. Neuropsychological theories seek to relate personality traits to individual differences in key brain systems. The principal source of evidence for these theories comes from studies that use psychophysiological recording techniques to investigate the functioning of the brain. Theories typically start from a 'conceptual nervous system': a simplified account of the most relevant brain systems for understanding personality. Leading theorists include Hans Eysenck (emphasising arousal systems), Jeffrey Gray (emphasising reward and punishment systems)

and Marvin Zuckerman (emphasising multiple neurotransmitter and hormonal systems).

2. Various psychophysiological techniques are used in personality research. Central nervous system activity can be recorded directly, using the EEG. An important variant of this technique is the recording of EPs, the averaged waveform seen in response to a controlled stimulus, that presents a regular pattern of positive and negative waves. Indices of the autonomic nervous system, such as skin conductance and heart rate may also be recorded. Increasingly, researchers are using modern brain scanning techniques that allow personality to be linked to the activity of specific brain regions, during some mental activity.

3. Much empirical work has been directed towards Eysenck's arousal theory, which links extraversion to (low) arousability of a reticulo-cortical circuit, neuroticism to arousability of a limbic-cortical circuit, and psychoticism to a fight–flight system. The basic assumptions of arousal theory have been criticised, and it may be too simplistic to accommodate the multiple activating systems of the brain. Experimental studies provide some modest support for the hypothesis that introverts are more easily aroused than extraverts, but there are various inconsistencies in the data. Careful attention to methodology is essential to obtain replicable results. Arousal theory may only explain some of the psychophysiological correlates of extraversion, and has had little success as an account of neuroticism.

4. Recently, Gray's RST has become increasingly prominent. It proposes that impulsivity (similar to extraversion) relates to a Behavioural Activation System sensitive to reward signals, whereas anxiety (similar to neuroticism) relates to a Behavioural Inhibition System sensitive to punishment signals. Psychophysiological studies show that motivational stimuli may indeed moderate the effects of personality on response. However, little consistent evidence for RST has so far been obtained from psychophysiology, although behavioural paradigms provide some support. The theory may require modification to accommodate interaction between different brain systems.

5. There are some trends among current studies that point to successful strategies for future research on the biology of personality traits. First, genetic covariance studies (e.g., Kirk et al., 2001; chapter 6) offer a new method for finding variance shared by personality traits and biological variables. These can provide firm starting points for further mechanistic research. Second, studies that combine personality traits and cognitive processing models in the setting of functional brain imaging provide richer, more tractable findings than those studies which study people at rest (e.g., Gray and Braver, 2002). Such studies might help to link personality to the brain via cognitive processing theories. Third, studies that examine personality, genetics and brain imaging together help to understand the cerebral mechanisms through which genetic contributions to personality traits might act (Hariri et al., 2002; chapter 6). In summary, if it

can be demonstrated that personality trait scores and genetic polymorphisms point to the same cerebral activation signatures in response to well-conceived cognitive and/or emotional processing demands then a psychobiological understanding of personality will begin in earnest. However, it is still an open question whether neuroscience theories of personality can provide a full account of the behavioural expressions of traits. Some researchers believe that the whole of trait psychology may ultimately be reducible to neuroscience explanations, whereas others believe that complementary psychological explanations will always be necessary.

Further reading

Matthews, G. and Gilliland, K. (1999) The personality theories of H. J. Eysenck and J. A. Gray: a comparative review. *Personality and Individual Differences*, 26, 583–626.

Pickering, A. D., Corr, P. J., Powell, J. H., Kumari, V., Thornton, J. C. and Gray, J. A. (1997) Individual differences in reactions to reinforcing stimuli are neither black nor white: to what extent are they Gray? In H. Nyborg (ed.), *The scientific study of human nature: tribute to Hans J. Eysenck at eighty*, pp. 36–67. London: Elsevier Science.

Stelmack, R. M. (1997) The psychophysics and psychophysiology of extraversion and arousal. In H. Nyborg (ed.), *The scientific study of human nature: tribute to Hans J. Eysenck at eighty*, pp. 388–403. New York: Elsevier Science.

8 The social psychology of traits

Social-psychological approaches have played a major role in personality psychology. In the modern era, the two most influential theorists are Albert Bandura (e.g., 1997) and Walter Mischel (e.g., 1999). Bandura's studies of modelling (e.g., Bandura and Walter, 1963) showed how social learning processes could generate dispositions, such as tendencies towards aggression. However, such dispositions were seen as dynamic rather than static, in that they undergo ongoing modification as a consequence of interaction with the environment. Mischel also emphasised social learning and dynamic person–environment interaction. His personality theory is also known for its emphasis on the situation: individuals may display consistent behaviours in specific situations, consistencies that are not related to conventional traits. The relationship between these approaches and trait theory has often been thorny: as discussed in chapter 2, Mischel's (1968) critique of trait theory was seen, in his words (Mischel, 1999, p. 39), 'as a glove hurled to the ground'. As Mischel (1999) also points out, the two disciplines of personality psychology had previously been unified in constructive collaboration. At the present time, there is increased interest in whether – and if so, how – a new unity between the two disciplines may be forged.

From the trait perspective, there is renewed interest in social learning approaches because of evidence that links traits to the explanatory constructs of social learning theorists. We can readily show correlations between traits such as extraversion and neuroticism, and indices of cognitive appraisal, self-efficacy and self-reflective cognition (Matthews, Schwean et al., 2000). Could these data be pointing us towards the sources of the environmental influences on traits indicated by behaviour genetic studies? Could it be that individual differences in social learning processes, such as development of beliefs about the self, shape personality traits (and vice versa)? Perhaps extraversion is influenced by exposure to outgoing role models, by parental approval of sociable behaviours, and by internalisation of an 'extraverted' self-identity. Such a perspective might also help us to explain how traits influence social behaviours.

In this chapter we examine the relationship between social psychology and the study of personality traits. However, it is important to recognise that social psychology is itself a multifaceted discipline that includes at least two different approaches to personality. The first approach is *social constructivism*, the idea that 'personality' is not a property of the individual at all, but a mutually negotiated meaning attached to social discourse. The second approach is *social-cognitive* (Kunda, 1999). It assumes that people represent social knowledge in the form of cognitive structures, such as schemas, that guide the individual's processing of the social stimuli provided by other people, and, hence, social interaction. Bandura and Mischel have both applied the social-cognitive approach in attempting to describe the internal processes that give coherence to the personality of the individual. In trying to span the divide between different disciplines, we can start building the bridge from either end. Next, we will look in outline at how we might take these two social-psychological conceptions of personality as a starting point for understanding traits. We will also consider how we might start with trait concepts, and work towards a social-psychological understanding.

Social constructivism

The constructivist approach views people as active participants in social encounters, focusing on meaning as jointly constructed through interaction between the participants. It sees natural science methods as unsuitable for investigating 'meaning', and emphasises the use of qualitative data. It lends itself to studies of the interplay between the individual and social and political contexts; for example, feminist psychology is exclusively constructivist in outlook. Hence, it tends to be inimical to trait theory. 'Aggression', in the constructivist view, is not a fixed attribute of an individual, but a construction of meaning placed upon a social interaction. Such a construction is interpersonal in several senses. It may depend on a shared, possibly culture-specific belief that certain actions should be labelled as aggressive. It may also depend on a negotiation of meaning between participants. For example, a statement by the 'aggressor' that he or she acted in self-defence might lead to a re-evaluation of the events. There may also be a sense in which the 'victim' contributed to the construction by accepting the role of victim. As Hampson (1988) has suggested, personality may then be located 'between' rather than 'within' people.

Harré and Gillett (1994) describe personality as the outcome of the person's attempt to fashion a coherent psychological life from everyday 'discourses': symbolic interactions within a framework of conventions and relationships. Their prescription for personality research is unequivocally idiographic: 'a detailed, empathic, and individualized understanding of the way someone has construed and come to organize their own location in a range of discourses' (Harré and Gillett, 1994, p. 142). Hence, to try to quantify an individual's aggressiveness would be crass. What is important is to understand the personal significance of acts which might be construed as 'aggressive', and the psychological and social factors influencing the construction.

Harré and Gillett's (1994) theory is evidently a dead end so far as trait models are concerned. A more interesting constructivist theory that makes some contact with trait theory has been advanced by Hampson (1988). She distinguishes three components of personality: actor, observer and self-observer. The 'actor' refers to the individual's internal characteristics and dispositions, as conventionally studied by trait psychologists. The 'observer' describes another person's assignation of meaning to the actor's behaviour. The 'self-observer' is the actor in another guise. The person not only emits behaviours, but constructs meanings for them. Moreover, the person is often aware of being observed, and forms beliefs about the ways in which his or her behaviour is being evaluated by the observer. Two people in conversation will each fill all three roles as they communicate with one another. Personality may be seen as arising out of this complex interplay; according to Hampson (1988), participants aim to arrive at a mutually satisfactory construction of reality.

One of the main planks of constructivist personality theory is evidence that the personality of the individual appears to vary dynamically according to the cues provided by others (see Hampson, 1988). We can all think of instances of jovial, Santa Claus-like individuals who seem to have an extraverting effect on people around them. Conversely, people in elevators often behave so as to discourage conversation and other signs of extraversion. The constructivist view is that the extraversion is a situationally negotiated construct, such that one's own extraversion may be influenced by cues that others wish one to be extraverted, or, as at a party, that the shared identity of a group is based on extraverted attitudes and behaviours. However, such observations do not necessarily force us to think in terms of personality as inter- rather than intra-personal. Moderation of personality (or rather its outward signs) may be a special case of person × situation interaction, in which the situation is dependent upon the traits of the individuals concerned. It is plausible that the social cues a situation provides depend on the extraversion scores of the participants. If so, there is nothing particularly surprising about introverts showing extraverted behaviour if sufficiently strongly cued by the situation to be talkative, assertive and so on. We might also find that, even if introverts show extraverted behaviour at a party, extraverts become even more extraverted, or execute extraverted behaviours more effectively. There is nothing in contemporary trait theory which states that social behaviour is unaffected by social cues, or by interaction between traits and those cues. As Deary (1993b) has stated, 'Most of the results of the constructivist approach appeared to be compatible with an interpretation that says that constructivism describes how traits (important, biologically based phenomena) are picked up and inferred by individuals. In other words, it is not personality itself that is being constructed, but our perception of its truth – and that is a very weak form of constructivism indeed.'

Social-cognitive approaches to personality

From the social-cognitive perspective, the individual is 'programmed' by experience with processing routines and items of knowledge stored in memory, which allow him or her to handle social encounters (Matthews, Schwean et al., 2000).

Some of these program elements are available to consciousness, whereas others, such as routines for reacting to non-verbal social stimuli, may be largely unconscious. Individual differences in personality result from individual differences in the program elements and operation. For example, an aggressive person might be one whose interpretive routines are biased towards the detection of hostility and threat in others, and who has a large and accessible store of information about inflicting injury on others (e.g., Dodge, 2000). These biases may also be situation-specific: sensitivity to hostility may be linked to specific contexts. As researchers, we can then seek methods for unravelling the programming, and identifying elements, such as knowledge in long-term memory, which may be responsible for consistencies in behaviour over time, and observable 'traits'. This approach is well-suited to the development of cognitive psychological models of the processes used by people to interpret and react to social stimuli. It is also compatible with experimental methods and rigour of natural science. However, to constructivist social psychologists, it risks sacrificing realism in pursuit of this rigour.

This view of personality presents an intriguing mixture of similarities and differences with trait research. It shares the idea of an inner locus of personality, introduced in chapter 1, i.e., that people possess core qualities that influence surface behaviours. It also shares the idea of at least some stability in behaviour: people's social-cognitive dispositions are represented in long-term memory, and so change relatively slowly. Like trait theory, the social-cognitive approach is concerned too with issues of *coherence* of personality; how is it that individual differences in beliefs, emotions, motivations and behaviours are interrelated and integrated? Table 8.1 lists three aspects of coherence described by Cervone and Shoda (1999). There are also important differences in theoretical perspective. In particular, Cervone and Shoda (1999, p. 10) state that:

> Coherence across time is revealed not only in stability of action, but in meaningful patterns of change when people face changing environmental demands . . . Coherence across contexts is revealed not only in stable mean levels of response, but in variations in cognition and action from one context to another . . . Further, when consistency in response is observed, it is found across sets of situations that vary idiosyncratically from person to person and that often bear little relation to nomothetic trait categories.

Interestingly, different social-cognitive theorists arrive at different opinions of the compatibility of such models with trait theory. Mischel (1999) sees dispositions and processing dynamics as complementary facets of the same personality system. 'The dispositional qualities of individuals are represented in the personality system in terms of particular enduring structures in the organization among cognitive-affective mediating units available to the person' (Mischel, 1999, p. 56). In chapter 2, we discussed the Mischel and Shoda (1995) CAPS model that describes the dynamic operation of these units in detail. Mischel's point is that there may be mappings to be found between conventional traits and this more fine-grained, contextualised account of personality structure. By contrast,

Table 8.1 *Three aspects of personality coherence, within social-cognitive theory*

Organisation among multiple personality processes
Interrelationship of multiple psychological processes: e.g., the individual's typical
    patterns of emotion and cognition

Coherence in overt response
Patterns of behaviour that generalise across space and time; i.e., behavioural consistency
    and temporal stability of behaviour (in some contexts)

Coherence in subjective experience
The person's experience of having a unitary self and finding personal meaning in their life
    story, expressed in a stable sense of preferences, values and self-perceptions

Source Cervone and Shoda (1999)

Cervone (1999; Caprara and Cervone, 2000) cautions against an integration of the
two approaches, in that, in his view, trait theories fail to identify causal mechanisms, and they offer no explanation for the cross-situational consistencies shown
by individuals. We will return to these arguments again in the concluding section
of this chapter.

Traits and social behaviour

Social psychologists do not have a monopoly on explanations for social behaviour.
Trait theorists have long been concerned with individual differences in social behaviour (Furnham and Heaven, 1999). Traits that represent the person's characteristic style of interacting with others are, of course, an essential part of conventional
trait models such as those of Eysenck and the five factor model. Extraversion, for
example, has an important social component: the extravert is typically more sociable, gregarious and assertive. Extraversion has considerable validity as a predictor
of social behaviour; when placed in social situations with strangers, extraverts
are more likely to initiate conversations than introverts (Thorne, 1987; Argyle,
Martin and Crosland, 1989). They also joke more and ask more questions. We saw
in chapter 4 how extraversion, happiness and social skills may be closely linked
(Argyle and Lu, 1990b). Agreeableness is defined entirely by social qualities such
as kindness and trustfulness. Trapnell and Wiggins (1990) identify two specifically interpersonal traits, Dominance and Nurturance, which correspond to extraversion and agreeableness respectively. Two similar, broad interpersonal traits –
'diffidence versus dominance' and 'nastiness versus niceness' – were found in
a combined, confirmatory factor analysis of the NEO-FFI, the Bedford-Foulds
Personality Deviance Scales and the Spielberger State-Trait Anger Inventory
(Whiteman et al., 2001). Conscientiousness appears, in part, to reflect acceptance
of societal values, as expressed through qualities such as dutifulness and orderli-
ness. McCrae (1996) cites evidence that openness relates to qualities of interpersonal interaction such as understanding and adapting to others' perspectives, and to

expressing egalitarian rather than traditional family values. There are also narrower 'social' traits such as guilt, shame and embarrassment (Klass, 1990), which relate to neuroticism.

There is little doubt that traits predict social behaviour, although social-cognitive researchers contend that contextualised and/or idiographic personality measures predict a larger part of the variance. The next question is how these social-psychological correlates of traits are to be explained. Traditionally, biological theories of traits have explained their effects on social behaviour by reference to conditioning processes. For example, neurotic extraverts may be more prone to delinquent behaviour because they are more sensitive to reward signals than to punishment signals (Gray, 1981). Cloninger's three temperament traits of harm avoidance, reward dependence, and novelty seeking are hypothesised to derive from evolutionary-relevant social activity underpinned by specific neural circuits and learning mechanisms (see chapters 1 and 11). However, while basic conditioning mechanisms may contribute to social learning, it is unlikely that they are the only, or even the most important influence.

A social-psychological agenda for trait psychology

Our introductory overview demonstrates overlap between the concerns of trait theory and of the social-psychological conception of personality, especially in its social-cognitive form. Furthermore, cognitive theory suggests mechanisms that may influence the development of personality, and the expression of personality traits as individual differences in social behaviour. If people encode knowledge about social encounters in long-term memory, this knowledge may be sufficiently stable over time to provide the basis for traits. Perhaps an agreeable person is someone who has stable beliefs that other people are generally benevolent (cognition), and that it is important to have amicable relations with others (motivation). The person may also have a repertoire of skills for appearing as friendly to others (behavioural skills).

In the remainder of this chapter, we take several steps necessary to develop the idea that traits are associated with individual differences in social cognition:

1 First, we explore how social-cognitive processes may influence the *development* of personality traits, mediating the environmental influences that are shown to be important by the behaviour-genetic research reviewed in chapter 6. The assumption is that development builds stable social and self-knowledge. These knowledge structures provide a cognitive core to personality, within the interactionist framework described in chapter 2. We must investigate how stable social knowledge is acquired from social learning, rather than simpler processes such as conditioning.

2 If personality resides in stable knowledge structures, then social-cognitive models should tell us how traits influence social behaviours in specific contexts. We must find sources of long-term consistency that will support the stability of traits and individual differences in behaviour. Social-cognitive theories describe

stable knowledge structures, such as the 'self-schema', that encode beliefs and procedural skills relevant to a variety of important types of situation. These theories also describe how person and situation factors interact in the short term, as external cues influence which knowledge elements are 'activated', so as to influence behaviour.

3 Next, we must show that individual differences in stable social knowledge may be conceptualised, at least partially, in nomothetic rather than idiographic terms, so as to explain the data on associations between traits and social behaviour. Here, we are hindered by the traditional antagonism of the two fields of enquiry, and the reluctance of researchers to engage with the constructs of the 'enemy' camp. Fortunately, recent work on Agreeableness provides a model for relating traits to social-psychological constructs, to the probable benefit of both approaches. We will review the relevant studies, though, as yet, theory development is sketchy.

4 Another approach to treating social knowledge nomothetically is to operationalise traits that directly represent social psychological constructs, such as cultural values and attitudes towards others. We will briefly outline some exemplary research.

5 In the final section of this chapter, we review the prospects for integrating trait and social-psychological models of personality.

Personality development: social-psychological perspectives

The social-psychological approach suggests that one source of stable personality dispositions is the child's early learning and socialisation. It seems plausible that a happy childhood may encourage traits such as extraversion and agreeableness, whereas the maltreated child might be more prone to neuroticism. However, as discussed in chapter 3, personality development is a two-way street. The external social environment may influence personality development, but the child also actively interacts with and shapes its social experience. In this section we consider how person–situation interactions operating over long time periods of months or years may mould the child's personality. We look first at some general principles for the role of person–situation interaction in personality development, followed by two influential areas of research: self-efficacy and attachment styles.

Interactionist perspectives on development

A popular view is that the self originates in caregiver–child interactions. The infant graduates from coordinated, reciprocal transactions with the mother, such as those of feeding routines, to developing internal working models of the self (e.g., Bretherton, 1988). Initially, interaction is centred on the infant's biological needs and simple emotional transactions, such as mutual smiling. As the child matures, interaction becomes more dependent on language, and on the child's growing

Table 8.2 *Stages of development of the social self*

Age period	Self-regulation	Social expressions
0–12 months (infancy)	Use of simple behavioural strategies such as self-soothing responses and gaze aversion; also much reliance on caregiver	Social games and turn-taking. Instrumental use of social (e.g., fake crying to get attention)
12–30 months (toddler period)	Emergence of self-awareness and use of language	Early forms of empathy and voluntary prosocial and antisocial behaviour
2½ years–5 years (pre-school)	Symbolic understanding of self and others	Increased insight into other people leads to increased sensitivity to social feedback and readiness to act to influence others
5 years–10 years (early and middle school years)	Increasing self-reliance, and use of problem-solving strategies	Improving social skills and awareness of social norms
10+ years (later school years)	Increasing self-knowledge and self-insight, leading to increasing self-regulative sophistication	Increasingly skilful use of self-presentation strategies and management of relationships and social roles

Source Adapted and simplified from Saarni (1999)

capacity for self-regulation, for example, through use of emotional displays to attract caregiver attention and concern (Denham, 1998). In school-age children, self-reflective thought, sensitivity to the opinions of others and social comparison become increasingly important in the development of the self-schema (Saarni, 1999). Children also develop increasing self-control, in being able to translate self-knowledge into action, through deferring gratification for long-term benefit, for example (Metcalfe and Mischel, 1999). In the older child, social interaction with peers, teachers and other adults also plays an increasing role in shaping the sense of self. Table 8.2 shows, in simplified form, how the self develops, and how increasingly sophisticated self-regulation is expressed in social behaviour (Saarni, 1999).

The development of the self is frequently seen from a purely social-psychological perspective. For example, Saarni (1999, 2000), a social constructivist, believes that social exposure influences how the child gives meaning to events. The individual's development reflects a social history, i.e., immersion in cultural beliefs (often transmitted via narrative and discourse), observation of important others, and reinforcement from significant others. The ability of the child to assign meaning becomes progressively more sophisticated as cognitive and emotional development progresses, as indicated in table 8.2. Throughout, the process is essentially one of learning to construct meaning, on the basis of perception of one's social role within specific contexts.

However, this constructivist perspective neglects the possibility that the factors of temperament discussed in chapter 3 systematically influence the social learning process. In fact, there is evidence that temperament (as a precursor to personality traits) influences the behaviour of both child and caregiver in their mutual interaction (Bates and McFadyen-Ketchum, 2000). The child's temperament influences whether the child reacts to adult anger with displays of negative emotion (Davies and Cummings, 1995), and how compliant the child is to maternal instructions (Kochanska et al., 2001). Conversely, mothers who lack positive emotionality tend to have young children who are emotionally dysregulated (Zahn-Waxler et al., 1984). These bidirectional paths may have the capacity to lead to mutually dysfunctional interactions in which 'difficult', distress-prone children elicit suboptimal parenting, and vice versa, with adverse consequences for subsequent social development. Whatever the idiographic content of the child's social development, it seems that (as also discussed in chapter 3) dimensions of temperament influence the child's style of interaction with its social environment. Box 8.1 illustrates the different processes that may contribute to the development of the emotional aspects of personality. Furthermore, interaction is supported by biological as well as social mechanisms, especially in infancy. Emotional interactions with the care-giver may influence the development of the neural circuits involved in emotional awareness and regulation (Taylor, Bagby and Parker, 1999).

Box 8.1 Temperament and social learning: development of emotional competence

The development of emotional competence appears to depend on multiple levels of interaction between the child and its social environment, that become progressively more sophisticated as the child develops and acquires more advanced cognitive and social skills. The figure below shows three levels identified in a recent review (Zeidner, Matthews, Roberts and McCann, 2003):

1 *Development of temperament.* The quality of the infant's interaction with the caregiver shapes the emotional aspects of temperament; maltreated infants may develop aggressive or inhibited temperament, together with deficits in emotion expression and emotion regulation (e.g., Southam-Gerow and Kendall, 2002). Conversely, the child's temperament influences caregiver behaviour. The distress-prone infant may be clingy, whiny or otherwise 'difficult', which may cause frustration or neglect by the caregiver.

2 *Development of social-emotional skills.* As the child acquires greater linguistic abilities, the way the caregiver (and others) instruct the child influences the child's personality, along with modelling. For example, more empathic and emotionally open parents tend to have more empathic and expressive children (e.g., Gottman, 2001). Again, the relationship is

bidirectional: the child's empathy may influence how warm and expressive the parent is (Zhou et al., 2002).

3 *Development of emotional self-awareness*. Older children acquire metacognitive abilities that allow them to reflect about their own emotions. The conversations that children have with adults and peers about emotions help to build styles of emotional self-regulation that may be related to personality traits. For example, an exaggerated concern with negative emotions (excessive metacognition) may contribute to neuroticism (Matthews, Schwean et al., 2001), whereas children coached in strategies for dealing with their own negative feelings may be more stress-resistant (Gottman, 2001).

The figure suggests that temperament, influenced by genes, biases subsequent emotional development, with continuing mutual interaction between levels. For example, higher levels of emotion regulation may feed back into temperament, and eventually into adult personality. The social learning processes indicated in the figure also interact with the child's biological constitution, as further discussed by Zeidner, Matthews et al. (2003).

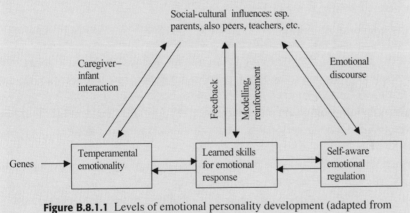

Figure B.8.1.1 Levels of emotional personality development (adapted from Zeidner, Matthews et al., in press)

It is important also to appreciate that the environment changes along with the child. Caspi and Bem (1990) identify three types of person–environment interaction which tend to promote continuity in personality through childhood and adulthood:

1 *Reactive interaction* refers to individual differences in filtering and interpreting environmental stimuli, controlled by cognitive structures such as the self-schema. Children may develop characteristic styles of cognitions about themselves and the outside world.

2 *Evocative interaction* refers to feedback loops that link children's behaviour to the reactions of others. For example, if aggressive children expect others to be hostile (Schwean and Saklofske, 1995), they may show suspicion and aggression

in social interaction, thereby promoting the hostility expected, and generating a self-fulfilling prophecy.

3 *Proactive interaction* refers to the active choice and construction of environments. Swann's (1997) self-verification principle suggests that individuals tend to shape interaction in accord with their self-concepts, which promotes temporal stability of the self-concept, and, in consequence, stability of behaviour. People may be motivated to construct environments around themselves which tend to verify their self-beliefs, even if these are negative (Swann, Stein-Seroussi and McNulty, 1992).

Such interactive processes may contribute to the temporal continuity of the Big Five and other traits. As discussed in chapter 3, temperament and personality show some changeability during childhood, becoming increasingly stable during the adult years (Caspi and Roberts, 2001). In addition to direct constitutional effects, stability may also reflect people's ability to create environmental 'niches' for themselves that match their personality. For example, high neuroticism scorers may tend to seek out or create stressful encounters (Bolger and Schilling, 1991; see also chapter 9) which feed back into maintenance of a more neurotic personality. Extraverts are more prone than introverts to attend parties and social events (Furnham, 1981), which may help to confirm the personal significance of socialising, and to build the social skills and self-efficacy which contribute to enjoyment of social events. Kohn and Schooler (1983) discuss an instance of proactive interaction which may relate to the Big Five Openness dimension. Intellectually flexible and self-directed men tend to choose jobs requiring complex work, which in turn enhances their flexibility and self-directedness. People also tend to form friendships with those of similar personality, in which mutual traits are reinforced. In sports clubs, high levels of extraversion expressed in practical jokes and rumbustiousness which would normally cause offence to others may be tolerated or even encouraged. Similarly, delinquent behaviour may be maintained, in part, through the tendency of delinquents to belong to delinquent peer groups (Patterson, 1988).

Development of self-efficacy

Bandura's social learning theory has been applied to personality development, framed within an interactionist model termed *reciprocal determinism*. Within a given situation, the person chooses how to act, but the action is then modified by the feedback received, so that person and environment mutually shape one another. Bandura's (e.g., 1999) later writings propose the more complex notion of triadic reciprocal causation, which distinguishes three mutually interacting elements: behaviour (B), internal personal factors (P) and the external environment (E), as shown in figure 8.1. The 'person' is broken down into B and P elements to emphasise that beliefs and intentions shape behaviour (P → B), and, reciprocally, feedback from actions influences thought and affect (B → P). Similarly, the environment interacts reciprocally with both internal thoughts and overt behaviours.

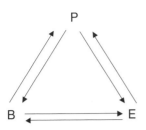

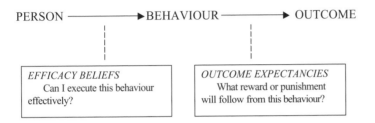

Figure 8.1 Triadic reciprocal relationships between behaviour (B), internal personal factors (P) and the external environment (E), according to Bandura (1999)

PERSON ————————▶BEHAVIOUR————————▶ OUTCOME

| *EFFICACY BELIEFS* | *OUTCOME EXPECTANCIES* |
| Can I execute this behaviour effectively? | What reward or punishment will follow from this behaviour? |

Figure 8.2 Bandura's distinction between outcome expectations and self-efficacy perceptions

Bandura (1997, 1999) links the self to *agency*, i.e., to a system for self-regulation capable of operating proactively, rather than just reacting passively to stimuli. Within the triadic model, the P element is supported by various self-related cognitions, but Bandura emphasises especially the role of perceived *self-efficacy*, i.e., beliefs about whether personally significant activities can be performed successfully. Self-efficacy influences choice of activities, motivation and cognitions and emotions during task performance. It is important to realise that self-efficacy is not just some generalised optimism. Bandura distinguishes self-efficacy from outcome expectancies (see figure 8.2). Self-efficacy refers to beliefs about whether the person can execute an action, which is different from beliefs about whether that action will lead to a desired outcome. Bandura sees self-efficacy as specific to particular domains or contexts, but other researchers have developed generalised measures that assess overall confidence across a variety of different situations (Chen, Gully and Eden, 2001). Self-efficacy is distinct from self-esteem, i.e., a global sense of self-worth, although measures of the two constructs are inter-correlated (Stanley and Murphy, 1997). To complicate the issue, it seems that self-esteem measures actually comprise two dimensions, one relating to self-liking, and one to self-competence (Tafarodi and Swann, 2001). Self-competence might be expected to overlap with self-efficacy.

Self-efficacy beliefs are influenced by a variety of factors, including, unsurprisingly, the person's previous success and failure experiences on the activity concerned. Some of these factors are specifically social, such as modelling. The vicarious experience of observing a model succeeding through sustained effort increases the likelihood of the observer imitating that course of action in similar contexts. Bandura's classic studies of the modelling of aggressive behaviours of young children showed how this process may contribute to personality development. What children learn is not only that violence may pay, but that they have a good chance of personally profiting from violence themselves. Another important influence is social persuasion; encouraging or discouraging statements from others, perhaps accompanied by actual social support or impedance. Finally, physical and arousal states such as anxiety may signal lack of efficacy, so enhancing physical and emotional status may increase efficacy beliefs.

There is considerable experimental evidence demonstrating that measures of self-efficacy, typically linked to some specific context, are predictive of more effective behaviour (see Caprara and Cervone, 2000, for a review). Such measures have been developed to assess self-efficacy in arenas such as interacting with the opposite sex, control of food intake, resisting peer pressure and managing emotion. A meta-analysis of 114 studies, with a total n of 21,616 (Stajkovic and Luthans, 1998), showed a mean correlation of 0.38 between self-efficacy and work performance, a predictive validity that exceeds that typical for personality traits (see Barrick and Mount, 1991; chapter 13). Caprara and Cervone (2000) review studies suggesting that self-efficacy is more strongly related to behaviour than is self-esteem. A meta-analysis of studies of work performance (Judge and Bono, 2001) showed that the mean correlation was 0.26 for self-esteem, and 0.23 for self-efficacy, contrary to this view. However, the meta-analysis focused on generalised self-efficacy; context-linked self-efficacy may be more predictive, as the Stajkovic and Luthans meta-analysis suggested. Another reviewer (Zimmerman, 2000) claims that, in educational contexts, academic self-efficacy measures are more predictive of performance than closely related constructs including outcome expectancies, positive self-concept (similar to self-esteem) and perceived control. Zimmerman suggests that effects of self-efficacy may be mediated by motivational variables such as activity choice and persistence, together with more effective study skills.

Self-efficacy measures have considerable predictive validity. They also appear to measure dispositional qualities, as evidenced by high test–retest reliabilities for measures in a variety of different domains (e.g., Steffen et al., 2002). Thus, self-efficacy beliefs might be related to broad traits such as the Big Five. Several reliable measures of generalised self-efficacy have indeed been developed (Jerusalem and Schwarzer, 1989; Lee and Bobko, 1994; Chen, Gulley and Eden, 2001): see table 8.3 for some sample items. It appears that self-efficacy relates to several traits, including extraversion, emotional stability (e.g., Young and Bradley, 1998), and conscientiousness (C). Chen, Casper and Cortina (2001) report a meta-analysis that found an average correlation of 0.21 between C and various occupational self-efficacy measures. They also showed that self-efficacy mediated beneficial effects of high C on occupational performance (see chapter 13), at least for low-complexity tasks for which effort may be more important than skill. Self-efficacy may also relate to tolerance of stress (see also chapter 9). Deary et al.

Table 8.3 *Sample items for generalized self-efficacy*

1. I can always manage to solve difficult problems if I try hard enough.
2. If someone opposes me, I can find the ways and means to get what I want.
3. I am certain that I can accomplish my goals.
4. I am confident that I could deal efficiently with unexpected events.

Source Jerusalem and Schwarzer (1989)

(1996) found that senior doctors with lower N and higher C scores report significantly more personal achievement and personal confidence in their work. Effects of C were mediated via a task-oriented coping style, another trait-like concept which is related to self-efficacy (Holahan, Moos and Schaefer, 1996). High N individuals exhibit a range of negative self-perceptions, to the extent that N may be difficult to distinguish from reduced self-efficacy and low self-esteem (Judge et al., 2002).

The data just reviewed suggest that generalised self-efficacy may be a narrow or midlevel trait that contributes a social-psychological component to several higher-order traits. However, social-cognitive theorists typically have a different point of view. Bandura (1999) and Cervone (2000) argue that self-efficacy beliefs are highly context-specific, so that it is not meaningful to aggregate them across situations. However, the strength of cross-contextual correlations in efficacy perceptions is unclear. Cervone (2000) shows idiosyncratic individual differences in self-efficacy in different situations, but these findings do not preclude the operation of general biases. Even if personal and situational characteristics are normally in mutual dynamic interaction (reciprocal determinism), the trait concept remains valid if two conditions are met. First, the person's self-cognitions should be sufficiently correlated across situations to provide a degree of cross-situational consistency. Second, efficacy beliefs should be sufficiently slow to change in response to environmental feedback to demonstrate traitlike stability.

Bandura's model itself suggests several possible sources of cross-situational correlation. First, the environments to which the child is exposed may be correlated; parents may be skilled in choosing environments in which the child can succeed. Second, data on modelling suggest that learning generalises across different situations, though the extent of generalisation is poorly quantified. Third, verbal persuasion may be expressed globally, as when a child is told it is a complete failure. Furthermore, domain-specific and generalised efficacy are likely to be dynamically linked. Success in many domains is likely to breed a generalised confidence, which in turn is likely to raise self-efficacy perceptions when dealing with new challenges. There is also nothing in trait theory that denies the importance of context-linked dispositions; anxiety research comfortably accommodates both general trait anxiety and anxiousness linked to specific contexts such as test anxiety. Similarly, dispositional self-efficacy may be conceptualised in both generalised form and in terms of contexts such as academic and social self-efficacy (Young and Bradley, 1998). As Cervone (2000) states, a part of the variance in

Table 8.4 *Use of the 'strange situations' paradigm to classify attachment style in young children*

Attachment style	Behavioural pattern
Secure	Willing to explore unfamiliar environment, but seeks proximity with mother when she returns after being absent. Generally cooperative and calm.
Anxious-avoidant	Shows little overt distress during separation, but remains distant from mother when she returns.
Anxious-resistant	Responds to separation with stress, anxiety and anger. Responds to reunion after separation from mother by seeking proximity but not physical contact.

Source Ainsworth et al. (1978)

self-efficacy beliefs at the level of the individual may well be idiosyncratic, and best studied idiographically. At the same time, there may be general biases across and within broad-contexts that can be conceptualised as traits, and linked to existing trait dimensions.

Individual differences in attachment

Another social-psychological perspective on continuity of personality from childhood to adulthood comes from Bowlby's (1984) attachment theory. Bowlby saw the bond between caregiver and child as a kind of prototype for later adult relationships. The attachment process builds on the biologically based needs of child and parent, to form mental representations of parental interactions. After the first few years, attachment relates increasingly to the behavioural organisation of the child, and it becomes increasingly stable and resistant to change. One interpretation of attachment is that it affects self-related schemas: the child may believe that he or she is unwanted by others (Main, Kaplan and Cassidy, 1985). Hence, the poorly attached child may have difficulties in adult intimate relationships.

In the present context, the interesting aspect of attachment theory is that it supports measurement of fairly reliable and stable individual differences. Ainsworth et al. (1978) developed the 'strange situations' paradigm (see table 8.4) that classifies the child's attachment style on the basis of the child's behaviour in situations involving exposure to strangers, and short separations from the mother, followed by reunion. On this basis, about 70 per cent of infants are classified as secure, 20 per cent as anxious-avoidant, and 10 per cent as anxious-resistant. Various studies show that parenting behaviour relates to attachment; in particular, maternal sensitivity seems to produce secure attachment (DeWolff and Van Ijzendoorn, 1997). However, correlations between parenting style and attachment may also reflect the correlated genotypes of mother and child, as opposed to a direct causal link, and there may be multiple routes by which maternal behaviour influences the child (Raval et al., 2001).

In adults, attachment style is assessed not by coding of observed behaviours, but by the person's retrospective ratings of their childhood attachment experiences, assessed by structured interview or questionnaire. Van Ijzendoorn (1995) has reviewed research on the Adult Attachment Interview protocol, which allows adults' mental representations to be categorised as secure ('autonomous'), anxious-avoidant ('dismissing') or anxious-resistant ('preoccupied'). The interview data show trait-like stability over time, although scores show some sensitivity to life events. They also show validity in predicting criteria such as quality of parents' relationships with their children, parents' responsiveness to infants' attachment signals (Van Ijzendoorn, 1995), beliefs about love and attitudes towards intimate relationships (Shaver and Hazan, 1994). In one ingenious study (Fraley and Shaver, 1998), couples were unobtrusively observed at airports. Their scores on an attachment questionnaire completed beforehand predicted some aspects of their separation behaviour, such as distress (in women).

Most studies have shown fairly high stability of attachment classification (concordance rates of 70–90 per cent) in adults over periods of one to twelve years (Zimmerman and Becker-Stoll, 2002). However, studies of the stability of attachment from infancy to adulthood produce conflicting results, with some authors questioning whether there is any individual stability, as opposed to stability of environmental factors (Lewis, 2001; see also chapter 3). Zimmerman and Becker-Stoll (2002) point out that failure to show stability may reflect methodological factors relating to the differences between behavioural observation and retrospective interview methods. There is also considerable psychometric uncertainty over the status of adult attachment measures, with limited agreement between different measures, poor reliabilities for some instruments, and little justification for treating attachment as a categorical rather than a dimensional variable (Baeckstroem and Holmes, 2001; Stein et al., 2002). A final difficulty is that people seem to show different types of attachment in different relationships, calling into question the consistency of attachment behaviour (Ross and Spinner, 2001).

Several studies have correlated measures of adult attachment style with personality scales, including scales for the FFM (e.g., Carver, 1997; Mickelson, Kessler and Shaver, 1997; Baeckstroem and Holmes, 2001). Secure attachment seems to relate most reliably to extraversion, with some evidence also for associations between low neuroticism, high self-esteem and openness, depending on the measures used. Both types of insecure attachment (avoidant and resistant-preoccupied) are fairly reliably related to neuroticism and related traits, and also, in most studies, to introversion. Carver (1997) found that agreeableness related positively to secure attachment and negatively to avoidant attachment. These are tantalising but inconclusive findings, because these cross-sectional studies have not addressed attachment and personality developmentally. Could it be that early attachment experiences influence temperament and personality? Perhaps (consistent with psychodynamic theories) the infant's difficulties in bonding with the mother lead to dysfunctional relationships later in life. Or, could temperament influence how the infant responds to the caregiver, so that temperament is a causal influence on both attachment and adult personality? Answers to these questions would elucidate the role of early child–parent relationships on subsequent personality development.

Consistencies in social knowledge and cognition

So far, we have looked at socialisation processes over the long term. The message has been that childhood experiences such as bonding with parents and mastering the challenges of everyday life build stable beliefs, attitudes and expectancies, that may provide a basis for adult personality. The socialisation process should be seen dynamically, such that personality (or temperament) feeds back to influence what the child learns from its social encounters. In this section, we look in more detail at sources of consistency in social behaviour in the adult. Social-cognitive theory tells us something about the knowledge structures or 'schemas' built by long-term socialisation, which represent the person's social understanding and behavioural tendencies. It also describes how the influence of schemas on behaviour is moderated by situational cues, consistent with the interactionist models of personality discussed in chapter 2. In this section, we look at how theories of social knowledge explain consistency and inconsistency in behaviour, followed by an account of person–situation interaction.

The self-schema

We consider first what social-cognitive psychological theory has to say about possible sources of consistency in behaviour. Perhaps the single most important concept is that of the schema. The idea derives originally from Bartlett's (1932) studies of memory for short stories. He showed that subjects tended to use their general beliefs about the story, the schema, to reconstruct details, often incorrectly. More generally, a schema is typically described as a structured set of items of abstract or generic information (e.g., Neisser, 1967). The information may pertain to any object or category, but social psychologists are typically concerned with schemata for the self, other people, social roles and so forth. Schemata reside in long-term memory and are resistant to change, thus providing a source of consistency. They are active, in that they guide processes such as recall from memory, attention and action.

The best-known application of schema theory in social psychology is to the person's self-concept. According to Markus (1977), people develop a self-schema, an internal working model of the self. The schema shapes both interpersonal processes, such as evaluating and interacting with others, and intrapersonal processes of self-understanding and motivation. Markus (1977) provided experimental evidence in support of the hypothesis by showing that processing of self-referent information appears to be particularly efficient. The concept has not been without its difficulties. For example, it is unclear that self-beliefs are actually stored in a schema-like structure (Segal, 1988). Wells and Matthews (1994) suggest that 'procedural knowledge' which is not directly accessible to conscious awareness is more important in self-related processing than verbal propositions about the self, or 'declarative knowledge'. It has also proved difficult to show that processing of self-referent information is privileged, although many researchers favour this view. It seems that trait beliefs are not simply a post hoc reconstruction from memories of one's behaviour; abstract beliefs about one's traits are represented independently from autobiographical memories (Klein and Loftus, 1993).

The self-schema is often seen as fundamentally 'interpersonal' (Markus and Cross, 1990), for several reasons. First, awareness of self and beliefs about the self are a product of social interaction. Other people are the most important source of information about the self. From direct feedback and other indirect signals, people form beliefs about how others see them, termed 'reflective appraisals' (Sullivan, 1940). These appraisals are not necessarily accepted as accurate, but are particularly influential for socially defined characteristics such as attractiveness (Felson, 1985). People tend to form opinions concerning how they are viewed by other people in general (De Paulo et al., 1987), which in turn may influence behaviour, through a kind of self-fulfilling prophecy. Self-knowledge is often integrated with beliefs about interpersonal relationships within a 'relational schema' (Baldwin, 2001). Attachment processes in childhood may influence the development of relational schemas that encode the person's understanding of close relationships (Baldwin, 2001). Downey and Feldman (1996) identified a trait-like construct of rejection sensitivity, relating to expectancies of rejection in close interpersonal relationships. Downey and Feldman's studies showed that rejection-sensitive individuals are indeed prone to feelings of rejection when exposed to ambiguous interpersonal behaviour, and that such persons are at greater risk of breaking up with their partner.

Second, other people are the primary vehicle through which social and cultural values are internalised, such that the person identifies with the common beliefs of those around them. Third, explicit comparison of oneself with others also serves to shape the self (Festinger, 1954). Comparisons with others provide information on the person's social worth, and indicate how the person may improve themselves (Wood, 1989). Comparisons with a person of differing attainments may either be a source of threat, or a source of self-enhancement. Indeed, there are multiple motivations for social comparison. People actively seek information that will raise self-esteem (Baumeister, 1998), described as *self-enhancement*. They also seek information that will maintain a consistent self-concept, even if that self-referent information is negative, a motive for *self-verification* (Swann, 1997). This motive is likely to contribute to stability of personality. Thus, there is a motivational tension between the search for 'disagreeable truth or what fits our fancy' (Pervin, 2002, p. 169).

Evidently, the self-schema concept lends itself to both normative and idiographic research. Much of the research in this area assumes that the elements of the self-schema are highly context-dependent; a person might have high self-esteem in one context, but low self-esteem in another (Caprara and Cervone, 2000). Markus and Cross (1990) discuss the concept of possible selves; diverse representations of selves one would like to be, and feared future selves one is afraid of becoming. Perspectives of this kind have been explored through idiographic research, although it is unclear whether this proliferation of self-systems is amenable to measurement or scientifically rigorous investigation. As Bandura (1999) notes, we could think of an athlete as having a tennis self and a golfing self, further subdivided into a driving self, a fairway self and a putting self. Rather than fractionate selves endlessly, it is better to conceive of a single self that can call upon different self-regulatory mechanisms.

Nevertheless, self-schemas may include more global self-referent beliefs that influence behaviour across many situations. For example, work on clinical depression (Clark and Beck, 1999) suggests that depressed individuals are characterised by the inclusion of negative self-beliefs in the schema. They believe themselves to be worthless, ineffectual and with dismal future prospects. A scale representing negativity of the self-schema might then relate to a depressive trait, spanning mild depression in normal individuals as well as the clinical disorder. In fact, neuroticism appears to relate to the negativity of self-beliefs in many different contexts (Wells and Matthews, 1994; Matthews, Schwean et al., 2000), although there is considerable variance in the content of beliefs in different high N individuals. We look at some traits said to relate directly to the self below. Box 8.2 illustrates how some of the concepts we have discussed apply to the personality trait of shyness, which correlates with neuroticism and introversion, but is distinct from them (Briggs, 1988). The inhibited temperament, discussed in chapter 6, may provide a developmental basis.

Other sources of consistency

Imagined future selves. The self-schema is the best-known social-psychological construct which may generate temporal and cross-situational consistency, but not the only one. Cantor and Zirkel (1990) have drawn attention to the importance of integrating cognitive and motivational constructs. They point out that constructs such as the person's imagined future selves indicate the importance of temporal awareness and goal-striving over extended periods of time. Abstract goals such as personal fulfillment or high achievement must be attained through creative engagement in specific tasks or projects. Implementation of such tasks requires the acquisition of relevant knowledge and processing routines, so that cognition and motivation are inextricably linked in somewhat schema-like structures. Personality then attains continuity from long-term projects (Emmons, 1996), as in the case of a painter who devotes his or her life to art. However, some projects may be less enduring; Cantor and Kihlstrom (1987) discuss tasks which relate to a particular life period or transition. Obtaining formal educational qualifications, for example, is primarily (though not exclusively) a concern of young people.

Box 8.2 Social-psychological bases for shyness

Shyness refers to social anxiety, and may be looked at both dispositionally and situationally. Validation studies show that shyness as a trait influences various social behaviours, including frequency and length of verbal utterances, eye contact and social skills deficits such as difficulties in decoding the meanings of social interaction (see Bruch, 2001, for a review). According to Crozier and Alden (2001), 'there seems to be too much of the self in shyness', i.e., the person is over-preoccupied with the impression they make on others, as shown, for example, by correlations with the public self-consciousness trait discussed below. Empirical studies have suggested various more specific social-psychological constructs that relate to shyness (see Bruch, 2001; Leary, 2001).

Self-perceptions and self-schema. Shy people tend to rate themselves as negatively, both generally (e.g., low self-esteem, low physical attractiveness) and in relation to social competence. Shy people see themselves as lacking self-efficacy in interpersonal settings and lacking social skills, for example, in presenting themselves favourably. Although research data suggest some skills deficit in shyness, it is likely that shyness leads to exaggeration of such difficulties.

Relational schemas. Shy people may represent their expectancies of social interaction in terms of negative outcomes, such as being criticised, ignored or disrespected. Such relational schemas will bias evaluation of social interaction (e.g., interpreting quietness as rejection), provide a 'script' for the person's behaviour (e.g., being ready to terminate the conversation) and bias self-evaluation (e.g., as socially inept).

Self-protective motivations. In social encounters, shy persons tend to be motivated by self-protection goals, such as avoiding disapproval, rather than seeking rewarding interactions. Self-effacing behaviours may be a consequence of such motivations. Shy people may avoid personal disclosure and intimacy, because of the risk of criticism and rejection.

Taken together, these interrelated social-cognitive attributes of the shy personality help to explain its behavioural expressions. In pathological or clinical cases of social anxiety disorder, they also provide a basis for cognitive-behavioural therapies that seek to build social self-efficacy and challenge dysfunctional self-related cognitions (Wells, 1997).

Interpersonal script. Another relevant construct is termed by Cantor and Zirkel (1990) the 'interpersonal script', which is a 'mental model' of how a social encounter should proceed. Just as we have expectations about the sequence of events in a restaurant or shop, we may also have scripts for generic encounters such as going on a date or attending a job interview, and for our interactions with specific other individuals. People who know one another well may have shared scripts which pattern their interaction. As with schemas, it seems possible to focus on both nomothetic and idiographic aspects of interpersonal scripts. In the former case, we might be able to rank-order individuals' scripts in terms of various qualities such as friendliness, social conformity, verbal expressiveness and so forth. In a very aggressive person, for example, confrontation may be 'written into' the script for a wide variety of social interactions.

Sources of inconsistency

Thus far, we have focused on sources of continuity in social processes and knowledge structures which might give rise to an observable 'trait'. However, social psychology also provides reasons why personality may vary over short time periods and across contexts. A major source of inconsistency is the process of active negotiation of personality which takes place in social interaction. According to Hampson (1988), the characteristics that a person brings to a social encounter, such as self-beliefs, personal projects and interpersonal scripts, are only a starting point for the context-dependent personality which emerges through social interaction. Schlenker and Weigold (1989) suggest that during interaction, individuals attempt to develop 'self-identifications', images of identity within specific contexts. The person attempts to arrive at a compromise between achieving their aims in the context, being accepted by others, and conforming to social and cultural norms. Hence, there is nothing necessarily fixed about personality at all, as any aspect of personality is open to re-negotiation. Apparent consistency of behaviour could as easily be attributed to consistency in the social settings to which the person is exposed as to any internal characteristic. Personality is always somewhat provisional, and dependent on sanction by others.

Snyder (1984, 1992) reviews several studies which show that personality is susceptible to social feedback, such that individuals tend to behave so as to elicit reactions consistent with their beliefs. For example, in telephone conversation, men elicit more friendly and sociable behaviour from a woman they believe to be attractive rather than unattractive. Presumably, the men's beliefs influence their verbal communication, which, in turn, influences the women's behaviour. Hypotheses about the personality of another person also influence social interaction. Snyder (1992) suggests that such 'behavioural confirmation' effects serve motivations such as getting to know the other, and getting along with the other. Experimental studies show that when other motivations are engaged, such as expressing personal attributes or defending threatening identities, behavioural confirmation is inhibited, and may even be replaced by behavioural disconfirmation. For example, if someone believes the other person thinks them dislikeable, they may make a particular effort to be pleasant.

The weakness of Schlenker and Weigold's (1989) position is that there may, in fact, be consistent individual differences in the self-identifications individuals arrive at across situations. For example, Coyne (1985) has identified a characteristic cycle of interaction between depressed and non-depressed individuals. Depressed patients fail to provide the verbal and non-verbal positive signals to others which normally maintain conversations, such as showing interest in the other person's point of view. So, the non-depressed person finds the interaction increasingly non-rewarding and also makes increasingly negative signals; talking to a depressed person may be upsetting, boring or frustrating. In other words, the two participants jointly negotiate a shared 'depressive' personality through their mutually unsatisfactory interaction. This example indicates the importance of taking into account sources of both consistency and inconsistency. The depressed individual's style of interaction, derived from stable negative self-beliefs, leads to conversations with others being characterised by consistency. For the non-depressed person, whose conversational style is driven mainly by the depressive, the interaction is one in which situational factors are dominant. Hence, it is futile to suggest that either person or situation factors are of more importance in social behaviour; we must necessarily adopt some form of interactionism. Furthermore, traits may relate to characteristic (though context-sensitive) styles of self-identification or other social motivations. Snyder (1992) speculates that Neuroticism has some overlap with defence of threatened identities, Extraversion and Agreeableness with regulating interaction, Openness with acquiring knowledge, and Conscientiousness with expressing personal attributes.

The interactionist perspective: the role of social cues

So far, we have seen that stable social knowledge provides a possible basis for trait stability. In addition, the role of social knowledge in controlling behaviour is sensitive to situational factors. For example, on the basis of Snyder's (1992) work, it seems that a man speaking to a woman might access different elements of knowledge, depending on whether the situation is perceived as an opportunity for intimacy or as a business meeting. The man's personality, accordingly, would appear as either flirtatious or business-like, depending on the situational cues. This social-cognitive perspective is highly compatible with the interactionist position described in chapter 2. Flirtatious behaviour depends on both the person having some stable schema or knowledge of how to act flirtatiously, and on situational cues that allow that knowledge to influence behaviour. Next, we consider in more detail how such person × situation interactions may be conceptualised by social cognitive theorists.

Higgins (1989, 1996) proposed a theory of personality and self-knowledge that addresses person–situation interaction from a social-psychological perspective. Self-knowledge is held as information in long-term memory, and so provides a potential source of consistency. However, knowledge may be potentially *available* but not actually *accessible*. At one level, people differ in the availability of self-knowledge, i.e., the self-beliefs and acquired skills that are capable of guiding social cognition and action. However, in a given situation, only certain self-beliefs are accessible to awareness, and some elements of social knowledge cannot be retrieved. For example, most of us have probably experienced loss of confidence in a difficult situation of some kind, and failed to express ourselves as well as we might in other circumstances. Higgins (1989) suggests that items of knowledge vary in how 'activated' or excited they are; knowledge items must reach a certain level of activation to influence conscious cognition. Situational influences tend to activate congruent knowledge. As discussed in chapter 5, several studies show that when subjects are exposed to personality information, this priming manipulation may lead to unconscious biasing of their judgements of the personality of others.

An important type of knowledge is social standards; internalised beliefs concerning social norms and personal standards. For example, people have 'ideal self-guides' which represent their hopes and aspirations, and 'ought self-guides' which refer to concepts of their social duties and moral responsibilities. They also internalise beliefs about how others see their aspirations and responsibilities. Like Rogers (1951; see chapter 5), Higgins (1989, 1996) believes that discrepancies between the perceived actual self and ideal or ought self-guides are associated with emotional distress: depression when the person fails to live up to ideals, and anxiety when responsibilities are infringed. However, just as with other self-knowledge, the self-guide must be accessed to influence behaviour, so that the effect of the self-guide varies across situations. Such processes may generate a variety of types of person–situation interaction. In Snyder's (1992) studies, we might suppose that male beliefs about female attractiveness bias the accessibility of conversational skills and routines, 'chat-up lines', and the like. The resulting behaviour influences the situational context for the female, which similarly biases her access to knowledge, and subsequent behaviour. Hence, person × situation interaction is dynamic; the accessibility of any item of self-knowledge varies as the encounter unfolds.

This analysis shows how social-cognitive theory complements the modern, interactionist forms of trait theory. Traits may be associated with self-beliefs and action tendencies that are latent, represented as schemas in long-term memory. Activation of schemas (or other knowledge structures) by situational cues supports person × situation interaction. Individuals differ in both the availability of knowledge, and in the extent to which knowledge is chronically accessible (Higgins, 1996). A person high in N might have availability of negative self-beliefs, but only intermittent accessibility, allowing normal social function. However, during some episode of personal failure, negative self-beliefs may become chronically accessible, so that the person may continually ruminate about their shortcomings, leading to clinical depression. There are at least two challenges to such an approach. The first challenge comes from social-cognitive personality theory itself, which supposes that self-knowledge should be conceptualised on a contextual or even idiographic basis (e.g. Caprara and Cervone, 2000), rather than on a nomothetic basis. This challenge may be met by showing that traits are related to consistency in social behaviour across different contexts. The second challenge is whether latent self-knowledge is amenable to measurement, especially by questionnaire. Can the person access the core elements of their self-beliefs while answering questions in a neutral setting? By its nature, latent self-knowledge is difficult to measure directly.

However, operationalising specific aspects or components of self-knowledge may allow the formulation and testing of hypotheses. For example, work on depression has specified some specific beliefs, such as hopelessness, that may mediate the effects of depression on behaviour (Clark and Beck, 1999).

Traits and processes: agreeableness and social behaviour

The literature reviewed demonstrates that there may be no fundamental incompatibility between social cognitive theory and the trait approach. Indeed, social cognitive theory might, in principle, help to elucidate the nature of traits with a strong social component. In this section, we apply this idea to the Agreeableness (A) trait, which has been seen as the trait most closely concerned with interpersonal relationships (Graziano, Jensen-Campbell and Hair, 1996). The contrast between adopting an affiliative, cooperative stance towards others, as opposed to being competitive and confrontive, is seen as a fundamental aspect of social relations (Wiggins and Trapnell, 1996). Within the Five Factor Model, A contrasts qualities such as altruism, cooperativeness, trust and tender-mindedness with being unsympathetic and inconsiderate (though not necessarily actively hostile). In this section, we look at two issues. First, how does A relate to indices of social behaviour? Second, how can we use social-cognitive theory to explain these associations?

Agreeableness and social behaviour

Superficially, we would expect more agreeable individuals to enjoy more positive interpersonal relationships than those low in A. Indeed, there is evidence that high A individuals enjoy a higher quality of social interaction both in general (Asendorpf, 1998), and in specific social interactions investigated in the laboratory (Berry and Sherman, 2000). Conversely, low A relates to more frequent conflicts with others (Suls, Martin and David, 1998), and to aggressive behaviour (Caprara, Barbaranelli and Zimbardo, 1996). The effects of agreeableness on social behaviour can be traced back to childhood, as evidenced by associations with popularity and reduced victimisation by peers (Jensen-Campbell et al., 2002).

A is important also in forming intimate relationships and marriage. Botwin et al. (1997) found that, together with openness/intellect, agreeableness is one of the most important traits that people look for in choosing a partner. This study also showed that high A was the strongest personality predictor of marital and sexual satisfaction. Conversely, low A is the Big Five trait linked most strongly to anger and upset in married couples (Buss, 1991), although neuroticism is also implicated in marital dissatisfaction (Furnham and Heaven, 1999).

In other contexts, there may be disadvantages to being highly agreeable. Suls et al. (1998) used evidence from a diary study to show that agreeableness relates to higher levels of distress experienced following interpersonal conflict. Similarly, high A individuals experience a greater decrease in self-esteem in conflict situations than do low A persons (Barrett and Pietromonaco, 1997). More agreeable persons may also be vulnerable to dependency in social relationships, especially if they are also high in neuroticism (Bornstein and Cecero, 2000). Dependency is a form of abnormal personality characterised by an excessive need to be taken care of, expressed in submissive and clinging behaviour. In business, high A individuals benefit from a superior capacity for teamwork (Neuman and Wright, 1999), but they may suffer as a result of lack of competitiveness in group settings (Graziano, Hair and Finch, 1997).

Cognitive substrate of agreeableness

How could we explain these social-psychological correlates of A? In general, the models reviewed above imply that A may relate to the content of schemas for handling relationships (cf. Baldwin, 2001). More specifically, these schemas may represent trait-characteristic *beliefs* about relationships (e.g., 'other people are generally benevolent'), and *motivations* (e.g., wishing to maintain good relations with others), and styles of *action* (e.g., social skills for affiliative behaviours). Although research in this area is sparse, there is a burgeoning empirical literature that relates A to constructs of this kind. It is important to note that the social processes associated with A are not necessarily accessible to consciousness; more behavioural studies are required to investigate unconscious processes.

Perhaps the simplest hypothesis is that A is associated with social perceptions (Jensen-Campbell and Graziano, 2001). Consistent with this hypothesis, a study conducted in an experimentally controlled small-group setting showed that A correlates with greater acceptance of both self and others (Hurley, 1998). Similarly, high A persons report lower perceptions of conflict in everyday settings monitored by use of a diary study (Barrett and Pietromonaco, 1997), and see themselves as being relatively less competitive than others (Graziano, Hair and Finch, 1997). Turning to aggressive personality, as a correlate of low A, we find evidence for distortions of appraisal, in the form of exaggerated beliefs in the hostility and malevolence of other people (Matthews, Schwean et al., 2000). Olson and Evans (1999) investigated how social appraisals contribute to mood-regulation. An important appraisal process is comparison of self with others: 'downward comparison' of oneself with people of inferior status may promote greater self-esteem and happiness. Olson and Evans (1999) quote Schopenhauer:

> The best consolation in misfortune or affliction of any kind will be the thought of other people who are in a still worse plight than yourself; and this is a form of consolation open to every one.

Olson and Evans correlated the Big Five with use of downward comparison, which was linked to low A; perhaps these individuals are most likely to enjoy the misfortunes of others. In addition, high A individuals experienced loss of positive affect following upward comparison (i.e., with people of higher status). Perhaps highly agreeable persons tend to be somewhat deferential and submissive, rendering them vulnerable to unfavourable upward comparisons. The low A person may be more thick-skinned. Whiteman et al. (2001), however, found near-zero correlations between NEO-FFI A and submissiveness.

Agreeableness has also been linked to motivation and action. In general, high A is associated with motives for maintaining positive interpersonal relations (Jensen-Campbell and Graziano, 2001). These authors conducted a diary-based study of adolescents that investigated the role of A in conflict-resolution. They found that both self- and teacher-rated agreeableness predicted the tactics reported in conflict resolution. High A was linked to use of compromise, and to avoidance of physical force and threats. Moreover, A was negatively correlated with 'walking away' from conflict, implying a need to maintain interpersonal engagement. In adults, a further diary study showed an association between A and 'loyalty', i.e., maintaining relations despite problems, and, conversely, a negative association with 'exit' from social interaction (Berry, Willingham and Thayer, 2000). Similarly, Antonioni (1999) showed that high A persons use more integration and less domination in resolving conflict. Conversely, at the disagreeable end of the spectrum, aggression may be associated with the automatic access of confrontive behaviours in response to social problems (Rabiner et al., 1990). In an interesting study of nonverbal behaviour, Berry and Sherman Hansen (2000) videotaped pairs of students participating in social interaction. Independent observers coded their behaviours. High A related to greater visual attention, more 'open' body positions, and physical orientation of the body towards the other person. Low A participants showed more frequent negative facial expressions. High A was related to higher ratings of the overall quality of interaction, and this association was mediated by visual attention and body openness.

Overall, these studies show that agreeableness is associated with a variety of social-cognitive processes that influence whether a social encounter is affiliative or confrontational. These findings are compatible with high A and low A individuals differing in the content of the social knowledge they have in long-term memory. Whether these social-cognitive attributes are beneficial to the person or not depends on whether the situation calls for cooperation or competition. Further research is needed to develop and test such a theory in more detail. For example, it is unclear how much variance in social behaviour reflects the availability of knowledge in memory, and how much individual differences in accessing knowledge in specific situations. However, it is clear that agreeableness influences social cognition, and explaining the role of this trait is an essential component of the social psychology of interpersonal relationships.

'Social psychological' traits

In the previous section, we discussed how empirical studies allow us to relate a longstanding trait construct to social-psychological constructs. Another way to integrate these two approaches to personality is to operationalise as traits constructs taken directly from social-psychological theory. Next, we review some traits of this kind. It is convenient to divide them into two categories. The first concerns the person's stable social beliefs and attitudes. Such traits may reflect the qualitative content of schemas or other knowledge structures in long-term memory. The second category is that of traits related to the self, which may relate to the content of self-schemas.

Belief and attitude systems

Perhaps the best-known attitude-based trait is the authoritarian personality, seen as a coherent pattern of social and political attitudes (Adorno et al., 1950). In its original form, authoritarianism was associated with deference to authority figures, hostility towards those outside the dominant social group, such as ethnic minorities, and strong right-wing or even Fascist political beliefs. Adorno et al. devised a variety of scales for authoritarianism. The most successful was the F-scale, which measures 'potentiality for fascism', and has had some success in predicting criteria such as racial prejudice. Kline (1993) points out that the original F-scale was sensitive to acquiescence and social desirability response biases, and the items (which relate to the McCarthyite period of American history) are dated. He recommends an updated version of the F-scale, Altmeyer's (1981) Right-Wing Authoritarianism Scale.

Several difficulties have emerged for the authoritarianism construct. First, authoritarian attitudes such as prejudice may not simply be a function of the knowledge organisation of the individual; socio-cultural factors may be more important (Billig, 1976). Indices of national authoritarianism in the USA appear to be sensitive to economic hardship (Sales, 1973), so that it may be seen almost as a kind of group coping mechanism in the face of a threat to the group. Second, as Eysenck (1954) has pointed out, authoritarianism is not limited to right-wingers; Stalin would be as good an exemplar as Hitler of an extreme authoritarian. Third, its distinctiveness from broad personality traits is unclear. Kline and Cooper (1984) concluded from psychometric evidence that authoritarianism is the social expression of the obsessional personality, which relates to Conscientiousness. Authoritarianism scales are also substantially negatively correlated with Openness (MacCrae, 1996). Fourth, the psychological basis for authoritarianism is unclear. Originally, Adorno et al. (1950) related it to a psychoanalytic conception of excessive parental discipline causing the child to displace aggression from its parents to other, weaker individuals. However, as we saw in chapter 5, such hypotheses are difficult to test. A more promising hypothesis is cognitive in nature; that high F-scorers are characterised by low 'integrative complexity', so that they perceive the world in simplistic, stereotyped categories, and have little tolerance for ambiguity (Simonton, 1990).

Other traits relate directly to acceptance of cultural beliefs. Hui and Triandis (1986) discuss a dimension of collectivism vs individualism, which relates to adherence to group standards, and is higher in Asian than in American samples (see also Triandis, 2001). A measure of the Protestant Work Ethic has been developed by Furnham (1990) which relates to beliefs such as the importance of attaining security through hard work and responsibility. It predicts a variety of occupational criteria including dissatisfaction with unemployment and retirement and attitudes to work (e.g., Mudrack, 1997).

A final example is provided by adherence to masculine or feminine sex roles. From the social psychological perspective, gender is socially constructed; children must learn the gender-appropriate behaviour and personal appearance of their particular culture. Bem (1981) suggested that gender role identification depends on a gender schema, which may differ from person to person. The Bem Sex Role Inventory (BSRI) (Bem, 1974) assesses the individual's strength of adherence to independent, culturally defined sex roles of femininity and masculinity, which result from gender-schematic processing. Bem views traditional sex roles as restrictive, such that a balance of masculinity and femininity ('androgyny') is psychologically healthy and allows greater flexibility of action. However, there is little evidence that androgyny is reliably related to mental health, and experimental work on the BSRI and gender-schematic processing have provided inconsistent results (Cook, 1985; Carson, 1989). On the other hand, gender role measures are valid as predictors of cognitive functioning, especially on tasks requiring visuo-spatial processing. Both masculinity and androgyny may be associated with superior performance (Hamilton, 1995). It is possible that individuals with more masculine gender schemata are more likely to take part in activities such as sports which develop spatial processing skills, although, as Hamilton (1995) indicates, there is little direct evidence that gender schemata are responsible for individual differences. Some limitations of the BSRI have also emerged. Factor analytic studies have generally confirmed that masculinity and femininity are distinct dimensions, but there is some inconsistency across studies in the factors obtained from the BSRI (Auster and Ohm, 2001). There is considerable overlap with the Big Five: Marusic and Bratko (1998) found that masculinity correlated at about 0.55 with extraversion, and femininity correlated at similar magnitude with agreeableness (in both genders: $n=464$). Masculinity also correlated at ~0.3 with high conscientiousness, low neuroticism and low agreeableness. Cultural norms for masculine and feminine behaviour have changed since its development (Auster and Ohm, 2001), and responses vary with context (Smith, Noll and Bryant, 1999), implying that the gender schema is dynamic and situational (consistent with social-psychological principles). On the other hand, masculinity and femininity have heritabilities similar to broad personality traits (Lippa and Hershberger, 1999): an ironic finding, given the original attribution of sex role to social learning.

Self-related traits

Some trait measures attempt to assess individual differences in the functions of the self. Perhaps the most widely used is the questionnaire developed by Fenigstein, Scheier and Buss (1975) to measure dispositional self-consciousness, the person's tendency to focus attention on the self. The questionnaire has three sub-scales relating to private self-consciousness (attention to internal thoughts and feelings), public self-consciousness (attention to outwardly observable aspects of the self) and social anxiety (attention to others' observations of the self). There is considerable empirical evidence for the validity of the scales (Carver and Scheier, 1981; Wells and Matthews, 1994).

Private self-consciousness seems to be distinct from the Big Five, although the other two scales tend to be quite highly correlated with neuroticism (see Wells and Matthews, 1994). Carver and Scheier (1981) have proposed a cybernetic theory of control of self-related functions which provides a theoretical basis for the dispositional self-consciousness construct. Self-attention serves to assess the individual's current status with respect to some behavioural standard, and to initiate action if the individual fails to meet the standard. The action may comprise either some active coping attempt or withdrawal and disengagement, depending on the chances of success. Dispositional self-consciousness may be particularly important as an influence on stress vulnerability, as discussed further in chapter 9.

There are a variety of other traits which explicitly relate to the self. Snyder (1979) has developed a self-monitoring scale, which, rather like Fenigstein et al.'s (1975) social anxiety dimension, relates sensitivity to the self-relevant cues provided by others. Other work is concerned with the relationship between 'personal' and 'social' selves. We might suppose that some people would view themselves as being highly personally autonomous, whereas others define themselves primarily in terms of group membership. Cheek and Hogan (1983) distinguish independent personal and social identity dimensions. The high personal identity individual is oriented towards achievement, whereas the high social identity person seeks group acceptance. As previously discussed, there are also widely used scales for dispositional self-esteem, although such scales may measure little more than a mixture of extraversion and low neuroticism (Kline, 1993; Judge et al., 2002).

A rapprochement between social psychology and trait theory?

The social psychological tradition has been of major importance to personality research, though not always to investigations of traits. The material reviewed in this chapter suggests that it is time for a rapprochement between social psychology and the trait approach. Considerable progress has been made along each of the steps necessary to link traits to social psychological constructs. Temperament and social-learning processes appear to be mutually influential, so we can start to describe how social-cognitive processes may mediate environmental effects on personality (within a dynamic, interactionist framework). Social-cognitive theory itself provides a rationale for stable mental structures ('schemas') that generate consistency of behaviour, in line with the assumptions of the inner locus and causal primacy of traits described in chapter 1. The role of situational cues in modifying the accessibility of self-knowledge accommodates trait × situation interaction: the situation determines which elements of self-knowledge control behaviour.

Social psychological theory describes a variety of knowledge-based constructs that might relate to traits common to all individuals. We focused on Agreeableness, but similar arguments apply to other traits. For example, extraversion relates to sets of beliefs cohering around social confidence, and neuroticism to beliefs about vulnerability to danger, especially social threat (Matthews, Schwean et al., 2000). Conscientiousness tends to relate to social conformity and a task-oriented coping style (Matthews, 1989; Deary et al., 1996). More narrowly defined traits such as self-consciousness, (generalised) self-efficacy and attachment style may also be important, together with traits relating to internalisation of cultural beliefs, such as the Protestant Work Ethic and individualism–collectivism. Of course, these traits overlap with broad traits such as the Big Five. Both broad and narrow traits may correspond to distinctive sets of beliefs, attitudes, action tendencies and social motivations that mediate their effects on social behaviour (Matthews, Schwean et al., 2000). We should also note that traits related to social desirability, discussed in chapter 13, may influence the person's style of self-presentation and management of the impression presented to others.

Unfortunately, the historical animosity between trait and social-psychological approaches continues to impede progress. There is growing interest in bridging the traditional divide, but old attitudes die hard. According to Bandura (1999, p. 202):

> There is little evidence that repackaging of traits in a fivefold format has produced any better prediction of human behaviour than do the traditional trait measures . . . which are not much to rave about. The inflated self-congratulatory claims of breakthrough stand in stark contrast to the paucity of empirical reality tests of predictiveness . . . Gains in social consensus among trait theorists about the number of supertraits without gains in predictive power hardly constitute an advance in the field of personality.

For Bandura (1999), the key problems are (1) that trait explanations are circular, because an aggregrated behavioural measure (i.e., the trait) is being used to explain behaviour, and (2) the personal determinants of behaviour are multiple processes whose operation is contextually determined (see also Caprara and Cervone, 2000). How much force do these criticisms have? We hope that Bandura's view that traits lack sufficient predictive power is countered by evidence throughout this book. The view that trait explanations are circular seems to misrepresent trait theory, which, from Allport's (1937) time, has always been concerned as much with underlying mechanisms for trait action as with descriptive schemes. (It is true that a selective reading of psychometric studies might not reflect these concerns.) Eysenck (1967) identified the causal influence of brain systems as critical to theory, and Costa and McCrae (1992) also see the theoretical basis for traits as an essential argument for their relevance. As Mischel (1999) recognises, temperament may influence the development of specific cognitive-affective units, and so applying social-psychological methods to trait psychology may contribute to a more sophisticated understanding of traits as latent causal agents, rather than manifest regularities of behaviour.

The context-dependence of much of the variance in individual differences in behaviour is a more substantial issue. Evidently, individuals show idiographic stabilities in behaviour that cannot be explained by nomothetic traits (Cervone and Shoda, 1999). Furthermore, dispositional factors may vary systematically from situation to situation, requiring contextualised assessments of personality. Both observations may be accommodated within trait theory, in that, first, trait models have always recognised that some variance is idiographic (Allport, 1937), and, second, trait theory includes contextualised trait measures, such as test anxiety scales. Human social environments have sufficient structure that we can identify specific contexts, such as being evaluated, being in conflict and being romantically attached, and operationalise appropriate dispositional measures. As Mischel (1999) describes, dispositions may be analysed at different levels, and there is a place for both nomothetic and idiographic approaches. Dispositions are indeed a 'foundation stone in personality psychology' (Mischel, 1999, p. 52), and dispositions may be represented in social-cognitive terms as distinct, stable patterns of cognitive-affective units. These patterns define how the disposition is related to processing dynamics and enactment of behaviours, subject to the moderating role of situational cues.

In suggesting this rapprochement, we must point out that many socially oriented researchers would not share the assumptions made that (1) social knowledge can be (partially) characterised in terms of nomothetic dimensions (e.g., Cervone and Caprara, 2000), and (2) social knowledge is supported by cognitive structures within the individual. Hence, there are three alternative positions which might be taken. If we accept the first, but not the second assumption, we arrive at a position similar to that of Markus and Cross (1989), who wish to move away from self-structures as causal influences on behaviour. While we may still refer to nomothetic constructs such as self-esteem or androgyny, understanding of such constructs requires understanding of the dynamic interaction between people. If we accept the second assumption, but not the first, we arrive at an idiographic trait psychology. It is meaningful to assign causal status to self-beliefs, etc., but such beliefs resist nomothetic classification. Such an approach would be compatible with the idiographic methods discussed in chapter 5. If both assumptions are rejected, we have a radical constructivist approach such as that of Harré and Gillett (1994), representing, in our view, the retrograde step of replacing the 'Hall of Fame' with a hall of mirrors.

Finally, one of the themes of this book is that personality researchers have made great advances in bridging Cronbach's (1957) divide between differential and ex-perimental psychology. We look forward to research which crosses the equally gaping chasm between social psychological and natural science approaches to personality. To the trait researcher, the lack of contact between much of the social psychological research and the trait approach is frustrating. Social psychology pro-vides a wealth of constructs which are open to operationalisation and measurement, and might substantially enrich understanding of traits. Careful experimental work is required to investigate whether social knowledge should be assigned causal status. There are at least three causal possibilities:

1 Traits might be causally antecedent to social knowledge, as factors biasing basic social learning processes, as in the psychobiological theories of Eysenck (1967) and Gray (1991). Threat sensitivity might lead to more negative self- and social cognitions, for example.
2 Social knowledge might be causally antecedent to traits, if it is long-term memory that controls personality. A negative self-schema might produce the various manifestations of neuroticism, for example (similar to Beck's 1967 theory of depression).
3 There may be some dynamic, reciprocal relationship between traits and social knowledge: biases in basic processes and in knowledge structures may be mutually interdependent (e.g., Zeidner et al., 2003). For example, biases in various levels of processing of threat may contribute to building a negative self-schema, which, in turn, feeds back into further biasing of processing.

Much work remains to be done on the construct validity of the different social-psychological constructs and how they fit into the nomological network with traits. Wells and Matthews (1994) point out that there is a variety of qualitatively different cognitive models capable of explaining the origin of reportable self-beliefs, which are difficult to distinguish experimentally. Studies are also needed which directly pit biological and social-cognitive explanations for specific phenomena against one another. It is also conceivable that consciously available self-beliefs are epiphenomenal to brain processes; like a sports commentator, the 'stream-of-consciousness' may be removed from the field of play. Social psychology may also be prone to over-complicate the origins of self-awareness. According to Gazzaniga (1994, p. 203) '. . . one does not learn to be conscious. When the brain starts to function, up it comes, just like steam out of a turbine.'

Conclusions

1. Both trait theories and social-psychological accounts of personality seek to explain individual differences in social behaviours such as forming friendships, acting aggressively and conforming to social and cultural standards. Trait theory supposes that these behaviours show some cross-situational consistency, that relate to both broad and narrow traits. Social-psychological theories can be loosely subdivided into constructivist and social-cognitive theories. Constructivist theories suppose that personality is continuously created and recreated through discourse between people: it is located 'between' rather than 'within' persons. Social-cognitive theories assume that cognitive structures in long-term memory represent the person's social beliefs and motivations, giving consistency to behaviour. However, by contrast with trait theory, it is assumed that

this stable social knowledge is generally context-specific or even idiographic, and dependent on social learning.

2. Social-psychological approaches may be informative about the role of environmental factors in personality development. During childhood there is reciprocal interaction between the child and its social environment. The behaviour of others, especially caregivers, influences social knowledge and hence personality. Conversely, the child's own behaviour influences how others behave ('difficult' children may elicit suboptimal parenting) and the social environments to which the child is exposed ('inhibited' children may avoid strangers). Two trait-like constructs that may be linked to the quality of the child's social interactions are self-efficacy and attachment style. Self-efficacy refers to the person's confidence that they can execute actions that will allow them to master environmental challenges. Dispositional self-efficacy is predictive of various criteria, although there has been controversy over the meaningfulness of generalised self-efficacy measures (as opposed to measures linked to a specific context, such as work). Attachment style refers to the security of the child's bond with its parents. Despite some psychometric difficulties, measures of attachment style have some validity as predictors of adult social relationships.

3. Social-cognitive theory provides accounts of both consistencies and inconsistencies in social behaviour. Stable knowledge structures, such as the 'self-schema', encode beliefs and procedural skills. The extent to which items of social knowledge control behaviour in a specific situation depends both on the content of stable knowledge (availability) and on the extent to which social cues activate knowledge in the situation (accessibility). There is increasing evidence that some elements of social knowledge may be accessible across different situations, supporting behavioural consistency that may relate to traits. However, most social psychologists emphasise the contextual nature of social knowledge.

4. Broad traits, such as the Big Five, may relate to elements of social knowledge. We illustrated the growing convergence between trait and social-cognitive approaches by reviewing empirical studies of Agreeableness (A) and social behaviour. A relates positively to affiliative and cooperative behaviours, but negatively to aggression and performance in competitive settings. Further studies show that A is related to basic social-cognitive processes such as social perception, social comparison and choice of behavioural tactics for dealing with conflict.

5. Various narrower or midlevel traits also appear to have a social-psychological basis. Some traits refer to beliefs and attitudes that are known to be central to cultural values, such as authoritarianism and individualism–collectivism. Other traits describe properties of the self. These traits include self-consciousness and self-esteem. Such traits may describe the contents of self-knowledge, although it remains unclear whether self-knowledge that is inaccessible to consciousness may be validly assessed by questionnaire.

6. The evidence reviewed in this chapter suggests that developmental interaction with caregivers and others builds stable self-knowledge. Some of this knowledge controls behaviour across multiple situations and may provide a cognitive core to personality traits. Other elements of self-knowledge are nomothetic but linked to specific contexts (e.g. test anxiety), whereas further elements are entirely idiographic. Hence, the traditional antagonism between trait and social-psychological approaches to personality is misplaced, and both branches of inquiry may learn from one another.

Further reading

Boekarts, M., Pintrich, P. R. and Zeidner, M. (eds.) (2000) *Handbook of self-regulation*. New York: Academic.

Caprara, G. V. and Cervone, D. (2000) *Personality: determinants, dynamics, and potentials*. Cambridge: Cambridge University Press.

Furnham, A. and Heaven, P. (1999) *Personality and social behaviour*. London: Arnold.

Consequences and applications

9 Stress

Stress is a necessary part of life, but the impact it has on people varies, depending partly on their personality traits. In this chapter, we discuss how personality, stress reactions, styles of cognitive appraisal and coping relate to stress vulnerability and emotional problems arising from stress. The most straightforward research on personality and stress is correlational in nature. As we shall see, there is abundant evidence that shows traits, especially neuroticism (N), are associated with high levels of stress symptoms, including mental disorders. Beyond correlational studies, there are several more difficult issues. One issue is whether high N is truly a causative factor on stress outcomes: perhaps increased N is simply a concomitant of stress, with no direct causal influence. A second theme which we will develop is that 'stress' refers to a multitude of concepts that may be only loosely related, including exposure to disturbing events, physiological response to threat, biases in cognition and disruption of everyday social interaction. A third theme is that of person–situation interaction in the stress process, consistent with the interactionist approaches to personality reviewed in chapter 2.

Defining stress

It is useful to begin with some definitions of stress. Because the term 'stress' is imprecise, it is interpreted in many different ways. Therefore, below, we give a brief overview of the concept of 'stress' before we consider, in the rest of the chapter, how it relates to personality traits. Stress can be thought of in three main ways (Matthews, 2000b; Sarafino, 2002):

(1) *As a stimulus (stressor)*. This is an external event that is threatening and potentially damaging (Baum, 1990). Lazarus and Cohen (1977) break such stressors into three categories: (1) cataclysmic, such as natural disasters or terrorist attacks; (2) personal, such as the death of a partner; and (3) daily hassles, which are more minor but also more persistent and frequent (e.g., having to get the children up, fed and to school on time).

(2) *As a response (strain)*. This is the feeling of nervousness that arises from having to attend an interview or give a speech, for example. The response involves

emotional and cognitive components as well as physical reactions (e.g., rapid heart beat or sweating). It may also have motivational elements, such as the apathy and loss of interest that accompany 'burn-out'.

(3) *As a process (transaction).* The stressor and the strain have a different impact on a person depending on the characteristics of the person and the environment in which the stressor exists (e.g., Cox, 1978; Lazarus and Folkman, 1984; Lazarus, 1999). This approach takes into account the fact that the same external events will have different effects depending on the person experiencing them. This view is summed up neatly by Carroll (1992): 'stress, like beauty, lies in the eye of the beholder' (p. 5). It also views the person as an active agent who tries to *cope* with external demands using various strategies. Thus, the stress process has a cyclical aspect, as the person tries to cope with stressors, and reacts to the changing external situation. The process may sometimes run in a loop: a stressor poses a threat, which causes a feeling of strain or nervousness, which, if the person fails to cope adequately with the stressor, feeds back into further stress symptoms.

In short, although in one sense 'stress' may refer only to a particular event, within psychology it is more usually understood as the transaction between the environmental stressor and the individual. Broadly, stress is the result of a mismatch between the demands of a given situation and the individual's perceived ability to deal with those demands (e.g., Lazarus and Folkman, 1984; Cox and Ferguson, 1991; Lazarus, 1999). However, to make further progress, it is important to operationalise the different processes and outcomes that contribute to the stress process. As a start, it is important to differentiate (1) 'stressors' or external events that potentially elicit psychological disturbance, (2) outcomes or symptoms, such as anxiety or abnormal behaviour, and (3) physiological and psychological processes that may intervene between the potentially stressful stimulus and the subsequent stress response (Matthews, 2000b). Personality might influence each of these constructs, i.e., (1) structuring people's lives in ways that precipitate more frequent life events, (2) biasing processes such as coping, and (3) controlling the magnitude of stress response.

Measuring stress

Reliable and valid measurement of stress responses is critical for personality research. Physiologically, stress is indicated in a number of ways: rapid heart beat, sweating, raised blood pressure and raised levels of circulating 'stress hormones' (e.g., cortisol) in the blood. Many of the 'arousal' indices discussed in chapter 7 may also be used to index the stress response. These reactions are easy to measure in controlled settings, by exposing the person to a stressful task (such as public speaking). More commonly, stress is measured by self-report questionnaire: from reporting of major life events or daily hassles to specific measures of occupational stress (e.g., Holmes and Rahe, 1967; Kanner et al., 1981; Karasek and Theorell,

1990). As discussed in chapter 4, subjective stress has emotional, cognitive and motivational aspects (Matthews, Campbell et al., 2002). In some studies both physiological and self-report measures are used, thus allowing the validation of the questionnaire against a physiological measure, or, not infrequently, showing dissociation of physiological and self-report responses (e.g., Huwe, Hennig and Netter, 1998).

The remainder of this chapter is organised as follows. First, we discuss studies that directly investigate individual differences in physical reactivity to stressors. Next, we outline the evidence that traits, especially N, relate to stress vulnerability, assessed as both subclinical stress symptoms, and mental disorders. These correlational studies naturally raise the issue of causality, and we proceed to review the evidence for a causal role for N in the stress process. Next, we turn to more theoretically oriented research based upon the transactional definition of stress, that investigates how biases in appraisal and coping may mediate effects of N on stress outcomes. Related research has been directed towards the hypothesis that traits may have protective 'stress-buffering' effects when the person is exposed to adverse life events. Finally, we interrelate some of the themes of this chapter, by looking a dynamic, transactional model of how N relates to emotional pathology.

Stress and physiological reactivity

There is some evidence to suggest that physiological reactions to stress are different between individuals: some are highly reactive, and some are less reactive. For instance, heart rate responses are exaggerated in people who are stress prone (e.g., Carroll, 1992). Before explaining this further, however, we briefly describe the basic biology of the stress response, with particular reference to Cannon's (1929) 'fight-or-flight' phenomenon and Selye's (1976) work on the general adaptation syndrome (GAS).

According to Selye's (1976) model, when a person is confronted with a stressful situation, the body prepares for either running away from or confronting the stressor. This is known as 'alarm' or Stage 1, of the GAS. In Stage 1, the body's 'hypothalamus–pituitary–adrenal axis' is activated: the hypothalamus stimulates the pituitary gland to secrete ACTH (adrenocorticotropic hormone), which then causes epinephrine (adrenalin), norepinephrine and cortisol to be released from the adrenal glands into the bloodstream. These hormones cause the characteristic sweating, rise in blood pressure and increased heart rate – symptoms we can easily identify with nervousness – that help the body either to 'fight' or to 'flee' (Cannon, 1929). In the second stage (resistance), the body tries to adjust to the still-present stressor. The level of arousal drops (but not back to normal levels) and hormone stores are replenished. The increased arousal may not be apparent to outside observers, but in this stage the body is weakened and the person may be more prone to mental or physical health problems. Finally, if the stressor continues, in the third stage (exhaustion), the body's resources are totally depleted and health problems, even death (if the stressor is extreme), are much more likely to occur.

Selye (1976) postulated that the general adaptation syndrome is non-specific, and that the same set of reactions occurs in response to physical or emotional stressors. The strength of the reaction, however, does vary depending on how stressful the event is judged to be (Sarafino, 2002). As we will see later in the chapter, the cognitive appraisal of the same event may be quite different in two people. For example, a person who is afraid of flying may consider going on a far-flung holiday to be extremely stressful, whereas a person who likes flying may consider the holiday travelling to be much less stressful. In addition, physiological responses to the same stressor (which may be either a physical or mental stressor) differ across individuals (e.g., Carroll, 1992; Steptoe et al., 2000; Marsland et al., 2001). That is, the biological stress response itself reflects multiple dimensions of individual differences, at least some of which dimensions are closely related both to personality and cognitive appraisal mechanisms.

Individual differences in the physiological stress response

Some researchers have found that individual differences in physiological reactivity to stress are stable over time: people who have exaggerated responses on one occasion are likely to do so on other occasions. Carroll et al. (1984) studied young male students who were asked to play a video game. Those with the greatest increases in heart rate in response to the task still showed greater responsivity when doing the same task each day for four days; those with the lowest responses continued to have low reactivity. In a second study using video games as the stressor, heart-rate reactions were found to be stable between the baseline task and the same task given again, twenty months later (Turner et al., 1986). Other studies have demonstrated that there is differential stress hormone release (cortisol) in subjects subjected to a mental stressor in the laboratory (Roy, Kirschbaum and Steptoe, 2001), which is stable across tasks. Low stress hormone reactors remained low, and high reactors remained high, across the tasks. A similar study examining blood pressure and immune response found that individuals differed reliably in their level of physiological activation to a mental stressor (an arithmetic task and a mirror-tracing task; Steptoe et al., 2001). There is uncertainty as to whether physiological hyper-reactivity is innate or not, but some studies of the genetic contribution to reactivity (using twin pairs) have shown that heart-rate reactivity may have a biological basis (Carroll et al., 1985). Research in this area is difficult to carry out, in part because of the challenges of replicating 'real-life' situations inside the laboratory; however, studies of teachers have shown that the teachers' physiological reactions to episodes of work rated as being under low personal control show similar patterns to physiological reactions to uncontrollable laboratory tasks (Steptoe, 2001).

As outlined in Box 9.1, the genetic contribution to traits may be expressed through various aspects of stress vulnerability. However, it has proved difficult

Box 9.1 A genetic contribution to coping?

Coping styles are related to personality. For example, people high in neuroticism have a tendency to use emotion-focused, passive coping strategies, and highly conscientious people tend to use active, problem-focused coping strategies (Watson and Hubbard, 1996). As we have shown in chapter 6, personality traits are partly heritable, so it is possible that genetic contributions to coping are mediated by personality traits. However, there is some evidence to suggest that there is a genetic basis for coping styles that is separate from personality (Kendler et al., 1991; Mellins et al., 1996; Busjahn et al., 1999). In a study based at Humboldt University in Berlin, Busjahn et al. studied 212 pairs of monozygotic and dizygotic twins. They assessed coping styles using a self-report scale, finding associations between neuroticism and emotion-focused coping, as expected. They also found that their four coping factors (defence, emotion, substitution and active coping) all showed evidence of genetic variance; some of the subscales also showed evidence for shared genetic and environmental effects. Few such studies of coping style have been conducted, but future research could help elucidate the role that genetic factors have on both personality and coping styles.

to relate physiological reactivity to the standard personality traits (see also chapter 7). For example, although high N individuals are more reactive to stressors emotionally, one study showed a reduced cortisol response in this group, perhaps because the HPA is 'downregulated' to prevent harmful overactivation (McCleery and Goodwin, 2001), an idea similar to the TMI concept discussed in chapter 7. In addition to studies of the physiological stress response, personality and cognitive predictors of stress proneness in individuals have been widely researched – and have been greatly facilitated by the resurgence of trait theory and psychometrically sound measures of traits. It is to this research that we turn next.

Neuroticism and stress vulnerability

Personality traits are consistently related to measures of well-being (Diener et al., 1999), and the trait that has been found to be most salient for stress reactions is neuroticism (N). In some senses, high N in itself can be considered to be a form of stress proneness: a high N individual's persistent worry, feelings of inadequacy, tension and nervousness are unpleasant, stressful feelings. However, this does not mean that emotionally stable people never feel stressed, merely that stress is less a feature of their everyday lives than it is for someone who is emotionally labile. Major events such as bereavement, divorce or loss of job will almost always elicit some stress response, although the magnitude of the response may vary with personality. In this section we look, successively, at (1) N

Table 9.1 *Correlations between neuroticism, extraversion and scales of the General Health Questionnaire, in two student samples*

		GHQ scale			
	Total score	Somatic symptoms	Social dysfunction	Depression	Anxiety/insomnia
Undergraduates (*n* = 77)					
Neuroticism	59**	29**	32**	57**	68**
Extraversion	−32**	−19	−31**	−23*	−25*
Postgraduates (*n* = 214)					
Neuroticism	53**	40**	30**	42**	54**
Extraversion	−25**	−16*	−27**	−21**	−22**

Note *P<.05, **P<.01
Source Mohamed (1996)

and everyday, relatively minor stress symptoms, (2) N and emotional disorder and (3) the causal status of N.

Neuroticism and stress outcomes in everyday life

Much evidence shows that high N relates to various indices of subclinical stress in everyday life, consistent with the robust associations between N and states of negative affect noted in chapter 4. N also relates to lower life satisfaction and subjective well-being (e.g., DeNeve and Cooper, 1998), and to job dissatisfaction and strain indices of job strain (Tokar, Fischer and Subich, 1998; see also chapter 13). Various instruments may be used to assess longer-lasting emotional disturbance. Goldberg's (1978) General Health Questionnaire (GHQ) is widely used to detect recent deterioration in a person's well-being, and it can also be used to screen individuals for possible psychiatric disorder. Two studies of undergraduate and postgraduate students (Mohamed, 1996; Matthews, Schwean et al., 2000) found that N was consistently related to overall levels of stress symptoms, as shown in table 9.1. N was also associated with the different symptoms assessed by the four subscales of the GHQ, with the highest correlations being for anxiety and depression subscales. Correlations with somatic or physical symptoms of ill-health, and with social dysfunction in everyday life, were rather lower. Although introversion was related to stress symptoms, the strengths of the relationships are considerably weaker. Deary et al. (1996) reported similar associations between N and GHQ dimensions, and showed that the introversion–GHQ correlations fell to non-significant levels when N was partialled out. A special source of stress for university students is homesickness, whose relationship to N is described in Box 9.2. High N vehicle drivers are also prone to stress in the form of anger, irritation, anxiety and lack of confidence (Matthews, Dorn and Glendon, 1991).

Box 9.2 Homesickness, stress and personality in students

Homesickness is surprisingly common amongst both male and female university students. Estimates of the incidence of homesickness in first-year students range from 39 to 72 per cent (Brewin, Furnham and Howes, 1989). Homesickness can interfere with academic work; homesick students report higher levels of absent-mindedness, cognitive failure and late handing in of work (Fisher, 1989). Individual differences in homesickness may be reliably assessed with Fisher's (1989) Dundee Relocation Inventory (DRI). Mohamed (1996) obtained measures of appraisal and coping style from 214 postgraduate students, together with personality scores. Subjects high in neuroticism and introversion tended to be more homesick. A pessimistic style of appraisal and adoption of confrontive and self-critical coping strategies were also associated with homesickness. Further analysis showed that the two personality variables of neuroticism and extraversion together predicted 20 per cent of the variance in homesickness. However, when individual differences in appraisal and coping were statistically controlled, the variance explained by personality dropped to 4 per cent. Students who are high in N and low in E appear to be susceptible to homesickness largely because of their somewhat dysfunctional cognitive stress processes.

Anxiety and depression are not the only symptoms experienced more often by people high in neuroticism; those high in N are also more sensitive to adverse emotional reactions to the various hassles and upsets of everyday life. Bolger and Schilling (1991) had 339 subjects provide daily reports of minor stressful events and mood for six weeks. High N subjects reported higher emotional distress than low N subjects following stressful events – for example, work overload or financial troubles. Arguments with a child or spouse were stressful for all respondents, but were particularly distressing for high N subjects (see figure 9.1). Students, too, show a similar pattern: in 119 medical students, neuroticism was related to two of five different 'daily hassles' measures (Vollrath, 2000). However, while the daily hassles measures were relatively stable over time, personality traits were not the strongest predictors of hassles; there was also some evidence that hassles predicted later levels of neuroticism.

There is evidence too that N may be associated with behavioural disturbances attributed, in part, to stress. High N subjects report they are more prone to cognitive failures: everyday errors such as switching on an empty bottle. Another correlate of N is sexual problems such as nervousness, guilt and inhibition (Kennedy et al., 1999). Neuroticism is also associated with difficulties in interacting with other people and poorer quality social relationships (Berry, Willingham and Thayer, 2000). For example, neuroticism seems to predispose people to marital problems (O'Leary and Smith, 1991) and to shyness (Crozier, 1982). Neuroticism also tends to be high in certain types of criminal, such as those who are socially inadequate (Eysenck, Rust and Eysenck, 1977), and in alcoholics and drug users

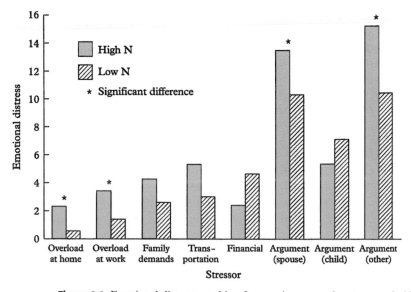

Figure 9.1 Emotional distress resulting from various everyday stressors in high and low neuroticism subjects
Source Bolger and Schilling, 1991

(Furnham, 1992). A three-year longitudinal study (Jessor, Turbin and Costa, 1998) found that low self-esteem and hopelessness, both traits linked to N, related negatively to various indices of social adjustment in adolescents. These effects were moderated by protective factors, such as having attitudes intolerant of deviance and having conventional role models. It has also been suggested that deviance may be best predicted by narrow traits such as impulsivity, rather than the broad traits of the Big Five (Heaven, 1996). Also, individual differences in deviance may relate primarily to psychoticism and related traits, rather than to stress vulnerability (Furnham and Heaven, 1999).

Vulnerability to psychiatric symptoms

It is well known that psychiatric patients diagnosed with severe depression or generalised anxiety are more likely to have high neuroticism or negative affectivity, sometimes accompanied by lower extraversion (Eysenck and Eysenck, 1985; Clark, Watson and Mineka, 1994). The correlation between N and symptom level is highly robust: Levenson et al. (1988) obtained correlations of 0.3–0.4 between N and a variety of psychiatric symptoms in a study of a community sample, in which symptom level was assessed ten years after N was measured. Some studies also suggest that N acts as a predisposing factor for major depression (Bagby et al., 1995; Surtees and Wainwright, 1996). Indeed, the tendency for depression and anxiety disorders to be 'comorbid' (occur together) may in part be attributed to the influence of N across a range of disorders (Bienvenu et al., 2001). Beyond anxiety and depression, N is elevated in a variety of disorders, including substance abuse (Martin and Sher, 1994), eating disorders (Goldner et al., 1999), and sleep

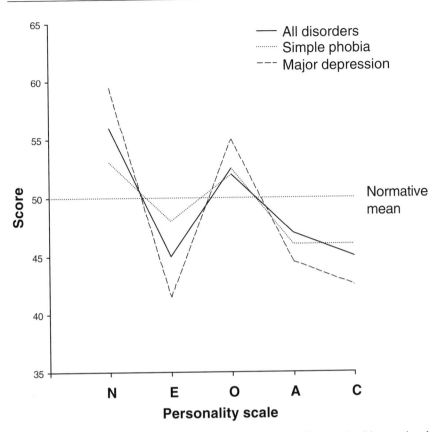

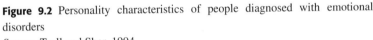

Figure 9.2 Personality characteristics of people diagnosed with emotional disorders
Source Trull and Sher, 1994

disorders (Dorsey and Bootzin, 1997). In a study of abnormal personality, Austin and Deary (2000) found evidence for a general distress factor highly correlated with N, and related to the majority of personality disorders, as discussed further in chapter 11. An informative study conducted by Trull and Sher (1994) investigated the role of the Big Five in various anxiety and mood disorders. They administered a diagnostic interview to 468 young adults to establish whether they had ever met psychiatric criteria for the disorders of interest, according to the DSM-III clinical diagnostic system. Respondents also completed the NEO-PI-R. As shown in figure 9.2, those individuals classified as having suffered from a disorder differed in personality from those who had not. The personality profiles varied somewhat across disorders, but there was a clear general pattern of high N, together with low E, low C, low A and high O. Low A and low C may be associated with difficulties in social functioning, whereas the high O person may perhaps be over-sensitive. Figure 9.2 also shows profiles for two specific disorders: major depression and simple phobia. The depression group showed larger deviations from the normative value of 50, but the profiles were qualitatively similar. Individuals diagnosed with agoraphobia, social phobia and post-traumatic stress disorder also showed similar profiles.

Medical students and medical professionals are not immune from these effects. In a longitudinal investigation of medical students, neuroticism was a significant predictor of maladaptive perfectionism (excess worry about being evaluated), depression and hopelessness (Enns et al., 2001). In studies of mental-health problems in young doctors, it was found that neuroticism, perceived stress, overwork and emotional pressure, and perceived stress outside of work, all measured when the doctors were medical students, were predictive of symptoms of anxiety and depression early on in the doctors' careers (Tyssen and Vaglum, 2002).

Similar patterns have also been observed in older people. Ormel, Oldehinkel and Brilman (2001) found that elderly men and women who had both high neuroticism and severe difficulties in everyday life were at significantly increased risk of depression. The occurrence of a stressful life event, such as death of a spouse, further increased the risk of depression, but only in those who were initially high on neuroticism and difficulties. In addition, high neuroticism in conjunction with mildly stressful life events was associated with the recurrence of depression. In the Longitudinal Aging Study Amsterdam, subjects who were most at risk of becoming chronically anxious over three years were those who were high in neuroticism at baseline; factors that contributed in addition to neuroticism were severe life events, such as the death of a partner (De Beurs et al., 2000). Carers are under a specific and chronic source of stress: does neuroticism contribute to development of anxiety and depression in carers? Spousal caregivers of dementia patients took part in a year-long study that investigated their psychological health at baseline and at a twelve-month follow-up in relation to personality traits (Vedhara et al., 2001). Neuroticism, perceived stress, anxiety and depression were all assessed. N was associated with increased reports of stress and greater likelihood of depression and anxiety at both baseline and twelve-month follow-up.

The problem of subjectivity: causal relationships between neuroticism and stress

High N individuals report dissatisfaction in a variety of areas of everyday life, but there is a problem with data based on self-reports, which will surface at several points in this chapter and the next. It is often unclear whether the distress associated with neuroticism is mainly subjective, or whether it relates to objectively measurable difficulties with life (e.g., Stone and Costa, 1991). For example, it is unclear whether neurotics actually commit more everyday errors, or whether they simply tend to remember their errors or interpret their actions as mistaken. Similarly, it is uncertain whether high N subjects simply derive less pleasure from social interactions, or whether their style of conversation and interaction is itself somewhat dysfunctional. There is some evidence for associations between N and objective behaviours. Daly (1978) showed that trait anxious (i.e., high N) individuals tend to avoid gazing at the listener when talking. When listening, anxiety is associated with either eye gaze avoidance or fixity of gaze on the speaker. Such patterns of eye contact may well be disconcerting for the person conversing with the neurotic, and impede social interaction. In general, caution is necessary in interpreting self-report data, although there may well be some degree of interaction between neuroticism, subjective distress and observable behaviours.

In principle, neuroticism might be either a cause or a symptom of unpleasant life experiences, mental disorders and behavioural problems. We might naively suppose that N is correlated with stress symptoms because high N subjects are more prone to adverse emotional and behavioural reactions following a major life event such as bereavement. However, the converse causal link is also possible: neuroticism may be a symptom rather than a cause. Perhaps high levels of neuroticism tend to develop after the life event has taken place, as one element of the various stress symptoms triggered by the event. Distinguishing these causal possibilities in a cross-sectional study conducted after the event is difficult, because neuroticism may influence the person's memory and evaluation of the event. Note that when we describe neuroticism as a 'cause', we are referring to the package of underlying physiological and/or psychological structures from which the surface characteristics of neuroticism (such as negative affect) emerge, rather than the surface characteristics themselves (see chapter 1).

Causality is best investigated through longitudinal studies, in which both personality and stress outcomes are assessed on two or more occasions some time apart. Structural modelling of longitudinal data may be used to test whether or not high neuroticism actually precedes stress symptoms. In fact, longitudinal studies of neuroticism and distress provide mixed results. Studies of reactions to everyday life stressors provide convincing evidence for N being a cause of stress symptoms. Ormel and Wohlfarth (1991) report a longitudinal study of 296 Dutch adults. After intitial asessement of N, at time T0, they administered a battery of stress-related measures on two further occasions, six and seven years after measurement of N (times T1 and T2). They distinguished endogenous and exogenous adverse life events. Endogenous life events are those strongly influenced by the person's own behaviour, such as serious marital discord, whereas exogenous events such as illness are predominantly due to external factors. Figure 9.3 shows a part of the causal model fitted to the data, in which N directly influences psychological distress and frequency of endogenous life events six or seven years later. Life events also have some independent, but relatively weak, effects on distress.

A somewhat similar study run by Magnus et al. (1993) measured both objective events (verifiable by external observers, such as divorce) and subjective events. Study participants were assessed once at the beginning of a four-year follow-up, and once at the end of the follow-up. In contrast to Ormel and Wohlfarth (1991), Magnus et al. found that neuroticism was more strongly related to objective than to subjective life events. The model that best fitted that data was a causal one, in which neuroticism influenced future negative events, but in which the events had no effect on neuroticism. They suggest two mechanisms for these relationships. First, neurotics react to a wider variety of events in a negative way. Second, high

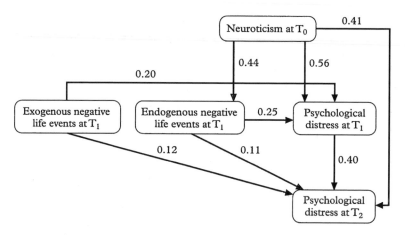

Figure 9.3 Part of a causal model of the effects of neuroticism and negative life events on psychological distress
- Only significant paths are shown
- $T_1 = T_0 + 6$ years, $T_2 = T_0 + 7$ years
- Paths to life situation change omitted

Source Ormel and Wohlfarth, 1991

N individuals 'bring it on themselves', in that their difficulties in social interaction may actually initiate negative events such as divorce, loss of job and so forth. This mechanism is consistent with the association between N and greater exposure to negative life events (Bolger and Schilling, 1991; Kardum and Krapic, 2001). Thus, although causal relationships between N and stress symptoms may well be complex, there does seem to be a direct causal link between neuroticism and subsequent stress reactions.

In the clinical field, there are conflicting viewpoints. One influential article (Barnett and Gotlib, 1988) reviewed studies of neuroticism and treatment for depression, concluding that, although elevated during the depressive episode, levels of N recovered to normal levels as the person recovered from the disorder. Thus high N appeared to be a concomitant of clinical depression, rather than a cause of disorder. However, social introversion remained high following treatment, suggesting that this trait might represent a persistent vulnerability factor. More recent research presents a rather different picture. Santor, Bagby and Joffe (1997) and Bienvenu et al. (2001) reported that people in remission from major depression exceeded the normative mean for N by over 1 standard deviation. In a twelve-year study of depression, Surtees and Wainwright (1996) showed that, out of many clinical, demographic and social measures taken at baseline, the strongest predictors of eventual poor clinical outcome were two personality traits: neuroticism, and low self-confidence measured by the Personality Deviance Scales (Deary, Bedford and Fowkes, 1995).

A recent article (Harkness et al., 2002) discusses evidence from studies of 'double depression', that is the coexistence of clinical major depression with chronic minor depression (dysthymia). People unfortunate enough to fall into this category are at particular risk of relapse following treatment. Harkness et al. (2002) studied patients in remission, and found that 'double depressives' were higher in neuroticism (and also lower in agreeableness) than patients who had experienced major depression alone. Both groups showed similar levels of depressive symptomatology and mood, so the comparison was not confounded with severity of depression. The effect of neuroticism was dependent on one of the six primary facets measured by the NEO-PI-R: Angry Hostility. Harkness et al. (2002) suggest that 'double depressives' may be frustrated and disaffected. The study also confirmed personality change as depression remits: N (except for Angry Hostility) declined, whereas E and C increased. Somewhat similarly, Piedmont (2001) showed decreased N, and increased E, C and A in a sample of ninety-nine people given treatment for drug addiction. Changes in N, C and A were maintained at fifteen-month follow-up. Thus, personality and emotional disorder seem to show some reciprocity; personality may predispose the person to disorder, but the onset of the disorder influences personality.

Transactional perspectives on personality and stress: mediator and moderator hypotheses

It is clear that the trait of neuroticism is related to facets of what we call stress in everyday language. The next step is to consider theoretical frameworks for stress research that help us explain these relationships. Of particular interest are transactional theories of stress, which propose that stress arises out of the dynamic interaction between person and environment. The cognitive processes of appraisal and coping play a central part in formal models of this kind.

Transactional models of stress: appraisal

The transactional approach to stress (e.g., Cox and Ferguson, 1991; Lazarus, 1999) sees stress as arising out of significant encounters or transactions between the person and the physical and social environment. As described briefly above, stress is generated when the person appraises the demands of the environment as difficult or impossible to cope with successfully. The student anticipating exam failure, the spouse confronting irretrievable marital failure, and the worker sacked with little chance of finding alternative employment are all examples of people in situations that are highly likely to be considered stressful. According to Lazarus (1991), the cognitive processing associated with stressful transactions may be understood at two levels, macro and micro. As we saw in chapter 4, at the macro level, emotional distress may be a function of the individual's perception of the meaning of the situation, or its 'core relational theme'. That is, anxiety may arise when facing the 'core relational theme' of threat, and sadness is the response when the event's underlying 'theme' is one of irrevocable loss.

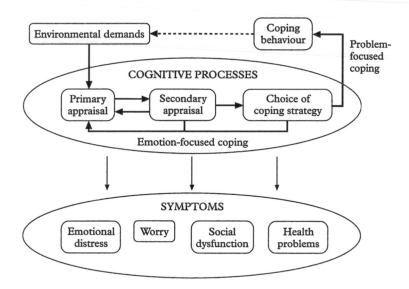

Figure 9.4 The transactional model of stress: symptoms result from negative appraisals and ineffective coping

At the micro level, various specific cognitive processes that may contribute to stress can be identified (Lazarus and Folkman, 1984). The individual's appraisals or evaluations of the situation are of great importance: Lazarus and Folkman draw a distinction between primary appraisal (the evaluation of the threat of the situation) and secondary appraisal (the evaluation of one's ability to cope with the situation successfully). For example, extreme optimists may appraise events in such a way that they find a silver lining in almost any situation, protecting them against stress, whereas pessimists may find even minor hassles and upsets stress inducing. Evaluation of the situation as beyond one's personal control is particularly likely to induce stressful feelings. In addition, people generally make active efforts to cope with the demands of threatening situations (Lazarus and Folkman, 1984), with varying degrees of success. An executive who is facing the possibility of redundancy may respond by working longer hours, or by drinking heavily. Figure 9.4 illustrates the transactional model of the stress process. Appraisal of demands leads to coping that may either feed back into the appraisal process (emotion-focus) or may aim to change external demands through behaviour (problem-focus). Stress-related appraisals and unsuccessful coping may generate a cascade of possible stress outcomes: physiological arousal (such as increased heart rate), health problems, difficulties with social relationships, or cognitive and behavioural disturbance. As figure 9.4 shows, it is uncertain whether there is any close correspondence between specific processes and specific symptoms. Appraisal and efforts at coping vary dynamically as the event develops and unfolds, so that the symptoms of stress vary depending on both the situation and the person. The cognitive appraisal of a stressful situation plays an important part in the dynamic relationship between the negative situation and the level of distress that is reported (Garnefski, Kraaj and Spinhoven, 2001).

Coping

Most psychometric studies of individual differences in cognitive stress processes have been directed towards the different types (dimensions) of coping (see Zeidner and Endler, 1996). These studies seek to investigate whether there are common set patterns to people's self-reported strategies for dealing with stressful situations. As with personality traits, there is more agreement on broad rather than narrow dimensions of coping. Most researchers would accept that there are three broad dimensions of coping: problem-focused coping, emotion-focused coping, and avoidance (Cox and Ferguson, 1991). Problem- (or task-) focused coping describes efforts to change the objective external situation, often by making and following a plan of action (for example, a student drawing up and sticking to an exam revision timetable). Emotion-focused coping refers to strategies in which the person tries to change their thoughts and feelings about the distressing event, perhaps by trying to learn something from it, to 'look on the bright side', or to express their negative emotions (a student who tells a friend of their worries or who decides the result doesn't really matter that much). Avoidance coping involves trying to evade the problem, perhaps by suppressing thoughts about it, distracting oneself with other activities and by actively removing oneself from the stressful situation (here, the student might go to the pub instead of revising, or perhaps not even turn up for the exam). Endler and Parker's (1990) Coping Inventory for Stressful Situations (CISS) assesses these three broad coping dimensions very reliably (typical reliability coefficients are 0.8–0.9). Many believe that problem-focused coping is more effective than either emotion-focused or avoidance coping, although the empirical evidence is complex (Zeidner and Saklofske, 1996). Lazarus and Folkman (1984) emphasise that the efficacy of a given strategy depends on the nature of the stressful situation and on the individual's ability to use their chosen strategy in that situation. For instance, problem-focused coping may be effective when dealing with exams and revision, and avoidance less so; however, in the case of a phobia about snakes, avoidance could be a very effective solution most of the time.

Traits and the transactional model

The transactional model suggests two rather different research avenues, related to the important conceptual distinction between *mediation* and *moderation*. A mediating variable is one that directly links two other variables, so that it transmits the effect of one variable on the other, making up a causal chain. Thus we might say that life events cause perceptions of lack of control that cause depression. In this case, lack of control mediates the effect of life events on depression. By contrast, a moderator variable changes the relationship between two other variables (quantitatively or qualitatively). For example, the relationship between life events and depression may be moderated by social support, such that the effect of life events on depression is strong when social support is low, but life events have little effect on depression when social support is high. Thus, while mediation deals exclusively with linear relationships, moderation implies that two variables have an *interactive* effect on the third. Research also tends to have rather different aims, depending on whether it is focused on mediation or moderation. Mediation research tends to be theory driven, because finding a mediating variable is informative about intervening processes and mechanisms, e.g., for adverse effects of life events. By contrast, moderator research, though still linked to theory, is particularly informative about variation in empirical findings across different circumstances, e.g., when life events are predictive of depression, and when they are not.

Figure 9.5 illustrates typical mediation and moderation research questions in the study of traits and stress. The mediation hypothesis is that trait effects are mediated by individual differences in appraisal and coping. Perhaps, for example, it is the negative outlook and ineffective coping of high N persons that generates higher levels of stress symptoms. The critical test here is whether the association between N and stress outcome remains significant, with the mediators statistically controlled (by partial correlation, multiple regression or structural equation modelling), i.e., whether there is a *direct* effect of N, as well as the indirect effect dependent on the mediators. A more complete model might also include life events as a further independent variable, influencing the mediators independently of N (i.e., no interaction between N and life events).

The moderation hypothesis is that certain personality characteristics may act as a buffer or shield that protects the person against the impact of adverse events (see lower part of figure 9.5). For example, as shown in figure 9.5, low N (emotional stability) may not have much influence during times of low stress, but helps to protect the individual in times of high stress. In this case, personality should be strongly related to stress outcomes in stressful circumstances (i.e., many life events), but only weakly related to outcomes when life events and hassles are infrequent. The moderator hypothesis is not necessarily correct. Personality factors may indeed simply introduce a general bias, so that the high N person, for example, shows higher levels of stress outcomes irrespective of events. The critical test is whether there is a statistical interaction between N and level of life events (as independent variables) in their effects on stress outcomes. If their effects are additive, there is no moderator effect. Demonstrating a moderator effect might lead to a subsequent search for mechanisms, i.e., whether some traits may help people to appraise demanding situations as fairly non-threatening or controllable.

It is difficult to say whether neuroticism operates primarily as a general biasing factor, or as a moderator factor. Evidence can be found in support of both points of view. As discussed in chapter 4, an influential school of thought sees negative affect as integral to neuroticism (e.g., Lucas and Diener, 2000). Indeed, substantial correlations between N and negative mood are often found in apparently neutral settings (Matthews and Gilliland, 1999). In contrast, the studies of life events

a) Example of a mediating hypothesis

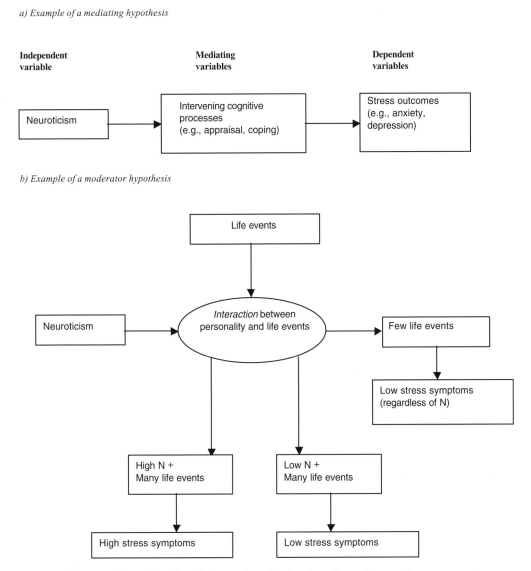

Figure 9.5 Examples of mediation and moderation hypotheses in research on traits and stress

reviewed above suggest hyper-reactivity to adverse events on the part of high N persons. Consistent with a moderator hypothesis, neuroticism relates to a larger, more prolonged stress response. Perhaps both hypotheses are correct, i.e., that N is associated with some more negative baseline of mood and stress symptoms, *and* that N moderates affective responses to stressors. In the subsections which follow, we look, first, at possible cognitive mediators of the effect of N on stress outcome, and, second, at effects of additional traits (which may involve mediation or moderation).

Table 9.2 *Empirical demonstrations of negative appraisals in neurotic and trait anxious individuals*

Study	Major finding
Butler and Mathews (1987)	Trait anxious subjects prior to an exam rate negative events as more probable
Smith and Sarason (1975)	Trait anxious subjects interpret experimentally controlled feedback as more negative
Greenberg and Alloy (1989)	Trait anxious subjects compare themselves unfavourably with their friends
Gallagher (1990)	Neurotic subjects appraise academic stressors as more threatening
De Paulo et al. (1987)	Neurotic subjects believe they make a poor impression in social interaction
Penley and Tomaka (2002)	Neurotic subjects rate their coping ability and performance lower, when required to make a speech

Mediators of neuroticism

If neuroticism does have some causal effects on stress symptoms, we may ask whether these effects are mediated by individual differences in style of appraisal and coping, as the transactional model of stress might suggest. Are individuals high in N more stress prone because they tend to appraise events more negatively, and adopt ineffective coping strategies? If so, we would expect to find correlations between neuroticism, appraisal and coping. Table 9.2 summarises studies suggesting that neuroticism and trait anxiety correlate with negative appraisals of various potential stressors, and of personal capabilities. N relates to a pessimistic style of appraisal in both performance testing and social contexts. Such beliefs are often unrealistic, and may contribute to sensitivity to stress. For example, high N individuals tend to perceive themselves as lonely, although their social networks are actually as well developed as those of emotionally stable individuals (Stokes and McKirnan, 1989).

Similarly, neuroticism is also associated with characteristic choices of coping strategy. N correlates with less use of problem-focused and more use of emotion-focused and avoidance strategies (e.g., McCrae and Costa, 1986; Endler and Parker, 1990; Deary et al., 1996; Brebner, 2001). McCrae and Costa (1986) also showed that the coping strategies favoured by neurotics were typically rated as being ineffective in dealing with stressful events. However, such results do not necessarily imply that coping strategies mediate the neuroticism–stress association. Bolger (1990) tested the mediation hypothesis directly. He had fifty pre-medical students report their coping strategies in the thirty-five days leading up to an examination. Coping was measured with the Folkman and Lazarus (1988) Ways of Coping questionnaire, which assesses seven coping dimensions. Neuroticism predicted greater increases in anxiety in the final week before the examination. The model

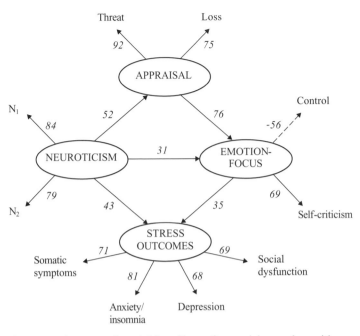

Figure 9.6 A structural model for effects of neuroticism and cognitive process variables on stress outcomes
Note Path coefficients are standardised; error variances for variables and latent factors are omitted. Note that the latent neuroticism factor is defined by two short N scales, representing even- and odd-number items on the full N scale
Source Matthews, Derryberry et al., 2000

suggests that this effect was mediated by greater use of escape-avoidance in high N students, which was the coping dimension most strongly related to anxiety change. Similarly, Deary et al. (1996) demonstrated mediating effects of emotion-oriented coping between neuroticism and job-related stress in a large group of senior doctors.

Figure 9.6 shows a more complex structural model for effects of N (data from Mohamed, 1996, reanalysed by Matthews, Derryberry and Siegle, 2000). This study used averaged ratings of appraisal and coping for different kinds of stressors to which students may be exposed. The ratings were found to be consistent across stressors, demonstrating consistency in cognition across different situations. The best-fitting model in this study suggested partial mediation of the effect of N by the cognitive process variables. Similar to Deary et al. (1996), a part of the influence of N on stress outcomes (measured with the GHQ) was mediated by emotion-focused coping. However, the effect of N on emotion-focus was itself partially mediated by more negative appraisals in high N persons. Furthermore, there was a significant direct path from N to stress outcomes, unmediated by cognition. Some part of the effect of N is unexplained here; it may represent some noncognitive, physiologically mediated influence of N on the outcome variables, or unconscious cognitive biases linked to N, or consciously accessible cognitions that were not measured in the study. Matthews, Derryberry and Siegle (2000) also reported that relationships between N and acute responses to performing demanding tasks (distress and worry) were fully mediated by situational appraisal and coping.

Additional traits for stress vulnerability

There is little doubt that neuroticism is the trait most strongly implicated in severe emotional distress, but other dimensions may be important too (see Matthews et al., 2003), as we shall now discuss.

Extraversion

The Big Five trait of Extraversion has been shown to be modestly related to better mental health in a variety of studies (e.g, Levenson et al., 1988; Bienvenu et al., 2001), perhaps because extraverts' tendency to use problem-focused coping strategies (McCrae and Costa, 1986; Kardum and Krapi, 2001; Penley and Tomaka, 2002) may help them to maintain high self-esteem and to deal with life events more effectively. Eysenck and Eysenck (1985) suggest that extraversion has a moderating effect on the expression of neuroticism. Neurotic introverts are prone to emotional disturbance, whereas neurotic extraverts tend to exhibit behavioural problems. It is somewhat unclear whether E acts as a stress buffer that moderates the impact of events, or whether E is associated with some general bias towards better adjustment, irrespective of life circumstances. Other, narrower traits have been explicitly proposed as stress buffers. In the remainder of this section we present studies on some of these traits that may relate to reduced (or amplified) stress vulnerability.

Hardiness

The construct of hardiness was developed by Kobasa (1982), as a possible personality-based stress buffer. It is a trait-like measure of stress resistance: a putative moderator of stress. Hardiness has three components: belief in personal control over events, commitment to full involvement in life and enjoyment of challenge and opportunity. Evidence for the importance of hardiness in stress reactions is mixed. Hardiness has been found to moderate relationships between stress and depression, and to interact with social support (Pengilly and Dowd, 2000), but other investigators have not found evidence that hardy individuals are less distressed by adverse events (Cohen and Edwards, 1989). The psychometric properties of hardiness have also been called into question: hardiness, when measured using negatively worded items, is confounded with neuroticism; however, its factor structure and associations with well-being are more robust when positively worded items are used to measure the construct (Sinclair and Tetrick, 2000).

Locus of control

Another construct proposed as a moderator of stress reactions is locus of control (Rotter, 1966). People with an internal locus believe that events in life are controlled by their own actions, whereas those with an external locus attribute the outcomes of events to outside factors such as luck. People with an external locus appear to be prone to a variety of symptoms of stress including emotional distress, job dissatisfaction, burn-out and low self-esteem (e.g., Kasl, 1989). Some studies have suggested a moderator effect of locus of control, such that externals are particularly vulnerable to stress symptoms due to frequent or severe negative life events, but, overall, the evidence is rather mixed (Hurrell and Murphy, 1991). As with hardiness, there are psychometric problems with the locus of control construct, associated with an uncertain factor structure, and of confounding with neuroticism and other traits (see Hurrell and Murphy, 1991; Smith and Williams, 1992; Kline, 1993). Moreover, research on personality traits in relation to locus of control may yield findings that are apparently contradictory to findings from research into motivations or cognitions in relation to locus of control; this is because neither trait nor cognition models, on their own, are fully complete (Code and Langan-Fox, 2001). Locus of control has been shown in some studies to alter according to the context (Sarafino, 2002); this also contributes to mixed findings concerning locus of control and stress outcomes.

Optimism and hope

A third trait that has been extensively researched is optimism–pessimism. Dispositional optimism (a trait) is a generalised expectancy for positive outcomes (Scheier et al., 1986). Optimism may also be considered to be an 'explanatory style' (Buchanan and Seligman, 1995). People's explanations for events in their lives differ: some people may explain events in an optimistic light, and others in a more pessimistic light. Dispositional and explanatory-style optimism are related, and are also associated with the construct of hope (Peterson, 2000). Higher optimism (and greater hope) relates to better mental health, perceptions of increased control over stressful situations (such as a competitive event; Wilson, Raglin and Pritchard, 2002), and more effective coping (Scheier, Carver and Bridges, 1994; Carver and Scheier, 2000). It has also been linked to positive mood, to academic and job success and to popularity (Peterson, 2000). Unlike hardiness and locus of control, there is some evidence that optimism may predict reduced levels of stress even with neuroticism controlled (Scheier, Carver and Bridges, 1994). Some research has suggested that the relationship between optimism and stress is mediated by coping, and that optimistic individuals are more likely to choose problem-focused coping strategies (Carver et al., 1993; Pakenham and Rinaldis, 2001).

Optimism and pessimism are not necessarily mutually exclusive: it has been shown that people may be optimistic on a grand scale but more pessimistic concerning specific events (Peterson, 2000). There are also signs that an over-optimistic outlook ('unrealistic optimism', Weinstein, 1989) is personally dangerous, because it may lead to an underestimation of risk, especially risks associated with health (e.g., the risk of contracting AIDS or lung cancer). Over-optimism may also have other correlates; people with overly positive self-evaluations tend to have poor social skills and to be maladjusted (Colvin, Block and Funder, 1995). In sum, optimism has the potential to protect people from becoming depressed when faced with potential stressors, but it may not be helpful in every situation.

Dispositional self-consciousness

Private self-consciousness refers to a chronic tendency towards reflecting about the self. It is measured by an acceptably reliable scale developed by Fenigstein et al. (1975), and it is not highly related to the Big Five measures (Zuckerman et al., 1993). Self-consciousness is elevated in a variety of emotional disorders and in experimentally induced negative mood states (Ingram, 1990). Subjects high in self-consciousness tend to use the emotion-focused strategy of ruminating about problems, and to neglect direct coping, particularly if the controllability of the situation is unclear (Matthews and Wells, 1996). Self-conscious people seem to have difficulty in diverting their attention from thinking about themselves to thinking about the needs of the situation. Hamlet, Shakespeare's morose prince of Denmark, exemplifies the idea that habitual self-preoccupation and introspection lead to stress. In his famous soliloquy, 'to be or not to be . . .' (Act III, Scene 2), he muses on 'Whether 'tis nobler in the mind to suffer the slings and arrows of outrageous fortune [i.e., emotion-focused coping] or take arms against a sea of troubles, and by opposing end them [confrontive problem-focused coping?]'. Hamlet recognises the paralysing effects of too much introspection later in the same speech: 'And thus the native hue of resolution is sicklied o'er with the pale cast of thought . . .' Ironically, his later efforts at active coping lead to tragedy and his own death.

Matthews, Mohamed and Lochrie (1998) demonstrated similar effects empirically. Low self-focused subjects who appraise situations as open to change tend to use problem-focused strategies, and so match coping to the situation adaptively. However, under the same circumstances, high self-focused individuals prefer the emotion-focused strategy of reappraisal, which, Hamlet-like, may lead to prevarication and failure to act. Below, we describe a theory of negative emotion and cognition that sees self-focus as a key element of a cognitive-attentional syndrome associated with distress, dysfunctional coping and disruption of performance (Wells and Matthews, 1994).

Resources influencing secondary cognitive appraisal

Individuals must evaluate a situation in order to decide whether it is stressful or not. We have shown above that extraversion, high hardiness or optimism, or low self-consciousness, may help people to evaluate situations as being not very stressful (primary appraisal). In secondary appraisal, people are evaluating whether they have adequate resources to deal with the demand (e.g., Lazarus, 1999). There are several factors that may influence secondary appraisal: social support networks, self-esteem, or sense of control over the situation. The distinction between factors that influence secondary and primary appraisal is somewhat artificial, for it is obvious that they are interrelated (optimism, for instance, affects both primary and secondary appraisal processes). However, it is useful to discuss them separately to maintain clarity.

Social support

Perceived availability of social support – compassion and assistance given by other people or organisations (e.g., Cobb, 1976) – can have an important influence on how stressful an event is judged to be, and on the ultimate impact of that event. In a study of social adjustment in eighty-four chronically ill adolescents (aged thirteen to sixteen) and their parents, it was found that the adolescents' coping style, locus of control and social support accounted for about 25 per cent of the variance in 'social adjustment' factors (e.g., social activities, social self-esteem and global self-esteem) (Meijer et al., 2002). The study was cross-sectional, so it is impossible to tease out the separate effects of 'seeking social support' from the effects of having a well-developed social network in the first place. However, studies of adults have also shown that social support is stress-buffering: people asked to speak publicly show lower heart rate responses if there is a supportive person with them (Lepore, Allen and Evan, 1993; Uchino and Garvey, 1997). It is clear, however, that social support availability does not stand alone: it is related to personality traits. People higher in N are more likely to have (or report) unsatisfactory support networks (Miyamoto et al., 2001), and higher extraversion is related to increased social support (Swickert et al., 2002).

Spiritual or religious coping

Related to social support, but also to optimism, hope and coping, is spiritual or religious coping. Some studies have demonstrated that people who use spiritual or religious beliefs to help them cope with stress are more likely to have good mental health and to be happy (Myers, 2000). Kim and Seidlitz (2002) studied spirituality, daily stress, mood and physical symptoms in 113 American university students, over a two-month period. Greater spirituality was found to buffer the adverse effects of stress, even after controlling for coping strategies. Similarly, Kamya (2000) found that spiritual well-being and hardiness were strong predictors of self-esteem in 105 social work students, with self-esteem important for coping with the demands of social work. As with hardiness and locus of control, however, spirituality – especially involvement in organised religion – is linked to other stress-buffers, in particular, to social support systems (Ellison, Gay and Glass, 1989). Religious groups often encourage people to be hopeful and optimistic in the face of difficulties (Myers, 2000), two other attributes that help people deal with stress.

Spirituality may relate to traits: a recent meta-analysis (Saroglou, 2002), established some reliable relationships between religion and the Big Five, although the author also cautioned that effect sizes were small (typically 0.1–0.2). Extraversion, agreeableness and conscientiousness were linked to greater religiosity. Open, mature religion and spirituality were associated with lower neuroticism and higher openness. Both these traits were also inversely correlated with religious fundamentalism; those high in agreeableness were also more likely to espouse fundamentalism. Causality is unclear in these studies. Traits may influence a person's preference for religion, and, alternatively, religious values may influence personality. Possibly, religious beliefs account for a small part of the variance in relationships between traits and stress outcomes, although the effect sizes reported by Saroglou (2002) appear too small to support a major role for religiosity in trait effects. Alternatively, it may be better to see spirituality as a sixth factor of personality (Piedmont, 1999), although its validity as a predictor of stress vulnerability has not been systematically explored.

Neuroticism, stress and emotional disorders: a self-regulative perspective

Thus far, we have established the criterion validity of N as a predictor of individual differences in various indices of stress. The central role of N is apparent from several different lines of evidence: correlations between N and various forms of stress outcome (including mental disorders), the link between N and life events, and correlations between N and numerous cognitive biases. We may also remain hopeful that research will eventually identify physiological correlates of N that contribute to stress vulnerability, although, so far, the evidence is equivocal (Matthews and Gilliland, 1999; see chapter 7). There is also evidence that high N may have at least some causal effects, as a predictor of future distress (e.g., Magnus et al., 1993). However, we have also seen that (in line with interactionism), the transactional model of stress proposes a *dynamic* view of person–situation interaction. Personality may bias responses to stress, but so too do situational factors feed back into personality change. As we saw in discussing causality previously, mental disorder seems to elevate N, as well as producing other personality changes such as decreased E and C (Harkness et al., 2002). In this section, we present a dynamic perspective on N, and its role as a vulnerability factor in mental illness.

The theoretical basis here is provided by the idea of self-regulation (Carver and Scheier, 1990). The person is seen as a cybernetic system that aims to fulfill personal goals within a changing external environment. Discrepancies between preferred and actual status (similar to appraisals) drive compensatory efforts intended to reduce the discrepancy (similar to coping). We outline here a theory of individual differences in self-regulation (Wells and Matthews, 1994; Matthews and Wells, 1999; Matthews, Derryberry et al., 2000; Matthews, Schwean et al., 2000; Wells, 2000) that provides a dynamic account of neuroticism and its role in mental disorders.

Any comprehensive model of neuroticism needs several parts. First, we must accept that the trait is distributed across multiple, independent processes (cf. Suls's, 2001, idea of the 'neurotic cascade'). In the next subsection, we distinguish some of these different processes. Second, we must describe how the processes operate together as part of an integrated, functional system for self-regulation. In the following subsection, we discuss how the cognitive building blocks may be assembled to make up a 'cognitive architecture' for self-regulation. Third, we must specify how the system can malfunction to the point of generating major pathology, an issue to be addressed in the final subsection.

Building a self-regulative model: basic constructs

It is well known that cognitive models of stress are prone to excessive proliferation of constructs, limiting testability and generality. A partial solution to the problem is to distinguish sets of processes functionally, i.e., in terms of what the process does to support the overall goal of self-regulation. On this basis, processes may be distinguished as follows (Matthews, Schwean et al., 2000; Wells and Matthews, in press):

Self-knowledge. As discussed in chapter 8, traits may be linked to the content of stable self-beliefs, such as the self-schema. Wells and Matthews (1994) related emotional disorder to procedural as well as to declarative knowledge, i.e., the person's typical plans and acquired skills for dealing with demanding situations. The anxious person may be 'primed' to deal with threat by attempting to avoid the feared situation, for example. High N persons are distinguished both by overtly negative self-beliefs (see also chapter 8), and by their stable tendencies towards maladaptive management of difficult situations (Matthews, Schwean et al., 2000).

Cognitive stress processes. As the transactional model of stress describes, demanding events elicit active attempts to understand and manage the stressor. Processing of this kind is typically 'controlled', in being flexible and context-sensitive, requiring mental effort, and accessible to consciousness. We have already described appraisal and coping as two aspects of processing of this kind. Wells (2000) emphasises also the importance of *metacognition*, i.e., thoughts about one's own thoughts, feelings and mental images. Clinical patients often show a heightened concern with their own thoughts and feelings, so that they become preoccupied with their own negative thoughts. For example, Generalised Anxiety Disorder (GAD) patients worry that their own worries are frequent and difficult to control (meta-worry).

We have already reviewed the evidence that ties N to situational appraisals and coping (noting that associations 'in-situation' are often weaker than those with general styles of coping, for example). In addition, evidence is accumulating that links N (or its close relation, trait anxiety) to metacognition. For example, high N persons tend to monitor their mood state frequently (Swinkels and Giuliano, 1995), and they worry about their own worries (Wells, 1994). Trait anxious subjects show heightened levels of concern about numerous aspects of their own thinking, as measured by the Meta-Cognitions Questionnaire (Cartwright-Hatton and Wells, 1997); for example, beliefs that thoughts are uncontrollable and dangerous.

Lower-level processes. Other stress processes are more 'automatic' in nature, in that they are reflexively triggered by stimuli, irrespective of the personal context, and may not be accessible to consciousness. Traumatised war veterans, for example, may find that a car backfiring activates images of combat, or even an aggressive response. In the clinical context, it then becomes important to identify 'environmental triggers' that elicit threatening thoughts and images (Wells, 2000). The extent to which neuroticism and anxiety are associated with inbuilt, automatic biases towards selective attention to threatening stimuli is a controversial issue (Matthews and Wells, 1999). Biases assumed to be automatic often turn out to be dependent on voluntarily chosen strategies (Matthews and Wells, 2000; see also chapter 12). However, a conservative view is that trait anxiety and neuroticism relate to both 'controlled' and 'automatic' biases (Mathews and Mackintosh, 1998). Furthermore, work on the attentional correlates of these traits inspired by neuropsychology suggests that they may relate to specific brain systems for attentional modulation of motivation, such as slow disengagement from sources of threat stimuli (Derryberry and Reed, 1997).

Neuroticism within the S-REF model

The Wells and Matthews (1994) self-regulative model placed the various processes we have described within a common cognitive architecture, the Self-Regulative Executive Function (S-REF) model. The operation of the architecture is shown in figure 9.7. Lower-level processing of external events or internal thoughts triggers intrusive thoughts that signal a threat to well-being, and initiates attempts at self-regulation (e.g., neutralising the threat). These attempts are performed by the executive system at the core of the model (the S-REF), which seeks to evaluate the nature of the discrepancy, and select and implement an appropriate coping strategy. To do so, the executive accesses the store of stable self-knowledge, retrieving schematic information that makes sense of the situation, and generic plans for coping that provide the basis for correcting the discrepancy. As previously described, coping efforts may be directed towards thoughts and feelings (emotion-focus and avoidance), or they may comprise overt behaviours that alter external reality (problem-focus). If coping is appraised as successful, then the executive system terminates its activities.

The model incorporates several dynamic aspects. Matthews, Campbell et al. (2002) point out that dysfunctional cognitions will tend to *propagate*. That is, appraisals of elevated threat and poor personal coping abilities, will tend to elicit ineffectual coping strategies, such as self-criticism, which, in turn, will lead to poorer objective outcomes of the encounter, feeding back into further negative appraisals.

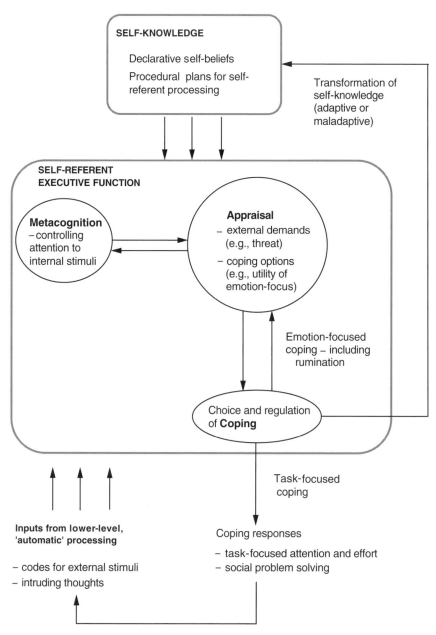

Figure 9.7 An outline of the S-REF model of emotional distress and self-regulation
Source Wells and Matthews (1994); Matthews and Wells (1999)

Thus, some consistency in individual differences develops, even though the various processes are functionally distinct. Wells and Matthews (1994) describe 'vicious circles' that serve to maintain pathology. Indeed, the difference between 'normal' and 'abnormal' anxiety may be the extent to which these maladaptive dynamic processes develop, perpetuating the negative affect. Internally, emotion-focused coping may operate on the contents of self-knowledge, either maladaptively (e.g., elaboration of negative self-beliefs) or adaptively (e.g., storage of successful ways of dealing with a problem). *Rumination* is a form of emotion-focused coping that leads to more elaborated representations of negative beliefs and stressful events, making negative self-referent information more easily accessed, and so perpetuating maladaptive self-knowledge (Matthews and Wells, in press). Failure to integrate memories of a traumatic event into more general self-knowledge has been implicated in the aetiology of Post-Traumatic Stress Disorder (PTSD), for example (Feeny and Foa, in press).

External ly, the person's ways of coping may interact with the situation so as to perpetuate rather than solve the problem. Depressed persons, for example, because of their tendencies to complain and denigrate themselves, tend to make poor companions. These behaviours may discourage others from maintaining social contact with the depressed person, maintaining that person's self-perception as socially isolated (Coyne, 1983). Likewise, anxiety patients may engage in 'safety behaviours', such as avoiding feared situations, that prevent them from ever acquiring the coping skills they require (Wells, 2000).

Thus, within the S-REF model, neuroticism may be seen as a general property of the system as a whole, as well as an influence on the various individual processing elements. Furthermore, consistent with evidence on the role of low N as a stress buffer, interaction with the external environment plays a critical role in stress vulnerability. The metacognitive and coping styles characteristic of high N are liable to interfere with successful resolution of problems. We could even take a more radically ecological view of neuroticism, and locate some part of stress vulnerability in the external environments that high N persons create for themselves (cf. Magnus et al., 1993): lack of effective social support, sources of interpersonal conflict and persistence of external threats (cf. Suls, 2001). Although we focus on N here, we note that other related but narrower traits may relate to more specific aspects of the cognitive architecture. For example, self-esteem may relate especially to self-appraisals, self-efficacy to secondary appraisals of personal coping abilities, and dispositional self-focus to the likelihood of self-referent executive processing being initiated. Models of this kind may thus reconcile narrow traits, as biases in specific functions, with broad traits, referring to overall system functioning.

Vulnerability factors in mental disorder

Several accounts of vulnerability to emotional disorders are compatible with the S-REF model in identifying stable dysfunctional self-knowledge (both declarative and procedural) as a key vulnerability factor (Ingram, Miranda and Segal, 1998;

Clark and Beck, 1999). We can look at the aetiological role of self-knowledge over both longer and short time spans (Ingram et al., 1998). In the long term, research is concerned with how learning, especially in childhood, may lead to the acquisition of potentially harmful self-beliefs and coping styles. As discussed in previous chapters, aspects of temperament linked to neuroticism (e.g., distress proneness) may bias these learning processes (Zeidner et al., 2003), creating a latent vulnerability, that may be activated by stressful events. In the short term, the emphasis is on study of how dysfunctional self-knowledge promotes maladaptive response to stressors and demands, as a consequence of biases in processes such as self-appraisal, metacognition and coping.

According to the account given by the S-REF model, neuroticism may be linked to multiple self-regulative biases that increase the likelihood of clinical disorder. There is an extensive literature on cognitive vulnerability factors (see Ingram, Miranda and Segal, 1998; Clark and Beck, 1999; Alloy and Riskind, in press, for reviews), much of which is concerned with the possible aetiological role of dys-functional self-beliefs. Various methods are used to establish causality, including longitudinal designs, demonstrating persisting cognitive abnormality in recovered patients, and structural equation modelling. We will give some illustrative exam-ples of research that suggest a causal role for some of the self-regulative constructs that we have described, focusing especially on styles of processing that may be both harmful and linked to neuroticism and related traits.

Research has been directed towards constructs that overlap with the self-referent executive processing syndrome of perseverative worry and rumination. The most extensive work has been conducted by Nolen-Hoeksema (e.g., 2000), using a measure of 'ruminative response style' that refers to a trait of dealing with nega-tive emotions by reflecting on them. Nolen-Hoeksema's longitudinal studies have confirmed that dispositional rumination predicts future clinical anxiety and depres-sion. Bagby and Parker (2001) showed that Nolen-Hoeksema's scale for ruminative response style actually comprises two distinct factors of symptom-focused rumi-nation (e.g., thinking about negative emotions) and self-focused rumination (e.g., thinking about why you are experiencing negative emotions). Consistent with the S-REF model, self-focused rumination rather than symptom-focused rumination was linked to anxiety and depression. Similarly, Holeva, Tarrier and Wells (2001) showed that dispositional worry predicted development of PTSD following trauma (road-traffic accidents), in a longitudinal, two-wave study. Worry at time 1 pre-dicted PTSD at time 2 (four to six months later), even with acute stress disorder at time 1 controlled.

Another focus for empirical research is the role of coping. A longitudinal study of 154 former psychiatric outpatients in Norway (Vollrath et al., 1996; Vollrath, Alnæs and Torgersen, 1998) found that coping style measures predicted clinical syndromes assessed six or seven years later. Active goal-oriented coping (similar to task-focus) was predictive of a lower incidence of pathology; as previously noted, worry and rumination tend to block this form of coping (Matthews and Wells, in press). Valentiner et al. (1996) conducting a study of coping among female assault victims: coping through 'wishful thinking' (e.g., self-blame and denial by fantasy) predicted severity of trauma symptoms three months after the assault. These coping strategies may interfere with the adaptive restructuring of self-knowledge needed to come to terms with the traumatic event. Similarly, Morgan, Matthews and Winton (1995), in a study of flood victims, found that emotion-focused coping was related to trauma symptoms even with appraised severity of the event controlled.

Other processes implicated as causal factors include metacognition and attentional bias. Reiss and McNally (1985) developed a trait measure for 'anxiety sensitivity', i.e., beliefs that somatic arousal is harmful. This is a metacognitive trait because it refers to beliefs about internal anxiety symptoms. Research reviewed by Schmidt and Woolaway-Bickel (in press) suggests that high anxiety sensitivity acts as one of several risk factors for panic disorder. The patient is prone to misattribute normal bodily sensations to a catastrophic event, such as a heart attack. In PTSD, the trauma victim's interpretation of symptoms such as intrusive thoughts contribute to the severity of the disorder, over and above frequency of intrusions (Ehlers and Clark, 2000). Finally, although evidence is a little limited, some studies implicate attentional bias towards threat as a risk factor for anxiety (McLeod et al., 2002) and depression (McCabe, Gotlib and Martin, 2000).

To summarise, emotional disorders typically relate to multiple cognitive risk factors associated with high N, as well to the person's biological constitution. Cognitive risk factors create a latent vulnerability that may be expressed as chronic negative affect or 'dysthymia' (Harkness et al., 2000). Typically, self-regulation, even in high N persons, is sufficently effective in controlling environmental demands that trait change is minor. However, when exposed to especially stressful events, the person is more likely to develop the more severe cognitive, emotional and behavioural disturbances that define clinical disorders. These conditions may produce elevated levels of N and other personality changes (Barnett and Gotlib, 1988; Piedmont, 2001; Harkness et al., 2002). One of the key factors that produces trait change may be personality–situation interaction that strengthens and elaborates dysfunctional negative cognitions (Matthews and Wells, 2000), such as the styles of social interaction characteristic of depressives, that may indeed cause others to avoid or criticise the depressed person. Cycles of rumination that perpetuate negative self-beliefs may be important in clinical anxiety, as well as depression (Matthews and Wells, in press).

Conclusions

1. 'Stress' is   may be defined as a stimulus
   (e.g., life e   autonomic arousal), or as a
   dynamic tr   *Lp*   ent, supported by cognitions
   such as appraisal and coping. Personality factors may influence what kind of
   life events the person experiences, and how responsive the person is to stressful events. Traits may also bias appraisal and coping processes, influencing

adaptation to demanding events. At a physiological level, stress is often related to Selye's 'General Adaptation System', although this generalised stress response is now seen as over-simplified. There are systematic individual differences in physiological reactivity, which may have a genetic basis. It remains to be seen how closely these physiological processes relate to personality.

2. The single most important personality factor that influences stress vulnerability is neuroticism. High N individuals show a range of elevated stress responses and outcomes in everyday life, including negative mood, distress following life events and behavioural disturbances. Various groups of psychiatric patients also show high levels of N, especially those diagnosed with anxiety and mood disorders. These correlational findings do not indicate whether high N is a cause or an effect of life disturbance. Longitudinal studies of life stress suggest that N is indeed a causal factor, both directly, and through increasing exposure to adverse events. For clinical disorders, the picture is more complex. It seems that high N is indeed a risk factor for emotional disorder, but N also becomes elevated as a consequence of the disorder, suggesting a reciprocal relationship between N and mental illness. Treatment for mental illness may lower N, as well as producing changes on other traits.

3. One route to greater theoretical understanding of the effects of N on stress outcomes is to relate N to the transactional model of stress. This model supposes that adverse outcomes reflect negative appraisals of personal coping ability and control, and the impact of the coping strategies used to manage the situation. One application of the transactional model to personality is the search for mediator variables, processes that may transmit the effect of personality on stress outcome. High N relates to various biases, such as negative self-appraisal and use of self-critical emotion-focused coping, that may feed into greater levels of stress outcome. A second application is the search for personality factors that are moderator variables in the stress process, i.e., variables that may shield or buffer the person from the effects of adverse life events. Emotional stability may play a role of this kind, but other personality factors have been implicated too, including extraversion, hardiness, internal locus of control, optimism and (low) dispositional self-consciousness. Social support and spirituality are examples of buffering factors that are not themselves traits, but are linked to personality.

4. Beyond mediator and moderator effects, the transactional model suggests a dynamic perspective on personality effects on stress. We outlined a self-regulative model of this kind, the S-REF model, that seeks to explain both normal stress processes and emotional pathology. The model assumes that people actively regulate the status of the self, using automatic and controlled processing, and retrieval of information held in long-term memory. Neuroticism may relate to multiple biases in these self-regulative processes, which together are associated with difficulties in adaptive coping, leading to negative emotion, worry and other stress symptoms. Research on cognitive risk factors for mental

disorder confirms this view of neuroticism as a latent risk factor for mental disorder. Pathology is most likely when the person develops maladaptive cycles of cognition that perpetuate negative self-beliefs (e.g., rumination), or maladaptive cycles of interaction with the outside world (e.g., social withdrawal).

Further reading

Lazarus, R. S. (1999) *Stress and emotion: a new synthesis*. New York: Springer.

Peterson, C. (2000) The future of optimism. *American Psychologist, 55*, 44–55.

Surtees, P. G. and Wainwright, N. W. J. (1996) Fragile states of mind: neuroticism, vulnerability and the long-term outcome of depression. *British Journal of Psychiatry,* 169, 338–47.

10 Traits and health

Introduction

It is a popular notion that personality traits may influence the state of a person's physical health. The image of the stressed, aggressive businessman being liable to have a heart attack is so common as to have become a cliché, yet, as we shall see, it has little evidential basis. If personality traits do influence health, then this is one of the prime reasons to measure personality traits in medical settings. However, there are difficulties in establishing the true nature of the relationship between personality and health, including measurement, the distinction between subjectively reported symptoms and objective signs of illness, and the direction of causation. In addition, it is virtually impossible to assess the amount of risk that personality traits pose on their own – the separate impact they might have over and above that of poverty or working conditions, for example. The best solution is to try to design studies and use statistical analyses that are appropriate to the study of complex interactions. In this chapter we first discuss models of personality and health, then go on to describe more specific areas such as personality, stress and heart disease. Finally, we briefly discuss the connection between personality and clinically defined 'psychosomatic' disorders such as irritable bowel syndrome and globus pharyngis.

Models of the association between personality and health

We begin by reviewing possible causal relationships between personality and health. Figure 10.1 shows four of the main ways in which health status and personality might be linked (Suls and Rittenhouse, 1990; Smith and Williams, 1992). The first possibility makes the strongest assumptions about the importance of personality traits; traits may represent biologically based differences that partly cause different illness outcomes. For instance, if neuroticism represents differentially sensitive autonomic responsivity, as discussed in chapter 9, then one might expect disorders such as hypertension, which are under autonomic control, to be related to neuroticism differences. Second, the relationship between traits and illness might be correlational rather than causal; for instance, the same biological processes might underlie traits and illness outcomes without either being causally related to the other. Perhaps, for instance, a particular gene makes someone susceptible to

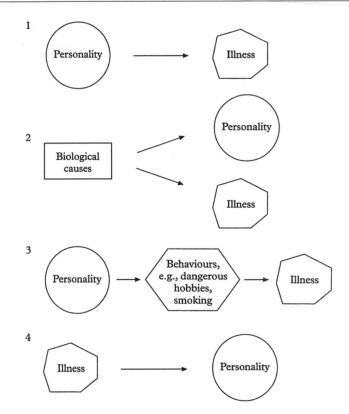

Figure 10.1 Four causal models for associations between health and personality

coronary heart disease and also predisposes them towards increased hostility, but it is not the increased hostility that is *causing* the higher risk of coronary heart disease.

Third, it is possible that traits lead to behaviours that, in turn, lead to health differences. If certain personality traits dispose people to take up dangerous hobbies, or to take dangerous drugs, then an indirect association between personality and health might be established. This model would offer clearer preventive strategies than model 1; behaviour is likely to be easier to change than the biological basis of a trait. Fourth, illnesses may cause personality changes; any trait differences between groups suffering from an illness and matched controls could be caused by an illness-induced change in personality. A chronic illness might conceivably lower extraversion, through decreasing the likelihood that a person will feel up to going out to socialise, and raise neuroticism, because of the greater difficulty of coping with day-to-day activities.

Research has tended to focus on one aspect of the model at a time, which may oversimplify the complex interrelationships that are likely to exist (Friedman, 2000). Friedman notes that disease prevention interventions are often aimed at adults at a single point in time, with little attention to the life-span trajectories along which the individuals are already travelling. For example, adults may be urged by public health campaigns to limit drinking and to stay out of the sun, exhorted by ads to take legal drugs but avoid illegal drugs . . . The results often are that people . . . conclude that everything is bad for you and so nothing need be done. (p. 1090)

He goes on to explain how personality and health relationships can be explored more appropriately using a wide array of psychosocial measures and outcomes in longitudinal studies (and ideally, studies that follow people from childhood onwards).

In summary, a correlation between personality and health outcomes can mean a number of different things. Establishing a robust association between personality and health is only the beginning of the process; beyond that, further investigation of pathways and mechanisms is necessary before we can fully understand such associations. Methodologically, the best studies are those in which personality traits are assessed before the onset of illness, so that the temporal relationship between putative cause (personality) and effect (disease outcome) can be established. In addition, we need to make a distinction between objectively and subjectively measured health outcomes. This does not mean that the psychological associations between personality and subjective outcomes, or personality and psychosomatic illnesses, are of no interest; rather, the more clearly we understand the relationships, the better it is for health prevention and treatment efficacy. In addition, if traits are associated with objective health outcomes, this provides further evidence for their status as valid psychobiological constructs.

Personality and longevity

Does personality predict how long we will live? Box 10.1 describes the remarkable study by Friedman and colleagues (1993; 1995) that found that longevity was associated with high conscientiousness and low levels of optimism in childhood (as rated by parents). Lower conscientiousness was also associated with a range of health-related behaviours such as smoking, alcohol consumption and social and work stability (Friedman et al., 1995). Other studies have been conducted into the mechanism of a conscientiousness–health association; for instance, conscientiousness is associated with greater compliance with medical advice (Christensen et al., 1999) and to uptake of breast cancer screening (Siegler et al., 1995). Friedman et al.'s (1993) findings regarding longevity imply that the more widely studied association between neuroticism and health may be too narrow a focus for personality–health research. However, very few studies have studied such a definite outcome as age at death, and we now turn to other health outcomes.

Box 10.1 Conscientious children live longer; cheerful children die younger

Does childhood personality predict longevity? That was the daring question asked by Friedman et al. (1993; 1995). They used data from the Terman Life-Cycle Study of Children begun in 1921–2. Over 1,500 academically bright, mostly white, male and female children were followed from about age eleven at five- to ten-year intervals, and those still alive are still being studied. At the beginning of the study one of each child's parents was asked to rate the child's personality on a number of traits. Friedman et al. (1993; 1995) combined the trait ratings statistically to form the following factors, which were designed to be as close as possible to the Big Five personality dimensions: Sociability (like Extraversion-Surgency), High Self-Esteem, High Motivation (like Neuroticism), Conscientiousness-Social Dependability (like Conscientiousness), Cheerfulness, Activity and Permanence of Moods. These variables, rated at age eleven, were used to predict whether individuals lived to age seventy. The study had an impressively low attrition rate of less than 10 per cent. Controlling for sex, survival analysis and logistic regression techniques were used to predict the dichotomous dependent variable (alive or dead). Of the six personality variables, conscientiousness (P<0.001) and cheerfulness (P<0.01) predicted longevity. Conscientious children were more likely to be alive at age seventy, and cheerful children less so. The authors suggested that conscientious individuals might be more likely to form better health habits and comply with medical advice; they might also have more functional coping mechanisms.

Heart disease

The most studied interface between personality and illness is the case of coronary heart disease (CHD), a narrowing of the arteries that supply blood to the heart, which predisposes to myocardial infarction ('heart attack') and angina. As long ago as 1910, in his Lumleian lectures on angina pectoris, Sir William Osler asserted that 'it is not the delicate neurotic person who is prone to angina, but the robust, the vigorous in mind and body, the keen and ambitious man, the indicator of whose engines is always at "full speed ahead."' Interest in this particular mind–body relationship has continued throughout the twentieth century and into the twenty-first.

Although the techniques for measuring both personality and heart disease advanced rapidly and significantly during the last century, allowing investigators to be more precise in methodology and findings, the hypotheses concerning the psychosomatic nature of CHD, and researchers' conclusions, have remained remarkably similar. H. Flanders Dunbar, physician and psychiatrist, and the founder of the modern-day field of 'Psychosomatic Medicine', wrote, in 1938:

> Important in the psychic situation of organic heart patients is the absence of a definite correlation between the seriousness of the illness and the subjective experience of it. In striking contrast to the objective findings, [organic heart] patients show little or no consciousness of the disease . . . complaints (shortness of breath on exertion, etc.) are minimized . . . On the contrary, in the 'heart neurotics' we usually find a marked subjective experience of illness referred to heart or circulatory system. We have to acknowledge that, in spite of negative organic findings, the subjective experience of the illness may greatly endanger the work-capacity. With these patients it is in the psychic condition of the personality that we must look for the cause of the subjective complaints. (p. 208)

The distinction between subjective symptoms and objective outcomes was raised as an important issue in the previous chapter on stress, and arises again throughout this chapter. It is clear from Dunbar's (1938) review that the medical profession's attitude towards patients who have pain that cannot be linked to an 'organic' (bodily) cause was as much of a problem then as it is now, and she cautioned:

> In our heart patients, psyche and soma are particularly closely intertwined . . . the psychic condition is more important for happiness in life and subjective work-capacity than a perhaps seriously damaged circulatory system. (p. 209)

The discussion of this issue continues still, despite the hundreds, if not thousands, of studies conducted since Dunbar's time. For example, Costa and McCrae (1987) described the problem of the 'neuroticism artefact' in health psychology research as a growing consensus, and Watson and Pennebaker (1989) found that high neuroticism scorers

> complain of angina, but show no evidence of greater coronary risk or pathology . . . In general, they complain about their health but show no hard evidence of poorer health or increased mortality.

But again, there is a voice of caution about the attitude taken towards people who are reporting symptoms: Adler and Matthews (1994) assert that the association between neuroticism and illness should not be written off as a nuisance factor, arguing that high N people suffer more physical discomfort and that self-reported health, in any case, is an important medical outcome. As we discuss below, there is increasing evidence from recent studies that neuroticism may be implicated in some objective diseases, as well as psychosomatic disorders.

What remains clear is that in studying personality and heart disease, it is vital that the outcomes of angina (which may be diagnosed on the basis of symptoms alone) and myocardial infarction (which is an objectively verifiable, organic outcome) are kept separate, and not treated as if they were the same. Otherwise, the trait predictors of the two outcomes will be confused, and we will be able to offer no insight into effective prevention or treatment of either condition.

Personality and myocardial infarction

Building on the research from earlier in the century, and from observations in their clinical practice, Friedman and Rosenman (1974) formulated the concept of the 'Type A Behaviour pattern'. They noted that their coronary heart disease patients displayed the 'Type A pattern' of brisk body movements, fist clenching in conversation, explosive and hurried speech, upper chest breathing, lack of bodily relaxation, aggressiveness, drive to dominate and achieve goals, and a tendency to be workaholic. They set out to investigate, in systematic, longitudinal research, whether this pattern could predict incident myocardial infarction.

An early success for the Type A personality came from the Western Collaborative Group Study (Rosenman et al., 1975). The study followed 3,154 initially healthy men, aged between thirty-nine and fifty-nine years, for eight and a half years. According to the results of structured interviews, 1,589 were classified as having Type A personalities; 1,565 were Type B. Death rates from CHD were 2.92 per 1,000 person-years for the type A group and 1.32 for the Type B group. Type A individuals were about twice as likely to suffer myocardial infarction; they were also about twice as likely to suffer from angina pectoris. The risk from the Type A pattern was comparable with, and independent of, more traditional risk factors for CHD such as family history of heart disease, smoking and high blood pressure.

However, studies at the latter end of the twentieth century were more equivocal, or negative. Ragland and Brand (1988) reported the twenty-two-year follow-up of the men in the Western Collaborative Group Study. They found that people with Type B personality were likely to have a second heart attack earlier than Type A individuals. In addition, Type As were no more likely, at the twenty-two-year follow-up, to have a fatal heart attack than Type Bs. Another large prospective trial, the Framingham Study (Haynes, Feinleib and Kannel, 1980), found that Type A personality was predictive of myocardial infarction only in certain occupational groups. The Multiple Risk Factor Intervention Trial (Shekelle et al., 1985), which studied 12,772 initially well men for a mean of 7.1 years, found no association between any kind of CHD and Type A personality using a questionnaire measure, the Jenkins Activity Survey (JAS), for the whole sample, and structured interviews for a sub-sample of over 3,000.

The overall significance of the large number of studies conducted has been periodically investigated using the statistical technique of meta-analysis, to assess how strong the underlying association between Type A and CHD actually is. One of the most widely cited is Booth-Kewley and Friedman's (1987) meta-analysis, which concluded that, at most, Type A behaviour might predict about 2 per cent of the variance in CHD, similar to other risk factors. Matthews (1988) indicated that the Booth-Kewley and Friedman meta-analysis had omitted some more recent studies and modified their conclusion by stating that the Type A effect in CHD was even less strong. Moreover, Type A only predicted CHD in population studies, not in high-risk studies. Both studies concluded that the Type A personality is really a composite, with some traits relevant to CHD, and some not. In general, it seemed that the workaholic aspect of Type A was not associated with CHD, but that the competitive, aggressive and impatient traits were more important. Methodological factors which may be associated with failure to find associations between Type A and CHD include the use of high risk populations, fatal myocardial infarction as the disease criterion, and use of self-report Type A measures (Miller et al., 1991).

Increasing integration of the Type A construct with standard personality models has produced three further interesting lines of research. First, the notion that Type A is a composite appears to be supported by psychometric studies of the main Type A measures. For example, distinct factors related to (1) time pressure or impatience, (2) hard-driving competitiveness, (3) speed and (4) emotional expression have been found in both the JAS (May and Kline, 1987) and another widely used measure, the Bortner Type A Scale (Deary et al., 1994). Second, it is clear that some aspects of the Type A conglomerate are associated with more conventional, better understood, personality factors, especially neuroticism and extraversion (Deary, MacLullich and Mardon, 1991). Third, the hostility factor appears to be the predictive core, or 'toxic element' of Type A as far as CHD is concerned (Helmer, Ragland and Syme, 1991; Johnston, 1993). Stone and Costa (1990) suggested that the hostility–CHD link might be related to the Agreeableness dimension of the Big Five model of personality. A meta-analysis of forty-five studies of hostility found that both self-reported and interview-rated hostility traits were associated with CHD, accounting for 3.2 per cent and 0.6 per cent of the disease variance, respectively (Miller et al., 1996). These effect sizes were confirmed in a later meta-analytic review (Myrtek, 2001). Opinion varies as to the importance of the effect from a clinical point of view, at least at present; Myrtek (2001), while noting that hostility is consistently associated with CHD, concludes that 'the effect size is so low that it has as yet no practical meaning for prediction and prevention'. The challenge for the future is to work out how best to use our knowledge about hostility and CHD for the optimum treatment of patients. Box 10.2 recounts a series of findings in the Edinburgh Artery Study that demonstrate the association between hostile traits and objective measures of CHD.

Cancer

It is depression and hopelessness (which share variance with neuroticism) that have been investigated most commonly in relation to cancer. There are three main lines of research: depression or hopelessness as risk factors for developing cancer, depression or hopelessness as modifiable behavioural factors that may influence either the patients' well-being, and depression or hopelessness as factors that influence the natural progression of the cancer after diagnosis. Although a great deal of research has been carried out, many 'positive' studies were methodologically weak (Anderson, 2002; Newell et al., 2002), leaving much doubt that these neuroticism-related factors influence the risk or progression of cancer. Given the confounding effect of neuroticism, it is not very surprising that results of studies

Box 10.2 Hostility and cardiovascular disease

In 1988, 1,592 men and women aged fifty-five to seventy-four were recruited to the Edinburgh Artery Study, a longitudinal cohort study of the prevalence, incidence and natural history of peripheral arterial disease (PAD) in the general population (Fowkes et al., 1991). The study group was physically examined at baseline and also filled in a comprehensive set of questionnaires to assess demographic and personality factors that were known or hypothesised to be related to the risk of PAD and coronary heart disease (CHD). PAD is atherosclerotic disease in the legs, and the extent of PAD not only is a marker of the severity of atherosclerosis throughout the body, but is also a predictor of cardiovascular events and deaths (Leng et al., 1996). Subclinical PAD – significant atherosclerosis in the legs that causes no symptoms – is an outcome measure that is less susceptible to the 'reverse causation' type of confounding that can affect studies of personality and CHD. In a series of analyses in the EAS, it was found that (1) increased hostility was cross-sectionally related to the severity of PAD (Deary et al., 1994); (2) higher levels of hostility were related to the progression of PAD over five years (Whiteman et al., 2000); and (3) 'submissiveness' (lack of dominance) was protective against incident, non-fatal myocardial infarction (Whiteman et al., 1997a, 1997b). Hostility was also found to be related to triglyceride levels in the blood (Fowkes et al., 1992) and to cigarette smoking and alcohol consumption (Whiteman et al., 1997a, 1997b). In all these cases, the personality effect, while independent, worked in conjunction with demographic and physical risk factors to increase risk – with personality accounting for approximately 2 per cent of the variance in either PAD or CHD; there was also an indication that some of hostility's effect acted through the health behaviours of smoking and alcohol consumption.

of depression and hopelessness and the objective outcome of cancer have been equivocal.

The initial question regards cancer incidence: are people with high levels of depression and hopelessness at greater risk of developing cancer? Two very large studies ($n=12,032$ and $n=89,491$) found no association between increased negative affectivity (neuroticism, hopelessness or depression) and the risk of any type of cancer (Dalton et al., 2002; Lillberg et al., 2002). Both of these studies were based in Scandinavia and both used data-linking systems to follow-up patients for twenty years or more. A few smaller studies have also been carried out to investigate this. For example, in a six-year longitudinal study of 2,428 men aged forty-two and sixty, moderate levels of hopelessness were associated with incident cancer (Everson et al., 1996). Men high in hopelessness were also at a threefold increased risk of dying from violence or injury (which are objective outcomes), and were more likely to have an incident myocardial infarction (another objective outcome). In this study the effects of hopelessness were not very specific to one type of disorder, but seemed to be associated with adverse health outcomes in general (and to unhealthy behaviours). However, the study was very small; its findings were interesting, but need replication in larger samples.

The second line of research is into hopelessness and depression and the clinical course of cancer after diagnosis. Watson et al. (1999) conducted an investigation into the impact of psychological factors on the prognosis of breast cancer. Women with early-stage breast cancer were recruited ($n=578$) and asked to complete a set of questionnaires that included the mental adjustment to cancer scale (MAC), the Courtauld Emotional Control scale (CEC) and the Hospital Anxiety and Depression Scale (HADS). The MAC assesses five dimensions: fighting spirit, hopelessness/helplessness, anxious preoccupation, fatalism and avoidance. The CEC assesses the extent to which people suppress negative emotions. Scores on these scales were divided into categories based on z-scores (mean of 0, standard deviation 1). HADS scores were divided into three: 0–7 (non-case); 8–10 (borderline case); and 11+ (case). In multiple regression models that were adjusted for severity of the disease, type of operation or chemotherapy and age, it was found that women who were high in helplessness/hopelessness at baseline ($n=91$) had a statistically significant 1.5 times greater chance of either relapsing or dying. Depression 'caseness' was associated with the risk of total mortality (hazard ratio 3.6), but not with relapse. However, only eleven women were in this category, so the finding must be considered tentative, even though it was 'statistically significant'. Despite having higher numbers of participants and increased power in comparison to similar earlier studies (e.g., Greer et al., 1979; Fawzy et al., 1993), this study's findings are not, in themselves, conclusive, and a wider body of evidence on the effect of hopelessness on survival in cancer is still needed.

The third line of study regarding psychosocial factors and cancer has been aimed at discovering what helps patients cope with their disease and maintain a good quality of life during their illness; it is sometimes found that interventions can improve cancer patients' quality of life (see meta-analysis by Meyer and Mark, 1995; and the review by Newell, Sanson-Fisher and Savolainen, 2002). There has been some debate concerning the best type of intervention – such as a peer support group versus an educational intervention by a trained nurse. Helgeson et al. (2001) conducted a randomised trial of 312 breast cancer patients who were randomised into one of four groups: an eight-week educational intervention led by experts, an eight-week peer-group discussion intervention, a combination of expert and peer-group meetings, and a control group. The women were followed up every few months for two years. Health-related quality of life at all waves of data collection was measured using the SF-36 Health Survey (Ware et al., 1993), which contains several scales, including general health, physical functioning, pain, mental health and social functioning. The educational intervention improved knowledge significantly more than the peer-group intervention, and the educational group, compared to the other groups, showed two-year sustained improvements in some of the dimensions: vitality, pain and physical functioning. The peer-group discussions were not superior to the control condition, although at only eight weeks, the intervention may have been too short to have a measurable effect. Other studies have noted that pre-morbid levels of neuroticism also affect quality of life reports in cancer patients (Ranchor et al., 2002), and that quality of life interventions are of greatest benefit to people who had high levels of depression at the time of diagnosis (McLachlan et al., 2001).

Despite the methodological difficulties in studying psychosocial factors and cancer, there are plausible biological pathways that could account for the relationship, in particular immune response (Fawzy et al., 1990). A meta-analytic review, however, of more than eighty-five trials of psychological interventions on immune function found that results were quite mixed (Miller and Cohen, 2001). The strongest evidence was for the effect of hypnosis on immune functioning; stress management and relaxation techniques showed little evidence of eliciting an improvement in immune function. Many of the trials, however, suffered from methodological difficulties (Anderson, 2002; Newell, Sanson-Fisher and Savolainen, 2002); until a larger, rigorously conducted set of studies is available, the complicated putative effects of psychological functioning on immune functioning – or on the risk or prognosis of cancer – will remain unclear. Box 10.3 outlines the

---

Box 10.3 Recommendations for research into psychosocial factors and cancer

Newell, Sanson-Fisher and Savolainen (2002) made several recommendations to advance the study of psychosocial intervention trials for cancer, which are summarised here:

1 Define the study population, determine eligibility and then randomly recruit from within that population or select every consecutive case.
2 Use a placebo intervention where possible, and ensure assessors are blinded as to patient's study group.
3 Use intention-to-treat analysis; that is, include the losses to follow-up in the analyses (in addition to trying to minimise losses to follow-up).

Adherence to these criteria would improve the quality of the trials, would allow comparability of studies and a much better understanding of whether there is or is not an effect of psychological interventions (Newell, Sanson-Fisher and Savolainen, 2002). Anderson (2002) also made further suggestions for epidemiological studies, including: paying careful attention to severity of disease at entry to the study; time since diagnosis; type of medical or surgical treatment received; widening the diversity of patients studied; the need to assess personality traits and pre-morbid levels of psychological distress. Without such improvements in study design and methodology, future research will not improve our knowledge regarding the putative effect of psychological factors on cancer incidence or prognosis (Newell et al., 2002; Anderson, 2002).

main recommendations from reviews of the research on psychosocial factors and cancer.

Neuroticism as a risk factor for multiple diseases

The focus of much research on heart disease and cancer has tended to obscure the possible role of traits in other serious diseases. Indeed, several studies implicate neuroticism as a predictor of various forms of ill-health (Kirmayer et al., 1994), although as previously noted, there are concerns that these findings simply represent a complaint-prone disposition. However, evidence is beginning to accumulate from prospective studies that links high N to conditions such as asthma (Huovinen, Kaprio and Koskenvuo, 2001) and gastrointestinal disorders (Drossman et al., 2000). There is still little convincing evidence that high neuroticism is directly implicated in vulnerability to CHD. However, following a first heart attack, neuroticism is associated with poorer prognosis and risk of subsequent death from cardiac disease (Denollet, 2000; Murberg, Bru and Aarsland, 2001).

A ten-year longitudinal study in progress in Heidelberg, using a community sample of around 5,000, aims to track the influence of personality on multiple diseases (Amelang, 1997). It will eventually use objective mortality indices, but, in preliminary analyses, self-reports have been used. Although self-reports have obvious disadvantages, there is increasing evidence from epidemiological studies that self-reports are quite accurate for diseases that are conceptually clear, severe and persistent, such as most major, life-threatening illnesses (Haapanen et al., 1997). Two recent reports on the Heidelberg study (Matthews et al., 2002; Yousfi et al., submitted) confirm that high N is correlated, cross-sectionally, with incidence of a wide variety of diseases, including CHD, hypertension, and gastric disorders, although effect sizes were small. In addition, levels of N were especially high in persons reporting multiple diseases. Indeed, Matthews et al. (2002) found that N was only a predictor of health in multiple-disease groups, and not in persons reporting a single disease. This finding suggests that N may be linked to a general susceptibility to disease, rather than to specific pathology (cf., Sanderman and Ranchor, 1997).

If N does correlate, modestly, with some general vulnerability, what might the mechanism be? The leading possibility is that the psychological stress vulnerability of persons high in N leads to loss of immune system function. Studies of the influence of infectious agents on antibody response suggest a link between stress and immune impairment (Cohen, Miller and Rabin, 2001). This argument is supported by two recent studies that demonstrate weaker immune response in high N persons, following vaccinations for the rubella virus (Morag et al., 1999) and hepatitis B (Marsland et al., 2001). Other causal mechanisms are, of course, possible, such as the 'complaint-prone' interpretation of high N. Possibly, N has an indirect effect via maladaptive health behaviours, although it seems that moderate anxiety and depression may have beneficial effects such as increased care-seeking (Mayne,

1999). We return to studies of stress and of health behaviours in the sections that follow.

Stress and health

Stress–health relationships are arguably the largest area of research within health psychology. In chapter 9, we discussed how stress is expressed in the body and how it is related to personality; these interrelationships are of great importance when considering the further link to health outcomes. At the beginning of this chapter, we briefly mentioned that the stereotype of the overworked stressed businessman getting a heart attack was a cliché with almost no evidence to support it. Why have we said that, and if stress does not increase the risk of heart attacks, is it related to health at all?

In this section, we look at the role of stress in some detail because, as we saw in chapter 9, various personality traits have been linked to stress vulnerability, which may also be expressed as health problems. Neuroticism plays a dual role here. On the one hand, stress or neuroticism may be linked to objective illness. However, given the link between N and stress (see chapter 9), N may act as a confounder of stress–disease associations. Outcomes relating to stress are widely varied: some self-report measures (e.g., 'are you under a lot of stress?') can be almost a proxy measure of neuroticism (Macleod et al., 2001). If, however, stress is measured in other ways (through raised cortisol levels, say), then the effects of stress on the body – and on objectively measured health outcomes – can be separated from the 'reporting effect' of neuroticism.

Stress and coronary disease

Findings on stress and coronary heart disease are extremely mixed: much more so even than findings on Type A, hostility, anger and coronary heart disease. As we have previously noted, however, 'stress' is a very broad term and ten studies examining stress and coronary heart disease could well be examining ten different psychological constructs in relation to coronary heart disease. This, added to the different outcomes that fall under the banner of 'coronary heart disease', makes it easy to see why the conclusions regarding stress and coronary heart disease are equivocal. This ambiguity is not reflected in lay perceptions of illness: people in hospital with a myocardial infarction most commonly cite stress as the cause of their heart attack (King, 2002). Such problems are neatly summed up by Stansfeld (2002), who notes that 'the problem with stress as a cause of illness is that it has too much face validity' (p. 1113): everyone feels stressed at times, and it is a too-easy leap to make to illnesses such as heart disease, which are not fully explained by other causes. Part of the problem is the construct of stress and its measurement.

Three typical studies illustrate the methodological differences: (1) a cross-sectional study of overall perceived stress and coronary heart disease risk factors

(Heslop et al., 2001); (2) a longitudinal cohort study of the effect of marital and work stress on the prognosis of female MI (heart attack) patients (Orth-Gomer et al., 2000); and (3) a longitudinal field study of job strain, stress hormone levels and anger in male and female teachers (Steptoe et al., 2000).

In the first study (Heslop et al., 2001), 5,848 men and 984 women recruited from workplaces in the west of Scotland were given physical examinations and asked to fill in a self-report, four-item stress questionnaire: the Reeder Stress Inventory (Reeder, Chapman and Coulson, 1968). It was found that higher levels of self-reported stress (e.g., one item reads: 'My daily activities are extremely trying and stressful') were associated with worse health behaviours such as smoking. When the levels of stress were analysed in relation to mortality, however, stress seemed to decrease the risk of death, particularly from smoking-related diseases such as CHD and lung cancer. The key to understanding the finding seemed to lie in confounding; when the analyses were adjusted for income and social position, the relationship between self-reported stress and risk of death was greatly attenuated. That is, higher stress was more likely to be reported by those in higher social class groups, who were, nonetheless, at lower risk of dying. The results were further complicated by the fact that within each social class group, those who smoked more were also more likely to report higher stress: however, the prevalence of smoking was higher in lower class groups and the effect of social position outweighed the effects of self-reported stress. Although the Reeder Stress Inventory has acceptable reliability and validity statistics, as a self-report measure of stressful feelings (as opposed to number or severity of life events), it is prone to confounding with the personality trait of neuroticism.

In the second study, 292 female patients aged thirty to sixty-five who were hospitalised with myocardial infarction (MI) were followed up for five years (Orth-Gomer et al., 2000). At baseline, work stress and marital stress were assessed using the Karasek demand–control questionnaire for work stress (Karasek et al., 1981) and a specially designed questionnaire on marital (or cohabitational) stress. The outcome measures were recurrent coronary events (either deaths or re-hospitalisation for MI). After adjustment for severity of initial illness, age, smoking, blood pressure and other relevant factors, it was found that marital stress, but not work stress, predicted recurrent events in these Swedish women. Interestingly, living alone posed no increased risk; the effect was limited to the quality of the marital or cohabitational relationship. Other large studies of job control that included both men and women, however, have found that higher job strain and lower job control are related to the risk of myocardial infarction and cardiac death (Bosma et al., 1997). Low job control in contrast to social class appeared to be the important risk factor; however, jobs that are paid less and have lower social status also tend to be jobs that allow the employees very little control over their own work.

The third study focused on mechanisms: forty-one male and sixty-four female schoolteachers were measured on job strain, anger and negative affect, and had their stress hormone (cortisol) levels monitored every two hours during a working day

(Steptoe et al., 2000). After adjustment for age and negative affect, it was found that cortisol levels were 22 per cent higher in the 'high job strain' group, and higher still in the group high on both job strain and anger. This study in particular shows that stress is not a stand-alone phenomenon; it interacts with other traits and emotions to have its effect.

Despite the mixed findings on stress it is apparent that physical factors alone are not sufficient to explain fully the risk of coronary heart disease: people have heart attacks even when they have been taking lipid-lowering drugs, they don't smoke, their weight is normal and their blood pressure is controlled. If there is a psychological factor that is associated with increased risk, and it is amenable to change, then medical practice has the potential to be improved. Reviews have reported that stress has been found to be associated with risk factor clustering (e.g., high stress, smoking, obesity and high blood pressure tend to occur together), with dysfunction of the lining of blood vessels, with insufficient oxygen reaching the heart, with heart arrhythmias and with ruptures of fatty plaques in coronary arteries and with blood clots (Merz et al., 2002). Very often, however, we see that social conditions can be more powerful and consistent predictors of ill-health than are psychological factors. That is not to say that psychological risk factors are not worth studying; but that our framework must also include social or economic factors. The evidence for the impact of socio-economic status (SES) on CHD is strong, and while some studies of SES and disease postulate that stress is the mediating mechanism between SES and CHD, Macleod and Davey Smith (2002) point out that 'stress is too general to usefully explain any social patterns of disease' (p. 1111). While the evidence for stress and CHD is equivocal, the idea is so pervasive that research will undoubtedly continue, hopefully following the call from Stansfeld (2002) that 'stress and health research needs to be pursued with the utmost rigour to discover the truth in a subtle, complex and seductive field' (p. 1116).

Stress and the common cold

Stress has also been implicated in a less serious, but highly prevalent disease: the common cold. In 276 volunteers who completed a questionnaire on life stress and who were then directly exposed to common cold viruses in the laboratory, severe chronic stress (such as long-term interpersonal difficulties) was associated with a much greater risk of developing a cold, after adjustment for social support, personality, health behaviours and immune response (Cohen et al., 1998). Similarly, Cobb and Steptoe (1996), in a fifteen-month study of 107 adults aged eighteen to sixty-five years, found that high life event stress increased the risk of getting a cold. In the three weeks just before the onset of illness, levels of perceived stress were higher than at other times. When Cobb and Steptoe analysed their findings to take account of other psychosocial factors, including coping, they found that the risk of respiratory illness with high life-event stress was reduced in people who used avoidant coping strategies. Other cohort studies have also documented the effect that stress has on susceptibility to the common cold: Takkoucche, Regueira and Gestal-Otero (2001) conducted a study of 1,149 staff and students of the University of Santiago, Spain. They measured four dimensions of stress – life events, negative and positive affect and perceived stress – finding that all four dimensions were related to increased risk of getting a cold. Participants in the highest quartile of negative affectivity were 3.7 times more likely than others to have a cold, with slightly lower risk ratios for other types of stress. Positive affect was protective: it reduced the likelihood (by 40 per cent) of getting a cold. The studies were careful to define the outcome as 'verified' colds – that is, they did not rely on individual's symptom reports alone, but on the judgement of a specially trained study researcher or nurse as to severity and duration of symptoms (eg., mucus production, fever, etc.). The evidence for stress increasing the risk of the common cold is quite consistent, although findings do vary according to the measure of stress and the way the cold is diagnosed.

Stress-buffers: optimism, hope, spirituality and happiness in relation to illness

If stress, in some cases, and 'negative' personality traits such as hostility or neuroticism are risk factors for illness, are there 'positive' aspects of personality that help protect people from illness and its effects? As we saw in the last chapter, coping styles are related to personality, and when it comes to health, things are no different. Stress, personality and coping styles interact to influence health: optimism, hope and hardiness are sometimes measured as traits, but are also considered methods of coping. What do we know about their effects on health? So far, similar to research on personality and cancer, the results are equivocal, partly as a result of construct, methodological and measurement difficulties.

Optimism is both an emotional and cognitive construct: a mood or feeling that things will turn out well, and a goal or motivation (Peterson, 2000). In his review, Peterson outlines the approaches to optimism as an individual differences variable with sub-constructs of dispositional versus situation-dependent optimism, optimism as an explanatory style, and optimism as an outlook of hope. In particular, Peterson notes that pessimism is not necessarily the polar opposite of optimism; that they can both have an effect on a person's outlook. Optimism as an explanatory style was found to protect against incident myocardial infarction and coronary heart disease death in 1,306 men followed up for ten years (Kubzansky et al., 2001), but not many studies were so careful about defining optimism or measuring disease objectively. Given these ambiguities, which also affect the related constructs of hope, faith and spirituality/religiosity, it is not surprising that research findings are mixed.

Other research has looked specifically at spirituality and/or religiosity, which are known to have beneficial effects on psychological well-being (Francis and Kaldor, 2002). It has also been noted that religious and spiritual coping are often important in helping people deal with a diagnosis of illness, especially serious illness such as

AIDS (Siegel and Schrimshaw, 2002). The question, then, is whether spirituality is associated with physical health outcomes. Blood pressure is one physical health marker that has been investigated in relation to spirituality or religious attendance, with almost all of the studies in this area finding that increased religiosity is associated with lower blood pressure levels (Koenig et al., 1988; Larson et al., 1989; Levin and Vanderpool, 1989; Livingston et al., 1991; Steffen et al., 2001). The results held even when confounding factors (age, socio-economic status or social network) were controlled. Koenig (1997) summarised the few studies of religiosity and heart disease, explaining that the initial evidence suggests that there could be a link, and that spirituality/religiosity are factors that should continue to be investigated in relation to heart disease – but at present the research is far from conclusive.

Happiness is another construct that is related to optimism. Argyle (1997) raises important issues when discussing happiness in relation to health – importantly, and reflecting model four at the beginning of this chapter – the possibility that health causes happiness rather than happiness causing health. In fact, there is evidence for such relationships working in both directions. Happier people have been found to live longer (Deeg and Zonneveld, 1989; Devins et al., 1990), and positive mood can have a beneficial effect on the immune system (Stone et al., 1987). In older people, high health satisfaction predicts subjective well-being (Willits and Crider, 1988) but the same caveat applies to this as to other research: self-reported or self-perceived health is not the same as objectively measured health, although objectively measured health also predicts life satisfaction (Brief et al., 1993). So, while there is some indication that optimism and related measures such as hope, spirituality and happiness have beneficial effects on health, rather than on coping processes, the research is at an early stage, and we do not yet understand the mechanism of such effects, if indeed they are found to be replicable associations.

Traits and health-related behaviours

Research findings regarding personality traits and health behaviour are fairly consistent. Two traits have tended to emerge as correlates and predictors of smoking and drinking: neuroticism (high) and sensation-seeking (high). Extraversion (high), hostility (high) and conscientiousness (low) have also been implicated as risk factors for these behaviours in some studies. Vollrath and Torgerson (2002), in a study of 683 university students, measured students on the Big Five personality dimensions and asked them to report their smoking and alcohol consumption. Smokers tended to be high on E, high on N and low on C – the key (moderating) trait being the low C. Being high on E or N alone did not predict smoking, but if this was combined with being low on C, the risk of being a smoker increased. In a sample of 343 Oregon community residents, conscientiousness was found to be an important predictor of perceptions of health risks associated with smoking, with personal smoking behaviour and with rules about smoking in the house (Hampson et al., 2000). Personality correlates of smoking and alcohol consumption have also been investigated in larger groups: in the Edinburgh Artery Study of 1,592 men and women aged fifty-five to seventy-four, both cigarette smoking and alcohol consumption were associated with increased levels of hostility (Whiteman et al., 1997), a finding that was presaged by results from large epidemiological studies in the USA (Scherwitz et al., 1992; Siegler, 1994).

Life course approaches to personality, stress and illness

There is a wide literature on social determinants of health that shows the importance of building models of illness susceptibility that can incorporate environmental, social, physical and psychological aspects of a person's lifetime. Hertzman et al. (2001), using data from 11,405 members of the 1958 British Birth Cohort, developed a model of lifecourse influences on self-reported health at age thirty-three, from birth onwards. Multiple regression models showed that early and later stage factors, in conjunction with contemporary societal factors, predicted self-rated health. Factors included birth weight, childhood socio-economic circumstances, social and emotional status at ages seven, eleven and sixteen, adulthood social and material circumstances, job strain, job insecurity, social network, marital status and emotional support. The factors were, individually, statistically significant predictors, and together, accounted for about 20 per cent of the variance in self-rated health. Hertzman and colleagues note the problematic outcome of using a one-item, self-report global rating of health as the outcome, although self-reports of this type have consistently been shown to be related to mortality (Wannamethee and Shaper, 1991; Idler and Benyamini, 1997).

Harper et al. (2002) studied lifecourse socio-economic position, education, occupation, and income in relation to adult hostility, hopelessness and depression in 2,585 Finnish men. Using multiple regression to model the associations, they found that higher hostility and hopelessness scores were related to both childhood and adulthood socio-economic circumstances: those who were more deprived also scored higher on hostility and hopelessness measures. A review of the contribution of social and demographic factors to health was carried out in the USA (Whitfield et al., 2002): ethnic group and socio-economic status, together with social support and personality, were found to have important effects on both self-reported and objectively measured health. Although they are not usually characterised as such, lifetime poverty and poor working conditions could be considered to be a special kind of stress. Researchers have called for studies that will help clarify the relationships among socio-economic circumstances, personality traits and coping resources (Whitfield et al., 2002). Additionally, in order to grasp the true nature of any associations, it may be important to analyse broad traits (the five factors) in relation to general health measures, such as global self-ratings of health, and narrower traits (such as hostility) to narrower health measures (such as coronary heart disease); that is, macro-to-macro level and micro-to-micro level analyses (Wasylkiw and Fekken, 2002).

Friedman (2000) describes life span personality and health associations at three levels: 'dynamisms' (personality and health patterns that begin to develop in childhood), 'mechanisms' (personality in relation to health behaviours that, in turn, affect health) and 'tropisms' (person–situation interactions that involve either moving towards or away from healthy environments). Smoking and alcohol consumption may be involved at all three levels. For instance, *dynamic* factors include the child's temperament and family experiences. Are the child's parents smokers? What example do the child's neighbourhood, school and friends provide? Is the child naturally extravert or sensation seeking, and likely to try smoking? The smoking behaviour, once established, then may become both a behavioural and biological *mechanism* leading to poor physical, and perhaps, poor mental health. Finally, in both childhood and adulthood, a *tropism* could be a rebellious streak that leads a person into a health-damaging choice such as smoking; this pattern is then reinforced by the new situation created by being 'a smoker' and by new environmental and peer influences. Therefore, it is interesting to document associative and predictive personality factors for health behaviours and health outcomes, but analyses need to be able to take into account the broader context.

Models of psychosomatic illness

At a theoretical level, Watson and Pennebaker (1989) suggested that negative affectivity (and, therefore, neuroticism) be reconceptualised not just as an emotion-related trait, but something more general: a trait of somatopsychic distress. They suggested that the distinction between psychological and physical complaining is unnecessary and wrong, and that some people may have a general tendency toward self-reported distress of all kinds. Therefore, the exploration of the underlying common elements of the physical and psychological aspects of complaining must become a research priority. This conceptual reorientation of the place of neuroticism provides a useful introduction to the consideration of personality and psychosomatic illnesses. There is no absolute line between those illnesses which are purely physical and those that are purely psychosomatic, but a useful definition of a psychosomatic illness is one in which there are physical complaints but no identifiable physical cause for the symptoms after physical examination and investigations. Kellner (1991) includes the conditions shown in table 10.1 in his review of the commoner psychosomatic syndromes.

Widely varied studies have shown associations between psychosomatic illness and neuroticism. For example, patients with non-ulcer dyspepsia score higher on neuroticism than community controls (Talley et al., 1986). In studies of personality and other psychosomatic disorders the ubiquitous finding that high neuroticism relates to a general tendency towards more negative emotion is complemented by indicators of significant introversion effects. Kellner (1991) describes findings of high neuroticism and introversion in irritable bowel syndrome. The same personality pattern is found in other conditions such as non-ulcer dyspepsia (Dinan, Chua

Table 10.1 *Common psychosomatic conditions as reviewed by Kellner (1991)*

Fibromyalgia, fibrositis and myofascial pain syndrome
Chronic fatigue and chronic fatigue syndrome
Globus and fear of choking
Dysphagia and oesophageal motility disorders
Non-ulcer dyspepsia
Irritable bowel syndrome
Urethral syndrome
Behaviour-induced physiological changes: hyperventilation and aerophagia
Chronic pain syndromes

and Keeling, 1993) and globus pharyngis – a feeling of a lump in the throat in the absence of any detectable structural pathology (Deary, Wilson and Kelly, 1995).

Studies of specific psychosomatic disorders often find relationships between the given diagnosis (e.g, fibromyalgia or irritable bowel syndrome) and neuroticism, depression or anxiety (Kirmayer, Robbins and Paris, 1994; Katon, Sullivan and Walker, 2001; Koloski, Talley and Boyce, 2001). In addition to personality factors, childhood maltreatment and adult psychological trauma are implicated (Katon, Sullivan and Walker, 2001). It is also apparent that, while medically unexplained symptoms do cluster to form separate disorders such as chronic fatigue syndrome, fibromyalgia or irritable bowel syndrome, there is a latent factor – accounting for around 40 per cent of the variance – that underlies all the syndromes (Deary, 1999). Other studies have also described a similar pattern, noting the likelihood that a person with one disorder is more likely to display symptoms of another (Nimnuan et al., 2001).

In summary, psychosomatic conditions tend to occur in individuals with high levels of neuroticism; there is, in addition, some tendency towards introversion in these groups. Kirmayer, Robbins and Paris's (1994) review of the many personality traits said to predispose towards psychosomatic illness attempts to orient these around the five factor model of personality traits; it is clear from their account that there is much conceptual overlap between neuroticism and other health-related traits. More empirically, Marshall et al. (1994) have attempted to reduce the conceptual confusion among many supposedly health-related personality scales, and found that:

> First, most health-relevant dimensions and scales appear to be complex mixtures of broad personality domains. Second, variation in many health-related personality instruments is explained to a significant degree by the five-factor model. Third, two of the five personality domains (i.e., conscientiousness and openness) appear to be substantially neglected in health psychology research.

However, from their research it is clear that it is neuroticism, and then extraversion, that accounts for most of the variance in other health-related trait scales.

Conclusions

1. Two of the most widely investigated health-related personality traits are the Type A (coronary-prone) behaviour pattern and expressive hostility. The Type A pattern is a conglomerate, and meta-analyses and reviews consistently find that it is the expressive hostility part of the pattern that is related to the risk of incident myocardial infarction, accounting for around 2 per cent of the variance in disease. The biological mechanism of the association is still somewhat unclear. Hostility may cause damage directly through increased blood pressure and heart rate, and atherosclerotic build-up. Alternatively, it may contribute to general risk behaviours such as increased smoking or drinking, or reduced availability of social support.

2. Studies of depression/hopelessness and cancer have not documented any excess risk of cancer development, or any excess mortality after diagnosis, for people who are high on either dimension. However, depression and hopelessness are indicators of distress, and are important in quality of life after diagnosis. Expert-led educational support interventions, while not affecting disease outcome, are beneficial in reducing depression and increasing mental well-being, and are of particular benefit to those with high levels of depression at the start of the programme.

3. Neuroticism is associated with a wide range of poorer health outcomes. It is implicated in psychosomatic disorders, and some studies have shown that high N predicts poorer prognosis after myocardial infarction. Neuroticism is consistently associated with poorer self-reported health, but less consistently with objective measures of health, which could reflect the high N person's tendency to be 'distress-prone' either physically or mentally. However, high N has also been related to suppressed immune function, so there are biologically plausible mechanisms for observed relationships between N and poorer health. Neuroticism may also have health benefits, in that symptoms of illness – including serious illnesses such as cancer – are detected and reported earlier by high N compared to low N individuals.

4. The relationship between stress and disease is, as with N, unclear. Some well-defined types of stress, such as job strain/job control, are associated with objectively measured disease. Life events and self-reported stress have also been associated with a greater likelihood of suppressed immune response and increased risk of succumbing to the common cold. Study findings may depend on the way stress is measured as well as the outcome of interest, whether it be objective or subjective. Measuring the Big Five traits alongside stress may help 'control' for the overlapping variance with N, and give greater clarity to research findings.

5. Further investigations, with carefully delineated measures of N, stress and the Big Five traits, may help elucidate the dynamic, life-course effects of early

environments, health behaviour choices, immune functioning, and both subjective and objective measures of health and disease.

Further reading

Argyle, M. (1997) Is happiness a cause of health? *Psychology and Health*, 12, 769–781.

Friedman, H. S. (2000) Long-term relations of personality and health: dynamisms, mechanims, tropisms. *Journal of Personality*, 68, 1089–1107.

Miller, G. E., and Cohen, S. (2001) Psychological interventions and the immune system: a meta-analytic review and critique. *Health Psychology*, 20, 47–63.

11 Abnormal personality traits?

Dimensions of personality describe variations in behavioural dispositions in the population. Because most personality dimensions are normally distributed, it is easy to assume that 'abnormality' lies at the tails of the distributions. For example, people with very high Neuroticism scores might suffer much from anxiety, and those with very high Conscientiousness scores might be disablingly rigid. However, might there be qualitative, as opposed to statistical, differences between the bulk of the population and a few individuals with very unusual personalities? The concept of personality disorder or abnormal personality lies within the domain of psychiatry and clinical psychology. Strangely, although it alludes to human personality variation, until the 1990s personality disorder attracted relatively little interest from differential psychologists studying normal personality. Conversely, the largely medically oriented researchers in the field of personality disorders have until recently shown little interest in either normal personality dimensions or the techniques of differential psychology.

> Instead of benefiting from progress in the taxonomy of normal personality traits, psychiatric nosologists turned to medicine and biology rather than psychology for models for classifying psychopathology. They continue to do so because the philosophical assumptions underlying current psychiatric nosology . . . stipulate that psychiatry is a branch of medicine, that discrete categories of mental disorder exist, and that there is a clear distinction between normality and pathology. (Livesley, 2001b, p. 278–9)

It is commonplace for books on personality to make little or no mention of the research on personality disorders, let alone try to integrate normal and abnormal personality research, though there are exceptions (Buss and Larsen, 2002).

The research landscape of personality disorder that shapes this chapter is complex, and needs some sketching. Some of the main landmarks in this area are as follows.

Psychiatrists and clinical psychologists work with personality disorder concepts that form a typology. The principal taxonomic schemes for these typologies are described. Research work within this typological tradition, which supports and criticises it, is described.

There are several problems with these typologies that are becoming clearer and more serious as empirical research findings accumulate. Some key problems are described.

Several researchers in personality disorder have suggested that typologies of personality disorder, which originated within a clinical tradition, should be replaced with dimensions. Research on the possible dimensions of personality disorder is described. There is growing evidence for a four factor model of personality disorder, and for a greater number of more specific factors at lower levels in a hierarchical scheme.

There are different methods for seeking the dimensions of personality disorder, each of which is described. Some researchers work with present clinical schemes and attempt to treat clinical symptoms as test items, which they then analyse using psychometric methods. Some researchers create new items, not based on clinical classification schemes' criteria, and produce novel personality disorder dimensions. Some researchers examine the relationships between clinical personality disorder criteria and current factor models of normal personality, such as Eysenck's, Cloninger's and the five factor model. Similar dimensions of personality disorders emerge from these various approaches, and there are congruences between normal and abnormal personality trait models.

In addition to seeking the number and character of the principal traits that underlie variation in personality disorder, some researchers have instead concentrated on single, salient traits, such as psychopathy, schizotypy, borderline personality and narcissism. Examples of research on these narrow traits are given and discussed.

It is concluded that research on personality disorders is in a state of crisis. The current categorical schemes lack validity, but there is not yet agreement about whether to move to a dimensional system, or which one might be preferable.

Personality disorders – concept and classification

Some individuals who present to mental health professionals – because they suffer themselves or they cause others to suffer – show consistently maladaptive responses from late adolescence or even earlier. Unlike a mental illness, there is no clear pattern of remission and relapse, nor is there any gradual deterioration in behaviour. Instead of a mental disorder being superimposed upon a previously normal personality, it seems that mental disturbance in some individuals is a result of their lasting behavioural predispositions: their personality itself is awry.

History of personality disorder concepts

The concept and classification of disorders of personality might be said to stretch as far back as the ancient Greeks. Theophrastus (370–285 BC; see Rusten's, 1993, translation) described thirty types of arguably abnormal personalities, though the general approach of the book is a satirical description of types of behaving that are annoying, but rarely clinically disturbed. Since the beginning of the nineteenth century the concept of personality disorder has gradually broadened. At first it was centred around what we might recognise today as psychopathy or antisocial personality disorder. It now covers many modes of persistently aberrant behaviour. Berrios (1993) gave a useful account of the historical development of ideas in personality disorder that drew from many non-English texts. Although the French psychiatrist Pinel is often given the credit of originating the concept of personality disorder around 1809, his concept of '*manie sans delire*' was poorly understood by other clinicians. The central problem Pinel was trying to capture was those patients who showed outbursts of aggression in the absence of frank mental illness. The other term that is often cited as capturing what was later to become antisocial personality disorder – moral insanity – was coined by the English physician Pritchard. However, this was shown to be related to mood disorder rather than personality disorder (Whitlock, 1982). One of the group of problems captured by Koch's (1891) term 'psychopathic inferiority' was antisocial behaviour.

Schneider's book on *Psychopathic Personalities* in 1923 marks the beginning of modern ideas of abnormal personality. He recognised that some people suffered themselves or made others suffer as a result of their deviation from mean levels of personality attributes. Moreover, he described ten patterns of psychopathy, as follows: hyperthymic, depressive, insecure, fanatical, lacking in self-esteem, labile in affect, explosive, wicked, aboulic and asthenic (Berrios, 1993). The criticism that Schneider's ideas received at the time – of his disorders being tautological, a mix of psychological and social criteria, overlapping, and related to illness states – are all extant criticisms of modern personality disorder schemes. Henderson's *Psychopathic States* (1939) included three clusters of psychopathy: predominantly aggressive, passive and creative.

Classificatory schemes for personality disorder

As internationally recognised schemes of clinical classification grew and became based more and more on operational criteria, the types of personality disorder listed in clinical manuals became more settled. There are two classificatory schemes whose international influence is widespread: the American Psychiatric Association's *Diagnostic and Statistical Manual of Mental Disorders*, now in its 4th edition (DSM-IV; American Psychiatric Association, 1994, 2000); and the World Health Organisation's *International Classification of Diseases*, now in its 10th edition (ICD10; World Health Organisation, 1992, 1997). The DSM-IV system recognises ten disorders of personality and the ICD10 system lists nine. The lists are shown for comparison in table 11.1. The DSM-IV personality disorders are arranged in three clusters: odd–eccentric, dramatic–emotional and anxious–fearful (see table 11.2). The clusters and individual disorders in the DSM-IV scheme are the result of the deliberations of their Personality Disorders Work Group. This group of experts systematically reviews published literature, conducts data re-analyses and oversees field trials of the proposed criteria for each disorder. The adequacy of their deliberations to establish the validity of personality disorder categories was questioned (Farmer, 2000).

Table 11.1 *Titles of personality disorders recognised in the DSM-IV and ICD-10 classification systems*

DSM-IV	ICD10
Paranoid	Paranoid
Schizoid	Schizoid
Schizotypal	
Antisocial	Dyssocial
Borderline	Impulsive/Borderline
Histrionic	Histrionic
Narcissistic	
Avoidant	Anxious
Dependent	Dependent
Obsessive-compulsive	Anankastic

Table 11.2 *DSM-IV clusters of personality disorders*

Cluster A	Cluster B	Cluster C
Odd–eccentric	*Dramatic–emotional*	*Anxious–fearful*
Paranoid	Antisocial	Avoidant
Schizoid	Borderline	Dependent
Schizotypal	Histrionic	Obsessive–compulsive
	Narcissistic	

In the DSM-IV scheme, personality disorder is defined as 'an enduring pattern of inner experience and behaviour that deviates markedly from the expectations of the individual's culture, is pervasive and flexible, has an onset in adolescence or early adulthood, is stable over time, and leads to distress or impairment' (American Psychiatric Association, 1994). DSM-IV uses a multiaxial system to describe patients, and the ICD system has adopted one also. The first DSM axis is used for mental illness diagnoses, axis II includes the personality disorders and mental retardation, axis III documents general medical conditions, axis IV notes psychosocial and environmental problems, and axis V is a global assessment of functioning. Therefore, personality disorders are explicitly separated from psychiatric illnesses and may coexist with them. Moreover, individuals may be diagnosed as having more than one personality disorder. According to DSM-IV, before a specific abnormal personality type is diagnosed, a person's abnormal behaviour must: be broadly expressed, lead to distress or impaired functioning, be stable and of long duration, and not be due to mental illness or the effects of drugs or a physical medical condition. In other words, the behaviour must be trait-like.

Personality disorders, therefore, form a typology both in DSM-IV and in ICD10. Though classified in a separate axis, they are diagnosed like illnesses – one either has a personality disorder or one does not; there are no gradations. By contrast with

Table 11.3 *Brief definitions of the DSM-IV personality disorders*

Paranoid	A pattern of distrust and suspiciousness such that others' motives are interpreted as malevolent.
Schizoid	A pattern of detachment from social relationships and a restricted range of emotional expression.
Schizotypal	A pattern of acute discomfort in close relationships, cognitive or perceptual distortions and eccentricities of behaviour.
Antisocial	A pattern of disregard for, and violation of, the rights of others.
Borderline	A pattern of instability in interpersonal relationships, self image and affects, and marked impulsivity.
Histrionic	A pattern of excessive emotionality and attention seeking.
Narcissistic	A pattern of grandiosity, need for admiration and lack of empathy.
Avoidant	A pattern of social inhibition, feelings of inadequacy and hypersensitivity to negative evaluation.
Dependent	A pattern of submissive and clinging behaviour related to an excessive need to be taken care of.
Obsessive–compulsive	A pattern of preoccupation with orderliness, perfectionism, and control.

personality traits, one cannot have degrees of a personality disorder. A binary yes–no decision is made by the interviewing clinician with reference to the operational rules for each personality disorder. The DSM-IV manual makes repeated use of the term 'personality traits' (American Psychiatric Association, 1994, p. 630) to describe the individual features of personality disorders. Therefore, although the decision about whether someone does or does not have a personality disorder is binary, there is explicit recognition that there is a continuum of possibilities.

Personality disorders – descriptions of the individual disorders

A thumbnail sketch of each DSM-IV concept is provided in table 11.3. In addition, the more detailed criteria for three disorders, one from each of the three DSM-IV clusters, are shown in table 11.4. A wide range of behavioural abnormality is covered by the various disorders, and personality disorders represent the meeting place of many traditions of clinical research. Antisocial personality disorder arose after longitudinal studies of children with conduct disorder, borderline and narcissistic concepts come from the theories and clinical experience of psychodynamic psychotherapists, schizoid and obsessive–compulsive are in the tradition of European clinical phenomenology, avoidant personality disorder came from academic psychology, and schizotypal personality disorder arose from both psychodynamic studies and genetic research (Tyrer, Casey and Ferguson, 1991). Therefore, by contrast with the present situation in the dimensional theories of normal personality, the system that describes personality disorders is a raft on which many heterogeneous concepts have climbed. There has been no overarching theoretical scheme

Table 11.4 *Diagnostic criteria for schizotypal, antisocial and dependent personality disorders*

For schizotypal personality disorder *at least five or more of the following criteria must be met:*

1 Ideas of reference
2 Odd beliefs or magical thinking that influences behaviour and is inconsistent with subcultural norms
3 Unusual perceptual experiences, including bodily illusions
4 Odd thinking and speech
5 Suspiciousness or paranoid ideation
6 Inappropriate or constricted affect
7 Behaviour or appearance that is odd, eccentric or peculiar
8 Lack of close friends or confidants other than first degree relatives
9 Excessive social anxiety that does not diminish with familiarity and tends to be associated with paranoid fears rather than negative judgements about self

For antisocial personality disorder *three or more of the following criteria must be met:*

1 Failure to conform to social norms with respect to lawful behaviours as indicated by repeatedly performing acts that are grounds for arrest
2 Deceitfulness, as indicated by repeated lying, use of aliases, or conning others for profit or pleasure
3 Impulsivity or failure to plan ahead
4 Irritability and aggressiveness, as indicated by repeated physical fights or assaults
5 Reckless disregard for safety of self or others
6 Consistent irresponsibility, as indicated by repeated failure to sustain consistent work behaviour or honour financial obligations
7 Lack of remorse, as indicated by being indifferent to or rationalising having hurt, mistreated, or stolen from another

For dependent personality disorder *five or more of the following criteria must be met:*

1 Has difficulty in making everyday decisions without an excessive amount of advice and reassurance from others
2 Needs others to assume responsibility for most areas of his or her life
3 Has difficulty expressing disagreement with others because of fear of loss of support or approval
4 Has difficulty initiating projects or doing things on his or her own
5 Goes to excessive lengths to obtain nurturance and support from others, to the point of volunteering to do things that are unpleasant
6 Feels uncomfortable or helpless when alone because of exaggerated fears of being unable to care for himself or herself
7 Urgently seeks another relationship as a source of care and support when a close relationship ends
8 Is unrealistically preoccupied with fears of being left to take care of himself or herself

or integrated empirical base for the clusters or types of personality disorder found in the DSM or ICD systems (Farmer, 2000). Personality disorders – as assessed using ICD and DSM systems – are relatively common, occurring in about 9 per cent of adults in one community sample (Samuels et al., 2002). The highest prevalence was for DSM-IV antisocial personality disorder, which had a prevalence of 4.1 per cent.

Problems with personality disorders in current categorical systems

Here we highlight some of the problems with personality disorders and explain how the integration of personality disorders into the differential psychology tradition might resolve them. Critical overviews of the limitations of the categorical approaches to personality disorder may be found in Farmer (2000) and Ball (2001, and subsequent papers in the same journal issue), and Livesley (2001a, b). Also recommended is Kendell's (2002) argument that it is impossible, given present knowledge, to decide whether or not personality disorders are mental disorders.

The problems of labelling and tautology

In clinical practice a patient may be given the diagnosis of personality disorder after illness states have been excluded. Therefore, obtaining the diagnosis of personality disorder might signal merely that a person is considered to be untreatable. Moreover, whereas illness mitigates odd behaviour, in personality disorder the responsibility remains with the person. Lewis and Appleby's (1988) study, showing the devastating effects that a label of 'personality disorder' can have on psychiatrists' opinions of patients, is recounted in Box 11.1.

Box 11.1 The effect of receiving a personality diagnosis label on the way patients are perceived by psychiatrists

Lewis and Appleby (1988) considered the negative effects of labelling to be so severe that they recommended the whole system of personality disorder diagnosis be scrapped, though later, more systematic reviewers of the area disagree (Farmer, 2000). They based some of their criticisms of personality disorders on the mistaken belief that psychologists no longer used personality trait concepts because they had been proved unstable by Mischel in 1968. Nevertheless, their study brings home the power of personality diagnoses and the effect such a diagnosis has on clinicians. They sent one of six case vignettes to 240 practising psychiatrists. The vignettes are shown below. Psychiatrists were asked to rate the 'patients' on a number of statements. The effects of mentioning personality disorder were large, and subsequent judgements of the patient were always less favourable. According to the psychiatrists, patients with personality disorder were: likely to manipulate admission, unlikely to arouse sympathy, likely to take an overdose to seek attention, able to be discharged from outpatient follow up, unwanted in the doctor's clinic, difficult management problems, likely to annoy, unlikely to improve, in debt due to factors within their own control, not mentally ill, unlikely to merit health service time, unlikely to comply with treatment or complete it, unlikely to have a severe condition, not a suicide risk, not appropriate for antidepressants. Whether these responses are mere 'pejorative judgemental, rejecting attitudes' on behalf of the doctors or the result of accumulated wisdom having seen many patients with personality disorder (an hypothesis not entertained by the authors) it is clear that mention of personality disorder has a powerful effect on clinicians. For that reason it is important that the concepts should refer to real entities. Nevertheless, the authors were taken to task by Widiger (1989) who commented that Lewis and Appleby's results were:

consistent with and support the validity of the diagnosis. Persons with personality disorders do tend to be more manipulative, attention-seeking, and annoying. Some of these traits are used to make the diagnoses.

Lewis and Appleby's case vignettes

Case 1

A 34-year-old man is seen in outpatients. He complains of feeling depressed, and says he has been crying on his own at home. He is worried about whether he is having a nervous breakdown, and is requesting admission. He has thought of killing himself by taking an overdose of some tablets he has at home. He has taken one previous overdose, two years ago, and at that time he saw a psychiatrist who gave him a diagnosis of personality disorder. He has recently gone into debt and is concerned about how he will repay the money. He is finding it difficult to sleep and his GP has given him some nitrazepam. He thinks these have helped a little and is reluctant to give them up.

The other cases were modified from the first as follows:

Case 2

No previous diagnosis was mentioned.

Case 3

Previous diagnosis was given as depression.

Case 4

Information as for case I was given, but the subjects were told that the researchers were interested in the labelling effect of certain psychiatric diagnoses and were asked not to let themselves be affected by previous labels.

Case 5

Information as for case 2 was given, except that the patient was female.

Case 6

Information as for case 2 was given, except that the word 'man' in the opening sentence was changed to 'solicitor'.

Blackburn (1988) argued that members of any category should share a set of core characteristics. Within the set of criteria for antisocial personality disorder he found a mixture of trait terms and items that index examples of social behaviour. The latter items he viewed as existing within a moral frame of reference, whereas he insisted that personality disorders should identify personal characteristics which predict examples of social deviance (see Miller et al., 2001, below, for an example of this type of research). Following the classic arguments of Cleckley (1976), he argued that it is not the criminality, sexual deviation, alcoholism, etc., of the antisocial personality that should be the focus of criteria, rather it should be the personal characteristics of superficial charm, egocentricity, insincerity, affective poverty, etc. Blackburn suggested that a better descriptive system is needed for the universe of personality deviation and pointed towards a dimensional solution. In agreement with this suggestion, the research work on Hare's Psychopathy Checklist – Revised found that the items related to interpersonal style and affect had better discriminating power for the psychopathy construct than items related to social deviance (Cooke and Michie, 1997; Hare et al., 2000).

The problem of construct overlap

There is considerable overlap in personality disorders as conceived in the DSM systems (Farmer, 2000; Ball, 2001; Livesley, 2001b). The overlap is of at least three types. First, some of the criteria in the different personality disorders are very similar. Second, some personality disorders often occur together (co-morbidity). Third, some personality disorders show considerable co-occurrence with some axis I categories (mental illnesses).

Some operational criteria appear in more than one disorder (comparable with the same questionnaire item being used to index two supposedly distinct traits) (Livesley, 1987; Shea, 1995). As a result, borderline and histrionic personality disorders may occur together in as many as 46 per cent of patients (Tyrer, Casey and Ferguson, 1991). In a review of 180 patients with a discharge diagnosis of borderline personality disorder, Fyer et al. (1988) found that only 8 per cent had this diagnosis alone. The overlap between borderline personality disorder and affective disorder was up to 66 per cent, and they concluded that people diagnosed as borderline personality disorder were heterogeneous, with no clear separation from other concepts such as affective disorder and other personality disorders. These comprise what Farmer (2000, pp. 828–9) called problems of the 'horizontal organization' of personality disorders. He contended that there was too little research on the cross-loadings of personality disorders meaning that, whereas there was concern about the hierarchical structure of the DSM categories (the columnar loadings on factor analyses), there was less concern about their inter-correlations and redundancies (the row-based cross-loadings on factor analyses).

Aetiology, time course and distinctness fail to separate personality disorders and illness states. There are genetic and environmental contributions to both personality disorders and mental illnesses. Some personality disorders change while some illnesses are chronic (Seivewright, Tyrer and Johnson, 2002). There are axis I–II overlaps on the DSM system (Farmer, 2000). For example, Widiger and Shea (1991) found much overlap between the following axis I (mental illness)–axis II (personality disorder) pairs: schizotypal personality disorder and schizophrenia, borderline personality disorder and mood disorders, antisocial personality disorder and substance use disorders, and avoidant personality disorder and social phobia. The last pair provides a useful illustration. In the DSM-IV system social phobia is defined as:

> A marked and persistent fear of one or more social or performance situations in which the person is exposed to unfamiliar people or to possible scrutiny by others. The individual fears that he or she will act in a way (or show anxiety symptoms) that will be humiliating or embarrassing.

Avoidant personality disorder is defined as:

> A pervasive pattern of social inhibition, feelings of inadequacy, and hypersensitivity to negative evaluation, beginning by early adulthood and presenting in a variety of contexts.

Kendell (2002) cited this pair of disorders as an especially difficult problem in the separation of personality disorder and mental illness. The onset of social phobia is often in the late teens and the course unremitting and lifelong, so not even time-course criteria separate the 'personality disorder' from the 'illness'. Avoidant personality disorder traits might be treatable with the benzodiazepine drug alprazolam (Reich, Noyes and Yates, 1989), so the criterion of treatability does not separate them either.

Improving the validity of personality disorder constructs

Widiger and Shea (1991) considered five courses of action to remove personality disorder–mental illness overlaps. Here, they are considered in turn. A similar series of suggestions for the revision of current categorical systems was made by Farmer (2000). They are listed in table 11.5. First, it might be decided, for example, that social phobia should not be diagnosed in the presence of avoidant personality disorder, or that schizotypal disorder should not be diagnosed in the presence of schizophrenia. Any such decision is arbitrary and begs the question about whether either or both of the constructs is/are valid.

A second possibility is to move the position of a concept to another axis. For example, the cyclothymic personality disorder of DSM-II became cyclothymic disorder that is still among the axis I mood disorders in DSM-IV. Given the chronicity of cyclothymic disorder the placement in axis I cannot prevent the query as to whether it represents a personality dimension as opposed to an illness. Livesley (2001a) questioned more generally the separation of Axis I and II in the DSM system, as did Farmer (2000) and Kendell (2002).

Table 11.5 *Suggestions for revising the current categorical (e.g., DSM and ICD) systems for classifying personality disorders*

Suggestion	Rationale/explanation
Need a theoretical basis or rationale of delineation for each personality disorder.	A list of criterion features is insufficient.
Need greater consistency in the content of personality disorder criterion sets.	Some personality disorders have child and adult criteria; some are broad, some narrow; some address specific features; some address the construct more generally.
Need to revisit the Axis I–Axis II distinction.	There is Axis I–II overlap, and there might be links to super-ordinate constructs.
Consider applying psychometric test theory principles to decide upon sets of personality features and constructs.	Current personality disorders often have poor reliability, face validity, concurrent validity, discriminant validity, sensitivity and specificity.
Consider shift from categories to dimensions.	Dimensions are likely to be more reliable and valid.
Consider the methods used to assess personality disorders.	Over-use of verbal reports and interviews are a problem where individuals may lack insight about their own behaviour.
Consider replacing clusters with a more adequate hierarchical system of classifying personality disorders.	This might reduce co-morbidity.
Attempt to find features of personality disorder that are maximally discriminative and most central to the diagnostic concept.	This might reduce co-morbidity.
Do not revise the DSM system so frequently.	'in no other area of medicine are pathological conditions redefined before research studies are conducted on the conditions of interest' (p. 846)

Source After Farmer (2000)

The third solution was to remove overlapping criteria from disorders. Thus, one might extract the mood symptoms and the binge eating from borderline personality disorder to prevent its overlap with depression and eating disorder. However, not only might this alter the validity of the construct by arbitrarily removing core concepts, it is easily shown to be nonsensical. Imagine the same suggestion in physical medicine, whereby a scheme of diagnosing illnesses decided to remove all overlapping criteria. Thus, common symptoms like a high temperature or a fast pulse would be purged from all but one illness in order to separate categories. Instead, it might be better to consider Widiger and Shea's (1991) fourth suggestion and try to discover some differentiating criteria for particular disorders. For instance, an attempt might be made to discover whether there is a difference in the quality of low mood experienced in borderline personality disorders and depressives. Attempts to find the cores of the various personality disorder constructs have occurred, and have attracted the attention of differential psychologists to the field. Examples include Hare's research and the research of others on the essence of psychopathy (Hare et al., 2000; Cooke and Michie, 2001), Claridge's (1997; Rawlings, Claridge and Freeman, 2001) and others' work that attempts to define schizotypy, and Emmons's (1987) research on narcissism. Parker and Hadzi-Pavlovic (2001) attempted to refine the DSM descriptor sets by collecting self-report as well as witness data, and by eliminating descriptors that did not fit statistically with the relevant personality disorder concept.

Widiger and Shea's (1991) fifth suggestion for improving the validity of personality constructs – one that still had not been implemented and had to be made again in Farmer's (2000) and Ball's (2001) reviews a decade later – was to move to a dimensional system of personality disorder construct description and organisation, rather than a categorical one. Widiger and Shea alluded to the growing agreement within models of normal personality as to the principal dimensions, recognised that having a binary diagnostic cut-off is arbitrary, and acknowledged that it would be more informative if a person's personality problems were described in a multi-dimensional system. Others have suggested that the dimensional approach – relatively successful in finding a structure for normal personality traits – might be applied to personality disorders (Millon and Davis, 1995; Cloninger, 2000; Livesley and Jang, 2000). Tyrer (1995) expected the application of dimensional models to decrease the number of personality disorder constructs and provide a solution to the problem of overlap.

Disorder in the DSM system of personality disorder

The fluidity of the personality disorder classification system is prima facie evidence for its possible non-validity. Four of the eleven DSM-III-R personality disorder categories were new, viz. narcissistic, borderline, schizotypal and avoidant. DSM-IV no longer lists three personality disorders that existed in DSM-III-R, viz. sadistic, self-defeating and passive-aggressive.

The three broad DSM clusters do not emerge empirically. Analysis of the personality disorder symptoms/items produces from fifteen to thirty-nine specific traits of personality deviance (Widiger and Costa, 1994). The DSM cluster system does not cohere statistically or conceptually: narcissistic and antisocial are not 'dramatic, emotional or erratic'; passive-aggressive is not anxious or fearful; and schizoid is principally anhedonic rather than odd or eccentric. Only about half or fewer of the personality disorder criteria are assigned to the correct personality disorder category by clinicians, suggesting major problems with even the face validity of the criteria (Linde and Clark, 1998). Widiger and Costa (1994) discussed the vast differences in conceptual breadth entailed in the various disorders. Avoidant personality disorder captures a relatively narrow range of behaviours, whereas the concept of borderline personality disorder is broad, referring to aspects of identity, affect and impulsivity.

Most of the above problems, and others, were discussed by Farmer (2000, p. 285) who concluded that personality disorder, though now beyond mere 'committee consensus' is not yet at the stage where it can 'embrace an organizing theory'. In agreement with others, though, his principal suggestion was that the research on personality disorders should turn to psychometrics, with its concepts of test theory, dimensions, construct validity and hierarchical structure.

By the mid-to-late 1990s the agreement grew stronger that there were major problems with categorical systems of personality disorder classification (Livesley, 2001a, b). For example, Mulder and Joyce (1997) summarised that categories accrued by means of theory, opinion and history rather than data; too many categories occurred together, suggesting an uneconomical taxonomy; and there was little evidence for a strict behavioural discontinuity between normal and disordered personality. Seeking more balance, Ball (2001) argued that the international agreement on personality disorder categories embodied in DSM and ICD systems had some positive effects, such as facilitating communication and international research, and legitimising and standardising research and treatment efforts, though Livesley (2001b) disagreed that even these benefits were proven. The negative aspects acknowledged by Ball (2001) were those discussed above: the lack of reliability and validity for the personality disorder constructs; the excessive comorbidity; the lack of a theoretical scheme or valid hierarchy for the disorders; their poor convergent and discriminant validity; the arbitrary cut-offs imposed by adopting a categorical system; and the loss of information in non-prototypical cases of personality disorder.

All of this leaves the field of personality disorder in an odd position. For everyday clinical work and research, including diagnosis, treatment and prognosis, the DSM and ICD schemes are used, despite the fact that the constructs lack validity. Running in parallel with this work is an accumulating research programme which suggests that there might be a tractable, trait-based account of personality disorders. Livesley (2001b) made this latter point as follows,

The features of personality disorder are not organised into discrete diagnostic categories. Instead, putatively distinct diagnoses merge with each other and with normality. Evidence on these points has accumulated to the point that it can no longer be ignored. The implication is clear: individual differences in personality disorder are best represented by a dimensional system. Studies showing that the factorial structure of personality disorder traits is similar in clinical and non-clinical samples provide further support for this conclusion. (p. 278)

Are there abnormal personality traits?

Dimensional models of abnormal personality

The possibility that personality disorders might move from being categories within a typology to a series of dimensions was raised by many researchers (Presly and Walton, 1973; Livesley, 1986; Cloninger, 1987; Blackburn, 1988; Tyrer, Casey and Ferguson, 1991/3; Widiger and Shea, 1991; Costa and McCrae, 1992d). A pioneering study was conducted by Presly and Walton in 1973. They found that categories of personality disorder had low inter-rater reliabilities (Walton and

Presly, 1973) and, in view of the success that traits had in describing normal personality structure, they proposed a move to a dimensional system for personality disorders, stating that: 'the diagnostic process in psychiatry has been more impaired than need be the case, because illness and personality have not been differentiated as separate observational sectors'.

Utilising each symptom or criterion within each of the personality disorder categories as if they were trait indicators, Presly and Walton (1973) compiled a list of forty-two suitable items and had patients rated by three psychiatrists on each trait. None of the patients had an organic brain illness or chronic schizophrenia. Principal components analysis suggested four factors. The first factor had large loadings for egocentricity, lack of regard for the consequences of actions, inability to learn from experience, irresponsibility, impulsiveness, conscience defect, etc., and was called 'social deviance'. Factor 2 had positive loadings for timid, meek, submissive, avoidance of competition, indecisiveness and negative loadings for officiousness and need for attention, and was called 'submissiveness'. Factor 3 had positive loadings on stubbornness, over-independence, meticulousness, officiousness, detachment, suspiciousness, insensitivity and lack of suggestibility, and was thought to be a combination of 'schizoid' and 'obsessional' aspects of personality disorder. The final factor had loadings for ingratiation, need for attention, excess emotional display, unlikeability and insincerity, and was thought to represent 'hysterical personality' (a term no longer used in psychiatry). The authors recommended that a categorical system for diagnosing personality disorder should be scrapped.

> A co-ordinate dimensional approach is to be preferred, in order to encompass the wide differences in personality among patients as well as their similarities, and adequately to take account of the fact that personality traits must be considered a different order of phenomena from symptoms. (Presly and Walton, 1973, p. 275)

A similar attempt was made to derive dimensional traits from personality disorders by Widiger et al. (1987), who converted the eighty-one criteria covering the personality disorders into structured interview items with a nine-point scale. Each patient was then given a score on each personality disorder. This approach assumes that the various disorders represent valid conglomerations of items, an assumption not made by Presly and Walton (1973). In fact, the Cronbach alpha values for the scales were acceptable, except for the compulsive (0.08), schizotypal (0.45) and schizoid (0.38) categories. Of the sixty-five correlations among the various personality disorders, thirty-one were significant, the highest being dependent with avoidant (0.62) and histrionic with borderline (0.50). The scores for the personality disorders were subjected to multidimensional scaling resulting in three dimensions. Therefore, eleven categories of personality disorder were reduced to their positions on: social involvement, assertion-dominance, and anxious rumination versus behavioural acting out.

The economy of this three factor model, and Presly and Walton's (1973) four dimensional solution, is outdone by a model based on the two dimensions of interpersonal theory: hostile–friendly and dominant–submissive (O'Connor and Dyce, 2001). Blackburn (1988) construed the categories of personality disorder on these two dimensions. That two factors of this type might be very important for describing personality disorder, though not necessarily a complete system, was also suggested by a large-scale analysis of the Bedford and Foulds's (1978) Personality Deviance Scales (PDS). The PDS was intended to be a scheme for assessing personality disorder along the dimensions of intropunitiveness, extrapunitiveness and dominance. An analysis of the factorial structure of the PDS in over 1,500 non-psychiatric subjects found only two dimensions, hostility and submissiveness/low self-confidence (Deary, Bedford and Fowkes, 1995). Whiteman et al. (2001) found that, because of trait inter-correlations, the NEO-Five Factor Inventory could be represented at a higher level by these traits, also referred to as diffidence versus dominance, and nastiness versus niceness. They argued that these two dimensions can provide key constructs in personality theory and applications. The same two dimensions are used as general organising concepts for personality disorder by O'Connor and Dyce, who envisaged personality disorder to be based on rigidity and extremity (2001). Whereas it is not argued that these two dimensions can capture the variety of forms of abnormal personality, dependency is recognised as a key aspect of personality dysfunction (Bornstein and Cecero, 2000).

The research described above comprises early and partial attempts to describe the personality trait terms that might be useful in construing disorders of personality. We now turn to more comprehensive research programmes that envisage trait models of abnormal personality.

A dimensional model for the personality disorders

The work of Livesley and his colleagues provides a model for the transfer from categories to dimensions in personality disorder. A summary of their achievements is given in Box 11.2. Their painstaking research programme, contained in many publications, marries expertise in clinical psychiatry, differential psychology and biometric methods. They identified three stages in the validation of dimensions of personality disorder (Livesley and Schroeder, 1990). First, a theoretical classification must be constructed, whereby diagnoses are defined and diagnostic items are selected. Next, it must be shown that the diagnostic terms combine empirically to form the expected syndromes and entities. Third, external validity for the statistical grouping must be demonstrated in the form of clinical prediction, generalisation to other populations, and so forth. Their empirical starting point for converting personality disorder categories into dimensions was the list of 'symptoms' associated with each disorder. Although the categories might eventually disappear, they made the assumption that at least the symptoms captured the universe of disturbance that practitioners were meeting in patients. It makes sense not to ignore the hunches gathered over many years of clinical experience.

Box 11.2 Livesley and colleagues' research programme on the psychometric approach to personality disorder

It may reasonably be contended that the most prescient and the most comprehensive research on personality disorder dimensions originated from psychiatrists and psychologists who worked in Edinburgh, Scotland. The research of Walton and Presly (1973; and Presly and Walton, 1973) was based in the Royal Edinburgh Hospital. It found four dimensions among clinical personality disorders, as described in the text, and it stands alone among research at that time, and is well supported by later studies (e.g., Austin and Deary, 2000).

The decades-long work of Livesley (who originally worked as a psychiatrist in Edinburgh) and his colleagues at the University of British Columbia has no parallel in terms of scope, and is the best example of the combining of clinical and psychometric research. A useful account of the research programme is given in Jang, Livesley and Vernon (2002), from which this summary is taken.

Starting in the 1980s Livesley reviewed the clinical literature on personality disorders and collected descriptions of traits making up the relevant categories. These were reduced to about 100 traits. Self-report scales were composed to assess each trait. In the general population and in the clinical population the same fifteen narrow traits of personality disorder were found on factor analyses. These could be summarised as four broad factors, with similarities to four of the five factor model's traits: emotional dysregulation, dissocial behaviour, inhibitedness, and conscientiousness. They concluded that these findings supported 'a dimensional model of personality function: personality disorders are extreme variants of normal personality traits' (Jang, Livesley and Vernon, 2002, p. 2).

Further research on a revised scale – the Dimensional Assessment of Personality Pathology (DAPP) – produced a three-level hierarchical structure with sixty-nine specific traits, eighteen traits, and the same four higher-order factors. An example of the highly specific traits is that anxiety (one of the eighteen traits) divides into trait anxiety, rumination, guilt proneness and indecisiveness. Livesley and colleagues comment that models of 'normal' personality variation lack this three-level richness and that the normal assessment tools often have ceiling effects in their item content and responses that limit their ability to index abnormal-enough behaviours.

More recent research by this team has included genetically informative designs. All aspects of the DAPP personality disorder traits have proved substantially heritable in their twin studies. Heritability is similar in men and women, and probably higher in young adults than in older people. They have found evidence from genetic covariance approaches to state that 'the phenotypic structure of personality disorder closely corresponds to the underlying genetic architecture' (Jang, Livesley and Vernon, 2002, p. 2). Thus, they conclude, there appear to be four broad genetically influenced personality disorder dimensions. There are also genetic influences on the more specific traits once the influence from the higher-order traits has been removed. The DAPP scales are being revised in order to obtain genetically homogeneous scales, which is a landmark attempt to base phenotypic scales of personality on a valid biological basis.

Livesley and Schroeder's (1990) study of the DSM cluster A personality disorders (paranoid, schizoid and schizotypal) makes a good illustration. They began by examining the clinical literature for all possible descriptors applied to these diagnoses. After making lists of these descriptors they sent them to psychiatrists who were asked to rate each for prototypicality on a seven-point scale. Each psychiatrist saw items for only one personality disorder. After finding good agreement with respect to prototypicality, they constructed behavioural dimensions within each personality disorder diagnosis from highly prototypical items and scaled these from normality to pathology. An example of this intermediate stage was that there was very good agreement that suspiciousness was a highly prototypical dimension within the paranoid personality disorder. Therefore, items were written to capture this dimension, such as: 'When people do something nice for me, I wonder what their real motives are.' The list of dimensions within schizoid personality disorder were: low affiliation, avoidant attachment, defective social skills, self-absorption, restricted affectivity, social apprehensiveness, lack of empathy, and generalised hypersensitivity. Items relating to dimensions of all of the three cluster A diagnoses were given to patients with a diagnosis of personality disorder. They found good internal consistencies for each dimension within each personality disorder, and good dimension–diagnosis correlations. The dimensions within each personality disorder diagnosis were subjected to factor analysis. The paranoid dimensions yielded two factors, paranoid behaviours and fear of negative appraisal. The schizoid dimensions contained two factors, sensitivity and social avoidance. The schizotypal dimensions also had two factors, social avoidance and perceptual–cognitive distortion.

The last step taken by Livesley and Schroeder (1990) was to analyse the factor structure of all twenty-one dimensions pertaining to the three diagnostic categories. Four oblique factors were obtained: paranoid behaviours, social avoidance, perceptual–cognitive distortion and sensitivity. The correlations between factors ranged from 0.27 to 0.49. Thus, by contrast with other approaches to the proposed category-to-dimension shift in personality disorders, Livesley's solution was uneconomical in that three diagnoses yielded four factors. However, hierarchical factor analysis of these specific scales reduced the number of dimensions.

The scales used to measure behavioural dimensions of all of the DSM-III-R personality disorder categories contained almost 2,000 items initially (Livesley, 1986, 1987). To cover all diagnoses in the DSM personality disorder system Livesley's group, following the procedures described above, produced the Dimensional

Assessment of Personality Pathology-Basic Questionnaire (DAPP-BQ; Livesley, Jackson and Schroeder, 1992; Schroeder, Wormsworth and Livesley, 1992). This has eighteen relatively specific scales, assessed by 282 self-report items, as follows: affective lability, anxiousness, callousness, cognitive distortion, compulsivity, conduct problems, diffidence, identity problems, insecure attachment, interpersonal disesteem, intimacy problems, narcissism, passive oppositionality, rejection, restricted expression, self-harm, social avoidance, and stimulus seeking. In a landmark study, the DAPP was administered to 656 personality disorder patients, 939 healthy people, and 686 twin-pairs (Livesley, Jang and Vernon, 1998). All three samples showed that the eighteen specific scales combined, at a higher level, into the same four, broad factors of emotional dysregulation, dissocial behaviour, inhibitedness and compulsivity. Therefore, the same dimensions are found in clinical samples and healthy people.

The DAPP-BQ's construal of personality received some independent validation. The specific and higher-level traits of the DAPP-BQ were found to be highly convergent with Clark's Schedule for Nonadaptive and Adaptive Personality (Clark et al., 1996). This consensus on some core traits of personality disorder might herald a much-needed rationalisation of the many instruments used to assess personality disorder categories and traits (Hyler et al., 1990; Zimmerman, 1994).

Twin studies of the DAPP-BQ scales found substantial heritabilities in many of the scales (Livesley et al., 1993). Broad heritability (additive genetic factors and genetic dominance) contributed more than 50 per cent of the variance to affective lability, anxiousness, callousness, identity problems, narcissism, oppositionality, restricted expression, social avoidance, stimulus seeking and suspiciousness. The only dimensions for which the genetic contribution was small were conduct problems (0 per cent) and self-harm (29 per cent). The same research team found substantial heritabilities for most of the facets of personality disorder traits and concluded that these estimates are similar to those for normal personality dimensions (Jang, Livesley and Vernon, 2002).

This programme is among the most influential in international personality disorder research, for reasons that include the following: it pays attention to the universe of clinical phenomenology in personality disorder; it is well informed by psychometric and behaviour-genetic methods; it is well informed by and integrated with normal personality theories; it is empirically large in scale; and it includes clinical and normal population samples. We now show that it contributes to a growing consensus concerning the number and nature of personality disorder dimensions.

The four As model of personality disorder

The four higher-level, personality disorder constructs arrived at by Livesley and colleagues (e.g. Livesley, Jang, and Vernon, 1998; Jang, Livesley, and Vernon, 2002) find agreement from research teams that used different measurement instruments and examined different populations. As some discernible consensus emerges, so the four-construct model of abnormal personality has grown its own mnemonic, 'the four As': antisocial, asocial, asthenic and anankastic (Mulder and Joyce, 1997; Austin and Deary, 2000). Some of these terms are unfamiliar, reflecting the contrivance needed to assemble four terms beginning with the letter A. More transparently meaningful names for the factors follow, though they have less mnemonic force.

Mulder and Joyce (1997) administered the Structured Clinical Interview for DSM (the SCID-II Interview), which assesses DSM personality disorders, to psychiatric outpatients. Patients also completed Cloninger's Tridimensional Personality Questionnaire (TPQ) and the Eysenck Personality Questionnaire (EPQ). Their analyses were based on patients being rated on personality disorder categories, and how these correlated with TPQ and EPQ scale scores. They found four factors which brought personality disorders together in the following groups: antisocial, borderline, narcissistic, histrionic, passive–aggressive, paranoid (related to EQP-psychoticism and TPQ-novelty seeking) – *Antisocial*; schizoid (negatively related to TPQ-reward dependence) – *Asocial*; avoidant, dependent, self-defeating (related to TPQ-harm avoidance and EPQ neuroticism) – *Asthenic*; and obsessive–compulsive – *Anankastic*.

Deary et al. (1998) examined undergraduates on the self-report version of the SCID-II, which gives scores for each of the DSM personality disorders. They also administered the Eysenck Personality Questionnaire-Revised (EPQ-R). They factor-analysed the students' scores on the DSM-based personality disorders and the EPQ-R factors conjointly and obtained a four factor solution which brought together the following groups of concepts: avoidant, dependent, passive–aggressive, self-defeating, paranoid, schizotypal, histrionic and borderline (related to EPQ-R-neuroticism); passive–aggressive, narcissistic, and antisocial (related to EPQ-R-psychoticism and EPQ-R-lie scales); avoidant and histrionic (related positively and negatively, respectively, to EPQ-R-extraversion); and obsessive compulsive (related negatively to EPQ-R-psychoticism). These are similar to the four factors found by Mulder and Joyce (1997) and Livesley, Jang and Vernon (1998).

In a second report using the same data Austin and Deary (2000) argued that the DSM scales should not be trusted as a valid organising scheme for the personality disorder items in the SCID. Therefore, they carried out a factor analysis of the SCID items. One solution included eight factors. They gave each student a score on these eight factors and conjointly factor-analysed these scores with scores on the EQP-R factors. The rotated factor loadings are shown in table 11.6. Again, using perhaps more valid DSM-based scales – since they were based on an item-level analysis of the clinical personality disorder items – a four factor model emerges, which is arguably similar to the four As.

Another study arriving at a similar conclusion tested adult volunteers on the EPQ-R, NEO-PI-R and the DAPP-BQ (Larstone et al., 2002). They found four higher-order factors: emotional dysregulation, strongly related to neuroticism; inhibition, strongly related to (low) extraversion; obsessive–compulsive, strongly related to conscientiousness; and psychopathy, strongly related to (low) agreeableness (table 11.6 shows how these results accord with those of Austin and Deary,

Table 11.6 *Conjoint factor analysis personality disorder scales and factors from the Eysenck Personality Questionnaire-Revised (EPQ-R) and the NEU-PI-R (after Austin and Deary, 2000; Larstone et al., 2002)* [a]

	Factor 1	Factor 2	Factor 3	Factor 4
Austin and Deary (2000)				
EPQ-R scales				
Psychoticism		.78		−.39
Extraversion			.88	
Neuroticism	.82			
Lie Scale		−.68		
DSM-derived scales[b]				
Narcissistic	.61			
Antisocial		.76		
Suspicious avoidance		.47	−.58	
Need for others	.72			
Obsessive-compulsive				.92
Ego strength	−.73		.49	
Eccentric	.57			
Hostile obstructive	.52	.39		
Larstone et al. (2002)				
EPQ-R scales				
Psychoticism		.70		
Extraversion			.86	
Neuroticism	.71			
Lie Scale		−.56		
NEO-PI-R scales				
Neuroticism	.81			
Extraversion	−.35		.82	
Openness	−.50	.37		
Agreeableness	−.65	−.49		
Conscientiousness				.82
DAPP-BQ scales				
Emotional dysregulation	.84			
Dissocial behaviour		.72	.37	
Inhibition			−.78	
Compulsivity				.93
Possible association with 'Four As' model of personality disorder?	*Asthenic*	*Antisocial*	*Asocial*	*Anankastic*

[a] Only the major loadings (>.35) are shown. The factors are rotated factors using Varimax rotation.

[b] These scales were obtained after an item-level analysis of the self-report version of the DSM-based Structured Clinical Interview for DSM.

2000). This study has the advantages that it was not dependent on the questionable DSM personality disorder categories and employed two of the best-validated scales of normal personality variation.

At the highest level of organisation, therefore, there is growing agreement that four dimensions of personality disorder can be distinguished. The studies contributing to the consensus examined normal and various clinical groups; used clinical and normal personality scales; and used interviews and self-report scales. O'Connor and Dyce (1998) re-examined personality disorder data to investigate their fit with various models. They found poor fit to the interpersonal circle, and better fit to the DSM-IV and Cloninger's tridimensional theory. Stronger support was found for the five factor model and Cloninger's seven factor model. However, they concluded that 'a focus on just 4 factors seems preferable and sufficient'.

Individual dimensions of abnormal personality

The converging systems described above conceptualise the personality disorders in dimensional terms; their aim is an adequate and clinically useful taxonomy of dimensions. A different approach is taken by those researchers who see in a single personality disorder category a key clinical concept that should be validated. Psychopathy and schizotypy are described and discussed below as examples. There are sizeable, thriving literatures on other individual personality disorders, such as narcissistic (Rose, 2002) and borderline personality disorders (Hyman, 2002; Siever et al., 2002; Skodol, Gunderson et al., 2002; Skodol, Siever et al., 2002).

Psychopathy. One much-studied individual personality disorder concept is antisocial personality, or psychopathy. The concept is important and useful, especially as a predictor of criminal behaviour and violence (Cooke, Forth and Hare, 1998; Cooke and Michie, 2001), and relates to physiological processes (Hare, Cooke and Hart, 1999). Hare and his colleagues have sought a valid measure of the psychological concept of psychopathy which they, in agreement with Cleckley (1976), view as the key underlying concept in antisocial personality disorder (Hare, 1980). Hare's revised Psychopathy Checklist (PCL-R; Hare, 1991; Hare, Hart and Harpur, 1991; Hare et al., 2000; Cooke and Michie, 2001) contains twenty items, originally arranged in two oblique dimensions, shown in table 11.7. Factor 1 contains interpersonal and affective characteristics and factor 2 reflects the impulsive, antisocial and unstable lifestyle. Confirmatory factor-analytic studies (Cooke and Michie, 2001) of the PCL-R construe the items as a hierarchy: there is a superordinate psychopathy construct, which accounts for over 75 per cent of the total item variance; and three subfactors which correlate between 0.81 and 0.88 with the superordinate factor. The first two are a division of the old Factor 1 (table 11.7). The three are arrogant and deceitful interpersonal style, deficient affective experience, and impulsive and irresponsible behavioural style (Hare et al., 2000; Cooke and Michie, 2001). Hare and colleagues argued that the coverage of traits is better within their scale than within the clinical criteria for antisocial personality disorder. Scores on the scales correlate with scores on other scales aimed at antisocial personality

Table 11.7 *Items from Hare's Psychopathy Checklist-Revised*

Factor 1	Factor 2
[a]Glibness/superficial charm	[c]Need for stimulation/proneness to boredom
[a]Grandiose sense of self-worth	[c]Parasitic lifestyle
[a]Pathological lying	Poor behavioural controls
[a]Conning/manipulative	Early behaviour problems
[b]Lack of remorse or guilt	[c]Lack of realistic, long-term goals
[b]Shallow affect	[c]Impulsivity
[b]Callous/lack of empathy	[c]Irresponsibility
[b]Failure to accept responsibility for actions	Juvenile delinquency
	Revocation of conditional release
In addition:	
Promiscuous sexual behaviour	
Many short-term marital relationships	
Criminal versatility	

[a, b, c] Items in factors 1 (arrogant and deceitful interpersonal style), 2 (deficient affective experience), and 3 (impulsive and irresponsible behavioural style), respectively in Cooke and Michie's (2001) three factor model

disorder from the MMPI and MCMI, and predicted post-release behaviour among several studies of offenders. There is much predictive and criterion validity data with respect to the PCL-R's congruent associations with personality disorders, scores on indices of criminality, and the committing of violent offences and re-cidivism. Much of the predictive validity data are reviewed by Hare et al. (2000). Reviews indicate that psychopaths are four times as likely violently to re-offend after release from custody as non-psychopaths. The Psychopathy Checklist out-performs many other indicators as a predictor of violence, a finding replicated in several countries. Hart (1998) stated that psychopathy 'should be considered in any assessment of violence. It is empirically related to future violence, is theoretically important in the explanation of violence, and is pragmatically relevant in making decisions about risk management. Indeed, failure to consider psychopathy when conducting a risk assessment may be unreasonable (from a legal perspective) or unethical (from a professional perspective)' (pp. 368–9).

There are other psychopathy scales, such as the Psychopathic Personality Inventory, with a cogent factor structure and predictive validity (Edens, Poythress and Watkins, 2001). There are also cognitive and neurophysiological studies adding to the construct validity of psychopathy. In event-related potential (ERP) studies, psychopaths did not show the typical difference in amplitude of the P300 wave between target and non-target stimuli, nor the expected ERP differences between different verbal stimuli, and had larger centro-frontal negative waves in both studies (Kiehl, Hare, Liddle and McDonald, 1999; Kiehl, Hare, McDonald and Brink, 1999). Psychopaths show abnormal neural processing, as assessed by ERPs, during response inhibition tasks (Kiehl et al., 2000). Evidence from functional magnetic resonance imaging during an affective memory task suggested that the affective abnormalities in criminal psychopaths might have their origins in deficient or weakened inputs from limbic structures (Kiehl et al., 2001). A review of imaging studies in antisocial behaviour suggested that there might be disordered prefrontal circuitry (Bassarath, 2001).

Schizotypy. Another concept that has been studied in relative isolation is schizotypy, which is used by Venables (Raine and Green, 2002) and Claridge (1997) among many others as a dimensional propensity to develop psychotic disorders. Schizotypal personality disorder might be a mild form or a variant of schizophrenia (Dinn et al., 2002). The interface between schizotypal personality and schizophrenia has been called 'one of the most pressing and important questions in schizophrenia research today' (Raine and Green, 2002). The Schizotypal Personality Scale (STA) of the Schizotypal Traits Questionnaire was developed from the DSM version III criteria for schizotypal personality disorder (Claridge and Broks, 1984). The STA has four factors: magical thinking, paranoid suspiciousness and isolation, unusual perceptual experiences and social anxiety (Rawlings, Claridge and Freeman, 2001), though the second and fourth factors combine in other reports (Joseph and Peters, 1995). A difficulty in summarising research on schizotypy is that not only is there research on the schizotypal personality disorder and the STA, there are actually several different scales devised to measure schizotypy, and they do not have the same subfactors (Vollema and van den Bosch, 1995; Suhr and Spitznagel, 2001a). The schizotypy scale developed by Venables et al. (1990) tried to capture the fact that various research programmes suggested there might be positive and negative aspects of schizotypy. The positive aspects were magical ideation, perceptual aberration, schizophrenism and scores on STA. The negative aspects were physical and social anhedonia. They developed a scale that measured two uncorrelated factors: schizophrenism and anhedonia. High loading items on the schizophrenism scale included: 'sometimes people who I know well begin to look like strangers', 'I often have difficulties controlling my thoughts when I am thinking', and 'I often change between positive and negative feelings toward the same person.' High negative loading items on the anhedionia scale included: 'Beautiful scenery has been a great delight to me', 'A brisk walk has sometimes made me feel good all over', and 'Getting together with old friends has been one of my greatest pleasures.' Confirmatory factor analytic work by Venables and Rector (2000) suggested three factors: positive and negative schizotypy and social impairment. A combined analysis of several scales related to psychosis-proneness found four factors: aberrant perceptions and beliefs, cognitive disorganisation, introvertive anhedonia, and asocial behaviour (Claridge et al., 1996). This is an important area of research, i.e. defining and validating a personality predisposition to schizophrenia, one of the commonest and most devastating chronic illnesses. The questions addressed in this area are summarised by Raine and Green (2002). For example, it is not established whether some of the facets of schizotypy relate more to schizophrenic breakdown than others. The best validity exists for the positive and negative schizotypy facets of the construct (Vollema and van den Bosch, 1995). An example of validity studies, supporting the positive–negative schizotypy distinction, is that the negative aspects of schizotypy relate to executive function deficits in people with schizotypal disorder (Suhr and Spitznagel, 2001b) and in university students (Dinn, Harris, Aycicegi, Greene, and Andover, 2002).

Personality disorders and models of normal personality: integrating psychiatry and differential psychology?

Widiger et al. (1987) thought that the three dimensions of abnormal personality they had discovered 'have appeared throughout the history of the classification of normal personality'. They viewed their social involvement factor as similar to the affiliative dimension of the interpersonal circle, the self-other dimension of Millon, and perhaps even more so with the introversion–extraversion factor of Eysenck. Their assertion–dominance factor linked conceptually to the power–dominance factor of the interpersonal circle; previously identified by Leary and Wiggins (see Deary, Bedford and Fowkes, 1995). Therefore, the dominance factor appears in many schemes because it is also thought to be important in describing normal and abnormal personality in the results of Blackburn (1988) and in the Personality Deviance Scales' restructuring performed by Deary, Bedford and Fowkes (1995). Lastly, the anxious–rumination versus behavioural acting-out dimension was seen as similar to anxiety and impulsivity aspects of normal personality.

The five factor model as a basis for integration

There is congruence between the dimensions of personality reported by normal and personality-disordered groups (Livesley, Jang and Vernon, 1998). If the same dimensions are recovered, should the same structure be used to assess normal and abnormal personality? Could the five factor model be used in the assessment of personality disorder? Wiggins and Pincus (1989) used the NEO-PI to assess the five major dimensions of personality and the Minnesota Multiphasic Personality Inventory to assess dimensions of personality disorder, and found that the five factor model adequately covered aspects of personality disorder. Costa and McCrae (1990) found agreement between the five factor model and personality disorders as assessed by the Minnesota Multiphasic Personality Inventory and the Millon Clinical Multiaxial Inventory.

Schroeder, Wormsworth and Livesley (1992) administered their DAPP-BQ and the NEO-PI to 300 subjects in order to discover the degree to which personality disorder concepts might be captured within the five factor model. Reduction of the DAPP-BQ to a smaller number of dimensions was indicated because of the high degree of inter-correlation of many of the DAPP-BQ scales. When all scales were subjected to principal components analysis, five nearly orthogonal factors emerged. The rotated five factor structure is shown in table 11.8. With respect to

Table 11.8 *A combined analysis of the NEO-PI five factor model of normal personality traits and the DAPP-BQ sixteen factor model of personality disorders*

	Factor				
	1	2	3	4	5
NEO-PI Scales					
Neuroticism	84	−21	02	−16	−13
Extraversion	−18	72	−42	−05	08
Openness	−05	06	−41	09	−16
Agreeableness	−06	11	−09	86	01
Conscientiousness	−14	04	−05	08	94
DAPP-BQ Scales					
Anxiousness	83	−19	09	−11	06
Affective lability	68	−01	−17	−35	00
Diffidence	64	08	32	25	−07
Insecure attachment	61	22	−02	−10	04
Social avoidance	59	−15	42	−07	−09
Identity problems	58	−04	53	−14	−11
Narcissism	58	32	00	−29	−06
Stimulus seeking	−01	64	−03	−27	00
Restricted expression	15	01	81	03	−03
Intimacy problems	−11	−16	58	−12	−08
Interpersonal disesteem	11	09	19	−76	01
Rejection	11	32	−03	−62	05
Suspiciousness	30	10	32	−58	13
Conduct problems	12	16	−08	−48	−18
Compulsivity	12	06	13	−05	72
Passive oppositionality	51	09	22	−06	−55

resulting factors 1, 2, 4 and 5, the highest loadings are for factors from the NEO-PI. Neuroticism and eight of the DAPP factors load highly on factor 1. Extraversion and stimulus seeking define factor 2. Restricted expression, low extraversion and low openness define factor 3. Agreeableness and dimensions of the DAPP-BQ related to antisocial and paranoid personality disorder capture factor 4. Conscientiousness and compulsivity are the chief aspects of factor 5. Therefore, combining the two systems, the resulting five factors appear to capture dissatisfaction with self, stimulus seeking, difficulty with self disclosure, lack of regard and concern for others, and conscientiousness–compulsivity. The authors concluded that:

> the domain of personality pathology can be explained reasonably well within the five factor model of personality. Personality disorders are not characterised by functioning that differs in quality from normal functioning; rather personality disorder can be described with traits or dimensions that are descriptive of personality, both disordered and normal.

Their only reservation was that openness failed to load heavily on any factor. This was also found in their later study (Larstone et al., 2002) in which neuroticism, extraversion and conscientiousness from the NEO-PI-R were strongly loaded on the same factor, respectively, as the emotional dysregulation, inhibition, and compulsivity dimensions of the DAPP-BQ. Strong appeals for the marriage of personality disorders and the five factor model of normal personality have been made by Widiger and Trull (1992), Costa and McCrae (1992d) and Widiger and Costa (1994). Davis and Millon (1995, p. 389), emphasised that there is only 'partial overlap between these two universes of discourse' and that there is a distinctive contribution from clinical concepts in personality deviance.

To develop further the idea that the five factor model might provide an organising model for personality disorder Trull and Widiger (1997) developed a structured interview for the five factor model of personality (SIFFM). They tested a mixture of clinical and (mostly) college student subjects and used the Personality Disorder Questionnaire-Revised to assess personality disorder differences according to the DSM system (Trull, Widiger and Burr, 2001). They replicated the well-known finding that neuroticism domain scores related strongly to many personality disorders. Also, extraversion related negatively and strongly to avoidant and schizoid personality disorder scores. Of thirty correlations between the ten personality disorder scores and the SIFFM domains of openness, agreeableness and conscientiousness, none was greater than 0.3. Occasionally, facet scores on the SIFFM clearly performed better than the overall domain score. For example, there was a strong association between the trust facet of agreeableness and paranoid personality disorder scores. Reynolds and Clark (2001) showed that the NEO-PI-R facets improve upon the domain-level scores in predicting variance in interview ratings of DSM-IV personality disorders. The NEO-PI-R facets performed similarly to the Schedule for Nonadaptive and Adaptive Personality which was devised specifically for personality disorder assessment.

A further use of the five factor model as an organising framework for personality disorder focused on psychopathy (Miller et al., 2001). Experts were asked to rate a 'prototypical psychopath's' scores on the thirty NEO-PI-R traits. The similarity of each participant's profile to the typical psychopath's was then related to their NEO-PI-R scores. Correlations equal to or greater than 0.4 were found between the psychopathy resemblance index and: (-)N-self consciousness, E-assertiveness, E-activity, E-excitement-seeking, (-)A-straightforwardness, (-)A-compliance, (-)A-modesty. Resemblance to the psychopathy profile also correlated to self-reported psychopathy and to antisocial personality disorder symptoms, alcohol and drug use, and history of delinquent acts.

Though there are clear overlaps between the five factor model and personality disorders, it was Livesley's (2001b) assessment that trait models of normal personality are not directly applicable for clinical use; that the facet-level needs developing to capture clinical concepts; and that important aspects of personality disorder are missing from normal personality models. For example, although neuroticism could distinguish borderline and non-borderline patients, there were important aspects of borderline personality disorder not captured by the five factor model (Morey and Zanarini, 2000). Livesley (2001b) also concluded that, whereas there were four higher-order dimensions of personality disorder and these related to four of the five domains in the five factor model (excluding openness to experience), current findings on dimensions of personality disorder were equally consistent with various personality models, including Eysenck's (1987).

DSM-IV personality disorders and the Cloninger and Eysenck personality systems

The compilers of the DSM-IV system paid attention to findings from the psychometric study of normal and abnormal personality traits. For the first time, in the fourth revision of DSM, there was a section on dimensions in the chapter on personality disorders, and the American Psychiatric Association published a book examining the association between the five factor model of normal personality and personality disorders (Costa and Widiger, 1994). Many contributors to Livesley's (1995) encyclopaedic book on the DSM-IV personality disorders, including Shea (1995), stressed the need for a joint conceptualisation of personality disorders which absorbs what has been learned from psychometric studies of normal personality; especial emphasis is given to Eysenck's model, the five factor model and Cloninger's system.

Cloninger sought to combine categorical and dimensional approaches and to cover normal and abnormal traits within a single scheme. He originally proposed a three-dimensional scheme with personality traits that were linked to biological, genetic and neuroanatomical structures (Cloninger, 1987). His scheme has similarities in content with that of Eysenck and his general approach, which links evolutionary ideas, neurotransmitter systems and behavioural traits, and has resonances with that of Zuckerman (1991) and Gray (1987). The brain systems associated with his dimensions of novelty seeking, harm avoidance and reward dependence are shown in table 11.9. Molecular genetic evidence originally supported the suggestion that novelty seeking may be related to the brain's dopamine neurotransmitter system (Cloninger, Adolfsson and Svrakic, 1996). Cloninger was particularly influenced by the fact that factor analyses of personality disorders (with the Millon Clinical Multiaxial Inventory; Flynn and McMahon, 1984) and normal personality traits had found three broad dimensions akin to those of Eysenck.

Cloninger's economical system was increased to a seven factor model (Cloninger, Svrakic and Przybeck, 1993). In addition to the three independently heritable dimensions mentioned above he added another 'biological' dimension called persistence. Moreover, in recognition of humanistic ideas, he added three further dimensions that 'mature in adulthood and influence personal and social effectiveness by insight learning about self concepts'. These three concepts are called self-directedness, co-operativeness and transcendence, and relate, respectively, to the degree to which the person sees the self as autonomous, integrated with humanity and an integrated part of the universe. However, whereas the original

Table 11.9 *Brain systems associated with Cloninger's three-dimensional system for normal and abnormal personality*

Personality dimension	Main Neuro-transmitter	Brain system	Relevant stimuli	Behavioural response
Novelty seeking	Dopamine	Behavioural activation	Novelty	Exploratory pursuit
			Potential reward	Appetitive approach
			Potential relief of monotony or punishment	Active avoidance, escape
Harm avoidance	Serotonin	Behavioural inhibition	Conditioned signals for punishment, novelty or frustrative non-reward	Passive avoidance, extinction
Reward dependence	Noradrenalin	Behavioural maintenance	Conditioned signals for reward or relief of punishment	Resistance to extinction

three-dimensional model had largely orthogonal dimensions, there is more redundancy in Cloninger's seven factor model as measured by the Temperament and Character Inventory (TCI). Co-operativeness has high correlations with reward dependence and self-directedness, and there is a moderately large negative correlation between self-directedness and harm avoidance.

In an empirical test of the ability of the TCI to predict diagnoses of personality disorder, Svrakic et al. (1993) found that there were moderately large correlations between diagnoses in all of the DSM personality disorder clusters and the self-directedness and the co-operativeness scales of the TCI. This is yet more evidence for the importance of the dimensions of hostility and dominance/submission in personality disorder (cf. Blackburn, 1988; Deary, Bedford and Fowkes, 1995); the latter trait may be poorly indexed within Eysenck and Big Five models. Harm avoidance correlated moderately with DSM cluster C (anxious and fearful) diagnoses. Given the emphasis of worry, fatigue, fear and shyness in the harm avoidance scale this largely replicated the identification of this cluster with neuroticism. Novelty seeking correlated with cluster B (dramatic–emotional) diagnoses, which might reflect the association of impulsiveness and experimentation with antisocial personality disorder and extravagance with histrionic and narcissistic personality disorder. There was a modest negative correlation between reward dependence and cluster A (odd or eccentric) diagnoses. Reward dependence is related to attachment to others and sentiment and, given the detachment of the schizoid, especially, the correlation makes sense. Self-transcendence did not relate to diagnoses in any of the clusters.

In summary, the three original Cloninger scales have modest associations with particular DSM personality disorder clusters and with specific personality disorders within those clusters (see also Mulder and Joyce, 1997). The newer self-directedness and co-operativeness scales have promiscuous correlations with many personality disorder scales and may reflect the general importance of hostility and submissiveness in personality disorder. Cloninger (2000) suggested that these two scales, alongside affective stability, might be used practically to capture core features of personality disorder in a diagnostic scheme. However, co-operativeness and self-directedness are highly correlated and the latter is correlated with harm avoidance. The newer scales of persistence and self-transcendence do not relate to any personality disorder. The Cloninger system has congruences with many other normal personality systems. If it adds anything new it is to emphasise the need for a scale of self-directedness or dominance/submissiveness or will. However, there is much in the system that remains to be validated as the authors themselves noted. Indeed, the psychometric structure of the TPQ, which preceded the TCI, remains a matter of debate. Though Cloninger's factors are well recovered at the subscale level of analysis, analyses at the item level discover that up to half of the items fail to load satisfactorily on the appropriate, designated factor (Zohar et al., 2001).

O'Boyle (1995; O'Boyle and Holzer, 1992) reported shared variance between self-reported personality disorder – as assessed by the Personality Diagnostic Questionnaire–and Eysenck's three broad dimensions of normal personality. A joint factor analysis of the two instruments revealed three similar factors in two samples, one of medical students and one of patients in a substance abuse programme. The first factor had very high loadings for neuroticism and all of the personality disorders except antisocial and schizoid. A further factor linked psychoticism with antisocial personality. A third factor linked introversion with schizoid personality disorder. O'Boyle (1995) stated that the results were:

> consistent with the idea that personality disorder traits are variants of basic personality traits, and that personality disorder classification may be understood in terms of traditional personality dimensions . . . Specifically, the present results support the idea that Eysenck's dimensional components of personality can account for the various personality disorders. (p. 564)

The results of Deary and Austin (1999; Austin and Deary, 2000) and Larstone et al. (2002) afford a similar conclusion (see table 11.6). There are substantial, clear and replicable redundancies between Eysenck's personality scales and DSM personality disorders.

Conclusions

1. Over the years clinical impressions that there are individuals with disorders of personality have become organised as diagnostic systems. These systems have heterogeneous origins, are redundant and have not been validated. There is a growing recognition that a dimensional approach rather than a categorical approach might be appropriate for describing abnormal personality (Jackson

and Livesley, 1995; Widiger and Sanderson, 1995; Farmer, 2000; Livesley, 2001). There are several measurement instruments for assessing dimensions of personality disorder. That personality disorder research should benefit from the scientific advances in trait psychology is emphasised by Livesley (1995b) who stated that 'empirical research has begun to leapfrog DSM-IV, with the increasing use of dimensional models based on constructs that are very different from DSM diagnoses' (p. 504). The work from Livesley's team, having shown coherence of personality structure in normal and clinical populations, allowed them to conclude that it 'throws into question that [sic] validity of current approaches to classifying personality disorder' (Jang, Livesley and Vernon, 2002, p. 2). Farmer's (2000) conclusion about the state of research on categorical systems is even more negative, suggesting stagnation and a tragic conclusion.

> Although the use of literature reviews, data reanalyses, and field trials to inform modifications of [personality] disorder criteria represent a step towards an empirically-based classification, it is ultimately unsatisfactory as the concepts used as reference criteria for subsequent modification were primarily those concepts defined in accordance with previous editions of DSM. This incestuous approach to the refinement of psychiatric classification only adds to the reification and circularity already present within the DSM system, and makes it virtually impossible for future editions of DSM to substantially evolve beyond its predecessors. (p. 844)

Kendell's (2002) diagnosis of the state of personality disorder research is similar.

2. It is also apparent that personality disorders are conceptually heterogeneous, that information about them is limited, and that existing knowledge is largely derived from unrepresentative clinical populations. The clinical literature on personality disorders – indeed the basic concept of personality disorder – has few points of contact with the psychological literature on personality structure and development, and little is known of the cerebral mechanisms underlying personality traits.

3. When assessments of abnormal personality traits are made in non-clinical samples the structure of personality is similar to that found in clinical samples. This structure, at the highest level of organisation, often takes the form of four factors: asthenic, antisocial, asocial and anankastic.

4. There is significant redundancy between normal and abnormal personality dimensions and there are proposals to integrate the two fields of personality assessment. Eysenck's, Cloninger's and the five factor model's systems all show considerable overlap with personality disorders, whether they are based on categories or dimensions. It is not decided whether there is so much overlap that there should be some combined system for assessing normal and disordered personality. The two areas still retain largely distinct research profiles. There might

be room for some distinct dimensions of personality deviance. Joint studies of normal and abnormal personality traits in clinical and non-clinical samples reveal partial, but far from total, overlap, and it is not tenable to conclude that any current system of normal personality traits can 'account for' personality disorder variance.

5. The single, comprehensive world-class effort validly to organise and understand personality disorders as a whole is that of Livesley and colleagues at the University of British Columbia in Canada. Their research does not ignore accumulated clinical wisdom, is psychometrically sophisticated, is aware of models of normal personality dimensions, addresses aetiology and structure, and tests clinical and non-clinical groups. Their team has made suggestions for the diagnosis of personality disorder in which the presence of disorder is established first, and then an assessment of individual differences is made, with an emphasis on lower-order, specific personality disorder traits (Livesley and Jang, 2000).

6. Some psychometrically oriented psychologists have made a detailed and special study of clinically relevant dimensions such as psychopathy and schizotypy, akin to research on narrow traits with the field of normal personality. It remains to be seen how these dimensions will be integrated with dimensional and clinical instruments for assessing personality disorder characteristics in the round. The mapping of the domains of personality deviance will benefit from advances in normal personality research, but it may also be necessary to posit and research specific abnormal traits.

Further reading

American Psychiatric Association. (2000) *Diagnostic and statistical manual of mental disorders* (4th edition, Text Revision). Washington, DC: American Psychiatric Association.

Cooke, D. J., Forth, A and Hare, R. D. (1998) *Psychopathy: theory, research and implications for society*. Dordrecht, The Netherlands: Kluwer.

Costa, P. T., Jr. and Widiger, T. A. (eds.) (2002) *Personality disorders and the five-factor model of personality* (2nd edn). Washington, DC: American Psychological Association.

Livesley, W. J. (ed.) (2001) *Handbook of personality disorders*. New York: Guildford Press.

12 Personality, performance and information-processing

Studies of human performance provide one of the prime methods for investigating associations between traits and objective indices of behaviour. In the laboratory, we can design tasks that assess basic cognitive functions such as speed of reaction, short-term and long-term memory, and focused attention. We can then test whether personality traits predict speed, accuracy or qualitative style of performance on such tasks. Studies of this kind contribute broadly to construct validation, by showing that traits relate to *behavioural measures* that are conceptually linked to the trait. For example, a scale for impulsivity should predict a pattern of fast, inaccurate responding on speeded tasks – although we may have to design the task carefully to show the expected result. Demonstrations of this kind make a major contribution to showing that questionnaire measures of traits are assessing some genuine 'core' psychological quality, and not just some superficial response bias.

Performance research is also of considerable applied relevance, in that trait measures may be used to predict a person's competence in a particular job or activity. For example, personality may predict accidents in transportation and industrial settings. Most of us would be reluctant to fly in an aeroplane piloted by an individual with abnormally high sensation-seeking or psychopathic tendencies, and, in fact, some airlines use the MMPI in pilot selection, to screen out applicants who may be vulnerable to mental illness (see Dolgin and Gibb, 1989). At ground level, extraversion appears to relate to motor vehicle accident risk, perhaps because extraversion is related to impulsivity (Loo, 1979). Furnham (1992) reviewed the literature on accidents in occupational settings, and concluded that traits related to both E and N predict accident likelihood. The Big Five model is becoming increasingly popular as a framework guiding selection and assessment in occupational studies of personality (Matthews, 1997a). The present chapter focuses primarily on theoretical accounts of personality and performance, but we return to practical applications in chapter 13.

Performance studies and trait theory

Beyond general demonstrations that traits predict behaviour, performance studies are important both for developing the theory of personality traits, and for translating theory into practical applications. The starting point for theory is that behaviour is controlled by a large collection of distinct neural and psychological processes. Personality traits reflect individual differences in these processes, and performance studies can help us to isolate those processes that are critical for a particular trait.

Consider impulsive behaviour in a real-world situation such as vehicle driving; e.g., joining a busy multi-lane motorway from a slip-road (ramp). The driver must decide whether to continue driving, merging with oncoming traffic, or whether to stop and wait for a gap in the traffic. Impulsive drivers might merge when it was safer to stop, forcing other vehicles to brake or change lane. Decision-making here depends on at least two distinct processing stages. First, the driver forms some mental representation of the oncoming traffic, that specifies the position and trajectory of approaching vehicles. Second, the driver makes a judgement as to whether or not it is safe to begin a merging manoeuvre. Impulsivity in merging might be a consequence of either (or both) stages. Impulsivity might reflect lack of care in the initial evaluation and 'sizing-up' of the situation. Perhaps the impulsive driver only attends to the nearest vehicles, or attends to the location but not the speed of oncoming vehicles. Conversely, the impulsive driver might thoroughly evaluate the situation, but misjudge the consequences of failing to stop. The driver might realise that merging will force other vehicles to brake, but doesn't believe that there is a risk involved. In other words, impulsive personality might reflect either a tendency towards incomplete stimulus analysis, or a tendency to disregard the potential adverse consequences of rapid responses.

Laboratory studies help us to test these different hypotheses against one another. Broadly, we can set up tasks on which performance reflects either thoroughness of stimulus evaluation, or judgements of risk (but not both), and test whether impulsivity as a personality trait relates to stimulus processing or risk assessment. For example, Dickman and Meyer (1988) ran a study of impulsivity and reaction time that linked impulsivity to stimulus analysis (comparing stimulus features), but not to riskiness of response execution. We might also add a neurological dimension to such studies by, for example, using imaging techniques to test for individual differences in activity of the different areas of the brain during performance.

The attentive reader will notice that we have started to make some causal assumptions here, i.e., that personality influences processing functions, which in turn influence behaviour. Of course, we need to be cautious in assuming that an observed correlation between personality and performance reflects some direct causal effect of personality on processing. The interactionist perspective discussed in chapter 2 highlights the possible role of situational factors in shaping personality. Perhaps impulsive driving reflects not so much personality, but the kinds of training and on-road experiences the person has had. However – remembering that people actively choose and shape the situations to which they are exposed (Caspi and Bem, 1990) – we cannot entirely separate situational from personal influences. Drivers exercise choice over the traffic conditions which they experience. Some people avoid night-driving or freeway driving, whereas sensation-seekers may actively seek out risky experiences (Jonah, 1997).

Although we must be cautious in interpreting personality–performance correlations, the assumption that shapes much performance research is that personality traits influence fundamental cognitive processes, that can be investigated through measures of speed and accuracy taken in the laboratory. Understanding how traits relate to processes for attention, memory and speed of response may give us a broader understanding of how personality shapes behaviour. The influence of situational exposure and learning can be reduced by using simple laboratory tasks with abstract stimuli and responses. For example, we might investigate impulsivity using reaction-time tasks that require the respondent to press a button as quickly as possible in response to the illumination of a light-bulb, a task likely to be outside the person's immediate experience. We might still worry about generalisation from related real-world tasks, such as pressing the car accelerator pedal in response to a traffic light changing from red to green. Fortunately, skill learning tends to be fairly specific to the stimuli and responses involved. In addition, we can check for generalisation of personality–performance associations across different stimuli and responses. If the association appears robust across different task versions, we can have at least some confidence that it reflects some basic individual difference in task processing.

In this chapter, we will be primarily concerned with studies using simple tasks that aim to uncover fundamental processing biases linked to personality. We should not dismiss the potential role of experience and situation-specific learning, especially where real-world tasks are concerned. In addition, motivational factors may play a part. For example, impulsive drivers may not in fact differ from non-impulsive drivers in their processing of traffic stimuli. Instead, in line with the overlap between impulsivity and sensation-seeking (Zuckerman et al., 1993), they may enjoy risk-taking, leading to greater exposure to dangerous situations, and, consequently, to developing different driving skills, compared with the non-impulsive driver. Unfortunately, contextual and motivational factors have been rather neglected. Investigating these factors may require longitudinal studies that track how the effects of the person's interests and opportunities for skill acquisition feed into individual differences in performance. We will return to the interplay between person and environment in shaping performance later in the chapter.

Moderator factors: context-sensitivity and task-dependence

As the preceding discussion indicates, the simple demonstration of some correlation between a trait and performance is of rather limited value theoretically. Typically, any such correlation is open to a variety of different interpretations. A satisfactory theory needs to make predictions about *moderator factors* that influence whether or not a personality–performance correlation is observed. (As discussed in chapter 9, a moderator is a third variable that influences the association between two variables.) For example, suppose we have a theory of impulsivity that links the trait to incomplete stimulus analysis (cf. Dickman and Meyer, 1988). We might then predict that impulsivity will correlate with fast, inaccurate performance if we present the subject with a display containing many stimuli, or with a few complex stimuli, but not if the subject is required to respond to a single, simple stimulus that requires little analysis. The approach of using an explicit theory to predict the circumstances under which the trait will and will not relate to performance is much more powerful than simply formulating predictions on an ad hoc, intuitive basis.

Two kinds of moderator factor have been investigated in empirical studies. First, associations between traits and performance often depend on environmental factors such as the amount of stimulation or threat present during testing. A particular trait may be an advantage in some settings but a disadvantage in others. For example, both introverts and high neuroticism individuals tend to perform poorly on certain tasks only when the environment is arousing or stressful (Eysenck and Eysenck, 1985). Such *context-sensitivity* is an important focus for theory, and indicates the necessity of adopting an interactionist perspective. Context-sensitivity may sometimes indicate that situational learning is influencing individual differences, where 'context' refers to specific real-world settings. For example, if a trait measure is predictive of impulsivity only in the context of driving, we might suspect it assesses some index of beliefs and skills acquired during exposure to the driving task. By contrast, measures such as Zuckerman's (1977) sensation-seeking scale predict risk-taking in a variety of situations, including vehicle driving, dangerous sports and social situations, implying that some more fundamental processes are involved. A second type of moderator factor is the nature of the task itself. Typically, traits relate to a fairly complex patterning of performance, as we will now explain. Only certain tasks are sensitive to the trait, and a particular trait may have both beneficial and damaging effects on performance, depending on the task. Hence, *task-dependence* of associations between traits and performance is one of the major empirical findings which trait theory should explain.

Key traits in performance research

Many different traits, both broad and narrow, have been studied in relation to performance. Although, as discussed in chapter 13, the five factor model is becoming increasingly dominant in occupational psychology, the most systematic research has been conducted on traits from Eysenck's (e.g., 1967, 1997) personality theory. One important strand of research relates to extraversion and impulsivity, whereas a second focus concerns neuroticism and anxiety. Much of this chapter will be concerned with reviewing the effects of these traits on performance. We will contrast two theoretical approaches to understanding performance consequences of personality and their moderation by contextual and task factors. The first approach is psychobiological, exemplified by Eysenck's arousal theory, discussed in chapter 7. Perhaps performance differences between extraverts and introverts, for example, reflect individual differences in cortical arousal. The second, more recent approach is based on cognitive psychology. Personality effects may represent not so much generalised arousal, but, more likely, individual differences in specific information-processing functions, such as the capacity of working memory or the selectivity of attention. It is important also to look at what adaptive functions these individual differences may serve; for example, language skills, resistance to distraction, and high speed of response may support sociability, one of the primary characteristics of extraversion (Matthews, 1999).

We note briefly that space considerations prevent us reviewing other important traits. The third Eysenckian factor, psychoticism, is associated with a range of abnormalities in performance broadly similar to those found in schizophrenic patients (see Eysenck, 1992b, for a review). However, some of these effects seem to be more reliably related to measures of the schizotypal personality discussed in chapter 11 than to P itself. For example, Beech and Claridge (1987) used a 'negative priming' paradigm to show that schizotypy was associated with weakened inhibition in selective attention, but there were no significant effects of P in their study. Subsequent studies have fairly consistently found associations between schizotypy and reduced cognitive inhibition, which may contribute to the occurence of 'positive symptoms' of schizophrenia, such as hallucinations (Beech and Williams, 1997). We may also expect to see increased interest in performance correlates of the remaining Big Five factors. As we shall see in chapter 13, Conscientiousness is of interest as a predictor of better job performance, and investigators are beginning to run laboratory studies linking C to processes such as motivation to learn (Colquitt and Simmering, 1998).

Finally, we cannot review performance without at least a brief look at the relationship of personality to intelligence, i.e., general mental ability. Intelligence, as measured by conventional 'IQ' tests, is generally a more robust predictor of performance than personality. More intelligent individuals appear to have a general advantage in performance, although the magnitude of the advantage depends on the task. Contextual factors are of minor importance only. There is some overlap between personality and intelligence measures, although correlations are typically rather weak. Openness is probably the trait most strongly related to general intelligence measures (Ackerman and Heggestad, 1997). Personality and intelligence relate to rather separate spheres of differential psychology, but the limited overlap may be informative about how the person uses their cognitive capabilities in real-life settings, and we will look at their interrelationship towards the end of this chapter.

Theories of personality and performance

Psychobiological theories

In chapter 7, we laid out a rationale for treating personality traits as expressions of brain systems. Eysenck (1967, 1981), for example, linked extraversion to arousability of a cortico-reticular circuit, and neuroticism to arousability of the limbic system said to control emotion. We can build on this basic logic to make predictions about performance, provided that we can link individual differences in brain function to individual differences in performance. Thus, if we wish to use Eysenck's theory to predict performance, we need to know how cortical arousal relates to performance. According to the so-called Yerkes-Dodson Law (Yerkes and Dodson, 1908; Broadhurst, 1957) there is an inverted-U relationship between cortical arousal and performance, such that there is an optimal, moderate level of arousal for performance. That is, extremes of arousal, both high and low, tend to be associated with performance impairment. In addition, the optimum or ideal level is inversely related to task difficulty. Performance of easy tasks is best when arousal is relatively high, whereas a moderately low level of arousal is most favourable for difficult tasks. For example, we might need peace and quiet for reading a difficult journal article, but performing a routine clerical task might benefit from background music or other noise of moderate intensity.

If Eysenck (1967) was correct that extraverts tend to be low in cortical arousal (see chapter 7), compared with introverts, we can make some predictions. In fact, the theory predicts context-sensitivity of trait effects, i.e., that relationships between extraversion and performance will vary with the 'context' of whether people are generally high or low in arousal (see figure 12.1). Environmental factors, such as level of noise influence the person's arousal level, and, in turn, the most favourable baseline level of arousal for performance. For example, according to the Yerkes-Dodson Law, persons who are initially low in arousal will tend to perform better in noise, because they are less likely to become over-aroused. Hence, because extraverts tend to have chronically low arousal, they will tend to out-perform introverts in stimulating environments: introverts are more vulnerable than extraverts to becoming over-aroused, exceeding the optimal level. Conversely, extraverts will be disadvantaged in non-stimulating or de-arousing environments, being vulnerable to under-arousal. The Yerkes-Dodson Law also allows us to predict moderator effects related to task dependence, given that the optimum level of arousal varies with task difficulty, as shown in figure 12.1. In general, difficult tasks, that have a low optimum level of arousal, should favour extraverts, especially when the environment is stimulating so that introverts are highly over-aroused. Conversely, extraverts should be most prone to performance impairments on easy tasks in de-arousing situations, because of their tendency to be under-aroused.

In addition, arousal theory also makes various predictions concerning relationships between traits and basic psychological functions such as perception and conditioning that are considered to be minimally influenced by cognition (see Eysenck and Eysenck, 1985; Corr, Pickering and Gray, 1995). The tests of the theory have in some instances been successful, although there are also instances of predictive failure (see Corr et al., 1995; Matthews and Gilliland, 1999). For example, Shigehisa and Symons (1973) showed that visual stimulation lowers auditory thresholds in extraverts, but increases thresholds in introverts. There is also considerable evidence that introverts show more rapid associative conditioning than extraverts, provided that stimuli are not so strong that they elicit the

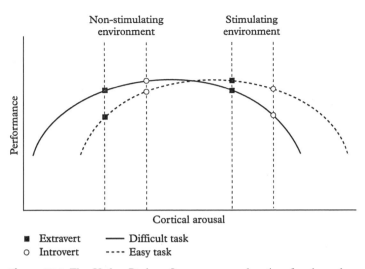

Non-stimulating
environment

Stimulating
environment

■ Extravert   —— Difficult task
o Introvert   ---- Easy task

Figure 12.1 The Yerkes-Dodson Law as an explanation for dependence of extraversion effects on task difficulty and level of environmental stimulation

protective 'transmarginal inhibition' discussed in chapter 7 (Levey and Martin, 1981; Matthews and Gilliland, 1999).

Arousal theory is not the only basis for predicting performance from psychobiological models. As we also saw in chapter 7, Gray's Reinforcement Sensitivity Theory (RST) links traits not so much to arousal but to motivational systems, with a punishment system supporting anxiety (the Behavioural Inhibition System or BIS), and a reward system supporting impulsivity (the Behavioural Activation System or BAS). Gray's theory is firmly based on animal studies that demonstrate the role of BIS and BAS in studies of conditioning to punishment and/or reward systems. This psychobiological orientation often makes it difficult to predict individual differences in human performance from the theory. Activation of the mainly subcortical structures involved in the BIS and BAS is known to generate cortical arousal, but it is unclear whether such activation has much effect on the more specific cortical circuits that support information-processing and higher-level cognition. Where RST is strongest is in predicting personality effects on simple learning and conditioning tasks, assumed to be controlled by similar brain structures to those supporting animal learning (Matthews and Gilliland, 1999). A prediction that is often made is that impulsives (and extraverts) should show stronger conditioning to signals of reward than low impulsives (and introverts). Also, high anxiety individuals (and high N persons) should show enhanced conditioning to signals of punishment.

Various studies have tested these predictions, with decidedly mixed results (see Matthews and Gilliland, 1999; Pickering et al., 1997 for reviews). As discussed in chapter 7, individual differences in behaviour may reflect the interaction of BIS and BAS (Corr, 2002). There is also the methodological problem that motivational manipulations may also influence arousal. Indeed, Gray's theory itself states that BIS and BAS activation feed into a noradrenergic arousal system, so that it is difficult to disentangle motivational and arousal-based effects. Broadly, some studies suggest that motivational signals are an important moderator of personality effects, as the Gray theory predicts, but the form of the personality x motivation interaction varies considerably from study to study (Matthews and Gilliland, 1999). Some applied studies are also consistent with Gray (1981), in suggesting that, in more complex learning paradigms, such as classroom learning, rewards may be more beneficial to extraverts than to introverts (see Pickering et al., 1995).

As discussed in chapter 7, arousal theory has been severely criticised, which weakens its attractiveness as a basis for explaining performance effects. Of particular importance is the critique from cognitive psychology (Eysenck, 1982). Hockey (1984) reviewed the status of arousal theory as an explanation for effects of stressors such as noise and heat on performance, but his reasoning is directly applicable to personality effects also. Arousal theory assumes that it is meaningful to characterise people as varying in overall performance efficiency, an assumption reminiscent of the Pavlovian view that the cortex can be described in terms of certain formal parameters such as strength of the nervous system (see chapter 3). However, Hockey showed that stressor effects are complex, and highly task-dependent. We cannot sensibly talk about the overall effect of stress on performance: each stressor is different. The patterns of performance change associated with individual stressors may be conceptualised by categorising tasks in terms of their demands on key elements of information-processing such as short-term memory (STM), selective attention and so forth. The precise processing demands of tasks are more important than their difficulty. A stressor might have very different effects on an attentional task and an STM task of equal difficulty, for example. The description of how a stressor affects a range of different tasks is known as its *cognitive patterning*. As we shall see, trait effects appear to be similarly dependent on information-processing, producing different patterns of performance change.

Cognitive psychological alternatives

At this point, we need to introduce the rather different view of individual differences in performance provided by cognitive psychology (see Matthews, Davies et al., 2000). This branch of psychology sees the person as resembling a very advanced robot, controlled by a digital computer. If we can discover the 'robot's' programs, then we can explain its behaviour. The person is thus seen as an information-processor. Sensory information is encoded in some abstract, symbolic form, such as a series of codes representing the meaning of a sentence. Computations are performed on these symbols that analyse their relevance, and may generate instructions that are sent to muscles to produce some response. The sequence of computations is controlled by some internal program. However, there is one critical difference between the brain and the typical desktop computer. Most computers have a single processor that implements program instructions on a serial, one-at-a-time, basis.

However, the brain comprises multiple processors, sometimes called *components* or *modules*, operating independently and in parallel, although communicating with one another. This gives us a view of task performance as controlled by a large number of distinct information-processing functions, such as short-term recall and selective attention processes, that may reflect not just different 'programs' but also different brain subsystems. Hence, it is entirely possible that a personality trait might be linked to some modules (subsystems) but not others, and so relate to performance of some tasks but not others. Thus, at their simplest, cognitive psychological studies of traits aim to provide descriptive information on which tasks are sensitive to the trait of interest. If we have a cognitive model of how the task is performed, then we can make inferences about which underlying processing components are associated with the trait. For example, a trait might be found to relate to memory but not to attentional processes.

A list of processing components is incomplete as a model of cognitive functioning. We also want to know how components are linked together into some overall, structured processing framework, referred to as a *cognitive architecture*. Such a framework aspires to be a kind of circuit diagram of the mind, showing how information flows between different processors, and how that flow is controlled so as to best meet the demands imposed by the task at hand. Of course, the complete architecture is alarmingly complex, and, currently, is not well understood. There are many competing candidate human cognitive architectures: Dawson (1998) listed twenty-four that 'attracted vibrant debates concerning the merits of each proposal'. However, cognitive psychologists have attempted to state some general principles that indicate how the multiplicity of processors may be organised so as to produce some coherent output. An influential idea is the distinction between upper and lower levels of control of processing (Norman and Shallice, 1985; Matthews, Davies et al., 2000). The lower level supports well-learnt, routine mental operations that can be executed with little conscious attention. It is driven primarily by external stimuli, in a reflexive and 'automatic' fashion. The lower level is often conceptualised as a network (or set of networks) of interconnected units, processing information in parallel. The upper level operates as a supervisory executive that intervenes on a 'troubleshooting' basis when the task is novel or difficult. Processing sequences initiated and regulated by the upper level are sometimes referred to as controlled processing (Schneider, Dumais and Shiffrin, 1984). Controlled processing may require attentional resources or capacity, conceptualised here as a source of energisation for processing; insufficient resources leads to impairment of controlled processing.

Two features of this picture of the mind as an internally structured information-processing device are especially relevant in the performance context. First, performance is seen as controlled by both general- and special-purpose processing components. Driving a car might require both some specialised psychomotor skills for steering, together with general attentional capacity that could be diverted to other tasks such as talking to a passenger. A further example is provided by the important construct of working memory, which refers to the simultaneous storage and manipulation of information, such as remembering intermediate solutions when doing a mental arithmetic problem (Baddeley, 1986). (In contrast, short-term memory (STM) refers to retention with minimal additional processing.) We can assess working memory both as an integrated system or, alternatively, in terms of multiple components, such as the short-term retention facility provided by subvocal rehearsal of material (known as the phonological loop). Researchers have aimed to relate personality traits to both special- and general-purpose aspects of cognition. However, given that traits reflect rather general characteristics of the person, affecting a variety of behaviours, models that link traits to general components such as attentional resources or working memory tend to be more powerful and influential (e.g. Humphreys and Revelle, 1984).

A second feature of the information-processing metaphor is that it distinguishes involuntary and voluntary control of behaviour. By contrast, arousal theory encourages a rather passive view of the performer, and neglects the role of voluntarily selected strategies in controlling performance. Processing may be automatic to the extent that it is triggered without deliberate intent by incoming stimuli. As discussed in chapter 5, quite complex social behaviours may be influenced in this way. Voluntary behaviour is controlled by strategies or plans that are driven by some explicit goal. Often, processing of this kind is experienced as requiring mental effort. Personality may relate to both voluntary and involuntary aspects of performance. If we find some correlation between personality and performance, it might reflect either some 'in-built' bias in processing routines, or some deliberate strategic choice. Careful experimentation is required to distinguish these possibilities.

Cognitive neuroscience approaches

Arousal theory, as traditionally formulated, tends to neglect the cognitive level of description and the diversity of cognitive functions potentially sensitive to personality. Increasingly, researchers are employing methods based on cognitive neuroscience to link personality traits to more specific processes, that may be understood in both neurological and cognitive psychological terms. There is not, of course, any fundamental incompatibility between biological and cognitive models and, within a hierarchical model of the mind, information-processing may be seen as supported by neural activity. Cognitive psychology is becoming increasingly integrated with neuroscience, as researchers seek to localise specific processing components, and to specify how information-processing is supported by neural functioning. Personality studies have yet to fully capitalise on these advances, but there are some promising developments. For example, it is claimed that focusing attention narrowly is supported by left hemisphere structures, such as left posterior cingulate cortex, whereas right hemisphere involvement produces a more expansive focus. Tucker and Derryberry (1992) hypothesised that trait anxiety is associated with the left-hemisphere attentional focusing process. Consistent with this proposal, trait anxious individuals appear to show enhanced left-lateralisation of evoked potentials in response to visual stimuli (Dien, 1999).

Second, some researchers are using tasks that are believed to index specific brain systems. For example, Derryberry and Reed (1988) investigated attentional focusing in anxiety using a task believed to discriminate mechanisms for narrowing and broadening attention, described also as 'local' and 'global' mechanisms for attention. Stimuli are large letters composed of small letters, such as a large 'H' made up of small 'T's. Subjects in their study were required to respond to target letters as quickly as possible. When the target letter was large, there was no effect of trait anxiety on response time. However, when the target was one of the small letters making up the larger letter, anxious subjects were faster to respond. This effect was stronger when stimuli were presented to the right visual field, so that they were processed initially in the left hemisphere of the brain. Hence, these behavioural data are consistent with the neuropsychological data linking anxiety to the left-hemisphere attentional narrowing mechanism. The work of Derryberry and Reed provides a nice convergence between neuroscience and cognitive psychological approaches to understanding trait anxiety.

Third, there is interest in linking personality to individual differences in the operation of neural networks (Matthews, Derryberry et al., 2000). We can set up models of how a set of interconnected neuron-like units behaves once units representing some stimulus input become activated. Such models may be used to explore how individual differences in the spread of activation between units might underpin the effects of personality on performance (Matthews and Harley, 1993). Perhaps individual differences in response speed reflect whether information is transmitted rapidly or sluggishly, taking into account the functioning of the network as a whole. Similarly, Siegle (1999) suggested that the tendency of depressed and anxious persons to worry about problems reflects feedback between separate neural nets representing emotional and non-emotional aspects of information. Siegle (1999; Siegle and Ingram, 1997) showed that a simulation of this network model predicted real experimental data: e.g., how fast depressed individuals decide whether a word has positive or negative content. Siegle (1999) linked his simulated feedback processes to interaction between the limbic system and frontal lobes demonstrated neurophysiologically. Hence, such models may help to elucidate how neural processes support information-processing.

Extraversion–introversion and performance

The cognitive patterning of extraversion

Which type of person is the better performer: an extravert or an introvert? The answer is 'it depends': sometimes extraverts do better and sometimes introverts, depending on a whole range of task and contextual variables. A typical study is that of Eysenck and Eysenck (1979). They used a task popular with cognitive psychologists, the Sternberg memory scanning task, in which subjects search the contents of short-term memory to decide whether a probe stimulus matches a list

Table 12.1 *Cognitive patterning of extraversion-introversion effects on performance*

Cognitive function	Example study	Task	Result
Extraverts (Es) are better at			
Divided attention	Eysenck and Eysenck (1979)	Sternberg memory search	Es better at attention
Short term memory	Mangan and Hookway (1988)	Free recall of video sequences	Es better at immediate recall
Retrieval from semantic memory	Eysenck (1974)	Retrieve semantic category instances	Es faster at retrieving low dominance ('unusual') instances
Speech production	Dewaele and Furnham (2000)	Learning a second language	Es more fluent in production
Introverts (Is) are better at			
Visual vigilance	Harkins and Geen (1975)	Detection of line stimulus	Is show higher detection rate
Long-term memory	Howarth and Eysenck (1968)	Paired associate learning	Is better at delayed recall (thirty minutes, one day)
Problem-solving	Kumar and Kapila (1987)	Five 'insightful' problem-solving tasks	Is faster and more accurate

of items memorised previously. Manipulations of the task stimuli allow different aspects of information-processing to be investigated. In one condition, subjects were required to search for an exact match between the probe and one of the memorised items. In a second condition, subjects searched for a semantic match, such that the probe was an instance of one of a memorised list of categories (e.g. 'carrot' is an instance of 'vegetable'). In a third, dual-task condition, subjects were told to find an instance of either type of match, so that both the exact identity of the word and its meaning had to be processed. Extraversion effects were found mainly in this dual-task condition: introverts tended to be slower to respond than extraverts. From the variation of the effect of E across task conditions, Eysenck and Eysenck inferred that E has no general effect on memory search, but extraverts are superior at parallel processing or divided attention. This study also demonstrates how it is often convenient to treat extraverts and introverts as distinct 'types', although E–I is, of course, a continuous variable.

Table 12.1 illustrates the task-dependence of extraversion effects on performance, demonstrated in multiple studies (see Matthews, 1997b, for a review). Extraverts tend to show superior performance to introverts on some tasks, particularly relatively demanding tasks requiring divided attention, resistance to distraction or resistance to interference (Eysenck, 1982). For example, extraverts are less easily distracted than introverts by music, especially when it is complex, and presumably more attentionally demanding to process (Furnham and Allass, 1999). Extraverts may also have advantages in verbal information-processing that support their sociability. For example, extraverts are more fluent in speech pro-duction (Dewaele and Furnham, 1999), and more effective in constructive verbal communication (LePine and Van Dyne, 2001). Conversely, there are some tasks on which introverts perform better, such as vigilance, and certain kinds of problem-solving. Still other tasks, such as reaction-time tasks, do not appear to show any consistent effect of extraversion (Amelang and Ullwer, 1991). Extraversion may affect task strategy as well as performance efficiency; extraverts' lower response criterion (Koelega, 1992) and preference for speed over accuracy (Eysenck, 1967) suggest a risky, impulsive style of response. Brebner and Cooper (1985) charac-terise extraverts as 'geared to respond', and introverts as 'geared to inspect' (see Box 12.1 for an example study). Responsiveness may also have a motor component, in that extraversion consistently correlates with speed of movement in executing simple responses during reaction time studies (Doucet and Stelmack, 2000; Wickett and Vernon, 2000). The effects listed appear to generalise across a variety of envi-ronmental conditions. For example, Eysenck and Eysenck (1979) showed that the superiority of extraverts at parallel processing was unaffected by whether or not white noise was delivered during performance, so it was not arousal-dependent. These effects may generalise to applied contexts; relative to introverts, extraverted locomotive drivers show better detection of railway signal stimuli (Singh, 1989), extraverted post office trainees perform better on a demanding speeded mail-coding task (Matthews, Jones and Chamberlain, 1992), and extraverted subjects show better short-term recall of TV news broadcasts (Gunter and Furnham, 1986).

Studies of the context-sensitivity of relationships between E and performance have focused primarily on manipulations thought to influence arousal. Matthews (1992a) reviewed a series of studies showing that extraverts out-perform intro-verts in stimulating or stressful conditions, but introverts perform better under de-arousing conditions, such as sleep deprivation. These effects can be quite dra-matic, in that stressors may have qualitatively different effects in groups differing in E–I. Corcoran (1962, 1972) had subjects perform a tracking task on three succes-sive days of sleep deprivation. Sleep deprivation is considered one of the stronger arousal-reducing manipulations available to the researcher. However, as figure 12.2 shows, its effects are strikingly different in extraverted and introverted subjects, with extraverts showing a progressive deterioration in performance, whereas in-troverts' performance actually improves with increasing deprivation. The effect of sleep deprivation seems to generalise also to tasks requiring high-level cognition, such as logical reasoning (Blagrove and Akehurst, 2001). Conversely, arousing agents such as loud noise may have the reverse effect. Loud traffic noise (88 db (A)) actually improves mental arithmetic in extraverts, while impairing performance in introverts (Belojevic, Slepcevic and Jakovljevic, 2001). Context-sensitivity too may have applied relevance. In a study of vehicle driving, Fagerström and Lisper (1979) found that extraverts' attention derived more benefit than introverts' from arousing manipulations, ingestion of caffeine and use of the car radio. Conversely, extraverts appear to be more sensitive to harmful effects of drowsiness while driving (Verwey and Zaidel, 2000).

Box 12.1 Probing the cognitive architecture: extraversion and the response selection bottleneck

Cognitive psychology envisages a set of independent processing modules or components. Some of these components have been extensively studied, including the *response bottleneck* (Pashler, 1998), which limits the person's performance of two concurrent tasks. The response bottleneck is demonstrated in studies of the psychological refractory period (PRP). The subject must respond to two stimuli presented in quick succession. If the interstimulus interval (ISI) is less than a few hundred milliseconds, the second response is delayed. It appears that there is a response selection process that can only handle one incoming stimulus at a time. If, as in the PRP paradigm, a second stimulus is presented while response selection to the first is in progress, the second stimulus must 'wait in line', until the response selection process has concluded.

Brebner (1998) had subjects perform a reaction-time task in which they were required to discriminate between two light-emitting diodes. They responded to one light with the index finger of the right hand, and to the second light with the left index finger, as quickly as possible. On each trial, both lights were illuminated, but there was a delay (ISI) ranging from 175 ms to 650 ms between onsets of the first and second stimulus. Brebner showed the normal PRP effect: response to the second light was delayed at the shorter ISIs. Extraversion was measured prior to the study using the EPQ-R questionnaire. Brebner had previously argued that extraverts are more 'geared to respond' than introverts, and so he predicted a shorter PRP in extraverts than in introverts. This prediction was confirmed; the response selection process appeared to take about 60 ms less time to complete in extraverts compared with introverts.

The study is of special interest because it links personality to a discrete process (response selection) that has been thoroughly explored in cognitive-psychological experiments. Linking extraversion to faster response selection may also help to explain why extraverts may show faster response in real-world situations (Matthews, 1999). As further discussed in chapter 13, small biases in information-processing may feed forward into practically significant personality differences in real-world tasks requiring speeded response. At the same time, further experiments might be needed to show conclusively that extraversion relates to a processing bias rather than to strategy selection. Brebner (1998) raised the possibility that personality may influence preparatory processes that are known to influence reaction time.

Thus, to predict how (and whether) extraverts and introverts will differ in performance, we have to take into account both task demands and the level of stimulation provided by the environment. Extraversion effects may also be moderated by motivational factors, such as whether performance influences rewards or

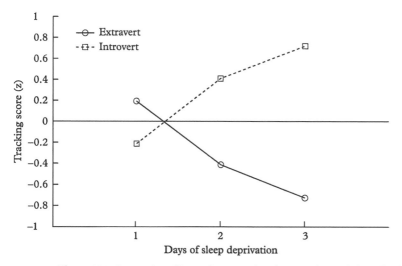

Figure 12.2 Interactive effects of extraversion–introversion and sleep deprivation on tracking performance
Source Corcoran, 1962

punishments, although reliable results are hard to obtain (Matthews and Gilliland, 1999). The complexity of extraversion effects suggests that there may be several independent mechanisms that are influenced by this personality trait.

Psychobiological explanations for cognitive patterning

Arousal theory seeks to explain these performance differences between extraverts and introverts as follows. Extraverts are superior at demanding attention and memory tasks because the difficulty of these tasks lowers the optimal level of cortical arousal for performance, and extraverts tend to be low in arousal. Extraverts' greater willingness to respond during performance may be a different kind of effect; a strategic attempt to raise arousal to the optimum by frequent responding (Eysenck, 1967). However, when scrutinised in detail, arousal explanations are often unsatisfactory; extraversion and task difficulty frequently fail to interact as predicted (Matthews, 1992a). Another problem is that some extraversion–introversion differences predicted from arousal theory are not obtained. Most arousing stressors tend to narrow the focus of attention (Hockey, 1984); i.e, attention becomes more selective and focused on the highest-priority stimuli. However, extraversion has no systematic effects on selectivity of attention (Matthews, 1992a), suggesting that extraverts do not behave like persons low in arousal.

At first glance, the tendency for extraverts to perform better than introverts in stimulating conditions is exactly as predicted by arousal theory. However, here too there are difficulties. First, studies measuring all three relevant constructs (extraversion, arousal and performance) fail to support the hypothesis that extraversion effects on performance are directly mediated by individual differences in arousal (e.g., Matthews, 1985, 1997b). The Eysenck and Eysenck (1985) theory predicts that subjects whose levels of cortical arousal are the same should show the same levels of performance. However, Matthews and Amelang (1993) showed that the relatively low arousal alpha state apparent in EEG recordings is associated with good performance in introverts but poor performance in extraverts. In other words, the same brain state has different consequences for performance in introverts and extraverts, a finding which is incompatible with conventional arousal theory, and a state-trait theory in which arousal/alpha state is the only causal influence on performance. Instead, it appears that the association between arousal and performance is qualitatively different in extraverted and introverted subjects. Matthews and Amelang (1993) suggest that there may be a positive association between arousal and performance in extraverts, but a negative arousal–performance association in introverts.

Second, the interaction between extraversion and arousal reverses in the evening; at this time of day, it is introverts rather than extraverts who tend to perform better under high arousal (Revelle et al., 1980; Matthews, 1985). Gray (1981, p. 258) colourfully described this finding as a 'dagger that goes to the heart of Eysenckian theory'. Revelle et al. (1980) suggested that the association between extraversion and arousal may vary with time of day, although Eysenck and Folkard (1980) questioned this hypothesis. Third, context-dependent effects are also task-dependent: extraversion and arousal do not show their characteristic interactive effect on all tasks. Matthews (1997b) characterised tasks sensitive to the interaction as those in which performance is influenced by simple, routine encoding operations which are somewhat 'automatic' in nature, and require little effortful deployment of attention. It is unclear how arousal theory can account for the restriction of the extraversion effect to tasks of this type. In general, individual differences in arousal may be related to performance, but in a more subtle and limited way than traditional arousal theory claims.

Cognitive explanations

Cognitive psychology tends to focus on the minutiæ of tasks and performance indices, so that it is best suited to explaining personality effects within specific paradigms, rather than offering the broad sweep provided by arousal theory. Several such 'mini-theories' of extraversion effects have been proposed. Eysenck (1982) proposed that extraverts typically have more attentional resources or capacity available than introverts, so they perform better on difficult tasks. This hypothesis explains extraverts' superiority on divided attention tasks, their ability to resist distraction, and, possibly, their advantage on difficult STM tasks. The resource hypothesis seems inconsistent with the poorer vigilance of extraverts. However, Matthews (1992a) pointed out that extraverts' performance superiority is most evident on verbal tasks, and they are most disadvantaged on visual vigilance tasks, whose demands tend to derive from low perceptual discriminability. Extraverts also tend to show poorer performance on visual perception tasks

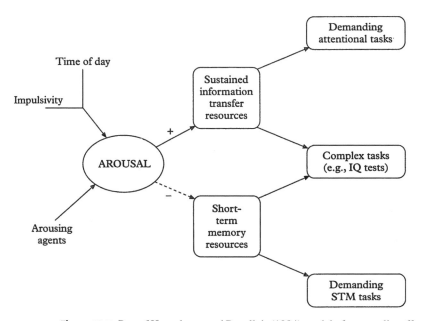

Figure 12.3 Part of Humphreys and Revelle's (1984) model of personality effects on performance

(Eysenck and Eysenck, 1985). Hence, extraverts may have more capacity specifically for processing verbal stimuli, but not for other types of task. Other researchers have addressed differences between extraverts and introverts in task strategy. Weinman (1987) presented data suggesting that extraverts are disadvantaged at complex problem-solving because they tend to adopt an 'impulsive exit strategy', curtailing processing of the problem prematurely. Similarly, extraverts are more likely to give up on a problem when it is difficult and frustrating (Cooper and Taylor, 1999).

The best-known cognitive theory of interactions between E and stress manipulations was put forward by Humphreys and Revelle (1984). Their theory is an ambitious attempt to explain effects of a variety of personality and environmental factors on attention and memory, and its details are beyond the scope of this chapter. In brief, they saw effects of E as driven primarily by impulsivity, one of the relatively narrow traits associated with the broad E factor. Impulsivity interacts with time of day to influence level of cortical arousal, as shown in figure 12.3. Arousal is also affected by arousing agents such as stimulant drugs and some environmental stressors. Arousal, in turn, tends to increase the availability of resources for attention-demanding tasks (sustained information transfer resources), but decreases resources for short-term retention. Hence, impulsivity (or extraversion) effects are mediated by tradeoffs in the availability of the two types of resource. For example, in the morning high impulsives/extraverts are low in arousal. This means they have plenty of STM resources, but few attentional resources. Increasing the arousal of these individuals tends to shift the balance towards greater attentional capacity, and improves their performance on tasks requiring attention. High impulsives/extraverts are expected to perform badly on attentional tasks such as vigilance, but their performance will be improved by arousing agents such as caffeine. The prediction that arousal should enhance performance of demanding attentional tasks has been supported in several studies (Matthews and Davies, 1998, 2001; Revelle, 1993), although other predictions derived from the model have been less successful (Matthews, 1992a), suggesting that it is in need of some revision.

Matthews (e.g. Matthews, Jones and Chamberlain, 1989) conducted a series of studies which systematically manipulated demands made by attentional tasks. Contrary to the Humphreys and Revelle (1984) theory, tasks making few demands on resources were more sensitive to interactive effects of extraversion and arousal than tasks believed to require many resources. Matthews and Harley (1993) proposed an alternative mechanism, that time of day, extraversion and arousal interactively affect the spread of activation in a semantic network. The spread of activation between semantically associated words such as 'doctor' and 'nurse' may be assessed by investigating semantic priming of lexical decision. On this task, the person must decide whether strings of letters are valid English words or non-words. Consistent with the spreading activation hypothesis, Matthews and Harley showed that extraversion and arousal influence semantic priming, i.e., the speeding of lexical processing resulting from prior presentation of a semantically related word. The mechanism concerned was investigated further by simulating the priming process, using a connectionist model based on a low-level array of interconnected elementary processing units. The simulation data suggested that extraversion and arousal might influence levels of random 'noise' or fluctuation in activation within the network. Matthews and Harley (1993) suggested that a variety of tasks requiring relatively routine 'bottom–up' data encoding may be sensitive to levels of random noise, but tasks requiring voluntary, 'top–down' control of performance may be more dependent on attentional resources and strategy, and so are insensitive to extraversion × arousal interactions.

Extraversion and performance: conclusions

The data reviewed suggest that arousal theory may provide a rough basis for predicting the task- and context-sensitivity of extraversion effects on performance. However, its predictions often break down in specific task paradigms, and it may be criticised on conceptual and methodological grounds. Possibly, improvements in methodology and in understanding of neural bases for cortical arousal may provide stronger support for the theory in the future. It may also be the case that arousal theory works better within subjects than between subjects (Anderson, 1994).

Cognitively oriented researchers have made considerable progress in relating specific extraversion effects to constructs in common use in cognitive psychology, such as attentional resources and semantic networks. Connectionist models (Matthews and Harley, 1993) may eventually bridge the gap between neural and

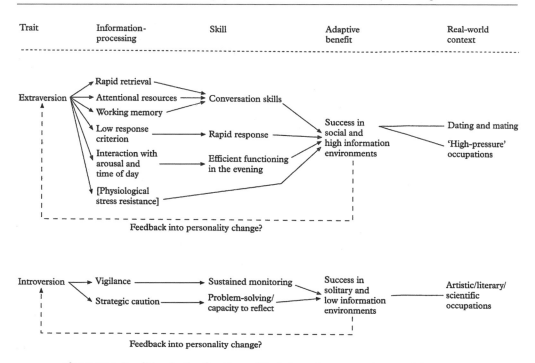

Trait	Information-processing	Skill	Adaptive benefit	Real-world context

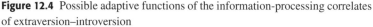

Figure 12.4 Possible adaptive functions of the information-processing correlates of extraversion–introversion

cognitive levels of description of personality effects. However, it is likely that there is no single information-processing mechanism which underlies all the various performance differences between extraverts and introverts which contribute to the overall cognitive patterning associated with the trait. Furthermore, it is hard to see why extraversion should relate to some of these mechanisms. For example, impulsiveness in performance seems broadly consonant with the general characteristics of the extravert, but it seems rather arbitrary and quirky that extraverts should benefit from high arousal in the morning, but not in the evening.

Although mapping the various associations between traits and information-processing functions is essential, the cognitive approach fails to provide a full explanation for cognitive patterning of traits (Matthews and Dorn, 1995). A deeper level of explanation is provided by taking an adaptive perspective; i.e., by asking how the information-processing correlates of extraversion help the extravert to perform extraverted behaviours successfully (see figure 12.4). For example, the superior verbal processing functions of extraversion may help the extravert in conversation with others, and facilitate the sociability which is a core aspect of the trait. The extravert's speed of retrieval of information from memory (Eysenck, 1981) is likely to give the extravert an advantage in multi-person conversation, in thinking of something to say before other participants. The apparently perplexing interactions between extraversion, arousal and time of day may support a mechanism for regulating activity during the day, which allows extraverts to function well in the evening, the time which provides most opportunity for social interaction (Matthews and Harley, 1993). The adaptive approach can accommodate psychobiological aspects of extraversion without making them central to the trait. Low arousability and insensitivity to punishment may confer a degree of physiological stress resistance on the extravert, which is advantageous in the high-stimulation environments this type of person prefers. Speculatively, the bundle of cognitive functions related to a given trait may have a causal effect on personality. We might imagine that a person who has difficulty in following a conversation and in thinking of things to say quickly, and who does not function well in the evening is likely to be disposed to introversion. Given that most cognitive functions are partially heritable, such a mechanism might allow transmission of genetic effects.

Trait anxiety, neuroticism and performance

Basic empirical findings

In this section, we consider performance correlates of trait anxiety and of neuroticism together, because of the high correlation between the two constructs. We also review work on test anxiety, which is only moderately correlated with N/trait anxiety. However, it is likely that it influences performance via the same mechanisms as the broader trait. Much of the initial work on anxiety was concerned with identifying which anxiety measures were most detrimental to performance. State anxiety is generally more harmful than trait anxiety (Spielberger, 1972), and worry is more damaging than emotionality (Morris et al., 1981) – as discussed in chapter 4, anxiety has both cognitive and emotional aspects. Task-dependence of anxiety effects was also demonstrated, with anxiety tending to improve performance on easy paired-associate learning tasks, but impairing performance when the task was difficult (Saltz and Hoehn, 1957; Eysenck, 1982; Zeidner, 1998).

Context-sensitivity has been shown in studies of both general anxiety and test anxiety. Manipulations which increase the subjects' feeling of evaluation, such as failure feedback or being informed that the task measures intelligence, tend to accentuate performance decrement in anxious individuals (Eysenck, 1982; Mueller, 1992). These results are particularly robust for test anxiety; under reassuring conditions, high test anxious subjects may actually do better than those low in test anxiety (Zeidner, 1998). An intriguing possibility is that some instances of task-dependence should actually be seen as context-sensitivity. Anxiety may impair difficult tasks not just because anxiety specifically impairs the processing which makes the task difficult, but because failure is more likely on difficult tasks, and failure increases state anxiety in high trait anxious subjects, leading to performance impairment (see Weiner and Schneider, 1971).

Eysenckian personality theory attributes effects of N (and, by implication, other related anxiety traits) to the Yerkes-Dodson Law. The emotional or 'visceral' arousal generated in high N subjects under stressful conditions also leads to increased cortical arousal. The tendency for high N/anxious subjects to perform relatively badly on difficult tasks, but (less reliably) well on easy tasks is exactly the task-dependence predicted by the Yerkes-Dodson Law. Humphreys and Revelle (1984) attribute detrimental effects of anxiety on STM to the loss of resources for this kind of task resulting from high arousal. However, arousal theory has had limited impact as an explanation for N/anxiety effects, for two reasons. First, it is the cognitive elements of anxiety, such as worry and cognitive interference (see chapter 4), which relate to performance impairment. Second, while the arousal theorist can find some support from psychophysiological studies that extraversion relates to lower arousal or arousability (see chapter 7), psychophysiological studies of anxiety and N consistently fail to show any reliable link (Fahrenberg et al., 1983). Test anxiety is unrelated to autonomic nervous system arousal even under evaluative conditions (Holroyd and Appel, 1980).

Hence, in this section, we are concerned with cognitive psychological studies of anxiety. We will focus on two aspects of the 'cognitive patterning' of anxiety: performance impairment on cognitively demanding tasks, and bias in selective attention towards threatening stimuli. We examine the evidence on task-dependence of effects which helps to choose between 'mini-theories' of specific phenomena, and we also consider the wider implications of this performance research. Some of the performance correlates of anxiety are beyond the scope of this chapter. Anxiety may, under different circumstances, relate to both caution and impulsivity in response (see Wallace, Newman and Bachorowski, 1991). Sports psychologists have carried out extensive research on the anxiety effects on the motor and cognitive–motor skills required for sports (see Tenenbaum and Bar-Eli, 1995).

Anxiety and performance impairment

In principle, it should be possible to examine anxiety effects across a range of difficult tasks varying in their exact information-processing demands. The nature of the tasks sensitive to the anxiety would then provide clues to the particular processes sensitive to impairment by anxiety. In fact, efforts of this kind have stimulated rather different theoretical views. Eysenck (1992) proposed that active, working memory is one of the cognitive functions most sensitive to anxiety; worry-related processing uses up working memory capacity. There are a variety of studies suggesting that the magnitude of anxiety-related performance deficits increases with the complexity of short-term retention tasks (e.g. Darke, 1988), or when a dual-task manipulation is used to increase demands on working memory (Ashcraft and Kirk, 2001). Worry associated with anxiety may especially impair the integrated short-term storage and processing functions central to the working memory concept. The weakness of this hypothesis is that anxiety also seems to impair tasks making few demands on working memory, such as visual signal detection tasks (Geen, 1985).

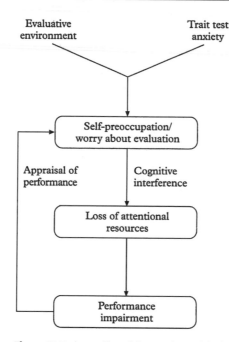

Figure 12.5 An outline of Sarason's model of test anxiety effects on performance

Alternatively, anxiety may divert attentional resources from the task at hand to worry-related processing, leading to an insufficiency of resources for the task at hand (Sarason et al., 1995). Consistent with the transactional model of stress, Sarason et al. (1995) claimed that anxious subjects worry because they appraise themselves as incompetent. Figure 12.5 illustrates Sarason's model. This hypothesis, of course, explains anxiety deficits on attentional tasks, such as slower reaction time (RT) to probe stimuli presented during performance of some other, primary task (Eysenck, 1992, p. 141), and the greater distractibility of anxious subjects (Eysenck, 1988). Relating anxiety to lack of attentional resources has the converse problem to the working memory hypothesis; i.e., it has difficulty explaining dependence of anxiety effects on high working memory demands (e.g., Darke, 1988). It might be supposed that working memory tasks are also attentionally demanding, so that anxious subjects cannot attend to the task effectively when working memory is overloaded. Attentional hypotheses have also been advanced to explain effects of other negative affect variables correlated with N. For example, depression impairs tasks requiring controlled processing, which is resource-limited, but has little effect on tasks requiring automatic processing, which requires few resources (Hartlage et al., 1993). Finally, anxiety and depression are associated with reluctance to adopt active, effortful strategies (Mueller, 1992). One attractive explanation for these diverse findings is that anxiety produces some general disruption of central executive functioning (Ashcraft and Kirk, 2001), whose exact effects on performance depend on the task and the person's choice of strategy.

Anxiety and attentional bias

Trait anxious individuals show a bias towards attending to threatening stimuli. The most robust evidence for attentional bias is provided by studies of the emotional Stroop test. By analogy with the conventional colour-word Stroop, subjects are required to name the ink colours of emotion-related words. The words may be printed in a list on large cards, or they may be singly presented on a VDU. In a pioneering study, Watts et al. (1986) presented spider phobics with several appropriately matched word-lists to colour-name. They included a list of neutral words, a list of general emotional words, and a list of words associated with spiders, such as 'web' and 'tarantula'. The spider phobics were as fast as controls on the first two lists, but their colour-naming of the spider-related words was slowed. It appeared that their selective attention was biased towards processing the meaning of the spider words, even though they were instructed to focus attention on the colour of the word, not on its semantic content. In a whole range of affective disorders, attention is biased towards words which match the patients' personal concerns (Matthews and Harley, 1996). Emotional Stroop effects have also been demonstrated in non-clinical samples of trait anxious or neurotic individuals, who tend to be slow to name anxiety-related words when in anxious states (Richards et al., 1992; Egloff and Hock, 2001).

Various other paradigms also demonstrate anxiety-related biases. In general, bias is more reliable when the task has an element of attentional selection, rather than simply requiring stimulus encoding (MacLeod, 1999). One technique for investigating selective attention is to present a pair of words, one threatening and one non-threatening, followed by a 'dot-probe' stimulus in the same position as one of the two words. Speed of response to the dot-probe indicates which of the two words was being attended. MacLeod and Mathews (1988) found that high trait anxiety students tend to focus their attention on the threatening word, especially in the week before an important examination. Another technique is to have subjects listen to homophones, words which when spoken have two alternative spellings or meanings (e.g., 'poll' and 'pole'). Eysenck, MacLeod and Mathews (1987) had subjects write down homophones, forcing them to select one of the alternatives. When one alternative was threatening (e.g., 'die' vs 'dye'), trait anxious individuals tended to write down the threatening word. Box 12.2 describes a recent study that links anxiety to a bias in thinking – making predictive inferences from sentences.

Selective attention is controlled by various, distinct mechanisms. Recent work in this area has tried to tease apart some of the different processing components that might be especially sensitive to anxiety. We give one example here. One issue is whether anxiety affects the shifting of attention towards threatening stimuli, as they appear in the visual field, or, alternatively, whether anxiety influences the *disengagement* or withdrawal of attention from a threat stimulus, following attentional focusing. These two mechanisms are distinguished neuropsychologically (Derryberry and Reed, 1997). Fox et al. (2001) used an attentional cueing paradigm

Box 12.2 Jumping to conclusions? Anxiety and predictive inference

When reading or hearing a descriptive passage of text, people form inferences about how the episode described will finish. We might expect that anxious individuals would show a bias towards expecting more negative events. Calvo and Castillo (2001) tested this prediction using a *predictive inference* paradigm. That is, subjects read initial context sentences liable to generate an expectancy, followed by a target word that was congruent or incongruent with expectation. In addition, the context might describe a threatening or non-threatening event. For example, the context might describe a van approaching a child running into the street (threatening), followed by a sentence beginning *The van **ran over** . . .* (congruent) or *The van **avoided** . . .* (incongruent).

In a series of studies, Calvo and Castillo (2001) assessed the latency of naming the target word (i.e., the bold words in the example). In general, a predictive context facilitated naming speed, consistent with the idea that people form inferences as they read material. In addition, trait anxiety related to greater predictive facilitating of naming when the material read was threatening, implying that anxious persons are especially prone to infer negative outcomes to threatening events. The study is a nice example of how the anxiety-related bias towards threatening cognitions shown in highly artificial paradigms also occurs in a setting closer to natural language processing. It suggests that trait anxious persons may be liable to jump to unduly negative conclusions when reading or listening to others.

Calvo and Castillo (2001) also varied the time delay between context and subsequent word. They found the trait anxiety effect only at the relatively long delay of 1050 ms, but not at shorter delays of 50 ms and 550 ms. These data suggest that the bias shown by trait anxious subjects reflects a voluntary, strategic process, rather than an automatic bias, consistent with the S-REF theory of anxiety (Wells and Matthews, 1994). Calvo has reached similar conclusions about other linguistic biases, for example interpreting ambiguous words (Calvo, Eysenck and Castillo, 1997).

to test whether these two processes were differentially sensitive to anxiety. In one condition, they found that anxiety did not influence how effectively a threatening word drew attention to a location on a VDU screen. In a second condition, they found that anxious subjects were slow to disengage attention from a threat stimulus, when they were required to move the focus of attention to another stimulus presented at a different location. This and other studies suggest that anxiety is associated not so much with the initial focus of attention on threatening stimuli, but with a tendency to 'lock onto' threatening stimuli after they have been focused upon (Derryberry and Reed, 1997).

There has also been interest in demonstrating differences between the processing biases associated with anxiety and depression, both constructs closely related to N. It has been argued that selection biases in attention are restricted to anxiety, and are not found in depressed individuals (Williams et al., 1988). Conversely, mood-congruent biases in memory, in which distressed individuals show better recall of negative material, appear to be more robust in depressed subjects than anxious subjects. However, much of the evidence concerns clinical patient groups, and studies of non-clinical samples provide conflicting evidence (Wells and Matthews, 1994). Counter-examples to the Williams et al. hypothesis are demonstrations of the emotional Stroop effect in students with mild trait depression (Gotlib and McCann, 1984), and enhanced recall for negative self-referent trait descriptors in socially anxious subjects (Claeys, 1989). Neuroticism is associated with a similar memory bias (Martin, Ward and Clark, 1983).

Differing explanations for anxiety-related bias have been advanced by processing stage theory (Williams et al., 1988), hypervigilance theory (Eysenck, 1992) and Self-Referent Executive Function (SREF) theory (Wells and Matthews, 1994). Williams et al. (1988) proposed that anxiety affects early stages of processing associated with the automatic, unconscious encoding of information, whereas depression biases later stages during which consciously recognised stimuli are elaborated. Hence, anxiety tends to influence selective attention, whereas depression influences memory tasks dependent upon an elaborated memory trace, such as explicit recall. The most striking success of the theory comes from studies showing anxiety-related bias on Stroop stimuli so heavily masked the subject cannot consciously perceive them (Bradley et al., 1995). Wells and Matthews (1994) provided a critique of the theory which discusses evidence that anxiety influences voluntary rather than involuntary control of attention. They also question the methodological adequacy of masked Stroop studies; it is remarkably difficult to ensure that there is no 'leakage' of information from subliminal stimuli into consciousness. It is possible also that there are anxiety-related biases in both voluntary and involuntary attentional processes: Mathews and Mackintosh (1998) have presented a sophisticated theory of threat-sensitivity along these lines.

The other two theories suggest that there are qualitative differences in information-processing in high and low anxiety individuals. Eysenck's (1992) hypervigilance theory proposed that trait anxious subjects, particularly when high in state anxiety, tend to scan the environment for threat to an excessive degree. When a threat is detected, they tend to 'lock onto' the threat stimulus, and narrow the focus of attention. In contrast to Williams et al. (1988), Eysenck emphasised the role of voluntary control processes, in addition to pre-attentive bias; hypervigilance is driven in part by the person's secondary appraisal of personal threat vulnerability. However, the theory does not distinguish in detail involuntary and voluntary mechanisms for bias.

The final theory (Wells and Matthews, 1994; Matthews and Wells, 1999) identified emotional distress with a cognitive-attentional syndrome generated by a 'Self Referent Executive Function' (SREF), as described in chapter 9. This is a mode of controlled processing in which attention is self-focused, and processing effort is diverted to worry and ruminative emotion-focused coping. The syndrome includes the activation of strategies for allocation of attention which prioritise processing of threat-related stimuli, i.e., the person monitors for threats congruent with their personal concerns. The spider phobic is vigilant for spiders, people with social anxiety focus on the impression they are making on others, and so forth. Hence, attentional bias reflects the anxious or distressed person's choice of coping strategies for dealing with threat. One of the distinctive features of the theory is that it sees anxiety-related bias as driven by the person's voluntary choice of coping strategy (Matthews and Wells, 1996). Matthews and Harley (1996) presented a connectionist model of the emotional Stroop effect which demonstrates in detail how strategic mechanisms might function to bias response to this task.

Anxiety and performance: conclusions

As in the case of extraversion, cognitively oriented research has contributed much to providing an integrated perspective on how anxiety and neuroticism affect performance. Research is moving on from linking anxiety to rather general aspects of performance such as working memory and selective attention, to discriminating specific mechanisms that may be especially sensitive to anxiety, such as disengagement from threat. Increasingly, work of this kind is also linking processing functions to brain subsystems (Matthews, Derryberry and Siegle, 2000). Fine-grained description of the cognitive patterning of anxiety is essential, but leaves open the question of why anxiety should relate to some processing functions but not others. One view is that high trait anxiety is essentially a disorder that may be generated by maladaptive biases in key processes for handling threatening events. Eysenck (1992) suggested that the attentional bias associated with anxiety renders the individual susceptible to clinical anxiety disorders. Matthews and Dorn (1995) proposed an alternative view, that anxiety and N relate to an adaptive tradeoff (see figure 12.6). There may be advantages to being high in neuroticism when the environment is threatening but the threat stimuli are subtle or disguised, so that active monitoring for threat is required. Vigilance for threats may also to serve to maintain motivation in the absence of any immediate threat. However, high N also has clear adaptive costs, with respect to impaired performance on demanding tasks in stressful environments. Conversely, the low N person is particularly well suited to maintaining task-directed attention and performance under stress.

Personality and intelligence

It is only because of a recently conceived research field that a book on personality must consider the relationships between personality and intelligence. These two pillars of differential psychology have long stood separately but, with

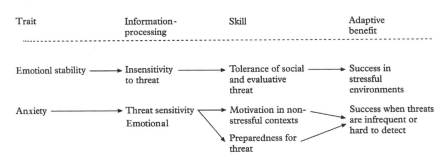

Figure 12.6 Possible adaptive benefits of emotional stability and anxiety

the increased interest in interactionist models of behaviour, it has occurred to trait theorists and others that the two concepts might usefully be studied in tandem to see whether there are associations and interactions that account for shared or supplementary variance, respectively, when they are used to predict human behaviour. Three books are partly or entirely devoted to this field of enquiry (Van Heck et al., 1993; Sternberg and Ruzgis, 1994; Saklofske and Zeidner, 1995). There are several types of relationship between personality traits and intelligence that may be of interest. First, personality may influence *performance* of intelligence tests, through its effects on attentional and memory functions. It is sometimes said that intelligence tests reflect how well a person *can* perform (maximal performance), whereas personality measures indicate how a person *typically* performs, in a given context, which may fall short of their intellectual potential (Ackerman and Heggestad, 1997). For example, anxiety may depress test scores through distracting attention from the task at hand, as discussed above. The sensitivity of intelligence tests to interactive effects of extraversion and arousal (e.g. Revelle et al., 1980) may also represent the effects of these variables on attention. Hence, personality and intelligence may influence behaviours interactively: optimal performance may depend on both underlying intellectual aptitude, and personality factors that allow that aptitude to be translated into effective behaviour. Eysenck (1994a, 1995) has urged researchers to follow up some of the more interesting possibilities for the empirical interaction of personality and intelligence: that personality variables can affect performance indicators on cognitive tests; that personality might affect cognitive performance and achievement differently at different stages of childhood; that introversion–extraversion might affect cognitive style; and that neuroticism has an effect when tests are done under stress.

Second, personality may be (modestly) related to underlying intellectual *competence;* perhaps certain traits facilitate or interfere with the acquisition of intellectual aptitudes. Block and Kremen (1996) developed a scale for ego-resiliency, a trait representing the capacity to exercise self-control effectively. More effective self-regulation would be expected to correlate with more effective acquisition of intellectual skills, and the ego-resiliency scale does indeed correlate with IQ. The role of self-regulation was demonstrated in a series of studies summarised by

Chiu, Hong and Dweck (1994). Equally bright groups of children who were either mastery-oriented (seeing problems as a challenge and persisting through difficulty) or helpless (tending to self-denigration, negative affect and giving up in difficulty) showed clear differences in problem-solving performance after failure. During 'impossible' problems mastery-oriented children resolved to concentrate better and come up with new strategies for solution, whereas helpless children doubted their own ability, became bored and engaged in irrelevant thoughts. In chapter 13, we will look at another approach to the overlap of personality and ability: the concept of 'emotional intelligence' as individual differences in competencies for recognising and managing emotion.

Third, traits may relate not so much to general intelligence as to more specific aspects of cognitive function that straddle the ability and personality domains. Personality may affect styles of cognition and learning (Furnham and Heaven, 1999). For example, the cognitive style of field-dependence is defined by sensitivity to contextual factors when making perceptual judgements. Crozier (1997) reported that field-dependence is related to agreeableness (warmth and affection), whereas field-independent individuals tend to be independent and manipulative.

We have already discussed how traits may influence information-processing functions, such as focused attention, that may play some modest role in intelligence test performance. Hence, in the remainder of this section, we will look, first, at the psychometric overlap between personality and ability traits, and, second, at creativity, as a somewhat specialised cognitive ability that may relate to both personality and intelligence.

Empirical associations between personality and intelligence

Broadly speaking, there are no simple, sizeable correlations between intelligence test scores and any of the major personality dimensions (Eysenck, 1994a; Brebner and Stough, 1995). Ackerman and Heggestad's (1997) meta-analytic review of the correlations between ten aspects of ability and twenty different dimensions/facets of personality found few consistent associations with coefficients greater than ± 1. There were small (<1) positive associations between ability and extraversion, and negative associations (<0.2) between ability and psychoticism. Openness was somewhat more predictive of ability, correlating at about 0.3 with general intelligence. However, O was more strongly related to the acquired cognitive skills described as 'crystallised intelligence' than to the person's basic aptitude for abstract reasoning or 'fluid intelligence' (Goff and Ackerman, 1992). Similarly, O correlated at 0.28 with measures of achievement and specific topic knowledge (primarily in the arts: Rolfhus and Ackerman, 1996). Austin and Deary (e.g., Austin et al., 2002) have conducted several studies using large samples of British respondents that investigated the Eysenck personality traits. Generally, these traits were only weakly related to intelligence. For example, using a scale for the Eysenck traits, Austin et al. (2002) reported significant correlations of -0.15 and -0.19 between intelligence and N, and significant correlations of -0.09 and -0.14

between intelligence and P. In other samples, they confirmed that Openness was the strongest Big Five predictor of intelligence, with a correlation of about 0.35.

Austin, Deary and Gibson (1997) pointed out that there may be more subtle associations between personality and ability. For example, there might be non-linear relationships, or the correlations between personality traits might vary with ability level. Austin et al. (2002) failed to find any curvilinear personality–ability relationships, but they did establish that P and N appear to be positively correlated only in low intelligence individuals. It is unclear why personality structure should vary in this way (though see Austin et al., 1997), although it is possible that low intelligence persons have difficulties understanding some of the P and N items, which blurs the distinction between them.

How could associations between personality and intellectual competence come about? The possible causal mechanisms are not well understood, but one possibility is that personality influences the 'investment' of fluid intelligence in learning that establishes more crystallised skills (Cattell, 1971). Ackerman (1996) has developed a theory that focuses on how the person acquires knowledge of topic areas such as science, literature and arts. Intelligence is the primary influence on successful acquisition of specific intellectual skills and knowledge, but personality also plays a role via its effects on motivation. We have already discussed how personality may affect persistence following an initial failure (Chiu et al., 1994), for example. Openness is associated with motivations to engage in intellectual pursuits, which may explain why O correlates with crystallised intelligence and some aspects of knowledge (e.g. Rolfhus and Ackerman, 1996). There may be some dynamic interplay between personality and intelligence, in that successful mastery of intellectual skills might also promote intellectual interests and higher Openness.

Creativity and the personality–intelligence interface

Creativity is recognised as a broad ability distinct from general intelligence. It is assessed by tests such as thinking of many uses for objects (e.g., a brick). In cognitive-psychological terms, such tests are believed to reflect processes for retrieving information from long-term memory (M. W. Eysenck, 1982). It might seem a little simple-minded to assess creativity by such tests, but there is evidence that people who are creative in real life perform better on the tests (Eysenck, 1995). Of course, other abilities, such as being able to discriminate good and bad ideas, are also likely to be important in real-life creativity. Eysenck (1995) conceived of creative achievement as being influenced by fluid and crystallised intelligence, particular skills, environmental influences and personality variables such as internal motivation, confidence, nonconformity and originality. According to Zeidner (1995, p. 307), 'creativity holds an intermediate position between intelligence and personality, because creative productions imply both an *ability* to think fluently and flexibly and *inclination* to do so'.

Several personality factors appear to be implicated in creativity. A popular idea is that creative genius is linked to madness, and analyses of biographical material have reported rates of psychosis of around 30 per cent in great novelists, poets and painters (Karlsson, 1970). However, actual psychosis may depress both creativity and intelligence (Eysenck, 1995; Zeidner, 1995), and, as Eysenck (1995) indicated, creativity may be associated with pathological traits kept in check by positive attributes such as ego strength, mental flexibility and insight. Eysenck saw psychoticism as the most important trait for creativity. For example, Woody and Claridge (1977) found correlations of 0.3 to 0.4 between psychoticism and the number of uses the subject could think of for everyday objects, and larger associations (0.6 to 0.7) between psychoticism and the 'uniqueness' of the uses. In addition, highly creative individuals have high psychometric IQ test scores on average, and there appears to be a modest positive association (about 0.3) between intelligence test scores and productive creativity (that of artists, scientists, writers, etc.) and laboratory tests of creativity (Barron and Harrington, 1981). Across many fields of creative achievement Barron and Harrington (1981) found a core set of personality factors that were shared by creative individuals, as follows: 'high evaluation of aesthetic qualities in experience, broad interests, attraction to complexity, high energy, independence of judgement, autonomy, intuition, self-confidence, ability to resolve antinomies or to accommodate apparently opposite or conflicting traits in one's self-concept, and, finally, a firm sense of self as creative'.

In terms of the five factor model, real-life creativity, in a business setting, has been linked to openness to experience, neuroticism, extraversion, and low conscientiousness (Gelade, 1997). McCrae (1987) hypothesised that creativity was principally related to the openness dimension, and tested this in a samples ranging from sixty-five to 267 from the Baltimore Longitudinal Study of Aging. He found highly significant and consistent correlations of around 0.4 between scores on the personality trait of openness to experience (whether self-, peer-, or spouse-rated, and whether assessed by questionnaire or by adjective checklist) and total scores on a set of tests of divergent thinking. Other five factor model traits were correlated at near-zero levels with divergent thinking, and McCrae commented that 'creativity is uniquely related to openness to experience'. However, he did allow that different personality dimensions might come into play within different groups – creative painters are high in psychoticism, for example (Goetz and Goetz, 1979) – and that tests of creativity might correlate with other dimensions, such as extraversion and conscientiousness, when the test instructions change. Indeed, extraversion may influence attentional factors that promote effective test performance. Matthews (1996) found interactive effects of extraversion and arousal on creativity similar to those found with other attentional tasks; extraversion correlated with creativity test performance under high arousal. However, research on creativity has proved difficult because of the uncertain link between tests of divergent thinking and creativity in real life (Zeidner, 1995). As long as the outcome variable – in this case creativity as a trait and creative output – proves difficult to operationalise, the research will be less than definitive.

Conclusions

1. Both laboratory and real-world studies of performance contribute to establishing the predictive validity of personality traits. However, correlations between personality traits and performance vary with both the nature of the task performed, and with the context for performance. For example, a trait may be associated with better performance in a relaxing context, but poorer performance in a stressful context. This chapter focused especially on extraversion–introversion and neuroticism (including trait anxiety) as influences on performance.

2. There are different theoretical approaches to understanding why traits correlate with performance. Biological theories traditionally link traits to general aspects of brain functioning such as arousal, but they have difficulty in explaining why personality effects on performance depend on the precise information-processing demands of the task. Cognitive theories assume that performance is controlled by many distinct component processes, which may be differentially related to any given trait. Hence, each trait is associated with a cognitive patterning, a profile of processing strengths and weaknesses, as well as some processes that are not influenced by the trait. Recent cognitive neuroscience work is beginning to link the information-processing correlates of traits to specific brain systems controlling attention, memory and motor response.

3. Extraverts differ from introverts on various performance indices. Extraverts are relatively good at divided attention, verbal short-term recall, retrieval from memory and speech production, but relatively poor at vigilance, long-term memory and reflective problem-solving. Extraverts are also sometimes found to be more behaviourally impulsive than introverts. On some tasks, extraverts tend to perform better in high arousal contexts, whereas introverts benefit from low levels of stimulation. However, time of day also moderates these effects. Arousal theory provides an explanation for this context-dependence, by proposing that introverts tend to be over-aroused, whereas extraverts are suboptimally aroused. However, this explanation fails to explain the task-dependence of extravert–introvert differences. The cognitive-psychological approach allows us to link extraversion to a variety of specific information-processing mechanisms, but does not provide the 'big picture' of how these processing differences may shape personality in real-life settings. We may need an adaptive perspective on cognition, that sees the processing characteristics of the extravert, for example, as preparing the individual to handle high-pressure social environments.

4. Neuroticism and trait anxiety influence both the efficiency and the qualitative style of performance. Trait anxiety tends to be associated with poorer performance on demanding tasks. The mechanism for this effect appears to be cognitive: worries about the task interfere with performance by overloading attention or working memory. Anxiety is also associated with a bias in selective attention, i.e., sensitivity to threat-related stimuli or sources of stimuli, as

well as similar biases in judgement and reasoning. There are several, alternate cognitive explanations for enhanced processing of threat in anxious persons. Anxiety may be associated with an involuntary, automatic bias in threat processing, or with a use of voluntary strategies for monitoring stimuli for threat content. As with extraversion–introversion, individual differences in neuroticism/anxiety may reflect different adaptive specialisations. The low N person is equipped to function well under high levels of stress and cognitive demand, but the high N person may benefit when environmental threats are subtle or disguised, requiring high levels of vigilance for threat.

5. In general, ability factors such as general intelligence are a stronger influence on performance than personality traits. Psychometrically, traits are only weakly correlated with abilities, although openness correlates at about 0.30 with 'crystallised' intelligence (i.e., acquired intellectual skills). However, there may be more subtle interactions between personality and intelligence. Personality may influence performance on intelligence tests, for example, in arousing or dearousing contexts. Personality traits related to effective self-regulation may facilitate the development of ability. Traits may be related to cognitive qualities and styles that straddle the ability and personality domains, such as field-independence. One such quality may be creativity, in the sense of fluency and flexibility in generating ideas. High creativity is linked especially to the psychoticism trait, and also to openness and other traits. Creativity in real life may require both the mental flexibility and originality associated with psychoticism, as well as self-confidence and self-control that facilitate translating ideas into actual creative products such as literature or art.

Further reading

Matthews, G. (ed.) (1997) *Cognitive science perspectives on personality and emotion.* Amsterdam: Elsevier.

Saklofske, D. H. and Zeidner, M. (eds.) (1995) *International handbook of personality and intelligence.* New York: Plenum.

Zeidner, M. (1998) *Test anxiety: the state of the art.* New York: Plenum.

13 Applications of personality assessment

In this chapter, we consider the practical utility of personality assessment. How can we use the information provided by a personality questionnaire to help the individual or society? Personality is assessed in a variety of different contexts, including clinical, educational and occupational settings. In the first two applications, the aims of the assessment are often idiographic. The aim is to understand the unique personal circumstances that contribute to mental disorder or problem behaviour in the classroom. Personality assessment using standardised questionnaires is typically an adjunct to less formalised investigation; the trait scores of the client are themselves interpreted on the basis of clinical judgement. As we have seen in chapter 11, the typical clinical approach to diagnosis may underestimate the nomothetic predictive power of traits. In industrial and commercial settings, by contrast, there is more interest in using trait measures as a direct basis for decision-making, especially in selecting job applicants, although personality may also be treated idiographically, in career counselling for example.

This chapter is organised as follows. First, we review some principles of personality assessment, focusing on the applied issues confronting the practitioner: the choice of a trait questionnaire, evaluating the adequacy of questionnaires, and using trait information in professional practice. Next, we review clinical and developmental uses of trait assessment, before turning to organisational applications. We survey the validity of trait measures as predictors of performance and desirable behaviours in the workplace, supporting use of questionnaires in personnel selection. Additional applications include vocational and career guidance, and stress management. Finally, we will look at a new approach to assessment, the measurement of 'emotional intelligence', that has attracted much attention among both organisational psychologists and the general public.

Principles of trait assessment

In this section, we consider some of the challenges facing the practitioner working on personality-related issues. The outline here draws upon several more comprehensive accounts of personality assessment (Kline, 1993; Anastasi and Urbina, 1997; Lanyon and Goodstein, 1997). We assume what is called in clinical psychology the scientist-practitioner model. This means that, as well as practical skills, the applied psychologist has sufficient basic science training to formulate and test hypotheses, or to evaluate how well published studies conform to good scientific practice. Such a person may be called upon to deal with three related issues:

1 *Choice of questionnaire(s).* There is a bewildering array of published trait questionnaires that are potentially relevant to applied problems. How does the practitioner choose and evaluate the most useful instrument for his or her purposes? Personality questionnaires range from those that aim to assess general qualities, such as measures of the Big Five, to those that measure more narrowly drawn traits that may be critical in certain situations. There are no definite rules for choosing between the different questionnaires, but we will set out some of the issues involved.

2 *Evaluation of questionnaires.* Having chosen some questionnaires to evaluate, there are some well-established benchmarks that may used for comparing instruments. The first of these is reliability, referring to whether repeated measurements will give similar questionnaire scores (see chapter 1). However, a questionnaire may be reliable for the wrong reasons. In particular, it may assess some trivial response bias, such as a tendency to always answer 'Yes' to questions, than some genuine trait. The practitioner must be confident that scores are not seriously contaminated by biases of this kind. Finally, the questionnaire must assess some meaningful and relevant psychological construct: it must be valid. We will explore the evaluation of validity in more detail.

3 *Practical issues.* Even if the questionnaire is reliable, valid and relevant, using the trait information available for practical purposes is still a non-trivial task. We will consider two applied topics: use of questionnaire scores for practical decision-making, and ethical and legal issues in personality trait assessment.

Choice of questionnaire

Naturally, the practitioner needs an instrument relevant to the applied problem. For example, the personnel manager may need to assess a trait that influences job performance, or the clinician may be interested in assessing traits that will help with diagnosis of mental disorders. Beyond informal judgements of which traits seem most relevant to the problem, there are several choices to be made.

Comprehensive or targeted assessment?

The first decision is whether to assess some major domain of personality, or whether to target some more specific traits of particular relevance. The former case suggests use of a general instrument like the NEO-PI-R, 16PF or CPI, or questionnaires that aim to provide comprehensive assessment in some particular field. Clinicians may use the MMPI or MMPI-2, for example, to measure abnormal traits, and questionnaires such as the OPQ, discussed in chapter 1, are geared towards traits relevant to the workplace. The advantage of comprehensive assessment is that it samples a full range of constructs, and so it is especially useful in exploratory research. The disadvantage is that it may be uneconomic, in measuring constructs that may not be relevant. It may be more cost-effective to target a small number of critical traits for assessment, provided that previous research has established which traits are relevant, and which are irrelevant.

General or contextualised measurement? A further decision is whether to measure general attributes of personality, or attributes that refer to typical feelings and behaviour within some specified context. For example, sensation seeking can be measured either as a general trait, or using questionnaires that ask about enjoyment of danger in specific situations, such as vehicle driving. How narrowly the 'context' is to be defined is a further issue. We have seen in previous chapters that anxiety may be assessed as a general trait, or as anxiety proneness in broadly defined threatening contexts such as social and physical threat (Endler and Kocovski, 2001; see chapter 4), or in more narrowly defined contexts such as being tested, solving maths problems or working with computers (e.g., Zeidner, 1998). The advantage of general trait measures is that they allow findings to be integrated with the large bodies of relevant data and theory. The disadvantage is that contextualised measures may be more predictive of criteria, as we saw in the case of self-efficacy scales in chapter 8. However, the more specialised the scale, the more difficult it may be to interpret outcomes of studies within some more general theoretical framework.

Broad or narrow traits. A related choice concerns whether it is better to assess broad traits such as the Big Five, or narrower, 'midlevel' traits. Again, use of broad traits facilitates interpretation of data, and comparisons with other studies, but narrower traits may sometimes be more predictive. Of course, instruments like the NEO-PI-R, 16PF and OPQ provide both levels of analysis, although, as we noted in chapter 1, it is unlikely that any single instrument provides complete coverage of lower-level traits. When midlevel traits are preferred, it is desirable that something is known about their overlap with broader traits. For example, with traits related to stress vulnerability (see chapter 9), it is often unclear how much their predictive validity derives from the overlap with the broad trait of neuroticism, and how much is unique to the particular trait.

Evaluation of questionnaires

As discussed in chapter 1, it is essential that the questionnaire possesses good reliability, stability and validity. If it has subscales, their differentiation should be supported by factor analysis. Evaluation of internal consistency (i.e., reliability) and stability over time is straightforward: table 13.1 summarises definitions and techniques for calculating reliability. Generally, researchers take a reliability value of 0.7 as the minimum for research use, although 0.8 or more is preferable. Individual assessment requires a reliability of 0.9 or better. Determining factor structure may raise technical issues such as the nature of the factor structure to be used,

Table 13.1 *Definitions of reliability and stability*

General definition of *reliability*

The accuracy with which the test measures whatever it is that the test is measuring, so that
   measurements are *repeatable*.

Parallel form reliability

The correlation between two alternate or parallel forms of the test.

Split-half reliability

The correlation between the sums of the odd- and even-numbered items on the test.

Internal consistency

Estimate of reliability derived from inter-correlations of test items. Cronbach's alpha (α)
   is a common statistic used for this purpose.

Stability

The consistency of test scores over time: also called test–retest reliability. Time interval
   may be varied from 'immediate' to many years. Trait measures should show stability
   across periods of months and years.

although, if the factor structure is robust, choice of analytic method should have
minor effects only.

   Assessment of validity may be a little more complex, as we will now discuss.
Table 13.2 unpacks some different aspects of validity. As previously discussed,
the key element of validity is criterion validity – the ability of the questionnaire
to predict meaningful criteria such as emotional states, abnormal behaviours and
job performance. We may distinguish concurrent (present) and predictive (future)
validity as two different aspects of criterion validity. Both may be useful: the
clinician may want an index of current behavioural disturbance, while the personnel
manager needs to predict future job performance, following training. In any case,
the validity coefficient expresses how strongly the trait predicts the criterion. As
we discuss below, the trait may not be of much practical use if the coefficient is too
low. It is also important to establish whether the validity coefficient generalises
across different contexts; it is dangerous to assume that a single study establishes
validity, even if the coefficient is high.

   Face validity is the least important of the remaining aspects of validity, although lack of face validity may sometimes alienate respondents. Content validity
is especially important in the early stages of research, before the development
of a detailed nomological network (see chapter 1) that demonstrates the meaning of the construct from its relationships to other indices and behavioural
outcomes.

   Convergent and divergent validity are usually considered together. For example,
an extraversion–introversion scale should correlate moderately highly with related
constructs such as sociability and assertiveness (convergent validity): if it fails to do
so, the scale is probably not measuring extraversion. It should also show only small
correlations with other constructs that are known to be distinct from extraversion,

Table 13.2 *Definitions of validity*

General definition of *validity*

The extent to which the test measures some meaningful construct: i.e., the extent to which test scores are scientifically informative or practically useful.

Criterion validity. The extent to which the test correlates with some independent index believed to be related to the construct.

Concurrent validity. Criterion validity with respect to an index measured at the same time as the test is administered.

Predictive validity. Criterion validity with respect to an index measured at some future time, following test administration.

Validity coefficient. Size of the correlation between test and criterion (may be corrected for statistical artifacts).

Validity generalisation. The extent to which validity coefficients remain similar in different samples and situations.

Face validity. The extent to which test items superficially correspond to the construct.

Content validity. The extent to which test items are representative samplings of the construct.

Convergent validity. The extent to which the test correlates with other related scales.

Divergent validity. The extent to which the test is independent from other unrelated scales.

Incremental validity. The extent to which the test predicts criteria with other relevant constructs controlled.

Construct validity. The extent to which the test measures some scientifically meaningful construct – a somewhat ill-defined quality dependent on progressive research efforts.

such as neuroticism and intelligence (divergent validity). Establishing divergent validity is especially important in developing scales for new constructs, which, all too often, turn out to be similar to existing ones. Incremental validity is related to divergent validity. It refers to tests of whether the scale predicts criteria if other constructs correlated with both the scale and the criterion are statistically controlled, typically using partial correlation or multiple regression. If we had a new scale for stress vulnerability, incremental validity would be demonstrated if the scale predicted anxiety symptoms with neuroticism and extraversion controlled, for example.

Finally, as discussed in chapter 1, construct validity refers to the often elusive theoretical basis for the trait, and its psychological meaning. The relevance of theory to the practitioner varies according to the nature of the practical problem. Sometimes, prediction proceeds on an *actuarial* basis. That is, if we know that a battery of scales predicts performance on some job (with good validity generalisation), we can use the scales for personnel selection without too much concern about theory. However, this approach is often negated by the existence of *moderator* variables, that is, additional variables that influence the association between the trait scale and the criterion. For example, as we will discuss, correlations between traits and job performance depend critically on factors such as the nature of

Table 13.3 *Some common response styles*

Response style	Description	Countermeasures
Acquiescence	Tendency to answer questions positively, whatever the content	Balance items relating positively and negatively to the construct.
Deviance	Unusual, atypical responses	Avoid items with highly skewed response distributions. Indices of deviance may be indicators of psychopathology.
Extreme responding	Tendency to pick extreme response categories (e.g. 'strongly agree')	Correct using mathematical models.

the work, the stressfulness of the work environment, and the level of stimulation or arousal it affords. Although we can try to map out the influence of moderator variables empirically, prediction is enhanced when we can use theory to determine when a trait is or is not likely to be predictive.

Response bias

A general problem with personality questionnaires is that response may be influenced by various biases that do not relate to the construct the questionnaire aims to measure. Here, we will divide these biases into three types. *Response styles* describe biases in using the multiple-choice scales on the questionnaire that are unrelated to the actual content of items, such as tending to endorse items rather than reject them. *Impression management* describes deliberate attempts to present oneself as possessing, or not possessing, particular qualities, either by outright lying (faking) or by a more benign massaging of the truth. *Self-deception* refers to largely unconscious biasing of response to present a (usually) more favourable self-impression, for example by picking more socially desirable response alternatives.

Response styles. Table 13.3 summarises some common response styles, such as acquiescence (tending to answer 'yes') and extreme responding (tending to answer 'definitely' rather than 'somewhat'). On the whole, response styles are considered as a relatively minor nuisance, and, as the table shows, careful questionnaire design can minimise distortion of trait scores. However, in some cases confounding of trait scores with response style can lead to spurious correlations: in these cases, mathematical modelling may contribute to debiasing measurement of traits (Matthews and Oddy, 1997; Austin et al., 1998).

Impression management. In the formative years of personality assessment research, social desirability was conceptualised as a response set, and hence something of a nuisance. The tendency for individuals to present themselves favourably was detected empirically by using social desirability scales that appeared to measure stable dispositions (e.g., Crowne and Marlowe, 1960). Eysenck (e.g., 1967) introduced the 'Lie' scale that aimed to catch the liar out in refusing to admit to common faults, such as failing to keep promises. The researcher could then obtain a more valid estimate of other traits by statistically controlling for social desirability. Paulhus (1986) pointed out that self-presentation is partly deliberate and conscious, and partly unconscious, and these two aspects of social desirability should be distinguished. He suggests that deliberate manipulation of self-image, including lying, should be described as 'impression management', and distinguished from 'self-deception'. In a factor-analytic study, he found that traditional social desirability measures loaded on a self-deception factor, whereas scales linked more directly to deceit defined an 'impression management' factor. Dissimulation is an aspect of lack of integrity, which may relate to Conscientiousness (Ones, Viswesvaran and Schmidt, 1993). We should not be too surprised that respondents indulge in impression management, given the social psychological literature (see chapter 8) that describes how people are motivated to maintain and communicate a consistent self-image.

In occupational settings, impression management is directed towards presentation of the traits the job applicant thinks are required for the job. For example, an applicant for a sales position is unlikely to want to appear introverted, or a prospective marine timid. The extent to which impression management is a problem in practice may be investigated through experimental manipulations, such as instructing subjects to 'fake good', i.e., to present themselves as well as possible. Such instructions do have an effect. A meta-analytic review (Stanush, 1996) concluded that faking instructions change personality scores, especially Conscientiousness. However, trait scores also become more highly correlated with lie scales or social desirability measures, suggesting a test for the occurrence of faking in the sample as a whole. Other studies have explored the critical issue of whether impression management actually influences validity. In fact, although deliberate faking lowers validity in experimental studies, it appears to have relatively modest effects in real-life employment settings (Barrick and Mount, 1996; Stanush, 1996; Arthur, Woehr and Graziano, 2001), perhaps because the respondent fears being detected as a liar. Nevertheless, faking remains a concern, especially as fakers are liable to obtain especially high scores on desirable traits, and will thus be selected first for employment (Arthur et al., 2001).

Practical solutions include requiring additional corroborative evidence for high scorers (e.g., from interview) and/or concurrent measurement of social desirability, although the latter technique may penalise job applicants who are exceptionally ethical and genuinely have few faults (Arthur et al., 2001). Another technique sometimes used is forced-choice response, where items require the respondent to choose between equally attractive or unattractive, alternatives, e.g. 'My most important quality is being (a) confident or (b) honest.' Unfortunately, forced-choice questionnaires introduce statistical dependence between scales, because acceptance of one set of qualities implies rejection of others. Items similar to the example would lead to an artifactual negative correlation between confidence and honesty, for example. This undesirable statistical property leads to many problems in applied use (Bartram, 1996; Matthews and Oddy, 1997), although some practitioners feel that the advantages of forced choice may sometimes outweigh the disadvantages

Table 13.4 *Two kinds of self-favouring bias identified by Paulhus and John (1998)*

Type of bias	Value	Motive	Self-deceptive mechanism	Self-favouring bias on
Exaggeration of self-worth	Agency	need for Power	Egoistic bias	Extraversion Openness
Conformity to social norms	Communion	need for Approval	Moralistic bias	Agreeableness Conscientiousness

(Baron, 1996). Saville and Holdsworth, for example, publish a forced-choice version of the OPQ (see chapter 1), for use in situations where pressures to dissimulate are high.

In clinical contexts, the opposite problem applies. People may be motivated to fake disorders, for example to avoid criminal responsibility or to avoid military service. Again, there is evidence that normal individuals can at least sometimes succeed in faking disorders (Lanyon and Goodstein, 1997). Thus, questionnaires often include scales that aim to detect deliberate malingering or faking of psychiatric symptoms. These scales, included in both MMPI and NEO-PI-R, are quite successful in differentiating genuine clinical patients from normal subjects instructed to fake pathology (Berry et al., 2001; Bagby et al., 2002).

Self-deception. People are also prone to 'self-deception': attributing to themselves desirable characteristics they do not actually possess, like being invariably honest. People may also be defensive, in denying that they possess unattractive qualities. Moderate self-deception may even be healthy in promoting a positive self-image. However, narcissistic individuals appear to have a highly exaggerated sense of self-worth, that grades into personality disorder (Paulhus and John, 1998). These authors argue that self-deceptive traits are best treated as substantive personality traits that may be investigated in their own right as possible predictors of applied criteria. They may also partially overlap with the Big Five; narcissistic people tend to be disagreeable extraverts, for example. The Self-Deceptive Enhancement Scale (Paulhus, 1998) aims to measure the unconscious bias towards favourable self-promotion. It partitions bias into two subscales, one for self-enhancement, and one relating to denial of faults. Paulhus and John (1998; Paulhus, 2002) also claim that deliberate impression management also breaks down into factors related to accentuating the positive (e.g., bragging) and minimising the negative (e.g., defence of one's good name). Paulhus (1998) developed an Impression Management scale that measures such purposive self-distortions. Conscious and unconscious distortion may then relate to two basic motives or values, as represented in table 13.4.

Paulhus (2002) provides the most sophisticated account of self-deception yet proposed, but so far it has inspired limited empirical research. More work has been done on *repression*. Subjects with high social desirability but low trait anxiety are sometimes characterised as 'repressors', who may be unconsciously suppressing anxiety and negative self-beliefs (Weinberger, Schwartz and Davidson, 1979). Various studies (e.g. Derakshan and Eysenck, 2001) support the notion that repressors, although generally low in state anxiety, display physiological and be-havioural signs of anxiety in some threatening situations. However, such traits do raise measurement problems: the usual assessment of repressors in terms of two scales (social desirability, trait anxiety) designed for other purposes is inelegant, to say the least. Other work has focused on the measurement of defence mechanisms through projective tests, such as the TAT: such measures seem to have at least some validity as predictors of emotion and adjustment (Cramer, 2002). It remains to be seen whether unconscious styles of defence can be successfully measured by questionnaire.

Practical issues

We will briefly survey two areas in which the practitioner needs knowledge that goes beyond that offered by the standard personality textbook: (1) use of test scores in practical decision-making, and (2) ethical and legal issues in trait assessment.

Decision-making. We have seen that much research is focused on validity, and whether trait measures actually predict criteria. However, typically, the practitioner is not concerned so much with estimating correlations in a population, but making binary decisions on individuals. Should the client be diagnosed as schizophrenic or not? Should the job applicant be hired or not? If made on the basis of test scores, these decisions require a *cutting point*. On a clinical test, the cutting point defines the score necessary for the person to be diagnosed as disordered, for example.

Several authors (e.g., Messick, 1995; Anastasi and Urbina, 1997) have advocated a formal decision-making approach to setting the cutting point. For example, in a clinical diagnosis, there are four possible outcomes, as shown in figure 13.1, including two kinds of mistake that the clinician might make, falsely diagnosing the client as having a mental disorder (false positive), and failing to diagnose a genuinely disordered client (false negative). The best decision strategy depends on the costs and benefits attached to each outcome (*utilities*). For example, if personality assessment is used as a first step, prior to a more detailed interview, the cost of a false positive assessment is low (the clinician must spend time on the additional interview), but the cost of a false negative is high (the client will not receive much-needed treatment). These utilities can be used to develop a decision strategy that sets the cutting point relatively low, so that in cases of doubt, clients are likely to be fully interviewed, even though some of those interviewed will not be diagnosed with a disorder. Anastasi and Urbina (1997) provide a more detailed account of selection strategies.

Such evaluations must take into account several factors, including, but not limited to, the predictive validity of the test. One important factor is *base-rate*, i.e., how likely the practitioner is to arrive at the correct decision by chance. For example, if a job is very easy to perform, selecting applicants at random will work fairly well. There are special dangers attached to very low base rates in clinical settings. Imagine a diagnostic test for a rare phobia that only occurs in 1 per cent of the target population. Suppose the test is 90 per cent accurate. Out of every 1,000 people tested, ten will suffer from the phobia. Of these ten, nine will be

Diagnosis	Actual status	
	Disorder	Normal

Disorder	Correct diagnosis
	• *Benefit*: patient receives
	  treatment
		'False positive'
		• *Cost*: person receives
		  unnecessary treatment or
		  costly further tests

Normal	'False negative'
	• *Cost*: patient fails to received
	  needed treatment
		Correct recognition of normality
		• *Benefit*: person resumes normal
		  life

Figure 13.1 Four possible outcomes of clinical diagnosis, with costs and benefits

correctly diagnosed, and one will be misdiagnosed as 'normal'. Now consider the 990 people without the phobia. 891 (90 per cent) will be correctly diagnosed as healthy, but the remaining ninety-nine will be falsely diagnosed as phobic. In other words, most of the people diagnosed as phobic by the test (99 out of 108) will be free of the condition! In practice, diagnosis of disorders is not so difficult, because the selected nature of people tested (e.g., those choosing to consult their doctor about irrational fears) will ensure that the base rate is higher than in the general population.

In job selection, the problem is slightly different. The personnel manager does not have to 'diagnose' each applicant as competent or incompetent, but to select the best applicants to fill the available vacancies. In this case, decision-making proceeds on the basis of maximising the percentage of applicants who will meet minimum standards in criterion performance (see Anastasi and Urbana, 1997, for a more detailed account). There is a base rate reflecting the percentage of applicants who would be successful if selected at random. If the validity of the test is known, the *increase* in percentage of applicants who are competent may be calculated as an index of the usefulness of using the test in selection. This test utility depends on base rate, criterion validity and the selection ratio, i.e., the proportion of applicants to be hired. In general, test utility increases as the base rate gets closer to 50 per cent, and as criterion validity increases.

Selection ratio has a profound effect. If selection ratio is high (most applicants will be hired), even highly valid test produces only moderate improvements on chance. If selection ratio is low (few applicants will be hired), even a test of moderate validity will lead to substantial improvement over chance. One might conclude that personality assessment is more useful in a recession than during an economic boom. Anastasi and Urbana (1997) also review studies that have tried to relate validity to productivity gains, as a consequence of test use: when the selection ratio is low, gains for large organisations may amount to several million dollars.

Ethical and legal issues. The user of psychometric tests is, of course, bound by the same ethical principles as any other psychologist. The American Psychological

Table 13.5 *Some implications of the APA Ethics Code for assessment of personality traits*

9.0.1. *Bases for assessments*. Psychologists should base assessment on adequate and sufficient techniques. Hence, the test user must be able to justify the general relevance of assessing traits to the applied issue concerned.

9.0.2. *Use of assessments*. Psychologists should use instruments that are reliable and valid for members of the population tested. Tests should be scored and interpreted in the light of research evidence. Hence, the test user must be able to justify the use of particular trait measures in the applied context.

9.05. *Test construction*. Appropriate psychometric procedures and scientific or professional knowledge should be used in developing new tests. Naturally, new trait measures must meet these criteria.

9.06. *Interpreting assessment results*. Interpretation should take into account the purpose of the assessment as well as factors such as situational, personal, linguistic, and cultural differences between the psychologist and the testee that might influence interpretation. Hence, although trait assessment seeks to assess constructs that are robust across situations and cultures, the test user must be sensitive to possible contextual influences on scores.

9.07. *Obsolete tests and outdated test results*. Psychologists should not make recommendations using outdated tests and procedures. Of course, the user of modern trait measures will comply with this requirement. Users of older tests face the dilemma that there are no clear standards that establish when a test is to be considered obsolete or outdated.

9.10. *Explaining assessment results*. Where possible, psychologists should take reasonable steps to provide explanations of results to the individual or their representative. When this is not possible due to the nature of the professional relationship (e.g., security screenings), this fact should be explained to the person in advance. Published trait measures frequently include a feedback sheet given to the testee that explains their personality characteristics in every-day language. Of course, particular care is required in providing feedback on traits considered pathological.

Note This table paraphrases and comments on selected items of the APA Ethics Code. This table should not be used in place of the APA Ethics Code, which is available at http://www.apa.org/ethics/

Association (APA), 'Ethical Principles of Psychologists and Code of Conduct 2002' includes a section on assessment. Table 13.5 briefly summarises some of the obligations it places on the test user, with comments on their relevance to the assessment of traits. Other sections related to assessment deal with the need for informed consent, maintaining test security, release of test data and assessment by unqualified persons (which is discouraged).

Lanyon and Goodstein (1997) discuss some misuses of tests, which would be contra-indicated by the APA code. Naturally, it is unethical to use professionally a test whose validity has not been established. Even if the test has been systematically developed, problems may arise when there is no clear criterion for the construct that is assessed, and when tests are interpreted on the basis of common sense or the tester's personal insights. Such problems are often more acute for projective tests than for trait measures. More subtly, tests that are valid for one purpose may be misused in a different context. Lanyon and Goodstein point out that tests developed for use in psychiatric settings such as the Rorschach and MMPI may not be suitable as selection devices in industry, especially when administered by people with no clinical training. Several countries, including the UK, have formal systems for accrediting test users to counter such problems.

Ethical obligations are discharged within a legal framework, which, of course, differs from nation to nation, and, in the USA, from state to state. Laws typically deal with issues such as confidentiality and data protection, protection of privacy, and fairness in occupational selection. Naturally, the practitioner requires familiarity with such laws, especially in an increasingly litigious society. If a trait assessment is a factor in a job applicant not being hired or promoted, the psychologist may have to justify the relevance of the trait in court. Occasionally, legal decisions may seem capricious. In 1996, the police force of New London, Connecticut, obtained some notoriety for refusing employment to an applicant whose mental ability was deemed too high (corresponding to an IQ of about 125). The police department successfully argued in court that applicants who score too high could get bored with police work and leave soon after receiving costly training.

Arthur et al. (2001) review some legal implications of organisational personality assessment in the USA. They point out that personality measures may be less vulnerable than mental ability tests to the perception that they are unfair to minority applicants. Indeed, they quote a statement made by Hogan et al. (1996, p. 475):

> . . . we want to suggest in the strongest possible terms that the use of well-constructed measures of normal personality in preemployment screening will be a force for equal employment opportunity, social justice, and increased productivity.

This view is justified by the evidence for the validity of trait measures as predictors of occupational criteria, which we discuss below. However, Arthur et al. (2001) point out two unresolved problems in the occupational field. First, although fakers may be identified as having very high scores on desired traits, rejecting a job applicant because they score too highly might be difficult to justify legally. Second, the well-replicated sex differences in some personality traits (see chapter 3) lead to conflict between legal and scientific principles. The US Civil Rights Act specifically makes unlawful the use of score adjustments or differential cut-offs in the use of employment-related tests, on the basis of race, colour, religion, sex or national origin. (The intent here was primarily to prevent racial discrimination.) However, it is normal and scientifically justified practice in personality assessment to use separate norms for men and women, a procedure that in fact promotes fairness in occupational selection. It remains to be seen how this issue will play out in future court cases.

Educational and clinical applications

Educational psychology

Braden (1995) makes a useful distinction between educational psychologists, who are concerned with the psychological factors that influence learning, and school psychologists, who are concerned with abnormalities that may disrupt learning.

Table 13.6 *Some personality characteristics of various childhood disorders (see Kamphaus et al., 1995)*

Disorder	Personality characteristics
Childhood Depression	Excessive negative affect, low self-concept etc. (similar to adult depression)
Autism	Poorly socialised, lack of response to social stimuli
Substance abuse	Aggressiveness, impulsiveness
Schizophrenia	Thought disturbance, impaired social functioning, impoverished affect (similar to adult schizophrenia)
Attention-Deficit Hyperactivity Disorder	Hyperactivity, inattention, impulsiveness

These categories, of course, may overlap. Thus, the educational psychologist is often concerned with 'normal' individual differences, whereas the school psychologist focuses primarily on practical interventions for the 'problem' child. School psychologists may also be called on to identify gifted children, defined by intelligence and cognitive ability, rather than personality.

Educational psychologists thus conduct research that resembles much other trait research, apart from its focus on schoolchildren and college students. For example, several studies have found correlations between personality traits and academic achievement in students, typically measured by grade point average or examination results. Although there is some variation across studies, conscientiousness and emotional stability appear to promote better academic performance (see Furnham and Heaven, 1999, for a review). Extraverts do better at school, but introversion is an advantage at university, perhaps because of the greater emphasis on solitary study. The test anxiety research reviewed in chapter 12 is another example of educational research on traits, much of which is directed towards theoretical understanding of why test anxiety is detrimental to performance (Zeidner, 1998). Further work is involved in developing countermeasures, such as cognitive-attentional training, that the school psychologist can use to help children whose level of anxiety is crippling.

School psychologists typically use an array of assessment tools in evaluating those children who are brought to their attention, including clinical interviews, projective tests and ability tests in addition to personality assessment. Teachers and parents are also likely to be interviewed. Indeed, the school psychologist may work with clinicians in diagnosis and treatment of childhood mental disorders. Table 13.6 summarises selected conditions (Kamphaus et al., 1995), some of which, such as Attention-Deficit Hyperactivity Disorder (ADHD) are known primarily from childhood. Standardised assessments may be helpful in diagnosing the exact condition. For example, mental retardation, autism and schizophrenia may all be associated with social withdrawal, but children suffering from these conditions will show different patterns of intelligence and personality characteristics (see Schwean and Saklofske, 1999).

School psychologists may also contribute to the development of interventions for enhancing students' ability to learn and develop personally. Schunk and Ertmer (2000) describe programmes in which providing children with learning goals and progress feedback leads to increases in self-efficacy, which, as discussed in chapter 8, may be seen as a contextualised trait. On the other hand, the social experiment of trying to build the child's self-esteem, as a goal separate from building skills and accomplishments, is now seen as a failure (Stout, 2000). Some more ambitious programmes have sought to produce wide-ranging improvements in social, emotional and self-regulative skills. Such programmes, although not designed for this purpose, are now being seen as interventions that raise 'emotional intelligence', i.e., competencies in perceiving and managing the emotions of oneself and others. However, as Zeidner, Roberts and Matthews (2002) caution, these programmes typically suffer from a variety of shortcomings, such as poor design, lack of long-term follow-up and lack of systematic assessment. Indeed, one might recommend that if the goal is to produce substantial personality change, trait measures should be used as criteria.

Clinical psychology

Clinical practice, of course, is dominated by the judgement of the individual clinician, although there is an increasing movement towards more 'evidence-based' approaches that refer to the outcomes of nomothetic research. Personality assessment is thus important as one of several techniques that support the eventual diagnosis. In this section, we discuss the use of trait measures in diagnosis, and then briefly highlight some other clinical applications highlighted by Matthews et al. (1998). This section builds on the discussion of traits as predictors of mental disorder, ill health and abnormal personality set out in chapters 9 to 11.

Clinical diagnostic schemes like DSM-IV assume a *diathesis-stressor* model, in which personality characteristics create a vulnerability to disorder (the diathesis), which may be expressed as full-blown disorder as a result of precipitating events (the stressor). The dimensions of abnormal personality described in chapter 11 provide an account of underlying vulnerability. Clinicians use general personality questionnaires designed to assess these abnormalities of personality, such as the Minnesota Multiphasic Personality Inventory and the Millon Clinical Multiaxial Inventory. These questionnaires are supplemented by more specialised measures such as the Beck anxiety and depression scales. As discussed in chapter 11, the increasing evidence for convergence between abnormal and normal trait constructs is generating increased interest in the clinical applications of 'normal' personality measures such as the NEO-PI-R (e.g., Costa and Widiger, 2002).

A tension remains between the traditional clinical view of allocating patients to some discrete, categorical disorder, and the trait perspective, which suggests that patients may show graduated degrees of abnormality on several independent dimensions. Whichever questionnaire is used, the diagnosis cannot be made on trait scores alone. However, trait information may be an extremely useful aid to diagnosis, for example, antisocial personality disorder is unlikely if the person scores high in Agreeableness.

Thus, the clinician may use a standard trait questionnaire initially to obtain a first indication of the pathologies to which the person may be vulnerable. For example, high N and low E scores might indicate a vulnerability to anxiety and mood disorders. Next, the clinical interview, together with administration of more specialised questionnaires, indicates a likely diagnosis. The person might meet the detailed criteria for generalised anxiety disorders, but not phobia or obsessive-compulsive disorder. Finally, the clinician may develop an idiographic case conceptualisation, by, for example, probing the circumstances that elicit anxiety, the content of the patient's anxious thoughts, and how the person tries to avoid anxiety; factors that are unique to the individual (see Wells, 1997).

Some additional uses of trait measures are as follows (Harkness and Lilienfeld, 1997; Matthews et al., 1998):

Understanding the person and interpreting his or her problem. On the basis of the 'added value' principle (Costa and McCrae, 1992; chapter 1), trait assessment provides the clinician with a wealth of information on the likely characteristics, strengths and weaknesses of the client. The individual is not necessarily representative of the 'typical' trait description, but the trait information directs the clinician towards further probing of various potential problem areas. For example, a high score on N might usefully focus the clinician's attention on interpersonal difficulties (see chapter 8), excessive emotional and stress responses (see chapter 9) and on possibly 'psychosomatic' health complaints (see chapter 10). Understanding the person in the context of their dispositional traits may also help enhance clinical rapport and empathy. It may also help the clinician in explaining to the patient the nature of their vulnerabilities.

Selecting the type of therapy. The choice of therapy depends primarily on the clinician's skills and preferences in treating specific disorders, but personality assessment gives the clinician some scope for tailoring therapy to the individual. Interpersonally involved (high E) depressed patients may respond better to interpersonal therapy than to antidepressant medication; the opposite may be true for depressed introverts (Shea, 1988). Likewise, persons high in Openness to Experience (O) may respond favourably to unconventional forms of therapy (Miller, 1991). Conversely, the more conventional low O person may prefer and respond better to directive psychotherapies that offer behavioural techniques that teach concrete skills or practical techniques for relaxation. Box 13.1 illustrates this point for a narrow trait linked to neuroticism: alexithymia or difficulty in verbalising and understanding emotions. Matching the therapy to the client in this way may also help the clinician to explain its benefits, leading to greater compliance with the requirements of the treatment.

Box 13.1 Alexithymia

The concept of alexithymia originated with clinical observations that many patients suffering from so-called classical psychosomatic disorders showed an apparent inability to describe and explain their feelings. The term was coined by Sifneos (1972) to indicate difficulties verbalising emotion (*a* = lack, *lexis* = word, *thymos* = emotion). Currently, alexithymia is seen as a cluster of deficits in the experiencing, expression and regulation of emotions (see Parker, Taylor and Bagby, 2001, for a review). These authors identify the following components: (a) difficulty in identifying and describing emotions and distinguishing between feelings and the bodily sensations of arousal, (b) difficulty in describing feelings to other people, (c) constricted imaginal processes, as evidenced by a paucity of fantasies, and (d) a stimulus-bound externally oriented cognitive style, as evidenced by pre-occupation with the details of external events rather than inner emotional experiences. Clinically, alexithymia is common in a variety of emotional disorders.

Alexithymia can also be measured as a continuous trait in the normal population. The best-known instrument is the Toronto Alexithymia Scale (TAS-20: Bagby et al., 1994a), which has subscales corresponding to components (a), (b) and (d) described by Parker et al. (2001). It also overlaps with the Big Five, in relating to emotional distress (high N), low positive emotionality (low E) and a limited imagination (low O), but it appears to assess some unique configuration of traits (Luminet et al., 1999). High alexithymia is also implicated in stress vulnerability and suboptimal coping (Deary, Scott and Wilson, 1997).

Assessment of alexithymia may also be useful in clinical practice. In fact, alexithymia is bad news for the client on two counts (see Taylor, 2000). First, it may operate as a risk factor for a variety of pathologies, owing to the importance of effective emotion regulation in maintaining adjustment. Second, alexithymic patients tend to be hard to treat, especially using 'insight-oriented' therapies that involve talking about emotional problems. Several suggestions have been made for modifying therapies for alexithymics to reduce the need for sophisticated language-based understanding. These include group psychotherapy, behaviour therapy or working directly on the patient's skills in recognising and talking about emotions. As clinicians sometimes fail to recognise alexithymia, its assessment can make an important practical contribution.

However, the evidence that would support systematic use of personality assessment is not yet in place. Some commentators are insistent on the promise of trait measures. According to Harkness and Lilienfeld (1997, p. 349), 'the last forty years of individual differences research require the inclusion of personality trait assessment for the construction and implementation of any treatment plan that would lay claim to scientific status'. However, other commentators have pointed towards the lack of consistent evidence that personality factors moderate psychotherapeutic change (Petry, Tennen and Affleck, 2000), although rather few studies seem to have used modern trait scales together with a convincing rationale for traits influencing the outcome of the specific treatments implemented. Thus, the role of traits in treatment choice remains a topic for future research.

Anticipating the course of therapy. Personality assessment may help the clinician to judge the patient's prognosis. For example, it appears that outcomes may be poorer for patients especially high in N, and especially its 'angry hostility' component (Harkness et al., 2002). These authors found that depressed patients with this trait characteristic tended to remain in a state of chronic minor depression after the major depression had been treated, leaving them vulnerable to subsequent relapse and recurrence of pathology.

In addition, traits may indicate possible problems that may occur during the course of treatment. Individuals low in Conscientiousness may not be scrupulous in following treatments that require some self-direction; for example, recording moods, practising relaxation exercises, or even taking medication. Christensen and Smith (1995) confirmed that Conscientiousness is a predictor of adherence to medical regimens. The clinician may need to counter the lack of diligence of the low C patient by providing structure and motivation, and perhaps enlisting the assistance of family members in ensuring compliance and regular attendance at the clinic. Similarly, both high and low Agreeableness may carry risks (Matthews et al., 1998). The high A person is likely to be compliant, but may also be vulnerable to excessive dependency on the clinician, lack of assertiveness and inability to challenge the clinician's statements when appropriate. By contrast, the low A client may be prone to hostility and lack of co-operation, but may show a greater drive towards self-interested problem-solving.

Understanding the processes of pathology. A final advantage of personality assessment is that it provides the clinician with a systematic approach to organising the various pathological processes that are linked to personality (Wells and Matthews, 1994). For example, as discussed in chapters 9 and 12, high N relates to a multitude of disturbances in information-processing including biases in selective attention, self-judgement and retrieval from memory, and use of often ineffective coping strategies that perpetuate disorder. However, linking these various pathologies to traits allows them to be conceptualised as an integrated syndrome, that, theoretically, may be linked to the content of the self-schema (Matthews, Schwean et al., 2000). The syndrome of negative self-referent bias, i.e., of systematically underestimating one's ability to deal with threats and challenges, can then be addressed therapeutically (Wells and Matthews, 1994). Similarly, the cognitive symptoms of schizophrenia, such as hallucinations and delusions, may be a consequence of pathologies of selective attention, such as failure to inhibit intruding thoughts (Beech and Williams, 1997).

Personality and job performance

The principal application of assessment is to select job applicants whose personality will match the demands of the job, e.g., extraverts for sales positions, conscientious, emotionally stable individuals for police work, and so forth. Of course, selection must be justified on the basis that traits do actually predict important behaviours at work, especially job performance and counterproductive behaviours. The validity of trait measures in organisational settings has been an important, and controversial, issue for applied psychology. Although personality questionnaires are widely used in industry for selection and assessment (Kanfer et al., 1995; Matthews, 1997), popularity is no indication of validity; in some countries graphology and astrology are equally acceptable tools. We should note also that assessment of personality is usually combined with other validated techniques such as interviews, and behavioural tests performed in assessment centres.

There has been a long-running and sometimes heated debate on whether personality traits are in fact useful in predicting job performance and other organisational criteria. Two errors in reasoning are frequently committed. The first error is committed by enthusiasts for personality measures, who have been prone to 'cherry pick' isolated instances of some trait predicting performance, culled from large correlation matrices in which trait–performance associations are mostly non-significant. The error here is obvious: selected correlations may be significant due to chance.

The second characteristic error is that committed by critics of personality assessment, in pointing to the small magnitude of averaged correlations between traits and performance. A recent estimate of the mean correlation between Big Five traits and occupational criteria is a puny 0.03 (Barrick and Mount, 1991). Such procedures have exactly the same shortcomings identified by Eysenck and Eysenck (1980) in their rebuttal of Mischel's (1968) situationist critique (see chapter 2). No attempt is made to discriminate predicted and non-predicted correlations, and correlations are likely to be statistically attenuated due to factors such as restriction of range and unreliability of measures. Occupational criteria are frequently of rather low reliability (Ghiselli, 1973). There are also issues related to choosing criteria for performance: the person's usefulness to the organisation may reflect not just their performance on the main tasks assigned, but more intangible factors such as support of other workers, effective communication and personal initiative (Guion, 1997). Fortunately, recent years have produced several large-scale reviews which have sampled data systematically, corrected for statistical artifact, and distinguished exploratory and confirmatory findings. We will focus on meta-analyses based on the Big Five taxonomy, although midlevel and contextualised traits may also be very useful (see discussion of self-efficacy scales in chapter 8).

Meta-analyses of the Big Five

Two meta-analyses conducted in the early 1990s were especially influential. Barrick and Mount (1991) and Tett, Jackson and Rothstein (1991) surveyed large

Table 13.7 *Selected correlational data from three meta-analytic reviews of associations between the Big Five and occupational criteria*

Study	Measure	E	N	C	O	A
Barrick and Mount (1991)	Job proficiency	06	−04	13	02	04
	Training proficiency	26	−07	23	10	25
Tett et al. (1991)	Job proficiency (Confirmatory studies)	16	−22	18	33	27
Barrick et al. (2001)	Job proficiency	15	−13	27	07	13
	Training efficiency	28	−09	24	33	14
	Teamwork	16	−22	27	16	34

Note All correlations statistically corrected. Ns in Barrick and Mount (1991) analyses range from 9,454 to 12,893 (job proficiency), and from 2,700 to 3,685 (training proficiency). Ns for Tett et al. confirmatory studies range from 280 to 2,302. Ns in Barrick et al. (2001) range from from 48,100 to 23,225 (job proficiency), from 4,100 to 3,177 (training proficiency), and from 3,719 to 2,079 (teamwork)

numbers of studies, and conducted meta-analyses to establish average correlations between the Big Five and various occupational criteria, including performance. They report uncorrected and corrected coefficients, though they differ in the correction procedures used. Tett et al. (1991) also distinguished between confirmatory studies with an a priori theoretical rationale, from exploratory studies in which researchers were content to go fishing for whatever correlations reached significance empirically. However, Barrick and Mount (1991) considered a wider range of criteria than Tett et al. (1991), including training proficiency, for example, as well as job proficiency. Following some technical criticisms (Ones et al., 1994), Tett et al. (1994) reanalysed their data, finding slightly smaller correlations. Other meta-analyses have followed. Barrick, Mount and Judge (2001) present a 'meta-analysis of meta-analyses' that largely confirms the findings of the original studies. This review also extended the previous ones by including analyses of teamwork performance criteria.

Table 13.7 shows selected data (corrected correlations) from these studies. In general, the averaged trait–performance associations were fairly modest, with C the most consistent predictor of overall job proficiency. A large scale survey of European Union studies (Salgado, 1997) also identified C as the principal correlate of better job performance. In the various meta-analyses, E and O tended to relate more strongly to training performance than they did to actual job performance. Larger correlations were, in general, obtained from confirmatory studies, in which A and O had the largest positive correlations, and N was negatively related to performance. Barrick et al. (2001) also established several correlates of better teamwork: high A, high C and low N. These findings demonstrate that there are reliable associations between all five traits and performance criteria, particularly in confirmatory studies.

One might question the practical utility of these validity coefficients, but, in fact, even criterion validities of 0.2 or 0.3 may be practically useful (Rosenthal and Rubin, 1982). What is important is not so much the percentage of variance in the criterion predicted, but the improvement in decision-making resulting from the use of the trait measure (see above). Even small validities may produce substantial increases in the competence of applicants when selection must be stringent, so that perhaps only 5 per cent or 10 per cent of applicants will be hired (Anastasi and Urbina, 1997). Jensen (1980) characterises the validity ($\times$ 100) of a test or questionnaire as the average percentage gain in criterion performance resulting from use of the test in selection. Most personnel managers would be satisfied with the average 20–30 per cent gain in performance resulting from the use of a trait measure with a validity of 0.2–0.3. In addition, as we discuss below, traits predict not just performance but other important variables such as integrity (Ones et al., 1993) and vocational interests (Ackerman and Heggestad, 1997).

Interestingly, however, better job performance does not necessarily translate into greater career success. Boudreau, Boswell and Judge (2001) looked at predictors of external success, such as renumeration and job level, in samples of American and European executives. Surprisingly, Conscientiousness was mostly unrelated to success, and Agreeableness was negatively related to success in both samples: perhaps, nice guys do finish last, at least among executives. Among Americans only, neuroticism related to low success, and, among Europeans only, extraversion was a predictor of higher levels of success. Of course, findings might be different in different occupations. Box 13.2 describes another aspect of job success: leadership.

Box 13.2 Personality and leadership

What are the personality qualities that make an effective leader in industrial, military and political settings? Applied psychologists have devoted considerable evidence to this question. Various specialised questionnaires have been developed for this purpose (see Lanyon and Goodstein, 1997, for a review). They assess qualities such as influencing and inspiring others, setting and communicating long-term goals and strategies, and creative efforts that 'make things happen'. It is, of course, quite hard to validate such questionnaires, because objective indices of leadership success are rarely available. Typically, validation involves the use of either ratings of leadership made by others, or discrimination of groups such as top executives from managers in general.

Recently, there has been interest in using standard personality measures to predict leadership criteria. Judge et al. (2002) meta-analysed 222 correlations from 73 samples. Overall, the Big Five showed a multiple correlation of 0.48 with leadership. In order of magnitude, correlations for the traits were as follows: Extraversion=0.31, Conscientiousness=0.28, Openness to Experience=0.24, Neuroticism=−0.24, Agreeableness=0.08.

An interesting study of military leadership (Ployhart, Lim and Chan, 2001) distinguished between maximal performance – i.e., leadership in demanding conditions at an assessment centre – and typical performance – i.e., leadership rated for the three-month period of basic training. The study was concerned with *transformational* leadership, i.e., the ability of a Churchill or Gandhi to rise to a challenge by communicating a vision that motivates their followers to excel. Overall, the personality constructs explained 19 per cent and 12 per cent of the variance in maximum and typical performance, respectively. Consistent with the Judge et al. (2002) review, extraverts showed elevated levels of both maximal and typical leadership performance, relative to introverts. In addition, Openness predicted maximum performance and Neuroticism predicted lower typical performance. Ployhart et al. (2001) failed to confirm a predicted association between Conscientiousness and typical performance: possibly C is more important in business than in military settings. Of course, the varied personalities of historical transformational leaders (compare Gandhi and Churchill, for example) implies leaders may possess a variety of personality attributes (cf., Simonton, 2001).

Organisational correlates of personality: moderator variables

As already indicated, the interactionist approach implies that associations between personality and organisational criteria may vary according to various moderator variables. As Tett et al. (1994, 1999) suggest, mixing of positive and negative correlations in meta-analysis may provide an unduly pessimistic picture of the relevance of traits. Although the search for moderator variables is often unsystematic, detailed examination of the data provides some clues towards which factors may be important. C, the most consistent predictor of job performance, is generally insensitive to the moderating effects of other variables. For example, Barrick and Mount (1991) calculated corrected averaged correlations for five occupations separately, including professional, managerial and skilled/semi-skilled jobs. The correlation between C and performance hardly varied at all across these groups (range of rs: 0.20–0.23). C relates to generally beneficial motivational factors, such as goal setting and goal commitment, which may mediate effects of C on performance (Barrick, Mount and Strauss, 1993). However, Tett et al. (1999) identify some studies in which C was negatively associated with performance (e.g., innovation in health service employees), and suggest that high C may be a liability for jobs requiring expedient completion of numerous tasks and/or creative and artistic tendencies. In fact, it may be useful to distinguish different aspects of C. In a further meta-analysis, Hough (1992) divided C-like traits into narrower traits of Achievement and Dependability, and showed that Achievement showed the stronger associations with job proficiency, training success and educational success. C may also be important as a predictor of 'integrity': honesty, responsibility and reliability. Ones, Viswesvaran and Schmidt (1993) report a meta-analysis which demonstrated that personality measures related to integrity are good pre-dictors of job performance ($r = 0.35$) and counterproductive behaviours such as theft and absenteeism ($r = -.32$). Similarly, C also relates to being a good 'organisational citizen', i.e., being actively supportive of the organisation's aims (LePine, Erez and Johnson, 2002).

The predictive validity of other Big Five traits is more criterion-dependent. E, for example, is more strongly positively related to job performance in managerial occupations than in other jobs, as might be expected (Barrick and Mount, 1991; Barrick et al., 2001). Various studies have also linked E to sales performance (e.g., Barrick and Mount, 1991), but Barrick et al. (2001) were unable to con-firm that this association was greater than zero. Tett et al. (1999) suggest that in some sales settings, a soft-spoken, non-assertive approach may work better than overtly extraverted behaviours. We saw in chapter 12 that the association between extraversion and laboratory task performance may be positive, negative or zero depending on the precise nature of the task and contextual factors. The weak neg-ative association between N and performance is consistent with the experimental data; the relationship is likely to vary with environmental stress and cognitive com-plexity of the work performed. The association between N and poorer teamwork (Barrick et al., 2001) is consonant with the interpersonal difficulties typical of high N individuals, discussed in chapter 9.

Effects of A are contingent upon job demands: possibly, the high A worker does well when the job requires cooperation with others, but lacks the ruthless, compet-itive qualities sometimes necessary in business, as the Boudreau et al. (2001) find-ings suggest. CEOs are characterised by disagreeableness, for example (Matthews and Oddy, 1993). High A seems to relate to superior teamwork, but poorer cre-ativity and high-autonomy managerial performance (Hough, 1992; Barrick and Mount, 1993). Psychoticism, which relates to low A, seems to be associated with greater creativity in both laboratory and real-world settings (Eysenck, 1995). Fi-nally, O may be beneficial when the work environment offers greater change and variety. Matthews and Falconer (2002) found that customer service agents high in O found a work simulation more disengaging (i.e., tiring and boring).

Organisational psychology: further applications

In reviewing the relevant literature, Tokar, Fischer and Subich (1998) identify three other important areas of research, in addition to behavioural out-comes: choice-related processes (e.g., vocational interests), general career pro-cesses (e.g., changing career), and occupational satisfaction and well-being (e.g., job stress). We will briefly look at the applications of traits in each of these areas in turn.

Table 13.8 *Four trait complexes identified by Ackerman and Heggestad (1997)*

	Components		
Trait complex	Personality	Interests	Ability
Social	Extraversion, Well-being, Social Potency	Social, Enterprising	—
Clerical–conventional	Conscientiousness, Control, Traditionalism	Conventional	Perceptual Speed
Science–maths	—	Realistic, Investigative	Visual Perception, Maths reasoning
Intellectual–cultural	Openness to Experience, Absorption, Intellectual Engagement	Artistic, Investigative	Crystallised Intelligence, Ideational Fluency ('creativity')

Vocational choice

It is a fairly commonplace observation that people in different jobs differ in their typical personality characteristics, as indicated in chapter 1. The applied issue is whether we can go further, and use trait information in vocational guidance. The rationale for vocational guidance is provided by an idea that has been very influential in organisational psychology, that of person–environment fit (Schneider et al., 1997). It is supposed that workers will be happier and more productive if, first, the person possesses the aptitudes and skills needed for the job, and, second, if the job is congruent with the person's values and needs. For example, an achievement-striving individual needs a job providing opportunities for promotion and self-advancement. A popular theory in this area (Holland, 1997) describes six personality types that can be matched to occupational characteristics (see table 13.7). The fit between type and the person's actual job will influence job satisfaction and strain. Furnham's (1992) review of the area concluded that this prediction was quite well supported by evidence, although congruence appears to be only one of several factors influencing satisfaction. Low-paid drudgery is unattractive whatever one's personality.

Several authors have related Holland's descriptive scheme to the five factor model. Outcomes vary somewhat from study to study (see Tokar et al., 1998; and Larson, Rottinghaus and Borgen, 2002, for reviews). The most consistent relationships appear to link Extraversion to social and enterprising interests, and Openness to artistic and investigative interests. There is somewhat less consistent evidence relating emotional stability (low N) to realistic interests, Agreeableness to social interests and Conscientiousness to conventional interests. Ackerman and Heggestad (1997) describe four 'trait complexes' shown in table 13.8. These are rather loose associations of traits, but they suggest how it is useful to look at personality in relation to interests and abilities.

These findings suggest a place for trait measures in career counselling. Of course, there are already standard, validated measures of vocational interests, including the well-known Strong and Kuder inventories, as well as Holland's measure (see Anastasi and Urbina, 1997, for a review). It appears that vocational interests and traits, although overlapping, represent distinct constructs, and both may be useful in organisational psychology (Larson et al., 2002). According to Hammond (2001), assessment of the Big Five contributes to career counselling as follows, especially for clients seeking counselling because of career difficulties:

- Assisting the counsellor in understanding the client's internal experience
- Providing a context for understanding the client's concerns
- Aiding in anticipating potential difficulties in the course of career counselling
- Assisting the counsellor in developing a practical treatment plan.

On the 'added-value' principle (Costa and McCrae, 1992), trait measures provide information about adaptation to work environments that is not contained in interest measures. For example, given that the correlation between social extraversion and social interests at work is in the 0.3–0.4 range (e.g., Ackerman and Heggestad, 1997), we can readily find introverts with high social interests. However, the cognitive and emotional characteristics of these individuals (see chapters 8 and 10) may not equip them well for dealing with socially demanding environments. Counselling for these persons might encourage them to re-evaluate their career interests, and assess whether or not they have the requisite skills and aptitudes for their preferred vocation.

Career progression and change

A simple view is that the person's traits represent a stable pre-disposition that favours certain kinds of work. However, we can also take a more dynamic perspective by looking at how personality and career progression are interrelated over longer timespans. One area of research is concerned with *turnover*, i.e., how likely the person is to leave a job. Of course, people may have different motivations for changing job – such as better opportunities elsewhere – but, in general, turnover is linked to other counter-productive behaviours such as absenteeism (Salgado, 2002). Career progression may also be viewed from the interactionist perspective. Not only does personality influence work behaviours, but personality may change as the person becomes socialised into the work environment (Semmer and Schallberger, 1996).

In general, studies show that individuals high in Neuroticism and low in Conscientiousness are most likely to change jobs (Barrick and Mount, 1996; Tokar et al., 1998). In a meta-analytic study, Salgado (2002) cautioned that there were few data (four to five independent studies), but turnover correlated 0.25 with N and −0.24 with C. As discussed shortly, N may be associated with dissatisfaction with current work, and with lack of organisational commitment (Payne and Morrison, 2002). In a study of almost 2,000 executives, Boudreau et al. (2001) found that high

N was correlated with a greater frequency of searching for alternative employment. This study also found that job search was related to higher Agreeableness, Openness and Extraversion. As in some other studies (Tokar et al., 1998), extraversion effects were mediated by greater ambition. Among the unemployed, predictors of job search are rather different. Extraversion and Conscientiousness are the main predictors of both formal job search activities, and 'networking', i.e., contacting friends, acquaintances and others in search of useful information and contacts (Wanberg, Kanfer and Banas, 2001).

As with studies of vocational choice, these findings suggest a role of personality assessment in career guidance. Counselling might also be directed towards helping the person to deal with being assessed. Two recent studies show that personality variables relate to performance on standard assessment techniques. Stable extraverts seem to interview best (Cook, Vance and Spector, 2000), and also perform best on interpersonal exercises conducted during participation in a two-day management development assessment centre (Spector et al., 2000). Individuals high in Conscientiousness (and mental ability) performed best on cognitive exercises in the assessment centre (Spector et al., 2000). Findings also suggest that organisations might make use of trait information in their efforts to retain their more valuable staff. Interventions that reduce stress and dissatisfaction are likely to help the retention of high N individuals, whereas prevention of turnover in extraverts requires that these employees have sufficient outlets for their personal ambition.

Work satisfaction and stress

There have been extensive studies of personality factors in affective and cognitive reactions to work. We will deal with these fairly briefly, having already discussed personality and stress in chapter 9. In fact, the organisational studies concur with the conclusions of chapter 9, in that high N is the strongest personality predictor of stress responses in the workplace (Furnham, 1992; Tokar et al., 1998), including distress and worry (Matthews, Campbell et al., 2002) and self-reported health complaints (Mak and Mueller, 2001). High N is also associated with higher levels of work–family conflict, due to effects on both work stress and family stress (Stoeva, Chiu and Greenhaus, 2002).

There is also an extensive literature on personality correlates of job satisfaction and dissatisfaction. Job satisfaction is a major construct in organisational psychology, and several validated scales are widely used. It refers to both positive cognitions and emotions concerning work. Reviews of the literature (e.g., Tokar et al., 1998) have generally concluded that N is the broad personality trait most closely related to job dissatisfaction, although correlation magnitudes are sometimes low. In a meta-analysis, Judge and Bono (2001) reported that emotional stability correlated at 0.24 with job satisfaction. These authors also link job satisfaction to other, related traits described as 'core self-evaluations': self-esteem ($r = 0.26$), generalised self-efficacy ($r = 0.45$) and internal locus of control ($r = 0.32$).

Other traits are also implicated in job satisfaction; several authors link extraversion and/or positive affect to higher satisfaction (Brief, 1998). In a further meta-analysis, Judge, Heller and Mount (2002) reported estimated true score correlations between traits and job satisfaction of –0.29 for Neuroticism, 0.25 for Extraversion, 0.02 for Openness to Experience, 0.17 for Agreeableness, and 0.26 for Conscientiousness. Presumably, these correlations reflect the same mechanisms contributing to correlations between personality and indices of stress and emotion: biologically based affective predispositions, together with individual differences in how the person appraises and copes with workplace demands (e.g., Costa, 1996; Matthews, Campbell et al., 2002).

It is generally agreed that stress is a major problem in the workplace, as a consequence of absence, turnover, poor productivity, antisocial actions and ill-health (Spielberger and Reheiser, 1995). Often, interventions are at the workplace level, through environmental programmes that alleviate stress factors and enrich the content of work. In addition, the data we have reviewed suggest that interventions at the level of the individual may be targeted towards personnel most vulnerable to stress and dissatisfaction. Such interventions are typically directed towards appraisals and coping strategies (Brief, 1998), mechanisms that we have seen are implicated in stress vulnerability (see chapter 9). Thus, techniques such as relaxation, anger management and social skills training may be especially beneficial to individuals high in neuroticism. When a programme is implemented, the benefits of personality assessment are then similar to those in clinical practice, as described above.

A final thought is that the emotional needs of organisations and employees do not necessarily coincide. As the humourist Scott Adams (1996, p. 33) has pointed out, 'Employees like to feel their contributions are being valued. That's why managers try to avoid that sort of thing. With value comes self-esteem, and with self-esteem comes unreasonable demands for money.'

Emotional intelligence

In this section we turn to the applied utility of assessing emotional intelligence (EI). Broadly, EI refers to 'the ability to monitor one's own and others' emotions, to discriminate among them, and to use the information to guide one's thinking and actions' (Salovey and Mayer, 1990, p. 189). That is, the emotionally intelligent person can use their superior awareness and insight to deal more successfully with everyday life challenges. Especially in popular accounts (e.g., Goleman, 1995), EI has been seen as a general panacea to the woes of modern life. Mental illness, crime, youth delinquency and social disintegration may all be countered by training people to be more emotionally intelligent. These claims are unsubstantiated by evidence (see Matthews, Zeidner and Roberts, 2003, for a review). More realistically, emotional intelligence may represent a new sub-field of differential psychology that describes some significant personal attributes beyond conventional personality and ability constructs.

Emotional intelligence may be important in various areas of applied psychology, including clinical psychology (Parker, 2000) and educational psychology (Zeidner, Roberts and Matthews, 2002). For example, lack of emotional intelligence has been linked to the alexithymia construct described in Box 13.1. Here, we focus on its potential applications to organisational psychology. Many organisational psychologists consider that standard personality and ability measures fail to capture some of the qualities that are most important in working life, such as social awareness, understanding others, and effective communication (Gowing, 2001). By contrast, 'emotionally illiterate' individuals who needlessly antagonise co-workers and customers are damaging to the organisation.

The possibility that EI can be reliably and validly measured, and used for occupational selection, placement and assessment excites some organisational psychologists. As one pair of researchers has claimed: 'If the driving force of intelligence in twentieth-century business has been IQ, then . . . in the dawning twenty-first century it will be EQ' (Cooper and Sawaf, 1997, p. xxvii). Similarly, Watkin (2000) suggests, without empirical support: 'Use of EI for recruitment decisions leads to 90-percentile success rates.' He proceeds to claim that 'what distinguishes top performers in every field, in every industry sector, is not high IQ or technical expertise, it is EI' (p. 91). Goleman (1998) followed up his first best-seller with an account of EI in the workplace that listed twenty-five different competencies necessary for effective performance in the workplace, with different competencies believed to be required in different professions. Thus, confidentiality would presumably be important for loan officers and priests, while trust and empathy appear vital for psychotherapists, social workers and marriage counsellors.

In this section, we take a sober look at the prospects for assessment of EI in the workplace. First, we provide an overview of assessment issues. We will survey some of the instruments developed to measure EI, their psychometric properties, and their relationships with existing personality and ability measures. Second, we will consider the predictive validity and practical utility of EI scales: do they really provide useful information about the individual that could not be provided by conventional assessments?

Assessment of emotional intelligence

The first problem in assessing EI is deciding what we actually want to measure. Different authors present different conceptions of what it means to be 'emotionally intelligent', and some definitions are so broad as to include almost every positive quality other than conventional general intelligence (g). Mayer, Salovey and Caruso (2000) make a useful distinction between *ability* and *mixed* models of EI. Ability models, like their own, seek to define EI in terms of fairly well-defined aptitudes and skills for processing emotional information. As with established intelligence constructs, the presumption is that EI should be measured using objective performance tests, on which items have right-or-wrong answers. By contrast, mixed models conceptualise EI as a more diverse construct, including aspects of personality and motivation that facilitate dealing with emotional situations. Bar-On

(1997, 2000), for example, sees EI as an index of the person's overall capacity to adapt to demanding situations. Bar-On, and other mixed-model theorists, see self-reports and questionnaires as appropriate for measuring EI.

Whichever model is adopted, the development of a good test of EI is quite a challenge. The test must meet normal psychometric criteria. That is, it should be reliable, supported by factor analysis, and valid as a predictor of emotionally competent behaviour. Moreover, there is no point in reinventing the wheel: the test should measure a construct that is distinct from existing personality and ability variables. Tests based on the ability model (Mayer et al., 2000) must surmount the initial obstacle of constructing items that have clear right and wrong answers. The difficulties of doing so are well known. Many attempts to develop tests for the related construct of 'social intelligence' have failed because it is often debatable what actually constitutes 'socially intelligent' behaviour in many situations. Similarly, the 'emotionally intelligent' response to a real-life problem, such as resolving a dispute between two people, is unclear, or depends on the exact circumstances.

Mayer, Salovey and their colleagues (e.g., Mayer et al., 2000) have developed the two leading ability tests: the Multi-factor Emotional Intelligence Scale (MEIS) and its successor, the Mayer-Salovey-Caruso Emotional Intelligence Test (MSCEIT). Both are based on a four-branch conceptualisation of EI that distinguishes four different aspects of EI:

1 the ability to accurately perceive, appraise, and express emotions;
2 the ability to access or generate feelings that facilitate thought;
3 the ability to understand emotions and emotional knowledge;
4 the ability to regulate emotions to manage challenging situations and promote personal growth.

Each branch has several tests associated with it. Figure 13.2 shows a typical item from a test for the first branch (emotion perception). The respondent must judge what emotions are expressed in the face stimulus. Other tests require the person to associate pictures with emotions (branch 2), to describe typical progressions of emotion (branch 3), and to indicate how effective various courses of action would be in resolving difficult situations (branch 4). Mayer et al. (2000) suggest two solutions to the difficult problem of scoring the test responses. *Expert scoring* requires a team of experts, such as psychologists who study emotion, to decide the best answer to each question: high scorers on the test are those who agree with the experts. *Consensus scoring* requires that, first, a large set of test responses is collected from the population of interest. These normative data indicate the typical or modal response to each item. Subsequently, data are scored according to how close the respondent's answer is to the normative response. In effect, the more typical the response, the more emotionally intelligent it is deemed to be. The rationale for this seemingly odd procedure is that, it is claimed, the consensus opinion in large groups often appears to be optimal (Mayer et al., 2000). Of course, the two scoring methods should agree with one another. Roberts, Zeidner and

	Definitely not present				Definitely present
Anger	**1**	2	3	4	5
Sadness	**1**	2	3	4	5
Happiness	1	2	3	4	**5**
Disgust	**1**	2	3	4	5
Fear	1	**2**	3	4	5
Surprise	1	2	**3**	4	5

Figure 13.2 A sample item representing the face perception sub-test of the Multi-Factor Emotional Intelligence Scale

Note 'Best answers' (consensual scoring) are given in bold

Source Mayer et al. (2000)

Matthews (2001) showed rather mediocre convergence for the MEIS, but the two methods seem to show good agreement for the MSCEIT (Mayer et al., in press).

What, then, of the psychometric properties of the MEIS and MSCEIT? Generally, the scales of these instruments are tolerably reliable and stable over time, especially for overall score, and the factor structures seem consonant with the four-branch model (though some significant but relatively minor difficulties remain: Matthews et al., 2003; Roberts et al., 2001). Furthermore, whatever the Mayer-Salovey scales measure, it is something new, and distinct from existing constructs. Roberts et al. (2001), in a large sample ($n=704$), found a correlation of 0.32 with general intelligence measures, and only small correlations (<0.3) with the Big Five. Finally, studies have tested whether the MEIS relates meaningfully to criteria related to emotional competence (the MSCEIT is too new to have inspired much research on its external validity). A full review is beyond the scope of this chapter (see Matthews et al., 2003; Mayer et al., 2000). In general, although the MEIS does predict various criteria such as life happiness and low levels of deviant behaviour, correlation magnitudes are low (typically <0.3). However, these findings do justify further studies of the MEIS/MSCEIT as measures that add something new to psychological assessment.

Turning to mixed models, the process of test construction is much more akin to developing personality questionnaires. The test designer writes items that will sample the various qualities linked to EI by whatever definition of EI is being used. The most thorough development work of this kind has been conducted by Bar-On (1997, 2000). He has proposed five components of emotional intelligence. His EQ-i questionnaire includes fifteen scales that relate to one or other component, as illustrated in table 13.9. Although the five-factor structure does not seem to be reliable (Matthews et al., 2003; Petrides and Furnham, 2001), the scales are internally consistent and stable over time.

Unfortunately, the EQ-i shows poor 'convergent' and 'divergent' validity. Convergent validity means that the test should correlate highly with other related tests, as do the extraversion scales from the Eysenck Personality Questionnaire and NEO-PI-R. Bar-On (2000) reports a correlation of 0.46 between the MEIS and EQ-i, suggesting only moderate overlap: the two EI tests are not really measuring the same construct. Divergent validity means the test should *not* correlate highly with other distinct constructs. However, several studies have shown that the EQ-i fails this test. It is strongly correlated with measures of the Big Five (Dawda and Hart, 2000; Petrides and Furnham, 2001) and related traits (Newsome, Day and Catano, 2000). For example, Dawda and Hart (2000) report a correlation of −0.72 with Neuroticism, and Newsome et al. (2000) found a correlation of −0.77 with trait anxiety. Substantial correlations have also been found with high A, E and C (Dawda and Hart, 2000). Given this redundancy with the Big Five, it is not surprising that the EQ-i shows good criterion validity. For example (see Bar-On, 1997), it predicts the same set of coping characteristics (e.g. low emotion-focus, high task-focus) that are characteristic of low Neuroticism.

Another popular questionnaire, the Schutte Self Report Inventory (SSRI: Schutte et al., 1988) shows similar characteristics. It is internally consistent, but its internal factor structure is difficult to replicate (Petrides and Furnham, 2000). It is also highly correlated with the Big Five traits, though the pattern of correlation is a little different to the EQ-i (Saklofske, Austin and Minski, 2003). EI as defined by the SSRI tends to relate rather more strongly to E, and somewhat less to low N. Interestingly, Saklofske et al. (2003) showed incremental validity with respect to the Big Five in predicting criteria such as life satisfaction, but the additional variance explained was small. In sum, although questionnaires for 'emotional intelligence' may add something to existing personality scales, they largely assess existing constructs. However, it is possible that some elements of EI relate to a distinct primary personality trait (Petrides and Furnham, 2001).

Table 13.9 *EQ-i composite scales and sub-scales, with brief descriptions*

Composite/Subscale	Brief description
Intrapersonal	
Emotional self-awareness	Recognise and understand one's feelings
Assertiveness	Express feelings, thoughts and beliefs, and defend one's rights in a non-destructive manner
Self-regard	Understand, accept and respect oneself
Self-actualisation	Realise one's potential capacities
Independence	Self-directed, self-controlled and free of emotional dependency
Interpersonal	
Empathy	Aware and appreciative of the feelings of others
Interpersonal relationship	Establish and maintain satisfying relationships characterised by emotional closeness and mutual affection
Social responsibility	Co-operative and responsible member of one's social group
Adaptation	
Problem solving	Define problems and generate potentially effective solutions
Reality testing	Evaluate the correspondence between objective and subjective reality in realistic and 'well-grounded' fashion
Flexibility	Adjust emotions, thoughts and behaviours to changing conditions
Stress management	
Stress tolerance	Withstand adverse events, through positive, active coping
Impulse control	Resist or delay an impulse, drive or temptation to act
General mood	
Happiness	Feel satisfied with life, and enjoy oneself and being with others
Optimism	Maintain a positive attitude, even in the face of adversity

Source Bar-On (1997, 2000)

Applications to organisational psychology

As we have seen, organisational psychologists have high hopes for the applied utility of EI tests. Goleman, in collaboration with Boyatzis (Boyatzis, Goleman and Rhee, 2000), has developed the Emotional Competence Inventory (ECI) to assess EI in the workplace. Unfortunately, the evidence for its efficacy is almost all in the form of unpublished, sometimes confidential, reports, so its utility is unknown. Evidently, if EI is indeed the main quality required for success in the workplace (Goleman, 1998; Watkin, 2000), then it should be highly predictive of organisational criteria. There are some general grounds for caution. As previously discussed, correlations between standard personality measures and job performance are useful but modest (Barrick et al., 2001). It would be surprising if EI measures, especially those based on self-report, were dramatically more predictive. In addition, the more enthusiastic proponents of EI base their conclusions on remarkably little documented evidence (Zeidner, Matthews and Roberts, in press). Barrett at al.'s review (2001) concurs that much of the existing evidence bearing on the role of EI in occupational success is anecdotal, impressionistic, or collected by consulting companies and not published in the peer-reviewed literature.

The relatively small number of published studies, generally using questionnaire measures, give a better idea of what we can expect from EI scales (see Zeidner, Matthews and Roberts, in press, for a review). Bachman et al. (2000) hypothesised that emotional competencies enable account officers to achieve greater success in collections. In two rather small samples ($Ns < 40$), they did indeed show that more effective cash collectors scored more highly on the EQ-i than less effective officers. However, they failed to measure any of the personality factors with which the EQ-i is correlated.

Slaski and Cartwright (2002) studied 224 middle and senior managers from the UK's largest supermarket chain. The EQ-i was quite a good predictor of subjective qualities such as morale, distress and work satisfaction (rs were in the 0.4–0.6 range). In addition, management performance was gauged by assessments of immediate line managers who were asked to rate the frequency of specific behaviours such as setting objectives, planning and organising, and team work. Total EQ-i score was modestly related to managerial performance ($r = 0.22$). Again, no attempt was made to partial out personality variables confounded with the EQ-i. Thus, a decisive verdict on the utility of scales for EI must be delayed until more evidence is available, but, so far, findings are not particularly promising.

Conclusions

1. Personality trait measures are widely used in applied psychology, especially by clinical, educational and organisational psychologists. Typically, traits are administered together with other kinds of assessment, such as interviews. A variety of professional skills are needed in order to use trait questionnaires effectively. First, the practitioner must select a questionnaire, or questionnaires, that are appropriate for the applied problem, choosing between general and contextualised scales, and broad and narrow trait constructs, for example. Second, the practitioner must evaluate questionnaires against various accepted standards, such as reliability, validity and freedom from response bias. Third, assessment of traits must contribute to effective practical decision-making, for example in diagnosing clinical disorders, or in selecting job applicants. Decision-making requires consideration of the utilities of different choices, and an understanding of how validity, base rate and selection ratio influence the value of personality assessment. The practitioner must also be aware of ethical and legal issues, such as fairness in selection of job applicants.

2. Educational and clinical psychologists are often concerned with diagnosing and treating various forms of abnormality, ranging from relatively minor behaviour problems to clinical disorder. In the educational context, assessment of traits contributes both to understanding barriers to learning and performance, such as test anxiety, and to the diagnosis of childhood mental disorders. Clinical psychologists also use trait inventories to assist in diagnosis, most often using measures of abnormal personality such as the MMPI, but also general questionnaires such as the NEO-PI-R. In addition, assessment of traits may be useful in understanding the client, selecting therapies, anticipating treatment outcomes and understanding abnormalities of processing that underlie mental disorder.

3. In organisational psychology, the principal application of trait research is the selection of job applicants. This usage of traits requires that the trait is a valid predictor of performance on the job concerned, and the general validity of traits in this context has sometimes been challenged. There are various difficulties in assessing the criterion of validity of traits, related to measurement of job performance criteria, restriction of range in personality, and the role of moderator factors. However, recent meta-analyses have concluded that the major personality traits are indeed predictive of job performance, although correlations are typically modest. The most consistent predictor is Conscientiousness, which also relates to integrity and other desirable work behaviours. Other traits may also be predictive, depending on moderator variables such as the type of job. For example, Extraversion and Openness are especially predictive of performance during training.

4. Assessment of personality traits has additional applications in the workplace, supported by research. Traits are related to vocational interests and choices, so that assessment may contribute to career counselling. Longer-term career progression may also be related to personality: workers high in Neuroticism and low in Conscientiousness may be most likely to change jobs. Personality may also relate to the outcomes of other forms of assessment, such as interview and behavioural assessments. Counselling may help the job applicant make the best of their dispositional qualities. Personality traits, especially neuroticism, also relate to vulnerability to work stress, and so may be relevant to stress management programmes that focus on the individual's appraisals and coping resources.

5. A new field of personality assessment is concerned with 'emotional intelligence', defined by various competencies in perceiving and managing emotional situations. There are two main strategies for assessing EI. The first is to develop objective tests on which items have right or wrong answers, established by experts or by consensus judgement. Such tests have good divergent validity with respect to personality and mental ability, but, so far, there is only limited evidence for criterion validity. The second measurement strategy is to develop questionnaires, resembling personality questionnaires. In fact, instruments of

this kind have been shown to overlap substantially with existing scales, such that EI appears to be largely emotional stability, with additional contributions from Extraversion, Agreeableness and Conscientiousness. Assessment of EI has been seen as important for organisational psychology, because of the importance of 'emotional literacy' in the workplace. However, perhaps because of the difficulties in measuring the construct, there is little evidence so far to show that EI scales have much predictive validity over and above that provided by existing ability and personality tests.

Further reading

Barrick, M. R., Mount, M. K. and Judge, T. A. (2001) Personality and performance at the beginning of the new millennium: what do we know and where do we go next? *International Journal of Selection and Assessment*, 9, 9–30.

Costa, P. T., Jr. (1996). Work and personality: use of the NEO-PI-R in industrial/organizational psychology. *Applied Psychology: an International Review*, 45, 225–41.

Kline, P. (1993) *The handbook of psychological testing*. London: Routledge.

Matthews, G., Zeidner, M. and Roberts, R. D. (2003) *Emotional intelligence: science and myth*. Cambridge, MA: MIT Press.

14 Conclusions

Traits are alive and well. We contend that the research reviewed demonstrates that stable individual differences in personality are quantifiable and related to a variety of important criteria. Four key areas highlight the advances of contemporary trait research: psychometrics, biological bases, integration with mainstream psychology, and real-world applications. For each area, we will consider briefly both the accomplishments of trait research, and how future research might address remaining problems.

Psychometric issues

The current bullishness of trait psychologists begins with the slaying of the dragon of situationism, by exposure of the fallacies of Mischel's (1968) critique of traits (Eysenck and Eysenck, 1980), and increasingly sophisticated data on cross-situational behavioural consistency, cross-cultural generality and temporal stability (see chapters 2 and 3). We now have personalities again, and it is exciting to see their return (Goldberg, 1993). Furthermore, psychometricians have reduced competing structural models of broad 'superfactors' to a manageable number. Both Eysenck (1997) and proponents of the Big Five (Costa and McCrae, 1998; Saucier and Goldberg, 2002) have developed models with strong claims to validity, with some overlap with respect to the E and N factors. Possibly, the two models can be reconciled as alternative descriptions at different levels of generality, within a hierarchical personality model. Additional traits may also become elevated to superfactor status as research findings accumulate (Hogan and Hogan, 2002).

The way ahead is reasonably clear. At the psychometric level, advances in structural modelling are likely to provide better tools for choosing between alternative factor models. At the same time, most researchers agree with Eysenck (1992a) that psychometric evidence alone is insufficient to choose between different trait models. The development of internally consistent, stable trait measures, with good cross-cultural validity, such as those provided by the EPQ-R and NEO-PI-R, provides a solid platform for research on the predictive validity of traits. Traits are complemented by an increasing range of validated state constructs that may be investigated as dependent or mediating variables (see chapter 4). We anticipate more studies which use alternative trait measures to test contrasting theory-driven predictions. Previous research has delineated topic areas for which traits are demonstrably important. It is open to researchers to test which of the various dimensional models does the best job of predicting the criteria relevant to a topic by explicitly comparing the different measurement instruments. For example, it is evident that delinquent, antisocial behaviour relates to personality in both experimental and real-world paradigms (Furnham and Heaven, 1999). The Eysenckian might look to the P dimension to explain most of the criterion variance, the Cattellian to the Self-Control secondary factor, and the five factor model theorist to C and A. A clinician might prefer dimensions of personality disorder such as 'antisocial'. No single study will determine which trait theory provides the best explanation for the role of personality, but programmatic research should indicate which theory provides the most convincing nomological network. Whatever the outcome of comparative tests of different models, trait psychologists are now in a position to pursue 'normal science', testing clearly stated theories against one another and empirical data. We may anticipate a culling of weaker personality constructs, and a re-focus of research around those with demonstrable validity.

Biological bases of personality

One of the major advances of trait research has been the establishment of the heritability of traits, which necessarily implies that traits have at least some biological basis. The credit for this achievement goes to traditional behaviour genetic research using twin, family and adoption studies (see chapter 6). The future of genetic personality research, however, lies with large scale molecular genetic research which may reveal some of the specific DNA loci that contribute to personality dispositions (Plomin et al., 2001). This newer type of genetic research can give clues to the biological mechanisms that underlie personality traits (Goldman, 1996).

Progress in the psychophysiology of personality has been less dramatic, and has perhaps been hindered by an excessive focus on the problematic arousal construct. Psychobiological research on personality which is not inspired by arousal theory is often atheoretical, with significant results explained post hoc. This line of investigation is both driven and limited by the availability of psychobiological measures, and so is dependent on the sophistication of the techniques concerned. This strategy can only reveal meaningful findings about the bases of traits when the technique used does in fact assess variation in brain processes related to personality traits. Perhaps the regularity of some aspects of brain functioning can be assumed to exist, given the substantial genetic contribution to major traits. However, it is moot whether current techniques are adequate for accessing such patterning of brain function and its individual differences. On the positive side, the increased use of brain-imaging techniques in personality studies shows great promise for more satisfactory theory testing and development.

We saw in chapter 7 that replicable associations between traits and psychophysiological functioning have been found in certain, somewhat specialised experimental paradigms. In our opinion, such findings are promising, but do not yet serve to map out the major pathways from genes to individual differences in behaviour and subjective awareness. New technology, in the form of brain imaging techniques for specific ligands, informed by the links between genes and traits established in molecular genetic studies, may illuminate relationships between traits and brain function, although it is unlikely to provide complete or simple answers. A general difficulty is the complexity of the causal networks involved, both in tracing how multiple genes code for brain physiology, and in linking brain systems to behavioural regularities. We may reasonably infer that, even though traits are biologically based, a hard-nosed biological reductionism is unlikely to succeed in the foreseeable future. The hope of pioneers of the biological approach was that a small number of parameters or formal characteristics of brain functioning might be identified, which might be mapped one-to-one onto trait dimensions. For example, extraversion could be identified with cortical arousability or strength of the nervous system, which in turn would relate to specific genes. We tend to agree with Zuckerman (1991) that this hope may be forlorn, and that traits relate to interacting complexes of biological systems (see figure 7.5; Deary and Hettema, 1993). If substantial biological reductionism is theoretically possible, but impracticable, the alternative is to develop better psychological models of trait action, a task related to our next key area, integration with mainstream psychology.

We emphasise, nevertheless, that methodological failure of the psychophysiological project would not contradict the fact that personality has its bases partly in genetically influenced biological regularities in brain function. Researchers in this area may have to face the frustrating reality that, whereas we have established valid personality dimensions and the approximate, probably substantial genetic contributions to traits, there may for a long time exist a mechanistic chasm between these two achievements.

Integration with mainstream psychology

One of the features of the conventional, Hall of Fame personality textbook is the limited contact made with contemporary psychological theory in other areas. Personality psychology is based either on rather dated theories such as psychoanalysis, or, like humanistic psychology, it is something entirely distinct from other branches of psychology (see chapter 5). However, personality is investigated primarily through individual differences in psychological functioning and behaviour, so it is sensible to base our understanding on contemporary knowledge of the functions through which personality is expressed. Trait theory owes a considerable debt to physiologically oriented theorists such as Eysenck, Gray and Zuckerman, who have laboured to relate traits to contemporary neuropsychology. The psychophysiological approach has its limitations, but the research strategy of relating traits to an established model of functioning (e.g., a 'conceptual nervous system') is exemplary. As discussed previously, comparable research efforts are beginning to emerge using cognitive and social models of psychological functioning.

We see the use of contemporary psychological models as providing exciting prospects for future trait research. The 'cognitive revolution' which has transformed most areas of psychology has not yet fulfilled its potential for transforming trait psychology. It is perhaps not surprising that the prototypical cognitive psychological study, involving fine manipulations of specialised laboratory tasks, has had limited appeal to personality psychologists. However, the broader model of the person as information-processor is of wider relevance. This metaphor is becoming increasingly popular in social, clinical and developmental psychology. It is also highly compatible with current trends in the cognitive neuroscience of personality (Matthews, Derryberry and Siegle, 2000). The information-processing metaphor has made a major contribution to understanding how traits relate to stress and anxiety, as discussed in chapter 9, and, naturally, to research on traits and performance (see chapter 12). We anticipate further theoretical developments based on relating traits to individual differences in information-processing, especially in the field of social cognition and behaviour. Perhaps, then, personality psychology will catch up with its older sibling in the family of concepts studied by differential psychologists, viz. intelligence. Research in cognitive ability provides an excellent example of the coming together of psychology's two disciplines and contemporary research in mental ability is increasingly informed by cognitive psychological constructs (Deary, 2000).

Expanded contact between trait researchers and mainstream psychology is required to counter the criticism made of traits, that they are merely descriptive constructs, with no explanatory force. As we have seen, physiological trait theory is in principle capable of countering such criticisms. Individual differences in brain function are seen as the causal agent which influences psychophysiology, behaviour and responses to questionnaire items. We have also seen that physiological explanations are not in themselves sufficient, and must be supplemented by explanations at other levels of description. For example, we can use transactional models of stress (Lazarus and Folkman, 1984; Deary et al., 1996) to provide a 'conceptual information-processing system', within which styles of appraisal and coping processes may explain, at least partially, associations between neuroticism and stress symptoms (Wells and Matthews, 1994). A promising new frontier for research is to use social cognitive models as a framework for studying agreeableness (Graziano, Hair and Finch, 1997). In general, the aim is to move from seeing traits merely as descriptions of 'correlated habits of reaction' (Zuckerman, 1991) to identifying traits with patterns of individual differences in key physiological and social-cognitive variables that underpin both individual differences in behaviour and subjective awareness.

Applications of trait theory

Questionnaire measures of traits ask the respondent about everyday life, and theorists from Allport (1937) onwards have proposed that traits influence important real-world behaviours. This being so, a healthy trait psychology should contribute to applications of psychology, as discussed in chapter 13. The Big Five model in particular is increasingly providing a basic framework for applied studies, especially in industrial/organisational psychology. In clinical psychology, trait measures are increasingly important for diagnosis and other uses. Other important areas of application are educational psychology, in which traits related to anxiety and motivation are important (see Boekarts, 1995), and child psychopathology (see Southam-Gerow and Kendall, 2002, for a review of the contribution of temperament research).

Organisational psychologists' use of trait measures dates back to the 1900s (Kanfer et al., 1995). Interest in traits has been growing steadily in recent years, in line with the strengthening of the scientific case for traits. Roughly 50 per cent of UK business sector organisations use trait measures, primarily for recruitment and selection, but also for other purposes such as training and development and career counselling (Williams, 1994). Popularity does not indicate validity, but meta-analyses of Big Five data show that interest in trait measures as predictors of performance and other occupational criteria is well founded (chapter 13). The new construct of emotional intelligence has had considerable impact within organisational psychology, although, in this case, enthusiasm may exceed predictive validity (Zeidner, Matthews and Roberts, in press).

Some doubts about the modest magnitude of the criterion validity of traits may remain. However, we have seen that even quite small correlations may improve the quality of decision-making in selecting job applicants. Furthermore, modest correlations are generally the norm in psychology, unless both predictor and criterion assess similar constructs (e.g., two alternative measures of extraversion), as discussed in chapter 2. Funder and Ozer (1983) point out that effect size correlations between 0.30 and 0.40 characterise some of the most important experimental effects in social psychology, for example. It seems clear also that organisational psychologists are not reaping the full benefits of trait measures, through neglect of the task- and context-specificity of associations between traits and performance. The laboratory evidence on performance shows clearly that extraversion is sometimes an advantage and sometimes a hindrance, and use of extraversion measures in the workplace requires identification of the organisational and task variables which may moderate its effects on behaviour.

In clinical psychology the use of trait measures is increasingly bolstered by evidence of overlap between clinical and trait constructs (Costa and Widiger, 2002). Psychometric studies suggest that a substantial part of the variance in clinically oriented measures such as the MMPI is associated with the Big Five. Chapter 11 reviews the good convergence between the Big Five model and diagnostic categories for personality disorder: in particular, neuroticism is the common element to a variety of affective disorders related to negative affect. Neuroticism is a particularly potent predictor of everyday stress symptoms, and may also be relevant to treatment of physical health problems (see chapter 10). Eysenck (1992b) argued that many of the clinical features of psychotic disorders are apparent in subclinical form in high scorers on his Psychoticism scale. Evidence of this kind led McCrae and Costa (1986) to assert that the Big Five provide a general description of the individual's emotional, interpersonal, experiential and motivational styles, providing a starting point for the application of clinical judgements and skills.

Several issues remain to be resolved by future research, especially the causal status of traits. As we saw in chapter 9, longitudinal studies suggest that there is a subtle interplay between traits and clinical symptoms which requires careful modelling. The extent to which traits characteristic of normal populations should be supplemented by specifically abnormal traits remains open. For example, a factor-analysis of traits related to schizophrenia (Mason, 1995) identified a factor related to cognitive and perceptual abnormalities such as hallucinations which was quite distinct from the Eysenck traits, including P. A final difficulty which requires further research is the possible complexity of relationships between traits and disorders. Several traits may contribute to any particular condition. Mason (1995) found that all the Eysenck traits related to potential risk factors for schizophrenia: P and low L to impulsive non-conformity, N to cognitive disorganisation and low E to anhedonia. Furthermore, traits may interact: it is well established that neurotic introverts are prone to emotional problems, whereas neurotic extraverts tend to misbehave (Eysenck and Eysenck, 1985). A considerable research effort is required before the individual's vulnerability to clinical disorder can be ascertained with precision.

Thus, the application of traits must be tempered by realistic expectations about the amount of criterion variance that is actually predictable, in typical situations. We should not expect large correlations between single traits and occupational and clinical measures. It is enough to discover that traits can add significant and independent, albeit modest, increments to the variance in an outcome measure. It will often be the case that: (a) a small contribution to the variance of an outcome will have large implications over an extended period of time and/or when applied to a large sample of people; and (b) the modest contribution of trait(s) to prediction will not be bettered by any other psychological or sociological construct.

Towards a theory of traits

One of the messages of this book is that the evidence for predictive validity of traits is now overwhelming. In virtually every field of psychology, we find the traits correlate with individual differences in behaviour, subjective experience or physiology, often to a practically useful extent. However, this profusion of data requires some overarching theory which will integrate the different branches of trait research, a theory which, currently, does not exist. Nevertheless, there are various pointers towards what such a theory might look like, which we will summarise here.

First, we should deal with the objection that trait psychology is essentially atheoretical, and, at best, a means for actuarial prediction in applied settings (e.g., Cervone and Caprara, 2000). One of the complaints seen in the social-psychological literature is that traits are no more than redescriptions of behaviour, so that any 'explanation' of trait effects is circular (e.g., Bandura, 1999). This view is something of a canard. As we saw in chapter 1, from the outset, trait psychology assumed what we called the 'causal primacy' of traits. As a latent 'neuropsychic structure' (Allport, 1937), a trait moderates manifest behaviour: it is *not* a re-description of behaviour. No contemporary trait theorist believes that studies of traits should conclude once the optimal factor structure has been found. The search for a consistent structural model of traits is only the first step in theory construction, much as the periodic table in chemistry was the necessary foundation for the atomic theory of elements. Throughout this book, we have given examples of how researchers are linking traits to the processes that control behaviour, ranging from neural processes to high-level social-cognitive processes.

Next, we will outline three possible ground plans for designing a theory that will explain the multiplicity of correlates of the major traits. The first is the traditional strategy proposed by biological theorists, notably Eysenck (1997) and Gray (1991). Traits correspond to individual differences in a small number of key brain systems. The 'periodic table' of traits is essentially a map of brain systems. The second, multi-component approach focuses on the diversity of correlates of traits. It sees traits as collections of biases in neuropsychic functioning, that cannot be reduced to any single system. For example, social-cognitive accounts of stability in personality describe consistencies in a large number of specific processing components (e.g., Mischel, 1999). Studies of information-processing, reviewed in chapter 12, suggest a similiar view of personality as distributed across many independent processing functions. The third basis for theory design (Matthews, 1999) aims for a synthesis of the parsimony of traditional approaches and the more fine-grained account of empirical data offered by the multi-component approach. It supposes that traits represent individual differences in *adaptations* to major life challenges. That is, traits represent a functional organisation of multiple neural and cognitive processes that support management of the demands of specialised situations or environments; for example, the manifold attributes of extraversion support adaptation to socially challenging situations.

Traditional biological theories of personality

The latter part of the twentieth century was dominated by biological theories of personality inspired by the work of Hans Eysenck. His theory represented a scientific paradigm (see Eysenck, 1981), in the sense of providing a widely accepted framework for understanding personality traits. As discussed in chapter 7, the assumption was that personality traits corresponded closely to brain systems for arousal and motivation. The paradigm also received powerful support from the behaviour genetic studies reviewed in chapter 6. The hope of biological theorists was that they could trace a direct path from genes to brain systems to fundamental psychological processes to complex social behaviours. However, in the light of the complexity of psychophysiological data, this hope today looks a little optimistic (Matthews and Gilliland, 1999, 2001). Indeed, the basic assumption of one-to-one correspondence between brain systems and traits (isomorphism) has been challenged from within psychophysiology, notably by Zuckerman (1991).

Nevertheless, the idea that personality directly reflects variation in specific brain functions remains an influential and powerful approach. The biological approach is attractively parsimonious and, historically, it has stimulated many of the major fields of empirical research that demonstrate the validity of traits. The difficulties of biological theories in explaining the multifarious correlates of traits, and the moderator factors that influence those correlations, may be attributed to the measurement difficulties intrinsic to psychophysiology. New studies using brain-imaging techniques might conceivably identify neural substrates for traits with a precision that has not previously been possible. While traditional arousal theory is increasingly seen as simplistic (e.g., Robbins, 1998), the existence of distinct brain systems for reward and punishment is widely accepted (Gray and McNaughton, 2000). It is no coincidence that studies of Gray's Reinforcement Sensitivity Theory are at the forefront of contemporary psychophysiological research (e.g., Corr, 2002).

A similar philosophy supports psychological theories of extraversion and neuroticism that link these traits to positive and negative affect, respectively (Lucas and Diener, 2000; Watson, 2000). The assumption here is that we can use a major psychological construct, i.e., emotionality, as the sole basis for explaining traits. According to this view, the various expressions of extraversion, such as assertiveness, sociability and so forth, are all derived from the positive emotionality that represents the core of the trait (see chapter 4). Likewise, to be neurotic is to be prone to negative emotion. Again, this is an influential view that is open to empirical tests, although, in chapter 4, we argued that it does not fully explain the affective correlates of personality. It also begs the question of what factors control individual differences in emotionality. Proponents of this approach tend to assume that emotion is a fairly straightforward expression of brain systems, but this view does not do justice to the role of cognitive appraisal, coping and self-regulative processes, discussed in chapter 9. Like their biological counterparts, the emotionality theories are parsimonious, conceptually clear and readily testable. Whether they provide an adequate account of the full range of correlates of E and N is open to question. It is also unclear what single psychological or neural systems might explain other traits, such as C, A, and O.

Multi-component approaches

Traditional theories suppose that any behavioural correlate of the trait can ultimately be traced back to the core system that supports the trait: i.e., a 'tree' model, such that each branch converges on a common trunk. By contrast, multi-component theories suppose a 'thicket' model, such that any 'branch' (a behavioural expression) may be traced back to one of several independent 'trunks' (causal influences on personality). For example, a traditional theory might suppose that all the various manifestations of trait anxiety, such as subjective tension, worry, attentional bias, muscle tension and autonomic nervous system arousal may all be traced back to a common system for threat sensitivity. Multi-component models suppose that different manifestations actually reflect different underlying systems. For example, within a physiological instantiation of this approach we might relate anxiety to subcortical emotion generators, to frontal cortex systems for emotion regulation, and to parietal sites that control spatial orienting to threat (cf., Matthews, Derryberry and Siegle, 2000). As discussed in chapters 9 and 12, there are also multiple information-processing routines that may be linked to anxiety. In other words, there may be no master system for trait anxiety, which is controlled by multiple neural and cognitive components. Such a view is compatible with the emerging molecular genetics of personality, which posits multiple, independent genes as the basis for personality. It also fits with evolutionary–psychological approaches that suppose that behaviour is controlled by many independent modules (Tooby and Cosmides, 1992; see chapter 6). Mischel's (1999) CAPS model, described in chapter 2, also discriminates a multiplicity of cognitive, affective and motivational processes that may be linked to traits, within a very different theoretical perspective.

Developing multi-component approaches requires a more fine-grained mapping of the various processes that may, collectively, define the trait. Such an enterprise requires identifying not just biological processes that relate to traits, but also information-processing and higher-level cognitive-social constructs. A key idea is that *multi-levelled* trait explanations are required (Hettema and Deary, 1993): different phenomena require different kinds of explanation. Individual differences in the psychophysiological startle response might require an account of neural sensitivity to intense stimuli, whereas individual differences in coping with bereavement might require an understanding of the person's social identity (whether or not high-level social cognitions are ultimately reducible to biological explanations). Table 14.1 shows, informally, one scheme of this kind, that allocates empirical findings to different levels of explanation (see Matthews, 1997a, 2000a, for a formal model).

A further step organises empirical work on traits around such a multi-levelled scheme. Tables 14.2 and 14.3 illustrate how this can be done for the traits of extraversion and neuroticism, for some sample findings (see Matthews, 1999; and Matthews, Derryberry and Siegle, 2000, for more detailed accounts). In each case, the trait relates to biological substrates for behaviour, to individual differences in basic information-processing functions, and to the person's high-level understanding of the world and their role within it. Note also that, even within each level, the trait is associated with multiple, independent constructs (cf., Zuckerman, 1991). This view contrasts with traditional biological theories that seek one master system (e.g. the cortico-reticular loop) for each trait. These are tapestries half-woven. As

Table 14.1 *Three levels of explanation for trait psychology*

Level of explanation	Constructs	Empirical methods
Biological	Genes Brain systems	Molecular and behaviour genetics Psychophysiology Biological manipulations (e.g., drugs)

Information-processing	Basic cognitive processes
	  e.g., working memory,
	  attentional resources
		Experimental studies of task
		  performance, using objective
		  measures

*Volitional motivation and
  self-regulation*
	Stable self and social
	  knowledge, personal
	  meaning
		Experimental and field studies of
		  social cognition, appraisal and
		  coping: often using subjective
		  measures

Table 14.2 *Empirical findings regarding extraversion–introversion, allocated to different levels of explanation*

Level of explanation	Examples of empirical correlates and findings of extraversion
Biological	– Substantial inherited component – Low cortical arousability – Motor responsiveness (linked to Behavioural Activation System)
Information-processing	– Verbal divided attention – Poorer sustained attention – Moderation of effects of arousal on attention
Volitional motivation and self-regulation	– Strong social motivations and interests – Appraisal of events as challenging and controllable – Coping using task- or problem-focused strategies

Table 14.3 *Empirical findings regarding neuroticism–emotional stability, allocated to different levels of explanation*

Level of explanation	Examples of empirical findings
Biological	– Substantial inherited component – Biological stress vulnerability (e.g., health problems) – Sensitivity to punishment (linked to Behavioural Inhibition System)
Information-processing	– Vulnerability to attentional overload – Selective attention towards threat – Moderation of effects of stress on attention
Volitional motivation and self-regulation	– Self-protective motives (e.g., against social threat) – Appraisal of events as threatening – Coping using self-critical emotion-focused strategies

discussed previously, each area of research has its methodological and empirical controversies, and it may transpire that some of the threads have been misplaced. Nevertheless, the outline of the multi-levelled descriptive picture is appearing.

Thus, we can add process-oriented taxonomies of individual traits to structural taxonomies such as the five factor model. This approach portrays each trait as a multiple set of biases distributed across a range of biological and psychological processes. As discussed in chapter 12, each bias may be explained by a 'mini-theory'; for example, in the case of neuroticism (and trait anxiety), we can seek to explain attentional bias to threat in terms of very specific selective attentional processes. The multi-levelled perspective also provides a more satisfactory way to explain the real-world correlates of traits, such as emotion, stress response and social behaviours. Rather than making additional assumptions to squeeze the data into some arousal theory framework, for example, we can systematically test the different processes against one another as explanations for the gross correlates of personality. Biological and cognitive mediation hypotheses that explain personality–emotion correlations provide an example. At present, it is often unknown which type of explanation works best for a given phenomenon (individual differences in emotion are a case in point), but a process-based taxonomy points the way forward to resolving these issues by empirical test.

We can be fairly confident that future research will map traits to processes, and map processes to those behaviours that make a difference in real life. However, this achievement will not be the end of the road. There is a paradox in trait research that the more closely we look at traits at the process level, the harder they are to see. Extraversion–introversion emerges in factor analyses as an immovable pillar of trait psychology, but the magnitude of its correlations with measures of specific physiological and cognitive processes is typically quite small. How can such a dominant feature of the psychometric landscape be so elusive in these empirical studies? The answer from traditional approaches might be that researchers have not yet identified the critical neural processes that govern the trait, due to the difficulties of psychophysiological assessment. Next, we explore a second possibility, that we cannot straightforwardly reduce traits to a small number of basic mechanisms.

A cognitive-adaptive theory

As discussed in chapter 12, cognitive science emphasises not just information-processing models, but also the functional design of systems to pursue specific goals. It may be useful to think of traits as representing individual differences in design or *adaptation* (Buss, 1993; Matthews and Dorn, 1995). Traits indicate how well the individual is equipped to deal with the challenges common to most people's lives: e.g., maintaining personal safety, working with others and forming intimate relationships. We saw in chapter 12 that the physiological and cognitive characteristics of extraverts may give them advantages in social interaction. If so, we have not only a mini-theory for explaining social–behavioural correlates of extraversion, but a deeper understanding of the meaning of this trait. In a sense, extraversion 'is' fitness or preparedness for challenging social activity, supported by various acquired and/or inherited psychobiological and cognitive characteristics. Although the trait constitutes many small biases in multiple processes, the various levels of trait expression are unified in that they support a common adaptive goal (Matthews, 1999; Zeidner and Matthews, 2000). By analogy, designing a fast car is not simply a matter of installing a large engine. Multiple, independent parts must be designed to 'adapt' the car to high-speed operation, such as a streamlined body shell, a firm suspension and powerful brakes.

An adaptive theory links the 'component parts' of a specified trait to an adaptation, or fitness to manage some specialised environment or situation. What would such a theory look like? At the least, it should specify the following:

1 *Nature of component processes.* The theory should specify the various biases in neural and information-processing components that are characteristic of the trait.

2 *Sources of component processes.* The theory should, consistent with behaviour-genetic evidence, describe how genes and environmental influences shape these key processes during development.

3 *Acquired skills.* Real-world adaptation depends less on elementary component processes than on acquired skills (Ericsson, 1996). As we discussed in chapter 12, biases in elementary processes associated with traits promote individual differences in skill acquisition. For example, extraverts' advantages in language use feed into better social skills.

4 *Self-regulation.* Acquiring skills does not guarantee that they can be successfully executed when required; for example, test anxiety can block academic skills. The person is an active self-regulator who appraises his or her adaptive successes and failures, and tries to cope with failures to attain personal goals (see chapter 8). Self-regulative processes such as setting attainable goals and evaluating personal competence, together with the emotions generated by these processes, influence whether or not skills are deployed to maximum advantage.

5 *Key environments.* The theory must also specify the environments in which the trait is a determinant of adaptive success or failure; e.g., socially demanding environments in the case of extraversion.

6 *Adaptive behaviours.* The theory should describe the behaviours that influence goal attainment and adaptive success within the relevant environments. These include both behaviours directed towards some explicit goal (e.g., seeking a favour from another person) and behaviours that indirectly facilitate goal attainment by creating favourable internal and external conditions (e.g., maintaining a friendly demeanour).

7 *Dynamic factors.* As discussed in chapters 2 and 3, interaction with the environment feeds back into personality development: especially in childhood, but also in the adult. The theory should specify this dynamic person-situation interaction.

Figure 14.1 summarises a *cognitive-adaptive* theory of personality traits that follows these principles (Matthews, 1997b; Matthews, 1999; Zeidner and Matthews, 2000). It shows how different types or categories of personality components are

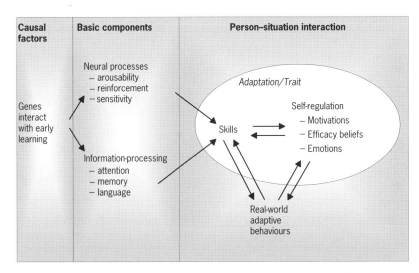

Figure 14.1 A cognitive-adaptive framework for understanding the processing basis for traits

interrelated. For simplicity, the figure does not try to present a full description of the many different specific components that might be located within each category. The left-hand part of the figure represents the basic building blocks of personality: individual differences in genotype and early learning feed into multiple components of neural function and information-processing. Thus, intrinsic to the trait is a prototypical pattern of typically small biases in neural and cognitive functioning. These patterns of processing differences provide a platform for subsequent personality development, depicted in the right-hand part of the figure. Processing biases influence the person's aptitude for acquiring skills, including cognitive skills such as problem-solving, to social skills for managing encounters with others, and to 'intrapersonal skills', such as maintaining focus when stressed or overloaded. These skills operate in tandem with self-regulation as the person seeks to use their capabilities in the service of some personal goal. Consistencies in self-regulation are supported by stable, self-referent memory structures such as schemas and scripts (Wells and Matthews, 1994; see chapters 8, 9 and 12). Self-regulative processing may facilitate or disrupt the application of skills, or it may generate other behaviours that act directly on the environment. For example, an anxious interviewee might experience distracting worries while attempting to answer a question (self-regulation disrupts skill). The person might also request more time to reflect (self-regulation acts on external environment, adaptively). The theory sees personality as being distributed across both acquired competencies, and across self-regulative dispositions that modulate the person–situation interaction.

The theory also specifies dynamic interaction between the person and the environment, which is an essential element of a larger theory. Successful adaptation, in the sense of beneficial person–environment interaction, in part reflects individual differences in neural and cognitive functioning feeding forward into superior skills. Extraverts have, so to speak, a natural advantage in demanding social

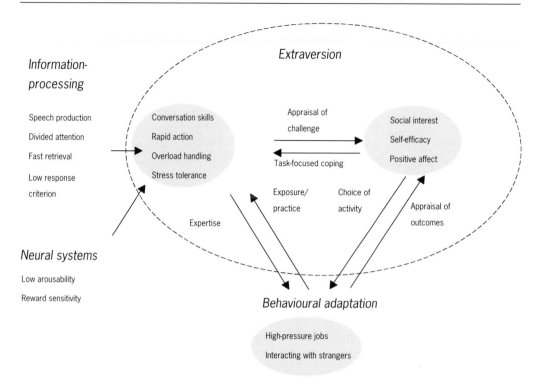

Figure 14.2 A cognitive-adaptive model of extraversion

settings, because their basic neural and cognitive attributes confer an advantage in acquiring the skills needed for those environments (irrespective of self-regulation). However, social-cognitive learning builds consistent styles of self-regulation (or self-knowledge), as discussed in chapter 8. For example, extraverts develop a self-concept that includes relatively high levels of self-esteem, self-efficacy and perceived control, with respect to social and cognitively challenging situations. Self-knowledge feeds back into skill acquisition and real-world adaptation.

In the well-adapted individual (e.g., the extravert engaged in demanding social activities), the dynamic interplay between skills, self-regulation and real-world behaviour operates harmoniously. Social ambitions, high social self-efficacy, and positive emotion encourage participation in social activities, affording further skill acquisition and positive outcomes, feeding back to maintain confidence. In addition, self-efficacy biases the person towards task-focused coping, leading to effective execution and deployment of skills. The trait might be seen as an emergent property of the 'adaptive triangle' (Matthews, 1999) of skills, self-knowledge and real-world adaptation. Trait stability results from the consistent influence of lower-level processing components, and the dynamic person–situation interaction which will tend to keep the person gravitating towards the situational 'niches' that are congruent with their skills and motivations. Figure 14.2 illustrates how these processes might work in extraverts (Matthews, 1999). As discussed in chapter 12, we

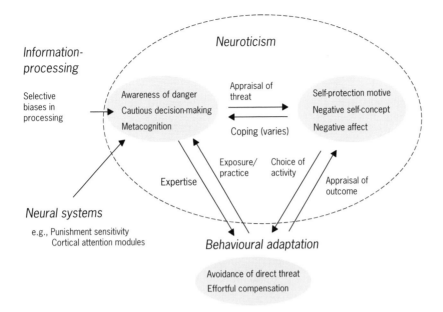

Figure 14.3 *Information-processing* — Selective biases in processing — *Neural systems* e.g., Punishment sensitivity, Cortical attention modules — *Neuroticism* — Awareness of danger, Cautious decision-making, Metacognition — Appraisal of threat, Coping (varies) — Self-protection motive, Negative self-concept, Negative affect — Expertise — Exposure/practice — Choice of activity — Appraisal of outcome — *Behavioural adaptation* — Avoidance of direct threat, Effortful compensation

Figure 14.3 A cognitive-adaptive model of neuroticism/trait anxiety

might construct a different adaptive triangle for introverts, focusing on skills and interests for more solitary pursuits.

Figure 14.3 shows a comparable adaptive triangle for neuroticism (Matthews, 1999; Matthews, Derryberry and Siegle, 2000). The assumption here is that the building blocks of N, such as biological and cognitive threat sensitivity, feed into an adaptation centred around self-protection motives, and perceptions of the self as inadequate to deal with threats, especially social threats. As discussed in chapter 12, this adaptation may indeed be adaptive in some settings, especially where delayed or subtle threats can be forestalled by compensatory effort and anticipation. However, it also risks a 'vicious circle' of maladaptation, in which difficulties at one vertex of the triangle provoke difficulties at the others, leading to stress or even mental disorder (see chapter 9). For example, excessive, self-critical emotion-focused coping may interfere with skill execution, leading to ineffective behavioural adaptation, and further emotion-focus. Similarly, emotion-focus may lead to avoidance of challenging situations, again with deleterious consequences. A cognitive-adaptive triangle for emotional stability would describe the processes building resilience under stress, and the capacity to prosper in threatening environments.

Of course, these figures are only schematic, and many of the details are open to challenge. However, the cognitive-adaptive model shows how the multifarious process-level correlates of traits may be organised around the fundamental adaptive issues of human life (Matthews, Zeidner and Roberts, 2003): personal security (Neuroticism), influence over others (Extraversion), co-operation vs competition (Agreeableness), self-advancement within society (Conscientiousness) and reliance on one's own intellect over received wisdom (Openness). Hence, as sets of neural, cognitive and social characteristics organised around adaptive goals, traits have scientific meaning which is not simply an arbitrary construction of the scientist.

Traits and the coherence of personality theory

The final issue to be addressed is how a theory of traits should be placed with regard to the wider field of personality, a field notorious for its lack of theoretical coherence. The question is currently especially acute because of the crumbling of the 'Berlin Wall' that formerly divided trait studies from social-psychological perspectives (Matthews and Gilliland, 1999). Trait psychologists increasingly are using the experimental paradigms of social psychology, and adopting some of its explanatory constructs (see chapter 8). Likewise, social psychologists are increasingly taking a serious look at how trait psychology relates to their own work (e.g., Cervone and Caprara, 2000; Mischel, 1999). Where will this new dialogue lead? Will there be some overall integration into a general theory of personality, or will the two approaches remain like distant cousins, meeting occasionally, but pursuing separate scientific lives?

Our position is that there is optimism for developing some broader personality theory to which traits are central, but which also includes elements of the social-psychological approach. The cause for optimism is that many of the central points of disagreement among theorists have been resolved, generally in favour of the trait approach. It is very clear from the empirical data reviewed that traits are substantially heritable, stable and predictive of behaviour across a wide variety of laboratory and real-world situations. It is difficult to see how social psychology can avoid some accommodation to these empirical realities. At the same time, trait psychology will continue to be enriched by infusions of ideas from social and cognitive psychology, including the importance of process-level analyses, representations of the self as a social being, and the role of social learning in constructing stable personality (see chapter 9). The largest of the remaining barriers towards integration appear to be the nature of constructs to be included in personality theory – the 'units of personality' (Pervin, 2002) – and the place of personal meaning in theory.

We have argued that traits permeate every aspect of personality, but, at the same time, personality is more than a bundle of trait characteristics. Even if the person's traits provide a general framework for personality, other factors such as culture, specific life experiences, learning and idiosyncrasies are undoubtedly important. Pervin (2002) differentiates traits, motives and cognitions as possible units of personality. Although historically relevant, this perspective may not be the most useful one for the future. As we have discussed, motivational and cognitive processes must be an important part of trait theory. Motives (e.g., need strengths) and cognitions (e.g., cognitive styles) can also themselves be operationalised as dispositions, and, as such, may represent somewhat separate spheres of differential psychology, whose interface with personality is open to exploration.

The more difficult issue is how we relate traits to more narrowly defined dispositional personality constructs. These are of two kinds: contextualised traits and idiographic qualities. Traits that refer to some specific context, such as self-efficacy at some activity, can be accommodated within a wider personality theory fairly straightforwardly. Constructs like test anxiety or job-related self-efficacy can be measured by validated questionnaires, and located psychometrically with respect to standard traits. So far, development of such constructs has proceeded on a fairly ad hoc basis. A more systematic approach to contextual and situational factors may be in order, though it is a familiar complaint of personality psychologists that the structure of situations is poorly understood. The work of Endler and Kocovski (2001), in differentiating anxiety traits that correspond to different classes of situational threat (e.g., social evaluation, physical danger), shows what can be accomplished within a limited domain. A focus on contextualised traits also suggests a more culturally grounded trait theory, as, to some extent, the salience of situational factors will vary cross-culturally: formal testing is a preoccupation of industrialised societies.

As Allport (1937) suggested, trait theory can accommodate idiographic traits, using methods such as those discussed in chapter 5, or through constructs such as personal projects (Cantor and Zirkel, 1990). Idiographic traits may also be essential to the self (Cervone, 1999), as discussed in chapter 8. At the same time, if the aim is to build a nomothetic science, the relevance of idiographic research is questionable, and this might be an area of inquiry that could be split off as a separate sub-discipline. Certainly, we cannot hope to map idiographic qualities psychometrically, as we can general and contextualised traits. On the other hand, if as Mischel (1999; see chapter 8) claims, dispositions reflect distinct, stable patterns of cognitive–affective units that may have idiographic content, the two conceptions of personality may be mutually supportive.

Another claim sometimes made by social psychologists is that only their approach can capture the fundamental nature of personality: how individuals understand the personal and interpersonal meaning of the events that shape their lives. This is, of course, a central theme of studies of the self. The criticism may be made gently, as in Strelau's (1983) separation of temperament (including most traits) from personality, or forcefully, as in Harre and Gillett's (1994) rejection of the whole concept. Social-cognitive theories that allow for some systematic variation in the contents of self-knowledge are something of a half-way house. At one level, the status of traits relates to the long-running philosophical debate between idealism and essentialism, which is expressed also in competing approaches to psychological theory (Brand, Egan and Deary, 1994). Like idealist philosophers, constructivists hold that 'beliefs create reality' (Hampson, 1988), and that meaning is constructed from other meanings. In contrast, trait psychology is based on the Aristotelian view that the human person has its own intrinsic essence. We have considered social constructivist criticisms of the trait approach already (chapter 8), so we will confine our further remarks largely to defending the place of traits at the core of personality theory.

Our claim is that adaptation, a process open to scientific study as outlined above, is central to the meanings individuals assign to their own personalities and life events. We suggest that, in Hampson's (1988) phrase, 'the theories we build about ourselves' are constrained, though not directly determined, by adaptive outcomes which have commonalities of meaning across all individuals and cultures, including outcomes relating to the areas of Power, Love, Work, Affect, and Intellect described by Goldberg (1990). Personal meaning for individuals high in Neuroticism is constrained by the experience of personal insecurity, negative affect and its cognitive concomitants. In the extreme case of clinical depression, cognitions of individuals show common features such as lack of self-worth and hopelessness which derive directly from the core beliefs and styles of erroneous reasoning characteristic of the condition (Beck, 1967). The information-processing machinery associated with these cognitive qualities is 'outside' the person's awareness, but serves to shape it. The negative beliefs are overly pessimistic, but not wholly illusory: depressives may be genuinely maladapted in problem-solving, attention, effortful action and interaction with others (Wells and Matthews, 1994). The patient's best efforts to think positively in a supportive social environment may not suffice to reverse the depression: it is not just a set of mental clothing to be put on and cast off at will (see Beck, 1967). Adaptive outcomes may be more varied in non-clinical, normally functioning individuals high in Neuroticism than in depressives, but, nevertheless, such individuals appear to have commonalities in style of cognitions of important life events, such as negative self-beliefs, which are likely to shape commonalities in personal meaning.

We suggest also that traits influence meanings derived from interpersonal interaction. People can, to some degree of accuracy, assess the adaptive status of others correctly. We are often able to judge which goals are personally important to someone else, and assess their success or failure in attaining those goals. Indeed, facial expression of emotion, which has a large degree of cross-cultural invariance, may have the function of signalling adaptive status to others, in a universal code (see Oatley and Johnson-Laird, 1987). As social beings, we could hardly survive without this capacity. The personality assessments of others are grounded in a reality common to self-assessments, consistent with the substantial correlations between self- and other-ratings of personality. Interaction with others is a key area of adaptation, and several of the Big Five may relate to predispositions to certain kinds of shared constructions. For example, depressed individuals are characterised by a style of interaction with others which tends to reinforce their negative self-beliefs (Coyne, 1985). Similarly, as discussed in chapter 8, individuals high in Agreeableness seek mutual positive regard and co-operation with others (e.g., Jensen-Campbell and Graziano, 2001). Longer-term social motives too may relate to traits. The high C individual may interpret their person–situation interactions in terms of a personal or societal mission, whereas the low C individual is more inclined to see the world as a basically disorganised place that rewards the opportunist. It is plausible that trait beliefs, rooted in the realities of adaptation, assist the person in finding and integrating meaning in disparate life experiences. Hence, there is a need for research on how traits relate to qualitative personal experience.

In conclusion, major advances have been made in developing psychometrically valid trait measures with good criterion and construct validity. A number of difficulties remain, such as competing structural models, weakness of psychophysiological evidence, delays in integrating trait research with mainstream psychology and limited predictive validity. There are grounds for optimism that such problems can be overcome by the normal scientific process of improving methodology and theory, and direct testing of alternative theories against one another. At the theoretical level, contemporary trait research increasingly draws on contemporary biological, cognitive and social-psychological science to describe Allport's (1937) underlying 'generalised neuropsychic systems' with increasing rigour and precision.

Our view is that understanding of traits is essential for understanding personality as a whole. This advocacy of traits is not a commitment to any one trait system, but to traits as a scientific construct central to psychology reflecting a regularity in nature. Personality is clearly more than just the sum total of the individual's trait values, and it may well be that individuals construct complex and idiosyncratic personal meanings upon the foundation provided by traits. Nevertheless, trait psychologists may well be able to make further inroads into understanding the personality of the individual by investigating styles of adaptation as the causal basis for trait action: the person's most salient adaptive challenges, and their perceived success in dealing with them. There is a fine balance to be struck between reductionism and wholism, identifying specific physiological and social-cognitive mechanisms contributing to trait action, without losing sight of the central, integrating features of traits. We look forward to a new science of personality in which understanding of traits plays a central role in shaping our understanding of the mental life of the individual.

Conclusions

1. The psychological science of personality traits has made major advances in recent years. Psychometric models of traits such as the five factor model provide robust constructs with considerable consensual support. The heritability of traits is firmly established, and further understanding of the biological bases of personality is expected from studies of molecular genetics and psychophysiology (especially brain-imaging). The constructs used by trait psychologists are increasingly well integrated with those of the mainstream psychology of neuroscience, cognitive science and social psychology. The applied relevance of assessment of personality traits is increasingly accepted, especially in organisational and clinical psychology. Many empirical and theoretical issues

remain to be resolved, but the strong foundation provided by existing research allows us to anticipate that normal scientific progress will address these issues successfully.

2. Trait psychology has sometimes been criticised for being atheoretical and overly empirical. This criticism has always been rather misinformed, but contemporary trait research is making rapid theoretical progress, as a consequence of integration with mainstream psychology. It is suggested that further progress requires a multi-levelled account of personality data, that accepts that observed linkages between traits and external criteria may require a variety of types of explanation. Different types of explanation refer to neuroscience, information-processing and high-level motivations and self-beliefs. We explored a cognitive-adaptive framework for personality that may serve to integrate the different levels at which traits are expressed. Thus, the various correlates of extraversion cohere around adaptation to demanding social environments, and the neuroticism seems to be linked to adaptation to threat.

An increasing dialogue between trait psychologists and social psychologists raises the issue of the place of trait theory in some overall theory of personality. It was proposed that trait theory provides a basis for a coherent personality theory that accommodates some of the traditional concerns of social psychological accounts of personality. Traits cannot be expected to explain everything about the individual's personality. However, the scope of trait theory may be expanded through an increasing focus on contextualised traits, and on patterns of idiographic thoughts and feelings that may relate to nomothetic dispositions. Trait psychology may also inform understanding of the meanings individuals assign to their own personalities and life events. The achievements of trait psychology so far give us confidence that the study of traits deserves to be placed at the heart of personality science.

References

Achenbach, T. M., McConaughy, S. H. and Howell, C. T. (1987) Child/adolescent behavioural and emotional problems: implications of cross-informant correlations for situational specificity. *Psychological Bulletin*, 101, 213–32.

Ackerman, P. L. (1996) A theory of adult intellectual development: Process, personality, interests, and knowledge. *Intelligence*, 22, 227–57.

Ackerman, P. L. and Heggestad, E. D. (1997) Intelligence, personality and interests: evidence for overlapping traits. *Psychological Bulletin*, 121, 219–45.

Adams, S. (1996) *The Dilbert Principle*. New York: HarperBusiness.

Adler, N. and Matthews, K. (1994) Health psychology: why do some people get sick and some stay well? *Annual Review of Psychology*, 45, 229–59.

Adorno, T. W., Frenkel-Brunswick, E., Levinson, D. J. and Sandford, R. N. (1950) *The authoritarian personality*. New York: Harper and Row.

Ainsworth, M. D. S., Blehar, M. C., Waters, E. and Wall, S. (1978) Patterns of attachment: a psychological study of the strange situation. Hillsdale, NJ: Lawrence Erlbaum.

Alison, L., Bennell, C., Mokros, A., Ormerod, D. (2002) The personality paradox in offender profiling – a theoretical review of the processes involved in deriving background characteristics from crime scene actions. *Psychology Public Policy and Law*, 8, 115–35.

Alloy, L. B. and Riskind, J. H. (eds.) (in press) *Cognitive vulnerability to emotional disorders*. Hillsdale, NJ: Lawrence Erlbaum.

Allport, G. W. (1937) *Personality: a psychological interpretation*. New York: Holt.
 (1961) *Pattern and growth in personality*. New York: Holt, Rinehart and Winston.

Allport, G. W. and Odbert, H. S. (1936) Trait names: a psycho-lexical study. *Psychological Monographs: General and Applied*, 47 (1, Whole issue 211).

Almagor, M., Tellegen, A. and Waller, N. G. (1995) The big seven model: a crosscultural replication and further exploration of the basic dimensions of natural language trait descriptors. *Journal of Personality and Social Psychology*, 69, 300–7.

Al-Mashaan, O. S. (2001) Job stress and job satisfaction and their relation to neuroticism, Type A behaviour, and locus of control among Kuwaiti personnel. *Psychological Reports*, 88, 1145–52.

Altmeyer, R. B. (1981) *Right-wing authoritarianism*. Winnipeg: University of Manitoba Press.

Aluja, A., Garcia, O. and Garcia, L. F. (2002) A comparative study of Zuckerman's three structural models for personality through the NEO-PI-R, ZKPQ-III-R, EPQ-RS and Goldberg's fifty-bipolar adjectives. *Personality and Individual Differences*, 33, 713–25.

Amelang M. (1997) Using personality variables to predict cancer and heart disease. *European Journal of Personality*, 11, 319–42.

Amelang, M. and Ullwer, U. (1991) Correlations between psychometric measures and psychophysiological as well as experimental variables in studies on extraversion and neuroticism. In J. Strelau and A. Angleitner (eds.) *Explorations in temperament*. New York: Plenum.

American Psychiatric Association (1994) *Diagnostic and statistical manual of mental disorders*. Washington, DC: American Psychiatric Association.

(2000) *Diagnostic and statistical manual of mental disorders*, 4th edition, Text Revision. Washington, DC: American Psychiatric Association.

Anastasi, A. and Urbina, S. (1997) *Psychological testing*, 7th edition. Upper Saddle River, NJ: Prentice Hall.

Anderson, B. L. (2002) Biobehavioral outcomes following psychological interventions for cancer patients. *Journal of Consulting and Clinical Psychology*, 70, 590–610.

Anderson, J. R. (1982) Acquisition of cognitive skill. *Psychological Review*, 89, 369–406.

Anderson, K. J. (1990) Arousal and the inverted-U hypothesis: a critique of Neiss's 'Reconceptualizing Arousal'. *Psychological Bulletin*, 107, 96–100.

(1994) Impulsivity, caffeine, and task difficulty: a within-subjects test of the Yerkes-Dodson Law. *Personality and Individual Differences*, 16, 813–29.

Anderson, M. (1992) *Intelligence and development: a cognitive theory*. Oxford: Blackwell.

Anderson, N. H. (1968) Likeableness ratings of 555 personality-trait words. *Journal of Personality and Social Psychology*, 9, 272–9.

Angleitner, A. and Wiggins, J. S. (eds.) (1986) *Personality assessment via questionnaires: current issues in theory and measurement*. Berlin: Springer-Verlag.

Angleitner, A., Ostendorf, F. and John, O. P. (1990) Towards a taxonomy of personality descriptors in German: a psycho-lexical study. *European Journal of Personality*, 4, 89–118.

Antonioni, D. (1999) Relationship between the Big Five personality factors and conflict management styles. *International Journal of Conflict Management*, 9, 336–55.

Argyle, M. (1997) Is happiness a cause of health? *Psychology and Health*, 12, 769–81.

Argyle, M. and Lu, L. (1990a) The happiness of extraverts. *Personality and Individual Differences*, 11, 1011–18.

(1990b) Happiness and social skills. *Personality and Individual Differences*, 11, 1255–62.

Argyle, M., Martin, M. and Crossland, J. (1989) Happiness as a function of personality and social encounters. In J. P. Forgas and J. M. Innes (eds.) *Recent advances in social psychology: an international perspective*. North Holland: Elsevier.

Arthur, W., Jr., Woehr, D. J. and Graziano, W. G. (2001) Personality testing in employment settings: problems and issues in the application of typical selection practices. *Personnel Review*, 30, 657–76.

Asendorpf, J. B. (1992) Beyond stability: predicting inter-individual differences in intra-individual change. *European Journal of Personality*, 6, 103–17.

(1998) Personality effects on social relationships. *Journal of Personality and Social Psychology*, 74, 1531–44.

Ashcraft, M. H. and Kirk, E. P. (2001) The relationships among working memory, math anxiety, and performance. *Journal of Experimental Psychology: General*, 130, 224–37.

Ashton, M. C. and Lee, K. (2002) Six independent factors of personality variation: a response to Saucier. *European Journal of Personality*, 16, 63–75.

Auster, C. J. and Ohm, S. C. (2000) Masculinity and femininity in contemporary American society: a reevaluation using the Bem Sex-Role Inventory. *Sex Roles*, 43, 499–528.

Austin, E. J. and Deary, I. J. (2000) The 'four As': a common framework for normal and abnormal personality? *Personality and Individual Differences*, 28, 977–95.

Austin, E. J., Deary, I. J. and Gibson, G. J. (1997) Relationships between ability and personality: three hypotheses tested. *Intelligence*, 25, 49–70.

Austin, E. J., Deary, I. J., Gibson, G. J., McGregor, M. J. and Dent, J. B. (1998) Individual response spread in self-report scales: personality correlations and consequences. *Personality and Individual Differences*, 24, 421–38.

Austin, E. J., Deary, I. J., Whiteman, M. C., Fowkes, F. G. R., Pedersen, N. L., Rabbitt, P., Bent, N. and McInnes, L. (2002) Relationships between ability and personality: does intelligence contribute positively to personal and social adjustment? *Personality and Individual Differences*, 32, 1391–411.

Avia, M. D., Sanz, J., Sanchez-Bernardos, M. L., Martinez-Arias, M. R., Silva, F. and Grana, J. L. (1995) The five-factor model-II. Relations of the NEO-PI with other personality variables. *Personality and Individual Differences*, 19, 81–98.

Bachman, J., Stein, S., Campbell, K. and Sitarenios, G. (2000) Emotional intelligence in the collection of debt. *International Journal of Selection and Assessment*, 8, 176–82.

Baddeley, A. (1986) *Working memory*. Oxford: Oxford University Press.

Baeckstroem, M. and Holmes, B. M. (2001) Measuring adult attachment: a construct validation of two self-report instruments. *Scandinavian Journal of Psychology*, 42, 79–86.

Bagby, R. M. and Parker, J. D. A. (2001) Relation of rumination and distraction with neuroticism and extraversion in a sample of patients with major depression. *Cognitive Therapy and Research*, 25, 91–102.

Bagby, R. M., Parker, J. D. A. and Taylor, G. J. (1994) The Twenty-Item Toronto Alexithymia Scale – I. Item selection and cross-validation of the factor structure. *Journal of Psychosomatic Research*, 38, 23–32.

Bagby, R. M., Joffe, R. T., Parker, J. D. A., Kalemba, V. and Harkness, K. L. (1995) Major depression and the five factor model of personality. *Journal of Personality Disorders*, 9, 224–34.

Bagby, R. M., Nicholson, R. A., Bacchiochi, J. R., Ryder, A. G. and Bury, A. S. (2002) The predictive capacity of the MMPI-2 and PAI validity scales and indexes to detect coached and uncoached feigning. *Journal of Personality Assessment*, 78, 69–86.

Baldwin, M. W. and Fergusson, P. (2001) Relational schemas: the activation of interpersonal knowledge structures in social anxiety. In W. R. Crozier and L. E. Alden (eds.), *International handbook of social anxiety: concepts, research and interventions relating to the self and shyness*, pp. 235–57. New York: Wiley.

Ball, S. A. (2001) Reconceptualizing personality disorder categories using personality trait dimensions. *Journal of Personality*, 69, 147–53.

Baltes, P. B. (1987) Theoretical propositions of life-span developmental psychology – on the dynamics between growth and decline. *Development Psychology*, 23, 611–26.

Bandura, A. (1997) *Self-efficacy: the exercise of control*. New York: W. H. Freeman and Co.

(1999) Social cognitive theory of personality. In D. Cervone and Y. Shoda (eds.) *The coherence of personality: social-cognitive bases of consistency, variability, and organization*, pp. 185–241. New York: Guilford Press.

Bandura, A. and Walter, R. H. (1963) *Social learning and personality development*. New York: Holt Rinehart and Winston.

Bannister, D. and Fransella, F. (1989) *Inquiring man: the psychology of personal constructs*. London: Routledge.

Bar-On, R. (1997) *The Emotional Intelligence Inventory (EQ-I): technical manual*. Toronto, Canada: Multi-Health Systems.

(2000) Emotional and social intelligence: Insights from the Emotional Quotient Inventory. In R. Bar-On and J. D. A. Parker (eds.), *The handbook of emotional intelligence*, pp. 363–88. San Francisco, CA: Jossey-Bass.

Bargh, J. A. (1997) The automaticity of everyday life. In R. S. Wyer, Jr. (ed.) *The automaticity of everyday life: advances in social cognition*, vol. 10, pp. 1–61. Mahwah, NJ: Lawrence Erlbaum Associates.

Bargh, J. A. and Pietromonaco, P. (1982) Automatic information processing and social perception: the influence of trait information presented outside of conscious awareness on impression formation. *Journal of Personality and Social Psychology*, 43, 437–49.

Bargh, J. A., Chen, M. and Burrows, L. (1996) Automaticity of social behavior: direct effects of trait construct and stereotype activation on action. *Journal of Personality and Social Psychology*, 71, 230–44.

Barnett, P. A. and Gotlib, I. H. (1988) Psychosocial functioning and depression: distinguishing among antecedents, concomitants, and consequences. *Psychological Bulletin*, 104, 97–126.

Baron, H. (1996) Strengths and limitations of ipsative measurement. *Journal of Occupational and Organizational Psychology*, 69, 49–56.

Barondes, S. H. (1993) *Molecules and mental illness*. New York: W. H. Freeman and Co.

Barrett, E. S. (1987) Impulsiveness and anxiety: information processing and electroencephalograph topography. *Journal of Research in Personality*, 21, 453–63.

Barrett, G. V., Miguel, R. F., Tan, J. A. and Hurd, J. M. (2001) Emotional Intelligence: the Madison Avenue approach to science and professional practice. Unpublished paper presented at the 16th annual meeting of the Society for Industrial and Organizational Psychology, San Diego, CA.

Barrett, L. F. and Pietromonaco, P. R. (1997) Accuracy of the five-factor model in predicting perceptions of daily social interactions. *Personality and Social Psychology Bulletin*, 23, 1173–87.

Barrett, P. and Kline, P. (1982) An item and radial parcel analysis of the 16PF questionnaire. *Personality and Individual Differences*, 3, 259–70.

Barrick, M. R. and Mount, M. K. (1991) The Big Five personality dimensions and job performance: a meta-analysis. *Personnel Psychology*, 44, 1–26.

(1993) Autonomy as a moderator of the relationships between the Big Five personality dimensions and job performance. *Journal of Applied Psychology*, 78, 111–18.

(1996) Effects of impression management and self-deception on the predictive validity of personality constructs. *Journal of Applied Psychology*, 81, 261–72.

Barrick, M. R., Mount, M. K. and Judge, T. A. (2001) Personality and performance at the beginning of the new millennium: what do we know and where do we go next? *International Journal of Selection and Assessment*, 9, 9–30.

Barrick, M. R., Mount, M. K. and Strauss, J. P. (1993) Conscientiousness and performance of sales representatives: test of the mediating effects of goal setting. *Journal of Applied Psychology*, 78, 715–22.

Barron, F. and Harrington, D. M. (1981) Creativity, intelligence and personality. *Annual Review of Psychology*, 32, 439–76.

Bartlett, F. C. (1932) *Remembering*. Cambridge University Press.

Barton, K., Dielman, T. E. and Cattell, R. B. (1971) The prediction of school grades from personality and IQ measures. *Personality*, 2, 325–33.

Bartram, D. (1996) The relationship between ipsatized and normative measures of personality. *Journal of Occupational and Organizational Psychology*, 69, 25–39.

Bartussek, D., Becker, G., Diedrich, O., Naumann, E. and Maier, S. (1996) Extraversion, neuroticism, and event-related potentials in response to emotional stimuli. *Personality and Individual Differences*, 20, 301–12.

Bassarath, L. (2001) Neuroimaging studies of antisocial behaviour. *Canadian Journal of Psychiatry*, 46, 728–32.

Bates, J. E. (1987) Temperament in infancy. In J. D. Osofsky (ed.), *Handbook of infant development* (2nd edn). New York: Wiley, pp. 1101–49.

Bates, J. E. and McFadyen-Ketchum, S. (2000) Temperament and parent–child relations as interacting factors in children's behavioral adjustment. In V. J. Molfese and D. L. Molfese (eds.), *Temperament and personality development across the life span*, pp. 141–76. Mahwah, NJ: Lawrence Erlbaum.

Baum, A. (1990) Stress, intrusive imagery, and chronic distress. *Health Psychology*, 9, 653–75.

Baumeister, R. F. (1998) The self. In D. T. Gilbert and S. T. Fiske (eds.), *The handbook of social psychology*, vol. 1 (4th edn), pp. 680–740. Boston, MA: McGraw-Hill.

Baumeister, R. F. and Leary, M. R. The need to belong: desire for interpersonal attachments as a fundamental human motivation. *Psychological Bulletin*, 117, 497–529.

Beck, A. T. (1967) *Depression: causes and treatment*. Philadelphia, PA: University of Pennsylvania Press.

Beck, A. T., Epstein, N., Harrison, R. P. and Emery, G. (1983) Development of the Sociotropy–Autonomy Scale: a measure of personality factors in psychopathology. Unpublished manuscript, University of Pennsylvania.

Bedford, A. and Deary, I. J. (1997) The Personal Disturbance Scale (DSSI/sAD): development, use and structure. *Personality and Individual Differences*, 22, 493–510.

Bedford, A. and Foulds, G. A. (1978) *Manual of the personality deviance scales*. Windsor, UK: NFER-Nelson.

Beech, A. and Claridge, G. (1987) Individual differences in negative priming: relations with schizotypal personality traits. *British Journal of Psychology*, 78, 349–56.

Beech, A. and Williams, L. (1997) Investigating cognitive processes in schizotypal personality and schizophrenia. In G. Matthews (ed.), *Cognitive science perspectives on personality and emotion*, pp. 475–502. Amsterdam: Elsevier.

Belojevic, G., Slepcevic, V. and Jakovljevic, B. (2001) Mental performance in noise: the role of introversion. *Journal of Environmental Psychology*, 21, 209–13.

Bem, D. J. (1972) Constructing cross-situational consistencies in behavior: some thoughts on Alker's critique of Mischel. *Journal of Personality*, 40, 17–26.

(1983) Further déjà vu in the search for cross-situational consistency: a reply to Mischel and Peake. *Psychological Review*, 90, 390–3.

Bem, D. J. and Allen, A. (1974) On predicting some of the people some of the time: the search for cross-situational consistencies in behavior. *Psychological Review*, 81, 506–20.

Bem, S. L. (1974) The measurement of psychological androgyny. *Journal of Consulting and Clinical Psychology*, 45, 196–205.

(1981) Gender schema theory: a cognitive account of sex typing. *Psychological Review*, 88, 354–64.

Benet, V. and Waller, N. G. (1995) The big seven factor model of personality description: evidence for its cross-cultural generality in a Spanish sample. *Journal of Personality and Social Psychology*, 69, 701–18.

Benjamin, J., Li., L., Patterson, C., Greenberg, B. D., Murphy, D. L. and Hamer, D. H. (1996) Population and familial association between the D4 dopamine receptor gene and measures of novelty seeking. *Nature Genetics*, 12, 81–4.

Benjamin, J., Osher, Y., Kotler, M., Gritsenko I., Nemanov, L., Belmaker, R. H. and Ebstein, R. P. (2000) Association between tridimensional personality questionnaire (TPQ) traits and three functional polymorphisms: dopamine receptor D4 (DRD4), serotonin transporter promoter region (5-HTTLPR) and catechol O-methyltransferase (COMT). *Molecular Psychiatry*, 5, 96–100.

Bentler, P. M. (1995) *EQS Structural equations program manual*. Encino, CA: Multivariate Software, Inc.

Berenbaum, H. and Williams, M. (1995) Personality and emotional reactivity. *Journal of Research in Personality*, 29, 24–34.

Bergeman, C. S., Plomin, R., McClearn, G. E., Pedersen, N. L. and Friberg, L. T. (1988) Genotype–environment interaction in personality development: identical twins reared apart. *Psychology and Aging*, 3, 399–406.

Berrettini, W. H. (2001) Molecular linkage studies of bipolar disorders. *Bipolar Disorders*, 3, 276–83.

Berrios, G. E. (1993) Personality disorders: a conceptual history. In P. Tyrer and G. Stein (eds.), *Personality disorder reviewed*. London: Gaskell.

Berry, D. S. and Sherman Hansen, J. (2000) Personality, nonverbal behavior, and interaction quality in female dyads. *Personality and Social Psychology Bulletin*, 26, 278–92.

Berry, D. S., Willingham, J. K. and Thayer, C. A. (2000) Affect and personality as predictors of conflict and closeness in young adults' friendships. *Journal of Research in Personality*, 34, 84–107.

Berry, D. T. R., Bagby, R. M., Smerz, J., Rinaldo, J. C., Caldwell-Andrews, A. and Baer, R. A. (2001) Effectiveness of NEO-PI-R research validity scales for discriminating analog malingering and genuine psychopathology. *Journal of Personality Assessment*, 76, 496–516.

Bienvenu, O. J., Brown, C., Samuels, J. F., Liang, K-Y., Costa, P. T., Eaton, W. W. and Nestadt, G. (2001) Normal personality traits and comorbidity among phobic, panic and major depressive disorders. *Psychiatry Research*, 102, 73–85.

Billig, M. (1976) *Social psychology and intergroup relations*. London: Academic.

Binswanger, L. (1963) *Being-in-the-world: selected papers of Ludwig Binswanger*. New York: Basic Books.

Blackburn, I. M., Cameron, C. M. and Deary, I. J. (1990) Individual differences and response to the Velten Mood Induction Procedure. *Personality and Individual Differences*, 11, 725–31.

Blackburn, R. (1988) On moral judgements and personality disorders: the myth of the psychopathic personality revisited. *British Journal of Psychiatry*, 153, 505–12.

Blagrove, M. and Akehurst, L. (2000) Personality and dream recall frequency: further negative findings. *Dreaming*, 10, 139–48.

(2001) Personality and the modulation of effects of sleep loss on mood and cognition. *Personality and Individual Differences*, 30, 819–28.

Blatt, S. J. and Maroudas, C. (1992) Convergences among psychoanalytic and cognitive-behavioral theories of depression. *Psychoanalytic Psychology*, 9, 157–90.

Block, J. (1995) A contrarian view of the five-factor approach to personality description. *Psychological Bulletin*, 117, 187–215.

Block, J. H. and Block, J. (1980) The role of ego-control and ego-resiliency in the organization of behaviour. In W. A. Collins (ed.), *Minnesota symposium on child psychology*, vol. 13, pp. 39–101. New York: Erlbaum.

Boekarts, M. (1995) The interface between intelligence and personality as determinants of classroom learning. In D. H. Saklofske and M. Zeidner (eds.), *International handbook of personality and intelligence*. New York: Plenum.

Bolger, E. A. and Schilling, E. A. (1991) Personality and the problems of everyday life: the role of neuroticism in exposure and reactivity to daily stressors. *Journal of Personality*, 59, 335–86.

Bolger, N. (1990) Coping as a personality process: a prospective study. *Journal of Personality and Social Psychology*, 59, 525–37.

Bond, A. J. (2001) Neurotransmitters, temperament and social functioning. *European Neuropsychopharmacology*, 11, 261–74.

Bond, M. H. (1979) Dimensions of personality used in perceiving peers: crosscultural comparisons of Hong Kong, Japanese, American, and Filipino university students. *International Journal of Psychology*, 14, 47–56.

Block, J. and Kremen (1996)
   (2000) Localizing the imperial outreach – the Big Five and more in Chinese culture. *American Behavioral Scientist*, 44, 63–72.

Booth-Kewley, S. and Friedman, H. S. (1987) Psychological predictors of heart disease: a quantitative review. *Psychological Bulletin*, 101, 343–62.

Borgatta, E. F. (1964) The structure of personality characteristics. *Behavioral Science*, 9, 8–17.

Borkenau, P., Riemann, R., Angleitner, A. and Spinath, F. (2001) Genetic and environmental influences on observed personality: evidence from the German Observational Study of Adult Twins. *Journal of Personality and Social Psychology*, 80, 655–68.

Bornstein, R. F. and Cecero, J. J. (2000) Deconstructing dependency in a five-factor world: a meta-analytic review. *Journal of Personality Assessment*, 74, 324–43.

Bosma, H., Marmot, M. G., Hemingway, H., Nicholson, A. C., Brunner, E. and Stansfeld, S. A. (1997) Low job control and risk of coronary heart disease in Whitehall II (prospective cohort) study. *British Medical Journal*, 314, 558–65.

Botwin, M. D., Buss, D. M. and Shackelford, T. K. (1997) Personality and mate preferences: five factors in mate selection and marital satisfaction. *Journal of Personality*, 65, 107–36.

Bouchard, T. J. (1993) Genetic and environmental influences on adult personality: evaluating the evidence. In J. Hettema and I. J. Deary (eds.), *Foundations of personality*. Dordrecht, The Netherlands: Kluwer.

   (1994) Genes, environment and personality. *Science*, 264, 1700–1.

Bouchard, T. J. and Loehlin, J. C. (2001) Genes, evolution, and personality. *Behavior Genetics*, 31, 243–73.

Bouchard, T. J. and Propping, P. (eds.) (1993) Twins as a tool of behavioral genetics. Chichester: Wiley.

Bouchard, T. J., Lykken, D. T., McGue, M., Segal, N. L. and Tellegen, A. (1990) Sources of human psychological differences: the Minnesota study of twins reared apart. *Science*, 250, 223–50.

Boudreau, J. W., Boswell, W. R. and Judge, T. A. (2001) Effects of personality on executive career success in the United States and Europe. *Journal of Vocational Behavior*, 2001, 53–81.

Boudreau, J. W., Boswell, W. R., Judge, T. A. and Bretz, R. D., Jr. (2001) Personality and cognitive ability as predictors of job search among employed managers. *Personnel Psychology*, 54, 25–50.

Bowen, D. D. (1973) Reported patterns in TAT measures of needs for achievement, affiliation, and power. *Journal of Personality Assessment*, 37, 424–30.

Bower, G. H. and Forgas, J. P. (2000) Affect, memory, and social cognition. In E. Eich, J. F. Kihlstrom, G. H. Bower and J. Forgas (eds.), *Cognition and emotion*, pp. 87–168. London: Oxford University Press.

Bowers, K. S. (1973) Situationism in psychology: an analysis and a critique. *Psychological Review*, 307–36.

Bowlby, J. (1984) *Attachment and loss*, vol. 1: *Attachment*. (Rev. edn). New York: Basic Books.

Boyatzis, R., Goleman, D. and Rhee, K. (2000) Clustering competence in Emotional intelligence: insights from the emotional competence inventory. In R. Bar-On and J. D. A. Parker (eds.), *Handbook of Emotional Intelligence*. San Francisco: Jossey-Bass.

Boyle, G. J. (1989) Re-examination of the major personality-type factors in the Cattell, Comrey, and Eysenck scales: were the factor solutions by Noller et al. optimal? *Personality and Individual Differences*, 10, 1289–99.

Braden, J. P. (1995) Intelligence and personality in school and educational psychology. In D. H. Saklofske and M. Zeidner (eds.), *International handbook of personality and intelligence*, pp. 621–50. New York: Plenum.

Bradley, B. P., Mogg, K., Millar, N. and White, J. (1995) Selective processing of negative information: effects of clinical anxiety, concurrent depression and awareness. *Journal of Abnormal Psychology*, 104, 532–6.

Brand, C. R. (1994) Open to experience – closed to intelligence: why the 'Big Five' are really the 'Comprehensive Six'. *European Journal of Personality*, 8, 299–31.

Brand, C. R. and Egan, V. G. (1989) The 'Big Five' dimensions of personality? Evidence from ipsative, adjectival self-attributions. *Personality and Individual Differences*, 10, 1165–71.

Brand, C., Egan, V. G. and Deary, I. J. (1993) Personality and general intelligence. In G. L. Van Heck, P. Bonaiuto, I. J. Deary and W. Nowack (eds.), *Personality psychology in Europe*, vol. 4, pp. 203–28. Tilburg: Tilburg University Press.

   (1994) Intelligence, personality and society: constructivist versus essentialist possibilities. In D. K. Detterman (ed.), *Current topics in human intelligence*, vol. 4: *Theories of intelligence*. Norwood, NJ: Ablex.

Brandstätter, H. (1994) Well-being and motivated person–environment fit: a time-sampling study of emotions. *European Journal of Personality*, 8, 75–94.

   (2001) Time sampling diary: an ecological approach to the study of emotions in everyday life. In H. Brandstätter and E. Andrzej (eds.), *Persons, situations and emotions: an ecological approach*, pp. 20–52. London: Oxford University Press.

Brebner, J. (1998) Extraversion and the psychological refractory period. *Personality and Individual Differences*, 25, 543–51.

(2001) Personality and stress coping. *Personality and Individual Differences*, 31, 317–27.

Brebner, J. and Cooper, C. (1985) A proposed unified model of extraversion. In J. T. Spence and C. E. Izard (eds.), *Motivation, emotion and personality*. Amsterdam: North-Holland.

Brebner, J. and Stough, C. (1995) Theoretical and empirical relationships between personality and intelligence. In D. H. Saklofske and M. Zeidner (eds.), *International handbook of personality and intelligence*. New York: Plenum.

Bretherton, I. (1988) Open communication and internal working models: their role in the development of attachment relationships. In *Nebraska Symposium on Motivation*, vol. 36. Lincoln, NE: University of Nebraska Press.

Brewin, C. R, Furnham, A. and Howes, M. (1989) Demographic and psychological determinants of homesickness and confiding among students. *British Journal of Psychology*, 80, 467–78.

Brief, A. P. (1998) *Attitudes in and around organizations*. Thousand Oaks, CA: Sage Pubications

Brief, A. P., Butcher, A. H., George, J. M. and Link, K. E. (1993) Integrating bottom–up and top–down theories of subjective well-being: the case of health. *Journal of Personality and Social Psychology*, 64, 646–53.

Briggs, S. R. (1988) Shyness: introversion or neuroticism? *Journal of Research in Personality*, 22, 290–307.

Broadhurst, P. L. (1957) Emotionality and the Yerkes-Dodson law. *Journal of Experimental Psychology*, 54, 345–52.

Brocke, B., Tasche, K. G. and Beauducel, A. (1997) Biopsychological foundations of extraversion: differential effort reactivity and state contol. *Personality and Individual Differences*, 22, 447–58.

Brody, N. (1988) *Personality: in search of individuality*. San Diego, CA: Academic.
   (1992) *Intelligence* (2nd edn.). New York: Academic.
   (1994) Heritability of traits. *Psychological Inquiry*, 5, 117–19.

Bruch, M. A. (2001) Shyness and social interaction. In W. R. Crozier and L. E. Alden (eds.), *International handbook of social anxiety: Concepts, research and interventions relating to the self and shyness*, pp. 195–215. New York: Wiley.

Brunner, H. G., Nelen, M., Breakefield, X. O., Ropers, H. H. and van Oost, B. A. (1993) Abnormal behavior associated with a point mutation in the structural gene for monoamine oxidase A. *Science*, 262, 578–80.

Bullock, W. A. and Gilliland, K. (1993) Eysenck's arousal theory of introversion–extraversion: a converging measure of investigation. *Journal of Personality and Social Psychology*, 64, 113–23.

Bunce, S. C., Larsen, R. J. and Cruz, M. (1993) Individual differences in the excitation transfer effect. *Personality and Individual Differences*, 15, 507–14.

Burton, R. (1837) *The anatomy of melancholy*, vol. 1. London: Longman, Rees and Co.

Busch, H. A., King, P. R. and Guttman, M. A. (1994) Interactional anxiety in an examination situation with French and English high school students: an empirical test of a composite predictor for state anxiety. *Personality and Individual Differences*, 17, 111–16.

Bush, G., Luu, P. and Posner, M. I. (2000) Cognitive and emotional influences in anterior cingulated cortex. *Trends in Cognitive Sciences*, 4, 215–22.

Busjahn, A., Faulhaber, H. D., Freier, K. and Luft, C. (1999) Genetic and environmental influences on coping styles: a twin study. *Psychosomatic Medicine*, 61, 469–75.

Buss, A. H. (1989) Personality as traits. *American Psychologist*, 44, 1378–88.

Buss, A. H. and Plomin, R. (1984) *Temperament: early developing personality traits.* Hillsdale, NJ: Erlbaum.

Buss, D. M. (1991) Conflict in married couples: personality predictors of anger and upset. *Journal of Personality*, 59, 663–88.

(1993) Strategic individual differences: the role of personality in creating and solving adaptive problems. In J. Hettema and I. J. Deary (eds.), *Foundations of personality.* Dordrecht, The Netherlands: Kluwer.

(1999) *Evolutionary psychology: the new science of mind.* Boston, MA: Allyn and Bacon.

(2001) Human nature and culture: an evolutionary psychological perspective. *Journal of Personality*, 69, 955–78.

Buss, D. M. and Craik, K. H. (1983) The act frequency approach to personality. *Psychological Review*, 90, 105–26.

Buss, D. M. and Greiling, H. (1999) Adaptive individual differences. *Journal of Personality*, 67, 209–42.

Buss, D. M. and Larsen, R. J. (2002) *Personality psychology: domains of knowledge about human nature.* Boston, MA: McGraw Hill.

Butler, G. and Mathews, A. (1987) Anticipatory anxiety and risk perception. *Cognitive Therapy and Research*, 91, 551–65.

Butler, J. M. and Haigh, G. V. (1954) Changes in the relation between selfconcepts and ideal concepts consequent upon client-centred counseling. In C. R. Rogers and R. F. Dymond (eds.), *Psychotherapy and personality change; co-ordinated studies in the client-centered approach*, pp. 55–76. Chicago, IL: University of Chicago Press.

Byrne, B. M. (2000) *Structural equation modeling with AMOS.* Mahwah, NJ: Lawrence Erlbaum.

Calvo, M. G. and Castillo, M. D. (2001) Bias in predictive inferences during reading. *Discourse Processes*, 32, 43–71.

Calvo, M. G., Eysenck, M. W. and Castillo, M. D. (1997) Interpretation bias in test anxiety: the time course of predictive inferences. *Cognition and Emotion*, 11, 43–63.

Campbell, D. T. and Fiske, D. W. (1959) Convergent and discriminant validation by the multitrait–multimethod matrix. *Psychological Bulletin*, 56, 81–105.

Canli, T., Zhao, Z., Kang, E. and Gross, J. (2001) An fMRI study of personality influences on brain reactivity to emotional stimuli. *Behavioral Neuroscience*, 115, 33–42.

Cannon, W. B. (1929) *Bodily changes in pain, hunger, fear and rage* (2nd edn). New York: Appleton.

Cantor, N. and Kihlstrom, J. F. (1987) *Personality and social intelligence.* Englewood Cliffs, NJ: Prentice-Hall.

Cantor, N. and Zirkel, S. (1990) Personality, cognition, and purposive behavior. In L. A. Pervin (ed.), *Handbook of personality: theory and research*, pp. 135–164. New York: Guilford.

Caprara, G. V. and Cervone, D. (2000) *Personality: determinants, dynamics, and potentials.* Cambridge: Cambridge University Press.

Caprara, G. V. and Perugini, M. (1994) Personality described by adjectives: generalizability of the Big Five to the Italian lexical context. *European Journal of Personality*, 8, 357–70.

Caprara, G. V., Barbaranelli, C. and Comrey, A. L. (1995) Factor analysis of the NEO-PI Inventory and the Comrey Personality Scales in an Italian sample. *Personality and Individual Differences*, 18, 193–200.

Caprara, G. V., Barbaranelli, C. and Zimbardo, P. G. (1996) Understanding the complexity of human aggression: affective, cognitive, and social dimensions of individual differences in propensity toward aggression. *European Journal of Personality*, 10, 133–55.

Carment, D. W., Miles, C. G. and Cervin, V. B. (1965) Persuasiveness and persuasibility as related to intelligence and extraversion. *British Journal of Social and Clinical Psychology*, 4, 17.

Carmichael, C. M. and McGue, M. (1994) A longitudinal study of personality change and stability. *Journal of Personality*, 62, 1–20.

Carr, H. A. and Kingsbury, F. A. (1938) The concept of traits. *Psychological Review*, 45, 497–524.

Carroll, D. (1984) *Biofeedback in practice*. London: Longman.

(1992) *Health psychology: stress, behaviour and disease*. London: Falmer Press.

Carroll, D., Hewitt, J. K., Last, K., Turner, J. R. and Sims, J. (1985) A twin study of cardiac reactivity and its relationship to parental blood pressure. *Physiology and Behavior*, 34, 103–6.

Carson, R. C. (1989) Personality. *Annual Review of Psychology*, 40, 227–48.

Cartwright-Hatton, S. and Wells, A. (1997) Beliefs about worry and intrusions: the Meta-Cognitions Questionnaire and its correlates. *Journal of Anxiety Disorders*, 11, 279–96.

Carver, C. S. (1997) Adult attachment and personality: converging evidence and a new measure. *Personality and Social Psychology Bulletin*, 23, 865–83.

Carver, C. S. and Scheier, M. F. (1981) *Attention and self-regulation: a control-theory approach to human behavior*. Berlin: Springer-Verlag.

(1990) Origins and functions of positive and negative affects: a control-process view. *Psychological Review*, 97, 19–35.

(2000) Autonomy and self regulation. *Psychological Inquiry*, 11, 284–91.

Carver, C. S. and White, T. (1994) Behavioral inhibition, behavioral activation and affective responses to impending reward and punishment: the BIS/BAS scales. *Journal of Personality and Social Psychology*, 67, 319–33.

Caspi, A. (2000) The child is the father of the man: personality continuities from childhood to adulthood. *Journal of Personality and Social Psychology*, 78, 158–72.

Caspi, A. and Bem, D. J. (1990) Personality continuity and change across the life course. In L. A. Pervin (ed.), *Handbook of personality: theory and research*, pp. 549–75. New York: Guilford.

Caspi, A. and Roberts, B. W. (2001) Personality development across the life course: the argument for change and continuity. *Psychological Inquiry*, 12, 49–66.

Caspi, A., McClay, J., Moffitt, T. E., Mill, J., Martin, J., Craig, I. W., Taylor, A. and Poulton, R. (2002) Role of genotype in the cycle of violence in maltreated children. *Science*, 297, 851–4.

Cattell, R. B. (1946) *Description and measurement of personality*. London: George Harrap.

(1971) *Abilities: their structure, growth and action*. New York: Houghton Mifflin.

(1973) *Personality and mood by questionnaire*. New York: Jossey Bass.

(1983) *Structured personality-learning theory: a wholistic multivariate research approach*. New York: Praeger.

Cattell, R. B. and Butcher, H. J. (1958) *The prediction of achievement and creativity*. New York: Bobbs Merrill.

Cattell, R. B. and Kline, P. (1977) *The scientific analysis of personality and motivation*. New York: Academic.

Cattell, R. B., Eber, H. W. and Tatsuoka, M. M. (1970) *Handbook for the sixteen personality factor questionnaire*. Champaign, IL: Institute for Personality and Ability Testing.

Cervone, D. (1999) Bottom-up explanation in personality psychology: the case of cross-situational coherence. In D. Cervone and Y. Shoda (eds.) *The coherence of personality: social-cognitive bases of consistency, variability, and organization*, pp. 303–41. New York: Guilford Press.

(2000) Thinking about self-efficacy. *Behavior Modification*, 24, 30–56.

Cervone, D. and Shoda, Y. (1999) Beyond traits in the study of personality coherence. *Psychological Science*, 8, 27–32.

Chartrand, T. L. and Bargh, J. A. (1999) The unbearable automaticity of being. *American Psychologist*, 54, 462–79.

(2002) Nonconscious motivations: their activation, operation, and consequences. In A. Tesser, D. A. Stapel and J. V. Wood (eds.), *Self and motivation: emerging psychological perspectives*, pp. 13–41. Washington, DC: American Psychological Association.

Cheek, J. M. and Hogan, R. (1983) Self-concepts, self-presentations, and moral judgements. In J. Suls and A. G. Greenwald (eds.), *Psychological perspectives on the self*, pp. 249–73. Hillsdale, NJ: Erlbaum.

Chen, M. and Bargh, J. A. (1997) Nonconscious behavioral confirmation processes: the self-fulfilling consequences of automatic stereotype activation. *Journal of Experimental Social Psychology*, 33, 541–60.

Chen, G. and Gully, S. (2001) Validation of a new general self-efficacy scale. *Organizational Research Methods*, 4, 62–63.

Chen, G., Casper, W. J. and Cortina, J. M. (2001) The roles of self-efficacy and task complexity in the relationships among cognitive ability, conscientiousness, and work-related performance: a meta-analytic examination. *Human Performance*, 14, 209–30.

Chernyshenko, O. S., Stark, S. and Chan, K. Y. (2001) Investigating the hierarchical structure of the fifth edition of the 16PF: an application of the Schmid-Leiman orthogonalization procedure. *Educational and Psychological Measurement*, 61, 290–302.

Chess, S. and Thomas, S. (1984) *Origins and evolution of behavior disorders*. New York: Brunner/Mazel.

Cheung, F. M., Leung, K., Zhang, J. X., Sun, H. F., Gan, Y. Q., Song, W. Z. and Xie, D. Indigenous Chinese personality constructs – is the five-factor model complete? *Journal of Cross-Cultural Psychology*, 32, 407–33.

Chipuer, H. M., Plomin, R., Pedersen, N. L., McClearn, G. E. and Nesselroade, J. R. (1993) Genetic influence on family environment: the role of personality. *Developmental Psychology*, 29, 110–18.

Chiu, C., Hong, Y. and Dweck, C. S. (1994) Toward an integrative model of personality and intelligence: a general framework and some preliminary steps. In R. J. Sternberg and P. Ruzgis (eds.), *Personality and intelligence*. Cambridge University Press.

Christensen, A. J. and Smith, T. W. (1995) Personality and patient adherence: Correlates of the five-factor model in renal analysis. *Journal of Behavioral Medicine*, 18, 305–13.

Christensen, A. J., Moran, P. J. and Wiebe, J. S. (1999) Assessment of irrational health beliefs: relation to health practices and medical regimen adherence. *Health Psychology*, 18, 169–76.

Claeys, W. (1989) Social anxiety, evaluative threat and incidental recall of trait words. *Anxiety Research*, 2, 27–43.

Claridge, G. (1997) *Schizotypy: implications for illness and health*. Oxford: Oxford University Press.

Claridge, G. and Broks, P. (1984) Schizotypy and hemisphere function: I. Theoretical considerations and the measurement of schizotypy. *Personality and Individual Differences*, 5, 633–48.

Claridge, G., McCreery, C., Mason, O., Bentall, R., Boyle, G. and Slade, P. (1996) The factor structure of 'schizotypal' traits: a large replication study. *British Journal of Clinical Psychology*, 35, 103–15.

Clark, D. A. and Beck, A. T. (1999) *Scientific foundations of cognitive theory and therapy of depression*. New York: Wiley

Clark, L. A. and Watson, D. (1988) Mood and the mundane: relations between daily life events and self-reported mood. *Journal of Personality and Social Psychology*, 54, 296–308.

(1991) Tripartite model of anxiety and depression: psychometric evidence and taxonomic implications. *Journal of Abnormal Psychology*, 100, 316–36.

Clark, L. A., Watson, D. and Mineka, S. (1994) Temperament, personality and the mood and anxiety disorders. *Journal of Abnormal Psychology*, 103, 103–16.

Clark, L. A., Livesley, W. J., Schroeder, M. L. and Irish, S. L. (1996) Convergence of two systems for assessing specific traits of personality disorder. *Psychological Assessment*, 8, 294–303.

Cleckley, H. (1976) *The mask of sanity* (6th edn.). St Louis, MO: Mosby.

Cloninger, C. R. (1987) A systematic method for clinical description and classification of personality. *Archives of General Psychiatry*, 44, 573–88.

(2000) A practical way to diagnose personality disorder: a proposal. *Journal of Personality Disorders*, 14, 99–108.

Cloninger, C. R., Adolfsson, R. and Svrakic, N. M. (1996) Mapping genes for human personality. *Nature Genetics*, 12, 3–4.

Cloninger, C. R., Svrakic, D. M. and Przybeck, T. R. (1993) A psychobiological model of temperament and character. *Archives of General Psychiatry*, 50, 975–90.

Clore, G. L. and Ortony, A. (2000) Cognition in emotion: always, sometimes, or never? In R. D. Lane and L. Nadel (eds.), *Cognitive neuroscience of emotion*, pp. 24–61. New York: Oxford University Press.

Cobb, J. M. T. and Steptoe, A. (1996) Psychosocial stress and susceptibility to upper respiratory tract illness in an adult population sample. *Psychosomatic Medicine*, 58, 404–12.

Code, S., and Langan-Fox, J. (2001) Motivation, cognitions, and traits: predicting occupational health, well-being, and performance. *Stress and Health*, 17, 159–74.

Cohen, S. and Edwards, J. (1989) Personality characteristics as moderators of the relationship betweeen stress and health. In R. W. Neufeld (ed.), *Advances in investigations of psychological stress*. New York: Wiley.

Cohen, S., Frank, E., Doyle, W. J., Skoner, D. P., Rabin, B. S. and Gwaltney, J. M. (1998) Types of stressors that increase susceptibility to the common cold in healthy adults. *Health Psychology*, 17, 214–23.

Coles, M. G. H., Gratton, G. and Fabiani, M. (1990) Event-related brain potentials. In J. T. Cacioppo and L. G. Tassinary (eds.), *Principles of psychophysiology: physical, social, and inferential elements*, pp. 413–55 Cambridge University Press.

Colquitt, J. A. and Simmering, M. J. (1998) Conscientiousness, goal orientation, and motivation to learn during the learning process: a longitudinal study. *Journal of Applied Psychology*, 83, 654–65.

Colvin, C. R., Block, J. and Funder, D. C. (1995) Overly positive self-evaluations and personality: negative implications for mental health. *Journal of Personality and Social Psychology*, 68, 1152–62.

Comrey, A. L. (1994) *Revised manual and handbook of interpretations for the Comrey Personality Scales*. San Diego, CA: EdITS Publishers.

Conley, J. J. (1984) The hierarchy of consistency: a review and model of longitudinal findings on adult individual differences in intelligence, personality and self-opinion. *Personality and Individual Differences*, 5, 11–26.

(1985) Longitudinal stability of personality traits: a multitrait–multimethod–multioccasion analysis. *Journal of Personality and Social Psychology*, 49, 1266–82.

Conn, S. R. and Rieke, M. L. (eds.) (1994) *The 16PF fifth edition technical manual*. Champaign, IL: Institute for Personality and Ability Testing.

Cook, E. P. (1985) *Psychological androgyny*. New York: Pergamon.

Cook, K. W., Vance, C. A. and Spector, P. E. (2000) The relation of candidate personality with selection-interview outcomes. *Journal of Applied Social Psychology*, 30, 867–85.

Cooke, D. J. and Michie, C. (1997) An item response theory evaluation of Hare's Psychopathy Checklist. *Psychological Assessment*, 9, 2–13.

(2001) Refining the construct of psychopathy: towards a hierarchical model. *Psychological Assessment*, 13, 171–88.

Cooke, D. J., Forth, A. and Hare, R. D. (1998) *Psychopathy: theory, research and implications for society*. Dordrecht, The Netherlands: Kluwer.

Cooper, R. K. and Sawaf, A. (1997) *Executive EQ: emotional intelligence in leaders and organizations*. New York: Grosset/Putnam.

Corcoran, D. W. J. (1962) Individual differences in performance after loss of sleep. Unpublished doctoral dissertation, University of Cambridge.

(1972) Studies of individual differences at the Applied Psychology Unit. In V. D. Nebylitsyn and J. A. Gray (eds.), *Biological bases of individual behaviour*. London: Academic.

Corr, P. J. (2001) Testing problems in J. A. Gray's personality theory: a commentary on Matthews and Gilliland (1999). *Personality and Individual Differences*, 30, 333–52.

(2002) J. A. Gray's Reinforcement Sensitivity Theory: tests of the joint subsystem hypothesis of anxiety and impulsivity. *Personality and Individual Differences*, 33, 511–32.

Corr, P. J. and Kumari, V. (2000) Individual differences in mood reactions to d-amphetamine: a test of three personality factors. *Journal of Psychopharmacology*, 14, 371–7.

Corr, P. J., Pickering, A. D. and Gray, J. A. (1995) Personality and reinforcement in associative and instrumental learning. *Personality and Individual Differences*, 19, 47–72.

Costa, P. T., Jr. (1996) Work and personality: use of the NEO-PI-R in industrial/organizational psychology. *Applied Psychology: An International Review*, 45, 225–41.

Costa, P. T., Jr. and McCrae, R. R. (1977) Age differences in personality structure revisited: studies in validity, stability and change. *Aging and Human Development*, 8, 261–75.

(1987) Neuroticism, somatic complaints, and disease: is the bark worse than the bite? *Journal of Personality*, 55, 299–316.

(1988) Personality in adulthood: a six-year longitudinal study of self-reports and spouse ratings on the NEO Personality Inventory. *Journal of Personality and Social Psychology*, 54, 853–63.

(1990) Personality disorders and the five-factor model of personality. *Journal of Personality Disorders*, 4, 362–71.

(1992a) *NEO PI-R Professional Manual*. Odessa, FL: Psychological Assessment Resources.

(1992b) Four ways five factors are basic. *Personality and Individual Differences*, 135, 653–65.

(1992c) Trait psychology comes of age. *Nebraska Symposium on Motivation*, 39, 169–204.

(1992d) The five factor model of personality and its relevance to personality disorders. *Journal of Personality Disorders*, 6, 343–59.

(1993) Bullish on personality psychology. *The Psychologist*, 6, 302–3.

(1994) Set like plaster? Evidence for the stability of adult personality. In T. Heatherton and J. Weinberger (eds.), *Can personality change?* Washington, DC: American Psychological Association.

(1995a) Primary traits of Eysenck's P-E-N system. *Journal of Personality and Social Psychology*, 69, 308–17.

(1995b) Solid ground on the wetlands of personality – a reply to Block. *Psychological Bulletin*, 117, 216–20.

Costa, P. T., Jr., Terraciano, A. and McCrae, R. R. (2001) Gender differences in personality traits across cultures: robust and surprising findings. *Journal of Personality and Social Psychology*, 81, 322–31.

Costa, P. T., Jr. and Widiger, T. A. (eds.) (1994) *Personality disorders and the five-factor model of personality*. Washington, DC: American Psychological Association.

Costa, P. T., Jr., McCrae, R. R. and Arenberg, D. (1980) Enduring dispositions in adult males. *Journal of Personality and Social Psychology*, 38, 793–800.

Costa, P. T., Jr., McCrae, R. R. and Dye, D. A. (1991) Facet scales for Agreeableness and Conscientiousness: a revision of the NEO Personality Inventory. *Personality and Individual Differences*, 12, 887–9.

Costa, P. T., Jr., Zonderman, A., Williams, R. and McCrae, R. R. (1985) Content and comprehensiveness in the MMPI: an item factor analysis in a normal adult sample. *Journal of Personality and Social Psychology*, 48, 925–33.

Costa, P. T., Jr. and Widiger, T. A. (eds.) (2002) *Personality disorders and the five-factor model of personality*, 2nd edn. Washington, DC: American Psychological Association.

Coté, S. and Moskowitz, D. S. (1998) On the dynamic covariation between interpersonal behavior and affect: prediction from neuroticism, extraversion, and agreeableness. *Journal of Personality and Social Psychology*, 75, 1032–46.

Cox, T. and Ferguson, E. (1991) Individual differences, stress and coping. In C. L. Cooper and R. Payne (eds.), *Personality and stress: individual differences in the coping process*, pp. 7–32. Chichester: Wiley.

Cox, T. and Mackay, C. (1985) The measurement of self-reported stress and arousal. *British Journal of Psychology*, 76, 183–6.

Cox-Fuenzalida, L.-G., Gilliland, K. and Swickert, R. J. (2001) Congruency of the relationship between extraversion and the brainstem auditory evoked response based on the EPI versus the EPQ. *Journal of Research in Personality*, 35, 117–26.

Coyne, J. C. (1985) Studying depressed persons' interactions with strangers and spouses. *Journal of Abnormal Psychology*, 85, 186–93.

Coyne, J. C. and Whiffen, V. E. (1995) Issues in personality as diathesis for depression: the case of sociotropy-dependency and autonomy-self-criticism. *Psychological Bulletin*, 118, 358–78.

Cramer, P. (2002) Defense mechanisms, behavior, and affect in young adulthood. *Journal of Personality*, 70, 103–26.

Crick, F. and Mitchison, G. (1995) REM sleep and neural nets. *Behavioral Brain Research*, 69, 147–55.

Cronbach, L. J. (1957) The two disciplines of scientific psychology. *American Psychologist*, 12, 671–84.

(1990) *Essentials of psychological testing* (5th edn.). New York: Harper and Row.

Crowne, D. P. and Marlowe, D. (1964) *The approval motive*. New York: Wiley.

Crozier, W. R. (1982) Explanations of social shyness. *Current Psychological Reviews*, 2, 47–60.

(1997) *Individual learners: personality differences in education*. New York: Routledge.

Crozier, W. R. and Alden, L. E. (2001) The social nature of social anxiety. In W. R. Crozier and L. E. Alden (eds.), *International handbook of social anxiety: concepts, research and interventions relating to the self and shyness*, pp. 1–20. New York: Wiley.

Curran, J. P. and Cattell, R. B. (1974) *The Eight State Questionnaire*. Champaign, IL: IPAT.

Dahl, A. A. (1995) Commentary on borderline personality disorder. In W. J. Livesley (ed.) *The DSM-IV Personality Disorders*. New York: Guilford.

Dalton, S. O., Mellemkjaer, L., Olsen, J. H., Mortensen, P. B. and Johansen, C. (2002) Depression and cancer risk: a register-based study of patients hospitalised with affective disorders, Denmark, 1969–1993. *American Journal of Epidemiology*, 155, 1088–95.

Daly, S. (1978) Behavioural correlates of social anxiety. *British Journal of Social and Clinical Psychology*, 17, 117–20.

Darke, S. (1988) Anxiety and working memory capacity. *Cognition and Emotion*, 2, 145–54.

Daruna, J. H., Karrer, R. and Rosen, A. J. (1985) Introversion, attention and the late positive component of event-related potentials. *Biological Psychology*, 20, 249–59.

Davies, P. T. and Cummings, E. M. (1995) Children's emotions as organizers of their reactions to interadult anger: a functionalist perspective. *Developmental Psychology*, 31, 677–684.

Davis, R. and Millon, T. (1995) On the importance of theory to a taxonomy of personality disorders. In W. J. Livesley (ed.), *The DSM-IV Personality Disorders*. New York: Guilford.

Dawda, D. and Hart, S. D. (2000) Assessing emotional intelligence: Reliability and validity of the Bar-On Emotional Quotient Inventory (EQ-i) in university students. *Personality and Individual Differences*, 28, 797–812.

Dawson, M. R. (1998) *Understanding cognitive science*. Oxford: Blackwell.

De Beurs, E., Beekman, A. T. F., Deeg, D. J. H., Van Dyck, R. and Van Tilburg, N. (2000) Predictors of change in anxiety symptoms of older persons: results from the Longitudinal Aging Study Amsterdam. *Psychological Medicine*, 30, 515–27.

(1977) Neuroticism and proxemic behaviour. *Perceptual and Motor skills*, 45, 51–5.

De Pascalis, V. and Speranza, O. (2000) Personality effects on attentional shifts to emotional charged cues: ERP, behavioural and HR data. *Personality and Individual Differences*, 29, 217–38.

De Pascalis, V., Fiore, A. D. and Sparita, A. (1996) Personality, event-related potential (ERP) and heart rate (HR): an investigation of Gray's theory. *Personality and Individual Differences*, 20, 733–46.

De Paulo, B. M., Kenny, D. A., Hoover, C. W., Webb, W. and Oliver, P. V. (1987) Accuracy of person perception: do people know what kinds of impressions they convey? *Journal of Personality and Social Psychology*, 52, 303–15.

De Raad, B. (1992) The replicability of the Big Five personality dimensions in three word-classes of the Dutch language. *European Journal of Personality*, 6, 15–30.

(2000) The big five personality factors: the psycholexical approach to personality. Seattle, WA: Hogrefe and Huber.

De Raad, B. and Perugini, M. (2002) *Big Five assessment*. Seattle, WA: Hogrefe and Huber.

De Raad, B. and Van Heck, G. L. (eds.) (1994) Special issue: the fifth of the Big Five. *European Journal of Personality*, 8, 225–56.

De Wolff, M. and van Ijzendoorn, M. H. (1997) Sensitivity and attachment: a meta-analysis on parental antecedents of infant attachment. *Child Development*, 68, 571–91.

Deary, I. J. (1993a) Behavioral genetics: variables, mechanisms and disorders. In J. Hettema and I. J. Deary (eds.), *Foundations of personality*. Dordrecht, The Netherlands: Kluwer.

(1993b) Book review of A. Gale and M. W. Eysenck (eds.) 'Handbook of individual differences: biological perspectives'. *Quarterly Journal of Experimental Psychology*, 46B, 413–15.

(1996) A (latent) big five personality model in 1915? A reanalysis of Webb's data. *Journal of Personality and Social Psychology*, 71, 992–5.

(1999) A taxonomy of medially unexplained symptoms. *Journal of Psychosomatic Research*, 47, 51–9.

(2000) *Looking down on human intelligence: from psychometrics to the brain*. Oxford: Oxford University Press.

Deary, I. J., Bedford, A. and Fowkes, F. G. R. (1995) The Personality Deviance Scales: their development, associations, factor structure and restructuring. *Personality and Individual Differences*, 19, 275–91.

Deary, I. J., MacLullich, A. M. J. and Mardon, J. (1991) Reporting of minor physical symptoms and family incidence of hypertension and heart disease – relationships with personality and Type A behaviour. *Personality and Individual Differences*, 12, 747–51.

Deary, I. J., Scott, S. and Wilson, J. A. (1997) Neuroticism, alexithymia, and medically unexplained symptoms. *Personality and Individual Differences*, 22, 551–64.

Deary, I. J., Wilson, J. A. and Kelly, S. W. (1995) Globus pharyngis, personality, and psychological distress in the general population. *Psychosomatics*, 36, 570–7.

Deary, I. J., Fowkes, F. G. R., Donnan, P. T. and Housley, E. (1994) Hostile personality and risks of peripheral arterial disease in the general population. *Psychosomatic Medicine*, 56, 197–202.

Deary, I. J., Peter, A., Austin, E. J. and Gibson, G. J. (1998) Personality traits and personality disorders. *British Journal of Psychology*, 89, 647–661.

Deary, I. J., Battersby, S., Whiteman, M. C., Connor, J. M., Fowkes, F. G. and Harmar, A. (1999) Neuroticism and polymorphisms in the serotonin transporter gene. *Psychological Medicine*, 29, 735–9.

Deary, I. J., Blenkin, H., Agius, R. M., Endler, N. S., Zealley, H. and Wood, R. (1996) Models of job-related stress and personal achievement among consultant doctors. *British Journal of Psychology*, 87, 3–29.

Deci, E. L. and Ryan, R. M. (2000) The "what" and "why" of goal pursuits: human needs and the self-determination of behavior. *Psychological Inquiry*, 11, 227–68.

Deeg, D. and van Zonneveld, R. (1989) Does happiness lengthen life? In R. Veenhoven (ed.), *How Harmful is Happiness?* Rotterdam: Rotterdam University Press.

Deffenbacher, J. L. (1980) Worry and emotionality in test anxiety. In I. G. Sarason (ed.), *Test anxiety: theory, research and applications*. Hillsdale, NJ: Erlbaum.

Deinzer, R., Steyer, R., Eid, M., Notz, P., Schwenkmezger, P., Ostendorf, F. and Neubauer, A. (1995) Situational effects in trait assessment: the FPI, NEO FFI and EPI questionnaires. *European Journal of Personality*, 9, 1–24.

Denham, S. A. (1998) *Emotional development in young children*. New York: Guilford Press.

DeNeve, K. M. and Cooper, H. (1998) The happy personality: a meta-analysis of 137 personality traits and subjective well-being. *Psychological Bulletin*, 124, 197–229.

Depue, R. A. and Collins, P. F. (1999) Neurobiology of the structure of personality: dopamine, facilitation of incentive motivation, and extraversion. *Behavioral and Brain Sciences*, 22, 491–533.

Derakshan, N. and Eysenck, M. W. (2001) Effects of focus of attention on physiological, behavioural, and reported state anxiety in repressors, low-anxious, high-anxious, and defensive high-anxious individuals. *Anxiety, Stress and Coping: An International Journal*, 14, 285–99.

Derryberry, D. and Reed, M. A. (1994) Temperament and attention: orienting toward and away from positive and negative signals. *Journal of Personality and Social Psychology*, 66, 1128–39.

(1997) Motivational and attentional components of personality. In G. Matthews (ed.), *Cognitive science perspectives on personality and emotion*, pp. 443–73. Amsterdam: Elsevier.

Derryberry, D. and Rothbart, M. K. (1988) Arousal, affective and attentional components of adult temperament. *Journal of Personality and Social Psychology*, 55, 953–66.

D'Esposito, M., Zarahn, E. and Aguirre, G. K. (1999) Event-related functional MRI: implications for cognitive psychology. *Psychological Bulletin*, 125, 155–64.

Devins, G. M., Ann, J., Mandin, H. and Paul, L. C. (1990) Psychosocial predictors of survival in end-stage renal disease. *Journal of Nervous and Mental Disease*, 178, 127–33.

Dewaele, J.-M. and Furnham, A. (1999) Extraversion: the unloved variable in applied linguistic research. *Language Learning*, 49, 509–44.

(2000) Personality and speech production: a pilot study of second language learners. *Personality and Individual Differences*, 28, 355–65.

Dickman, S. J. and Mayer, D. E. (1988) Impulsivity and speed-accuracy tradeoffs in information processing. *Journal of Personality and Social Psychology*, 54, 274–90.

Dien, J. (1999) Differential lateralization of trait anxiety and trait fearfulness: evoked potential correlates. *Personality and Individual Differences*, 26, 333–56.

Diener, E. and Biswas-Diener, R. (2002) Will money increase subjective well-being? *Social Indicators Research*, 57, 119–69.

Diener, E. and Larsen, R. J. (1984) Temporal stability and cross-situational consistency of affective, behavioral, and cognitive responses. *Journal of Personality and Social Psychology*, 47, 871–83.

Diener, E., Larsen, R. J., Levine, S. and Emmons, R. A. (1985) Intensity and frequency: dimensions underlying positive and negative affect. *Journal of Personality and Social Psychology*, 48, 1253–65.

Diener, E., Suh, E. M., Lucas, R. E. and Smith, H. L. (1999) Subjective well-being: three decades of progress. *Psychological Bulletin*, 125, 276–302.

Digman, J. M. and Takemoto-Chock, N. K. (1981) Factors in the natural language of personality: re-analysis, comparison and interpretation of six major studies. *Multivariate Behavioral Research*, 16, 149–70.

Dinan, T. G., Chua, A. S. B. and Keeling, P. W. N. (1993) Serotonin and physical illness: focus on non-ulcer dyspepsia. *Journal of Psychopharmacology*, 7 (Supplement), 126–30.

Dinn, W. M., Harris, C. L., Aycicegi, A., Greene, P. and Andover, M. S. (2002) Positive and negative schizotypy in a student sample: neurocognitive and clinical correlates. *Schizophrenia Research*, 56, 171–85.

Dishman, R. K., Nakamura, Y., Garcia, M. E., Thompson, R. W., Dunn, Andrea L. and Blair, S. N. (2000) Heart rate variability, trait anxiety, and perceived stress among physically fit men and women. *International Journal of Psychophysiology*, 37, 121–33.

Dodge, K. A. (2000) Conduct disorder. In A. J. Sameroff, M. Lewis and S. M. Miller (eds.), *Handbook of developmental psychopathology* (2nd edn.), pp. 447–463. New York: Kluwer Academic/Plenum.

Dolgin, D. L. and Gibb, G. D. (1989) Personality assessment in aviator selection. In R. S. Jensen (ed.), *Aviation psychology*, pp. 288–320. Brookfield, VT: Gower.

Dollard, J. and Miller, N. E. (1950) *Personality and psychotherapy: an analysis in terms of learning, thinking and culture*. New York: McGraw Hill.

Dorn, L. and Matthews, G. (1995) Prediction of mood and risk appraisals from trait measures: two studies of simulated driving. *European Journal of Personality*, 9, 25–42.

Dorsey, C. M. and Bootzin, R. R. (1997) Subjective and psychophysiologic insomnia: an examination of sleep tendency and personality. *Biological Psychiatry*, 41, 209–16.

Doucet, C. and Stelmack, R. M. (2000) An event-related potential analysis of extraversion and individual differences in cognitive processing speed and response execution. *Journal of Personality and Social Psychology*, 78, 956–64.

Downey, G. and Feldman, S. I. (1996) Implications of rejection sensitivity for intimate relationships. *Journal of Personality and Social Psychology*, 70, 1327–43.

Drossman, D. A., Leserman, J., Li, Z. M., Keefe, F., Hu, Y. J. B. and Toomey, T. C. (2000) Effects of coping on health outcome among women with gastrointestinal disorders. *Psychosomatic Medicine*, 62, 307–17.

Duffy, E. (1962) *Activation and behavior*. New York: Wiley.

Duggan, C. F., Lee, A. S. and Murray, R. M. (1990) Does personality predict long-term outcome in depression? *British Journal of Psychiatry*, 157, 19–24.

Duggan, C. F., Sham, P., Lee, A. S. and Murray, R. M. (1991) Does recurrent depression lead to a change in neuroticism? *Psychological Medicine*, 21, 985–90.

Dunbar, H. F. (1938) *Emotions and bodily changes: a survey of literature on psychosomatic interrelationships 1910–1933*, 2nd edn. New York: Columbia University Press.

Eagly, A. H. and Wood, W. (1999) The origins of sex differences in human behavior: evolved dispositions versus social roles. *American Psychologist*, 54, 408–23.

Eaves, L. J., Eysenck, H. J. and Martin, N. G. (1989) *Genes, culture and personality*. London: Academic.

Eaves, L. J., Heath, A. C., Neale, M. C., Hewitt, J. K. and Martin, N. G. (1998) Sex differences and non-additivity in the effects of genes on personality. *Twin Research*, 1, 131–7.

Ebmeier, K. P., Deary, I. J., O'Carroll, R. E., Prentice, N., Moffoott, A. P. R. and Goodwin, G. M. (1994) Personality associations with the uptake of the cerebral blood flow marker[99mTc]-exametazine estimated with single photon emission tomography. *Personality and Individual Differences*, 17, 587–95.

Ebstein, R. P., Benjamin, J. and Belmaker, R. H. (2000) Genetics of personality dimensions. *Current Opinion in Psychiatry*, 13, 617–22.

Ebstein, R. P., Novick, O., Umansky, R., Priel, B., Osher, Y., Blaine, D., Bennett, E. R., Nemanov, L., Katz, M. and Belmaker, R. H. (1996) Dopamine D_4 receptor (D_4DR) exon III polymorphism associated with the human personality trait of novelty seeking. *Nature Genetics*, 12, 78–80.

Edens, J. F., Poythress, N. G. and Watkins, M. M. (2001) Further validation of the Psychopathic Personality Inventory among offenders: personality and behavioral correlates. *Journal of Personality Disorders*, 15, 403–15.

Edman, G., Schalling, D. and Levander, S. E. (1983) Impulsivity and speed and errors in a reaction time task. A contribution to the construct validity of the concept of impulsivity. *Acta Psychologica*, 33, 1–8.

Egloff, B. and Hock, M. (2001) Interactive effects of state anxiety and trait anxiety on emotional Stroop interference. *Personality and Individual Differences*, 31, 875–82.

Ehlers, A. and Clark, D. M. (2000) A cognitive model of posttraumatic stress disorder. *Behaviour Research and Therapy*, 38, 319–45.

Eisenberg, N., Fabes, R. A. and Losoya, S. (1997) Emotional responding: regulation, social correlates, and socialization. In P. Salovey and D. J. Sluyter (eds.), *Emotional development and emotional intelligence: educational implications*, pp. 129–67. New York: Basic Books.

Ekehammar, B. (1974) Interactionism in personality from a historical perspective. *Psychological Bulletin*, 81, 1026–48.

Ellison, C. G., Gay, D. A. and Glass, T. A. (1989) Does religious commitment contribute to individual life satisfaction? *Journal of Health and Social Behavior*, 32, 80–99.

Emmons, R. A. (1987) Narcissism: theory and measurement. *Journal of Personality and Social Psychology*, 52, 11–17.

Emmons, R. A. and Diener, E. (1986) Influence of impulsivity and sociability on subjective well-being. *Journal of Personality and Social Psychology*, 50, 1211–15.

Endler, N. (1983) Interactionism: a personality model but not yet a theory. In M. M. Page (ed.), *Nebraska Symposium on Motivation* 1982: *personality – current theory and research*. Lincoln, NE: University of Nebraska Press.

(1989) The temperamental nature of personality. *European Journal of Personality*, 3, 151–65.

(1997) Stress, anxiety and coping: the multidimensional interaction model. *Canadian Psychology*, 38, 136–53.

Endler, N. S. and Kocovski, N. L. (2001) State and trait anxiety revisited. *Journal of Anxiety Disorders*, 15, 231–45.

Endler, N. and Parker, J. (1990) Multidimensional assessment of coping: a critical review. *Journal of Personality and Social Psychology*, 58, 844–54.

(1991) Personality research: theories, issues and methods. In M. Hersen, A. E. Kazdin and S. Bellak (eds.) *The clinical psychology handbook*. New York: Pergamon.

(1992) Interactionism revisited: reflections on the continuing crisis in the personality area. *European Journal of Personality*, 6, 177–98.

Endler, N., Edwards, J. M. and Vitelli, R. (1991) *Endler Multidimensional Anxiety Scales (EMAS): manual*. Los Angeles, CA: Western Psychological Services.

Endler, N., Parker, J. D. A, Bagby, R. M. and Cox, B. J. (1991) The multidimensionality of state and trait anxiety: the factor structure of the Endler Multidimensional Anxiety Scales. *Journal of Personality and Social Psychology*, 60, 919–26.

Enns, M. W., Cox, B. J., Sareen, J. and Freeman, P. (2001) Adaptive and maladaptive perfectionism in medical students: a longitudinal investigation. *Medical Education*, 35, 1034–42.

Epstein, S. (1977) Traits are alive and well. In D. Magnusson and N. S. Endler (eds.), *Personality at the crossroads*. Hillsdale, NJ: Lawrence Erlbaum Associates.

Ericsson, K. A. (1996) The acquisition of expert performance: an introduction to some of the issues. In K. A. Ericsson (ed.), *The road to excellence: the acquisition of expert performance in the arts and sciences, sports, and games*. Mahwah, NJ: Erlbaum.

Erikson, E. H. (1963) *Childhood and society*, 2nd edn. New York: Norton.

(1982) *The life cycle completed: a review*. New York: Norton.

Everson, S. A., Goldberg, D. E., Kaplan, G. A., Cohen, R. D., Pukkala, E., Tuomilehto, J. and Salonen, J. T. (1996) Hopelessness and risk of mortality and incidence of myocardial infarction and cancer. *Psychosomatic Medicine*, 58, 113–21.

Eysenck, H. J. (1954) *The psychology of politics*. London: Routledge and Kegan Paul.

(1957) *The dynamics of anxiety and hysteria*. London: Routledge and Kegan Paul.

(1967) *The biological basis of personality*. Springfield, IL.: Thomas.

(1969) *Personality structure and measurement*. London: Routledge and Kegan Paul.

(1970) *The structure of human personality* (3rd edn). London: Methuen.

(1976) *Sex and personality*. London: Open Books.

(1981) General features of the model. In H. J. Eysenck (ed.), A *model for personality*. Berlin, Germany: Springer.

(1985) *The decline and fall of the Freudian empire*. Harmondsworth: Penguin.

(1987) The definition of personality disorders and the criteria appropriate to their definition. *Journal of Personality Disorders*, 1, 211–19.

(1990) Genetic and environmental contributions to individual differences: the three major dimensions of personality. *Journal of Personality*, 58, 245–61.

(1991) Dimensions of personality: 16, 5 or 3? Criteria for a taxonomic paradigm. *Personality and Individual Differences*, 12, 773–90.

(1992a) Four ways the five factors are not basic. *Personality and Individual Differences*, 13, 667–73.

(1992b) The definition and measurement of psychoticism. *Personality and Individual Differences*, 13, 757–86.

(1993) From DNA to social behaviour: conditions for a paradigm of personality research. In J. Hettema and I. J. Deary (eds.), *Foundations of personality*. Dordrecht, The Netherlands: Kluwer.

(1994a) Personality and intelligence: psychometric and experimental approaches. In R. J. Sternberg and P. Ruzgis (eds.), *Personality and intelligence*. Cambridge University Press.

(1994b) Personality: biological foundations. In P. A. Vernon (ed.), *The neuropsychology of individual differences*, pp. 151–207. New York: Academic.

(1995) Creativity as a product of intelligence and personality. In D. H. Saklofske and M. Zeidner (eds.), *International handbook of personality and intelligence*. New York: Plenum.

(1997) Personality and experimental psychology: the unification of psychology and the possibility of a paradigm. *Journal of Personality and Social Psychology*, 73, 1224–37.

Eysenck, H. J. and Eysenck, M. W. (1985) *Personality and individual differences: a natural science approach*. New York: Plenum.

Eysenck, H. J. and Eysenck, S. B. G. (1969) *Personality structure and measurement*. London: Routledge and Kegan Paul.

(1982) Recent advances in the cross-cultural study of personality. In C. D. Spielberger and J. N. Butcher (eds.), *Advances in personality assessment*. Hillsdale, NJ: Erlbaum.

(1991) *The Eysenck Personality Questionnaire–Revised*. Sevenoaks: Hodder and Stoughton.

Eysenck, M. W. (1974) Individual differences in speed of retrieval from semantic memory. *Journal of Research in Personality*, 8, 307–23.

(1981) Learning, memory and personality. In H. J. Eysenck (ed.), *A model for personality*. Berlin: Springer.

(1982) *Attention and arousal: cognition and performance*. New York: Springer.

(1988) Anxiety and attention. *Anxiety Research*, 1, 9–15.

(1992) *Anxiety: the cognitive perspective*. Hillsdale, NJ: Erlbaum.

Eysenck, M. W. and Eysenck, H. J. (1980) Mischel and the concept of personality. *British Journal of Psychology*, 71, 191–204.

Eysenck, M. W. and Eysenck, M. C. (1979) Memory scanning, introversion–extraversion, and levels of processing. *Journal of Research in Personality*, 13, 305–15.

Eysenck, M. W. and Folkard, S. (1980) Personality, time of day, and caffeine: some theoretical and conceptual problems in Revelle et al. *Journal of Experimental Psychology: General*, 109, 32–41.

Eysenck, M. W., MacLeod, C. and Mathews, A. (1987) Cognitive functioning and anxiety. *Psychological Research*, 49, 189–95.

Eysenck, S. B. G., Barrett, P. T. and Barnes, G. E. (1993) A cross-cultural study of personality: Canada and England. *Personality and Individual Differences*, 14, 1–10.

Eysenck, S. B. G., Eysenck, H. J. and Barrett, P. T. (1985) A revised version of the Psychoticism scale. *Personality and Individual Differences*, 6, 21–9.

Eysenck, S. B. G., Makaremi, A. and Barrett, P. T. (1994) A cross-cultural study of personality: Iranian and English children. *Personality and Individual Differences*, 16, 203–10.

Eysenck, S. B. G., Rust, J. and Eysenck, H. J. (1977) Personality and the classification of adult offenders. *British Journal of Criminology*, 17, 169–79.

Fagerstrm, K. O. and Lisper, H. O. (1977) Effects of listening to car radio, experience, and personality of the driver on subsidiary reaction time and heart rate in a long-term driving task. In R. R. Mackie (ed.), *Vigilance*. New York: Plenum.

Fahrenberg, J. (1991) A differential psycho-physiology and the diagnosis of temperament. In J. Strelau and A. Angleitner (eds.), *Explorations in temperament*. London and New York: Plenum.

Fahrenberg, J., Walschburger, P., Foerster, F., Myrtek, M. and Muller, W. (1983) An evaluation of trait, state, and reaction aspects of activation processes. *Psychophysiology*, 20, 188–95.

Farmer, R. F. (2000) Issues in the assessment and conceptualization of personality disorders. *Clinical Psychology Review*, 20, 823–51.

Farthofer, A. and Brandstaetter, H. (2001) Extraversion and optimal level of arousal in high-risk work. In H. Brandstaetter and E. Andrzej (eds.), *Persons, situations and emotions: an ecological approach*, pp. 133–46. London: Oxford University Press.

Fawzy, F. I., Cousins, N., Fawzy, N. W., Kemeny, M. E., Elashoff, R. and Morton, D. (1990) A structured psychiatric intervention for cancer patients. I. Changes over time in methods of coping and affective disturbance. *Archives of General Psychiatry*, 47, 720–5.

Fawzy, F. I., Kemeny, M. E., Fawzy, N. W., Elashoff, R., Morton, D., Cousins, N. and Fahey, J. L. (1990) A structured psychiatric intervention for cancer patients: II. Changes over time in immunological measures. *Archives of General Psychiatry*, 47, 729–35.

Fawzy, F. I., Fawzy, N. W., Hyun, C. S., Elashoff, R., Guthrie, D., Fahey, J. L. and Morton, D. L. (1993) Malignant melanoma: effects of an early structured psychiatric intervention, coping and affective state on recurrence and survival 6 years later. *Archives of General Psychiatry*, 50, 681–9.

Feeney, N. C. and Foa, E. B. (in press) Cognitive vulnerability to PTSD. In L. B. Alloy and J. H. Riskind (eds.), *Cognitive vulnerability to emotional disorders*. Hillsdale, NJ: Erlbaum.

Feingold, A. (1994) Gender differences in personality – a metaanalysis. *Psychological Bulletin*, 116, 429–56.

Felson, R. B. (1985) Reflected appraisal and the development of self. *Social Psychology Quarterly*, 48, 71–8.

Fenigstein, A., Scheier, M. F. and Buss, A. H. (1975) Public and private selfconsciousness: assessment and theory. *Journal of Consulting and Clinical Psychology*, 43, 522–7.

Festinger, L. (1954) A theory of social comparison processes. *Human Relations*, 7, 117–40.

Finn, S. E. (1986) Stability of personality self-ratings over thirty years: evidence for an age/cohort interaction. *Journal of Personality and Social Psychology*, 50, 813–18.

Fisher, C. D. (2002) Antecedents and consequences of real-time affective reactions at work. *Motivation and Emotion*, 26, 3–30.

Fisher, S. (1989) *Homesickness, cognition and health*. Hillsdale, NJ: Erlbaum.

Fiske, D. W. (1949) Consistency of the factorial structures of personality ratings from different sources. *Journal of Abnormal and Social Psychology*, 44, 329–44.

Flint, J., Corley, R., DeFries, J. C., Fulker, D. W., Gray, J. A., Miller, S. and Collins, A. C. (1995) A simple genetic basis for a complex psychological trait in laboratory mice. *Science*, 269, 1432–5.

Floderus-Myrhed, B., Pedersen, N. and Rasmuson, I. (1980) Assessment of heritability for personality, based on a short form of the Eysenck Personality Inventory. *Behavior Genetics*, 10, 153–62.

Flynn, P. M. and McMahon, R. C. (1984) An investigation of the factor structure of the Millon Clinical Multiaxial Inventory. *Journal of Personality Assessment*, 48, 308–11.

Folkman, S. and Lazarus, R. S. (1988) *Manual for the ways of coping questionnaire*. Palo Alto, CA: Consulting Psychologists Press.

Forgas, J. P. (1995) Mood and judgement: the affect infusion model (AIM). *Psychological Bulletin*, 117, 39–66.

Forgays, D. G., Forgays, D. K. and Spielberger, C. D. (1997) Factor structure of the State-Trait Anger Expression Inventory for young adults. *Journal of Personality Assessment*, 69, 497–507.

Fowkes, F. G. R., Housley, E., Cawood, E. H. H., Macintyre, C. C. A., Ruckley, C. V. and Prescott, R. J. (1991) Edinburgh Artery Study: prevalence of asymptomatic and symptomatic peripheral arterial disease in the general population. *International Journal of Epidemiology*, 20, 384–92.

Fowkes, F. G. R., Leng, G. C., Donnan, P. T., Deary, I. J., Riemersma, R. A. and Housley, E. (1992) Serum cholesterol, triglycerides, and aggression in the general population. *The Lancet*, 340, 995–8.

Fowles, D. C., Roberts, R. and Nagel, K. (1977) The influence of introversion/extraversion on the skin conductance response to stress and stimulus intensity. *Journal of Research in Personality*, 11, 129–46.

Fox, E. (1996) Selective processing of threatening words in anxiety: the role of awareness. *Cognition and Emotion*, 10, 449–80.

Fox, E., Russo, R., Bowles, R. and Dutton, K. (2001) Do threatening stimuli draw or hold visual attention in subclinical anxiety? *Journal of Experimental Psychology: General*, 130, 681–700.

Fraley, R. C. and Shaver, P. R. (1998) Airport separations: a naturalistic study of adult attachment dynamics in separating couples. *Journal of Personality and Social Psychology*, 75, 1198–212.

Francis, L. J. and Kaldor, P. (2002) The relationship between psychological well-being and Christian faith and practice in an Australian population sample. *Journal for the Scientific Study of Religion*, 41, 179–84.

Freud, S. (1920) *Beyond the pleasure principle*. Standard edition, vol. 18. London: Hogarth Press, 1955.

Friedman, H. S. (2000) Long-term relations of personality and health: dynamisms, mechanims, tropisms. *Journal of Personality*, 68, 1089–107.

Friedman, H. S. and Booth-Kewley, S. (1987) The 'disease-prone personality': a metaanalytic view of the construct. *American Psychologist*, 42, 539–55.

Friedman, H. S., Tucker, J. S., Tomlinson-Keasey, C., Schwartz, J. E., Wingard, D. L. and Criqui, M. H. (1993) Does childhood personality predict longevity? *Journal of Personality and Social Psychology*, 65, 176–85.

Friedman, H. S., Tucker, J. S., Schwartz, J. E., Tomlinson-Keasey, C., Martin, L. R., Wingard, D. L. and Criqui, M. H. (1995) Psychosocial and behavioural predictors of longevity: the aging and death of the 'Termites'. *American Psychologist*, 50, 69–78.

Friedman, M. and Rosenman, R. H. (1974) *Type A behavior and your heart*. New York: Knopf.

Funder, D. C. (2001) Personality. *Annual Review of Psychology*, 52, 197–221.

Funder, D. C. and Colvin, C. R. (1988) Friends and strangers: acquaintanceship, agreement, and the accuracy of personality judgement. *Journal of Personality and Social Psychology*, 55, 149–58.

(1991) Explorations in behavioral consistency: properties of persons, situations and behaviors. *Journal of Personality and Social Psychology*, 60, 773–94.

Funder, D. C. and Ozer, D. J. (1983) Behavior as a function of the situation. *Journal of Personality and Social Psychology*, 44, 107–12.

Furnham, A. (1981) Personality and activity preference. *British Journal of Social Psychology*, 20, 57–60.

(1990) *The Protestant Work Ethic*. London: Routledge.

(1992) *Personality at work: the role of individual differences in the workplace*. London: Routledge.

Furnham, A. and Allass, K. (1999) The influence of musical distraction of varying complexity on the cognitive performance of extraverts and introverts. *European Journal of Personality*, 13, 27–38.

Furnham, A. and Heaven, P. (1999) *Personality and social behaviour*. London: Arnold.

Furnham, A. Petrides, K. V. and Spencer-Bowdage, S. (2002) The effects of different types of social desirability on the identification of repressors. *Personality and Individual Differences*, 33, 119–30.

Fyer, M. R., Frances, A. J., Sulhvan, T., Hurt, S. W. and Clarkin, J. (1988) Comorbidity of borderline personality disorder. *Archives of General Psychiatry*, 45, 348–52.

Gale, A. (1981) EEG studies of extraversion–introversion: what's the next step? In R. Lynn (ed.), *Dimensions of personality: papers in honour of H. J. Eysenck*. Oxford: Pergamon.

Gale, A., Coles, M. and Blaydon, J. (1969) Extraversion–introversion and the EEG. *British Journal of Psychology*, 60, 209–23.

Gale, A. and Edwards, J. (1986) Individual differences. In M. G. H. Coles, E. Donchin and S. W. Porges (eds.), *Psychophysiology: systems, processes, and applications*. New York: Guilford Press.

Gale, A., Edwards, J., Morris, P., Moore, R. and Forrester, D. (2001) Extraversion–introversion, neuroticism–stability, and EEG indicators of positive and negative emphatic mood. *Personality and Individual Differences*, 30, 449–61.

Gallagher, D. J. (1990) Extraversion, neuroticism and appraisal of stressful academic events. *Personality and Individual Differences*, 11, 1053–8.

Galton, F. (1884) Measurement of character. *Fortnightly Review*, 36, 179–85.

Ganzer, V. J. (1968) Effects of audience presence and test anxiety on learning and retention in a serial learning situation. *Journal of Personality and Social Psychology*, 8, 194–9.

Gardner, H. (1983) *Frames of mind: the theory of multiple intelligences*. New York: Basic Books.

Garnefski, N., Kraaj, V. and Spinhoven, P. (2001) Negative life events, cognitive emotion regulation and emotional problems. *Personality and Individual Differences*, 30, 1311–27.

Gatzke-Kopp, L. M., Raine, A., Loeber, R., Stouthamer-Loeber, M. and Steinhauer, S. R. (2002) Serious delinquent behaviour, sensation seeking, and electrodermal arousal. *Journal of Abnormal Child Psychology*, 30, 477–86.

Gazzaniga, M. S. (1994) *Nature's mind: the biological roots of thinking, emotions, sexuality, language and intelligence*. Harmondsworth: Penguin.

Geen, R. G. (1985) Test anxiety and visual vigilance. *Journal of Personality and Social Psychology*, 49, 963–70.

Gelade, G. A. (1997) Creativity in conflict: the personality of the commercial creative. *Journal of Genetic Psychology*, 158, 67–78.

Gendolla, G. H. E. and Kruesken, J. (2001) Mood state and cardiovascular response in active coping with an affect-regulative challenge. *International Journal of Psychophysiology*, 41, 169–80.

Gerrards-Hesse, A., Spies K. and Hesse, F. W. (1994) Experimental inductions of emotional states and their effectiveness: a review. *British Journal of Psychology*, 85, 55–78.

Ghiselli, E. E. (1973) The validity of aptitude tests in personnel selection. *Personnel Psychology*, 26, 461–77.

Goetz, K. O. and Goetz, K. (1979) Personality characteristics of successful artists. *Perceptual and Motor Skills*, 49, 919–24.

Goff, M. and Ackerman, P. L. (1992) Personality–intelligence relations: assessment of typical intellectual engagement. *Journal of Educational Psychology*, 84, 537–52.

Gold, A. E., MacLeod, K. M., Frier, B. M. and Deary, I. J. (1995) Changes in mood during acute hypoglycaemia in healthy participants. *Journal of Personality and Social Psychology*, 68, 498–504.

Goldberg, D. (1978) *The General Health Questionnaire*. Windsor: NFER-Nelson.

Goldberg, L. R. (1990) An alternative 'Description of personality': the Big-Five factor structure. *Journal of Personality and Social Psychology*, 59, 1216–29.

　(1992) The development of markers for the Big-Five factor structure. *Psychological Assessment*, 4, 26–42.

　(1993) The structure of phenotypic personality traits. *American Psychologist*, 48, 26–34.

　(1996) Evidence for the Big Five in analyses of familiar personality adjectives. *European Journal of Personality* 10, 61–77.

　(1999) A broad-bandwidth, public-domain, personality inventory measuring the lower-level facets of several Five Factor models. In I. Mervielde, I. J. Deary, F. de Fruyt, and F. Ostendorf (eds.), *Personality psychology in Europe*, vol. 7, pp. 7–28. Tilburg: Tilburg University Press.

Goldberg, L. R. and Saucier, G. (1995) So what do you propose we use instead? A reply to Block. *Psychological Bulletin*, 117, 221–5.

Goldman, D. (1996) High anxiety. *Science*, 274, 1483.

Goldner, E. M., Srikameswaran, S., Schroeder, M. L., Livesley, W. J. and Birmingham, C. L. (1999) Dimensional assessment of personality pathology in patients with eating disorders. *Psychiatry Research*, 85, 151–9.

Goleman, D. (1995) *Emotional intelligence*. New York: Bantam Books.

　(1998) *Working with emotional intelligence*. New York: Bantam Books.

Gorsuch, R. (1983) *Factor analysis*. London: Erlbaum.

Gotlib, I. H. and McCann, C. D. (1984) Construct accessibility and depression: an examination of cognitive and affective factors. *Journal of Personality and Social Psychology*, 47, 427–39.

Gottman, J. (2001) Meta-emotion, children's emotional intelligence, and buffering children from marital conflict. In C. D. Ryff and B. H. Singer (eds.), *Emotion, social relationships, and health*, pp. 23–40. New York: Oxford University Press

Gough, H. G. (1987) *California Personality Inventory Administrator's Guide*. Palo Alto, CA: Consulting Psychologists.

Gough, H. G. and Bradley, P. (1996) *The California Psychological Inventory manual*, 3rd edn. Palo Alto, CA: Consulting Psychologists Press.

Gowing, M. K. (2001) Measures of individual emotional competencies. In C. Cherniss and D. Goleman (eds.), *The emotionally intelligent workplace*, pp. 83–131. San Francisco: Jossey-Bass.

Gray, J. A. (1964) Strength of the nervous system and levels of arousal: a reinterpretation. In J. A. Gray (ed.), *Pavlov's topology*, pp. 289–366. Oxford: Pergamon.

(1981) A critique of Eysenck's theory of personality. In H. J. Eysenck (ed.), *A model for personality*. Berlin: Springer.

(1982) *The neuropsychology of anxiety: an enquiry into the functions of the septo-hippocampal system*. Oxford: Oxford University Press.

(1987) *The psychology of fear and stress*, 2nd edn. Cambridge: Cambridge University Press.

(1991) Neural systems, emotion and personality. In J. Madden IV (ed.), *Neurobiology of learning, emotion and affect*, pp. 273–306. New York: Raven Press.

Gray, J. A. and Braver, T. S. (2002) Personality predicts working-memory-related activation in the caudal anterior cingulate cortex. *Cognitive, Affective and Behavioral Neuroscience*, 2, 64–75.

Gray, J. A. and McNaughton, N. (2000) *The neuropsychology of anxiety: an enquiry into the functions of the septo-hippocampal system*, 2nd edn. Oxford: Oxford University Press.

Graziano, W. G., Hair, E. C. and Finch, J. F. (1997) Competitiveness mediates the link between personality and group performance. *Journal of Personality and Social Psychology*, 73, 1394–408.

Graziano, W. G., Jensen-Campbell, L. A. and Hair, E. C. (1996) Perceiving interpersonal conflict and reacting to it: the case for agreeableness. *Journal of Personality and Social Psychology*, 70, 820–35.

Green, D. P., Salovey, P. and Truax, K. M. (1999) Static, dynamic, and causative bipolarity of affect. *Journal of Personality and Social Psychology*, 76, 856–67.

Greenberg, B. D., Li, Q., Lucas, F. R, Hu, S., Sirota, L. A., Benjamin, J., Lesch, K. P., Hamer, D. and Murphy, D. L. (2000) Association between the serotonin transporter promoter polymorphism and personality traits in a primarily female population sample. *American Journal of Medical Genetics*, 96, 202–16.

Greenberg, M. S. and Alloy, L. B. (1989) Depression versus anxiety: processing of self- and other-referent information. *Cognition and Emotion*, 3, 207–23.

Greenwald, A. G. (1982) Social psychology from the perspective of the self. In J. Suls (ed.), *Psychological perspectives on the self*, vol. 1, pp. 151–81, Hillsdale, NJ: Erlbaum.

Greer, S., Morris, T. and Pettingale, K. W. (1979) Psychological response to breast cancer, effect on outcome. *The Lancet*, 11, 785–7.

Greer, S., Moorey, S., Baruch, J. D., Watson, M., Robertson, B. M. and Mason, A. (1992) Adjuvant psychological therapy for patients with cancer: a prospective randomised trial. *British Medical Journal*, 304, 675–80.

Gross, J. J., Sutton, S. K. and Ketelaar, T. (1998) Relations between affect and personality: support for the affect-level and affective reactivity views. *Personality and Social Psychology Bulletin*, 24, 279–88.

Gruba, F. P. and Johnson, J. E. (1974) Contradictions within the self-concepts of schizophrenics. *Journal of Clinical Psychology*, 30, 253–4.

Grünbaum, A. (1984) *The philosophical foundations of psychoanalysis*. Berkeley: University of California Press.

Guion, R. M. (1997) Criterion measures and the criterion dilemma. In N. Anderson and P. Herriot (eds.), *International handbook of selection and appraisal*, 2nd edn. London: Wiley.

Gunderson, J. G., Ronningstam, E. and Smith, L. E. (1995) Narcissistic personality disorder. In W. J. Livesley (ed.), *The DSM IV Personality Disorders*. New York: Guilford.

Gunderson, J. G., Zanarini, M. C. and Kisiel, C. L. (1995) Borderline personality disorder. In W. J. Livesley (ed.), *The DSM IV Personality Disorders*. New York: Guilford.

Gunter, B. and Furnham, A. (1986) Sex and personality differences in recall of violent and non-violent news from three presentation modalities. *Personality and Individual Differences*, 6, 829–38.

Hagemann, D., Naumann, E., Luerken, A., Becker, G., Maier, S. and Bartussek, D. (1999) EEG asymmetry, dispositional mood and personality. *Personality and Individual Differences*, 27, 541–68.

Haier, R. J., Sokolski, K., Katz, M. and Buchsbaum, M. (1987) The study of personality with positron emission tomography. In J. Strelau and H. J. Eysenck (eds.), *Personality dimensions and arousal*. New York: Plenum.

Hamilton, C. J. (1995) Beyond sex differences in visuo-spatial processing: the impact of gender trait possession. *British Journal of Psychology*, 86, 1–20.

Hammond, M. S. (2001) The use of the Five-Factor Model of Personality as a therapeutic tool in career counseling. *Journal of Career Development*, 27, 153–65.

Hampson, S. E. (1988) *The construction of personality*, 2nd edn. London: Routledge.

(1992) The emergence of personality: a broader context for biological perspectives. In A. Gale and M. W. Eysenck (eds.), *Handbook of individual differences: biological perspectives*. Chichester: Wiley.

Hampson, S. E., Andrews, J. A., Barckley, M., Lichtenstein, E. and Lee, M. E. (2000) Conscientiousness, perceived risk, and risk-reduction behaviors: a preliminary study. *Health Psychology*, 19, 496–500.

Hare, R. D. (1980) A research scale for the assessment of psychopathy in criminal populations. *Personality and Individual Differences*, 1, 111–17.

(1991) *The Hare Psychopathy Checklist-Revised*. Toronto: Multi-Health Systems.

Hare, R. D., Cooke, D. J. and Hart, S. D. (1999) Psychopathy and sadistic personality disorder. In T. Millon and P. H. Blaney (eds.), *Oxford textbook of psychopathology*. Oxford: Oxford University Press.

Hare, R. D., Hart, S. D. and Harpur, T. J. (1991) Psychopathy and the DSM-IV criteria for antisocial personality disorder. *Journal of Abnormal Psychology*, 100, 391–8.

Hare, R. D., Clark, D., Grann, M. and Thornton, D. (2000) Psychopathy and the predictive validity of the PCL-R: an international perspective. *Behavioral Sciences and the Law*, 18, 623–45.

Hariri, A. R., Mattay, V. S., Tessitore, A., Kolachana, B., Fera, F., Goldman, D., Egan, M. F. and Weinberger, D. R. (2002) Serotonin transporter genetic variation and response of the human amygdala. *Science*, 297, 400–3.

Harkins, S. G. and Geen, R. G. (1975) Discriminability and criterion differences between extraverts and introverts during vigilance. *Journal of Research in Personality*, 9, 335–40.

Harkness, A. R. and Lilienfeld, S. O. (1997) Individual differences science for treatment planning: personality traits. *Psychological Assessment*, 9, 349–60.

Harkness, K. L., Bagby, R. M., Joffe, R. T. and Levitt, A. (2002) Major depression, chronic minor depression, and the Five-Factor Model of Personality. *European Journal of Personality*, 16, 271–81.

Harper, S., Lynch, J., Everson, S. A., Hillemeier, M. M., Raghunathan, T. E., Salonen, J. T. and Kaplan, G. A. (2002) Life course socio-economic conditions and adult psychosocial functioning. *International Journal of Epidemiology*, 31, 395–403.

Harré, R. and Gillett, G. (1994) *The discursive mind*. London: Sage.

Hart, S. D. (1998) The role of psychopathy in assessing risk for violence: conceptual and methodological issues. *Legal and Criminological Psychology*, 3, 121–37.

Hartlage, S., Alloy, L. B., Vazquez, C. and Dykman, B. (1993) Automatic and effortful processing in depression. *Psychological Bulletin*, 113, 247–78.

Hartshorne, H. and May, M. A. (1928) *Studies in deceit*. New York: Macmillan.

Haynes, S. G., Feinleib, M. and Kannel, W. B. (1980) The relationship of psychosocial factors to coronary heart disease in the Framingham study. III. Eight year incidence of coronary heart disease. *American Journal of Epidemiology*, 111, 37–58.

Heath, A. C. and Martin, N. G. (1990) Psychoticism as a dimension of personality: a multivariate genetic test of Eysenck and Eysenck's psychoticism construct. *Journal of Personality and Social Psychology*, 58, 111–21.

Heath, A. C., Cloninger, R. C. and Martin, N. G. (1994) Testing a model for the genetic structure of personality: a comparison of the personality systems of Cloninger and Eysenck. *Journal of Personality and Social Psychology*, 66, 762–75.

Heath, A. C., Neale, M. C., Kessler, R. C., Eaves, L. J. and Kendler, K. S. (1992) Evidence for genetic influences on personality from self-reports and informant ratings. *Journal of Personality and Social Psychology*, 63, 85–96.

Heatherton, T. F. and Polivy, J. (1991) Development of a scale for measuring state self-esteem. *Journal of Personality and Social Psychology*, 60, 895–910.

Heaven, P. C. L. (1996) Personality and self-reported delinquency: a longitudinal analysis. *Journal of Child Psychology and Psychiatry and Allied Disciplines*, 37, 747–51.

Heeger, D. J. and Ress, D. (2002) What does fMRI tell us about neuronal activity? *Nature Reviews Neuroscience*, 3, 142–51.

Helgeson, V. S., Cohen, S., Schulz, R. and Yasko, J. (2001) Long-term effects of educational and peer discussion group interventions on adjustment to breast cancer. *Health Psychology*, 20, 387–92.

Helmer, D. C., Ragland, D. R. and Syme, S. L. (1991) Hostility and coronary artery disease. *American Journal of Epidemiology*, 133, 112–22.

Helson, R. and Moane, G. (1987) Personality change in women from college to midlife. *Journal of Personality and Social Psychology*, 53, 176–86.

Helson, R. and Wink, P. (1992) Personality change in women from the early 40s to the early 50s. *Psychology and Aging*, 7, 46–55.

Helton, W. S., Dember, W. N., Warm, J. S. and Matthews, G. (1999) Optimism–pessimism and false failure feedback: effects on vigilance performance. *Current Psychology: Research and Review*, 18, 311–25.

Henderson, D. K. (1939) *Psychopathic states*. New York: Norton.

Hennessy, D. A., Wiesenthal, D. L. and Kohn, P. M. (2000) The influence of traffic congestion, daily hassles, and trait stress susceptibility on state driver stress: an interactive perspective. *Journal of Applied Behavioural Research*, 5, 162–79.

Hepburn, D. A., Deary, I. J., Munoz, M. and Frier, B. M. (1995) Physiological manipulation of psychometric mood factors using acute insulin-induced hypoglycaemia in humans. *Personaliy and Individual Differences*, 18, 385–91.

Hepburn, D. A., Deary, I. J., MacLeod, K. M. and Frier, B. M. (1996) Adrenaline and psychometric mood factors: a controlled case study of two patients with bilateral adrenalectomy. *Personality and Individual Differences*, 20, 451–5.

Herbst, J. H., Zonderman, A. B., McCrae, R. R. and Costa, P. T. (2001) Do the dimensions of the temperament and character inventory map a simple genetic architecture? Evidence from molecular genetics and factor analysis. *American Journal of Psychiatry*, 158, 1339–440.

Hertzman, C., Power, C., Matthews, S. and Manor, O. (2001) Using an interactive framework of society and lifecourse to explain self-rated health in early adulthood. *Social Science and Medicine*, 53, 1575–85.

Heslop, P., Smith G. D., Carroll, D., Macleod, J., Hyland, F. and Hart, C. (2001) Perceived stress and coronary risk factors: the contribution of socio-economic position. *British Journal of Health Psychology*, 6, 167–78.

Hettema, J. and Deary, I. J. (1993) Biological and social approaches to individuality: towards a common paradigm. In J. Hettema and I. J. Deary (eds.), *Foundations of personality*. Dordrecht, The Netherlands: Kluwer.

Hettema, J. and Kenrick, D. T. (1989) Biosocial interaction and individual adaptation. In J. Hettema (ed.), *Personality and environment: assessment of human adaptation*. Chichester: Wiley.

Heymans, G. and Wiersma, E. (1906) Beiträge zur speziellen Psychologie auf Grund einer Massenunter suchung. *Zeitschrift für Psychologie*, 42, 81–227.

Higgins, E. T. (1989) Self discrepancy: a theory relating self and affect. *Psychological Review*, 94, 319–40.

  (1990) Personality, social psychology, and person–situation relations: standards and knowledge activation as a common language. In L. A. Pervin (ed.), *Handbook of personality theory and research*, pp. 301–38. New York: Guilford.

  (1996) Knowledge activation: accessibility, applicability, and salience. In E. T. Higgins and A. W. Kruglanski (eds.), *Social psychology: handbook of basic principles*, pp. 133–68. New York: Guilford.

Higgins, E. T., King, G. A. and Mavin, G. H. (1982) Individual construct accessibility and subjective impressions and recall. *Journal of Personality and Social Psychology*, 43, 35–47.

Hilgard, E. R. (1980) The trilogy of mind: cognition, affection, and conation. *Journal of the History of the Behavioral Sciences*, 16, 107–17.

Hockey, G. R. J. (1984) Varieties of attentional state: the effects of the environment. In R. Parasuraman and D. R. Davies (eds.), *Varieties of attention*. New York: Academic.

Hodges, W. F. (1968) Effects of ego threat and threat of pain on state anxiety. *Journal of Personality and Social Psychology*, 8, 364–72.

Hofer, S. M. and Eber, H. W. (2002) Second-order factor structure of the Cattell Sixteen Personality Factor Questionnaire. In B. De Raad and M. Perugini (eds.), *Big Five Assessment*, pp. 397–409. Seattle, WA: Hogrefe and Huber.

Hoffman, L. W. (1991) The influence of family environment on personality: accounting for sibling differences. *Psychological Bulletin*, 110, 187–203.

Hofstede, W. K. B. (1990) The use of everyday personality language for scientific purposes. *European Journal of Personality*, 4, 77–88.

Hogan, J. (1986) *Hogan Personality Inventory Manual*. Minneapolis, MN: National Computer Systems.

Hogan, R. and Hogan, J. (2002) The Hogan Personality Inventory. In B. De Raad and M. Perugini (eds.), *Big Five Assessment*, pp. 329–51. Seattle, WA: Hogrefe and Huber.

Hogan, R., Hogan, J. and Roberts, B. W. (1996) Personality measurement and employment decisions: questions and answers. *American Psychologist*, 51, 469–77.

Holahan, C. J., Moos, R. H. and Schaefer, J. A. (1996) Coping, stress resistance, and growth: conceptualising adaptive functioning. In M. Zeidner and N. S. Endler (eds.), *Handbook of coping: theory, research, applications*, pp. 24–43. New York: Wiley.

Holender, D. (1986) Semantic activation without conscious identification in dichotic listening, parafoveal vision, and visual masking: a survey and appraisal. *Behavioral and Brain Sciences*, 9, 1–66.

Holeva, V., Tarrier, N. and Wells, A. (2001) Prevalence and predictors of acute stress disorder and PTSD following road traffic accidents: thought control strategies and social support. *Behavior Therapy*, 32, 65–83.

Holland, J. L. (1997) *Making vocational choices: a theory of vocational personalities and work environments*, 3rd edn. Odessa, FL: Psychological Assessment Resources.

Holmes, T. H. and Rahe, R. H. (1967) The Social Readjustment Rating Scale. *Journal of Psychosomatic Research*, 11, 213–18.

Holroyd, K. A and Appel, M. A. (1980) Test anxiety and physiological responding. In I. G. Sarason (ed.), *Test anxiety theory, research and applications*. Hillsdale, NJ: Erlbaum.

Holt, R. R. (1985) The current state of psychoanalytic theory. *Psychoanalytic Psychology*, 2, 289–315.

Horney, K. (1950) *Neurosis and human growth*. New York: Norton.

Hough, L. M. (1992) The 'Big Five' personality variables – construct confusion: description versus prediction. *Human Performance*, 5, 139–55.

Howarth, E. and Eysenck, H. J. (1968) Extraversion, arousal, and paired-associate recall. *Journal of Experimental Research in Personality* 3, 114–16.

Howell, D. C. (1992) *Statistical methods for psychology*, 3rd edn. Belmont, CA: Duxbury Press.

(2002) *Statistics methods for psychology*, 5th edn. Boston, MA: Duxbury.

Hui, C. H. and Eriandis, H. C. (1986) Individualism–collectivism: a study of cross-cultural researchers. *Journal of Cross-Cultural Psychology*, 17, 255–48.

Humphreys, M. S. and Revelle, W. (1984) Personality, motivation and performance: a theory of the relationship between individual differences and information processing. *Psychological Review*, 91, 153–84.

Huovinen, E., Kaprio, J. and Koskenvuo, M. (2001) Asthma in relation to personality traits, life satisfaction, and stress: a prospective study among 11,000 adults. *Allergy*, 56, 971–7.

Hurley, J. R. (1998) Agency and communion as related to "Big Five" self-representations and subsequent behavior in small groups. *Journal of Psychology*, 32, 337–51.

Hurrell, J. J., Jr. and Murphy, L. R. (1991) Locus of control, job demands, and health. In C. L. Cooper and R. Payne (eds.), *Personality and stress: individual differences in the stress process*. Chichester: Wiley.

Huwe, S., Hennig, J. and Netter, P. (1998) Biological, emotional, behavioral, and coping reactions to examination stress in high and low state anxious subjects. *Anxiety, Stress and Coping: An International Journal*, 11, 47–65.

Hyler, S. E., Skodol, A. E., Kellman, H. D., Oldham, J. M. and Rosnick, L. (1990) Validity of the Personality Diagnostic Questionnaire-Revised: comparison with two structured interviews. *American Journal of Psychiatry*, 147, 1043–8.

Hyman, S. E. (2002) A new beginning for research on borderline personality disorder. *Biological Psychiatry*, 51, 933–5.

Idler, E. L. and Benyamini, Y. (1997) Self-rated health and mortality: a review of twenty-seven community studies. *Journal of Health and Social Behavior*, 38, 21–37.

Ingram, R. E. (1990) Self-focused attention in clinical disorders: review and a conceptual model. *Psychological Bulletin*, 107, 156–76.

Ingram, R. E., Miranda, J. and Segal, Z. V. (1998) *Cognitive vulnerability to depression*. New York: Guilford.

Jackson, D. N. and Livesley, W. J. (1995) Possible contributions from personality assessment to the classification of personality disorder. In W. J. Livesley (ed.), *The DSM IV Personality Disorders*. New York: Guilford.

Jang, K. L., Livesley, W. J. and Vernon, P. A. (1996) Heritability of the big five personality dimensions and their facets: a twin study. *Journal of Personality*, 64, 577–91.

Jang, K. L., Vernon, P. A. and Livesley, W. J. (2001) Behavioural-Genetic perspectives on personality function. *Canadian Journal of Psychiatry*, 46, 234–44.

(2002) The etiology of personality function: the University of British Columbia Twin Project. *Twin Research*, 5, 1–5.

Jang, K. L., Livesley, W. J., Vernon, P. A. and Jackson, D. N. (1996) *Heritability of personality disorder traits: a twin study*. Acta Psychiatrica Scandinavica, 94, 438–44.

Jang, K. L., Livesley, W. J., Angleitner, A., Riemann, R. and Vernon, P. A. (2002) Genetic and environmental influences on the covariance of facets defining the domains of the five-factor model of personality. *Personality and Individual Differences*, 33, 83–101.

Jensen, A. R. (1980) *Bias in mental testing*. London: Methuen.

Jensen-Campbell, L. A. and Graziano, W. G. (2001) Agreeableness as a moderator of interpersonal conflict. *Journal of Personality*, 69, 323–62.

Jensen-Campbell, L. A., Adams, R., Perry, D. G., Workman, K. A., Furdella, J. Q. and Egan, S. K. (2002) Agreeableness, extraversion, and peer relations in early adolescence: winning friends and deflecting aggression. *Journal of Research in Personality*, 36, 224–51.

Jerusalem, M. and Schwarzer, R. (1989) Anxiety and self-concept as antecedents of stress and coping: a longitudinal study with German and Turkish adolescents. *Personality and Individual Differences*, 10, 785–92.

Jessor, R., Turbin, M. S. and Costa, F. M. (1998) Risk and protection in successful outcomes among disadvantaged adolescents. *Applied Developmental Science*, 2, 194–208.

John, O. P., Hampson, S. E. and Goldberg, L. R. (1991) The basic level in personality trait hierarchies: studies of trait and accessibility in different contexts. *Journal of Personality and Social Psychology*, 60, 348–61.

Johnson, D. L., Wiebe, J. S., Gold, S. M., Andreasen, N. C., Hichwa, R. D., Watkins, G. L. and Boles Ponto, L. L. (1999) Cerebral blood flow and personality: a positron emission tomography study. *American Journal of Psychiatry*, 156, 252–7.

Johnson, J. A. (1999) Persons in situations: distinguishing new wine from old wine in new bottles. *European Journal of Personality*, 13, 443–53.

Johnston, D. W. (1993) The current status of the coronary-prone behavior pattern. *Journal of the Royal Society of Medicine*, 86, 406–9.

Jonah, B. A. (1997) Sensation seeking and risky driving: a review and synthesis of the literature. *Accident Analysis and Prevention*, 29, 651–65.

Jöreskog, K. G. (1973) A general method for estimating a linear structural equation system. In A. S. Goldberger and O. D. Duncan (eds.), *Structural equation models in the social sciences*, pp. 85–112. New York: Seminar Press.

Joseph, J. (2002) Separated twins and the genetics of personality differences: a critique. *American Journal of Psychology*, 114, 1–30.

Joseph, S. and Peters, E. R. (1995) Factor structure of schizotypy with normal subjects: a replication of Hewitt and Claridge 1989. *Personality and Individual Differences*, 18, 437–40.

Judge, T. A. and Bono, J. E. (2001) Relationship of core self-evaluations traits – self-esteem, generalized self-efficacy, locus of control, and emotional stability – with job satisfaction and job performance: a meta-analysis. *Journal of Applied Psychology*, 86, 80–92.

Judge, T. A., Heller, D. and Mount, M. K. (2002) Five-factor model of personality and job satisfaction: a meta-analysis. *Journal of Applied Psychology*, 87, 530–41.

Judge, T. A., Bono, J. E., Ilies, R. and Gerhardt, M. W. (2002) Personality and leadership: a qualitative and quantitative review. *Journal of Applied Psychology*, 765–80.

Judge, T. A., Erez, A., Bono, J. E. and Thoresen, C. J. (2002) Are measures of self-esteem, neuroticism, locus of control, and generalized self-efficacy indicators of a common core construct? *Journal of Personality and Social Psychology*, 83, 693–710.

Jung, C. G. (1948) On psychic energy. *Collected works*, vol. 8. Princeton, NJ: Princeton University Press, 1960.

Kagan, J. (1989) Temperamental contributions to social behaviour. *American Psychologist*, 44, 668–74.

Kagan, J., Reznick, J. S. and Snidman, N. (1988) Biological bases of childhood shyness. *Science*, 240, 167–71.

Kamphaus, R. W., Morgan, A. W., Cox, M. R. and Powell, R. M. (1995) Personality and intelligence in the psychodiagnostic process: the emergence of diagnostic schedules. In D. H. Saklofske and M. Zeidner (eds.), *International handbook of personality and intelligence*, pp. 525–44. New York: Plenum.

Kamya, H. A. (2000) Hardiness and spiritual well-being among social work students: implications for social work education. *Journal of Social Work Education*, 36, 231–40.

Kanfer, R., Ackerman, P. L., Murtha, T. and Goff, M. (1995) Personality and intelligence in industrial and organisational psychology. In D. H. Saklofske and M. Zeidner (eds.), *International handbook of personality and intelligence*. New York: Plenum.

Kanner, A. D., Coyne, J. C., Schaefer, C. and Lazarus, R. S. (1981) Comparison of two modes of stress measurement: daily hassles and uplifts versus major life events. *Journal of Behavioral Medicine*, 4, 1–39.

Karasek, R. A. and Theorell, T. (1990) *Healthy work*. New York: Basic Books.

Karasek, R., Baker, D., Marxer, F., Ahlbom, A. and Theorell, T. (1981) Job decision latitude, job demands, and cardiovascular disease – a prospective study of Swedish men. *American Journal of Public Health*, 71, 694–705.

Kardum, I. and Krapic, N. (2001) Personality traits, stressful life events, and coping styles in early adolescence. *Personality and Individual Differences*, 30, 503–15.

Karlsson, J. I. (1970) Genetic association of giftedness and creativity with schizophrenia, *Heredity*, 66, 171–82.

Kasl, S. V. (1989) An epidemiological perspective on the role of control in health. In S. L. Sauter, J. J. Hurrell, Jr. and C. L. Cooper (eds.), *Job control and worker health*, pp. 161–89. Chichester: Wiley.

Katon, W., Sullivan, M. and Walker, E. (2001) Medical symptoms without identified pathology: relationship to psychiatric disorders, childhood and adult trauma, and personality traits. *Annals of Internal Medicine*, 134, 917–25 (Part 2 Suppl.S).

Kellner, R. (1991) *Psychosomatic syndromes and somatic symptoms*. Washington, DC: American Psychiatric Press.

Kelly, E. L. (1955) Consistency of the adult personality. *American Psychologist*, 10, 659–81.

Kelly, G. A. (1955) *The psychology of personal constructs*. New York: Norton.

Kendell, R. E. (2002) The distinction between personality disorder and mental illness. *British Journal of Psychiatry*, 180, 110–15.

Kendler, K. S. and Hewitt, J. (1992) The structure of self-report schizotypy in twins. *Journal of Personality Disorders*, 6, 1–17.

Kendler, K. S., Kessler, R. C., Heath, A. C., Neale, M. C. and Eaves, L. J. (1991) Coping – a genetic epidemiologic investigation. *Psychological Medicine*, 21, 337–46.

Kennedy, S. H., Dickens, S. E., Eisfeld, B. S. and Bagby, R. M. (1999) Sexual dysfunction before antidepressant therapy in major depression. *Journal of Affective Disorders*, 56, 201–8.

Kenrick, D. T. and Funder, D. C. (1988) Profiting from controversy: lessons from the person–situation debate. *American Psychologist*, 43, 23–34.

Kenrick, D. T. and Stringfield, D. O. (1980) Personality traits and the eye of the beholder: crossing some traditional philosophical boundaries in the search for consistency in all of the people. *Psychological Review*, 87, 88–104.

Kiehl, K. A., Hare, R. D., Liddle, P. F. and McDonald, J. J. (1999) Reduced P300 responses in criminal psychopaths during a visual oddball task. *Biological Psychiatry*, 45, 1498–507.

Kiehl, K. A., Hare, R. D., McDonald, J. J. and Brink, J. (1999) Semantic and affective processing in psychopaths: an event-related potential (ERP) study. *Psychophysiology*, 36, 765–74.

Kiehl, K. A., Smith, A. M., Hare, R. D. and Liddle, P. F. (2000) An event-related potential investigation of response inhibition in schizophrenia and psychopathy. *Biological Psychiatry*, 48, 210–21.

Kiehl, K. A., Smith, A. M., Hare, R. D., Mendrek, A., Forster, B. B., Brink, J. and Liddle, P. F. (2001) Limbic abnormalities in affective processing by criminal psychopaths as revealed by functional magnetic resonance imaging. *Biological Psychiatry*, 50, 677–84.

Kihlstrom, J. F. (1987) Introduction to the special issue: integrating personality and social psychology. *Journal of Personality and Social Psychology*, 53, 989–92.

(1999) The psychological unconscious. In L. A. Pervin and O. P. John (eds.), *Handbook of personality: theory and research*, 2nd edn, pp. 424–42. New York: Guilford.

Kihlstrom, J. F. and Cantor, N. (1984) Mental representations of the self. In L. Berkowitz (ed.), *Advances in experimental social psychology*, vol. 17, pp. 1–47. New York: Academic.

Kim, Y. and Seidlitz, L. (2002) Spirituality moderates the effect of stress on emotional and physical adjustment. *Personality and Individual Differences*, 32, 1377–90.

King, R. (2002) Illness attributions and myocardial infarction: the influence of gender and socio-economic circumstances on illness beliefs. *Journal of Advanced Nursing*, 37, 431–8.

Kirk, K. M., Whitfield, J. B., Pang, D., Heath, A. C. and Martin, N. G. (2001) Genetic covariation of neuroticism with monoamine oxidase activity and smoking. *American Journal of Medical Genetics (Neuropsychiatric Genetics)*, 105, 700–6.

Kirmayer, L. J., Robbins, J. M. and Paris, J. (1994) Somatoform disorders: personality and the social matrix of somatic distress. *Journal of Abnormal Psychology*, 103, 125–36.

Kirschbaum, C., Pirke, K.-M. and Hellhammer, H. (1993) The 'Trier Social Stress Test' – a tool for investigating psychobiological stress responses in a laboratory setting. *Neuropsychobiology*, 28, 76–81.

Kitayama, S. (1997) Affective influence in perception: some implications of the amplification model. In G. Matthews (ed.), *Cognitive science perspectives on personality and emotion*, pp. 193–258. Amsterdam: Elsevier Science.

Klass, E. T. (1990) Guilt, shame and embarrassment: cognitive–behavioral approaches. In H. Leitenberg (ed.), *Handbook of social evaluation and anxiety*, pp. 385–414. New York: Plenum.

Klein, S. B. and Loftus, J. (1993) The mental representation of trait and autobiographical knowledge about the self. In T. K. Srull and R. S. Wyer, Jr. (eds.), *Advances in social cognition*, vol. 5. *The representation of trait and autobiographical knowledge about the self*, pp. 1–50. Hillsdale, NJ: Erlbaum.

Kline, P. (1981) *Fact and fantasy in Freudian theory*, 2nd edn. London: Methuen.

(1993) *The handbook of psychological testing*. London: Routledge.

(1994) *An easy guide to factor analysis*. London: Routledge.

(2000) *A psychometric primer*. London: Free Association.

Kline, P. and Cooper, P. (1984) A factorial analysis of the authoritarian character. *British Journal of Psychology*, 75, 171–6.

Kline, P. and Lapham, S. (1991) The validity of the PPQ: a study of its factor structure and its relationship to the EPQ. *Personality and Individual Differences*, 12, 631–6.

Klonowicz, T. (1987) Reactivity and the control of arousal. In J. Strelau and H. J. Eysenck (eds.), *Personality dimensions and arousal*, pp. 183–96. New York: Plenum.

Knyazev, G. G., Slobodskaya, H. R. and Wilson, G. D. (2002) Psychophysiological correlates of behvioural inhibition and activation. *Personality and Individual Differences*, 33, 647–60.

Kobasa, S. C. (1982) Commitment and coping in stress resistance among lawyers. *Journal of Personality and Social Psychology*, 42, 168–77.

Koch, J. A. (1891) *Die Psychopathischen Minder wertigkeiten*. Ravensburg: Maier.

Kochanska, G., Coy, K. C. and Murray, K. T. (2001) The development of self-regulation in the first four years of life. *Child Development*, 72, 1091–111.

(2002)

Koelega, H. S. (1992) Exraversion and vigilance performance: thirty years of inconsistencies. *Psychological Bulletin*, 112, 239–58.

Koenig, H. G. (1997) *Is religion good for your health? The effects of religion on physical and mental health*. London: Haworth Press.

Koenig, H. G., George, L. K., Hays, J. C., Larson, D. B., Cohen, H. J. and Blazer, D. B. (1998) The relationship between religious activities and blood pressure in older adults. *International Journal of Psychiatric Medicine*, 28, 189–213.

Kohn, M. and Schooler, C. (1983) *Work and personality: an inquiry into social stratification*. Norwood, NJ: Ablex.

Koloski, N. A., Talley, N. J. and Boyce, P. M. (2001) Predictors of health care seeking for irritable bowel syndrome and nonulcer dyspepsia: a critical review of the literature on symptom and psychosocial factors. *American Journal of Gastroenterology*, 96, 1340–9.

Krueger, J. W., Bouchard, T. J. and McGue, M. (2002) The personalities of twins: just ordinary folks. *Twin Research*, 5, 125–31.

Krueger, R. F. (2000) Phenotypic, genetic, and nonshared environmental parallels in the structure of personality: a view from the Multidimensional Personality Questionnaire. *Journal of Personality and Social Psychology*, 79, 1057–67.

Krug, S. E. and Johns, E. F. (1986) A large-scale cross-validation of second-order personality structure defined by the 16PF. *Psychological Reports*, 59, 683–93.

Kubzansky, L. D., Sparrow, D., Vokonas, P. and Kawachi, I. (2001) Is the glass half empty or half full? A prospective study of optimism and coronary heart disease in the normative aging study. *Psychosomatic Mecicine*, 63, 910–16.

Kuhn, T. S. (1962) *The structure of scientific revolutions*. Chicago, IL: University of Chicago Press.

Kumar, D. and Kapila, A. (1987) Problem solving as a function of extraversion and masculinity. *Personality and Individual Differences*, 8, 129–32.

Kunda, Z. (1999) *Social cognition: making sense of people*. Cambridge, MA: MIT Press.

Kunimoto, C., Miller, J. and Pashler, H. (2001) Confidence and accuracy of near-threshold discrimination responses. *Consciousness and Cognition: An International Journal*, 10, 294–340.

Lacey, J. I. (1967) Somatic response patterning and stress: some revisions of activation theory. In M. H. Appleby and R. Turnbull (eds.), *Psychological stress*. New York: Appleton-Century-Crofts.

Laing, R. D. (1965) *The divided self*. Harmondsworth: Penguin.

Lakatos, I. (1970) Falsification and the methodology of scientific research programmes. In I. Lakatos and A. Musgrave (eds.), *Criticism and the growth of knowledge*, pp. 91–196. Cambridge University Press.

(1976) *Proofs and refutations*. Cambridge: Cambridge University Press.

Lake, R. I., Eaves, L. J., Maes, H. H., Heath, A. C. and Martin, N. G. (2000) Further evidence against environmental transmission of individual differences in neuroticism from a collaborative study of 45,850 twins and relatives on two continents. *Behavior Genetics*, 30, 223–33.

Lamiell, J. T. (1981) Toward an idiothetic psychology of personality. *American Psychologist*, 36, 276–89.

Langinvainio, H., Kaprio, J., Koskenvuo, M. and Lonnqvist, J. (1984) Finnish twins reared apart. Vol. III: Personality factors. *Acta Geneticae Medicae et Gemellologiae*, 33, 259–64.

Lanyon, R. I. and Goodstein, L. (1997) *Personality assessment*, 3rd edn. New York: Wiley.

Larson, D. B., Koenig, H. G., Kaplan, B. H., Greenbert, R. S., Logue, E. and Tyroler, H. A. (1989) The impact of religion on men's blood pressure. *Journal of Religion and Health*, 28, 265–78.

Larson, L. M., Rottinghaus, P. J. and Borgen, F. H. (2002) Meta-analyses of Big Six interests and Big Five personality factors. *Journal of Vocational Behavior*, 61, 217–39.

Larsen, R. J. and Diener, E. (1992) Promises and problems with the circumplex model of emotion. In M. S. Clark (ed.), *Emotion*, pp. 25–59. Thousand Oaks, CA: Sage Publications.

Larsen, R. J. and Ketelaar, T. (1991) Personality and susceptibility to positive and negative emotional states. *Journal of Personality and Social Psychology*, 61, 132–40.

Larsen, R. J. and Sinnett, L. M. (1991) Meta-analysis of experimental manipulations: some factors affecting the Velten mood induction procedure. *Personality and Social Psychology Bulletin*, 17, 323–34.

Larstone, R. M., Jang, K. L., Livesley, W. J., Vernon, P. A. and Wolf, H. (2002) The relationship between Eysenck's P-E-N model of personality, and traits delineating personality dysfunction. *Personality and Individual Differences*, 33, 25–37.

Lazarus, R. S. (1991) *Emotion and adaptation*. Oxford: Oxford University Press.

Lazarus, R. S. and Cohen, J. P. (1977) Environmental stress. In I. Altman and J. F. Wohlwill (eds.), *Human behavior and the environment: current theory and research.* New York: Plenum.

(1999) *Stress and emotion: a new synthesis*. New York: Springer.

(2000) Does the positive psychology movement have legs? *Psychological Inquiry*, 14.

Lazarus, R. S. and Folkman, S. (1984) *Stress, Appraisal and Coping*. New York: Springer.

Leary, M. R. (2001) Shyness and the self: attentional, motivational, and cognitive self-processes in social anxiety and inhibition. In W. R. Crozier and L. E. Alden (eds.), *International handbook of social anxiety: Concepts, research and interventions relating to the self and shyness*, pp. 217–34. New York: Wiley.

Lee, C. and Bobko, J. (1994) Self-efficacy beliefs: comparison of five measures. *Journal of Applied Psychology*, 79, 364–9.

Leng, G. C., Lee, A. J., Fowkes, F. G. R., Whiteman, M., Dunbar, J., Housley, E. and Ruckley, C. V. (1996) Incidence, natural history and asymptomatic peripheral arterial disease in the general population. *International Journal of Epidemiology*, 25, 1172–81.

Leon, G. R., Gillum, B., Gillum, R. and Gouze, M. (1979) Personality stability and change over a thirty year period – middle to old age. *Journal of Consulting and Clinical Psychology*, 47, 517–24.

LePine, J. A. and Van Dyne, L. (2001) Voice and cooperative behaviour as contrasting forms of contextual performance: Evidence of differential relationships with Big Five personality characteristics and cognitive ability. *Journal of Applied Psychology*, 86, 326–36.

LePine, J. A., Erez, A. and Johnson, D. E. (2002) The nature and dimensionality of organizational citizenship behavior: a critical review and meta-analysis. *Journal of Applied Psychology*, 87, 52–65.

Lepore, S. J., Allen, K. A. M. and Evans, G. W. (1993) Social support lowers cardiovascular reactivity to an acute stressor. *Psychosomatic Medicine*, 55, 518–24.

Lesch, K.-P., Bengel, D., Heils, A., Sabol, S. Z., Greenberg, B. D., Petri, S., Benjamin, J., Muller, C. R., Hamer, D. H. and Murphy, D. L. (1996) Association of anxiety-related traits with a polymorphism in the serotonin transporter gene regulatory region. *Science*, 274, 1527–31.

Levenson, M. R., Aldwin, C. M., Bosse, R. and Spiro, A., III. (1988) Emotionality and mental health: longitudinal findings from the normative aging study. *Journal of Abnormal Psychology*, 97, 94–6.

Levey, A. B. and Martin, I. (1981) Personality and conditioning. In H. J. Eysenck (ed.), *A model for personality*. Berlin: Springer.

Levin, J. S. and Vanderpool, H. Y. (1989) Is religion therapeutically significant for hypertension? *Social Science and Medicine*, 29, 69–78.

Lewis, G. and Appleby, L. (1988) Personality disorder: the patients psychiatrists dislike. *British Journal of Psychiatry*, 153, 44–9.

Lewis, M. (2001) Issues in the study of personality development. *Psychological Inquiry*, 12, 67–83.

Lieberman, M. D. and Rosenthal, R. (2001) Why introverts can't always tell who likes them: multitasking and nonverbal decoding. *Journal of Personality and Social Psychology*, 80, 294–310.

Lillberg, K., Verkasalo, P. K., Kaprio, J., Teppo, L., Helenius, H. and Koskenvuo, M. (2002) A prospective study of life satisfaction, neuroticism and breast cancer risk (Finland). *Cancer Causes and Control*, 13, 191–8.

Linde, J. A. and Clark, L. A. (1998) Diagnostic assignment of criteria: clinicians and the DSM-IV. *Journal of Personality Disorders*, 12, 126–37.

Lippa, R. and Hershberger, S. (1999) Genetic and environmental influences on individual differences in masculinity, femininity, and gender diagnosticity: analyzing data from a classic twin study. *Journal of Personality*, 67, 127–55.

Livesley, W. J. (1986) Trait and behavioral prototypes of personality disorder. *American Journal of Psychiatry*, 144, 728–32.

(1987) Systematic approach to the delineation of personality disorders. *American Journal of Psychiatry*, 144, 772–7.

(1995) Past achievements and future directions. In W. J. Livesley (ed.), *The DSM IV Personality Disorders*. New York: Guilford.

(2001a) Conceptual and taxonomic issues. In W. J. Livesley (ed.), *Handbook of personality disorders*, pp. 3–38. New York: Guilford.

(2001b) Commentary on reconceptualizing personality disorder categories using trait dimensions. *Journal of Personality*, 69, 277–86.

Livesley, W. J. (ed.) (1995) *The DSM IV Personality Disorders*. New York: Guilford.

Livesley, W. J. and Jackson, D. N. (1992) Guidelines for developing, evaluating, and revising the classification of personality disorders. *Journal of Nervous and Mental Disease*, 180, 609–18.

Livesley, W. J. and Jang, K. L. (2000) Toward an empirically based classification of personality disorder. *Journal of Personality Disorders*, 14, 137–51.

Livesley, W. J. and Schroeder, M. L. (1990) Dimensions of personality disorder: the DSM-III-R cluster A diagnoses. *Journal of Nervous and Mental Disease*, 178, 627–35.

Livesley, W. J., Jackson, D. N. and Schroeder, M. L. (1992) Factorial structure of traits delineating personality disorders in clinical and general population samples. *Journal of Abnormal Psychology*, 101, 432–40.

Livesley, W. J., Jang, K. L. and Vernon, P. A. (1998) The phenotypic and genetic architecture of traits delineating personality disorder. *Archives of General Psychiatry*, 55, 941–8.

Livesley, W. J., Sang, K. L., Jackson, D. N. and Vernon, P. A. (1993) Genetic and environmental contributions to dimensions of personality disorder. *American Journal of Psychiatry*, 150, 1826–31.

Livingston, I. L., Levine, D. M. and Moore, R. D. (1991) Social integration and African American intraracial variation in blood pressure. *Ethnicity and Disease*, 1, 135–49.

Loehlin, J. C. (1986) Heredity, environment, and the Thurstone Temperament Schedule. *Behavior Genetics*, 16, 599–603.

(1992) *Genes and environment in personality development*. Newbury Park, CA: Sage.

(1998) *Latent variable models: an introduction to factor, path, and structural analysis*, 3rd edn. Mahwah, NJ: Erlbaum.

Loehlin, J. C. and Nichols, R. C. (1976) *Heredity, environment and personality*. Austin, TX: University of Texas Press.

Loehlin, J. C., Willerman, L. and Horn, J. M. (1985) Personality resemblances in adoptive families: a ten year follow-up. *Journal of Personality and Social Psychology*, 53, 961–9.

Loevinger, J. (1997) Stages of personality development. In R. Hogan and J. A. Johnson (eds.), *Handbook of personality psychology*, pp. 199–208. San Diego, CA: Academic.

Loo, R. (1979) Role of primary personality factors in the perception of traffic signs and driver violations and accidents. *Accident Analysis and Prevention*, 11, 125–7.

Lu, L., Gilmour, R. and Kao, S. F. (2001) Cultural values and happiness: an East–West dialogue. *Journal of Social Psychology*, 141, 477–93.

Lucas, R. and Diener, E. (2000) Personality and subjective well-being across the life span. In V. J. Molfese and D. L. Molfese (eds.), *Temperament and personality development across the life span*, pp. 211–34. Mahwah, NJ: Erlbaum.

Lucas, R. E., Diener, E. and Suh, E. (1996) Discriminant validity of well-being measures. *Journal of Personality and Social Psychology*, 71, 616–28.

Luminet, O., Bagby, R. M., Wagner, H., Taylor, G. J. and Parker, J. D. A. (1999) Relation between alexithymia and the five-factor model of personality: a facet-level analysis. *Journal of Personality Assessment*, 73, 345–58.

Lykken, D. T., McGue, M., Tellegen, A. and Bouchard, T. J. (1992) Emergenesis: genetic traits that may not run in families. *American Psychologist*, 47, 1565–77.

Lynn, R. and Martin, T. (1995) National differences for thirty-seven nations in extraversion, neuroticism, psychoticism and economic, demographic and other correlates. *Personality and Individual Differences*, 19, 403–6.

MacDonald, K. (1998) Evolution, culture, and the five-factor model. *Journal of Cross-Cultural Psychology*, 29, 119–49.

Mackay, C. J. (1980) The measurement of mood and psychophysiological activity using self-report techniques. In I. Martin and P. H. Venables (eds.), *Techniques of psychophysiology*. New York: Wiley.

MacLeod, C. (1999) Anxiety and anxiety disorders. In T. Dalgleish and M. J. Power (eds), *Handbook of cognition and emotion*, pp. 447–77. New York: Wiley.

MacLeod, C. and Matthews, A. (1988) Anxiety and the allocation of attention to threat. *Quarterly Journal of Experimental Psychology*, 38A, 659–70.

(1991) Cognitive-experimental approaches to the emotional disorders. In P. R. Martin (ed.), *Handbook of behaviour therapy and psychological science: an integrative approach*. Oxford: Pergamon.

MacLeod, C., Rutherford, E., Campbell, L., Ebsworthy, G. and Holker, L. (2002) Selective attention and emotional vulnerability: assessing the causal basis of their association through the experimental manipulation of attentional bias. *Journal of Abnormal Psychology*, 111, 107–23.

Macleod, J. and Davey Smith, G. (2002) Stress and the heart, fifty years of progress? *International Journal of Epidemiology*, 31, 1111–13.

Macleod, J., Smith, G. D., Heslop, P., Metcalfe, C., Carroll, D. and Hart, C. (2001) Are the effects of psychosocial exposures attributable to confounding? Evidence from a prospective observational study on psychological stress and mortality. *Journal of Epidemiology and Community Health*, 55, 878–84.

MacMillan, M. (1997) *Freud evaluated: the completed arc*. Cambridge, MA: MIT Press. (2001) The reliability and validity of Freud's methods of free association and interpretation. *Psychological Inquiry*, 12, 167–75.

Magnus, K., Diener, E., Fujita, F. and Pavot, W. (1993) Extraversion and neuroticism as predictors of objective life events: a longitudinal analysis. *Journal of Personality and Social Psychology*, 65, 1046–53.

Magnusson, D. (1988) *Individual development from an interactional perspective: a longitudinal study*. Hillsdale, NJ: Erlbaum.

Magnusson, D. and Endler, N. S. (1977) Interactional psychology: present status and future prospects. In D. Magnusson and N. S. Endler (eds.), *Personality at the crossroads*. Hillsdale, NJ: Lawrence Erlbaum Associates.

Main, M., Kaplan, K. and Cassidy, J. (1985) Security in infancy, childhood and adulthood: a move to the level of representation. In I. Bretherton and E. Waters (eds.), *Growing points of attachment theory and research. Monographs of the Society for Research in Child Development*, 50 (102, Serial No. 209), 66–104.

Mak, A. S. and Mueller, J. (2001) Negative affectivity, perceived occupational stress and health during organisational restructuring: a follow-up study. *Psychology and Health*, 16, 125–37.

Malhotra, A. K., Virkkunen, M., Rooney, W., Eggert, M., Linnoila, M. and Goldman, D. (1996) The association between the dopamine D4 receptor (D4DR) 16 amino acid repeat polymorphism and novelty seeking. *Molecular Psychiatry*, 1, 388–91.

Mangan, G. L. (1982) *The biology of human personality*. Oxford: Pergamon.

Mangan, G. L. and Hookway, D. (1988) Perception and recall of aversive material as a function of personality type. *Personality and Individual Differences*, 9, 289–95.

Mann, C. C. (1994) Behavioral genetics in transition. *Science*, 264, 1686–9.

Markus, H. (1977) Self-schemata and processing information about the self. *Journal of Personality and Social Psychology*, 35, 63–78.

Markus, H. and Cross, S. (1990) The interpersonal self. In L. A. Pervin (ed.), *Handbook of personality: theory and research*, pp. 576–608. New York: Guilford.

Marshall, E. (1994) Highs and lows on the research roller coaster. *Science*, 264, 1693–5.

Marshall, G. N., Wortman, C. B., Vickers, R. R., Kusulas, J. W. and Hervig, L. K. (1994) The five factor model of personality as a framework for personality health research. *Journal of Personality and Social Psychology*, 67, 278–86.

Marsland, A. L., Cohen, S., Rabin, B. S. and Manuck, S. B. (2001) Associations between stress, trait negative affect, acute immune reactivity, and antibody response to hepatitis B injection in healthy young adults. *Health Psychology*, 20, 4–11.

Martin, E. D. and Sher, K. J. (1994) Family history of alcoholism, alcohol use disorders and the five-factor model of personality. *Journal of Studies on Alcohol*, 55, 81–90.

Martin, L. R. and Friedman, H. S. (2000) Comparing personality scales across time: an illustrative study of validity and consistency in life-span archival data. *Journal of Personality*, 68, 85–110.

Martin, M., Ward, J. C. and Clark, D. M. (1983) Neuroticism and the recall of positive and negative personality information. *Behaviour Research and Therapy*, 21, 495–503.

Martin, N. G. and Jardine, R. (1986) Eysenck's contribution to behaviour genetics. In S. Modgil and C. Modgil (eds.), *Hans Eysenck: consensus and controversy*. Philadelphia, PA: Falmer.

Martin, R. P., Wisenbaker, J. and Hattunen, M. (1994) Review of factor analytical studies of temperament measures based on the Thomas-Chess structural model: implications for the Big Five. In C. F. Halverson Jr., G. A. Kohnstamm and R. P. Martin (eds.), *The developing structure of temperament and personality from infancy to adulthood*, pp. 157–72. Hillsdale, NJ: Erlbaum.

Martin, S. E., Engleman, H. M., Deary, I. J. and Douglas, N. J. (1996) The effect of sleep fragmentation on daytime function. *American Journal of Respiratory and Critical Care Medicine*, 153, 1328–32.

Martin, S. E., Wraith, P. K., Deary, I. J. and Douglas, N. J. (1997) The effect of nonvisible sleep fragmentation on daytime function. *American Journal of Respiratory and Critical Care Medicine*, 155, 1596–601.

Marusic, I. and Bratko, D. (1998) Relations of masculinity and femininity with personality dimensions of the five-factor model. *Sex Roles*, 38, 29–44.

Maslow, A. (1971) *The farther reaches of human nature*. New York: Viking Press.

Mason, O. (1995) A confirmatory factor analysis of the structure of schizotypy. *European Journal of Personality*, 9, 271–82.

Mathews, A. and Mackintosh, B. (1998) A cognitive model of selective processing in anxiety. *Cognitive Therapy and Research*, 22, 539–60.

Matthews, G. (1985) The effects of extraversion and arousal on intelligence test performance. *British Journal of Psychology*, 76, 479–93.

  (1986) The interactive effects of extraversion and arousal on performance: are creativity tests anomalous? *Personality and Individual Differences*, 7, 751–61.

  (1988) Morningness–eveningness as a dimension of personality: trait, state and psychophysiological correlates. *European Journal of Personality*, 2, 277–93.

  (1989) The factor structure of the 16PF: twelve primary and three secondary factors. *Personality and Individual Differences*, 10, 931–40.

  (1992a) Extraversion. In A. P. Smith and D. M. Jones (eds.), *Handbook of human performance*, vol. 3. *State and trait*. London: Academic.

  (1992b) Mood. In A. P. Smith and D. M. Jones (eds.), *Handbook of human performance*, vol. 3. *State and trait*. London: Academic.

  (1997a) The Big Five as a framework for personality assessment. In N. Anderson and P. Herriot (eds.), *Handbook of selection and appraisal*, 2nd edn. London: Wiley.

  (1997b) Extraversion, emotion and performance: a cognitive-adaptive model. In G. Matthews (ed.), *Cognitive science perspectives on personality and emotion*, pp. 339–442. Amsterdam: Elsevier.

  (1999) Personality and skill: a cognitive-adaptive framework. In P. L. Ackerman, P. C. Kyllonen and R. D. Roberts (eds.), *The future of learning and individual differences research: processes, traits, and content*, pp. 251–70. Washington, DC: American Psychological Association.

  (2000a) A cognitive science critique of biological theories of personality traits. *History and Philosophy of Psychology*, 2, 1–17.

  (2000b) Stress and emotion: Physiology, cognition and health. In D. S. Gupta and R. M. Gupta (eds.), *Psychology for psychiatrists*, pp. 143–74. London: Whurr Publishers.

(2001) Levels of transaction: a cognitive science framework for operator stress. In P. A. Hancock and P. A. Desmond (eds.), *Stress, workload and fatigue*, pp. 5–33. Mahwah, NJ: Erlbaum.

(2002) Towards a transactional ergonomics for driver stress and fatigue. *Theoretical Issues in Ergonomics Science*, 3, 195–211.

Matthews, G. and Amelang, M. (1993) Extraversion, arousal theory and performance: a study of individual differences in the EEG. *Personality and Individual Differences*, 14, 347–64.

Matthews, G. and Davies, D. R. (1998) Arousal and vigilance: the role of task factors. In R. B. Hoffman, M. F. Sherrick and J. S. Warm (eds.), *Viewing psychology as a whole: the integrative science of William N. Dember*, pp. 113–44. Washington, DC: American Psychological Association.

(2001) Individual differences in energetic arousal and sustained attention: A dual-task study. *Personality and Individual Differences*, 31, 575–89.

Matthews, G. and Desmond, P. A. (2002) Task-induced fatigue states and simulated driving performance. *Quarterly Journal of Experimental Psychology*, 55A, 659–86.

Matthews, G. and Dorn, L. (1995) Cognitive and attentional processes in personality and intelligence. In D. H. Saklofske and M. Zeidner (eds.), *International handbook of personality and intelligence*, pp. 367–96. New York: Plenum.

Matthews, G., Dorn, L. and Glendon, A. I. (1991) Personality correlates of driver stress. *Personality and Individual Differences*, 12, 535–49.

Matthews, G. and Falconer, S. (2000) Individual differences in task-induced stress in customer service personnel. In *Proceedings of the Human Factors and Ergonomics Society 44th Annual Meeting*. Santa Monica, CA: Human Factors and Ergonomics Society.

(2002) Personality, coping and task-induced stress in customer service personnel. In *Proceedings of the Human Factors and Ergonomics Society 46th Annual Meeting*. Santa Monica, CA: Human Factors and Ergonomics Society.

Matthews, G. and Gilliland, K. (1999) The personality theories of H. J. Eysenck and J. A. Gray: a comparative review. *Personality and Individual Differences*, 26, 583–626.

(2001) Personality, biology and cognitive science: a reply to Corr (2000). *Personality and Individual Differences*, 30, 353–62.

Matthews, G. and Harley, T. A. (1993) Effects of extraversion and self-report arousal on semantic priming: a connectionist approach. *Journal of Personality and Social Psychology*, 65, 735–56.

(1996) Connectionist models of emotional distress and attentional bias. *Cognition and Emotion*, 10, 561–600.

Matthews, G., Coyle, K. and Craig, A. (1990) Multiple factors of cognitive failure and their relationships with stress vulnerability. *Journal of Psychopathology and Behavioral Assessment*, 12, 49–64.

Matthews, G., Davies, D. R. and Lees, J. L. (1990) Arousal, extroversion, and individual differences in resource availability. *Journal of Personality and Social Psychology*, 59, 150–68.

Matthews, G., Derryberry, D. and Siegle, G. J. (2000) Personality and emotion: cognitive science perspectives. In S. E. Hampson (ed.), *Advances in personality psychology*, vol. 1, pp. 199–237. London: Routledge.

Matthews, G. and Oddy, K. (1993) Recovery of major personality dimensions from trait adjective data. *Personality and Individual Differences*, 15, 419–31.

(1997) Ipsative and normative scales in adjectival measurement of personality: problems of bias and discrepancy. *International Journal of Selection and Assessment*, 5, 169–82.

Matthews, G. and Ryan, H. (1994) The expression of the 'premenstrual syndrome' in measures of mood and sustained attention. *Ergonomics*, 37, 1407–18.

Matthews, G. and Stanton, N. (1994) Item and scale factor analyses of the Occupational Personality Questionnaire. *Personality and Individual Differences*, 16, 733–43.

Matthews, G. and Wells, A. (1996) Attentional processes, coping strategies and clinical intervention. In M. Zeidner and N. S. Endler (eds.), *Handbook of coping: theory, research, applications*, pp. 573–601. New York: Wiley.

(1999) The cognitive science of attention and emotion. In T. Dalgleish and M. Power (eds.), *Handbook of cognition and emotion*, pp. 171–92. New York: Wiley.

(2000) Attention, automaticity and affective disorder. *Behavior Modification*, 24, 69–93.

(in press) Rumination, depression, and metacognition: The S-REF model. In C. Papageorgiou and A. Wells (eds.), *Rumination: nature, theory, and treatment of negative thinking in depression*. Chichester: Wiley.

Matthews, G. and Westerman, S. J. (1994) Energy and tension as predictors of controlled visual and memory search. *Personality and Individual Differences*, 17, 617–26.

Matthews, G. and Zeidner, M. (in press) A reappraisal of traits and states: Self-regulation, adaptation and the trilogy of mind. In D. Dai and R. J. Sternberg (eds.), *Motivation, emotion, and cognition: integrative perspectives on intellectual functioning and development*. Mahwah, NJ: Erlbaum.

Matthews, G., Campbell, S. and Falconer, S. (2001) Assessment of motivational states in performance environments. In *Proceedings of the Human Factors and Ergonomics Society 45th Annual Meeting*, pp. 906–10. Santa Monica, CA: Human Factors and Ergonomics Society.

Matthews, G., Jones, D. M. and Chamberlain, A. G. (1989) Interactive effects of extraversion and arousal on attentional task performance: multiple resources or encoding processes? *Journal of Personality and Social Psychology*, 56, 629–39.

(1990) Refining the measurement of mood: the UWIST Mood Adjective Checklist. *British Journal of Psychology*, 81, 17–42.

(1992) Predictors of individual differences in mail coding skills, and their variation with ability level. *Journal of Applied Psychology*, 77, 406–18.

Matthews, G., Mohamed, A. and Lochrie, B. (1994) Self-reports of coping and appraisal as predictors of chronic and acute stress. Paper presented to the 23rd IAAP International Congress of Applied Psychology, Madrid, Spain, July 1994.

(1998) Dispositional self-focus of attention and individual differences in appraisal and coping. In J. Bermudez, A. M. Perez, A. Sanchez-Elvira and G. L. van Heck (eds.), *Personality psychology in Europe*, vol. 6., pp. 335–50. Tilburg: Tilburg University Press.

Matthews, G., Pitcaithly, D. and Mann, R. L. E. (1995) Mood, neuroticism and the encoding of affective words. *Cognitive Therapy and Research*, 19, 563–87.

Matthews, G., Davies, D. R., Westerman, S. J. and Stammers, R. B. (2000) *Human performance: cognition, stress and individual differences*. London: Psychology Press.

Matthews G., Yousfi S., Schmidt-Rathjens C. and Amelang M. (2002) Personality variable differences between disease clusters. *European Journal of Personality*, 16, 1–21.

Matthews, G., Saklofske, D. H., Costa, P. T., Jr., Deary, I. J. and Zeidner, M. (1998) Dimensional models of personality: a framework for systematic clinical assessment. *European Journal of Psychological Assessment*, 14, 35–48.

Matthews, G., Schwean, V. L., Campbell, S. E., Saklofske, D. H. and Mohamed, A. A. R. (2000) Personality, self-regulation and adaptation: a cognitive-social framework. In M. Boekarts, P. R. Pintrich and M. Zeidner (eds.), *Handbook of self-regulation*, pp. 171–207. New York: Academic.

Matthews, G., Joyner, L., Gilliland, K., Campbell, S. E., Huggins, J. and Falconer, S. (1999) Validation of a comprehensive stress state questionnaire: towards a state 'Big Three'? In I. Mervielde, I. J. Deary, F. De Fruyt and F. Ostendorf (eds.), *Personality psychology in Europe*, vol. 7, pp. 335–50. Tilburg: Tilburg University Press.

Matthews, G., Campbell, S. E., Falconer, S., Joyner, L., Huggins, J., Gilliland, K., Grier, R. and Warm, J. S. (2002) Fundamental dimensions of subjective state in performance settings: task engagement, distress and worry. *Emotion*, 2, 315–40.

Matthews, G., Zeidner, M. and Roberts, R. D. (2003) *Emotional intelligence: science and myth*. Cambridge, MA: MIT Press.

Matthews, K. A. (1988) Coronary heart disease and Type A behaviors: update on an alternative to the Booth-Kewley and Friedman (1987) quantitative review. *Psychological Bulletin*, 104, 373–80.

May, J. and Kline, P. (1987) Extraversion, neuroticism, obsessionality and the Type A behavior pattern. *British Journal of Medical Psychology*, 60, 253–9.

Mayer, B. and Merckelbach, H. (1999) Do subliminal priming effects on emotion have clinical potential? *Anxiety, Stress and Coping: An International Journal*, 12, 217–29.

Mayer, J. D., Frasier Chabot, H. and Carlsmith, K. M. (1997) Conation, affect, and cognition in personality. In G. Matthews (ed.), *Cognitive science perspectives on personality and emotion*, pp. 31–63. Amsterdam: Elsevier Science.

Mayer, J. D., Salovey, P. and Caruso, D. R. (2000) Competing models of emotional intelligence. In R. J. Sternberg (ed.), *Handbook of human intelligence*, 2nd edn. New York: Cambridge University Press.

Mayer, J. D., Salovey, P., Caruso, D. R. and Sitarenios, G. (in press) Modeling and measuring emotional intelligence with the MSCEIT V2.0. *Emotion*.

Mayer, J. D., Salovey, P., Gomberg-Kaufman, S. and Blainey, K. (1991) A broader conception of mood experience. *Journal of Personality and Social Psychology*, 60, 100–11.

Mayo, P. R. (1989) A further study of the personality-congruent recall effect. *Personality and Individual Differences*, 10, 247–52.

McAdams, D. P. (1999) Motives. In V. J. Derlega and B. A. Winstead (eds.), *Personality: contemporary theory and research*, 2nd edn, pp. 162–94. New York: Wadsworth.

McCabe, S. B., Gotlib, I. H. and Martin, R. A. (2000) Cognitive vulnerability for depression: deployment of attention as a function of history of depression and current mood state. *Cognitive Therapy and Research*, 24, 427–44.

McCleery, J. M. and Goodwin, G. M. (2001) High and low neuroticism predict different cortisol responses to the combined dexamethasone-CRH test. *Biological Psychiatry*, 49, 410–15.

McClelland, D. C. (1961) *The achieving society*. Princeton, NJ: Van Nostrand.

(1985) *Human motivation*. Glenview, IL: Scott, Foresman.

McCrae, R. R. (1987) Creativity, divergent thinking, and openness to experience. *Journal of Personality and Social Psychology*, 52, 1258–65.

(1993) Moderated analyses of longitudinal personality stability. *Journal of Personality and Social Psychology*, 65, 577–85.

(1996) Social consequences of experiential openness. *Psychological Bulletin*, 120, 323–37.

(2001) Trait psychology and culture: exploring intercultural comparison. *Journal of Personality*, 69, 819–46.

(1991) Adding *Liebe und Arbeit:* the full five-factor model and well-being. *Personality and Social Psychology Bulletin*, 17, 227–32.

(1994) The stability of personality: observations and evaluations. *Current Directions in Psychological Science*, 3, 173–5.

(1995) Positive and negative valence within the five-factor model. *Journal of Research in Personality*, 29, 443–60.

(1997) Personality trait structure as a human universal. *American Psychologist*, 52, 509–16.

McCrae, R. R. and Costa, P. T. (1986) Personality, coping, and coping effectiveness in an adult sample. *Journal of Personality*, 54, 385–405.

(1989) Reinterpreting the Myers-Briggs Type Indicator from the perspective of the five-factor model of personality. *Journal of Personality*, 57, 17–40.

McCrae, R. R., Costa, P. T., del Pilar, G. H., Rolland, J. P. and Parker, W. D. (1998) Cross-cultural assessment of the five factor model: the Revised NEO Personality Inventory. *Journal of Cross-Cultural Psychology*, 29, 171–188.

McCrae, R. R., Jang, K. L., Livesley, W. J., Riemann, R. and Angleitner, A. (2001) Sources of structure: genetic, environmental, and artifactual influences on the covariation of personality traits. *Journal of Personality*, 69, 511–35.

McCrae, R. R., Zonderman, A. B., Bond, M. H., Costa, P. T., Jr. and Paunonen, S. V. (1996) Evaluating replicability of factors in the revised NEO Personality Inventory: confirmatory factor analysis versus procrustes rotation. *Journal of Personality and Social Psychology*, 70, 552–66.

McCrae, R. R., Costa, P. T., Ostendorf, F., Angleitner, A., Hrebícková, M., Avia, M. D., Sanz, J., Sánchez-Bernardos, M. L., Kusdil, M. E., Woodfield, R., Saunders, P. R. and Smith, P. B. (2000) Nature over nurture: temperament, personality, and life span development. *Journal of Personality and Social Psychology*, 78, 173–86.

McCrae, R. R., Costa, P. T., Pedroso de Lima, M., Simoes, A., Ostendorf, F., Angleitner, A., Marusic, I., Bratko, D., Caprara, G. V., Barbaranelli, C., Chae, J. H. and Piedmont, R. L. (1999) Age differences in personality across the adult lifespan: parallels in five cultures. *Developmental Psychology*, 35, 466–77.

McCrimmon, R. J., Frier, B. M. and Deary, I. J. (1999) Appraisal of mood and personality during hypoglycemia in human subjects. *Physiology and Behavior*, 67, 1999.

McDougall, W. (1930) The hormic psychology. In C. Murchison (ed.), *Psychologies of 1930*, pp. 3–36. Worcester, MA: Clark University Press.

McFadden, S. H. (1999) Religion, personality and aging: a life span perspective. *Journal of Personality*, 67, 1081–104.

McGinnies, E. M. (1949) Emotionality and perceptual defense. *Psychological Review*, 56, 471–82.

McGue, M., Bacon, S. and Lykken, D. T. (1993) Personality stability and change in early adulthood: a behavioral genetic analysis. *Developmental Psychology*, 29, 96–109.

McLachlan, S. A., Allenloy, A., Matthews, J., Wirth, A., Kissane, D., Bishop, M., Beresford, J. and Zalcberg, J. (2001) Randomized trial of coordinated psychosocial interventions based on patient self-assessments versus standard care to improve the psychosocial functioning of patients with cancer. *Journal of Clinical Oncology*, 19, 4117–25.

Mealey, L. (1995) The sociobiology of sociopathy: an integrated evolutionary model. *Behavioral and Brain Sciences*, 18, 523–99.

Meijer, S. A., Sinnema, G., Bijstra, J. O., Mellenbergh, G. J. and Wolters, W. H. G. (2002) Coping styles and locus of control as predictors for psychological adjustment of adolescents with a chronic illness. *Social Science and Medicine*, 54, 1453–61.

Mellins, C. A., Gatz, M. and Baker, L. (1996) Children's methods of coping with stress: a twin study of genetic and environmental influences. *Journal of Child Psychology and psychiatry and Allied Disciplines*, 37, 721–30.

Mendoza-Denton, R., Ayduk, O., Mischel, W., Shoda, Y. and Testa, L. (2001) Person x situation interactionism in self-encoding (I am . . . when . . .): implications for affect regulation and social information processing. *Journal of Personality and Social Psychology*, 80, 533–44.

Mervielde, I., Buyst, V. and De Fruyt, F. (1995) The validity of the Big-Five as a model for teachers' ratings of individual differences among children aged 4–12 years. *Personality and Individual Differences*, 18, 525–34.

Merz, C. N. B., Dwyer, J., Nortstrom, C. K., Walton, K. G., Salerno, J. W. and Schneider, R. H. (2002) Psychosocial stress and cardiovascular disease: pathophysiological links. *Behavioral Medicine*, 27, 141–7.

Messick, S. (1995) Validity of psychological assessment: validation of inferences from persons' responses and performances as scientific inquiry into score meaning. *American Psychologist*, 50, 741–9.

Meyer, T. J. and Mark, M. M. (1995) Effects of psychosocial interventions with adult cancer patients – a meta-analysis of randomised experiments. *Health Psychology*, 14, 101–8.

Meyer, T. J. and Shack (1989)

Mickelson, K. D., Kessler, R. C. and Shaver, P. R. (1997) Adult attachment in a nationally representative sample. *Journal of Personality and Social Psychology*, 73, 1092–106.

Miller, G. (2000) Mental traits as fitness indicators: expanding evolutionary psychology's adaptationism. *Annals of the New York Academy of Sciences*, 907, 62–74.

(2001) *The mating mind*. London: Vintage.

Miller, G. E. and Cohen, S. (2001) Psychological interventions and the immune system: a meta-analytic review and critique. *Health Psychology*, 20, 47–63.

Miller, J. D., Lynam, D. R., Widiger, T. A. and Leukefeld, C. (2001) Personality disorders as extreme variants of common personality dimensions: can the five factor model adequately represent psychopathy? *Journal of Personality*, 69, 253–76.

Miller, T. (1991) The psychotherapeutic utility of the five-factor model of personality: a clinician's experience. *Journal of Personality Assessment*, 57, 414–33.

Miller, T. Q., Smith, T. W., Turner, C. W., Guijarro, M. L. and Hallet, A. J. (1996) A meta-analytic review of research on hostility and physical health. *Psychological Bulletin*, 119, 322–48.

Miller, T. Q., Turner, C. W., Tindale, R. S., Posavac, E. J. and Dugoni, B. L. (1991) Reasons for the trend toward null findings in research on Type A behavior. *Psychological Bulletin*, 110, 469–85.

Millon, T. and Davis, R. (1995) Conceptions of personality disorders: historical perspectives, the DSMs, and future directions. In W. J. Livesley (ed.), *The DSM IV Personality Disorders*. New York: Guilford.

Mischel, W. (1968) *Personality and assessment*. New York: Wiley.

(1973) Toward a cognitive, social learning reconceptualization of personality. *Psychological Review*, 80, 252–83.

(1983) Delay of gratification as process and as person variable in development. In D. Magnusson and V. P. Allen (eds.), *Human development: an interactional perspective*. New York: Academic.

(1999) Personality coherence and dispositions in a cognitive-affective personality (CAPS) approach. In D. Cervone and Y. Shoda (eds.), *The coherence of personality: social-cognitive bases of consistency, variability, and organization*, pp. 37–60. New York: Guilford.

Mischel, W. and Metcalfe, J. (1999) A hot/cool-system analysis of delay of gratification: dynamics of willpower. *Psychological Review*, 106, 3–19.

Mischel, W. and Peake, P. K. (1982) Beyond déjà vu in the search for crosssituational consistency. *Psychological Review*, 89, 730–55.

Mischel, W. and Shoda, Y. (1995) A cognitive-affective system theory of personality: reconceptualizing situations, dispositions, dynamics, and invariance in personality structure. *Psychological Review*, 102, 246–68.

Miyamoto, R. H., Hishinuma, E. S., Nishimura, S. T., Nahulu, L. B., Andrade, N. N., Goebert, D. A. and Carlton, B. S. (2001) Path models linking correlates of self-esteem in a multi-ethnic adolescent sample. *Personality and Individual Differences*, 31, 701–12.

Moffitt, T. E., Silva, P. A., Lynam, D. R. and Henry, B. (1994) Self-reported delinquency at age eighteen. In J. Junger-Tas and G. J. Terlouw (eds.), *The international self-report delinquency project*, pp. 356–71. The Hague: Ministry of Justice of the Netherlands.

Mohamed, A. A. R. (1996) Stress processes in British and overseas students. Unpublished doctoral dissertation, University of Dundee.

Morag, M., Morag, A., Reichenberg, A., Lerer, B. and Yirmiya, R. (1999) Psychological variables as predictors of rubella antibody titers and fatigue – a prospective, double blind study. *Journal of Psychiatric Research*, 33, 389–95.

Morey, L. C. and Zanarini, M. C. (2000) Borderline personality: traits and disorder. *Journal of Abnormal Psychology*, 109, 733–7.

Morgan, I. A., Matthews, G. and Winton, M. (1995) Coping and personality as predictors of post-traumatic intrusions, numbing, avoidance and general distress: a study of victims of the Perth flood. *Behavioural and Cognitive Psychotherapy*, 23, 251–64.

Morris, L. W. and Liebert, R. M. (1969) Effects of anxiety on timed and untimed intelligence tests: another look. *Journal of Consulting and Clinical Psychology*, 33, 240–4.

Morris, L. W., Davis, M. A. and Hutchings, C. H. (1981) Cognitive and emotional components of anxiety: literature review and a revised worry–emotionality scale. *Journal of Educational Psychology*, 73, 541–55.

Morrone, J. V., Depue, R. A., Scherer, A. J. and White, T. L. (2000) Film-induced incentive motivation and positive activation in relation to agentic and affiliative components of extraversion. *Personality and Individual Differences*, 29, 199–216.

Moskowitz, D. S. (1988) Cross-situational generality in the laboratory: dominance and friendliness. *Journal of Personality and Social Psychology*, 54, 829–39.

Moskowitz, D. S. and Cote, S. (1995) Do interpersonal traits predict affect? A comparison of three models. *Journal of Personality and Social Psychology*, 69, 915–24.

Moskowitz, D. S. and Schwartz, J. C. (1982) Validity comparison of behavior counts and ratings by knowledgeable informants. *Journal of Personality and Social Psychology*, 42, 518–28.

Mudrack, P. E. (1997) Protestant work-ethic dimensions and work orientations. *Personality and Individual Differences*, 23, 217–25.

Mueller, J. H. (1992) Anxiety and performance. In A. P. Smith and D. M. Jones (eds.), *Handbook of human performance*, vol. 3. *State and trait*. London: Academic.

Mulder, R. T. and Joyce, P. R. (1997) Temperament and the structure of personality disorder symptoms. *Psychological Medicine*, 27, 99–106.

Munafo, M. R., Clark, T. G., Moore, L. R., Payne, E., Walton, R. and Flint, J. (2003) Genetic polymorphisms and personality in healthy adults: a systematic review and metaanalysis. *Molecular Psychiatry*.

Murray, H. (1938) *Explorations in personality*. New York: Oxford University Press.

Musson, D. J. (2001) Male and female Anglican clergy: gender reversal on the 16PF5? *Review of Religious Research*, 43, 175–83.

Myers, D. G. (2000) The funds, friends, and faith of happy people. *American Psychologist*, 55, 56–67.

Myrtek, M. (2001) Meta-analyses of prospective studies on coronary heart disease, type A personality, and hostility. *International Journal of Cardiology*, 79, 245–51.

Naveteur, J. and Freixa i Baqué, E. (1987) Individual differences in electrodermal activity as a function of subjects' anxiety. *Personality and Individual Differences*, 8, 615–26.

    (1992) Anxiety and inhibition: a psychophysiological approach. In D. G. Forgays, T. Sosnowski and K. Wrzesniewski (eds.), *Anxiety: recent developments in cognitive, psychophysiological, and health research*, pp. 143–51. Washington, DC: Hemisphere.

Neely, J. H. (1991) Semantic priming effects in visual word recognition: a selective review of current findings and theories. In D. E. Besner and G. Humphreys (eds.), *Basic processes in reading*, pp. 264–336. Hillsdale, NJ: Erlbaum.

Neiss, R. (1988) Reconceptualizing arousal: psychobiological states in motor performance. *Psychological Bulletin*, 103, 345–66.

Neisser, U. (1967) *Cognitive psychology*. New York: Appleton-Century-Crofts.

Nemanick, R. C., Jr. and Munz, D. C. (1997) Extraversion and neuroticism, trait mood, and state affect: a hierarchical relationship? *Journal of Social Behavior and Personality*, 12, 1079–92.

Neugarten, B. L. (1964) Personality change over the adult years. In J. E. Birren (ed.), *Relations of development and aging*. Springfield, IL: Charles C. Thomas.

Neuman, G. A. and Wright, J. (1999) Team effectiveness: beyond skills and cognitive ability. *Journal of Applied Psychology*, 84, 376–89.

Newell, S. A., Sanson-Fisher, R. W. and Savolainen, N. J. (2002) Systematic review of psychological therapies for cancer patients: overview and recommendations for future research. *Journal of the National Cancer Institute*, 94, 558–84.

Newman, J. P., Patterson, C. M. and Kosson, D. S. (1987) Response perseveration in psychopaths. *Journal of Abnormal Psychology*, 96, 145–8.

Newsome, S., Day, A. L. and Catano, V. M. (2000) Assessing the predictive validity of emotional intelligence. *Personality and Individual Differences*, 29, 1005–16.

Nichols, S. L. and Newman, J. P. (1986) Effects of punishment on response latency in extraverts. *Journal of Personality and Social Psychology*, 50, 624–30.

Nigg, J. T. and Goldsmith, H. H. (1994) Genetics of personality disorders: perspectives from personality and psychopathology research. *Psychological Bulletin*, 115, 346–80.

Nimnuan, C., Rabe-Hesketh, S., Wessely, S. and Hotopf, M. (2001) How many functional somatic syndromes? *Journal of Psychosomatic Research*, 51, 549–57.

Nolen-Hoeksema, S. (2000) The role of rumination in depressive disorders and mixed anxiety/depressive symptoms. *Journal of Abnormal Psychology*, 109, 504–11.

Noller, P., Law, H. G. and Comrey, A. L. (1987) Cattell, Comrey, and Eysenck personality factors compared: more evidence for five robust factors. *Journal of Personality and Social Psychology*, 53, 775–82.

Norman, D. A. and Shallice, T. (1985) Attention to action: willed and automatic control of behaviour. In R. J. Davidson, G. E. Schwartz and D. Shapiro (eds.), *Consciousness and self-regulation: advances in research*, vol. 4. New York: Plenum.

Norman, W. T. (1963) Toward an adequate taxonomy of personality attributes: replicated factor structure in peer nomination personality ratings. *Journal of Abnormal and Social Psychology*, 66, 574–88.

Nowlis, V. (1965) Research with the Mood Adjective Check List. In S. S. Tomkins and C. E. Izard (eds.), *Affect, cognition, and personality*, pp. 352–89. New York: Springer.

O'Connor, B. P. (2002) A quantitative review of the comprehensiveness of the five-factor model in relation to popular personality inventories. *Assessment*, 9, 188–203.

O'Connor, B. P. and Dyce, J. A. (1998a) A test of models of personality disorder configuration. *Journal of Abnormal Psychology*, 107, 3–16.

(1998b) Rigid and extreme: a geometric representation of personality disorders in five factor model space. *Journal of Personality and Social Psychology*, 81, 1119–30.

Oatley, K. and Johnson-Laird, P. (1987) towards a cognitive theory of emotions. *Cognition and Emotion*, 1, 29–50.

(1996) The communicative theory of emotions: empirical tests, mental models, and implications for social interaction. In L. L. Martin and A. Tesser (eds.), *Striving and feeling: interactions among goals, affect, and self-regulation*, pp. 363–93. Hillsdale, NJ: Erlbaum.

O'Boyle, M. (1995) DSM-III-R and Eysenck personality measures among patients in a substance abuse programme. *Personality and Individual Differences*, 18, 561–5.

O'Boyle, M. and Holzer, C. (1992) DSM-III-R personality disorders and Eysenck's personality dimensions. *Personality and Individual Differences*, 13, 1157–9.

O'Gorman, J. G. (1984) Extraversion and the EEG: I. An evaluation of Gale's hypothesis. *Biological Psychology*, 19, 113–27.

O'Gorman, J. G. and Lloyd, J. E. M. (1987) Extraversion, impulsiveness, and EEG alpha activity. *Personality and Individual Differences*, 8, 169–74.

O'Gorman, J. G. and Malisse, L. R. (1984) Extraversion and the EEG: 11. a test of Gale's hypothesis. *Biological Psychology*, 15, 113–27.

O'Leary, K. D. and Smith, D. A. (1991) Marital interactions. *Annual Review of Psychology*, 42, 191–212.

Oishi, S., Schimmack, U. and Diener, E. (2001) Pleasures and subjective well-being. *European Journal of Personality*, 15, 153–67.

Olson, B. D. and Evans, D. L. (1999) The role of the Big Five personality dimensions in the direction and affective consequences of everyday social comparisons. *Personality and Social Psychology Bulletin*, 25, 1498–1508.

Ones, D. S., Viswesvaran, C. and Schmidt, F. L. (1993) Comprehensive metaanalysis of integrity test validities: findings and implications for personnel selection and theories of job performance [Monograph]. *Journal of Applied Psychology*, 78, 679–703.

Ones, D. S., Mount, M. K., Barrick, M. R. and Hunter, J. E. (1994) Personality and job performance: a critique of the Tett, Jackson and Rothstein (1991) meta-analysis. *Personnel Psychology*, 47, 147–56.

Ormel, J. and Wohlfardh, T. (1991) How neuroticism, long-term difficulties, and life situation change influence psychological distress: a longitudinal model. *Journal of Personality and Social Psychology*, 60, 744–55.

Ormel, J., Oldehinkel, A. J. and Brilman, E. I. (2001) The interplay and etiological continuity of neuroticism, difficulties, and life events in the etiology of major and subsyndromal, first and recurrent depressive episodes in later life. *American Journal of Psychiatry*, 158, 885–91.

Orth-Gomer, K., Wamala, S. P., Horsten, M., Schenk-Gustafsson, K., Schneiderman, N. and Mittelman, M. A. (2000) Marital stress worsens prognosis in women with coronary heart disease – The Stockholm Female Coronary Risk Study. *Journal of the American Medical Association*, 284, 3008–14.

Osler, W. (1910) The Lumleian lectures on angina pectoris. *The Lancet*, 1, 839–44.

Ostendorf, F. and Angleitner, A. (1994) Reflections on different labels for Factor V. *European Journal of Personality*, 8, 341–50.

Pakenham, K. I. and Rinaldis, M. (2001) The role of illness, resources, appraisal, and coping strategies in adjustment to HIV/AIDS: the direct and buffering effects. *Journal of Behavioral Medicine*, 24, 259–79.

Panicker, S. and Parasuraman, R. (1998) The neurochemical basis of attention. In I. Singh and Raja Parasuraman (eds.), *Human cognition: a multidisciplinary perspective*. Thousand Oaks, CA: Sage Publications.

Parker, G. and Hadzi-Pavlovic, D. (2001) A question of style: refining the dimensions of personality disorder style. *Journal of Personality Disorders*, 15, 300–18.

Parker, J. D. A. (2000) Emotional intelligence: clinical and therapeutic implications. In R. Bar-On and J. D. A. Parker (eds.), *Handbook of emotional intelligence*, pp. 490–504. San Francisco, CA: Jossey-Bass.

Parker, J. D. A., Taylor, G. J. and Bagby, R. M. (2001) The relationship between emotional intelligence and alexithymia. *Personality and Individual Differences*, 30, 107–15.

Parkinson, B., Totterdell, P., Briner, R. B. and Reynolds, S. (1996) *Changing moods: the psychology of mood and mood regulation*. London: Longman.

Pashler, H. (1998) *The psychology of attention*. Cambridge, MA: MIT Press.

Patrick, C. J., Curtin, J. J. and Tellegen, A. (2002) Development and validation of a brief form of the Multidimensional Personality Questionnaire. *Psychological Assessment*, 14, 150–63.

Patterson, G. R. (1988) Family process: loops, levels, and linkages. In N. Bolger, A. Caspi, G. Downey and M. Moorehouse (eds.), *Persons in context: developmental processes*, pp. 114–51. New York: Cambridge University Press.

Paulhus, D. L. (1986) Self-deception and impression management in test responses. In A. Angleitner and J. S. Wiggins (eds.), *Personality assessment via questionnaire*, pp. 143–65. New York: Springer.

(1998) *Manual for the Balanced Inventory of Desirable Responding (BIDR-7)*. Toronto, Ontario: Multi-Health Systems.

(2002) Socially desirable responding: the evolution of a construct. In H. I. Braun and D. N. Jackson (eds.), *The role of constructs in psychological and educational measurement*, pp. 49–69. Mahwah, NJ: Erlbaum.

Paulhus, D. L. and John, O. P. (1998) Egoistic and moralistic biases in self-perception: The interplay of self-deceptive styles with basic traits and motives. *Journal of Personality*, 66, 1025–60.

Paunonen, S. V. and Jackson, D. N. (2000) What is beyond the big five? Plenty! *Journal of Personality*, 68, 821–35.

Paunonen, S. V., Jackson, D. N., Trzebinski, J. and Forsterling, F. (1992) Personality structure across cultures: a multimethod evaluation. *Journal of Personality and Social Psychology*, 62, 447–56.

Pavot, W., Diener, E. and Fujita, F. (1990) Extraversion and happiness. *Personality and Individual Differences*, 11, 1299–306.

Payne, R. L. and Morrison, D. (2002) The differential effects of negative affectivity on measures of well-being versus job satisfaction and organizational commitment. *Anxiety and Coping: An International Journal*, 15, 231–44.

Pedersen, N., Plomin, R., McClearn, G. E. and Friberg, L. (1988) Neuroticism, extraversion, and related traits in adult twins reared apart and reared together. *Journal of Personality and Social Psychology*, 55, 950–7.

Pengilly, J. W. and Dowd, E. T. (2000) Hardiness and social support as moderators of stress. *Journal of Clinical Psychology*, 56, 813–20.

Penley, J. A. and Tomaka, J. (2002) Associations among the Big Five, emotional responses, and coping with acute stress. *Personality and Individual Differences*, 32, 1215–28.

Perugini, M. and Di Blas, L. (2002) The Big Five Marker Scales (BFMS) and the Italian ABC5 taxonomy: analyses from an etic-emic perspective. In B. De Raad and M. Perugini (eds.), *Big Five Assessment*, pp. 281–304. Seattle, WA: Hogrefe and Huber.

Pervin, L. A. (1985) Personality: current controversies, issues and directions. *Annual Review of Psychology*, 36, 83–114.

(1994) A critical analysis of current trait theory. *Psychological Inquiry*, 5, 103–13.

(2002) *Current controversies and issues in personality*, 3rd edn. New York: Guilford.

Pervin, L. A. (ed.) (1990) *Handbook of personality: theory and research*. New York: Guilford.

Peterson, C. (2000) The future of optimism. *American Psychologist*, 55, 44–55.

Petrides, K. V. and Furnham, A. (2000) On the dimensional structure of emotional intelligence. *Personality and Individual Differences*, 29, 313–20.

(2001) Trait emotional intelligence: Psychometric investigation with reference to established trait taxonomies. *European Journal of Personality*, 15, 425–48.

Petry, N. M., Tennen, H. and Affleck, G. (2000) Stalking the elusive client variable in psychotherapy research. In C. R. Snyder and R. E. Ingram (eds.), *Handbook of psychological change: psychotherapy processes and practices for the twenty-first century*, pp. 88–108. New York: John Wiley.

Pfohl, B. (1995) Histrionic personality disorder. In W. J. Livesley (ed.), *The DSM IV Personality Disorders*. New York: Guilford.

Pickering, A. D., Corr, P. J., Powell, J. H., Kumari, V., Thornton, J. C. and Gray, J. A. (1997) Individual differences in reactions to reinforcing stimuli are neither black nor white: to what extent are they Gray? In H. Nyborg (ed.), *The scientific study of human nature: tribute to Hans J. Eysenck at eighty*, pp. 36–67. London: Elsevier Science.

Piedmont, R. (1999) Does spirituality represent the sixth factor of personality? Spiritual transcendence and the Five-Factor Model. *Journal of Personality*, 67, 985–1013.

(2001) Cracking the plaster cast: big five personality change during intensive outpatient counseling. *Journal of Research in Personality*, 35, 500–20.

Picton, T. W. (1992) The P300 wave of the human event-related potential. *Journal of Clinical Neurophysiology*, 9, 456–19.

Pinker, S. (1994) *The language instinct*. London: Penguin.

Plomin, R. and Daniels, D. (1987) Why are children in the same family so different from each other? *Behavioral and Brain Sciences*, 10, 44–55.

Plomin, R. and Nesselroade, J. R. (1990) Behavioral genetics and personality change. *Journal of Personality*, 58, 191–219.

Plomin, R., Asbury, K. and Dunn, J. (2001) Why are children in the same family so different? Nonshared environment a decade later. *Canadian Journal of Psychiatry*, 46, 225–33.

Plomin, R., Owen, M. J. and McGuffin, P. (1994) The genetic basis of complex human behaviors. *Science*, 264, 1733–9.

Plomin, R., DeFries, J. C., McClearn, G. E. and McGuffin, P. (2001) *Behavioral Genetics*, 4th edn. New York: Worth.

Plomin, R., Corley, R., Caspi, A., Fulker, D. W. and DeFries, J. C. (1998) Adoption results for self-reported personality: not much nature or nurture? *Journal of Personality and Social Psychology*, 75, 211–18.

Ployhart, R. E., Lim, B.-C. and Chan, K.-Y. (2001) Exploring relations between typical and maximum performance ratings and the five factor model of personality. *Personnel Psychology*, 54, 809–43.

Pogue-Geile, M., Ferrell, R., Deka, R., Debski, T. and Manuck, S. (1998) Human novelty seeking personality traits and dopamine D4 receptor polymorphisms: a twin and genetic association study. *American Journal of Medical Genetics*, 81, 44–8.

Polich, J. and Kok, A. (1995) Cognitive and biological determinants of P300: an integrative review. *Biological Psychology*, 41, 103–46.

Popper, K. (1957) *The poverty of historicism*. London: Routledge and Kegan Paul.

Posner, M. I. and Rodhbart, M. K. (2000) Developing mechanisms of self-regulation. *Development and Psychopathology*, 12, 427–41.

  (1991) Attentional mechanisms and conscious experience. In A. D. Milner and M. D. Rugg (eds.), *The neuropsychology of consciousness*. New York: Academic.

Powell, G. E. (1981) A survey of the effects of brain lesions upon personality. In H. J. Eysenck (ed.), *A model for personality*. Berlin: Springer.

Presly, A. S. and Walton, H. J. (1973) Dimensions of abnormal personality. *British Journal of Psychiatry*, 122, 269–76.

Price, R. A., Vandenberg, S. G., Iyer, H. and Williams, J. S. (1982) Components of variation in normal personality. *Journal of Personality and Social Psychology*, 43, 328–40.

Pryse-Phillips, W. (1969) *Epilepsy*. Bristol: John Wright.

Quinlan, P. T., Lane, J., Moore, K. L., Aspen, J., Rycroft, J. A. and O'Brien, D. C. (2000) The acute physiological and mood effects of tea and coffee: the role of caffeine level. *Pharmacology, Biochemistry and Behaviour*, 66, 19–28.

Rabiner, D. L., Lenhart, L. and Lochman, J. E. (1990) Automatic versus reflective social problem solving in relation to children's sociometric status. *Developmental Psychology*, 26, 1010–16.

Ragland, D. R. and Brand, R. J. (1988) Coronary heart disease mortality in the Western Collaborative Group Study: follow-up experience of twenty-two years. *American Journal of Epidemiology*, 127, 462–75.

Raine, A. and Green, M. F. (2002) Schizophrenia and schizotypal personality: a tribute to Peter H. Venables. *Schizophrenia Research*, 54, 1–5.

Ranchor, A. V., Sanderman, R., Steptoe, A., Wardle, J., Miedma, I. and Ormel, J. (2002) Premorbid predictors of psychological adjustment to cancer. *Quality of life research*, 11, 101–13.

Raval, V., Goldberg, S., Atkinson, L., Benoit, D., Myhal, N., Poulton, L. and Zwiers, M. (2001) Maternal attachment, maternal responsiveness and infant attachment. *Infant Behavior and Development*, 24, 281–304.

Rawlings, D., Claridge, G. and Freeman, J. L. (2001) Principal components analysis of the Schizotypal Personality Scale (STA) and the Borderline Personality Scale (STB). *Personality and Individual Differences*, 31, 409–19.

Reich, J., Noyes, R. and Yates, W. (1989) Alprazolam treatment of avoidant personality traits in social phobic patients. *Journal of Clinical Psychiatry*, 50, 91–5.

Reis, H. T., Sheldon, K. M., Gable, S. L., Roscoe, J. and Ryan, R. M. (2000) Daily well-being: the role of autonomy, competence, and relatedness. *Personality and Social Psychology Bulletin*, 26, 419–35.

Reisenzein, R. (1994) Pleasure-arousal theory and the intensity of emotions. *Journal of Personality and Social Psychology*, 67, 525–39.

Reiss, S. and McNally, R. J. (1985) Expectancy model of fear. In S. Reiss and R. R. Bootzin (eds.), *Theoretical issues in behavior therapy*, pp. 107–21. San Diego, CA: Academic Press.

Reiss, D., Neiderhiser, J. M., Hetherington, E. M. and Plomin, R. (2000) *The relationship code: deciphering genetic and social influences on adolescent development*. Cambridge, MA: Harvard University Press.

Revelle, W. (1993) Individual differences in personality and motivation: 'noncognitive' determinants of cognitive performance. In A. Baddeley and L. Weiskrantz (eds.), *Attention: selection, awareness and control*, pp. 346–73. Oxford: Oxford University Press.

Revelle, W., Amaral, P. and Turriff, S. (1976) Introversion/extraversion, time stress, and caffeine: effect on verbal performance. *Science*, 192, 149–50.

Revelle, W., Humphreys, M. S., Simon, L. and Gilliland, K. (1980) The interactive effect of personality, time of day and caffeine: a test of the arousal model. *Journal of Experimental Psychology: General*, 109, 1–31.

Reynolds, S. K. and Clark, L. A. (2001) Predicting dimensions of personality disorder from domains and facets of the five factor model. *Journal of Personality*, 69, 199–222.

Richards, A., French, C. C., Johnson, W., Naparstek, J. and Williams, J. (1992) Effects of mood manipulation and anxiety on performance of an emotional Stroop task. *British Journal of Psychology*, 83, 479–91.

Riemann, R., Angleitner, A. and Strelau, J. (1997) Genetic and environmental influences on personality: a study of twins reared together using self and peer-report NEO-FFI scales. *Journal of Personality*, 65, 449–76.

Robbins, T. W. (1998) Arousal and attention: Psychopharmacological and neuropsychological studies in experimental animals. In R. Parasuraman (ed.), *The attentive brain*, pp. 189–220. Cambridge, MA: MIT Press.

Roberts, B. W., Caspi, A. and Moffitt, T. E. (2001) The kids are alright: growth and stability in personality development from adolescence to adulthood. *Journal of Personality and Social Psychology*, 81, 670–83.

Roberts, R. D., Zeidner, M. and Matthews, G. (2001) Does emotional intelligence meet traditional standards for an intelligence? Some new data and conclusions. *Emotion*, 1, 196–231.

Robins, R. W., John, O. P. and Caspi, A. (1994) Major dimensions of personality in early adolescence: the Big Five and beyond. In C. F. Halverson Jr., G. A. Kohnstamm and

R. P. Martin (eds.), *The developing structure of temperament and personality from infancy to adulthood*, pp. 267–91. Hillsdale, NJ: Erlbaum.

Rogers, C. R. (1951) *Client-centred therapy; its current practice, implications, and theory.* Boston: Houghton Mifflin.

Rolfhus, E. L. and Ackerman, P. L. (1996) Self-report knowledge: at the crossroads of ability, interest, and personality. *Journal of Educational Psychology*, 88, 174–88.

Rose, P. (2002) The happy and unhappy faces of narcissism. *Personality and Individual Differences*, 33, 379–91.

Rose, R. J. (1995) Genes and human behavior. *Annual Review of Psychology*, 46, 625–54.

Rose, R. J., Koskenvuo, M., Kaprio, J., Sarna, S. and Langinvainio, H. (1988) Shared genes, shared experiences, and similarity of personality. *Journal of Personality and Social Psychology*, 54, 161–71.

Rosenthal, R. and Rubin, D. B. (1982) A simple, general purpose display of magnitude of experimental effect. *Journal of Educational Psychology*, 74, 166–9.

Rosenman, R. H., Brand, R., Jenkins, D., Friedman, M., Straus, R. and Wurm, M. (1975) Coronary heart disease in the Western Collaborative Group Study: final follow-up of eight and a half years. *Journal of the American Medical Association*, 233, 872–7.

Ross, L. R. and Spinner, B. (2001) General and specific attachment representations in adulthood: is there a relationship? *Journal of Social and Personal Relationships*, 18, 747–66.

Rothbart, M. K. (1988) Temperament and the development of inhibited approach. *Child Development*, 59, 1241–50.

Rothbart, M. K. and Bates, J. E. (1998) Temperament. In N. Eisenberg (ed.), *Handbook of child psychology*, vol. 3, *Social, emotional and personality development*, 5th edn, pp. 105–76. New York: Wiley.

Rothbart, M. K., Derryberry, D. and Hershey, K. (2000) Stability of temperament in childhood: laboratory infant assessment to parent report at seven years. In V. J. Molfese and D. L. Molfese (eds.), *Temperament and personality development across the life span*, pp. 85–119. Mahwah, NJ: Erlbaum.

Rothbart, M. K., Ahadi, S. A., Hershey, K. L. and Fisher, P. (2001) Investigations of temperament at three to seven years: the Children's Behavior Questionnaire. *Child Development*, 72, 1394–408.

Rotter, J. B. (1966) Generalized expectancies for internal versus external control of reinforcement. *Psychological Monographs*, 80, 1–28.

Rowe, D. C. (1990) As the twig is bent? The myth of child-rearing influences on personality development. *Journal of Counseling and Development*, 68, 606–11.

Roy, M. P., Kirschbaum, C. and Steptoe, A. (2001) Psychological, cardiovascular, and metabolic correlates of individual differences in cortisol stress recovery in young men. *Psychoneuroendocrinology*, 26, 375–91.

Royce, J. R. and Powell, A. (1983) *Theory of personality and individual differences: factors, systems and processes.* Englewood Cliffs: Prentice Hall.

Runyan, W. M. (1983) Idiographic goals and methods in the study of lives. *Journal of Personality*, 51, 413–37.

Russell, J. A. (1979) Affective space is bipolar. *Journal of Personality and Social Psychology*, 37, 345–56.

Russell, J. A. and Feldman Barrett, L. (1999) Core affect, prototypical emotional episodes, and other things called emotion: dissecting the elephant. *Journal of Personality and Social Psychology*, 76, 805–19.

Rusten, J. (ed.) (1993) *Theophrastus: characters*. Cambridge, MA: Harvard University Press.

Rusting, C. L. and Larsen, R. J. (1997) Extraversion, neuroticism, and susceptibility to positive and negative affect: a test of two theoretical models. *Personality and Individual Differences*, 22, 607–12.

(1999) Clarifying Gray's theory of personality: a response to Pickering, Corr and Gray. *Personality and Individual Differences*, 26, 367–72.

Ryan, R. M. and Deci, E. L. (2000) The darker and brighter sides of human existence: basic psychological needs as a unifying concept. *Psychological Inquiry*, 11, 319–38.

Saarni, C. (1999) *The development of emotional competence*. New York: Guilford.

(2000) Emotional competence: a developmental perspective. In R. Bar-On and J. D. A. Parker (eds.), *The handbook of emotional intelligence*, pp. 68–91. San Francisco, CA: Jossey-Bass.

Saklofske, D. H. and Zeidner, M. (eds.) (1995) *International handbook of personality and intelligence*. New York: Plenum.

Saklofske, D. H., Austin, E. J. and Minski, P. S. (2003) Factor structure and validity of a trait emotional intelligence measure. *Personality and Individual Differences*, 34, 707–21.

Sales, S. M. (1973) Threat as a factor in authoritarianism: an analysis of archival data. *Journal of Personality and Social Psychology*, 28, 44–57.

Salgado, J. F. (1997) The five factor model of personality and job performance in the European Community. *Journal of Applied Psychology*, 82, 30–43.

(2002) The Big Five personality dimensions and counterproductive behaviors. *International Journal of Selection and Assessment*, 10, 117–25.

Salovey, P. and Mayer, J. D. (1990) Emotional intelligence. *Imagination, Cognition and Personality*, 9, 185–211.

Salovey, P., Mayer, J. D. and Caruso, D. (2002) The positive psychology of emotional intelligence. In C. R. Snyder and S. J. Lopez (eds.), *Handbook of positive psychology*, pp. 159–71. New York: Oxford University Press.

Saltz, E. and Hoehn, A. J. (1957) A test of the Taylor-Spence theory of anxiety. *Journal of Abnormal and Social Psychology*, 54, 114–17.

Samuels, J., Eaton, W. W., Bienvenu, O. J., Brown, C. H., Costa, P. T. and Nestadt, G. (2002) Prevalence and correlates of personality disorders in a community sample. *British Journal of Psychiatry*, 180, 536–42.

Sanderman, R. and Ranchor, A. V. (1994) Stability of personality traits and psychological distress over six years. *Perceptual and Motor Skills*, 78, 89–90.

Santor, D. A., Bagby, R. M. and Joffe, R. T. (1997) Evaluating stability and change in personality and depression. *Journal of Personality and Social Psychology*, 73, 1354–62.

Sarafino, E. P. (2002) *Health psychology: biopsychosocial interactions*, 4th edn. New York: John Wiley and Sons.

Sarason, I. G. (1984) Stress, anxiety, and cognitive interference: reactions to tests. *Journal of Personality and Social Psychology*, 46, 929–38.

Sarason, I. G., Sarason, B. R. and Pierce, G. R. (1995) Cognitive interference: at the intelligence–personality crossroads. In D. H. Saklofske and M. Zeidner (eds.), *International handbook of personality and intelligence*. New York: Plenum.

Sarason, I. G., Sarason, B. R., Keefe, D. E., Hayes, B. E. and Shearin, E. N. (1986) Cognitive interference: situational determinants and traitlike characteristics. *Journal of Personality and Social Psychology*, 31, 215–26.

Saroglou, V. (2002) Religion and the five factors of personality: a meta-analytic review. *Personality and Individual Differences*, 32, 15–25.

Saucier, G. and Goldberg, L. R. (1996) Evidence for the Big Five in analyses of familiar English personality adjectives. *European Journal of Personality*, 10, 61–17.

(1998) What is beyond the big five? *Journal of Personality*, 66, 495–524.

(2001) Lexical studies of indigenous personality factors: premises, products and prospects. *Journal of Personality*, 69, 847–79.

Saucier, G. and Ostendorf, F. (1999) Hierarchical subcomponents of the Big Five personality factors: a cross-language replication. *Journal of Personality and Social Psychology*, 76, 613–27.

Saudino, K. J., Pedersen, N. L., Lichtenstein, P. and McClearn, G. E. (1997) Can personality explain genetic influences on life events? *Journal of Personality and Social Psychology*, 72, 196–206.

Saville, P., Holdsworth, R., Nyfield, G., Cramp, L. and Mabey, W. (1984) *The Occupational Personality Questionnaires (OPQ)*. London: Saville and Holdsworth (UK) Ltd.

Saville, P., Sik, G., Nyfield, G., Hackston, J. and MacIver, R. (1996) A demonstration of the validity of the Occupational Personality Questionnaire (OPQ) in the measurement of job competencies across time and in separate organisations. *Applied Psychology: An International Review*, 45, 243–62.

Sawa, A. and Snyder, S. H. (2002) Schizophrenia: diverse approaches to a complex disease. *Science*, 296, 692–5.

Scarr, S. (1987) Three cheers for behavior genetics: winning the war and losing our identity. *Behavior Genetics*, 17, 219–28.

Scarr, S., Webber, P. L., Weinberg, R. L. and Wittig, M. A. (1981) Personality resemblance among adolescents and their parents in biologically related and adoptive families. *Journal of Personality and Social Psychology*, 40, 885–98.

Schachter, S. and Singer, J. E. (1962) Cognitive, social, and physiological determinants of emotional state. *Psychological Review*, 69, 379–99.

Schaubroeck, J. and Ganster, D. C. (1991) Associations among stress-related individual differences. In C. L. Cooper and R. Payne (eds.), *Personality and stress: individual differences in the stress process*. Chichester: Wiley.

Scheier, M. F. and Carver, C. S. (1992) Effects of optimism on psychological and physical well-being: Theoretical overview and empirical update. *Cognitive Therapy and Research*, 16, 201–28.

Scheier, M. F., Carver, C. S. and Bridges, M. W. (1994) Distinguishing optimism from neuroticism (and trait anxiety, self-mastery, and self-esteem): a reevaluation of the Life Orientation test. *Journal of Personality and Social Psychology*, 67, 1063–18.

Scherer, K. R. (2001) Appraisal considered as a process of multilevel sequential checking. In K. R. Scherer, A. Schorr and T. Johnstone (eds.), *Appraisal processes in emotion: theory, methods, research*, pp. 92–120. London: Oxford University Press.

Scherwitz, L. W., Perkins, L. L., Chesney, M. A., Hughes, G. H., Sidney, S. and Manolio, T. A. (1992) Hostility and health behaviors in young adults: the CARDIA Study. *American Journal of Epidemiology*, 136, 136–45.

Schimmack, U. and Grob, A. (2000) Dimensional models of core affect: A quantitative comparison by means of structural equation modeling. *European Journal of Personality*, 14, 325–45.

Schimmack, U. and Reisenzein, R. (2003) Experiencing activation: Energetic arousal and tense arousal are not mixtures of valence and activation. *Emotion*, 2, 412–17.

Schimmack, U., Boeckenholt, U. and Reisenzein, R. (2002) Response styles in affect ratings: making a mountain out of a molehill. *Journal of Personality Assessment*, 78, 461–83.

Schimmack, U., Radhakrishnan, P., Oishi, S., Dzokoto, V. and Ahadi, S. (2002) Culture, personality, and subjective well-being: integrating process models of life satisfaction. *Journal of Personality and Social Psychology*, 82, 582–93.

Schlenker, B. R. and Weigold, M. F. (1989) Goals and the self-identification process: constructing desired identities. In L. A. Pervin (ed.), *Goal concepts in personality and social psychology*, pp. 243–90. Hillsdale, NJ: Erlbaum.

Schmitt, D. P. and Buss, D. M. (2000) Sexual dimensions of personality description: beyond or subsumed by the Big Five. *Journal of Research in Personality*, 34, 141–77.

Schmidt, L. A., Fox, N. A., Rubin, K. H., Hus, S. and Hamer, D. H. (2002) Molecular genetics of shyness and aggression in preschoolers. *Personality and Individual Differences*, 33, 227–38.

Schmidt, N. B. and Woolaway-Bickel, K. (in press) Cognitive vulnerability to panic disorder. In L. B. Alloy and J. H. Riskind (eds.), *Cognitive vulnerability to emotional disorders*. Hillsdale, NJ: Erlbaum.

Schneider, B., Kristof-Brown, A. L., Goldstein, H. W. and Smith, D. B. (1997) What is this thing called fit? In N. Anderson and P. Herriott (eds.), *International handbook of selection and assessment*, pp. 393–412. Chichester: Wiley.

Schneider, K. (1923) *Psychopathic personalities*. London: Cassell.

Schneider, W., Dumais, S. T. and Shiffrin, R. M. (1984) Automatic and control processing and attention. In R. Parasuraman and D. R. Davies (eds.), *Varieties of attention*. New York: Academic.

Schredl, M. (2002) Dream recall frequency and openness to experience: A negative finding. *Personality and Individual Differences*, 33, 1285–9.

Schredl, M., Nuernberg, C. and Weiler, S. (1995) Dream recall, attitude towards dreams, and personality. *Personality and Individual Differences*, 20, 613–18.

Schredl, M., Kronenberg, G., Nonnell, P. and Heuser, I. (2001) Dream recall, nightmare frequency, and nocturnal panic attacks in patients with panic disorder. *Journal of Nervous and Mental Disease*, 189, 559–62.

Schroeder, M. L., Wormsworth, J. A. and Livesley, W. J. (1992) Dimensions of personality disorder and their relationships to the big five dimensions of personality. *Psychological Assessment*, 4, 47–53.

Schuerger, J. M., Zarrella, K. L. and Hotz, A. S. (1989) Factors that influence the temporal stability of personality by questionnaire. *Journal of Personality and Social Psychology*, 56, 777–83.

Schunk, D. H. and Ertmer, P. A. (2000) Self-regulation and academic learning: self-efficacy enhancing interventions. In M. Boekaerts, P. R. Pintrich and M. Zeidner (eds.), *Handbook of self-regulation*, pp. 631–49. San Diego, CA: Academic.

Schutte, N. S., Malouff, J. M., Hall, L. E., Haggerty, D. J., Cooper, J. T., Golden, C. J. and Dornheim, L. (1998) Development and validation of a measure of emotional intelligence. *Personality and Individual Differences*, 25, 167–77.

Schwean, V. L. and Saklofske, D. H. (1995) A cognitive-social description of exceptional children. In D. H. Saklofske and M. Zeidner (eds.), *International handbook of personality and intelligence*, pp. 185–204. New York: Plenum.

Schwean, V. L. and Saklofske, D. H. (eds.) (1999) *Handbook of psychosocial characteristics of exceptional children*. New York: Plenum.

Sedikides, C. (1992) Mood as a determinant of attentional focus. *Cognition and Emotion*, 6, 129–48.

Segal, N. L. (1999) *Entwined lives: twins and what they tell us about human behavior*. New York: Dutton.

Segal, Z. V. (1988) Appraisal of the self-schema construct in cognitive models of depression. *Psychological Bulletin*, 103, 147–62.

Seiveright, H., Tyrer, P. and Johnson, T. (2002) Change in personality status in neurotic disorders. *Lancet*, 359, 2253–4.

Seligman, M. E. M. and Csikszentmihalyi, M. (2000) Positive psychology: an introduction. *American Psychologist*, 55, 5–14.

Selye, H. (1976) *Stress in Health and Disease*. Reading, MA: Butterworth.

Semmer, N. and Schallberger, U. (1996) Selection, socialisation, and mutual adaptation: resolving discrepancies between people and work. *Applied Psychology: An International Journal*, 45, 263–88.

Shaver, P. R. and Hazan, C. (1994) *Attachment*. In A. L. Weber and J. H. Harvey (eds.), *Perspectives on close relationships*, pp. 110–30. Boston, MA: Allyn and Bacon.

Shea, M. T. (1995) Interrelationships among categories of personality disorders. In W. J. Livesley (ed.), *The DSM IV Personality Disorders*. New York: Guilford.

(1988) Interpersonal styles and short-term therapy for depression. Paper presented at the meeting of the American Psychological Association, Atlanta, GA.

Shekelle, R. B., Hulley, S. B., Neaton, J. D., Billings, J. H., Borhani, N. O., Gerace, T. A., Jacobs, D. R., Lasser, N. L., Mittlemark, M. B. and Stamler, J. (1985) The MRFIT behavior pattern study. 11. Type A behavior and incidence of coronary heart disease. *American Journal of Epidemiology*, 122, 559–70.

Sheldon, K. M. and Kasser, T. (2001) Goals, congruence, and positive well-being: new empirical support for humanistic theories. *Journal of Humanistic Psychology*, 41, 30–50.

Shields, J. (1962) *Monozygotic twins: brought up apart and brought up together*. London: Oxford University Press.

Shigehisa, T. and Symons, J. R. (1973) Effects of intensity of visual stimulation on auditory sensitivity in relation to personality. *British Journal of Psychology*, 64, 205–13.

Shoda, Y., LeeTiernan, S. and Mischel, W. (2002) Personality as a dynamical system: emergence of stability and distinctiveness from intra- and interpersonal interactions. *Personality and Social Psychology Review*, 6, 316–25.

Siegel, K. and Schrimshaw, E. W. (2002) The perceived benefits of religious and spiritual coping among older adults living with HIV/AIDS. *Journal for the Scientific Study of Religion*, 41, 91–202.

Siegle, G. J. (1999) A neural network model of attention biases in depression. In E. Ruppin, J. Reggia and D. Glanzman (eds.), *Progress in Brain Research*, vol. 121, pp. 415–41. New York: Elsevier.

Siegle, G. J. and Ingram, R. E. (1997) Modeling individual differences in negative information processing biases. In G. Matthews (ed.), *Cognitive science perspectives on personality and emotion*, pp. 301–53. Amsterdam: Elsevier.

Siegler, I. C. (1994) Hostility and risk: demographic and lifestyle variables. In Siegman, A. W. and Smith, T. W. (eds.), *Anger, hostility and the heart*. London: Erlbaum.

Siegler, I. C., Feaganes, J. R. and Rimer, B. K. (1995) Predictors of adoption of mammography in women under age fifty. *Health Psychology*, 14, 274–8.

Siegler, I. C., Welsh, K. A., Dawson, D. V., Fillenbaum, G. G., Earl, N. L., Kaplan, E. B. and Clark, C. M. (1991) Ratings of personality change in patients being evaluated for memory disorders. *Alzheimer Disease and Associated Disorders*, 5, 240–50.

Siever, L. J., Bernstein, D. P. and Silverman, J. M. (1995) Schizotypal personality disorder. In W. J. Livesley (ed.), *The DSM IV personality disorders*. New York: Guilford.

Siever, L. J., Torgersen, S., Gunderson, J. G., Livesley, W. J. and Kendler, K. S. (2002) The borderline diagnosis III: identifying endophenotypes for genetic studies. *Biological Psychiatry*, 51, 964–8.

Sifneos, P. E. (1972) *Short-term psychotherapy and emotional crisis*. Cambridge, MA: Harvard University Press.

Silva, F., Avia, D., Sanz, J., Martinez-Arias, R., Grana, J. L. and Sanchez-Bernardos, L. (1994) *Personality and Individual Differences*, 17, 741–54.

Simonton, D. K. (1990) Personality and politics. In L. A. Pervin (ed.), *Handbook of personality: theory and research*, pp. 670–92. New York: Guilford.

   (2001) Kings, queens, and sultans: empirical studies of political leadership in European hereditary monarchies. In O. Feldman and L. Valenty (eds.), *Profiling political leaders: cross-cultural studies of personality and behaviour*, pp. 97–110. Westport, CT: Praeger.

Sinclair, R. R. and Tetrick, L. E. (2000) Implications of item wording for hardiness structure, relation with neuroticism, and stress buffering. *Journal of Research in Personality*, 34, 1–25.

Singh, I. L. (1989) Personality correlates and perceptual detectability of locomotive drivers. *Personality and Individual Differences*, 10, 1049–54.

Sjoberg, L., Svensson, E. and Persson, L.-O. (1979) The measurement of mood. *Scandinavian Journal of Psychology*, 20, 1–18.

Skodol, A. E., Gunderson, J. G., Pfohl, B., Widiger, T. A., Livesley, W. J. and Siever, L. J. (2002) The borderline diagnosis I: psychopathology comorbidity and personality structure. *Biological Psychiatry*, 51, 936–50.

Skodol, A. E., Siever, L. J., Livesley, W. J., Gunderson, J. G., Pfohl, B. and Widiger, T. A. (2002) The borderline diagnosis II: biology, genetics, and clinical course. *Biological Psychiatry*, 51, 951–63.

Slaski, M. and Cartwright, S. (2002) Health, performance and emotional intelligence: an exploratory study of retail managers. *Stress and Health*, 18, 63–8.

Slutske, W. S., Heath, A. C., Madden, P. A., Bucholz, K. K., Slatham, D. J. and Martin, N. G. (2002) Personality and genetic risk for alcohol dependence. *Journal of Abnormal Personality*, 111, 124–33.

Smith, B. D. (1983) Extraversion and electrodermal activity: arousability and the inverted U. *Personality and Individual Differences*, 4, 411–19.

Smith, B. D., Wilson, R. J. and Jones, B. E. (1983) Extraversion and multiple-levels of caffeine-induced arousal: effects of overhabituation and dishabituation. *Psychophysiology*, 20, 29–34.

Smith, B. D., Concannon, M., Campbell, S., Bozman, A. and Kline, R. (1990) Regression and criterion measures of habituation: a comparative analysis in extraverts and introverts. *Journal of Research in Personality*, 24, 123–32.

Smith, B. D., Davidson, R. A., Smith, D. L., Goldstein, H. and Perlstein, W. (1989) Sensation seeking and arousal: effects of strong stimulation on electrodermal activation and memory task performance. *Personality and Individual Differences*, 10, 671–9.

Smith, C. J., Noll, J. A. and Bryant, J. B. (1999) The effect of social context on gender self-concept. *Sex Roles*, 40, 499–512.

Smith, G. M. (1967) Usefulness of peer ratings in educational research. *Educational and Psychological Measurement*, 27, 967–84.

Smith, M. B. (1950) The phenomenological approach in personality theory: some critical remarks. *Journal of Abnormal and Social Psychology*, 45, 516–22.

Smith, R. E. and Sarason, I. G. (1975) Social anxiety and the evaluation of negative interpersonal feedback. *Journal of Consulting and Clinical Psychology*, 43, 429.

Smith, T. W. and Williams, P. G. (1992) Personality and health: advantages and limitations of the five-factor model. *Journal of Personality*, 60, 395–423.

Snyder, C. R., and Lopez, S. J. (2002) (eds.) *Handbook of positive psychology*. New York: Oxford University Press.

Snyder, M. (1979) Self-monitoring process. In L. Berkowitz (ed.), *Advances in experimental social psychology*, vol. 12, pp. 85–128. New York: Academic Press.

(1984) When belief creates reality. In L. Berkowitz (ed.), *Advances in experimental social psychology*, vol. 18, pp. 248–305. New York: Academic Press.

(1992) Motivational foundations of behavioral confirmation. In M. P. Zanna (ed.), *Advances in experimental social psychology*, vol. 25, pp. 67–114. New York: Academic Press.

Sokolowski, K., Schmalt, H.-D., Langens, T. A. and Puca, R. M. Assessing achievement, affiliation, and power motives all at once: the Multi-Motive Grid (MMG). *Journal of Personality Assessment*, 74, 126–45.

Southam-Gerow, M. A. and Kendall, P. C. (2002) Emotion regulation and understanding: implications for child psychopathology and therapy. *Clinical Psychology Review*, 22, 189–222.

Spearman, C. (1904) 'General intelligence', objectively determined and measured. *American Journal of Psychology*, 15, 201–93.

Spangler, W. D. (1992) Validity of questionnaire and TAT measures of need for achievement: two meta-analyses. *Psychological Bulletin*, 112, 140–54.

Spector, P. E., Schneider, J. R., Vance, C. A. and Hezlett, S. A. (2000) The relation of cognitive ability and personality traits to assessment center performance. *Journal of Applied Social Psychology*, 2000, 1474–91.

Spielberger, C. D. (1966) The effects of anxiety on complex learning and academic achievement. In C. D. Spielberger (ed.), *Anxiety and behavior*, pp. 3–20. London: Academic Press.

(1972) Anxiety as an emotional state. In C. D. Spielberger (ed.), *Anxiety: current trends in theory and research*, vol. 1. London: Academic Press.

Spielberger, C. D. and Reheiser, E. C. (1995) Measuring occupational stress: the Job Stress Survey. In R. Crandall and P. L. Perrewé (eds.), *Occupational stress: a handbook*, pp. 51–69. Washington, DC: Taylor and Francis.

Spielberger, C. D., Gorsuch, R. and Lushene, R. (1970) *The State Trait Anxiety Inventory (STAI) Manual*. Palo Alto, CA: Consulting Psychologists Press.

Spielberger, C. D., Jacobs, G. E., Russell, S. and Crane, R. S. (1983) The assessment of anger: the State-trait anger scale. In J. N. Butcher and C. D. Spielberger (eds.), *Advances in personality assessment*, vol. 2, pp. 159–85. Hillsdale, NJ: Erlbaum.

Spielberger, C. D., Sydeman, S. J., Owen, A. E. and Marsh, B. J. (1999) Measuring anxiety and anger with the State-Trait Anxiety Inventory (STAI) and the State-Trait Anger

Expression Inventory (STAXI). In M. E. Maruish (ed.), *The use of psychological testing for treatment planning and outcomes assessment*, 2nd edn, pp. 993–1021. Mahwah, NJ: Lawrence Erlbaum Associates.

Spielberger, C. D., Crane, R. S., Kearns, W. D., Pellegrin, K. L., Rickman, R. L. and Johnson, E. H. (1991) Anger and anxiety in essential hypertension. In C. D. Spielberger, I. G. Sarason, Z. Kulcsar and G. L. Van Heck (eds.), *Stress and emotion: anxiety, anger and curiosity*, vol. 14, pp. 265–83. New York: Hemisphere.

Stajkovic, A. D. and Luthans, F. (1998) Self-efficacy and work-related performance: a meta-analysis. *Psychological Bulletin*, 124, 240–61.

Stam, H. J. (1987) The psychology of control: a textural critique. In H. J. Stam, T. B. Rogers and K. J. Gergen (eds.), *The analysis of psychological theory: metapsychological perspectives*. Washington, DC: Hemisphere.

Stanley, K. D. and Murphy, M. R. (1997) A comparison of general self-efficacy with self-esteem. *Genetic, Social, and General Psychology Monographs*, 123, 79–99.

Stansfeld, S. A. (2002) The problem with stress: minds, hearts and disease. *International Journal of Epidemiology*, 31, 13–16.

Stanush, P. L. (1996) *Factors that influence the susceptibility of self-report inventories to distortion: a meta-analytic investigation*. Unpublished doctoral dissertation, Texas, A and M University.

Steffen, A. M., McKibbin, C., Zeiss, A. M., Gallagher-Thompson, D. and Bandura, A. (2002) The Revised Scale for Caregiving Self-Efficacy: reliability and validity studies. *Journals of Gerontology: Series B: Psychological Sciences and Social Sciences*, 57B, 74–86.

Steffen, P. R., Hinderliter, A. L., Blumenthal, J. A. and Sherwood, A. (2001) Religious coping, ethnicity, and ambulatory blood pressure. *Psychosomatic Medicine*, 63, 523–30.

Stein, H., Koontz, A. D., Fonagy, P., Allen, J. G., Fultz, J. B., Brethour, J. R., Jr., Allen, D. and Evans, R. B. (2002) Adult attachment: what are the underlying dimensions? *Psychology and Psychotherapy: Theory, Research and Practice*, 75, 77–91.

Stelmack, R. M. (1981) The psychophysiology of extraversion and neuroticism. In H. J. Eysenck (ed.), *A model for personality*. New York: Springer.

(1990) Biological bases of extraversion: psychophysiological evidence. *Journal of Personality*, 58, 293–311.

(1997) The psychophysics and psychophysiology of extraversion and arousal. In H. Nyborg (ed.), *The scientific study of human nature: tribute to Hans J. Eysenck at eighty*, pp. 388–403. New York: Elsevier Science.

Stelmack, R. M. and Houlihan, M. (1995) Event-related potentials, personality and intelligence: concepts, issues and evidence. In D. H. Saklofske and M. Zeidner (eds.), *International handbook of personality and intelligence*. New York: Plenum.

Stelmack, R. M. and Pivik, R. T. (1996) Extraversion and the effect of exercise on spinal motoneuronal excitability. *Personality and Individual Differences*, 21, 69–76.

Stelmack, R. M. and Stalikas, A. (1991) Galen and the humour theory of temperament. *Personality and Individual Differences*, 12, 255–63.

Stelmack, R. M., Houlihan, M. and McGarry-Roberts, P. A. (1993) Personality, reaction time, and event-related potentials. *Journal of Personality and Social Psychology*, 65, 399–409.

Stenberg, G. (1992) Personality and the EEG: arousal and emotional arousability. *Personality and Individual Differences*, 13, 1097–113.

(1994) Extraversion and the P300 in a visual classification task. *Personality and Individual Differences*, 16, 543–60.

Steptoe, A. (2001) Job control, perceptions of control, and cardiovascular activity – an analysis of ambulatory measures collected over the working day. *Journal of Psychosomatic Research*, 50, 57–63.

Steptoe, A., Cropley, M., Griffith, J. and Kirschbaum, C. (2000) Job strain and anger expression predict early morning elevations in salivary cortisol. *Psychosomatic Medicine*, 62, 286–92.

Steptoe, A., Willemsen, G., Owen, N., Flower, L. and Mohomed-Ali, V. (2001) Acute mental stress elicits delayed increases in circulating inflammatory cytokine levels. *Clinical Science*, 101, 185–92.

Sternberg, R. J. and Ruzgis, P. (eds.) (1994) *Personality and intelligence*. Cambridge: Cambridge University Press.

Stoeva, A. Z., Chiu, R. K. and Greenhaus, J. H. (2002) Negative affectivity, role stress, and work-family conflict. *Journal of Vocational Behavior*, 60, 1–16.

Stokes, J. P. and McKirnan, D. J. (1989) Affect and the social environment: the role of social support in depression and anxiety. In P. C. Kendall and D. Watson (eds.), *Anxiety and depression: distinctions and overlapping features*. New York: Academic.

Stone, A. A., Valdimarsdottir, H., Jandorf, L., Cox, D. S. and Neale, J. M. (1987) Evidence that secretory IgA antibody is associated with daily mood. *Journal of Personality and Social Psychology*, 52, 988–93.

Stone, S. V. and Costa, P. T., Jr. (1990) Disease-prone personality or distress-prone personality? In H. S. Friedman (ed.), *Personality and disease*. New York: Wiley.

Stout, M. (2000) *The feel-good curriculum: the dumbing down of America's kids in the name of self-esteem*. Cambridge, MA: Perseus Books.

Strelau, J. (1983) *Temperament, personality, activity*. London: Academic.

(1991) Are psychophysiological/psychophysical scores good candidates for diagnosing temperament/personality traits and for a demonstration of the construct validity of psychometrically measured traits? *European Journal of Personality*, 5, 323–42.

(2001) The concept and status of trait in research on temperament. *European Journal of Personality*, 15, 311–25.

Strelau, J. and Zawadzki, B. (1995) The formal characteristics of Behaviour Temperament Inventory (FCB-TI): validity studies. *European Journal of Personality*, 9, 207–29.

Suhr, J. A. and Spitznagel, M. B. (2001a) Factor versus cluster models of schizotypal traits. I: a comparison of unselected and highly schizotypal samples. *Schizophrenia Research*, 52, 231–9.

(2001b) Factor versus cluster models of schizotypal traits. II: relation to neuropsychological impairment. *Schizophrenia Research*, 52, 241–250.

Sullivan, H. S. (1940) *Conceptions of modern psychiatry*. New York: Norton.

Suls, J. (2001) Affect, stress, and personality. In J. P. Forgas (ed.), *Handbook of affect and social cognition*, pp. 392–409. Mahwah, NJ: Erlbaum.

Suls, J. and Rittenhouse, J. D. (1990) Models of linkages between personality and disease. In H. S. Friedman (ed.), *Personality and Disease*. New York: Wiley.

Suls, J., Martin, R. and David, J. P. (1998) Person–environment fit and its limits: agreeableness, neuroticism, and emotional reactivity to interpersonal conflict. *Personality and Social Psychology Bulletin*, 24, 88–98.

Surtees, P. G. and Wainwright, N. W. J. (1996) Fragile states of mind: neuroticism, vulnerability and the long-term outcome of depression. *British Journal of Psychiatry*, 169, 338–47.

Sutker, P. B. and Allain, A. N. (1983) Behavior and personality assessment in men labelled adaptive sociopaths. *Journal of Behavioral Assessment*, 5, 65–79.

Svrakic, D. M., Whitehead, C., Przybeck, T. R. and Cloninger, C. R. (1993) Differential diagnosis of personality disorders by the seven-factor model of temperament and character. *Archives of General Psychiatry*, 50, 991–9.

Swann, W. B., Jr. (1997) The trouble with change: self-verification and allegiance to the self. *Psychological Science*, 8, 177–80.

Swann, W. B., Jr., Stein-Seroussi, A. and McNulty, A. (1992) Outcasts in a white-lie society: the enigmatic worlds of people with negative self-conceptions. *Journal of Personality and Social Psychology*, 62, 618–24.

Swickert, R. J. and Gilliland, K. (1998) Relationship between the brainstem auditory evoked response and extraversion, impulsivity, and sociability. *Journal of Research in Personality*, 32, 314–30.

Swickert, R. J., Rosentreter, C. J., Hittner, J. B. and Mushrush, J. E. (2002) Extraversion, social support processes, and stress. *Personality and Individual Differences*, 32, 877–91.

Swinkels, A. and Giuliano, T. A. (1995) The measurement and conceptualization of mood awareness: monitoring and labeling one's mood states. *Personality and Social Psychology Bulletin*, 21, 934–49.

Szirmák, Z. and De Raad, B. (1994) Taxonomy and structure of Hungarian personality traits. *European Journal of Personality*, 8, 95–117.

Tafarodi, R. W. and Swann, W. B., Jr. (2001) Two-dimensional self-esteem: theory and measurement. *Personality and Individual Differences*, 2001, 653–73.

Takkouche, B., Regueira, C. and Gestal-Otero, J. J. (2001) A cohort study of stress and the common cold. *Epidemiology*, 12, 345–9.

Talley, N. J., Fung, L. H., Gilligan, I. J., McNeil, D. and Piper, D. W. (1986) Association of anxiety, neuroticism, and depression with dyspepsia of unknown cause. *Gastroenterology*, 90, 886–92.

Tambs, K., Sundet, J. M., Eaves, L., Solaas, M. H. and Berg, K. (1991) Pedigree analysis of Eysenck Personality Questionnaire (EPQ) scores in monozygotic (MZ) twin families. *Behavior Genetics*, 21, 369–82.

Taylor, G. J. (2000) Recent developments in alexithymia theory and research. *Canadian Journal of Psychiatry*, 45, 234–142.

Taylor, G. J., Parker, J. D. A. and Bagby, R. M. (1999) Emotional intelligence and the emotional brain: points of convergence and implications for psychoanalysis. *Journal of the American Academy of Psychoanalysis*, 27, 339–54.

Taylor, S. (1995) Commentary on borderline personality disorder. In W. J. Livesley (ed.), *The DSM-IV Personality Disorders*. New York: Guilford.

Tellegen, A. (1985) Structures of mood and personality and their relevance to assessing anxiety, with an emphasis on self-report. In A. H. Tuma and J. D. Maser (eds.), *Anxiety and the anxiety disorders*, pp. 681–706. Hillsdale, NJ: Erlbaum.

Tellegen, A., Lykken, D. T., Bouchard, T. J., Wilcox, K. J., Segal, N. L. and Rich, S. (1988) Personality similarity in twins reared apart and together. *Journal of Personality and Social Psychology*, 54, 1031–9.

Ten Berge, M. A. and De Raad, B. (1999) Taxonomies of situations from a trait psychological perspective: a review. *European Journal of Personality*, 13, 337–60.

Tenenbaum, G. and Bar-Eli, M. (1995) Personality and intellectual capabilities in sport psychology. In D. H. Saklofske and M. Zeidner (eds.), *International handbook of personality and intelligence*. New York: Plenum.

Terman, L. M. and Oden, M. H. (1947) *The gifted child grows up: twenty-five years' follow-up of a superior group*. Stanford, CA: Stanford University Press.

Tett, R. P., Jackson, D. N. and Rothstein, M. (1991) Personality measures as predictors of job performance: a meta-analytic review. *Personnel Psychology*, 44, 703–42.

(1994) Meta-analysis of personality-job performance relations: a reply to Ones, Mount, Berrick, and Hunter (1994) *Personnel Psychology*, 47, 157–72.

Tett, R. P., Jackson, D. N., Rothstein, M. and Reddon, J. R. (1999) Meta-analysis of bi-directional relations in personality-job performance research, *Human Performance*, 12, 1–129.

Thayer, R. E. (1978) Toward a psychological theory of multidimensional activation (arousal). *Motivation and Emotion*, 2, 1–34.

(1989) *The biopsychology of mood and arousal*. Oxford: Oxford University Press.

(1996) *The origin of everyday moods*. New York: Oxford University Press.

(2001) *Calm energy: how people regulate mood with food and exercise*. New York: Oxford University Press.

Thayer, R. E., Newman, J. R. and McClain, T. M. (1994) Self-regulation of mood: strategies for changing a bad mood, raising energy, and reducing tension. *Journal of Personality and Social Psychology*, 67, 910–25.

Thomas, A. and Chess, S. (1977) *Temperament and development*. New York: Brunner/Mazel.

Thomson, J. A. K. (1976) *The Ethics of Aristotle: the Nicomachean Ethics* (translation: rev. edn.). Harmondsworth: Penguin.

Thorne, A. (1987) The press of personality: a study of conversations between introverts and extraverts. *Journal of Personality and Social Psychology*, 53, 718–26.

Thurstone, L. L. (1947) *Multiple factor analysis*. Chicago, IL: Chicago University Press.

Todorov, A. and Bargh, J. A. (2002) Automatic sources of aggression. *Aggression and Violent Behavior*, 7, 53–68.

Tokar, D. M., Fischer, Ann R. and Subich, L. M. (1998) Personality and vocational behavior: a selective review of the literature, 1993–1997. *Journal of Vocational Behavior*, 53, 115–53.

Tooby, J. and Cosmides, L. (1992) Psychological foundations of culture. In J. Barkow, L. Cosmides and J. Tooby (eds.), *The adapted mind*, pp. 19–36. New York: Oxford University Press.

Torgersen, A. M. and Janson, H. (2002) Why do identical twins differ in personality: shared environment reconsidered. *Twin Research*, 5, 44–52.

Trapnell, P. D. and Wiggins, J. S. (1990) Extension of the Interpersonal Adjective Scales to include the Big Five dimensions of personality. *Journal of Personality and Social Psychology*, 37, 395–412.

Triandis, H. C. (1997) Cross-cultural perspectives on personality. In R. Hogan, A. Johnson and S. Briggs (eds.), *Handbook of Personality Psychology*, pp. 440–64. San Diego, CA: Academic Press.

(2001) Individualism–collectivism and personality. *Journal of Personality*, 69, 907–24.

Trull, T. J. and Sher, K. J. (1994) Relationship between the five-factor model of personality and Axis I disorders in a nonclinical sample. *Journal of Abnormal Psychology*, 103, 350–60.

Trull, T. J. and Widiger, T. A. (1997) *Structured interview for the five factor model of personality (SIFFM): professional manual*. Odessa, FL: Psychological Assessment Resources.

Trull, T. J., Widiger, T. A. and Burr, R. (1997) A structured interview for the assessment of the five factor model of personality: facet-level relations to the Axis II personality disorders. *Journal of Personality*, 69, 175–98.

Tucker, D. M. and Derryberry, D. (1992) Motivated attention: anxiety and the frontal executive mechanisms. *Neuropsychiatry, Neuropsychology, and Behavioral Neurology*, 5, 233–52.

Tupes, E. C. and Christal, R. E. (1961/1992) Recurrent personality factors based on trait ratings. Technical Report No. ASD-TR-61–97, US Air Force, Lackland US Air Force Base, TX. Reprinted in *Journal of Personality*, 60, 225–51.

Turkheimer, E. and Waldron, M. (2000) Nonshared environment: a theoretical, methodological and quantitative review. *Psychological Bulletin*, 126, 78–108.

Turner, J. R., Carroll, D., Sims, J., Hewitt, J. K. and Kelly, K. A. (1986) Temporal and intertask consistency of heart rate reactivity during active psychological challenge: a twin study. *Physiology and Behavior*, 38, 641–4.

Tyrer, P. (1995) Are personality disorders well classified in DSM-IV? In W. J. Livesley (ed.), *The DSM-IV Personality Disorders*. New York: Guilford.

Tyrer, P., Casey, P. and Ferguson, B. (1991) Personality disorder in perspective. *British Journal of Psychiatry*, 159, 463–71. (Reprinted under the same title in 1993 in P. Tyrer and G. Stein (eds.), *Personality disorder reviewed*. London: Gaskell.)

Tyssen, R. and Vaglum, P. (2002) Mental health problems among young doctors: an updated review of prospective studies. *Harvard Review of Psychiatry*, 10, 154–65.

Uchino, B. N. and Garvey, T. S. (1997) The availability of social support reduces cardiovascular reactivity to acute psychological stress. *Journal of Behavioral Medicine*, 20, 15–27.

Valentine, E. and Evans, C. (2001) The effects of solo singing, choral singing and swimming on mood and physiological indices. *British Journal of Medical Psychology*, 74, 115–20.

Valentiner, D. P., Foa, E. B., Riggs, D. S. and Gershuny, B. S. (1996) Coping strategies and posttraumatic stress disorder in female victims of sexual and nonsexual assault. *Journal of Abnormal Psychology*, 105, 455–8.

Van Heck, G. L. (1989) Situation concepts: definitions and classification. In P. Hettema (ed.), *Personality and environment: assessment of human adaptation*, pp. 53–69. Chichester: Wiley.

Van Heck, G. L., Bonaiuto, P., Deary, I. J. and Nowack, W. (eds.) (1993) *Personality psychology in Europe*, vol. 4. Tilburg, The Netherlands: Tilburg Universiy Press.

Van Ijzendoorn, M. H. (1995) Adult attachment representations, parental responsiveness, and infant attachment: a meta-analysis on the predictive validity of the Adult Attachment Interview. *Psychological Bulletin*, 117, 387–403.

Vedhara, K., Shanks, N., Wilcock, G. and Lightman, S. L. (2001) Correlates and predictors of self-reported psychological and physical morbidity in chronic caregiver stress. *Journal of Health Psychology*, 6, 101–19.

Venables, P. H. and Rector, N. A. (2000) The content and structure of schizotypy: a study using confirmatory factor analysis. *Schizophrenia Bulletin*, 26, 587–602.

Venables, P. H., Wilkins, S., Mitchell, D. A., Raine, A. and Bailes, K. (1990) A scale for the measurement of schizotypy. *Personality and Individual Differences*, 11, 481–95.

Verwey, W. B. and Zaidel, D. M. (2000) Predicting drowsiness accidents from personal attributes, eye blinks and ongoing driving behaviour. *Personality and Individual Differences*, 28, 123–42.

Viken, R. J., Rose, R. J., Kaprio, J. and Koskenvuo, M. (1994) A developmental-genetic study of adult personality: extraversion and neuroticism from eighteen to fifty-nine years of age. *Journal of Personality and Social Psychology*, 66, 722–30.

Vittersø, J. (2001) Personality traits and subjective well-being: emotional stability, not extraversion, is probably the important predictor. *Personality and Individual Differences*, 31, 903–14.

Vollema, M. G. and van den Bosch, R. J. (1995) The multidimensionality of schizotypy. *Schizophrenia Bulletin*, 21, 19–31.

Vollrath, M. (2000) Personality and hassles among university students: a three-year longitudinal study. *European Journal of Personality*, 14, 199–215.

Vollrath, M. and Torgerson, S. (2002) Who takes health risks? A probe into eight personality types. *Personality and Individual Differences*, 32, 1185–97.

Vollrath, M., Alnæas, R. and Torgersen, S. (1996) Differential effects of coping in mental disorders: a prospective study in psychiatric outpatients. *Journal of Clinical Psychology*, 52, 125–35.

(1998) Neuroticism, coping and change in MCMI-II clinical syndromes: test of a mediator model. *Scandinavian Journal of Psychology*, 39, 15–24.

Wallace, J. F., Newman, J. P. and Bachorowski, J.-A. (1991) Failures of response modulation: impulsive behaviour in anxious and impulsive individuals. *Journal of Research in Personality*, 25, 23–44.

Waller, N. G. (1999) Evaluating the structure of personality. In C. R. Cloninger (ed.), *Personality and psychopathology*, pp. 155–97. Washington, DC: American Psychiatric Press.

Walton, H. J. and Presly, A. S. (1973) Use of a category system in the diagnosis of abnormal personality. *British Journal of Psychiatry*, 122, 259–68.

Wanberg, C. R., Kanfer, R. and Banas, J. T. (2000) Predictors and outcomes of networking intensity among unemployed job seekers. *Journal of Applied Psychology*, 85, 491–503.

Wang, W. and Wang, Y.-H. (2001) Sensation seeking correlates of passive auditory P3 to a single stimulus. *Neuropsychologia*, 39, 1188–93.

Wannamethee, G. and Shaper, A. G. (1991) Self-assessment of health status and mortality in middle-aged British men. *International Journal of Epidemiology*, 20, 239–45.

Ware, J. E., Snow, K. K., Kosinski, M. and Gandek, B. (1993) *SF-36 Health survey manual and interpretation guide*. Boston, MA: The Health Institute, New England Medical Centre.

Wasylkiw, L. and Fekken, G. C. (2002) Personality and self-reported health: matching predictors and criteria. *Personality and Individual Differences*, 33, 607–20.

Watkin, C. (2000) Developing emotional intelligence. *International Journal of Selection and Assessment*, 2, 89–92.

Watson, D. (2000) *Mood and temperament*. New York: Guilford Press.

Watson, D. and Clark, L. A. (1992) On traits and temperament: general and specific factors of emotional experience and their relation to the five-factor model. *Journal of Personality*, 60, 441–76.

(1995) Depression and the melancholic temperament. *European Journal of Personality*, 9, 351–66.

(1997) Measurement and mismeasurement of mood: recurrent and emergent issues. *Journal of Personality Assessment*, 68, 267–96.

Watson, D. and Hubbard, B. (1996) Adaptational style and dispositional structure: coping in the context of the five-factor model. *Journal of Personality*, 64, 737–74.

Watson, D. and Pennebaker, J. W. (1989) Health complaints, stress, and distress: exploring the central role of negative affectivity. *Psychological Review*, 96, 234–54.

Watson, D. and Randolph (2001)

Watson, D. and Tellegen, A. (1985) Toward a consensual structure of mood. *Psychological Bulletin*, 98, 219–35.

Watson, D., Clark, L. A., McIntyre, C. W. and Hamaker, S. (1992) Affect, personality, and social activity. *Journal of Personality and Social Psychology*, 6, 1011–25.

Watson, D., Wiese, D., Vaidya, J. and Tellegen, A. (1999) The two general activation systems of affect: structural findings, evolutionary considerations, and psychobiological evidence. *Journal of Personality and Social Psychology*, 76, 820–38.

Watson, M., Haviland, J. S., Greer, S., Davidson, J. and Bliss, J. M. (1999) Influence of psychological response on survival in breast cancer: a population-based cohort study. *Lancet*, 354, 1331–6.

Watson, N. and Watts, R. H., Jr. (2001) The predictive strength of personal constructs versus conventional constructs: self-image disparity and neuroticism. *Journal of Personality*, 69, 121–45.

Watts, F. N., McKenna, F. P., Sharrock, R. and Tresize, L. (1986) Colour-naming of phobia-related words. *British Journal of Clinical Psychology*, 25, 253–61.

Webb, E. (1915) Character and intelligence. *British Journal of Psychology Monographs*, 1, 3, 199.

Weinberger, D. A. and Davidson, M. N. (1994) Styles of inhibiting emotional expression: distinguishing repressive coping from impression management. *Journal of Personality*, 62, 587–613.

Weinberger, D. A., Schwartz, G. E. and Davidson, J. R. (1979) Low-anxious, high-anxious, and repressive coping styles: psychometric patterns and behavioural and physiological responses to stress. *Journal of Abnormal Psychology*, 88, 369–80.

Weiner, B. and Schneider, K. (1971) Drive versus cognitive theory: a reply to Boor and Harmon. *Journal of Personality and Social Psychology*, 18, 258–62.

Weinman, J. (1987) Non-cognitive determinants of perceptual problem-solving strategies. *Personality and Individual Differences*, 8, 53–8.

Wells, A. (1997) *Cognitive therapy of anxiety disorders: a practice manual and conceptual guide*. Chichester: Wiley.

(2000) *Emotional disorders and metacognition: innovative cognitive therapy*. Chichester: Wiley.

Wells, A. and Matthews, G. (1994) *Attention and emotion: a clinical perspective*. Hove: Erlbaum.

Westen, D. (1999) The scientific status of unconscious processes: is Freud really dead? *Journal of the American Psychoanalytic Association*, 47, 1061–106.

Westen, D. and Gabbard, G. O. (1999) Psychoanalytic approaches to personality. In L. A. Pervin and O. P. John (eds.), *Handbook of personality: Theory and research*, 2nd edn. pp. 57–101. New York: Guilford.

White, R. W. (1959) Motivation reconsidered: the concept of competence. *Psychological Review*, 66, 297–333.

Whiteman, M. C., Deary, I. J. and Fowkes, F. G. R. (2000) Personality and Social predictors of atherosclerotic progression: Edinburgh Artery Study. *Psychosomatic Medicine*, 62, 703–14.

Whiteman, M. C., Fowkes, F. G. F., Deary, I. J. and Lee, A. J. (1997a) Hostility, cigarette smoking and alcohol consumption in the general population. *Social Science and Medicine*, 44, 1089–96.

(1997b) Submissiveness and protection from coronary heart disease in the general population: Edinburgh Artery Study. *The Lancet*, 350, 541–5.

Whiteman, M. C., Bedford, A., Grant, E., Fowkes, F. G. R. and Deary, I. J. (2001) The five-factor model (NEO-FFI) and the Personality Deviance Scales-Revised (PDS-R): going around in interpersonal circles. *Personality and Individual Differences*, 31, 259–67.

Whiteside, S. P. and Lynam, D. (2001) The Five Factor Model and impulsivity: using a structural model of personality to understand impulsivity. *Personality and Individual Differences*, 30, 669–89.

Whitfield, K. E., Weidner, G., Clark, R. and Anderson, N. B. (2002) Sociodemographic diversity and behavioural medicine. *Journal of Consulting and Clinical Psychology*, 70, 463–81.

Whitlock, F. A. (1982) A note on moral insanity and psychopathic disorders. *Bulletin of the Royal College of Psychiatrists*, 6, 57–9.

Wickett, J. C. and Vernon, P. A. (2000) Replicating the movement time-extraversion link . . . with a little help from IQ. *Personality and Individual Differences*, 28, 2, 205–15.

Widiger, T. A. (1989) Psychiatrists' responses to personality disorder. *British Journal of Psychiatry*, 154, 266.

Widiger, T. A. and Corbitt, E. M. (1995) Antisocial personality disorder. In W. J. Livesley (ed.), *The DSM-IV Personality Disorders*. New York: Guilford.

Widiger, T. A. and Costa, P. T., Jr. (1994) Personality and personality disorders. *Journal of Abnormal Psychology*, 103, 78–91.

Widiger, T. A. and Sanderson, C. J. (1995) Toward a dimensional model of personality disorders. In W. J. Livesley (ed.), *The DSM-IV Personality Disorders*. New York: Guilford.

Widiger, T. A. and Shea, T. (1991) Differentiation of Axis I and Axis II disorders. *Journal of Abnormal Psychology*, 100, 399–406.

Widiger, T. A. and Trull, T. J. (1992) Personality and psychopathology: an application of the five factor model. *Journal of Personality*, 60, 363–93.

Widiger, T. A., Trull, T. J., Hurt, S. W., Clarkin, J. and Frances, A. (1987) A multidimensional scaling of the DSM-III personality disorders. *Archives of General Psychiatry*, 44, 557–63.

Wiggins, J. S. and Pincus, A. L. (1989) Conceptions of personality disorders and dimensions of personality. *Psychological Assessment*, 1, 305–16.

Wiggins, J. S. and Trapnell, P. D. (1996) A dyadic-interactional perspective on the five-factor model. In J. S. Wiggins (ed.), *The five-factor model of personality: theoretical perspectives*, pp. 88–162. New York: Guilford.

Wilken, J. A., Smith, B. D., Tola, K. and Mann, M. (2000) Trait anxiety and prior exposure to non-stressful stimuli: effects on psychophysiological arousal and anxiety. *International Journal of Psychophysiology*, 37, 233–42.

Williams, D. G. (1989) Personality effects in current mood: pervasive or reactive? *Personality and Individual Differences*, 10, 941–8.

Williams, J. M. G., Watts, F. N., MacLeod, C. and Mathews, A. (1988) *Cognitive psychology and emotional disorders*. Chichester: Wiley.

Williams, L. M. (1995) Further evidence for a multidimensional personality disposition to schizophrenia in terms of cognitive inhibition. *British Journal of Clinical Psychology*, 34, 193–213.

Williams, R. S. (1994) Occupational testing: contemporary British practice. *The Psychologist*, 7, 11–13.

Willits, F. K. and Crider, D. M. (1988) Health rating and life satisfaction in the later middle years. *Journal of Gerontology*, 43, 172–6.

Wilson, G. S., Raglin, J. S. and Pritchard, M. E. (2002) Optimism, pessimism and pre-competition anxiety in college athletes. *Personality and Individual Differences*, 32, 893–902.

Wilson, J. A., Deary, I. J. and Maran, A. G. D. (1991) The persistence of symptoms in patients with globus pharyngis. *Clinical Otolaryngology*, 16, 202–5.

Wood, J. V. (1989) Theory and research concerning social comparisons of personal attributes. *Psychological Bulletin*, 106, 231–48.

Woody, E. and Claridge, G. (1977) Psychoticism and thinking. *British Journal of Social and Clinical Psychology*, 16, 241–8.

World Health Organisation (1992) *The ICD-10 Classification of mental and behavioural disorders: diagnostic criteria for research*. Geneva: World Health Organisation.

  (1997) *Multiaxial presentation of the ICD-10 for use in adult psychiatry*. Cambridge: Cambridge University Press.

Wright, J. C. and Mischel, W. (1987) A conditional approach to dispositional constructs: the local predictability of social behavior. *Journal of Personality and Social Psychology*, 53, 1159–77.

Wundt, W. (1897) *Grundriss der Psychologie* [Outlines of psychology]. Leipzig: Wilhelm Engelmann.

Yang, K. and Bond, M. H. (1990) Exploring implicit personality theories with indigenous or imported constructs: the Chinese case. *Journal of Personality and Social Psychology*, 58, 1087–95.

  (1993) Exploring the dimensions of Chinese person perception with indigenous and imported constructs: creating a culturally balanced scale. *International Journal of Psychology*, 28, 75–95.

Yang, S. Y. (2001) Conceptions of wisdom among Taiwanese Chinese. *Journal of Cross-Cultural Psychology*, 32, 662–80.

Yerkes, R. M. and Dodson, J. D. (1908) The relation of strength of stimulus to rapidity of habit-formation. *Journal of Comparative Neurology and Psychology*, 18, 459–82.

Yik, M. S. M. and Russell, J. A. (2001) Predicting the Big Two of affect from the Big Five of personality. *Journal of Research in Personality*, 35, 247–77.

Young, M. R. and Bradley, M. T. (1998) Social withdrawal: self-efficacy, happiness, and popularity in introverted and extroverted adolescents. *Canadian Journal of School Psychology*, 14, 21–35.

Zahn, T. P., Kruesi, M. J. P., Leonard, H. L. and Rapoport, J. L. (1994) Autonomic activity and reaction time in relation to extraversion and behavioral impulsivity in children and adolescents. *Personality and Individual Differences*, 16, 751–8.

Zahn-Waxler, C., Cummings, E. M., Mcknew, D. and Radke-Yarrow, M. (1984) Affective arousal and social interactions in young children of manic depressive parents. *Child Development*, 55, 112–22.

Zajonc, R. B. (1984) On the primacy of emotion. *American Psychologist,* 39, 117–23.

Zeidner, M. (1995) Personality trait correlates of intelligence. In D. H. Saklofske and M. Zeidner (eds.), *International handbook of personality and intelligence*. New York: Plenum.

(1998) *Test anxiety: the state of the art*. New York: Plenum.

Zeidner, M. and Matthews, G. (2000) Personality and intelligence. In R. J. Sternberg (ed.), *Handbook of human intelligence*, 2nd edn, pp. 581–610. Cambridge: Cambridge University Press.

Zeidner, M. and Endler, N. S. (eds.) (1996) *Handbook of coping: theory, research, applications*. New York: Wiley.

Zeidner, M. and Saklofske, D. (1996) Adaptive and maladaptive coping. In M. Zeidner and N. S. Endler (eds.), *Handbook of coping: theory, research, applications*, pp. 505–31. New York: Wiley.

Zeidner, M., Matthews, G. and Roberts, R. D. (in press) Emotional intelligence in the workplace: a critical review. *Applied Psychology: An International Journal*.

Zeidner, M., Roberts, R. D. and Matthews, G. (2002) Can emotional intelligence (EI) be schooled? A critical review. *Educational Psychologist*, 37, 215–31.

Zeidner, M., Matthews, G., Roberts, R. D. and McCann, C. (2003) Development of emotional intelligence: towards a multi-level investment model. *Human Development*, 46, 69–96.

Zelenski, J. M. and Larsen, R. J. (1999) Susceptibility to affect: a comparison of three personality taxonomies. *Journal of Personality*, 67, 761–91.

Zelenski, J. M. and Larsen, R. J. (2002) Predicting the future: how affect-related personality traits influence likelihood judgments of future events. *Personality and Social Psychology Bulletin*, 28, 1000–10.

Zhou, Q., Eisenberg, N., Losoya, S. H., Fabes, R. A., Reiser, M., Guthrie, I. K., Murphy, B. C., Cumberland, A. J. and Shepard, S. A. (2002) The relations of parental warmth and positive expressiveness to children's empathy-related responding and social functioning: a longitudinal study. *Child Development*, 73, 893–915.

Zimmerman, B. J. (2000) Self-efficacy: an essential motive to learn. *Contemporary Educational Psychology*, 25, 82–91.

Zimmerman, M. (1994) Diagnosing personality disorders: a review of issues and research methods. *Archives of General Psychiatry*, 51, 225–45.

Zimmermann, P. and Becker-Stoll, F. (2002) Stability of attachment representations during adolescence: the influence of ego-identity status. *Journal of Adolescence*, 25, 107–24.

Zinbarg, R. E. and Mohlman, J. (1998) Individual differences in the acquisition of affectively valenced associations. *Journal of Personality and Social Psychology*, 74, 1024–40.

Zohar, A. H., Lev-Ari, L., Benjamin, J., Ebstein, R., Lichtenberg, P. and Osher, Y. (2001) The psychometric properties of the Hebrew version of Cloninger's Tridimensional Personality Questionnaire. *Personality and Individual Differences*, 30, 1297–309.

Zuckerman, M. (1976) General and situation-specific traits and states: new approaches to assessment of anxiety and other constructs. In M. Zuckerman and C. D. Spielberger (eds.), *Emotions and anxiety: new concepts, methods and applications*, pp. 133–74. Hillsdale, NJ: Erlbaum.

(1979) *Sensation seeking beyond the optimal level of arousal.* Hillsdale, NJ: Erlbaum.

(1991) *Psychobiology of personality.* Cambridge: Cambridge University Press.

(1994) Diagnosing personality disorders: a review of issues and research methods. *Archives of General Psychiatry*, 51, 225–45.

(1995) Good and bad humors: biochemical bases of personality and its disorders. *Psychological Science*, 6, 325–32.

(1999) *Vulnerability to psychopathology: a biosocial model.* Washington, DC: American Psychological Association.

(2002) Zuckerman-Kuhlman Personality Questionnaire (ZKPQ): an alternative five-factorial model. In B. De Raad and M. Perugini (eds.), *Big Five Assessment*, pp. 377–96. Seattle, WA: Hogrefe and Huber.

Zuckerman, M. and Cloninger, C. R. (1996) Relationships between Cloninger's, Zuckerman's and Eysenck's dimensions of personality. *Personality and Individual Differences*, 21, 283–5.

Zuckerman, M., Kuhlman, D. M., Joireman, J., Teta, P. and Kraft, M. (1993) A comparison of three structural models for personality: the big three, the big five, and the alternative five. *Journal of Personality and Social Psychology*, 65, 757–68.

Zuckerman, M., Kuhlman, D. M., Thornquist, M. and Kiers, H. (1991) Five (or three) robust questionnaire scale factors of personality without culture. *Personality and Individual Differences*, 12, 929–41.

Zwick, W. and Velicer, W. (1986) Comparison of five rules for determining the number of components to retain. *Psychological Bulletin*, 99, 432–42.

Author index

Subject index